A Higher Score, Guaranteed

This book is the product of hundreds (thousands maybe?) of hours of test preparation and research, and represents the best system of preparation for the ACT exam on the market. Therefore, we want to back that up with a guarantee. If you, the student, complete this book, and the preparation does not help to improve your score, we will happily refund your money. Send an email to support@theactsystem.com to make arrangements, which will require images of the completed book, the original sales receipt, ACT scores before and after completing the book, and a written explanation.

All claims for refunds must be received within six months of original purchase.

The ACT *System*

A step-by-step, first-things-first, systematized, secret-free, no gimmicks, no tricks, no wasted time guide to the ACT test

Philip J Martin

Download Your *FREE* ACT System Cheat Sheets!

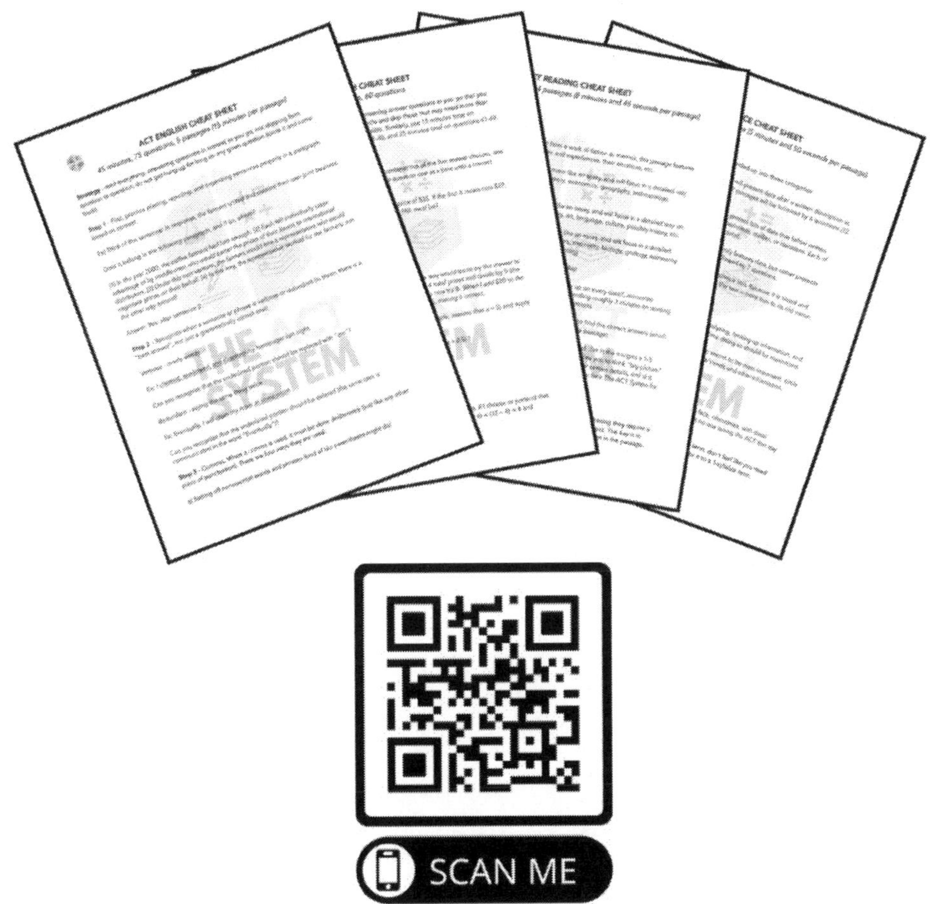

Scan the QR code above to receive your free ACT System cheat sheets, yours to print and use in your ACT preparation!

ACT® is a registered trademark of ACT, Inc

Published by Test Prep by Step, LLC

For special group pricing, please email support@theactsystem.com

ISBN: 9798859725779

www.theactsystem.com

www.philipmartinact.com

Table of Contents

Introduction

Have you looked through your average ACT prep book lately? It looks and feels more like the instruction manual for running a factory than it does a test preparation book. Frankly, you don't need to memorize or read about the technical names of the various types of ACT questions, their categories, the psychology behind the questions, etc. That knowledge is good for behind the scenes, but for you, it's a waste.

Also, if I hear another book or teacher promise to give all of the "tips, tricks, and secrets" to succeed on the ACT I think I'll scream. You don't need "tips, tricks, and secrets;" phrases like that are gimmicks that, at least I think, are big on promise but short on return. Not to mention, the ACT test makers are aware of each and every pattern and conceptions of patterns; as soon as it's circulated that "the shortest answer is almost always right," or whatever the case may be, the test makers will switch it up and defy the pattern. On the other hand, many other ACT books, instructors, and tutors are guilty of the sin of overanalyzing; this kind of instruction is so technical that reading it borders on punishment. Teachers have to remember that they aren't training teenagers to work for the ACT one day, but rather to take the test to the best of their abilities.

My thousands of hours ACT classroom experience (not including research and writing), on the other hand, have taught me that you, the student, need three things, especially when it comes to each of the ACT's 4 subject tests: content knowledge (especially in ACT English and Math), strategy, and skills, all reinforced by guided practice. This book will get you there without overanalyzing or appealing to cheap shortcuts.

Additionally, anxiety is already high enough, so why are so many students preparing for the ACT trying their hardest to memorize very specific, unlikely to be asked about rules? This, sadly, is what happens when ACT test preparation is detached from a professional instructor or course. For example, many students sweat over the who/whom distinction, when the odds of a question requiring your knowledge of this is less than 1%; many are researching whether or not the oxford comma (the second comma in a series) is required or optional, and are getting confused by the strong opinions of English teachers and counselors. These topics are important (more or less…closer to less), but unless you have already scored a 33 or higher in ACT English, they are a waste of mental energy. This same kind of misguided and misplaced stress is multiplied across all 4 subject tests. We'll get to some of these topics in this book, but in due time; we'll put them and the preparation they require where they belong.

The purpose of this book is clear: to focus your attention on the content and skills *most needed in ACT English, Math, Reading, and Science to raise your scores*, and to do so *one at a time*. In other words, those that, simply, are most tested across the 4 tests and across the ACT itself. The closer a Step is to Step 1, the more important; the further a Step is away from Step 1, the less important (and by less important, I simply mean less likely to be tested on ACT day). For example, you won't find the who/whom distinction anywhere near Step 1 of the ACT English section! As a Step is learned, it is continually refreshed throughout the book so as not to be forgotten, but rather built upon. This preparation culminates in two full-length practice tests for English, Math, Reading, and Science. These tests are important in that they put into practice what you have learned in the book and reveal where you still need work.

How to Use This Book

Use of this book is simple. Review the Step, then work your way through the practice that follows. The practice contains questions that reflect the current Step as well as previous Steps. Why not simply focus on this current Step's material only? Because again, we want to treat the ACT English, Math, Reading, and Science tests as cumulative, testing both skills (especially in ACT Reading and Science) and content (especially in ACT English and Math), and want to continually build upon the most important and work our way to least. This kind of guided *practice* (as opposed to blindly studying or binge watching YouTube videos) will reveal specific problem areas, thus heightening your focus.

In addition, the vast majority of the practice offered to you in this book is within the context of full-length passages. This is to train your mind to pay attention for that span of time and to become used to the real-life length of ACT English, Math, Reading, and Science passages. Following each practice section you will find a list of answers. However, the back of the book contains a written explanation for each and every question; these explanations review rules and strategy while giving the reasons behind each correct and incorrect answer.

In a time crunch? Don't have time to use this entire book from start to finish? In that case, complete as many steps as possible, then skip ahead to the two practice tests in Step 6 for ACT Math, Reading, and Science or in Step 7 for ACT English.

The ACT English *System*

Seven Steps to ACT English Perfection

Timing and Introduction

Each ACT English test is 5 passages in length, and you are given 45 minutes to complete the test. This equates to 9 minutes per passage. Before the final practice tests (which are comparable to real ACT English tests), we will return to timing because this is a crucial skill for the ACT exam. For the first six steps, however, timing will be inaccurate because the passages are customized to teach certain skills and content.

Overview and Basic Strategy

The ACT English Test is the first of four and is followed by Math, Reading, and Science, respectively. The English Test is designed to test just that: your ability to recognize either the *correct answer* (as in a question of grammar) or the *best answer* (as in a question of context).

It consists of 5 passages, or essays if you will. Each essay is roughly 340 words in length and contains 15 questions. Most of the questions reference an underlined portion of a sentence or sentences and ask you to choose the correct or best answer from four choices. Other questions may refer to a paragraph, asking for the best placement of a certain sentence or an appropriate sentence to finish or begin that paragraph. Further still, some questions refer to the passage as a whole, and could be categorized as something more like "reading comprehension."

Your best-bet basic strategy is this: <u>Answer questions as you go, but in context</u>. Read everything, and answer questions as you go. "Read everything," means <u>*do not*</u> skip over paragraphs, sentences, or pieces of sentences that are not underlined. You will need that information (more than you know!). "Answer questions as you go," means you should stop and answer questions while you read. However, this comes with a caveat: you will likely need greater context than just an underlined portion to answer a question correctly, such as the sentence as a whole, the sentence before, the sentence after, etc. More on that in a later lesson.

Question Breakdown

I break down ACT English questions into two types: grammar and context.

Grammar

Questions of grammar are questions that, like math, have a right or wrong answer. Take, for example, number 23 below:

I went to the grocery store today, I forgot to buy cheese.
23

This question is a question of grammar because, as written, *it is wrong*. In other words, the right answer doesn't depend on the flow of the paragraph, the author's intention, the greater context, the previous sentence, or the purpose of the essay or paragraph. There are a handful of ways that you can combine these two complete sentences (called *independent clauses*) into one, but no matter the way, we need one that is grammatically correct (*more on that later!*).

Context

You know how sometimes your teacher marks your answer wrong not because it is technically incorrect, but because it isn't the "best answer"? Well, ACT English does the same thing. Based on the sentence that the question is in, or the preceding sentence, or the sentence that follows, or the paragraph as a whole, or even the entire essay, there can be an answer that is *best* as opposed to just grammatically correct. Think about number 24 below:

I went to the grocery store today. Because of this, I forgot to buy cheese.
24

You will notice that "Because of this" is underlined. As an introductory, dependent clause, it is grammatically correct in that it is set off from the independent clause of the sentence ("I forgot to buy cheese"). But, does it *work*? Is it *the best* choice of words? It isn't going to the store, though, that *caused* me to forget to buy cheese. Can you think of a word or phrase that would be *best* to link these thoughts?

STEP 1

Sentences and Phrases in Context

It is undeniable that there is a skill that, if mastered, can move the needle on your ACT English score more than any other, and that is this: placing, rejecting, and organizing phrases and sentences properly in a paragraph based on greater context.

Again, it doesn't matter now if you know what that means or not; the purpose of the book is to teach you these things *through* practice.

Read the following paragraph:

> In the year 2000, the coffee farmers had had enough. Each felt individually taken advantage of by middle-men who would barter the prices of their beans to international distributors. Under this new venture, the farmers would hire a representative who would negotiate prices on their behalf. In this way, the representative worked for the farmers: not the other way around!

Notice anything missing? If not, *read it again, slowly*. Don't sweat if you don't: fortunately, the ACT English test is multiple choice, so you do not need to recognize these things blindly. But does something about this sentence strike you as odd? It should. You should be asking yourself this question: *what new venture*? You see, in the third sentence, "this new venture" is mentioned as something the farmers are doing. However, the venture has not yet been brought up or alluded to before that. This is the kind of recognition that is vital to your ACT English success.

The following page demonstrates how this paragraph might appear on the ACT. See if you can correctly place the sentence, and then try your ability to do so in the following paragraphs as well. If you want to test your abilities, cover up the questions in the right column, read the paragraphs, and ask yourself, "What does this paragraph need to function properly?"

In the year 2000, the coffee farmers had had enough. Each felt individually taken advantage of by middle-men who would barter the prices of their beans to international distributors. **|1|** Under this new venture, the farmers would hire a representative who would negotiate prices on their behalf. In this way, the representative worked for the farmers: not the other way around!

1. At this point, the author is considering adding the following true statement:

   In response, the farmers united and created their own, joint business.

   Should the writer make this addition here?

   A. Yes, because it creates feelings of sympathy in the reader.
   B. Yes, because it creates a logical transition to the next sentence.
   C. No, because the farmers' response is not relevant to the paragraph.
   D. No, because the information is already provided in the paragraph.

---

[1] To this day, the status of the Ivory-billed Woodpecker remains a mystery. [2] Some say that it has been spotted dozens of times. [3] I, on the other hand, prefer a position somewhere in between. [4] I believe my grandfather when he says that, as a young man, he spotted the bird, which today carries on indiscreetly as an endangered species. [5] Others maintain that the bird is extinct. **|2|**

2. For the sake of logic and cohesion, the best placement for Sentence 5 would be:

   F. where it is now.
   G. after Sentence 1.
   H. after Sentence 2.
   J. after Sentence 3.

|3| Well, did you also know that in 1484 he asked John II, King of Portugal, to finance his voyage? For various reasons, John II denied Columbus twice. This forced him to seek funding from neighboring Spain.

3. Given that all of the following statements are true, which one, if added here, would most effectively introduce the topic of this paragraph?

   A. You probably know that, as the rhyme goes, "In 1492 Columbus sailed the ocean blue."
   B. In the days of Christopher Columbus, most of Europe lived under a monarchy.
   C. Have you ever felt like a failure?
   D. Sailing seems timid and easy, but have you sailed across the open ocean?

Did it come naturally to you to see not only that each of these paragraphs was imperfect, but that each was missing something? If so, that is a good sign; follow that instinct! If not, the practice that follows in this Step will be beneficial and will teach you to notice clues that can help you nail down the answer.

Explanations

1. The correct answer is **B**. As we said on the previous page, and as written, there is simply no reference point for the phrase "this new venture," especially one that attributes it to farmers. Thus, the paragraph needs a sentence that does so. The "joint business" is this venture. The answer is not **A** because, while these positive feelings may exist, that is not the primary function of the sentence relative to the rest of the paragraph. The answer is not **C** because the farmer's response is relevant in that it itself *is* the venture. The answer is not **D** because the information is not provided in the paragraph, which is why it is needed.

2. The correct answer is **H**. This time, the question asked you to properly place a sentence. The sentence that needs proper placing begins with the word "Others." This is the context clue that you need to place it correctly. "Others"...compared to who or what? "Some," which is why this sentence pairs with Sentence 2 and, along with Sentence 2, forms a complete thought.

3. The correct answer is **A**. This time, the paragraph is searching for a sentence to properly introduce a paragraph. We need to look for clues that will help us to do two things: a) Link the proposed sentence to the second sentence, and b) Notice which sentence introduces the topic of the paragraph as a whole. Notice that the second sentence says, "did you *also* know..." That's our clue: we need an opening sentence that references our knowledge of a topic. This is why **A** is correct; it does just that and, if you read on, you'll notice that the rest of the paragraph is also about Columbus. The answer is not **B, C, or D** because none of them reference what we know about something. **D** may be tempting because it properly is in the second person (it is speaking to "you"), but the paragraph is not about the dangers of sailing.

Easy enough? I hope so. We'll put this skill to the test after a mini-lesson!

Step 1 Mini-Lesson: Yes or No

OK, I will admit that it feels a bit like cheating to tuck a mini-lesson into a greater lesson. But it is related and beneficial to do so here. Roughly three questions on every ACT English test your overall comprehension of an essay by asking you *Yes* or *No* after the essay has finished. These questions look something like this (I ask one here following a paragraph to get you thinking the right way; the subject of the essay is a fictional town, Shady Gulf, FL, and all it has to offer for tourists):

Visitors to the quaint beach town will be pleasantly surprised by the number of activities available to them. Many people, for example, have ridden a zip line. Few, however, have ever done so over beautiful bays that can sometimes feature dolphins or manatees. In addition, the In The Zone Arcade features more arcade games than any other single location in the entire state. Locals and tourists alike save up tickets won over weeks or months to trade them in for amazing prizes. If your summer plans are up in the air, pay a visit to Shady Gulf, FL; you'll be glad you did!

15. Suppose the author wishes to add a paragraph to the end of the essay about the biological differences between manatees and dolphins. Would such an addition be appropriate?

- **A.** Yes, because the reader is likely receptive to more information about these amazing sea creatures after reading about Shady Gulf, FL.
- **B.** Yes, because as it is currently written, the essay is incomplete.
- **C.** No, because the subject of the essay is Shady Gulf, FL, not the animal life in and around the town.
- **D.** No, because there is no mention in the essay of the sea life in and around Shady Gulf, FL.

The answer is **C**. The main reason I am teaching you about these comprehension questions is because your ability to get these questions correct on the ACT: 1) Will set you apart, as these questions are among the most missed, and 2) Depend upon a skill *that we are starting to practice now*. This skill is the ability to pay attention to the paragraph or essay as a whole while you read along answering questions.

On the pages that follow you will find passages and questions that test these skills. Do not worry if you do not have them perfected now…that is why you have this book! We are beginning to *build a skill.*

PASSAGE I

Flannery's Childhood Home

Those who know of the Southern Gothic writer Flannery O'Connor likely remember that she lived much of her life on a farm in Milledgeville, GA. It was on this farm where she lived as an adult, raising peacocks and writing stories. **|1|** However, the award-winning author spent her most formative years as a child in Savannah, a charming town on the East Coast of the same state. **|2|**

The charming home is tall and thin, reaching three stories in height, and overlooks Lafayette Square. Today, the square is shaded by beautiful oaks, but in the early 20th century (when the O'Connor family occupied the home) the square was completely grassed and served as a play space for the hundreds of school children who were educated in the area.

1. At this point, the author is considering adding the following true statement:

> Peacocks are male peafowl known for their beautiful plumage.

Should the writer make this addition here?

A. Yes, because it introduces a crucial distinction between peacocks and peahens.
B. Yes, because it creates a logical transition to the next sentence.
C. No, because the sentence detracts from the main focus of the paragraph.
D. No, because the information is already provided in the paragraph.

2. Given that all the choices are true, which one most effectively introduces the reader to the fact that the house she grew up in is still standing and open to the public?

F. The real estate market in Savannah, GA is thriving, as many prospective citizens seek work in the beautiful city.
G. Today, the writings of Flannery O' Connor continue to both shock and inspire readers of all ages.
H. Savannah, GA is a relatively short drive from Charleston, SC.
J. Her childhood home in that city is preserved to this day, and has in recent decades been converted into a museum.

|3| Flannery was one of these children, but her mother preferred to have friends over for play-dates rather than permit her only child to aimlessly roam around the square. [A] Thus she spent much of her time reading and playing with friends in rooms on the second floor. [B] When they were ready to take a break from these activities, Flannery would read out loud to her guests. [C] However, the stories she found most interesting (such as *Grimms' Fairy Tales*) were not the most appealing to the little girls who came to visit. [D] |4|

Flannery also spent time <u>dreaming about future fame</u>[5]. Though the space was small, it ran up against a back alley, which was primarily used by workers and servants; at the very least this space, meant first and foremost for growing different plants, must have been at least moderately entertaining for the young girl! However, the family also used the space to raise chickens. Flannery, an imaginative child, had other

3. The writer is considering deleting the preceding sentence. Should the sentence be kept or deleted?

   A. Kept, because it gives us a window into the everyday childhood environment of Flannery O'Connor.
   B. Kept, because it makes clear that trees are more valued today than in the past.
   C. Deleted, because it doesn't make clear whether or not Flannery O'Connor ever played soccer in the square.
   D. Deleted, because it it not specific enough about the century in which Flannery O'Connor was born.

4. The writer wants to add the following sentence to the preceding paragraph:

   > Like all girls their age, they would draw and play make-believe.

   This sentence would most logically be placed at:

   F. Point A.
   G. Point B.
   H. Point C.
   J. Point D.

5. Which choice best introduces the subject of the paragraph?

   A. NO CHANGE
   B. in the backyard garden.
   C. lounging in the backseat of their car.
   D. gathering eggs and cleaning the coop.

plans for them beyond laying eggs. |6| In fact, she was given a small taste of fame when a crew came to film the fowl she had trained to walk backwards!

[1] In those days, there was no air conditioning. [2] The most common reprieve from the heat was the simple opening of windows. [3] Today, fans of O'Connor speculate just what kinds of people and conversations she saw and overheard on the streets below her home. [4] Surely early inspirations for her over-the-top characters can be traced to this time and place. |7|

6. At this point, the author is considering adding the following true statement:

> Like other families of the time, the O'Connors would eat eggs and the chickens that laid them.

Should the writer make this addition here?

- **F.** Yes, because it shows how the O'Connor family was similar to other families.
- **G.** Yes, because it logically bridges the previous sentence to the rest of the paragraph.
- **H.** No, because at this point in the essay the reader does not need more information about Flannery O'Connor and her childhood home.
- **J.** No, because the information provided, while not explicitly stated, should be assumed to be true.

7. For the sake of the logic and coherence of this paragraph, Sentence 2 should be placed:

- **A.** where it is now.
- **B.** before Sentence 1.
- **C.** after Sentence 3.
- **D.** after Sentence 4.

Question 8 asks about the preceding passage as a whole.

8. Suppose the author's main purpose had been to compare and contrast the characters of Flannery O'Connor's fiction. Would this essay accomplish that purpose?

- **F.** Yes, because it discusses the kinds of people she likely heard outside her window.
- **G.** Yes, because the characters she created in Savannah stayed in her mind when she was forced to move to Milledgeville.
- **H.** No, because the essay describes the history of Savannah in tedious detail.
- **J.** No, because the essay provides an overview of her childhood home and what it was like to live there.

PASSAGE II

The Texas State Fair

[1]

They say that everything is bigger in Texas. I got to witness this first-hand when my family was vacationing in the Dallas area. It all began when my father playfully asked us children, "How about a turkey leg for dinner?" |9| My little brothers and I did not understand what he meant until we saw the spectacle for ourselves. [A]

[2]

We began to get excited when we heard our father's stomach rumbling. (10) We were going to the fair! After we parked the car we made our way through the hundreds of vendors lining the entrance. My brothers had to stop at every other booth, and they begged my mother and father to buy them all sorts of toys and pets we did not need. [B] Finally, we emerged into the open air and witnessed hundreds of rides and games to play.

9. The writer is considering deleting the preceding sentence. Should the sentence be kept or deleted?

A. Kept, because it deepens the reader's understanding of the father's desires.
B. Kept, because it helps to build anticipation that is fully realized in the next paragraph.
C. Deleted, because it adds a level of technical detail that is unnecessary at this point in the essay.
D. Deleted, because it detracts from the lighthearted tone of the rest of the paragraph.

10. Which choice most effectively explains the excitement of the children and logically coheres to the sentence that follows?

F. NO CHANGE
G. glimpsed a giant carousel from a distance.
H. fell asleep in the backseat, only to be awakened a few minutes later in a large parking lot.
J. when the excitement began to build.

[3]

My father bought us packs of little tickets, which were used as currency to get on the various rides. |11| My brothers used almost all of theirs on a small dragon roller coaster. [C] I, on the other hand, was looking for something a little more daring. It's not everyday that I get to choose from so many different thrills!

[4]

When I first laid eyes on the Starspinner 5000, I knew it was what I had been searching for. My father and I waited in line for what felt like an eternity. |12| Finally, when we reached the ticket-taker, we paid 4 tickets apiece, entered the large circle, and took our places. [D] We were instructed to stand with our backs to the padded walls, and we quickly learned why.

[5]

<u>All of a sudden the room started to spin</u>[13]: faster and faster it spun until we were pinned to the walls behind us. As we increased speed, the walls themselves slid upwards, lifting us up from the floor. At first I was worried for my father, thinking that at his age he couldn't handle it. However when I looked

11. At this point, the writer is considering adding the following true statement:

> Although my brothers chose cotton candy, the sweet smell of frying dough urged me to order a funnel cake topped with powdered sugar.

Should the statement be added here?

A. Yes, because it adds a fun detail to what is already a lighthearted essay.
B. Yes, because it answers previously raised questions about what the family would eat that evening.
C. No, because most readers are unfamiliar with food commonly found at a fair.
D. No, because it provides details that interrupt the logical flow of the paragraph.

12. If the writer were to delete the preceding sentence, the paragraph would primarily lose:

F. a transition from the narrator's initial desire to ride to the fulfillment of that same desire.
G. an unnecessary exaggeration.
H. a contextual detail that helps provide context for the fear that both father and daughter are experiencing.
J. a detail that teaches the reader that it takes time to count tickets and ensure you have enough of them to board the ride.

13. Which choice provides the most effective transition to Paragraph 5?

A. NO CHANGE
B. My stomach was churning
C. I could hear my father screaming with excitement next to me
D. I was seeing stars

over, he was grinning ear to ear. **|14|**

14. Given that all of the statements are true, which one, if added here, would best conclude the paragraph and the essay by referring back to the opening paragraph?

F. Maybe we should have ridden the carousel after all!
G. The book of tickets slipped out of his pocket, flew into the air, and were out of reach until the ride finally came to a complete stop.
H. "I think I'll skip out on the turkey leg!" he yelled, which made me chuckle.
J. My brothers had no idea what they were missing out on; dragon roller coasters could never create a thrill like this!

Questions 15 and 16 ask about the preceding passage as a whole.

15. The writer is considering adding the following sentence to the essay:

> To them, it was beyond exciting to go up and down the simple track at high speeds.

If the writer were to add this sentence, it would most logically be placed at:

A. Point A in Paragraph 1.
B. Point B in Paragraph 2.
C. Point C in Paragraph 3.
D. Point D in Paragraph 4.

16. Suppose the author's main purpose had been to write about a fun family memory as a gift for her father. Would this essay accomplish that purpose?

F. Yes, because the essay focuses on an exciting experience shared by the author and her father.
G. Yes, because the essay discusses many fun activities the family did together, such as snorkeling, camping, and playing charades.
H. No, because the essay is designed to scare readers away from riding the Starspinner 5000.
J. No, because the essay rarely mentions the author's father.

Step 1 Correct Answers

I'm going to go out on a limb here and guess that that wasn't the most fun you've ever had. It might have been a little painful, tense, and tedious, but that is good: *we are building a skill.* The format of each question is based on real, recent ACT English questions. Here are the answers for all 16 questions.

Passage I
1: C
2: J
3: A
4: G
5: B
6: J
7: A
8: J

Passage II
9: B
10: G
11: D
12: F
13: A
14: H
15: C
16: F

Stumped on any? You will find the explanations for each answer beginning on page 488.

STEP 2

Verbose and Redundant

In the last Step, we used context clues to correctly place or delete sentences or smaller phrases. Here, we will keep up the very basic idea that, on ACT English, there is often a *best* answer. Specifically, we will learn two new concepts (all while building upon Step 1):

Verbose - here's a rule of thumb: less is more. What does that mean? It means that if something necessary can be said in less words, it is better. Check out this sentence:

I chewed, swallowed, and digested my hamburger last night.

Any grammar errors? Nope. But notice anything wrong? Hopefully you see that the words "chewed, swallowed, and digested" could be replaced with one word: *ate*. Recognizing when phrases or sentences are overly wordy, or more specifically which combination of words says the right thing with the least number of words, is a fundamentally crucial skill to move the needle.

Redundant - one thing the ACT wants you to recognize is when an underlined portion is: a) Saying the same thing twice, and b) Being redundant (see what I did there?). Check out the following example:

Eventually, I will clean my room at some point.

At first glance this sentence seems fine. But do you notice the redundancy? "Eventually" and "at some point" are synonyms: they mean the same thing, and both imply that a day is coming in the future on which the author will clean his or her room. The ACT will want you to notice that this portion of the sentence should be deleted and the sentence should be ended after "room."

Step 2 Mini-Lesson: Best Word/Phrase Placement and Jumbled Words

We are working on recognizing *best* answers. Here's a strategy that you MUST be aware of: ***LISTEN***. That's odd advice for a test taken in a silent room, but if a group of words or a sentence "sounds" (in your mind, that is) off or strange, ***it probably is***. Even if you don't read a lot, you've absorbed a lot of well-written English over the course of your life. Here are two types of questions that test your ability to listen.

1) **Best Word or Phrase Placement** - One type of less-asked-about-but-related-question that I've seen is the *best* location of a word or phrase within a sentence. Check out this example:

Gilbert J. Smith, a reporter for the *Washington Wire*, reached a surprising conclusion after financially interviewing hundreds of successful business owners as to how to achieve lifetime stability: read often!

You should be asking yourself: how can someone financially interview another person? It doesn't really make sense. Thus, the ACT will want you to read and reread the sentence with the word or phrase in a proper place; in this case, one proper place for the adverb "financially" could be before "successful."

2) **The Jumbled Up Words** - A second type of less-asked-about-but-related-question that I've seen is the jumbled words kind of question. Look at this example:

My brother will be the one being coming near by to pick me up.

Umm…what? That should "sound" off, because it is. We need a less wordy phrase that actually makes sense to replace this jumble. That would be "be coming."

Without further ado, let's get into it; this book, after all, is about maximizing the productivity of your time. The following three passages test skills from Step 1 as well as the current Step.

PASSAGE I

Uluru

[1]

In late July, 1873, William Gosse spotted a large, almost mountainous rock rising from the Australian landscape in July.[1] He named it Ayers Rock after Sir Henry Ayers, who at the time was the Chief Secretary of South Australia. **|2|** Unbeknownst to Gosse, the rock already possessed a name: Uluru. **[A]** This latter name, it being Uluru,[3] was given to it by the Pitjantjatjara, the aboriginal people who regard the rock as sacred.

1. **A.** NO CHANGE
   B. landscape in late July.
   C. landscape in late July, 1873.
   D. landscape.

2. The writer is considering deleting the preceding sentence. Should the sentence be kept or deleted?

   F. Kept, because Ayers, as the discoverer of the rock, deserves more recognition.
   G. Kept, because it gives a detail that contrasts well with the formation's other name.
   H. Deleted, because it gives unnecessary details about Sir Henry Aires, which detracts from the paragraph's purpose.
   J. Deleted, because it it raises questions in the mind of the reader that are left unanswered.

3. **A.** NO CHANGE
   B. Uluru
   C. , it is Uluru,
   D. DELETE the underlined portion

[2]

Uluru is an inselberg, a hill or mountain composed of rock that emerges from the surrounding landscape like a mountain.[4] **[B]** Needless to say, one of the reasons Uluru is so attractive to tourists is its absolute segregation from other hills, peaks, or mountains. In fact, the closest and nearest[5] similar

4. **F.** NO CHANGE
   G. that surrounds it.
   H. while being made mostly of rock.
   J. in an isolated fashion.

5. **A.** NO CHANGE
   B. nearest, and closest
   C. closest
   D. most in proximity

formation is Mount Olga, which is pretty close by. 6

[3]

For the most part, Uluru is composed of arkose. [C] This is a type of sandstone, the composition of which is at least 25% feldspar. It is believed that Uluru is a remnant 7 of a mountain building event called the Peterman Orogeny. [D] While other smaller arkose formations have since dissipated, Uluru has survived the test of time that has passed by. 8

[4]

Many animal species are native to the park in and around Uluru. For example, 7 different species and types 9 of bats take advantage of the rock formation for roosting during the day, and at least 70 10 species of reptiles have been documented as well. |11| Some species, such as the black-flanked rock-wallaby and the common brushtail possum, are historically native to the area, but are locally extinct. That is not

6. Which choice most effectively illustrates the precise distance between Uluru and Mount Olga?

F. NO CHANGE
G. which lies 16 miles to the West.
H. which is not too far away.
J. which, by today's standards, is accessible by car.

7. A. NO CHANGE
B. remnant, meaning a leftover,
C. small remaining quantity of something
D. remnant, remainder, or leftover

8. F. NO CHANGE
G. time that has passed.
H. time.
J. time that, to this day, is still passing.

9. A. NO CHANGE
B. species
C. types:
D. categorical types

10. F. NO CHANGE
G. 70, or maybe more than 70,
H. 70, 71, 72, or maybe even more
J. as of today, up to, or perhaps exactly, 70

11. At this point, the writer is considering adding the following true statement:

Snakes are an example of a reptile.

Should the statement be added here?

A. Yes, because it answers a question asked earlier in the essay.
B. Yes, because it gives a detail that deepens the reader's understanding of the vast amount of animal life around Uluru.
C. No, because it gives a detail stated elsewhere in the paragraph.
D. No, because gives information about animal species and not about Uluru.

all: various species of bats also call Uluru home. **|12|**

[5]

In order to accommodate both the native history and English discovery of the inselberg, the Australian government named the rock Ayers Rock/Uluru in 1993. However, this was reversed in 2002 and it is <u>now and henceforth will be known as</u> [13] the Uluru/Ayers Rock. This dual name signals to tourists that the formation is of historical significance.

12. The writer is considering deleting the preceding sentence. Should the sentence be kept or deleted?

- **F.** Kept, because it details another species of animal that lives in or around Uluru.
- **G.** Kept, because it builds sympathy for Uluru and the animal species living there.
- **H.** Deleted, because it gives information that has already been stated elsewhere.
- **J.** Deleted, because the topic of the sentence fits better with an earlier paragraph

13.
- **A.** NO CHANGE
- **B.** now known as
- **C.** referred to by the name of
- **D.** called a name that is the result of this reversal:

Questions 14 and 15 ask about the preceding passage as a whole.

14. The writer is considering adding the following sentence to the essay:

> This episode took place as early as the Cambrian period 530 million years ago and as late as the Neoproterozoic Era 550 million years ago.

If the writer were to add this sentence, it would most logically be placed at:

- **F.** Point A in Paragraph 1.
- **G.** Point B in Paragraph 2.
- **H.** Point C in Paragraph 3.
- **J.** Point D in Paragraph 3.

15. Suppose the author's main purpose had been to write a brief essay about the history, importance, and geological makeup of an Australian landmark. Would this essay accomplish that purpose?

- **A.** Yes, because the essay details the author's firsthand experience visiting Uluru.
- **B.** Yes, because the essay speaks of Uluru's discovery, meaning, and scientific composition and importance.
- **C.** No, because, while the author mentions that Uluru is composed of arkose, he or she never discusses Uluru's history.
- **D.** No, because there is not enough information about Sir Henry Ayers, after whom the rock was named.

PASSAGE II

The Palace of Versailles

[1]

Extravagant palaces were a <u>common fixture</u> [16] of royalty throughout European history. Massive homes filled with expensive décor illustrated a monarch's

16.
- **F.** NO CHANGE
- **G.** commonly regular feature
- **H.** feature that was common
- **J.** regular, and ordinarily common

wealth, power, and money. They could often host opulent parties for hundreds of guests. Several of these centuries-old structures standing remain still today, and many have been re-purposed as historical landmarks or tourist attractions. |19|

[2]

Located near the village of Versailles in France, the Palace of Versailles uniquely stands apart for both its beauty and history. The Hall of Mirrors, a massive mirror-filled room built for entertaining, is perhaps the best-known large feature of the Palace. Other extravagant features include the massive Garden of Versailles and the Royal Opera. |22| With ornate statues and decorations around every corner of the Palace, the Palace of Versailles is often described as one of not only Europe's but the world's

17. A. NO CHANGE
    B. wealth and power.
    C. wealth, power, and control.
    D. powerful hoards of gold and money.

18. F. NO CHANGE
    G. today standing remain still,
    H. remain standing today,
    J. remain standing still today,

19. Given that all of the following statements are true, which one, if added here, would most effectively end Paragraph 1 and transition to Paragraph 2?

    A. While all of these former homes are significant, few are as well known as the Palace of Versailles.
    B. On the other hand, some of them have not survived the test of time and have been destroyed.
    C. Historical landmarks are all over Europe, and many of them have extravagant gardens.
    D. Many groups in and around not only Europe but the whole world are forming to raise funds to save many of these sites.

20. F. NO CHANGE
    G. stands apart
    H. stands uniquely
    J. stands

21. A. NO CHANGE
    B. Palace.
    C. feature of the Palace.
    D. giant, mountainous, humongous feature of the Palace.

22. If the writer were to delete the preceding sentence, the paragraph would primarily lose a statement that:

    F. makes clear the availability of the Palace to visitors.
    G. indicates the tragic implications for Europe if the Palace were to be forgotten.
    H. guides visitors as they tour the Palace from the Eastern half to Western half.
    J. concludes a summary of the grander features of the Palace.

23. A. NO CHANGE
    B. each and every decorated corner,
    C. each and every Palace corner,
    D. each corner,

most beatified and aesthetically pleasing places. 24

[3]

The beauty of the Palace of Versailles continues to attract visitors from all over. To this day, the Palace remains one of the most popular destinations in Europe. Travelers also come to learn about the historical significance of the Palace. |26| After the Revolution, the Palace saw many uses, including as a diplomatic meeting place. Heads of state would meet at the Palace to discuss global issues. Arguably the most famous diplomatic document signed within the Palace walls was the Treaty of Versailles, which ended World War I.

25

[4]

For roughly a century, the Palace of Versailles was only used as the home of the French monarch for about 100 years. In the years after the Revolution, the Palace went through disrepair and many phases of restoration. It has served as a museum, a diplomatic hall, and even a storage space. Today, the Palace of Versailles is a UNESCO World Heritage site and is open to visitors, roughly 8 million of which pass through its doors each year. All guests come to admire the Palace's splendor while learning about the

27 28

24. **F.** NO CHANGE
G. easy-on-the-eye
H. attractively pretty
J. beautiful

25. **A.** NO CHANGE
B. being one of the utmost
C. much like that of some of the most
D. to be among the highest

26. At this point, the writer is considering adding the following true statement:

> It was the seat of the French government from 1682 until the French Revolution in 1789.

Should the statement be added here?

F. Yes, because it provides specific evidence of the historical significance mentioned in the previous sentence.
G. Yes, because the author previously stated that it was the French Revolution that was responsible for the Palace's destruction.
H. No, because the beauty of the Palace has already been stressed enough in the essay.
J. No, because it fails to connect the preceding sentence to the sentence that follows in a logical way.

27. **A.** NO CHANGE
B. As a home for kings, queens, and other royalty, the Palace
C. The Palace
D. Palace

28. Which of the following placements for the underlined portion makes it clear that the physical condition of the Palace has improved and worsened multiple times since the French Revolution?

F. Where it is now
G. After the words *In the*
H. After the word *through*
J. Before the word *Palace*

history that took place within its four walls. [29]

29. A. NO CHANGE
   B. within.
   C. beneath its ceiling and above its floors.
   D. DELETE the underlined portion and end the sentence with a period

Question 30 asks about the preceding passage as a whole.

30. Suppose the author's main purpose had been to compare and contrast various historic European buildings. Would this essay accomplish that purpose?

   F. Yes, because the Palace of Versailles is one of many such buildings.
   G. Yes, because the first sentence of the essay mentions the "Extravagant palaces" of European history
   H. No, because only the Palace of Versailles is detailed and described in the essay.
   J. No, because the essay says nothing about other European palaces or buildings.

Step 2 Correct Answers

Passage I
1: D
2: G
3: D
4: J
5: C
6: G
7: A
8: H
9: B
10: F
11: D
12: H
13: B
14: J
15: B

Passage II
16: F
17: B
18: H
19: A
20: G
21: C
22: J
23: D
24: J
25: A
26: F
27: C
28: H
29: B
30: H

Stumped on any? You will find the explanations for each answer beginning on page 490.

STEP 3

Commas

We are now starting to enter the territory of what I defined before Step 1 as "grammar," meaning the kinds of questions that have a right or a wrong answer. In this case, we are talking about commas.

When I was in high school, I remember getting some advice from a counselor at my school about this. She said regarding commas, "When in doubt, take it out." However, I don't think that advice is very helpful. After all, it could very well be the case that you, the student, need to recognize that a comma (or two!) belongs when there is not one shown or used.

I have different advice: in ACT English, *every comma is **deliberate**.*

What does that mean?

That means that commas aren't thrown into sentences to create "pauses" just so people can take a breath. Of course commas create pauses in a sentence, but that doesn't mean that every pause *in your mind* or every pause *in your speech* needs a comma. It also doesn't mean that, just because a pause "sounds nice," that a comma belongs there or is *better* there. Again, with commas, we've left the realm of the *best* answer. Now, the ACT expects you to recognize the *correct* answer. Think about the following sentence:

There typically are a vast and overwhelming number of stainless-steel appliances that provide husbands and wives the ability to spend more of their time doing what they love to do and less of their time doing the things around the house that they do not want to do in just about 86.574% of households on the Southeastern point of reference on an official map of the Continental United States of America.

While that sentence makes almost no sense (I made it up off the top of my head), there is one thing about it you should know: it is grammatically correct, and it needs no commas. I'm trying to show you that just because a sentence could use a pause when spoken or even thought, it doesn't mean that one belongs on the written page.

The first time I wrote this Step, I had to remember that the purpose of this book is for you not to feel like you are reading a technical manual. I deleted pages of very specific rules about commas, phrases, etc. English teachers may not like that, but I want you to improve via *practice*. Thus, my explanations and lessons will be kept to an absolute minimum.

We will begin, of course, with the comma usage most likely to be tested on the ACT and end with the comma usage least likely to be tested (though still tested, and thus important).

1) Setting off nonessential words or phrases

The most-needed comma skill on recent ACT English tests is the ability to set off nonessential words or phrases with a pair of commas. In this case, commas act kind of like parentheses. The word or phrase that is offset is disruptive. Before we get to examples, think of it like this: imagine you are driving down the highway at 60 MPH and decide to take a detour off the main road to see the world's largest ball of yarn without stopping. You slow the car down as you exit and drive slowly past the yarn ball before getting back on the highway. The detour isn't essential to the trip you're taking, and you never stopped. That is what happens to a sentence when a nonessential word or phrase is inserted into it. Check out the following sentences. "Before" means no comma is necessary. "After" means a nonessential word or phrase has been added and has to be set off by commas.

Before: The Auburn Tigers are my favorite football team.

After: The Auburn Tigers**, not the Alabama Crimson Tide,** are my favorite football team.

Before: My neighbor has trophies scattered throughout her home.

After: My neighbor**, a former college athlete,** has trophies scattered throughout her home.

Before: There are no snakes in Ireland.

After: There are no snakes**, however,** in Ireland.

Your ability to spot these disruptive phrases, and to know that they are set off with commas (like parentheses…like this!) is comma necessity #1.

2) Setting off introductory word, adverb, or phrase, and setting off other dependent clauses

Before we begin, we need to define a couple of terms. I've mentioned them before, but now is the time to understand what these things mean. You may already know, and that's great, but in case you don't...

Independent Clause - for our purposes an independent clause is simply a complete thought or, you might say, a complete sentence; a thought that can stand alone as a sentence. We don't need to get too technical because this, after all, is an ACT English prep book and not a high school English book. Here are some examples of such clauses:

a) Claudia went to the grocery store.

b) One-third of hippopotamuses have no front teeth.

c) Getting nauseous is my new normal.

d) It rained on our wedding day.

Dependent Clause - for our purposes, when I say "dependent clause" I mean a phrase that can't stand alone as a sentence. Remember the strategy or advice to *listen* and simply determine which sounds strange? That can help you to identify when something is not a complete thought or sentence. Check out the following dependent clauses and notice how strange they are when treated like an independent thought or sentence.

a) Because she needed an ingredient for her recipe.

b) Despite brushing daily.

c) Whenever I eat shellfish.

d) Which is unfortunate.

It ought to irritate you a bit to see these clauses treated like complete sentences and ended with a period. That is the kind of recognition you will need to ace many ACT comma questions. Depending on how you try to combine clauses, they may or may not need commas.

a) Claudia went to the grocery store because she needed an ingredient for her recipe.

Because she needed an ingredient for her recipe, Claudia went to the grocery store.

b) One-third of hippopotamuses have no front teeth despite brushing daily.

Despite brushing daily, one-third of hippopotamuses have no front teeth

c) Getting nauseous is my new normal whenever I eat shellfish.

Whenever I eat shellfish, getting nauseous is my new normal.

d) It rained on our wedding day, which is unfortunate.

Putting the first three of these clauses at the beginning of sentences disrupts the flow; they need to be offset by a comma. Some clauses (like the last one that says "which is unfortunate") only work at the end of a sentence after a comma (in fact, unless it is beginning a question, the word "which" will usually come after a comma, and always if beginning a clause).

Again, *listen* to the sentence. Does it flow? Does it need a pit stop? We can talk all day about the hundreds of technical English rules regarding clauses and subordinating conjunctions and exceptions to rules, etc. That is not going to be helpful for most people because *practice creates recognition.*

One last thing about this comma usage: if a sentence begins with an adverb (usually they end in *ly*), it must be set off by a comma.

Incorrect: Unbelievably the cat lived to be 22 years old.

Correct: Unbelievably, the cat lived to be 22 years old.

PS I have no idea how many hippos are actually missing their front teeth.

3) Setting off adjectives in a series

Simple rule here: adjectives in a row that describe the same word often need commas to separate them. You don't need one after the last adjective. For example:

There's a mean, scary monster under my bed.

See what I did there? We need an adjective after "mean," but not after "scary." However, I said a second ago that this is "often" the case. There's an exception. If the adjective *can't be detached* from the noun, because it is essentially a part of the noun, it is treated like a part of the noun. This is better illustrated with an example:

It's not a monster. That's just my smelly little brother.

See how there's no adjective after the word "smelly"? That's because "little brother" itself acts like a noun. To test this, rearrange the adjectives in the phrase. If it still "works," you need commas. If not, you don't. Look at this example:

Before: That's just my smelly little brother.

After: That's just my little smelly brother.

The change doesn't work; now it sounds like my brother is physically little, like a leprechaun, instead of "younger." There are lots of noun/adjective combinations like this. Bowling ball. Cheddar cheese. Etc.

4) Combining two independent clauses

Use a comma to combine, essentially, two sentences into one. Before I get to an example, what must follow the comma is a conjunction, which can be remembered by the acronym FANBOYS (for, and, nor, but, or, yet, so). Let's combine these two sentences into one.

Before: I went to the grocery store. I forgot to buy cheese.

After: I went to the grocery store**, but** I forgot to buy cheese.

Simple enough. Remember that what might be asked for is the *correct* conjunction. If our new, complex sentence said this, it wouldn't make sense: "I went to the grocery store**, so** I forgot to buy cheese." **But** is the appropriate conjunction for this pair of clauses.

Step 3 Mini-Lesson: Linking Independent Clauses and Related Grammar

There are multiple ways to link two sentences together into one complex sentence. Let's look at those ways and the other ways to use the punctuation this brings us: semicolons, em dashes, and colons.

Semicolon

The semicolon has one use: to combine two independent clauses into one (but no FANBOYS allowed!)

Correct: I am tired of typing; writing is tedious.

Incorrect: I am tired of typing; and writing is tedious. *-can't have that "and" in there!*

Em-dash

This is just a long dash, like a double hyphen, this thing: —

You have to know it can do two things: combine independent clauses and replace parentheses.

Correct: I am tired of typing—writing is tedious.

Correct: The strength required to mountain climb—gained by months of training—is unbelievable.

Incorrect: The strength required to mountain climb, gained by months of training—is unbelievable.

Why incorrect? When used like parentheses, em dashes must come in pairs. The comma should be an —.

Colons

Colons have many uses (combine independent clauses, set off lists or quotes, set off dramatic nouns or phrases, etc.). Here's what you need to know: they *always* follow a complete sentence or thought.

Correct: I am tired of typing: writing is tedious!

Correct: I have three friends: Mom, Dad, and a tree.

Correct: The politician began his stump speech: "Please vote for me."

Correct: I reeled in the fish and couldn't believe what I caught: a shark!

Incorrect: Physical labor: believe me it is demanding! *-This colon doesn't follow a complete thought!*

OK....give the following practice your best shot! It is heavy on Step 3 but strengthens Steps 2 and 1!

PASSAGE I

Unity Through Tragedy

[1]

Like <u>many Americans I</u> [1] remember where I was on September 11, 2001. That day started off as normal as usual. I <u>woke up</u> [2] to an alarm at 6:15 AM, got ready for the school day, and was picked up by a <u>down the street good friend.</u> [3] I attended my high-school <u>classes unaware of what was happening in New York</u> [4] through mid-morning. [A]

[2]

When I arrived in English class, my teacher put aside the lesson for the day and simply turned on the television. **|5|** The first of the two towers of the World Trade Center had already been struck by the plane, and at this point there was speculation that this was no mere accident. Horrifyingly, I watched as the second tower was <u>struck, and</u> [6] as the Twin Towers then collapsed one after another.

1. **A.** NO CHANGE
B. many Americans, I
C. many, Americans I
D. many, Americans, I

2. **F.** NO CHANGE
G. rose up from my mattress
H. awoke up
J. woke up, not down,

3. **A.** NO CHANGE
B. down the street, good friend.
C. good friend down the street.
D. DELETE the underlined portion and end the sentence with a period.

4. **F.** NO CHANGE
G. classes unaware, of what was happening, in New York
H. classes unaware of what was, happening in, New York
J. classes, unaware of what was happening in New York,

5. At this point, the writer is considering adding the following true statement:

> In a 9th grade English class, a student can expect to study vocabulary and grammar, among other things.

Should the statement be added here?

A. Yes, because it provides much needed context for the author's lived reality.
B. Yes, because it creates a contrast between what was normal and the events of the day.
C. No, because the sentence shifts the focus of the paragraph away from the author's lived experience.
D. No, because the paragraph's focus is on Math class, not English class.

6. **F.** NO CHANGE
G. struck, but
H. struck
J. struck and

[3]

There are no words that can describe what happened to United America that day. It was a moment that defined a generation. [B] This is particularly true for the families of the nearly 3,000 Americans who lost their lives. However, what took place in the United States in the months following the terrorist attack is something that those not only my age, but also those from a generation before me—will never forget: unity.

7. **A.** NO CHANGE
   B. America
   C. the nation north of Mexico and south of Canada
   D. the United, America

8. **F.** NO CHANGE
   G. age but
   H. age—but
   J. age (but

9. **A.** NO CHANGE
   B. forget; unity.
   C. forget: being a united people.
   D. forget, unity.

[4]

Political squabbles, divergence of opinion, and differences in creed were all set to the side in favor of a simpler truer identity statement: *I am American!* [C] Honor due to veterans was renewed. American flags, once readily available at stores, were on backorder due to a seemingly unending demand at retail locations across the country.

10. **F.** NO CHANGE
    G. simpler, truer identity
    H. truer simpler identity
    J. identity, simpler truer,

11. **A.** NO CHANGE
    B. for American flags.
    C. when once they were easy to purchase.
    D. nationwide.

[5]

When I look back on that day, I am horrified at the atrocities that took place by the work and evil schemes of only a small handful of people. Because more than twenty years have passed since these awful, terrorist attacks, I have noticed, unfortunately,

12. **F.** NO CHANGE
    G. awful terrorist attacks,
    H. awful, terrorist, attacks,
    J. awful terrorist attacks

that the pride and unity [13] that strengthened in the months following has slowly faded away. [D] Many have forgotten that what unites a nation ought to transcend everyday and political differences.

13. **A.** NO CHANGE
B. pride, and unity,
C. pride, and unity
D. pride and unity,

Questions 14 and 15 ask about the preceding passage as a whole.

14. The writer is considering adding the following sentence to the essay:

> People of all walks of life came together over dinner.

If the writer were to add this sentence, it would most logically be placed at:

F. Point A in Paragraph 1.
G. Point B in Paragraph 3.
H. Point C in Paragraph 4.
J. Point D in Paragraph 5.

15. Suppose the author's main purpose had been to write a history of the United States of America. Would this essay accomplish that purpose?

A. Yes, because the essay details an important, though tragic, moment in American history.
B. Yes, because the essay is chronological like all historical accounts.
C. No, because the essay says nothing about events within the history of the United States.
D. No, because the essay describes only one event of American history from a personal perspective.

PASSAGE II

The Colosseum

Few archetypes of ancient civilization are better known than the Colosseum. An iconic symbol of Roman history the Colosseum, [16] was first constructed nearly 2000 years ago. Today, only about one-third of the original massive amphitheater still stands; what [17] does remain demonstrates the enormous scope of the original structure. Looking at the ruins, it is not

16. **F.** NO CHANGE
G. Roman, history the Colosseum
H. Roman history, the Colosseum
J. Roman, history, the Colosseum

17. Which of the following alternatives to the underlined portion would NOT be acceptable?

A. stands. What
B. stands—what
C. stands, but what
D. stands; but what

difficult to <u>imagine inside a mind</u> the size and majesty of the amphitheater at its peak.
18

Construction of the Colosseum first began around 70 A.D. under the <u>Roman Emperor Vespasian.</u> He decided to construct the amphitheater near the center of the city on the site of a palace that had been destroyed in the Great Fire of Rome. Funds for construction <u>were generated</u> by the Roman siege of Jerusalem in the same year. The Colosseum was fully constructed <u>after ten years</u> which was considered very fast for such a structure in the first century. **|22|**
19 20 21

The Colosseum is a free-standing stone structure. Builders used ancient forms of concrete to create certain <u>parts, pieces, and sections</u> of the main building. The <u>amphitheater, overall,</u> covers about 300,000 square feet. It once hosted gladiator battles, animal fights, mock military maneuvers, and other forms of popular entertainment. For centuries, the Colosseum was the largest amphitheater in the entire
23 24

18. **F.** NO CHANGE
G. imagine inside your mind
H. think up well
J. imagine

19. **A.** NO CHANGE
B. Roman, Emperor Vespasian.
C. emperor, Roman, Vespasian.
D. Vespasian, who was both Roman and an emperor.

20. **F.** NO CHANGE
G. were to be being gotten
H. being brought forth
J. generated, were those

21. **A.** NO CHANGE
B. after ten years;
C. after, ten years,
D. after ten years,

22. Given that all the choices are true, which one most effectively introduces the reader to the fact that the Colosseum was overseen by consecutive emperors?

F. The Emperor Vespasian was not born into a noble family by any stretch of the imagination, but earned his way to the throne by military prowess.
G. During this time, much of Europe, Northern Africa, and even parts of Asia were increasingly dominated by the Roman Empire.
H. Although Emperor Vespasian had died the year prior, it was his son, Emperor Titus, who opened the Colosseum with a large festival in 80 A.D.
J. Other projects on that scale often took decades or even centuries to fully construct.

23. **A.** NO CHANGE
B. parts, pieces, sections, and segments
C. parts, pieces and sections
D. parts

24. **F.** NO CHANGE
G. amphitheater, overall
H. amphitheater overall
J. amphitheater: overall,

world, and [25] remarkably could hold as many as 50,000 spectators at one time. However, in the 6th century, instability in the Western Roman Empire forced an end to its events. **|26|**

Over time, the Colosseum became abandoned entirely. Large parts were removed to provide stone for other construction projects, much [27] of the ornate construction—such as marble statues, [28] was taken away or destroyed. Weather and natural erosion also played a role in its slow ruination as the once bustling amphitheater faded slowly into antiquity. While some form of conservation of the Colosseum technically began in the 18th century. Actual [29] restoration did not begin until the mid-1990s. **|30|**

25. **A.** NO CHANGE
B. world, but
C. world and
D. world;

26. The writer is considering deleting the preceding sentence. Should the sentence be kept or deleted?

F. Kept, because it gives the reader deeper insight into world events.
G. Kept, because it fittingly describes how the Colosseum's flourishing activity was halted.
H. Deleted, because it shifts the focus of the essay away from the Colosseum.
J. Deleted, because it makes no mention of the Roman Emperor Titus and whether or not he attended the Colosseum regularly.

27. **A.** NO CHANGE
B. projects; much
C. projects much,
D. projects: much,

28. **F.** NO CHANGE
G. statues
H. statues:
J. statues—

29. **A.** NO CHANGE
B. began. In the 18th century, actual
C. began in the 18th century, actual
D. began, in the 18th century, actual

Question 30 asks about the preceding passage as a whole.

30. Given that all of the following statements are true, which one, if added here, would best conclude the paragraph and the essay by referring back to the opening paragraph?

F. Although repair is ongoing, the Colosseum continues to be one of history's most recognizable landmarks.
G. It is true, however, that weather continues to affect landmarks worldwide.
H. Ultimately, the Roman Empire would fall, although the city of Rome carries on.
J. It is up to all of us to pitch in, donate, and be a part of restoration projects worldwide

PASSAGE III

Stunt Kite

I used to think kites were boring or childish, but that changed when my uncle brought over a peculiar <u>kind of kite</u> [31] for us to fly together. When he began to set it <u>up I noticed something odd:</u> [32] instead of one string for height, this kite was controlled by two. As a heavy wind <u>blew over the field, we</u> [33] launched the kite, but unlike the lazy drifting of most I had flown, this kite shot into the air like a <u>very fast, rapid bullet.</u> [34] I knew then that something different was at hand.

I watched on in amazement and wide eyed as my uncle deftly controlled not only the height, but also <u>knew how to cause the kite to fly higher.</u> [35] This was done by controlling the <u>balance</u> [36] I could now see why he needed two strings: pulling on one string caused the kite to bank right, and pulling on the other string caused it to bank left. But that was not all, <u>for he</u> [37] could also do flips, dives, stalls, and other tricks.

<u>Suddenly as I was watching,</u> [38] the kite started to dive towards the ground. I shouted to

31. **A.** NO CHANGE
B. kind
C. type that was not that boring
D. variety of my uncle's

32. **F.** NO CHANGE
G. up, I noticed something: odd,
H. up I noticed: something odd
J. up, I noticed something odd:

33. **A.** NO CHANGE
B. blew, over the field, we
C. blew over, the field
D. DELETE the underlined portion.

34. **F.** NO CHANGE
G. bullet.
H. very fast rapid bullet.
J. bullet, quickly.

35. Which choice best emphasizes that the uncle possesses a control over the kite that is not limited merely to its distance from the ground?

A. NO CHANGE
B. where and in which direction the kite flew.
C. watched on in amazement by my side.
D. just how high the kite could fly.

36. **F.** NO CHANGE
G. balance and
H. balance, and
J. balance,

37. **A.** NO CHANGE
B. for, he
C. for, my uncle,
D. for he, my uncle,

38. **F.** NO CHANGE
G. Suddenly as I was watching
H. Suddenly, as I was watching,
J. Suddenly,

my uncle thinking, for a moment, he had lost control; he smiled, and when the kite was just a few feet from a crash landing, he pulled back hard. **|40|**

39. A. NO CHANGE
B. uncle thinking for a moment, he
C. uncle, thinking, for a moment, he
D. uncle, thinking for, a moment, he

40. At this point, the writer is considering adding the following true statement:

> The kite banked almost instantly and rocketed into the sky, averting disaster.

Should the statement be added here?

F. Yes, because the phrase "rocketed into the sky" pairs well with the rocket mentioned earlier in the paragraph.
G. Yes, because it fittingly closes the paragraph by stating that the kite did not crash.
H. No, because the reader can answer the question of whether or not the kite crashes for himself or herself.
J. No, because this paragraph's concluding sentence ought to create anticipation that leads into the next paragraph.

Soon my uncle put the strings in my hands, and with patience he spent the rest of the day teaching me how it is to fly the stunt kite. Within a few hours I could do amazing figure eights and dive bombs! Whenever I crashed, which happened more than a few times—my uncle used it as a teaching opportunity, encouraging me to pull with more or less force on one string or the other in a certain direction. Since that day I, though still a bit of an amateur, have gotten my own stunt kite and have had plenty of opportunities to hone my kite-flying skills. After years of stunt kite flying, it is hard to believe that I

41. A. NO CHANGE
B. how it were to fly
C. how to fly
D. how flying it were

42. F. NO CHANGE
G. figure, amazing eights
H. amazing, figure eights
J. amazing-figure-eights

43. A. NO CHANGE
B. I crashed, that
C. I crashed which
D. I crashed—which

44. F. NO CHANGE
G. Since that day, I, though
H. Since that day, though
J. Since that day, I though

once thought the hobby to be a boring one. **|45|**

Question 45 asks about the preceding passage as a whole.

45. Suppose the author's main purpose had been to share how he came to acquire a new hobby. Would this essay accomplish that purpose?

A. Yes, because the essay details how the author's uncle introduced him to stunt kite flying, a hobby he continued to learn.
B. Yes, because the essay compares and contrasts the various hobbies the author has tried over the course of many years.
C. No, because the essay never mentions that the author himself ever flies a stunt kite.
D. No, because the main focus of the essay is the author's uncle and his difficulty learning to fly a stunt kite.

Step 3 Correct Answers

Passage I
1: B
2: F
3: C
4: J
5: C
6: J
7: B
8: H
9: A
10: G
11: D
12: G
13: A
14: H
15: D

Passage II
16: H
17: D
18: J
19: A
20: F
21: D
22: H
23: D
24: F
25: C
26: G
27: B
28: J
29: C
30: F

Passage III
31: B
32: J
33: A
34: G
35: B
36: H
37: A
38: J
39: C
40: G
41: C
42: F
43: D
44: G
45: A

Stumped on any? You will find the explanations for each answer beginning on page 494
.

STEP 4

Verbs

We will break this Step down into two parts regarding verbs: subject/verb agreement and proper verb tense.

Subject/Verb Agreement

The ACT wants you to recognize which verb to properly match with a given subject, and which subject to properly match with a given verb. This is called "subject verb agreement" and is best illustrated with a few examples (see if you can correctly choose of the two choices in bold):

a) My dog's food, made of only the finest ingredients, **is/are** pretty expensive.

b) The pack of deer, made up of bucks, does, and fawns, **was/were** eating my grass.

c) The **snake/snakes**, which, if my wife would have known, would have scared her to death, was slithering through the front yard.

d) **Women/A woman** are more likely to buy a pair of shoes online.

Can you see in A/B which verb is correct, and in C/D which subject is correct? If you can't, it is helpful to strip away all nonessential material, prepositions, dependent clauses, etc. and simplify the sentence as much as you possibly can. The ACT will often put a distance between the subject and the verb to make it more difficult for you to find the correct answer.

a) My dog's food (***singular noun***)…**is** pretty expensive.

- Here, "ingredients" isn't what is expensive, but the singular "food"

b) The **pack** (***singular!***) of deer…**was** eating my grass.

c) The **snake**…**was slithering** (***singular verb***).

d) **Women are** (***plural verb***) more likely…

Verb Tense

Similarly, the ACT will test your ability to recognize the proper verb tense (for simplicity's sake, past, present, or future) that ought to be used in a sentence. For example:

a) All through the baseball game, Jacob would jump up and **drop/drops** his popcorn.

b) I am determined that, when I turn 16, I **will get/got** my driver's license.

c) My sister will drive to the store and, if they have fresh blueberries, **bought/will buy** me some.

d) My cat was walking along the fence until a stupid, aggressive terrier named "Chuck" ran up to her and **had been barking/barked**, causing her to jump down.

a) All through the baseball game, Jacob **would jump up** and **drop** his popcorn.

-Here, we are dealing with past tense (specifically past perfect); "drops" is present tense!

b) I **am determined** that, when I turn 16, **I will get** my driver's license.

c) My sister **will drive (*future tense*)** to the store and, if they have fresh blueberries, **will buy (*also future tense, thus correct*)** me some.

d) My cat **was walking *(past progressive)*** along the fence until a stupid, aggressive terrier named "Chuck" ran up to her and **barked**, causing her to jump down.

- "had been barking" (which is the past perfect progressive tense) would only work if it said, "My cat had been walking."

Think you can identify these and properly choose the correct verb or subject? I hope so, because that is the fourth most tested skill on the ACT.

Step 4 Mini-Lesson: Correct Vocabulary and Idioms

Vocabulary

On occasion, the ACT will ask a question that requires you to choose the correct word based on its actual meaning (vocabulary). You should be able to spot these based on the context of the sentence. However, the options are usually pretty similar sounding, which are designed to confuse you. Here is an example:

> The magician created an **illustration/allusion/elution/illusion** when he pretended to saw my little sister in half.

Here, we need the word of the four that means "something that appears one way but is in fact another." In this case, it is *illusion.*

This kind of thing (as we've touched on a bit) is also seen with (and within) *phrases*. In other words, some phrases sound very similar, but only one is correct based on the sentence's context. For example:

> The professional is **better then/more better than/more better then/better than** the amateur.

Here the ACT would be playing on the similar sounding nature of two different words (than/then) but also adding on your ability to identify the proper adjective or adjective phrase. Here, the correct choice would be: The professional is **better than** the amateur. This is because "more better" makes no sense and "then" implies time moving along (like, one thing happened, *then* another).

Idioms

In any language, there are groups of words that always go together. These are called idioms. The ACT may test your ability to be confident enough to choose words that always go together. Here is an example:

> **Once upon the time/Once on a time/Once upon a time/At one point upon a time** there was a princess who was kidnapped by a dragon.

Is there really anything grammatically better about "Once upon a time" compared to any of these other choices? Not really, but that is the phrase that is used to introduce fairy tales, so it is the correct option.

The following practice passages are heavy on Step 4, but include Steps 3, 2, and 1.

PASSAGE I

Norman Rockwell, American Artist

Some artists have chased trends or relied upon over-the-top details, colors, or gimmicks to garner attention. Norman Rockwell was not an artist of this sort. Rather[1] Rockwell acquired fame for his art due to his ability to create realistic pieces as to depicting[2] simple truths and situations in profound, yet straightforward, ways. **|3|**

In 1913, Rockwell was only 18 when he earned his paying, first job[4] as an artist. He was hired by the Boy Scouts of America and was paid $50 per month to produce a cover for their magazine *Boy's Life* and a set of illustrations for a story within it.[5] His first cover, *Scout at Ship's Wheel,* remains today[6] as one of his most valuable works.

1. A. NO CHANGE
   B. He rather
   C. He, rather,
   D. Rather,

2. F. NO CHANGE
   G. then depict
   H. that depicted
   J. of depicting

3. At this point, the author is considering adding the following true statement:

   > As is quoted in Beowulf, "Fame after death is the noblest of goals," and artists of all sorts have sought after this goal.

   Should the writer make this addition here?

   A. Yes, because the topic of the paragraph is how Rockwell carries on the traditions of various works.
   B. Yes, because the preceding sentence speaks about the fame the Rockwell was able to gain.
   C. No, because the sentence shifts the focus away from Rockwell and his art.
   D. No, because Rockwell was not famous after his death, which has previously been stated.

4. F. NO CHANGE
   G. his first paying job
   H. was paid
   J. he was being paid

5. A. NO CHANGE
   B. *Boy's Life*, all of which happened when Rockwell was only 18 years of age!
   C. *Boy's Life* and was only paid $50.
   D. *Boy's Life* for the Boy Scouts of America.

6. F. NO CHANGE
   G. still remains
   H. remains to this day
   J. remains

Amazingly, he was promoted [7] to art editor for the magazine prior to his 20th birthday. This was a role that he maintained for more than three years, and the Boy Scouts, even though he eventually stepped away, was featured often [8] in his work. For the following 47 years, Rockwell produced covers for *The Saturday Evening Post*, and was [9] frequently hired to do the same for various publications throughout his career.

Rockwell attempted to enlist [10] with the U.S. Navy during the first World War, but he turned away [11] for being underweight. That evening, he gorged himself on food and drink, returned to the recruiting office again the next day, and was deemed fit to join. Though he served as an artist who drew [12] for the military and never participated in combat, he was willing to serve in any capacity to help the cause. It was this same spirit that, coupled with a speech by President Roosevelt, inspired and motivated [13] him to to paint his now famous collection titled *Four Freedoms*.

Norman Rockwell would produce over 4,000 original pieces of art in his lifetime. Many of them depict aspects of American culture, but some (such as *The Problem We All Live With* and *Murder in Mississippi*) intend to [14] awaken the consciences of everyday Americans. Many of these pieces are held in Stockbridge, Massachusetts at the Norman

7. **A.** NO CHANGE
B. was being promoted
C. is promoted
D. was receiving a promotion

8. **F.** NO CHANGE
G. to be featured often
H. was often featured
J. were often featured

9. **A.** NO CHANGE
B. *Post*, he was
C. *Post* and was
D. *Post* and he was

10. **F.** NO CHANGE
G. exist
H. insist
J. in list

11. **A.** NO CHANGE
B. he was turned away
C. he turned them away
D. they, being turned away,

12. **F.** NO CHANGE
G. artist who draws
H. artist
J. artist drawing

13. **A.** NO CHANGE
B. was an absolute inspiration for
C. pushed him inwardly
D. moved

14. **F.** NO CHANGE
G. intend
H. intends to
J. intends

Rockwell Museum, which houses the largest collection of his work.

Question 15 asks about the preceding passage as a whole.

15. Suppose the author's main purpose had been to write a brief essay focusing on the history of American art. Would this essay accomplish that purpose?

- **A.** Yes, because Norman Rockwell was an American artist, and the museum that safeguards much of his work is in America as well.
- **B.** Yes, because although the essay focuses mostly on one artist, the essay is written chronologically.
- **C.** No, because Norman Rockwell, while having lived most of his life in America, was born in Toronto, Canada.
- **D.** No, because the essay focuses on the life and art of one artist alone.

PASSAGE II

The Challenger Deep

It has been said that there is only one place on planet earth that is yet to be thoroughly explored, and that were [16] its oceans. This is certainly true of the deepest and farthest down area [17] of the ocean: the Mariana Trench, which is over a mile deeper than Mount Everest is tall. The deepest part of this trench is called *Challenger Deep*; but only [18] a handful of brave souls have descended to the bottom of *Challenger Deep* in protective research submarines.

16. **F.** NO CHANGE
G. that is
H. that being
J. which are

17. **A.** NO CHANGE
B. deepest area
C. more deeper and farther down area
D. area

18. **F.** NO CHANGE
G. *Deep*, only
H. *Deep*; and only
J. *Deep*; only

The first manned visit to the bottom of the Mariana Trench occurred[19] in 1960 by Don Walsh of the United States and Jacques Piccard of Switzerland. They descended over 10,900 meters into the *Challenger Deep*; despite hearing a loud *crack* on the way down, they decided to carry on.[20] At the bottom, Walsh and Piccard claimed to have observe[21] a flatfish, which scientists dispute, and other marine life as well. When the pair discovered cracks in the windows of the vessel, they cut their voyage shortly[22] and ascended to the surface.

Incredibly[23] the next explorer to reach the bottom of the *Challenger Deep* did not do so until over 50 years after Walsh and Picard. This happened in 2012 when filmmaker James Cameron, known for directing movies such as *The Terminator* and *Avatar*, descended alone by himself[24] in a submarine he designed himself. Despite the failure of a few instruments on the way down due to the extreme pressure—the[25] dive was a success. Cameron spent a

19. **A.** NO CHANGE
B. Trench, having occurred
C. Trench is sure to occur
D. Trench is hoping to be occurring

20. Given that all of the choices are true, which of the following phrases most effectively communicates not only the danger of the voyage, but the courage of the two explorers?

F. NO CHANGE
G. this is nearly seven miles below the surface of the ocean.
H. there are numerable dangerous creatures in the ocean, such as sharks, rays, and jellyfish.
J. as the pair descended—which took a few hours—they busied themselves by monitoring equipment and gauges.

21. **A.** NO CHANGE
B. have observed
C. claiming to observe
D. claimed to have observed

22. **F.** NO CHANGE
G. cut their voyage short
H. were cutting their voyage shortly
J. cut their voyage low

23. **A.** NO CHANGE
B. The incredible Cameron
C. Incredibly,
D. In an incredible way

24. **F.** NO CHANGE
G. solo
H. without anyone else
J. solitarily and companionless

25. **A.** NO CHANGE
B. pressure: the
C. pressure, the
D. pressure, and the

total of three <u>hours, on the ocean floor.</u> 26

As of 2021, these are the only three people to have reached the deepest, darkest point in the ocean, <u>which is</u> 27 nine less than the number of people to have walked on the moon! **|28|** Needless to say, the age of exploration is far from over. What creatures and other wonders of nature <u>waited</u> 29 to be discovered in the depths of the Mariana Trench? It will be up to a new generation of explorers to find out.

26. **F.** NO CHANGE
G. hours—on the ocean floor.
H. hours on the ocean floor.
J. down there.

27. **A.** NO CHANGE
B. which were
C. which will be
D. which was to be

28. At this point, the writer is considering adding the following true statement:

> Neil Armstrong was the first man to walk on the moon; perhaps he was an inspiration to Walsh and Piccard.

Should the statement be added here?

F. Yes, because it helps the reader make connections between various explorers.
G. Yes, because the paragraph questions the identities of those who have landed on the moon.
H. No, because the information is irrelevant and distracts from the essay's primary focus.
J. No, because the essay makes no mention of if Walsh, Piccard, and Cameron ever had aspirations to explore the moon.

29. **A.** NO CHANGE
B. have waited
C. are waiting
D. is

Question 30 asks about the preceding passage as a whole.

30. Suppose the author's main purpose had been to explain in depth the technology behind and the purposes of various instruments aboard protective submarines. Would this essay accomplish that purpose?

F. Yes, because to reach the *Challenger Deep*, precision instruments are necessary.
G. Yes, because the author mentions how Cameron's submarine lost instruments as it descended.
H. No, because although the essay mentions such instruments, it fails to describe them in detail.
J. No, because the essay proved that such instruments are unnecessary and a burden to explorers.

PASSAGE III

The Pont du Gard

[1]

Visitors, to France, are [31] likely to see the Eiffel Tower, the Louvre Museum, or Notre Dame Cathedral. However, there is a site in Southern France that deserves recognition from both visitors and natives alike: the Pont du Gard, having to be [32] an aqueduct bridge estimated to be over 2,000 years old.

[A] The bridge crosses the Gardon River, and [33] today is listed as a UNESCO World Heritage Site.

[2]

Aqueducts were constructed by the Romans throughout their empire. [34] Their primary purpose was to carry [35] water from one location to another using gravity alone. [B] The Pont du Gard aqueduct is a supreme example of the brilliance of Roman engineering. The bridge, though over 900 feet in length, can descend [36] merely 1 inch from one side to the other!

[3]

Another architectural, noteworthy feature [37] of the bridge worthy of note is its arches, of which there are

31. **A.** NO CHANGE
B. Visitors to France are
C. Visitors, to France are
D. Visitors to France,

32. **F.** NO CHANGE
G. Gard, which will be
H. Gard, which was
J. Gard, which is

33. **A.** NO CHANGE
B. River and
C. River—
D. River, but

34. **F.** NO CHANGE
G. all of their occupied land.
H. the regions of Europe, West Asia, and Northern Africa that they had conquered.
J. the places that they could claim as their territory.

35. Which of the following alternatives to the underlined portion would NOT be acceptable?

A. the delivery of
B. delivering
C. to deliver
D. having delivered

36. **F.** NO CHANGE
G. descend
H. is descending
J. descends

37. **A.** NO CHANGE
B. noteworthy, architectural feature
C. noteworthy feature
D. architectural feature

three tires. The lowest and middle rows contain 6 and 11 arches, respectively, all of which are over 65 feet in height. The top layer contains 35 smaller arches, each of which reaches a height of 23 feet. Due to its ability to undoubtedly distribute weight and force, it is the arch that has contributed to the longevity of the Pont du Gard. [C]

[4]

The actual composition of the bridge is also astonishing. The stones that make up the Pont du Gard were precisely cut into blocks designed to perfectly stack up one on top of the other really high. These limestone bricks were immensely heavy, weighing up to six tons apiece. [D] However, the Romans had mastered the ability to lift such blocks by a system of cranes and pulleys.

[5]

With the fall of the Roman Empire came the end of the Pont du Gard as an aqueduct; maintenance proved too difficult for peoples and governments throughout history. Its use as a toll bridge throughout

38. F. NO CHANGE
G. tiers.
H. tears.
J. tries.

39. A. NO CHANGE
B. arches respectively, all of which
C. arches, respectively all of which,
D. arches respectively all of which

40. Which of the following placements for the underlined portion makes it clear that the timeless nature of the aqueduct can be attributed primarily to the arch?

F. Where it is now
G. After the word *has*
H. After the word *distribute*
J. After the word *longevity*

41. Which choice most effectively provides further evidence for the notion that Roman engineering was brilliant and ahead of its time?

A. NO CHANGE
B. and imprecisely fit together.
C. fit together without the use of mortar.
D. withstand rain and wind but not the test of time.

42. F. NO CHANGE
G. proves
H. continues to prove
J. will have proved

the centuries, on the other hand, has guaranteed some
43

level of maintenance. |44|

43. **A.** NO CHANGE
B. will guarantee
C. guaranteeing
D. to guarantee

44. Given that all of the following statements are true, which one, if added here, would best conclude the paragraph and the essay?

F. Toll bridges are found all over the world.
G. It is not too difficult to imagine that maintaining bridges takes skilled engineers.
H. Ultimately, it is up to each one of us to remember all of the reasons for the fall of Rome.
J. Today, the Pont du Gard is legally protected, and will hopefully survive for the enjoyment of future generations.

Question 45 asks about the preceding passage as a whole.

45. The writer is considering adding the following sentence to the essay:

> Aqueducts were thus meticulously constructed to run at a slight incline from the point of water to a populated end point.

If the writer were to add this sentence, it would most logically be placed at:

A. Point A in Paragraph 1.
B. Point B in Paragraph 2.
C. Point C in Paragraph 3.
D. Point D in Paragraph 4.

Step 4 Correct Answers

Passage I	Passage II	Passage III
1: D	16: G	31: B
2: H	17: B	32: J
3: C	18: J	33: B
4: G	19: A	34: F
5: A	20: F	35: D
6: J	21: D	36: J
7: A	22: G	37: D
8: J	23: C	38: G
9: C	24: G	39: A
10: F	25: C	40: G
11: B	26: H	41: C
12: H	27: A	42: F
13: D	28: H	43: A
14: F	29: C	44: J
15: D	30: H	45: B

Stumped on any? You will find the explanations for each answer beginning on page 500.

STEP 5

Sentence Structure and Meaning

Here, the phrase "sentence structure and meaning" is being used broadly. Yes, anything that affects a sentence could probably be grouped under this umbrella. However, I am referring to a couple of specific problems the ACT wants you to identify: a) Punctuation and word use that makes something a non-sentence, and b) identifying words and phrases that actually give a sentence the meaning that is intended or needed.

Sentence Structure

Let's keep this simple. Sometimes, the wording of a sentence renders it not a sentence at all, but rather some kind of sentence fragment, run on, or nonsense. For example:

> When the Beatles, who had built up an overseas audience, famously landed in America, they brought a nation along with its knees.

Read that sentence again; remember the skill to *listen*? Does that "sound" like a sentence that functions to you? Did they bring a nation to America, as well as bring along some knees on the plane? That doesn't make sense. It is nonsense. The sentence of course should say, "...they brought a nation to its knees."

Here's another example:

> Although they never found the treasure they were looking for, the pirates discovered caves. Previously unknown to man; today they are known as "Blackbeard's Caverns."

This is the kind of questions in which students are quick to put "NO CHANGE" because the period that comes after "caves" forms a complete sentence. However, the second sentence beginning with "Previously unknown" makes no sense at all. The semicolon in the second sentence is unchangeable, so something about the underlined portion has to be changed. That is why the sentence should say, "Although they never found the treasure they were looking for, the pirates discovered caves previously unknown to man; today they are known as Blackbeard's Caverns."

You see? The main skill you need is the ability to *listen* to the sentence and spy out nonsense.

Sentence Meaning

The skill that helps you determine whether or not a sentence belongs, or whether or not a phrase is the right phrase, or where a certain word belongs in a sentence (Step 1) is the same skill that is necessary here: *identifying the BEST answer based on context.* In other words, a sentence or a group of sentences *need* to say one thing *based on context*, but say something different. The ACT is testing here your ability to identify the *best* answer, but on a smaller scale, or sometimes the only possible correct answer. Let's break this into three smaller categories: a) Correct transitions ("connector words") between sentences or clauses, b) Correct pronoun use, and c) Correct prepositional phrase use.

a) Correct transitions - words or phrases to connect sentences or clauses

Transitions are words or phrases like "However," "Because," "For this reason," "Instead," etc. These phrases *transition* thoughts and create a relationship between sentences. You need to be able to identify which one is the *best* based on context. Here is an example:

The pirate was going to sail the Seven Seas. Because of this, he went to the mall.

Nothing grammatically incorrect here; the problem is one of context. What is needed is a word or phrase to begin the second sentence that implies contrast between the two sentences. As it is written, it makes it sound like the pirate's initial plan to sail *caused him* to go to the mall. But surely that's not what is being implied; what we need instead is a word or phrase to start the second sentence that tells the reader that there was a change of plan. Thus, it should say something like this: "The pirate was going to sail the Seven Seas. Instead, he went to the mall."

b) Correct pronoun use

A pronoun is a word (like he, she, them, those, etc.) that refers to a person or persons or thing or things. A singular pronoun (like "it") can only refer to a singular thing (like "the watermelon"), and of course a plural pronoun (like "them") can only refer to plural things (like "the seeds in the watermelon"). Sometimes, it is a choice between the proper use of singular pronouns (it, he, etc.) or plural ones (them, those, they, etc.). Here is an example:

> The way you know if you've stumbled across a pirate treasure chest filled with gold coins and silver goblets is to examine them closely.

At first it seems like there is nothing wrong here. "Them" is a plural pronoun, and we have plural nouns like "coins" and "goblets." However, what needs to be examined closely? Not the coins and goblets, but the chest itself, thus the appropriate choice would be "it," not "them."

This can also come up with the essay's "POV", or Point of View. For example, look at these two sentences:

> I am going to the concert; I don't care what Mom says. She thinks I'm too young, but I have something to say to that: "She's a teenager now!"

Nothing grammatical here, but does the pronoun *she* really work there? No; the essay and sentence are in first person ("I"), and I don't think the daughter is telling her Mom that *she* (the mother) is a teenager now. Thus, what is need there is this: "I'm a teenager now!"

c) Correct prepositional phrase use

Just like identifying the proper phrase in a sentence earlier, we can apply that same thinking to a smaller kind of phrase, a prepositional phrase. Prepositions are things like "at," "to," "under," etc., and they specify something's action or location. Thus, you might say, "I looked *under the bed* for a monster," or, "My sister plays solitaire *in the house* *in her room* *by the window*. All of those phrases work, but check out this example:

> Scurvy, which results from Vitamin C deficiency, is a common problem among pirates, who forget to pack oranges at their suitcases.

Well, do you pack something "at" a suitcase? No, of course this should read, "…who forget to pack oranges *in* their suitcases."

Step 5 Mini-Lesson: Modifying Clauses

You know that adjectives can describe a noun (the green ball), and adverbs can describe a verb or how something is done (she kicked the ball aggressively). However, there is a clause that does this: a modifying clause. Look at the following example, which is written correctly:

Watching television in the evenings, Dad relaxes in the chair.

What is underlined here is called a "modifying clause," and it *modifies* (or you could say, describes) what comes immediately after the comma: "Dad." It is clear from the sentence that *Dad* relaxes in his chair *by watching television*. What would happen, however, if we rewrote it like this?

Watching television in the evenings, the chair is where Dad relaxes.

Do you see what's wrong? The way that it is written, it sounds like *the chair* (which comes immediately after the comma) is *watching television in the evenings*. Unless your chair is alive and has eyeballs, I doubt it is watching television. Can you see what is wrong, then, with these three examples?

a) Admiring the clouds, the sky seemed different that day.

b) After winning The Masters for the first time, the success of Tiger Woods seemed inevitable.

c) Leaning over to touch my toes, my fitness needed some work.

All three of them make the same mistake: what comes after the comma in each is incapable of the *modifying clause* that comes before the comma. In a), the problem is that "the sky" can't admire the clouds. In b) the problem is that "the success of Tiger Woods" didn't win The Masters. In c), "my fitness" didn't lean over to touch my toes. They should look like this (keeping the modifying clauses the same):

a) Admiring the clouds, he noticed that the sky seemed different that day.

b) After winning The Masters for the first time, Tiger Woods seemed destined for success.

c) Leaning over to touch my toes, I noticed that my fitness needed some work.

The following practice passages are heavier on Step 5, but includes of course Steps 4, 3, 2, and 1.

PASSAGE I

Steve Irwin, Crocodile Hunter

Crikey! is an exclamation you've probably heard, but does he [1] know who popularized the word? His name was Steve Irwin, and he gained international fame through his television series *The Crocodile Hunter*. Which [2] aired worldwide for over a decade. Steve was a native Australian whose fun-loving and addictive personality gained and raptured the attention of the world. [3]

Steve never enjoyed the spotlight or sought after attention from other people [4], but he was happy if it was a means to promote his conservation efforts. His philosophy was: simple, [5] if you show people how wonderful nature is, you won't have to preach environmentalism to them. Thus, [6] Steve was willing to flash his trademark smile and confront wild (and sometimes dangerous) animals for the cameras.

Steve learned to work with all kinds of animals, even crocodiles, as a young boy. Because, his parents were the owners [7] of the Australia Zoo, a 700 acre

1. **A.** NO CHANGE
B. do he
C. do you
D. does you

2. **F.** NO CHANGE
G. *Hunter*, which
H. *Hunter*, this
J. *Hunter*; which

3. **A.** NO CHANGE
B. in the world.
C. at the entire world.
D. of the whole world.

4. **F.** NO CHANGE
G. them
H. it
J. attention

5. **A.** NO CHANGE
B. was; simple,
C. was simple,
D. was simple:

6. Which of the following alternatives to the underlined portion would NOT be acceptable?

F. Rather,
G. Because of this,
H. Hence,
J. For this reason,

7. **A.** NO CHANGE
B. Because his parents were the owners
C. Because, his parents, were the owners
D. Because they owned

facility in Queensland, he had access to them all. |8|

Eventually, Steve gained ownership of the zoo and

8. At this point, the author is considering adding the following true statement:

    This included crocodiles, which are some of the most dangerous and fear-inducing animals on the planet.

    Should the writer make this addition here?

    F. Yes, because it foreshadows Steve's future work with crocodiles.
    G. Yes, because it helps to further induce fear in the reader, which is the primary purpose of the paragraph as a whole.
    H. No, because, as is stated earlier in the essay, the Australia Zoo never held crocodiles because they were too dangerous.
    J. No, because the sentence is redundant and distracts the reader from the paragraph's purpose.

shares [9] it with his wife, Terri. The couple was so

9. **A.** NO CHANGE
    B. shared
    C. share
    D. to share

unwaveringly committed to the cause of [10]

10. **F.** NO CHANGE
    G. at a cause for
    H. for the cause at
    J. from a cause to

environmentalism that all of the dollars [11] generated by

11. **A.** NO CHANGE
    B. the entire sum of all the money
    C. the funds
    D. DELETE the underlined portion

television and other media funneled were they [12] back into the zoo.

12. **F.** NO CHANGE
    G. were funneled
    H. funneled are
    J. will be funneled

Irwin was also a man of great courage and love of people. In 2003 he was filming a documentary on sea lions in Mexico. Upon hearing a message come through the radio saying that two scuba divers were missing in the area, the search was on, and the crew got to work. [13] They were able to assist one of the missing divers, who was found perched on a rock.

13. **A.** NO CHANGE
    B. A message hearing came through the radio, two scuba divers were missing, and the search was on in the area by the crew.
    C. The crew heard a message, it came through the radio, saying that two scuba divers were missing in the area, and they stopped production to help in the search.
    D. A message came through the radio saying that two scuba divers were missing in the area, and immediately the crew aided in the search.

Tragically, Steve lost his life at the young age of 54 in 2006 filming [14] around the Great Barrier Reef, and while snorkeling in shallow waters, he was pierced by a stingray barb. The world mourned the loss of the man who many saw as the face of worldwide conservation efforts. **|15|**

14. **F.** NO CHANGE
G. 54 in 2006, filming
H. 54. In 2006 filming,
J. 54. In 2006, he was filming

15. Given that all of the following statements are true, which one, if added here, would best conclude the paragraph and the essay?

A. You can still carry on Steve's legacy by visiting the Australia Zoo, which, to this day, is owned and operated by Terri and their two children.
B. Conservation has grown in popularity over the last few decades.
C. To this day, crocodiles remain popular with children across the world, and any zoo that has them is sure to draw a crowd (and maybe a camera as well)!
D. The Great Barrier Reef, located off of the coast of Australia, is under legal protection, and is home to countless animal species.

PASSAGE II

The Theory of Beauty

I don't see sunsets in the same way others do. This is within [16] the forest, a stream, a sunrise, or the night sky as well. What most people see when they look at any of these beautiful sights is just that: one sight. I on the other hand, have [17] trained myself to first breakdown a scene into colors and shapes, then to find the contrasts, then finally to see the bigger picture. I have had this innate ability since a young

16. **F.** NO CHANGE
G. true of
H. to become
J. only about

17. **A.** NO CHANGE
B. I on the other hand have
C. I, on the other hand, have
D. I, on the other hand have

age, and it has led me [18] to study the theory of art.

One topic in art of all forms that has long fascinated me is the question of beauty and its relationship with color. [19] There are colors and combinations of colors that, when isolated, appear very beautiful indeed, but others [20] however, appear ugly or detestable. Most people would rather stare at a gradient of blue morphing into yellow than at a swirl of grey and black that intermixes, [21] for example. However, if one adds a pattern of pink into the grey/black image, the beholder's inclinations change dramatically; all of a sudden, they find [22] it to be beautiful.

Interesting: preferences [23] in aesthetics go far beyond colors and appear to be universal. For example, architecture that displays skill, curves, arches, and both acute and obtuse angles are preferred by most when compared to a simple building that is built in its entirety in right angles. [24] I find this fascinating because right angles are not only common, but is [25] both efficient and simple in the construction of a building.

I have studied the world of color and art. With intensity [26] and interest over the course of a lifetime. I

18. **F.** NO CHANGE
G. has lead me
H. will lead me
J. have led me

19. Which choice best introduces the subject of the paragraph and the rest of the essay?
A. NO CHANGE
B. is whether or not people recognize the true beauty in others.
C. is the theme of piercing light in the history of film.
D. is how people, like myself, have come to be interested in this topic in the first place.

20. **F.** NO CHANGE
G. indeed, but, others,
H. indeed but others
J. indeed, but others,

21. **A.** NO CHANGE
B. black,
C. black which intermixes
D. mixing up black

22. **F.** NO CHANGE
G. they found
H. he or she found
J. he or she finds

23. **A.** NO CHANGE
B. Interesting preferences,
C. Preferences interestingly
D. Interestingly, preferences

24. **F.** NO CHANGE
G. of right angles.
H. at right angles.
J. for right angles.

25. **A.** NO CHANGE
B. but they are
C. for is
D. for they are

26. **F.** NO CHANGE
G. and art with intensity
H. and art, with intensity
J. and intense art

have designed the interiors of some of the world's most magnificent and grandiose homes. I have consulted over the construction [27] of magnificent galleries and headquarters for Fortune 500 companies. I have given lectures on the topic on every continent except for the Southernmost, really icy landmass. [28] In short, I have a lot of experience in the world of art. I have, therefore, concluded that beauty is not just something in the eye of the beholder, nor is it merely a matter of opinion. Beauty *exists*, and we [29] human beings are hardwired not only to see it, notice it, or create it, but to experience it.

27. **A.** NO CHANGE
B. on top of the construction
C. in the construction
D. under construction

28. **F.** NO CHANGE
G. but Antarctica.
H. apart from the continent down there.
J. except for Antarctica, which is at the Southernmost tip of the globe.

29. **A.** NO CHANGE
B. but all the
C. although every
D. and, in total, the

Question 30 asks about the preceding passage as a whole.

30. Suppose the author's main purpose had been to explain to a friend why she found the study of the theories of art and beauty to be both fascinating and worthwhile. Would this essay accomplish that purpose?

F. Yes, because the essay is written from a first person point of view and uses color and architecture as examples of topics in these fields.
G. Yes, because the essay is not written in the form of an essay, but rather it takes the form of a letter addressed to a friend.
H. No, because the author insists that beauty is not in the "eye of the beholder," thus other people have to experience beauty in their own time.
J. No, because the author clearly states that the intermixing of various colors can be both "ugly and detestable."

PASSAGE III

An Inventor's Childhood

Alexander Graham Bell is best known for his invention of the telephone. **|31|** There were three aspects of his childhood that all came together to make his future breakthrough possible. There [32] was his mother's hearing disability and his father's work. Second, his parents and neighbors supported his curiosities and inventing spirit inside of him. [33] Lastly, he possessed a natural genius that he refused to squander, rather, [34] he used it for good.

Alexander's mother was nearly deaf. [35] This more than anything awakened his curiosity about human speaking and hearing. Even so, [36] as a boy, he developed a talent for voice throwing and ventriloquism that happily entertained family and friends in addition. His [37] father, uncle, and grandfather were all specialists in elocution and teaching communication to the deaf. It seemed that the future

31. At this point, the author is considering adding the following true statement:

> In many respects, it was his upbringing that prepared him for this triumphant invention.

Should the writer make this addition here?

- **A.** Yes, because Alexander Graham Bell invented the telephone as a child, as is stated later in the paragraph.
- **B.** Yes, because it transitions the subject of the essay to Bell's childhood.
- **C.** No, because the sentence implies that the invention of the telephone was "triumphant," an opinion not yet established in the essay.
- **D.** No, because the sentences that follow make no mention of his upbringing.

32.
- **F.** NO CHANGE
- **G.** Although, there
- **H.** First, there
- **J.** Except, there

33.
- **A.** NO CHANGE
- **B.** inventing spirit.
- **C.** the inventing spirit inside of him.
- **D.** a spirit of invention that had taken root in his spirit.

34.
- **F.** NO CHANGE
- **G.** squander rather:
- **H.** squander—rather
- **J.** squander; rather,

35.
- **A.** NO CHANGE
- **B.** very close to being unable to hear at all.
- **C.** almost unable to listen to everything.
- **D.** practically finding it impossible to hear.

36.
- **F.** NO CHANGE
- **G.** On the other hand,
- **H.** In fact,
- **J.** Be that as it may,

37.
- **A.** NO CHANGE
- **B.** friends, in addition, his
- **C.** friends in addition his
- **D.** friends. In addition, his

inventor of the telephone was one way or another destined <u>of working over</u> 38 the realm of hearing.

Alexander's parents also encouraged him to invent, to tinker, and <u>he finds</u> 39 solutions to problems from an early age. His curiosity about the natural world was <u>tremendous, by commonly gathering</u> 40 plant species and use them in science experiments.

<u>Growing up in Scotland, a flour mill was run by Alexander's neighbors, the Herdman family.</u> 41 Ben Herdman was his best friend, and Alexander spent a lot of time around their operation. At the age of 12, young Alexander invented a dehusking device that <u>was used by the family</u> 42 for a number of years in their mill. As a sort of reward or payment, Mr. Herdman created a space in which the two boys could invent and run science experiments.

It was clear to all that young Alexander had a brilliant mind. <u>In fact with no training</u> 43 he mastered the piano when he was but a child. Alexander was the type of boy who had the intelligence to do whatever he wanted, as long as he worked hard. Because of his mother's hearing issues, Alexander was naturally fascinated with acoustics, and thus applied <u>her</u> 44 genius

38. F. NO CHANGE
G. to work within
H. within to work inside of
J. to be working all in

39. A. NO CHANGE
B. he found
C. he was finding
D. to find

40. F. NO CHANGE
G. tremendous, and by commonly gathering
H. tremendous; he would commonly gather
J. tremendous, for to be commonly gather

41. A. NO CHANGE
B. Running a flour mill, Alexander grew up next to the family in Scotland that did so: the Herdman family.
C. Growing up in Scotland, Alexander was neighbors with the Herdman family, who ran a flour mill.
D. Being neighbors with Alexander, the flour mill was run by the Herdman family in Scotland.

42. F. NO CHANGE
G. were used by the family
H. to be in use with the family
J. was using the family

43. A. NO CHANGE
B. In fact, with no training,
C. As a matter of fact: with no training,
D. With no, in fact, training,

44. F. NO CHANGE
G. their
H. his or her
J. his

to that particular field. **|45|**

45. Given that all of the statements are true, which one, if added here, would best conclude the paragraph and the essay by referring back to the opening paragraph?

A. Children are capable of more than society gives them credit for.
B. As they say, "The family that plays together, stays together," and as Alexander became better at the piano, the closer his family became.
C. If Alexander had never invented the dehusking device for his neighbors, it is unlikely the telephone would have ever been invented.
D. As a consequence, everyone benefits from Alexander Graham Bell's breakthrough invention.

Step 5 Correct Answers

Passage I	Passage II	Passage III
1: C	16: G	31: B
2: G	17: C	32: H
3: A	18: F	33: B
4: H	19: A	34: J
5: D	20: J	35: A
6: F	21: B	36: H
7: B	22: J	37: D
8: J	23: D	38: G
9: B	24: H	39: D
10: F	25: B	40: H
11: C	26: G	41: C
12: G	27: C	42: F
13: D	28: G	43: B
14: J	29: A	44: J
15: A	30: F	45: D

Stumped on any? You will find the explanations for each answer beginning on page 506.

STEP 6

The Rest - All of the Little Things

If you've made it to this point, you have come very far. What is left to learn represents 4-6% of questions on recent ACT English tests. This is also why I wrote this book: to put this stuff last to show how little it is asked. Why would you, as a student, spend an hour memorizing the difference between "less" and "fewer" when, odds are, you won't even have one question on ACT test day that tests your knowledge of this? It makes no sense, unless you've made it to this point.

This Step does not have a mini-lesson at the end of it because, well, the entire Step is made up of mini-lessons.

Apostrophes

a) Possessives (to show possession or ownership)

Apostrophes are used to show possession; here are the different situations that could come up with this.

i) Add an apostrophe and 's' to singular nouns and plural nouns that do not end in 's'

ex) The **cat's** paws were white. ex) This store sells **women's** shoes.

ii) Add an apostrophe to a plural noun that already ends in 's'

ex) The **kids'** toys are there. (This refers to the toys that belong to multiple kids)

ex) The **hyenas'** prey was eaten (This refers to the prey that was eaten by multiple hyenas)

iii) Make both nouns possessive for individual possession; make the final noun possessive for joint possession.

ex) **Ben's** and **Bob's** hats are red. (This says that Ben has a red hat and Bob also has a red hat)

ex) Kim and **Carla's** birthday party is today. (This says that Kim and Carla are having a joint party)

b) Contractions (combining words)

Add an apostrophe to represent missing letters when words are joined (like do + not = **don't**).

Special Case - Its vs It's vs Its'

i) **Its** is the possessive for of "it." ex) **Its** leg was injured.

ii) **It's** is the contraction for "it is" or "it has." ex) **It's** time for bed. ex) **It's** been a long day.

iii) **Its'** is not a word in English. Don't use it. Ever.

They're vs Their vs There

i) **They're** is a contraction. If it can be replaced with "they are," then this is correct.

ex) **They're** trying to escape from jail.

ii) **Their** is possessive. Plural subjects own something; if possession is being implied, this is correct.

ex) Are you going to **their** house for dinner?

iii) **There** has a couple of uses. It can denote a location, for example (it is synonymous with "that place"). It is also used as a pronoun to place a conjugation of the verb "to be" (is/are/were/will be/etc.) before a subject.

ex) The fox lives over **there**.

ex) **There** will be no reason to go out tonight.

Who vs Whom

Here is how the rule is stated: *who* goes where *he* goes, and *whom* goes where *him* goes. In other words if you can rephrase the sentence to put in the pronoun *he* or *him*, or if you can rephrase the sentence as a question in which the answer is either *he* or *him*, then you can be sure as to which to use.

ex) Remember **who/whom** you are speaking to.

Rephrase: Are you speaking to ***he**, or are you speaking to **him***? You would say, " I am speaking to **him**", which is why the answer is **whom**. (Remember whom you are speaking to).

ex) **Who/whom** stole the cookie?

Rephrase: Did ***he*** steal the cookie, or did ***him*** steal the cookie? You would say, "**He** stole the cookie", which is why the answer is **who**. (Who stole the cookie?).

To vs Too

To is a preposition; too means "very" or "also" or "as well".

ex) It is **too** wet outside, so I will not be walking **to** the store.

Good vs Well

Good is an adjective (it describes a noun), and well is an adverb (it describes how something is done).

ex) This is a **good** snack. There's a **good** chance I'll get a 36 on the ACT.

ex) I did **well** on the ACT. How are you? I'm **well**, how are you?

Than vs Then

I believe we covered this, but just to review. Than is used to compare things; then is used to show the passage of time.

ex) I am older **than** my twin brother. I was born, and **then** he was born.

Between vs Among

Between is used when referring to being between only 2 things or persons; among is used when there are more than 2 things or persons.

ex) The policeman, though **among** a large crowd, stood **between** the bad guy and the victim.

Lie vs Lay

Lie is something a subject does to itself; lay is something done to something else.

ex) I'm going to **lie** down. (It is *lie* because I am doing it to myself).

ex) He is going to **lay** the book on the table. (It is *lay* because he is doing it to something else).

Less vs Fewer

Use fewer for things that can be numbered or counted; use less for something that can't be numbered.

ex) Because I had 2 gallons of milk to buy, I used the "Ten Items or **Fewer**" checkout line.

ex) There are **fewer** cars in my garage than my neighbor's.

ex) There is **less** Vitamin C in a banana than an orange. (You can't count the number of Vitamin C's).

ex) The Gulf of Mexico has **less** water than the Atlantic Ocean.

Affect vs Effect

For ACT purposes, remember affect is a verb and effect is a noun. To remember this, think of the phrase "cause and effect," which is about 2 nouns.

ex) The previous mayor had a negative **effect** on the city because he **affected** it in the wrong way.

Further vs Farther

Farther is a word that is always used to identify a distance. Further is used to indicate an additional amount of something that was done, is being done, must be done, etc.

ex) New York City is **farther** from my house than Atlanta.

ex) Scientists need to research **further** into the COVID pandemic.

ex) The athlete needs **further** training if she is to finish in first place.

Last Semicolon Use

Up to this point I've been saying there's a prime way to use a semicolon: to combine independent clauses. Guaranteed, you will have to know *that* on ACT day! However, a semicolon can also be used to set off items in a list, like commas can. All you could ever need to know is that if a sentence is setting off items in a list with semicolons, you can't switch punctuation to commas or something else.

ex) The writers on my bookshelf include Flannery O'Connor, a National Book Award winner**;** Walker Percy, who won the same award**;** and C.S. Lewis, British author who preceded the other two.

That's a lot of little things. Like I said, you will have 3-5 questions that test your knowledge of the above material, but if mastery of these small rules is all that's left for you, then get to work on the following practice passages!

While heavy on Step 6, each of the following 2 passages contains at least one question type from Steps 1-5 to keep you on top of it!

PASSAGE I

Mammoth Cave

[1]

Mammoth <u>Cave located in Kentucky</u> [1] is the longest cave system in the world. No other surveyed cave <u>matches its massive</u> [2] size. Researchers who have explored the cave have mapped out a total of around 360 miles but <u>estimates the total length</u> [3] of the cave to be roughly 3 times longer! [A] To put that into perspective, that is just about 40 miles <u>further than</u> [4] the <u>distance between</u> [5] Boston and Atlanta.

[2]

The limestone rock beds that make up Mammoth Cave have existed for about 350 million years. <u>However, the caves'</u> [6] passages did not begin to form until 10-15 million years ago. [B] Over the passage of millions of years, water gradually widened those small cracks, which <u>become less</u> [7] in number as they widened into passageways. The limestone walls actually accelerated the erosion: as the water moved <u>through. The limestone,</u> [8] it actively dissolved minerals in the rock, speeding the process. Eventually, the cracks became passages large enough for humans to enter <u>into, because they were now big enough</u> [9].

1. **A.** NO CHANGE
B. Cave in Kentucky where it is located
C. Cave, located in Kentucky,
D. Cave located, in Kentucky,

2. **F.** NO CHANGE
G. can match it's massive
H. matches it's massive
J. is able to matches its massive

3. **A.** NO CHANGE
B. estimate, the total length,
C. estimates, the total length,
D. estimate the total length

4. **F.** NO CHANGE
G. further then
H. farther than
J. farther then

5. **A.** NO CHANGE
B. distances between
C. distance among
D. distances among

6. **F.** NO CHANGE
G. However the caves'
H. However, the cave's
J. However, the cave's,

7. **A.** NO CHANGE
B. become fewer
C. became less
D. became fewer

8. **F.** NO CHANGE
G. through the limestone,
H. through, the limestone,
J. through. The limestone

9. **A.** NO CHANGE
B. into the large caves.
C. into.
D. into over time.

[3]

Apart from its unique, massive size, Mammoth Cave also has a unique history. Early Native Americans, <u>whom were</u> [10] truly the first to actually discover the cave, used it as shelter during certain times of the year as a way to escape the elements. These tribes also <u>used it</u> [11] as a primitive mine as early as 3000 years ago, extracting mirabilite, epsomite, and gypsum. [C] How these minerals were used by the Native Americans is still unclear, but they did leave behind some <u>of they're</u> [12] possessions that, today, are considered rare and valuable artifacts. There is also evidence that Mammoth Cave may also have had a more solemn use; members of the tribe <u>will lay</u> [13] the body of a deceased companion within the cave to protect it from predators while it was prepared for burial.

10. **F.** NO CHANGE
G. who are
H. whom are
J. who were

11. **A.** NO CHANGE
B. to use them
C. used them
D. using it

12. **F.** NO CHANGE
G. of them
H. of there
J. of their

13. **A.** NO CHANGE
B. will lie
C. would lay
D. would lie

[4]

Mammoth Cave officially became a National Park in 1941. At that time, only 40 miles of passageway had been mapped. **|14|** In the time since, however, surveyors have made huge leaps in understanding the cave system. [D] Although researchers now comprehend the massive scope of the cave in much greater detail, archaeologists and other scientists continue to study Mammoth Cave, hoping to gain further insight into both how it was

14. The writer is considering deleting the preceding sentence. Should the sentence be kept or deleted?

F. Kept, because otherwise the reader is unable to infer that Mammoth Cave is now believed to be the largest cave system in the world.
G. Kept, because it gives the reader a benchmark for understanding just how far research has come since 1941.
H. Deleted, because it portrays the researchers working within the cave system prior to 1941 as incapable.
J. Deleted, because it shifts the focus of the paragraph away from a broad understanding of the cave's history to one that focuses on detail.

formed and how it has been used since.

Question 15 asks about the preceding passage as a whole.

15. The writer is considering adding the following sentence to the essay:

> At that time, flowing water entered the rock bed through small cracks and eroded the stone.

If the writer were to add this sentence, it would most logically be placed at:

A. Point A in Paragraph 1.
B. Point B in Paragraph 2.
C. Point C in Paragraph 3.
D. Point D in Paragraph 4.

PASSAGE II

Nikola Tesla

Few inventors have gained the type of notoriety <u>as if Nikola Tesla.</u> [16] He was a brilliant and capable inventor who pioneered many of the technological concepts society relies on today. Though Tesla may have been misunderstood in his own time, history indicates that the <u>overall more work</u> [17] and inventions of Nikola Tesla deserve respect and admiration.

<u>Throughout his life, Tesla dedicated himself to science and technological pursuits.</u> [18]

16. F. NO CHANGE
G. as Nikola Tesla have.
H. that Nikola Tesla has.
J. being like Nikola Tesla.

17. A. NO CHANGE
B. overall work well
C. overall well work
D. overall good work

18. F. NO CHANGE
G. Being dedicated, science and technological pursuits were the lifelong focus of Tesla.
H. As a scientist, technological pursuits were Tesla's dedication throughout his life.
J. From the beginning of his career in science, pursuits of a kind of technological type of focus of Tesla were what he was dedicated in pursuit of.

Nikola Tesla was born in Croatia in 1856. He had humble <u>beginnings, so his mother</u> [19] ran the family farm, and his father worked for the church. However, his early years were indicative of the future he would have: he was a bright student; he studied at the Technical University of <u>Graz, and</u> [20] he flourished at the University of Prague. In 1884 Tesla emigrated to the United States and took a job as an engineer at Thomas Edison's electric company. During his employment under Edison, Tesla was often undervalued. Edison once promised to pay Tesla $50,000 for an improved invention design. **|21|**

Unfortunately, <u>Tesla's and Edison's</u> [22] lifelong <u>rivalry against each other</u> [23] was established by this slight. Tesla moved on, and would go on to partner

19. A. NO CHANGE
B. beginnings; his mother
C. beginnings, which explains why she
D. beginnings and his mother

20. F. NO CHANGE
G. Graz, but
H. Graz, however,
J. Graz; and

21. At this point, the writer is considering adding the following true statement:

> When Tesla delivered, Edison refused to pay, telling Tesla that he "did not understand our American humor."

Should the statement be added here?

A. Yes, because, without it, readers will not understand what the author meant when he wrote that "Tesla was often undervalued."
B. Yes, because it gives the reader insight into the nature of American humor, which is understandably different than that Tesla would have been used to.
C. No, because the preceding sentence fittingly ends the paragraph and transitions to the following paragraph.
D. No, because the sentence shifts the focus of the essay away from Nicola Tesla and to economics.

22. F. NO CHANGE
G. Tesla and Edison's
H. Teslas' and Edisons'
J. Teslas and Edisons

23. A. NO CHANGE
B. rivalry
C. rivalry, one being rivals with the other,
D. competition between one another

with another electricity magnate, George [24] Westinghouse, whom he saw [25] Tesla's potential. With the backing of Westinghouse's company, Tesla was able to experiment and develop some of his best inventions. It was while working for Westinghouse that Tesla created designs for oscillators, meters, and transformers; derivatives of these creations were first attributed to Edison, though they were Tesla's. [26]

Tesla's most significant contribution to society may have been the development of his Alternating Current method of generating electricity, which is still used to deliver power to homes [27] and businesses today. Despite his enormous contributions, Tesla's unconventional eccentricities became overwhelming, and they found it [28] difficult to find funding. He continued to work on inventions until he died in 1943. It was not until after Tesla's death that the value of many of his discoveries came to light. One thing is for sure: Nikola [29] Tesla was one of the foremost brilliant people of his day and age. [30]

24. **F.** NO CHANGE
G. magnet,
H. manage,
J. magenta,

25. **A.** NO CHANGE
B. whom saw
C. who he saw
D. who saw

26. Given that all of the choices are accurate, which one most clearly communicates that Tesla's inventions have had a lasting effect within the realm of technology?

F. NO CHANGE
G. were used for a brief time before, ultimately, they were phased out.
H. are still used in many electronic devices produced today.
J. were also created while Tesla was with Westinghouse.

27. **A.** NO CHANGE
B. too homes
C. too, homes
D. to the homes

28. **F.** NO CHANGE
G. he found it
H. they were finding it
J. he having found it

29. **A.** NO CHANGE
B. to be for sure, and Nikola
C. for sure, is that Nikola
D. for sure, Nikola

30. **F.** NO CHANGE
G. intellectual individuals of the early twentieth century.
H. smart inventors to have lived when he did.
J. geniuses of his time.

Step 6 Correct Answers

Passage I
1: C
2: F
3: D
4: H
5: A
6: H
7: D
8: G
9: C
10: J
11: A
12: J
13: C
14: G
15: B

Passage II
16: H
17: D
18: F
19: B
20: J
21: A
22: G
23: B
24: F
25: D
26: H
27: A
28: G
29: A
30: J

Stumped on any? You will find the explanations for each answer beginning on page 511.

STEP 7

Full-Length Practice Tests

I hope you have found this book so far to be valuable. My goal was to root your ACT English preparation in just that: *preparation*, meaning specifically ordered preparation that puts first things first and last things last.

What follows now is two complete, full-length ACT English practice tests. Let's quickly review strategies (not content) before you set that timer and dive in.

1) "Listen"

Unless English is your second language, you have been listening to English your entire life. That means that you probably have good instincts. Even if you don't read a lot (which you should; want to improve on all aspects of the ACT? READ! I don't mean read classic novels, but anything written professionally: sports articles, fashion magazines, horror stories, etc.), every advertisement you've ever encountered on the radio, the internet, or live TV was written by people who know the English language, and this is especially true of anything your teachers have ever made you read in school. What I'm trying to say is this: *trust your gut; if something "sounds" weird, it probably is*. Just reading all four examples in context can often help you identify the correct or best answer, even if you can't pinpoint the exact reason why.

2) Answer questions as you go, but in context

By now you should know that you can't skip sentences or paragraphs that have no questions tied to them. This is, of course, true because there are always *context* questions waiting around the corner. Maybe you will need to identify the correct sentence to go at the end of the paragraph, maybe you will need to know the greater purpose of the entire essay, maybe you will need to choose the correct transition ("connector" word or phrase, like "Because of this" or "On the other hand"), or maybe you will need to identify the correct verb tense. Whatever the case is, context is key. Even when only one or two words are underlined, <u>like this,</u> it is still important for you to read the underlined portion within the entirety of the sentence.

3) Circle and return

Especially in ACT English and Math, there are questions that fall into the category of "maybe later." This simply means that you will probably be able to identify a question that will require a bit more time than normal; if you foresee that you will have to spend 1, 2, or 3 minutes on a question to get it right (like having to reread an essay to figure out the author's purpose, having to arrange sentences in a paragraph, etc.), then you should circle it, skip it (or temporarily guess), and come back at the end of the test with your spare time.

Closing Notes

a) You have 45 minutes to complete 5 passages and 75 questions. That gives you 9 minutes per passage. Get a watch and keep time *on your own*. Make this a habit; don't count on there being a clock in front of you on ACT day. Make sure you're finishing Passage I prior to 9 minutes having passed, Passage II prior to 18 minutes having passed, etc.

b) There is nothing in the directions you need to know. Read them, if you like, before you start the 45 minute timer. However, certainly don't read them on test day. They never change.

c) Of course, guess on every question; there is no penalty for guessing.

PRACTICE TEST 1

45 Minutes, 75 Questions

DIRECTIONS: In the five passages that follow, certain words and phrases are underlined and numbered. In the right-hand column, you will find alternatives for the underlined part. In most cases, you are to choose the one that best expresses the idea, makes the statement appropriate for standard written English, or is worded most consistently with the style and tone of the passage as a whole. If you think the original version is best, choose "NO CHANGE." In some cases, you will find in the right-hand column a question about the underlined part. You are to choose the best answer to the question.

You will also find questions about a section of the passage, or about the passage as a whole. These questions do not refer to an underlined portion of the passage, but rather are identified by a number or numbers in a box.

For each question, choose the alternative you consider best and fill in the corresponding oval on your answer document. Read each passage through once before you begin to answer the questions that accompany it. For many of the questions, you must read several sentences beyond the question to determine the answer. Be sure that you have read far enough ahead each time you choose an alternative.

PASSAGE I

Fallingwater

[1]

Most would agree that a boulder bulging through the living room floor are considered [1] a waste of valuable space. After all, there is very little practical use, save for sitting on it [2] or covering it up with some kind of blanket or other throw, for a large rock in the home. [A] However, for the famous American architect Frank Lloyd Wright, and [3] his client Edgar Kauffman, such a feature was the perfect way to demonstrate the affect [4] that the natural world can have on the structures built by man. [B]

1. **A.** NO CHANGE
   B. were
   C. is
   D. do appear to be

2. **F.** NO CHANGE
   G. use save for sitting on it
   H. use, save for sitting on it,
   J. use save for sitting on it,

3. **A.** NO CHANGE
   B. architect, Frank Lloyd Wright, and
   C. architect Frank Lloyd Wright; and
   D. architect Frank Lloyd Wright and

4. **F.** NO CHANGE
   G. effecting
   H. affecting
   J. effect

[2]

[1] Built over a [5] waterfall in Southwestern Pennsylvania, Fallingwater draws over 100,000 visitors annually and has been praised by numerous institutions of American public life as a site with a view like few homes in America [6]. [2] Fallingwater is the name of this home, and yes, any guest will easily see the purposeful unity of nature and architecture. [3] Thus, most students of the home are stunned to learn that Wright drew the initial plans in less than two hours. |7|

5. **A.** NO CHANGE
   B. Fallingwater is constructed over a
   C. The home is constructed over a
   D. It will be over a

6. Which choice best stresses the extensive recognition of the importance of Fallingwater?

   F. NO CHANGE
   G. that the original owners cherished.
   H. with historic and cultural significance.
   J. with unprecedented access to an unending supply of fresh water.

7. Which sequence of sentences makes this paragraph most logical?

   A. NO CHANGE
   B. 3, 1, 2
   C. 1, 3, 2
   D. 2, 1, 3

[3]

A first draft of the plans, which called for a home above the falls, [8] did not suit the desires of Kauffman, who had wanted a home below the waterfall so that he could enjoy the view. [C] As a result, [9] he came around to the bird's-eye view idea, but he continued to butt heads with Wright throughout the process of construction. At one point, Kauffman, [10] thought the space set out for his personal desk, a tiny plot in the corner of his bedroom, that was [11] too small. [D] On another occasion, Kauffman sought an engineer's opinions of one of Wright's designs. When the latter threatened to quit the job over this, Kauffman relented, apologized, and had the report permanently

8. **F.** NO CHANGE
   G. Kauffman was not thrilled with these initial plans, for they
   H. The plans first drafted cost Kauffman his view; thus, they
   J. These initial plans

9. **A.** NO CHANGE
   B. However,
   C. Because of this,
   D. Otherwise,

10. **F.** NO CHANGE
    G. Kauffman point,
    H. point, Kauffman
    J. point—Kauffman

11. **A.** NO CHANGE
    B. to be
    C. it was
    D. DELETE the underlined portion

sealed up in an unknown wall of the house, which he [12] read again. [13]

12. **F.** NO CHANGE
G. by being
H. he
J. never to be

13. At this point, the writer is considering adding the following true statement:

> Not only the walls of the home, but the foundation and roof are sturdily built.

Should the writer make this addition here?

A. Yes, because it supports the idea already stated that it is unlikely that the plans will be accessed ever again.
B. Yes, because it provides further evidence that Wright was not only a skilled architect, but also hired the best builders.
C. No, because it provides information about Fallingwater's construction that is not relevant at this point in the essay.
D. No, because it contradicts facts about the construction of the home presented earlier in the essay.

[4]

Having been used for more than 25 years [14] by the Kauffman family as a weekend getaway. When this time of personal use came to an end, the home was donated to the Western Pennsylvania Conservancy so that it could be maintained and appreciated by all. Fallingwater is not only a masterpiece of American architecture, but is proof that, sometimes, the struggle for beauty is just that: a struggle.

14. **F.** NO CHANGE
G. Fallingwater was used for over 25 years
H. While its use only lasted 25 years
J. Though its using only spanned 25 years

Question 15 asks about the preceding passage as a whole.

15. The writer is considering adding the following sentence to the essay:

> This prompted Kauffman to contact Wright and ask if there was even enough room to write his architect a check!

If the writer were to add this sentence, it would most logically be placed at:

A. Point A in Paragraph 1.
B. Point B in Paragraph 1.
C. Point C in Paragraph 3.
D. Point D in Paragraph 3.

PASSAGE II

Turn Out the Lights!

[1]

We saw the men sprinting from the beach in the direction of the restaurant where my siblings and I were <u>dining. They shouted,</u> [16] "Turn off the lights!" Needless to say, I was confused. How was I to finish my dessert if I couldn't see it? [A] How could a <u>restaurant operate, with waitstaff crashing</u> [17] into walls and drinks spilling across tables? Thankfully the out-of-breath men <u>clarify</u> [18] what they meant for the restaurant staff: sea turtles were hatching and would be confused by the restaurant's lights.

16. **F.** NO CHANGE
    G. dining, shouted,
    H. dining shouting
    J. dining, they were shouting,

17. **A.** NO CHANGE
    B. restaurant operate with waitstaff crashing
    C. restaurant operate with waitstaff crashing,
    D. restaurant operate, with waitstaff crashing,

18. **F.** NO CHANGE
    G. were to clarify
    H. are clarifying
    J. clarified

[2]

Sea turtle eggs hatch most often at nighttime when the air is <u>cooler, which had</u> [19] the added benefit of shielding them from many predators, such as birds. <u>Once</u> [20] the turtle is triggered by the temperature change, it breaks free of sand and shell and follows its instinct to find the ocean. [B] When a beach is <u>completely darkened,</u> [21] such as they were before the invention of electricity, the turtles are drawn by the moon's reflection shimmering off of the water. This is why, when a turtle hatches, it can be led in the wrong direction by bright <u>lights further</u> [22] inland.

19. **A.** NO CHANGE
    B. cooler, which, having
    C. cooler, which has
    D. cooler, had

20. **F.** NO CHANGE
    G. All at once,
    H. This is beneficial because
    J. Because of instinct, the turtle is ready for it,

21. **A.** NO CHANGE
    B. finally enveloped entirely and completely in darkness,
    C. in a situation in which the sun is no longer shining upon it,
    D. dark, like at nighttime when the air is cooler, and

22. **F.** NO CHANGE
    G. those lights further
    H. lights farther
    J. lights that went farther

[3]

Thankfully, everyone in the restaurant understood what had to be done.[23] The diner quickly darkened and dozens of curious and eager patrons (including ourselves) laid down[24] enough cash to cover the bill and the tip onto the tabletop. [C] We rushed from the restaurant down to the beach to catch a glimpse of a wonderful spectacle few ever get to witness. **|25|**

[4]

We arrived just in the time.[26] [D] More and more lights were turned off in all directions. Some on-the-spot volunteers even used black garbage bags on nearby piers that did not have a simple on-off switch to darken bait lights.[27] I felt transported to a different time, one free of light pollution in which humans and animals lived in complete harmony. I witnessed the fluorescent moon glaring off of the soft waves and, like the baby turtles, felt drawn,[28] to it myself.

23. **A.** NO CHANGE
B. comprehended in their minds the steps that had to be taken.
C. had a knowledgable sense to do certain things and avoid others.
D. succumbed to their intuition as to the things to do and the things not to do.

24. **F.** NO CHANGE
G. lied down
H. lay with
J. lied within

25. If the writer were to delete the preceding sentence, the paragraph would primarily lose a statement that:

A. emphasizes the tremendous effort people take all over the world to care for animals.
B. restates why sea turtle eggs hatch most of the time during the night.
C. provides a crucial detail in the flow of the story being told.
D. helps to overcome prejudice against animal life that burdens human beings.

26. **F.** NO CHANGE
G. just in time.
H. in the time.
J. just within time.

27. The best placement for the underlined portion (adjusting for capitalization as necessary) would be:

A. where it is now.
B. before the word *Some*.
C. after the word *bags*.
D. after the word *nearby*.

28. **F.** NO CHANGE
G. turtles felt drawn,
H. turtles, felt drawn
J. turtles felt drawn

Questions 29 and 30 ask about the preceding passage as a whole.

29. The writer is considering adding the following sentence to the essay:

> Hundreds of baby turtles were waddling towards the ocean.

If the writer were to add this sentence, it would most logically be placed at:

A. Point A in Paragraph 1.
B. Point B in Paragraph 2.
C. Point C in Paragraph 3.
D. Point D in Paragraph 4.

30. Suppose the author's main purpose had been to record the details and scientific background of a rare and meaningful personal experience. Would this essay accomplish that purpose?

F. Yes, because the essay describes the author's interest in studying marine biology, and how that interest led her to study sea turtles.
G. Yes, because the essay bolsters an encounter with sea turtles with facts about the animal's instincts, particularly when hatching.
H. No, because the essay focuses too little on sea turtles and their habitat and too much on the author's feelings about the animal.
J. No, because the essay indicates that a person can be dismissive of the sea turtle when, in reality, all have an obligation to vulnerable animal species.

PASSAGE III

Jefferson and Lewis

Thomas Jefferson is a former American <u>president known for many</u> [31] things, and rightly so. The man who authored <u>the words that make up, the Declaration of Independence, became America's third</u> [32] president beginning in 1801, during which time he radically expanded the territory of the United States. This included the Louisiana Purchase from <u>France, this</u> [33] acquisition nearly doubled the size of the nation. The purchase bolstered Jefferson's ambitions to catalogue

31. **A.** NO CHANGE
B. president, which is known for
C. president that known
D. president knowing for

32. **F.** NO CHANGE
G. the words, that make up the Declaration of Independence became America's third
H. the words that make up the Declaration of Independence, became America's third
J. the words that make up the Declaration of Independence became America's third

33. **A.** NO CHANGE
B. France
C. France:
D. France; because

a route from the East Coast to the Pacific Ocean. **|34|**

34. Which of the following statements, if added here, would provide the best transition to the discussion of how Jefferson tapped Lewis to lead this expedition?

F. Much of the West Coast, however, was not under American control.
G. Jefferson was a busy man.
H. The Pacific Ocean was on the West Coast.
J. What he needed most was the right man for the job.

Jefferson acquired funds from Congress in the amount of $2,324 to pay for the expedition, <u>and he</u> [35] tapped Army Captain Meriwether Lewis as its leader. Lewis then chose Willam Clark to help him lead the now famous Lewis and Clark Expedition. <u>Because Lewis boasted many</u> [36] of the qualities necessary to traverse the continent, there was much he did not know. <u>Because of this,</u> [37] President Jefferson sent him to various experts to acquire skills that could prove <u>important or even life-saving.</u> [38]

35. A. NO CHANGE
B. which he
C. it
D. Jefferson having been

36. F. NO CHANGE
G. Having to explain many
H. Although Lewis possessed many
J. Lewis, needing a change, still had many

37. A. NO CHANGE
B. Because of this, experts were needed, and
C. Because of, and having been caused by, this,
D. Because of this (that there were many things Lewis did not know),

38. Which choice best stresses the seriousness of the training Lewis would receive?

F. NO CHANGE
G. to his friends he was a Renaissance man.
H. his critics wrong.
J. a fun entry into knowledge of all kinds.

Lewis was first sent to study medicine **|39|** . Soon

39. At this point, the writer is considering adding the following true phrase:

> as a student of the physician Benjamin Rush in Philadelphia

Should the writer make this addition?

A. Yes, because the reader needs to know that Lewis studied medicine.
B. Yes, because it gives credibility to his study and follows the pattern of the paragraph.
C. No, because it makes Lewis seem unqualified for his expedition.
D. No, because it is too specific of a detail for this point in the essay.

after, Lewis tutored Andrew Ellicot, under[40] an expert in astronomy and navigation. Then, he learned the science of cataloguing plant and animal specimens from Benjamin Barton, latitude and longitude computations from Robert Patterson, and the science of fossils from Caspar Wistar. Though capable of learning such a vast array of knowledge, Lewis's intellect also showed[41] that he was both willing and eager. This explains the additional hours that he sat[42] studying in the vast library of Monticello, Jefferson's personal home. |43|

The expedition set out from St. Charles, Missouri on May 21, 1804 with as many as 45 members in their party. The journey, however adventurous, proved difficult for obvious reasons, and the group faced challenges beyond the modern imagination. Conversely,[44] only one brave explorer, Sergeant Charles Floyd, lost his life. In November of 1805, due in no small part to Lewis' vast training and knowledge, Jefferson got his wish: Lewis, Clark, and the men under their command finally reached the Pacific Ocean.[45]

40. The best placement for the underlined portion would be:

- **F.** where it is now.
- **G.** after the word *Soon.*
- **H.** after the word *and.*
- **J.** after the word *tutored.*

41.
- **A.** NO CHANGE
- **B.** Lewis's willingness to learn displayed
- **C.** Lewis, in addition, demonstrated
- **D.** multiple subjects were learned to show

42.
- **F.** NO CHANGE
- **G.** used up
- **H.** spent
- **J.** blew through

43. If the writer were to delete the preceding sentence, the essay would primarily lose a statement that:

- **A.** highlights the jealousy Jefferson must have had for Lewis.
- **B.** argues for the addition of libraries to most, if not all, homes.
- **C.** shows that Lewis was willing to go above and beyond the minimum requirements.
- **D.** demonstrates Jefferson's love of learning.

44.
- **F.** NO CHANGE
- **G.** Miraculously,
- **H.** Suspiciously,
- **J.** Uniquely,

45. Given that all the choices are true, which one best concludes this sentence and the essay as a whole?

- **A.** NO CHANGE
- **B.** the Louisiana Purchase was worth the cost.
- **C.** his library would need a new book to catalogue the adventures.
- **D.** adventure, like learning, is the work of a lifetime.

PASSAGE IV

The Eastern Indigo Snake

[1]

Though my friends are timid around[46] snakes, I find them fascinating. This is probably because my father is a biologist and professor at the local university.[47] I grew up visiting him in his office and spending hours among the reptiles housed in a nearby building on campus. This is why, when finally allowed as a teenager to be his intern; I was[48] honored to be asked to be a part of the Eastern Indigo Snake Reintroduction Project and I'm eager[49] to help in any way I could. [A]

[2]

The Eastern Indigo Snake is not only the longest species of snake, native[50] to the United States, but in all of North America. [B] It is also non-venomous and plays an important role in the balance of life in those[51] across Florida, Southern Georgia, Alabama, and Mississippi. However, they have never been found in Arkansas.[52] Decades have gone by between sightings in areas they once inhabited in large numbers.

46. Which choice most clearly contrasts the author's feelings towards snakes with that of her friends?

F. NO CHANGE
G. terrified of
H. not the biggest fans of
J. enamored by

47. Given that all the choices are accurate, which one best connects this sentence to the information that follows in the next sentence?

A. NO CHANGE
B. took me camping all throughout childhood.
C. had a book of snakes that he kept on the bookshelf in his office.
D. told me many stories growing up that featured snakes, in both good and evil ways.

48. **F.** NO CHANGE
G. intern, I was
H. intern. I was
J. intern, then I was

49. **A.** NO CHANGE
B. eager
C. eagerly
D. eager in my desire

50. **F.** NO CHANGE
G. species of snake native
H. species, of snake native,
J. species, of snake, native

51. **A.** NO CHANGE
B. forests
C. them
D. all of them

52. Given that all the choices are accurate, which one best provides information about the Eastern Indigo Snake that is most clearly relevant at this point in the essay?

F. NO CHANGE
G. they eat small mammals and reptiles.
H. they are not the longest snakes in the world.
J. the species is critically endangered.

[3]

This new endeavor, a collaborative effort between biologists representing various organizations (such as zoos, government agencies, and universities) throughout the Southeastern United States whom shared the urgency to protect this endangered species.

Longleaf, Pine forests that had been restored over time to meet the particular needs of the Eastern Indigo, such as habitat, prey, and isolation from human interference, were preferable. Finally, a forest in Southern Alabama was selected. [C] When the day of release finally came, I was beyond excited. [57]

53. A. NO CHANGE
B. endeavor, having been
C. endeavor had been
D. endeavor was

54. F. NO CHANGE
G. they that
H. who
J. which

55. A. NO CHANGE
B. Longleaf Pine forests that had been restored
C. Longleaf Pine forests, that had been restored
D. Longleaf Pine forests, that had been restored,

56. Given that all the choices are accurate, which one most effectively transitions the essay from a focus on research to a focus on the actual release of the snakes back into the wild?

F. NO CHANGE
G. Eastern Indigo Snakes need the right habitat.
H. The researchers needed time to select the correct forest.
J. The Longleaf Pine is a tree found in many different states, especially in the Southeast.

57. At this point, the writer is considering adding the following sentence:

> My father teaches biology at a local university, and he and I spent a lot of time together around reptiles.

Given that the information is true, should the writer make this addition here?

A. Yes, because it gives the reader necessary background information about the writer.
B. Yes, because it clarifies why the writer is personally involved in the project.
C. No, because it repeats information about the writer that is provided earlier in the essay.
D. No, because it suggests that the writer was a part of the project.

[4]

The team, including myself, hiked miles deep into the forest carrying a dozen of the endangered reptiles that had been carefully chosen for reintroduction. When we arrived to the preselected location, my father lifted a beautiful snake from its cage, but instead of letting it slither away, he handed it to me. "You do the honor," he said. [D] I would never see this snake again, but as it got away, since that is why we were there, from my loving hands, I knew we had done the best we could for this endangered species.

58. F. NO CHANGE
G. slithered off, thesnaked I mean,
H. escaped
J. wriggled, slithered, and went out

Questions 59 and 60 ask about the preceding passage as a whole.

59. The writer is considering adding the following sentence to the essay:

It is black but boasts a beautiful blue or purple sheen that flashes as it slithers through the sunlight.

If the writer were to add this sentence, it would most logically be placed at:

A. Point A in Paragraph 1.
B. Point B in Paragraph 2.
C. Point C in Paragraph 3.
D. Point D in Paragraph 4.

60. Suppose the author's main purpose had been to recount a meaningful participation in an important project. Would this essay accomplish that purpose?

F. Yes, because it recalls how the author personally organized a serious and enduring effort to restore Longleaf Pine forests.
G. Yes, because it describes how the author helped to begin the restoration of an endangered species.
H. No, because the author is writing about an effort that involved only her father and not her personally.
J. No, because the essay provides plenty of evidence to show that the author was forced to participate, making it less meaningful.

PASSAGE V

Fred "Nall" Hollis

When Fred <u>Hollis nicknamed Nall,</u> [61] graduated from high school in a small town with a population of less than 10,000 people, it would have been nearly impossible for him to <u>foresee</u> [62] the international acclaim that would one day be his. Nall's artwork has been featured across Europe, particularly in Italy, and is famous for elevating the frame of a piece to a new <u>level of artistic genius</u> [63] by incorporating it into the art

61. **A.** NO CHANGE
B. Hollis, nicknamed Nall,
C. Hollis nicknamed Nall
D. Hollis, nicknamed Nall

62. **F.** NO CHANGE
G. foresee into the future
H. foresee—having grown up in an area with a very low population—
J. foresee back then

63. Given that all the choices are accurate, which one most strongly suggests that Nall's art is both unique and beautiful?

A. NO CHANGE
B. area
C. status that is really good
D. group to be recognized

itself. It's [64] almost impossible to pass by one of Nall's breathtaking pieces without stopping to contemplate the beauty and purpose in every detail. [65]

After graduating from college, Nall was admitted to the School of Fine Arts in Paris, here [66] he learned to further harness his natural artistic ability. He spent a great deal of time traveling as well in these early days, visiting a variety of cultures being [67] as Mexico, India, and North Africa. After having a number of pieces incorporated [68] in both America and Europe, he trained under artistic legend Salvador Dalí.

Any observer of Nall's most famous pieces can see the influence of Dalí's surrealism. However, Nall seems to tamper the absurdity in his own images with the beauty of mosaics, color, and order. [69] For example, a human character may be depicted in black and white—with [70] lovely hints of color to highlight their

64. **F.** NO CHANGE
G. Its
H. Its'
J. They're

65. If the writer were to delete the underlined portion (adjusting the punctuation as needed), the essay would primarily lose:

A. a reason to pass by one of Nall's pieces without stopping.
B. the idea that Nall creates beautiful art.
C. details that create irony given that he is from a small town.
D. the reasons why a person would stop to think and wonder about a Nall piece.

66. **F.** NO CHANGE
G. Paris and
H. Paris; here
J. Paris

67. **A.** NO CHANGE
B. those being
C. much
D. such

68. **F.** NO CHANGE
G. featured
H. seasoned
J. underwhelmed

69. Given that all of the choices are true, which one most effectively leads the reader from the first sentence of this paragraph to the information that follows in the paragraph?

A. NO CHANGE
B. As a matter of fact, there is speculation that Dalí is actually the artist who created many of Nall's early pieces.
C. Many of these pieces of art ended up on public display in Europe.
D. On the other hand, maybe Dalí had no influence on Nall after all.

70. **F.** NO CHANGE
G. white with
H. white:
J. white with,

features. Oftentimes, these human features are out of proportion, creating in the distorted observer a sense of wonder.[71] However, the absurdity and distortion are further transformed as they are framed in by a beautiful array of wood, tile, or some other combination of bright materials, some of which make their way into and become a part of the art itself.

His art has undoubtedly become famous,[72] Nall has not forgotten his small town roots. In fact, they[73] still owns and operates a studio in his home state, from which he creates pieces[74] for local museums and hotels featuring and inspired by the beauty of the area. All in all, Fred Hollis is living proof that artistic ability can be found anywhere and, as long as it is nurtured, can blossom into something truly inspiring.

71. Which choice provides the clearest indication that the person discerning Nall's contorted art is often in awe?

A. NO CHANGE
B. These distorted human features often create in the observer a sense of wonder out of proportion.
C. Oftentimes, these human features are out of proportion or distorted, creating in the observer a sense of wonder.
D. The observer, out of proportion and distorted, is often in wonder at these human features.

72. **F.** NO CHANGE
G. Without a doubt, Nall's art is famous throughout the world,
H. He became famous,
J. Although his art has become famous,

73. **A.** NO CHANGE
B. there
C. he or she
D. he

74. **F.** NO CHANGE
G. artfully crafts works of art
H. brings art into existence
J. designs and produces examples of his art

Question 75 asks about the preceding passage as a whole.

75. Suppose the writer's main purpose had been to explain the reasons why, how, and when various art galleries around the world displayed Nall's work. Would this essay accomplish that purpose?

A. Yes, because the essay clearly states that Nall's work was shown in Europe.
B. Yes, because the author traveled extensively around the world to countries like Mexico and India.
C. No, because although the writer mentions Nall's art being shown in Europe, the writer does not elaborate on when or how any specific gallery did so.
D. No, because the writer never mentions any international attention that Nall's art was able to garner.

PRACTICE TEST 2

45 Minutes, 75 Questions

PASSAGE I

Goodall and the Chimps

[1]

When Jane Goodall entered the Gombe Stream National Reserve in Tanzania, she was determined to make history, and that she did.[1] While she is known today as a woman who made headway in a scientific field dominated mostly by men; she would prefer[2] to be known by the body of knowledge she produced and cultivated during her time.[3] Much of what we know about chimpanzees is the direct result of Goodall's efforts.

[2]

One groundbreaking observation of it[4] was tool use among the primates. She watched as one chimp, inserting repetitively into the mounds of termites grass that was tall, for example.[5] The termites would climb the stalk, which the chimpanzee would remove from the mound.[6] The insects that came up with the

1. A. NO CHANGE
   B. did earn a spot in history.
   C. did do when she entered the reserve.
   D. did, her name being Jane Goodall.

2. F. NO CHANGE
   G. men, preferring
   H. men, but she would prefer
   J. men, she would prefer

3. Which choice best portrays Goodall's work as the result of years of difficulty and strife?
   A. NO CHANGE
   B. by her blood, sweat, and tears.
   C. by working.
   D. through hard work.

4. F. NO CHANGE
   G. hers
   H. theirs
   J. ours

5. A. NO CHANGE
   B. over and over insert, for example, stalks of tall grass into where the termites lived.
   C. with tall stalks inserted in there, where termites are living.
   D. for example, repeatedly inserted tall stalks of grass into termite mounds.

6. The writer is considering deleting the underlined portion (adjusting the punctuation as needed). Should the underlined portion be kept or deleted?
   F. Kept, because otherwise we would not know the type of ape she saw hunting termites.
   G. Kept, because it provides a necessary step in the tool use observed by Goodall.
   H. Deleted, because it repeats a detail provided earlier in the paragraph.
   J. Deleted, because it shifts the focus of the paragraph away from what Goodall observed.

stalk got eaten [7].

7. Given that all the choices are accurate, which one best emphasizes the chimpanzee's nature as hunter?

A. NO CHANGE
B. didn't live for much longer.
C. were swallowed.
D. fell victim to the hungry predator.

[3]

Another discovery of Goodall's was that chimpanzees eat meat. Up to that time, it was believed that chimps ate a mostly vegetarian diet supplemented by the consumption of [8] some insects. However, on one occasion, Goodall witnessed a hunting group climb a tree, and surround [9] a colobus monkey, with which they shared a habitat. [A] The aggressive apes blocked off all possible exits for the colobus while one among the group singlehandedly killed the monkey. The chimps then shared [10] the carcass with one another.

8. Which of the following alternatives to the underlined portion would NOT be acceptable?

F. the eating of
G. the combustion of
H. the ingestion of
J. DELETE the underlined portion.

9. A. NO CHANGE
B. climb a tree, and surround,
C. climb, a tree, and surround
D. climb a tree and surround

10. F. NO CHANGE
G. having a share of
H. in sharing with
J. share

[4]

One probable reason that Goodall was able to make such strides, with the chimpanzees [11] is because she named them. At the time, it was customary to number animals. Goodall, on the other hand, found joy in assigning names to them, *David Greybeard*, *Fifi*, and *Mr. McGregor* being a few examples. [B] This helped her to bond [12] with them, and thus to live among the troupe for so long a time.

11. A. NO CHANGE
B. make such strides, with the chimpanzees,
C. make such strides with the chimpanzees,
D. make such strides with the chimpanzees

12. F. NO CHANGE
G. form a deep, heartfelt connection
H. grow really close
J. share a bond

[5]

When Goodall first arrived, a chimp titled [13] Goliath was the alpha male. [C] Sadly, Goodall was attacked on a regular basis by a very aggressive male chimpanzee named Frodo. When Frodo became the

13. A. NO CHANGE
B. named
C. known by
D. designated

alpha male, Goodall knew that it was time for her to step away from the troupe. [D]

Questions 14 and 15 ask about the preceding passage as a whole.

14. Upon reviewing the essay and finding that some information has been left out, the writer composes the following sentence incorporating that information:

> He was succeeded by Mike, a cunning primate with a thirst for power.

If the writer were to add this sentence, it would most logically be placed at:

F. Point A in Paragraph 3.
G. Point B in Paragraph 4.
H. Point C in Paragraph 5.
J. Point D in Paragraph 5.

15. Suppose the writer's main purpose had been to highlight the contributions to the knowledge of animals by a scientist. Would this essay accomplish that purpose?

A. Yes, because the essay centers on Jane Goodall, and details her comprehensive study of the chimpanzees.
B. Yes, because the essay compares and contrasts the scientific achievements of various researchers over time.
C. No, because Jane Goodall, though a scientist, did not conduct research among the chimpanzees, but merely observed them.
D. No, because the writer focuses more on the emotional reactions of chimpanzees to stimuli as opposed to the scientist behind it.

PASSAGE II

A Fishing Memory

When my grandfather woke me on those early mornings, he always did so in a <u>gentle, yet urgent,</u> [16] fashion. I would take a deep breath, roll out of the bed, and stare <u>from</u> [17] the dark morning that awaited outside my window. <u>I always had a sense that the fish knew that we were coming.</u> [18]

Every evening before one of our fishing trips he would rig each fishing pole from scratch. He checked the drag, the strength of the line, the knots that held

16. F. NO CHANGE
G. gentle yet urgent
H. gentle yet urgent,
J. gentle, yet urgent

17. A. NO CHANGE
B. behind
C. into
D. above

18. Given that all of the choices are true, which one best concludes this paragraph and transitions to the following paragraph?

F. NO CHANGE
G. Then, I got back into bed.
H. We were ready to go, our tackle and poles having been prepared in advance.
J. The darkness was thick and intimidating.

the treble hooks, and the weights. "Can I help, Grandpa?" I'd ask, <u>and</u> [19] even though he never needed it, he'd let me be his assistant.

<u>After all that work,</u> [20] we would be well on our way in the boat. Grandpa's favorite spot was a <u>large oil rig</u> [21] about a mile off the coast of the island. There was never need for an anchor: <u>he was simply tying</u> [22] a rope to the structure and we were ready to fish. <u>Carefully,</u> [23] he would hook my line up with a shrimp, and because we would arrive before the changing of the tides, we always set ourselves up for the greatest possibility of success. |**24**|

[1] In other words, it was a thrill every time no matter how big or small the catch might be. [2] It

19. **A.** NO CHANGE
B. therefore,
C. as a matter of fact,
D. DELETE the underlined portion.

20. Given that all of the choices are accurate, which one most effectively introduces the paragraph by returning to the topic of the essay's opening paragraph?

F. NO CHANGE
G. Due to unforeseen weather,
H. Before first light,
J. With the fishing poles ready,

21. **A.** NO CHANGE
B. large oil rig,
C. large oil, rig,
D. large, oil rig

22. **F.** NO CHANGE
G. to tie simply he would
H. he would simply tie
J. tying he did simply

23. Which choice best emphasizes the grandfather's delight in fishing with his grandson?

A. NO CHANGE
B. Unexpectedly,
C. Excitedly,
D. Dutifully,

24. At this point, the writer is considering adding the following true statement:

> Shrimp are decapod crustaceans, and because there are thousands of species around the world, they are commonly eaten by a vast variety of fish.

Should the writer make this addition here?

F. Yes, because it answers a rhetorical question raised earlier in the paragraph.
G. Yes, because it transitions the preceding paragraph to the paragraph that follows.
H. No, because the sentence implies that the pair are going to successfully catch fish.
J. No, because it detracts from the story that is being told as the essay progresses.

seemed the fish were always biting, for we would fill (25) our ice chest with Speckled Trout, White Trout, Sheepshead, Mangrove Snapper, Redfish, Flounder, and a kind (26) of other delicious fish. [3] Though I enjoyed the taste of a deep-fried fillet from any one of these, my favorite part, quality time not included, (27) was never knowing what we would pull from the water. |28|

I remember fighting a large fish for what seemed like hours as the sun was rising. Workers on the rig gathered above us to see what a visiting kid from the Midwest might pull in after such a battle. |29| When the fish was just below the surface, the line snapped and the pole recoiled; I tried to keep calm under the watchful gaze of the workers. Though I missed the big one, which I had on the line for a very long time, (30) Grandpa was able to cheer me up by speculating as to what kind of fish it might have been.

25. **A.** NO CHANGE
B. they filled
C. we were to be filling
D. we would filling

26. **F.** NO CHANGE
G. lack
H. type
J. variety

27. **A.** NO CHANGE
B. part quality time not included,
C. part, quality time not included
D. part quality time not included

28. Which of the following sequences of sentences makes this paragraph most logical?

F. NO CHANGE
G. 2, 3, 1
H. 1, 3, 2
J. 3, 2, 1

29. If the writer were to replace the word *battle* with the word *try* in the preceding sentence, the sentence would primarily lose a word that:

A. emphasizes the difficulty and length of time it took to reel in the fish.
B. restates a theme introduced in the first paragraph.
C. understates how tiresome it was to get the fish into the boat.
D. fails to transition the sentence to the one that follows.

30. The writer is considering deleting the underlined portion (adjusting the punctuation as needed). Should the underlined portion be kept or deleted?

F. Kept, because it adds a dramatic detail that makes the story more relatable.
G. Kept, because without it the reader would assume that the fish got away quickly.
H. Deleted, because it restates a fact that has been stated elsewhere in the paragraph.
J. Deleted, because it fails to mention the reaction of the group of workers who were watching.

PASSAGE III

The Sailing Stones

Visitors to the American West have no shortage of potential sites to visit, from lively cities like Portland, OR and Las Vegas, NV to the Redwood forests of California, any vacation to the area is sure to be, as one may experience, too short. One rarity, however, has been on the receiving end of growing interest in recent years: sailing stones.

Sailing stones are a natural phenomenon in which, from the point of view of the casual observer, stones appear to have been walking or sailing across the desert. This movement, trails that sometimes swerve smoothly or, on occasion, cut at sharp angles. These trails eventually end at the base of a large stone, thus giving the allusion that the stone has been moving of its own accord. To the untrained eye, it looks as if the stones have been moving by themselves through the sand.

The stones are indeed moving across the desert, but there is a scientific explanation. During cold

31. **A.** NO CHANGE
B. visit from,
C. visit. From
D. visit from

32. **F.** NO CHANGE
G. be, most definitely,
H. be, though it may be obvious,
J. be

33. **A.** NO CHANGE
B. changing
C. illuminating
D. taking

34. Which choice best suggests that the sailing stones are difficult to explain because they are not man-made?

F. NO CHANGE
G. thing that happens
H. logically consistent happening
J. neat event

35. **A.** NO CHANGE
B. movement, which creates
C. movement creates
D. movement to create

36. **F.** NO CHANGE
G. giving the elusion
H. giving the illusion
J. giving the effusion

37. **A.** NO CHANGE
B. More recently, these stones have been getting a lot of attention.
C. All of this happens naturally.
D. DELETE the underlined portion.

38. **F.** NO CHANGE
G. moving
H. moves about
J. moved around

nights, sheets of ice form on the desert floor. |39| The sheets are broken up on sunny days. When this breakup is accompanied, the[40] ice is pushed across the desert floor and against the base of the stone, thus pushing the stone itself.

This process is known as ice shove. Although ice shove is a buildup of ice in areas one might expect,[41] such as the arctic—scientists have shown that even if there is very little ice involved, and even if it is occurring in the desert, ice buildup combined with gusts of wind still though technically[42] qualifies as an example of ice shove.

Throughout the 20th century there was much speculation as to the cause of the stones' movements. Some hypothesized that movement of mud was to blame the others[43] theorized that something more supernatural or extraterrestrial was at work. Thankfully a handful of serious scientists sought a more accurate explanation. Now, all whom[44] travel far to catch a glimpse of the sailing stones benefit from the scientists' thorough research. |45|

39. If the writer were to delete the preceding sentence, the essay would primarily lose a sentence that:

A. describes every detail in the water cycle.
B. distracts from the paragraph's purpose.
C. rightly contrasts cold nights with hot days.
D. explains how ice comes to be in the desert.

40. **F.** NO CHANGE
G. accompanied through wind, the
H. accompanied with the
J. accompanied by high wind speeds, the

41. **A.** NO CHANGE
B. expect—
C. expect:
D. expect

42. **F.** NO CHANGE
G. on the contrary, though technically,
H. though technically altogether
J. technically

43. **A.** NO CHANGE
B. blame, and though others
C. blame, while others
D. blame

44. **F.** NO CHANGE
G. themselves whom
H. who
J. they

45. The writer is considering deleting the preceding sentence. Should this sentence be kept or deleted?

A. Kept, because it reinforces that scientists must do their research wholeheartedly.
B. Kept, because it fittingly ends the essay by linking with the first paragraph.
C. Deleted, because it shifts the focus from the stones to tourists who visit the stones.
D. Deleted, because it presumes that everyone will eventually see the stones firsthand.

PASSAGE IV

The Moai of Easter Island

Easter Island sits in the Pacific Ocean off the coast of Chile; of which [46] it is a special territory. Its name stems from the first European visit to the island, which occurred, on Easter Sunday [47] in 1722. Though its history and isolation from the mainland are of interest to many, the most academically appealing aspect of the island, not to mention its most mysterious: is its [48] Moai.

Moai are large human figures carved from stone and are thought to represent ancestors of natives. The average stone's and its [49] height and weight is about 13 feet and 12 tonnes, respectively; [50] though they vary in size. Characteristic of each statue is an oversized head, nose, and chin. They carve [51] from a quarry called Rano Raraku, which is an inactive volcanic crater [52] on the Western side of the island.

While nearly half of all Moai remain at the site of the quarry, hundreds [53] of statues were transported around the island between the years 1250 and 1500. This has led to an immense amount of pillow talk [54] as to the means of the transportation, a mystery deepened by the fact that the island was nearly

46. **F.** NO CHANGE
G. Chile of which
H. Chile, and which
J. Chile, of which

47. **A.** NO CHANGE
B. island, which occurred on Easter Sunday,
C. island, which occurred on Easter Sunday
D. island which occurred on Easter Sunday

48. **F.** NO CHANGE
G. mysterious, is its,
H. mysterious, is its
J. mysterious is its

49. **A.** NO CHANGE
B. stones' and its
C. stone's
D. stones

50. **F.** NO CHANGE
G. respectively,
H. respectively
J. respectively, and

51. **A.** NO CHANGE
B. are carving
C. do the carving
D. were carved

52. **F.** NO CHANGE
G. inactive, volcanic, crater
H. inactive, volcanic crater
J. inactive volcanic crater,

53. **A.** NO CHANGE
B. quarry—hundreds
C. quarry. Hundreds
D. quarry hundreds

54. **F.** NO CHANGE
G. conjecturing of guesses
H. people talking and chatting
J. speculation

treeless when Europeans first arrived in the 18th century.
[55]

One hypothesis is that the stones were rolled across lubricated logs. Although men pulled on the stones by rope, others lifted logs from the back of the line to the front so that the stone could continue rolling in the direction of its final destination. A scientific analysis has shown that at one time, the island was very wooded indeed |57| .
[56]

A second hypothesis about the transportation of the Moai, however, has been gaining a steady following among many anthropologists. This theory postulates that ropes were tied to the carved statues by the natives while they were upright. As men pulled on the enormous statues, others would rock the statue back and forth to the rhythm of a chant or song. Slowly, the statues would "walk" across the island. No matter how them were transported from Rano Raraku across the island, all can appreciate their beauty, mystery, and history.
[58] [59] [60]

55. Which of the following alternatives to the underlined portion would NOT be acceptable?

A. landed
B. came
C. reached the shore
D. glanced

56. F. NO CHANGE
G. While
H. However
J. Contrary to popular belief

57. At this point, the writer is considering adding the following information:

which would lend credence to this theory

Should the writer make this addition here?

A. Yes, because otherwise the reader would not know that the island was once wooded.
B. Yes, because it connects the fact of the island's wooded past to the hypothesis put forward by the paragraph.
C. No, because the paragraph has nothing to do with historical theory.
D. No, because it fails to provide a credible source for the scientific analysis already mentioned in the sentence.

58. F. NO CHANGE
G. have been gaining
H. have gained
J. gains

59. A. NO CHANGE
B. statues
C. previously carved statues
D. statues, previously carved,

60. F. NO CHANGE
G. the Moai
H. it
J. all they

PASSAGE V

John Hart, Unsung Hero

[1]

Stories of <u>that long ago American war</u> 61 and the heroism of many of the nation's founders abound. <u>On the contrary, most</u> 62 are familiar with Thomas Jefferson, George Washington, Benjamin Franklin, John Adams, and John Hancock, to name a few, but they are not the only ones who took risks <u>instead of</u> 63 so great a nation. [A] There were 56 total signers of the Declaration of Independence—many of whom fly under the radar—including <u>some person</u> 64 from New Jersey. |65|

[2]

John Hart was the son of a farmer and owned hundreds of acres of farmland himself in Hunterdon County, a rural area north of Trenton. [B] As a politician who had penned his name to the parchment that declared the sovereignty of the American <u>colonies; Hart</u> 66 was a wanted man when the British army closed in on his home in December of the same year.

61. **A.** NO CHANGE
B. the American Revolution
C. all of the fighting that started in 1776
D. all the shots fired and battles waged over the states

62. **F.** NO CHANGE
G. As a result, most
H. In conclusion, most
J. Most

63. **A.** NO CHANGE
B. on behalf of
C. to the detriment of
D. rather

64. Which choice best fits the tone of the essay and most strongly introduces the subject of the essay as a man whose story is worthy of being told?

F. NO CHANGE
G. a man
H. an unsung hero
J. a great citizen

65. At this point, the writer is considering adding the following true statement:

> George Washington embarked on his famous crossing of the Delaware into New Jersey in the winter of 1777.

Should the writer make this addition here?

A. Yes, because it ties in well with the more famous signers of the Declaration mentioned earlier in the paragraph.
B. Yes, because it provides historical evidence for the important role New Jersey played in the American Revolution.
C. No, because it is only loosely related to the information provided in the first paragraph.
D. No, because the first paragraph makes no mention of George Washington.

66. **F.** NO CHANGE
G. colonies, Hart
H. colonies, but Hart
J. colonies. Hart

[3]

After entrusting the safety of his children to a family that lived near him, Hart was forced into the Sourland Mountains, where he hid among the rocks and in caves for over a month. [C] His empty farm was raided and damaged by troops. Not finding Hart at home, the British hunted him like an animal throughout the surrounding area, but to no avail: Hart, though in his 60's, was able to elude their efforts to track him down. [D]

[4]

[1] Finally, American troops retook Trenton; after living in terrible conditions for such a long time, the relief of returning home was incredible. [2] For example, prior to the Battle of Monmouth, Hart's abundant farmland was used as camping grounds for Washington's patriot army. [3] Its even said that Washington himself dined one night with his cosigner of the Declaration. [4] Over a year later the war was ongoing, and Hart was still doing his part. [72]

[5]

Sadly, Hart would not live to see the end of the Revolutionary War. He passed away peacefully in 1779 there and was buried in the local churchyard.

67. **A.** NO CHANGE
B. group of people under one roof nearby
C. family in the general vicinity
D. local family

68. **F.** NO CHANGE
G. to hide
H. be hiding
J. were to hide

69. Given that all of the choices are accurate, which one most effectively dramatizes the situation at hand and stresses the urgency of Hart's circumstances?

A. NO CHANGE
B. the troops searched far and wide
C. enemy forces took a good look
D. soldiers in red uniforms checked out some places

70. **F.** NO CHANGE
G. Hart was relieved and able to return to his home.
H. home was waiting for Hart, who was relieved.
J. the caves were traded for the home Hart was used to, which explains just how relieved he truly was.

71. **A.** NO CHANGE
B. They
C. It's
D. Its'

72. For the sake of logic and cohesion, Sentence 4 should be placed:

F. where it is now.
G. before Sentence 1.
H. after Sentence 1.
J. after Sentence 2.

73. **A.** NO CHANGE
B. there is hope that Hart will be remembered
C. under his own roof and in his own bed
D. at his home

Since Hart had donated <u>the land to build the church</u> [74] in the first place, it was a fitting burial for a generous and courageous man.

74. **F.** NO CHANGE
G. the land, to build the church,
H. the land to build the church,
J. the land to build, the church,

Question 75 asks about the preceding passage as a whole.

75. At this point, the writer is considering adding the following information:

> He had thirteen children, but sadly his wife passed away in October of 1776, relatively soon after Independence Day earlier that summer.

If the writer were to add this sentence, it would most logically be placed at:

A. Point A in Paragraph 1.
B. Point B in Paragraph 2.
C. Point C in Paragraph 3.
D. Point D in Paragraph 3.

Step 7 Correct Answers

Practice Test 1

Passage I	Passage II	Passage III	Passage IV	Passage V
1: C	16: F	31: A	46: G	61: B
2: F	17: B	32: J	47: A	62: F
3: D	18: J	33: C	48: G	63: A
4: J	19: C	34: J	49: B	64: F
5: A	20: F	35: A	50: G	65: D
6: H	21: A	36: H	51: B	66: H
7: D	22: H	37: A	52: J	67: D
8: J	23: A	38: F	53: D	68: G
9: B	24: F	39: B	54: H	69: A
10: H	25: C	40: J	55: B	70: G
11: B	26: G	41: C	56: F	71: C
12: J	27: C	42: H	57: C	72: J
13: C	28: H	43: C	58: H	73: D
14: G	29: D	44: G	59: B	74: F
15: D	30: G	45: A	60: G	75: C

Practice Test 2

Passage I	Passage II	Passage III	Passage IV	Passage V
1: A	16: F	31: C	46: J	61: B
2: J	17: C	32: J	47: C	62: J
3: B	18: H	33: A	48: H	63: B
4: G	19: A	34: F	49: C	64: H
5: D	20: H	35: C	50: G	65: C
6: G	21: A	36: H	51: D	66: G
7: D	22: H	37: D	52: F	67: D
8: G	23: C	38: F	53: A	68: F
9: D	24: J	39: D	54: J	69: A
10: F	25: A	40: J	55: D	70: G
11: D	26: J	41: B	56: G	71: C
12: F	27: A	42: J	57: B	72: H
13: B	28: G	43: C	58: F	73: D
14: H	29: A	44: H	59: B	74: F
15: A	30: H	45: B	60: G	75: B

Stumped on any? You will find the explanations for each answer beginning on page 515 (Practice Test 1) and 523 (Practice Test 2).

The ACT Math *System*

Six Steps to ACT Math Perfection

Introduction

My more than 1,000 hours of ACT classroom experience have taught me that you, the student, need three things when it comes to the ACT Math test: content knowledge, strategy, and skills. *The ACT Math System* book will get you there. We're not going to waste your time by having you try to memorize very specific, unlikely to be asked about math rules and equations. For example, many students I have tutored and taught have obsessed over memorizing the Quadratic Formula or the Law of Cosines or the formula of an ellipse. Don't get me wrong, knowing those things is *good*, but I would bet the cost of 1,000 of these books that you do not *need* to know any of those three on your next ACT Math test. Even on questions where you *think* that one of those or some other obscure formula is necessary, I can bet that it, indeed, is not.

The purpose of this portion of the book is to focus your attention on the content and skills *most needed in ACT Math to raise your score*, and to do so *one at a time*. In other words, those that, simply, are most tested across the ACT Math test. The closer a Step is to Step 1, the more important; the further a Step is away from Step 1, the less important (and by less important, I simply mean less likely to be tested on ACT day). You'll notice that Steps 1 and 2 focus on strategy. This is intentional, as in my experience, strategy on the ACT Math test is the most important skill to acquire to move the needle on your ACT Math score. Once these are acquired, it's time for content. You'll notice that I have broken ACT Math content up into two categories: ACT Math *Have to Know* (which features all of the ACT Math content that is guaranteed to be asked about on your next ACT Math test) and ACT Math *Good to Know* (ACT Math content that is *likely* to appear on your next ACT Math test, but not *guaranteed*). There are a total of 120 questions to practice exclusively as a part of the ACT Math *Have to Know* lessons (60 questions as you go, and another 60 in a *Have to Know* practice test). This preparation, in combination with the questions to answer as you go in the ACT Math *Good to Know* section, culminates in two full-length practice tests (the final Step!).

How to Use This Section of the Book

Use of this section of *The ACT System* book is simple. Review the Step, then work your way through the practice that follows. The book is laid out to ensure that you put first-things-first, thus it is crucial to begin at the beginning.

In addition, most of the practice offered to you in *The ACT Math System* is within the context of full-length passages (there are 3 full-length tests of 180 problems in this format). This is to train your mind to pay attention for that span of time and to become used to the real-life length of ACT Math passages. The remaining questions follow specific content lessons, but are formatted exactly like the ACT Math test (even the practice questions are formatted like the actual ACT with the questions on the left and space on the right hand side of the page for you to use like scratch paper). Following each practice section, you will find a list of answers. However, the back of the book contains a written explanation for each and every question; these explanations review rules and strategy while explaining the proper way (or ways, if there are multiple strategies to use) to solve the problem.

In a time crunch? Don't have time to use this entire part of the book from start to finish? In that case, complete as many steps as possible, then skip ahead to the two practice tests in Step 6.

The ACT Math Test - Overview and Basics

The ACT Math Test is the second of four and is preceded by English, then followed by Reading and Science, respectively. The ACT Math test is designed to test your ability to recall learned material from middle and high school, to apply learned material in a variety of situations, and to think logically and cohesively.

The ACT Math test is the longest of all four subject tests. You are given 60 minutes to answer 60 questions that test your knowledge and abilities across a wide-range of math topics. This ranges from pre-Algebra concepts such as calculating percentages and mean, median, and mode to concepts in Trigonometry like recognizing changes in the graphs of sine and cosine....and everything in between.

As the test moves along, the questions generally increase in difficulty. This isn't linear. In other words, it isn't guaranteed that question 10 is more difficult than question 9 or 8, or that question 59 is more difficult than question 58 or 57. This means that this is a good time to talk about...

Pacing

The best way to think about the increase in difficulty is like this: questions 1-20 are the easiest block of questions on the test, questions 21-40 are of middle difficulty, and questions 41-60 are the most challenging on the test. Number 58 might be of more medium difficulty, for example, but as a whole, the final third that it is in is the most difficult group.

Your knowledge of this increase in difficulty is very important for this reason: pacing (more on this and strategy in Step 1). Though it may seem that you should allocate one minute for each question (you are given 60 minutes for 60 questions, after all), that's really not accurate. You should be spending roughly 15 minutes *total* on questions 1-20, 20 minutes *total* on questions 21-40, and 25 minutes *total* on the harder group, questions 41-60.

Mindset

The ACT Math test is an easy test to get depressed about because there are going to be math concepts that you don't remember and definitions that you've forgotten. Again, that's the purpose of this book: to increase your knowledge and familiarity of a wide range of math topics, beginning with the ACT Math that you *have to know*, followed by the math that is *good to know*.

However, just because you miss or can't remember a bunch of questions, don't sweat it during the test. Again, a 31 out of 60 in school would be a failing grade, but on the ACT that score would earn you a 22.

Question Types

In general, there are three or four types of ACT Math questions.

- First, there are questions that give you a diagram or shape or describe some kind of diagram or shape. Of course, if a diagram or shape is being described in words, *draw it out!* Failing to do so will lead to simple mistakes.

- Second, there are problems that give you a math question within some sort of story or real life example. There is a lesson in Step 3 about this kind of question since it is so common, so more on that later!

- Third, there are problems that, like in school, simply test your math abilities without either of the above. You'll find examples of this type throughout the book, but in order of importance.

- Lastly, there are some problems that I'd call concept problems in which it won't matter how much time you dedicate to them: either you know them or you don't. Again, the more important, the earlier it will appear in the book.

There are plenty of examples of all four forthcoming in this book!

Calculator Policy

The ACT is always changing its calculator policy to exclude more and more newer, very advanced kinds of calculators. Graphing calculators are allowed, including the standard TI-84; in general, if it's allowed in math class, it's allowed on the ACT. See the ACT's website for more information if you have a specific question about a particular kind of calculator. However, I do think that too many students think, "If I don't have a graphing calculator, I'm going to do terribly!" However, I can only *really* think of one possible (not even guaranteed to be on the test) ACT Math question that this could be true about (and even then, there are other, possibly simpler ways to solve it).

STEP 1

The ACT Math Two Pass Strategy

ACT Math Strategy

60 Minutes, 60 Questions

If you've taken the ACT before, there is a good chance you had the following common experience. When the proctor says, "You may begin," you start the ACT Math test at number one; then, when you're finished with that one, you move on to number two; then, when you're finished with this problem, you move on to number three, and so on.

Then, sometime around question 45 or 50, you hear the proctor shout out, "5 minutes remaining."

You now rush to answer questions that maybe you can get with time that's left and guess on a bunch and kind of go back and glance over questions that you wanted to return to if there was time. Then, during the break that follows the math test you start to question your life choices because you feel so flustered.

There is a much better, calmer, and simpler way to go through the ACT Math test. Traditionally, it is called the *Two Pass Strategy*. It is easy to implement, and I guarantee you are already familiar with the basic idea. I remember a few years ago a student who was in one of my ACT classes sought me out to say that his math score increased 4 or 5 points by simply putting the following strategy into effect (I think he would have done better if he had had a book like this one to order his content knowledge, but I digress…).

Here is the basic idea: for our purposes, there are **three types** of ACT Math questions.

First, there are questions you can probably get right in about a minute or less. For the *Two Pass Strategy*, simply answer these questions right away. My guess is that, for the average student, this is probably 30-40 of the 60 questions. For more advanced students, maybe this is 45-50 out of 60.

Second, there are questions that you *kind of* recognize; maybe you know what's being asked, but you can't quite put your finger on it. In other words, these questions would probably take you over a minute to solve or boil down to an educated guess. As you can hopefully see, questions in this category might take some time, and so you don't want to use up all of it at first. Simply circle these questions, and with spare time at the end, come back to them! My guess is that, for the average student, there are probably 15 of these kinds of questions on the ACT Math test.

Third, there are questions that test concepts in math that you have never heard or have completely left your mind. No matter how much time you spend on these questions, there is a 0% chance that you could come up with the correct answer on your own. For these questions, just *guess*, and save yourself the time. I'd say that, for the average student, there are roughly 5 of these on any given ACT Math test.

This isn't a novel concept; I would bet that you have circled and skipped questions on final exams or other important tests looking to come back to them with spare time at the end. The difference is that if you employ this strategy on ACT Math, you are likely to circle and skip a lot of them. That's OK; you aren't neglecting them. You will return to them with all of the time you have stockpiled.

But why? Why do all this circling and skipping? In the previous lesson I stressed that the first 20 math problems are the easiest third, the middle 20 of middle difficulty, and the final 20 math problems are the most difficult.

However, like I also said, that does NOT mean that number 59 is the 2nd most difficult math problem, or that number 55 is the 6th most difficult math problem, or that number 52 is the 9th most difficult problem, or that 50 is the 11th most difficult problem, or that 47 is the 14th most difficult problem. If these 5 problems are problems that you could get right in a minute or less, wouldn't it be a shame if you didn't give yourself a chance to get to them? With the Two Pass Strategy, you give yourself a chance at them.

In fact, let me break down for you what could happen if you guess on 5 questions you could get right if you simply gave yourself a chance.

If you were to guess on those 5 problems, on average you would get only 1 correct (since in ACT Math, unlike the other three ACT tests, there are 5 answer choices; more on that later). However, if you save yourself time to work them well, and if you get all 5 correct, you could raise your ACT Math score from an 18 to a 21, from a 21 to a 24, or a 27 to a 30. That bump in Math will more than likely raise your overall ACT score by 1 point.

To sum up, the best ACT Math strategy requires you to do one of three things with each math question: answer it, circle it, or guess. This will give you a chance to answer each question correctly. No more frantic guessing when the proctor shouts out "5 minutes remaining!"

You'll have 3 opportunities to apply this strategy to a full-length practice test in this book.

STEP 2

The Four ACT Math Mini-Strategies

There is no doubt that mastering your time (correct pacing on early questions, circling and skipping with the *Two Pass Strategy* as already discussed, etc.) is **THE** ACT Math strategy. However, there are what I like to call *mini-strategies* that can help you get questions correct along the way (and definitely save you time as well!). Most ACT tutors identify three of these strategies, but I add a fourth regarding the calculator that is a crucial time-saver and represents a mindset you must have about the ACT Math test.

Mini-Strategy #1: Backsolving

The first such strategy is called *Backsolving*. You may have noticed that each ACT Math question features not 4, but 5 options. This makes it unique; every question on every other test only has options A/B/C/D and F/G/H/J, but the math test adds a fifth option for each question: A/B/C/D/**E** or F/G/H/J/**K**. This isn't an accident, and it isn't arbitrary. It seems unfair; most students who I've taught think it's just another way for the ACT (and life as a whole) to make things unnecessarily harder.

The reason for the 5 answer choices, however, is not to make your life more miserable, but rather because of the math strategy that I want to teach you today. *Backsolving* simply means instead of solving the math problem in front of you forwards like you would on a typical math quiz, test, or homework assignment at school, you try out each of the answers one at a time to see which one is the correct answer.

In other words, we are taking advantage of the fact that this is a multiple choice test, and out of the 5 answer choices sitting in front of you, one of them has to work. In some situations, why not just try them out one at a time? Let's analyze the following question using the *Backsolving* strategy to show you how it's done!

ex. A restaurant wants its 5 entrees to average a price of $35. If the first 4 meals cost $29, $55, $39, and $32, what must the price of the fifth meal be?

A. $15
B. $20
C. $27
D. $30
E. $35

Traditionally, you would solve this problem by setting up an equation with one missing variable, x, and isolate the x on one side of the equation to solve. Doing that here would also be relatively simple. However, my purpose is simply to walk you through how *Backsolving* works. To use this mini-strategy, choose one of the answer choices and simply see if it is correct. You can begin with choice A and move down, or with choice E and move up, or even better, you can begin with choice C to determine if you need a bigger number and move down or a smaller number and move up. This works since most of the time ACT Math answers are listed in numerical (usually ascending, though sometimes descending) order.

Let's try C: $27. When I add $27 to the other 4 meal prices and divide by 5 (the total meals) I get an average of $36.40. That is too high, so I need a lower meal price. Let's now try B: $20. When I add $20 to the other 4 meal prices and divide by 5, I get an average of $35…that's it!

My purpose in creating this problem was not to make a difficult problem (it is obviously not too difficult!) but to illustrate the basics of *Backsolving*, a strategy that is beneficial in two ways: first, it can often save you precious time, and second, it can also be used in problems in which the mathematics is more difficult.

Here are three additional example questions. Give them a shot yourself first, and then see if you can figure out just how the questions can be solved backwards: trying out each answer choice one at a time. Explanations for each of these three examples can be found at the back of the book, which include detailed explanations for how *Backsolving* can be utilized for each one.

1. Sophie would like to average 30 points scored per game over the first five basketball games of her senior season. In her first four games, Sophie scored 19, 27, 34, and 27 points, respectively. How many points must Sophie score in her next game to achieve her goal of averaging 30 points per game?

   A. 30
   B. 33
   C. 34
   D. 43
   E. 44

2. Which of the following (x, y) pairs is a solution for the equation $y + \frac{1}{2}x = 3$?

F. $(-4, 5)$
G. $(1.5, 0)$
H. $(0, -3)$
J. $(0.5, 4)$
K. $(-2, 2)$

3. A certain manufacturing plant produces a set amount of baseball bats every year. It is found, upon inspection, that 1 out of every 60 bats produced is considered damaged. Additionally, it is found that 3 out of every 4 damaged bats is considered *permanently* damaged and cannot be repaired. If the plant's manufacturing produces 3,150 baseball bats that are *permanently* damaged every year, then how many baseball bats are produced each year?

A. 14,175
B. 25,200
C. 141,750
D. 252,000
E. 567,000

Mini-Strategy #2: Picking Numbers

The second such strategy is called *Picking Numbers*, which involves choosing numbers (such as pretending a variable like x to be equal to 5) to apply to a question and its answers, then looking for a match. Usually these kinds of questions involve variables, taking advantage of the fact that, of the 5 choices, one of them must be correct. You plug the numbers you've picked into the question, then you apply the same numbers to the answers, and if the values match up, you've found the correct answer.

Let's analyze the following question using *Picking Numbers* simply to illustrate the strategy:

2. What is the product of the expressions $(3x - 4)$ and $(2x + 0.5)$?

F. $6x^2 - 6.5x - 2$
G. $6x^2 - 9.5x - 2$
H. $6x^2 - 8x + 2$
J. $5x^2 + 10.5x - 3.5$
K. $5x^2 + 10.5x - 4.5$

Now, let's just pretend like you don't know how to multiply these two expressions (which, if you did, would be the fastest way to solve this particular problem). What to do? Well, notice that the question and the answers both have the variable x. If I choose a value for x and plug it into both the question's expressions and its answers, I will get the same number value. Let's pretend then that $x = 4$ (in *Picking Numbers*, avoid $x = 0$, $x = 1$, and $x = -1$). When I plug $x = 4$ into both of the question's expressions, I now am looking for the product of $(3x - 4) = (3 \cdot 4 - 4) = (12 - 4) = 8$ and $(2x + 0.5) = (2 \cdot 4 + 0.5) = (8 + 0.5) = 8.5$. Well, $8 \times 8.5 = 68$. Now, apply $x = 4$ to each answer choice and find which also equals 68.

Start with F: $6x^2 - 6.5x - 2 = 6(4^2) - 6.5(4) - 2 = 96 - 26 - 2 = 68$, which matches! F is correct!

Let's take a look at a few more examples where this strategy can work so that you can understand this strategy well. Most of these involve variables (like x or y or a or b, etc.), as you can see, but one does not.

Just like the *Backsolving* examples, try them out yourself first, then see the *Picking Numbers* explanations that can be found in the back of the book for a more detailed analysis.

4. Which of the following is equivalent to $(\frac{x^2 - 5x - 6}{x + 1}) + x + 1$?

F. $x - 5$

G. $2x - 5$

H. $x^2 - 5x - 6$

J. $x^2 - 4x - 5$

K. $\frac{(2x - 5)}{(x + 1)}$

5. What is the average of the expressions $3a^2 - 7$, $2a^2 + 1$, $-4a^2 + 12$, and $3a^2 - 2$?

A. $-a^2 + 1$

B. $\frac{1}{2}a^2 + 1$

C. $a^2 + \frac{1}{2}$

D. $-a^2 + \frac{1}{2}$

E. $a^2 + 1$

6. Between Monday and Tuesday, the number of people in line to buy ice cream at a brand new ice cream store increased by 35%. Between Tuesday and Wednesday, the number of people in line increased by an additional 40%. What was the combined percent increase of people in line to buy ice cream between Monday and Wednesday ?

F. 40%
G. 76%
H. 85%
J. 89%
K. 99%

7. If a, b, c, and d are all positive real numbers and if $a^{-2} > b^{-2} > c^{-2} > d^{-2}$, then which of the following numbers has the least value ?

A. a
B. b
C. c
D. d
E. Cannot be determined from the given information

Mini-Strategy #3: Drawn to Scale

Perhaps I've said already that it is a waste of time for you to read the directions before any of the four ACT tests, and that is absolutely true. There is one line in one of the tests however, the ACT Math test, that is worth mentioning. Here is what it says: "Illustrative figures are NOT necessarily drawn to scale."

What does that mean? That means that, according to the ACT's own directions, you the student can't assume that just because one line is 5 units long, and a second line looks to be exactly twice its size, it is exactly or just about twice its size. Or, if an angle looks to be around 45 degrees, you the student can't assume that it is somewhere around 45 degrees.

The reason the ACT is saying this is not because it's true, but to cover their tracks in case something isn't drawn to scale. Thus, the third ACT Math mini-strategy worth a lesson is this: although the ACT *says* that figures are not drawn to scale, in reality *they are*. If a line *looks* to be about 7 units long, it *is* about 7 units long. If an angle *looks* to be obtuse, it *is* obtuse.

Let's say the following diagram was put on an ACT test and you were asked, based on a lot of factors, to find the length of segment $\overline{DE}$.

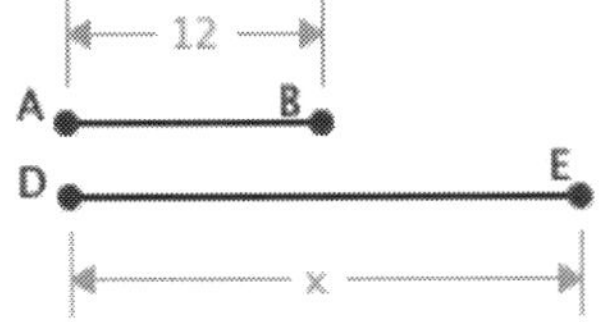

It could be that this segment is the side of a larger shape, like the leg of a triangle, or it could be that it is a piece of a larger line segment. No matter what, if you know that segment $\overline{AB}$ is 12, and can't figure out the math do determine the length of $\overline{DE}$, then you can at least remember that segments like this are actually drawn to scale. If $\overline{AB}$ is 12, you can reasonably determine that $\overline{DE}$ is somewhere between 22 and 26. If you want to be even more accurate, then use the side of your answer sheet like a ruler; put your answer sheet up against the first segment, mark it as "12," then compare it to the segment you don't know to determine an approximate length.

We can use the same kind of thinking with angles. No matter what the question stem tells you about this triangle below, let's assume that you simply can't determine the math behind how to figure out the measure of angle Θ. At a minimum, however, we *can* determine a few things about it. Although the ACT tells us that this figure is not necessarily drawn to scale, we can know for certain that *it is*. Thus, we know right off the bat that it is an obtuse angle. If we draw a 90 degree angle and a 135 degree angle on top of it, we might be able to figure out that it's somewhere between the two. It's possible that this kind of thinking can accelerate achieving of the correct answer.

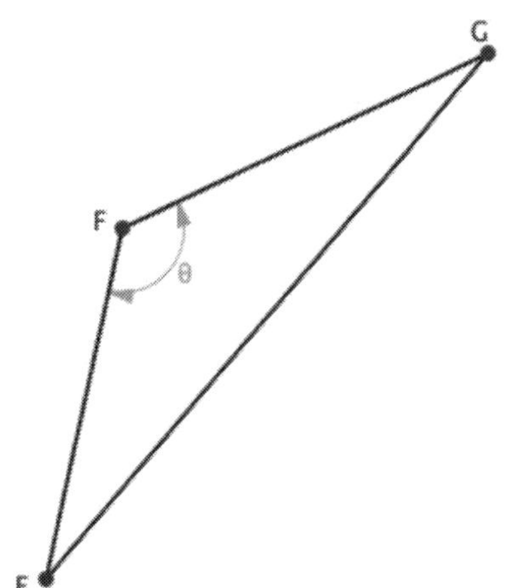

Solve the problem that follows and see if you can determine the correct answer by simply employing the *Drawn to Scale* mini-strategy; you might be surprised at just how often it can help you achieve a correct answer on the actual ACT Math test!

8. In parallelogram *ABCD* shown below, points *F*, *D*, *C*, and *E* form a straight line. Given the angle measures as shown in the figure, what is the measure of $\angle ACB$?

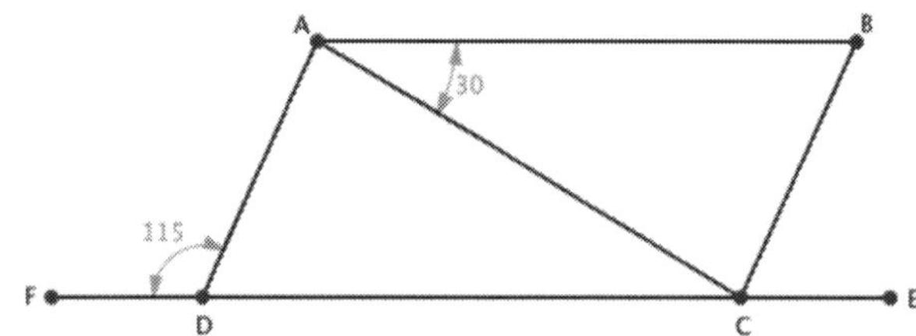

F. 30°
G. 45°
H. 85°
J. 115°
K. 145°

Mini-Strategy #4: The Calculator

This fourth strategy is the reminder you absolutely need before the ACT Math test. It needs to be restated: use your calculator to save yourself precious time! Don't do on paper what can be done in a fraction of the time on the calculator! Think about a math problem that asks you to add a bunch of fractions, for example, like this: $\frac{2}{7} + \frac{4}{23} + \frac{5}{111} = ?$

Here's the problem: you've been trained probably since grade school that in order to solve this problem, you must first find a common denominator, then add the terms, then simplify the final result. I have no idea what such a common denominator might be, since I just made up this problem while typing, but finding it might have been your first instinct, too. Sure enough, all of the answer choices will be in fraction form as well, let's say, further making it seem like I would need to find the common denominator of 7, 23, and 111. Well I know what I am *not doing*: finding a common denominator. Why?

There is this amazing thing that can solve this problem in a matter of seconds: *the calculator!* No matter what type you have, you can type this into it: $(2 \div 7) + (4 \div 23) + (5 \div 111) =$

Sure enough, this comes out to equal to 0.505 when rounded to the nearest thousandths place. This is where a bit of *Backsolving* comes in: try out each answer choice in the calculator too until you get a decimal equivalent that matches. *Voila!* The math problem that took you 4 minutes to solve in Algebra I is now reduced to one that takes 20 seconds thanks to the calculator! No fancy calculator needed, either; you don't need to be able to demand from your calculator an answer in the form of a fraction. Just match the decimal equivalents.

Again, on the ACT, there is no partial credit for showing your work. If anything, there is *less* credit for showing your work when you don't have to, since this will cost you precious time!

Try this out on the following two examples; see if you can use the calculator straight through.

9. What is $\frac{4}{17} + \frac{1}{2} + \frac{1}{68}$?

A. $\frac{6}{17}$

B. $\frac{1}{3}$

C. $\frac{25}{34}$

D. $\frac{3}{4}$

E. $\frac{7}{9}$

10. Which of the following inequalities orders the numbers 0.3, $\frac{1}{3}$, and 0.04 from greatest to least?

F. $0.3 > \frac{1}{3} > 0.04$

G. $\frac{1}{3} > 0.3 > 0.04$

H. $0.04 > \frac{1}{3} > 0.3$

J. $0.04 > 0.3 > \frac{1}{3}$

K. $0.3 > 0.04 > \frac{1}{3}$

Step 2 Correct Answers

Backsolving:	Picking Numbers:	Drawn to Scale:	The Calculator:
1: D	4: G	8: H	9: D
2: F	5: E		10: G
3: D	6: J		
	7: A		

Mini-Strategies Practice answer explanations begin on page 532.

STEP 3

ACT Math Have to Know

ACT Math Have to Know Introduction

I recently read an article online listing something like a dozen math concepts you need to know and practice to perform well on the ACT. I noticed right away, however, that whoever wrote this article did *not* do their homework over the actual ACT test because the article prioritized a few math concepts that really aren't asked about that often on the ACT itself.

I have spent hours and hours (and hours and hours...) analyzing ACT Math tests, cataloging the types of math knowledge and abilities that are most important or asked about, and those that are least important or asked about. The lessons that follow are broken up into two categories: *Have to Know* (Steps 3 and 4) and *Good to Know* (Step 5). *Have to Know* means that, beyond a doubt, multiple ACT Math questions test this ability or knowledge, even if only as one step among a few to get a question correct. It is crucial that you understand the *Have to Know* concepts first. *Good to Know* means that it is very likely that you will have at least one ACT Math question testing this topic or ability, though it's not guaranteed.

This doesn't mean that I'll cover every basic concept in math. I'm taking it for granted that you know how to graph (that you know what the (x, y) coordinate plane is, that the origin is at (0, 0), that to graph point (2, 5) means you move two to the right then up 5, etc.) and that you know how to add, multiply, divide, and subtract, and that you know how to find the square root of a number (among other basics).

There's a third category that I'm not getting into with its own series of lessons, and I'm calling that category *Possibly Might Have to Know*, which consists of math concepts that you are very unlikely to see on the average ACT Math test. If you are near a 36 in ACT Math, then I'd recommend pouring over ACT Math practice tests in search of questions you do not know as one approach to bumping up that final point or two. For the rest of us, let's begin with what's most important and make our way. However, I'm ***not*** going to ignore these types of questions completely; I'll sprinkle as many of these little *Possibly Might Have to Know* topics as I can into the example questions as we go.

Have to Know #1: Writing Expressions/Equations from Word Problems

An added difficulty to the ACT Math test is that *many* of the math problems are wrapped up in little stories. It could be a story of how Roberta wanted to purchase 10 different gift cards for her 10 friends, or about how Timothy is walking at a rate of 3 MPH down the road to his aunt's house. These problems get a name; they're called *modeling* problems because they attempt to "model" a real life example (though I can't imagine it is terribly realistic to find nearly $10 in change on the ground on your walk home from school). You'll read that I'll call them either modeling problems or story problems.

One of the top two or three ACT skills is your ability to: 1) read a modeling problem, and 2) translate the story into an actual math problem, most likely an Algebra problem. If you're having difficulty with these problems, keep in mind that the actual question, aka what the question is requiring of you, is always the last sentence of the paragraph. Many students who struggle here, therefore, find it helpful to read the last sentence (the actual question) first or to reread it to make sure they get it. Here are a few examples to try:

1. Cliff wants to have a 150 foot fence installed around his pool and deck area. Baldwin Fence, Inc. charges a $600 fee, plus a set amount per foot of fence. Baldwin Fence, Inc. has given Cliff an estimate of $1,950 to install the fence around his pool and deck area. What is the set amount the company will charge per foot of fence?

A. $4.00
B. $9.00
C. $12.25
D. $13.00
E. $17.00

2. A 4-foot-by-7-foot white board was installed on the 10-foot-by-9-foot wall of Mrs. Thomas's English classroom. What is the area, in square feet, of the part of the wall that is not covered by the white board?

F. 28
G. 62
H. 72
J. 88
K. 90

3. Horatio reads online that, in order to make a very strong cup of coffee, he needs to drip $\frac{2}{3}$ cups of water over $1\frac{1}{4}$ tablespoons of coffee grounds. Horatio measures that his coffee mug can hold $2\frac{1}{2}$ cups of water without spilling. If Horatio uses the same ratio of water to coffee grounds as called for by the instructions he found on the internet, then how many tablespoons of coffee grounds will he need to use?

A. $2\frac{1}{12}$
B. $4\frac{11}{16}$
C. $4\frac{3}{4}$
D. $5\frac{1}{3}$
E. $5\frac{31}{32}$

4. Bernard has \$1,200 invested in Stock A, and his sister Kathleen has \$1,230 invested in Stock B. It is projected that Stock A will increase by \$1 in value every day and that Stock B will increase by \$0.50 in value every day. If projections are accurate, in about how many days will the two investments be valued at the same amount?

F. 15
G. 30
H. 40
J. 55
K. 60

Have to Know #2: Simplifying Expressions and Order of Operations

When I taught Algebra I, I remember giving my students countless problems in which they had to simplify expressions. Sometimes this involved negative exponents, and sometimes it involved going through the order of operations and then adding like terms when possible. Skills like this are extremely important for the ACT, but you have an advantage that my students didn't: *Picking Numbers*.

Many students have memorized an acronym to help them remember the order of operations: PEMDAS, which stands for: Parentheses, Exponents, Multiplication, Division, Addition, and Subtraction. For our purposes, let's just remember this rule: be really careful when you have to simplify! Careless mistakes are more likely to cost students questions than a failure to memorize PEMDAS ever would.

Before I get to a few examples, I will say that these examples feature a few ideas that are good to review in math, though in regards to the ACT itself they don't need their own separate lesson. These are: multiplying variables with exponents, what to do with negative exponents, raising exponents to an additional power, how to divide one fraction by another, and factoring trinomials.

5. Which of the following expressions is equivalent to $y(6-y)-y(y+9)$?

A. $-2y^2-3y$
B. $2y-3y^2$
C. $-y^2+y-45$
D. $3y^2+2y$
E. $-y^2-9y$

6. If x and y are positive real numbers, which of the following expressions is equivalent to $\dfrac{(3x^{-2}\sqrt{y})^4}{x^2y^{-5}}$?

F. $81y^7$

G. $\dfrac{27y^7}{x^4}$

H. $\dfrac{81}{x^7y^3}$

J. $\dfrac{3y^4}{x^6}$

K. $\dfrac{81y^7}{x^{10}}$

7. Which of the following expressions is equivalent to $\dfrac{\frac{a}{4}+\frac{1}{3}}{\frac{1}{2}-\frac{1}{3}}$?

A. $\dfrac{3a+4}{2}$

B. $\dfrac{a+6}{5}$

C. $\dfrac{2a+3}{2}$

D. $\dfrac{a-1}{2}$

E. $\dfrac{a}{2}$

8. Which of the following expressions is equivalent to $\dfrac{(x^2+5x+4)(x-8)}{(x^2-7x-8)(x+2)}$?

F. $\dfrac{x+8}{x-2}$

G. $\dfrac{2x+4}{x-8}$

H. $\dfrac{x+4}{x+2}$

J. $\dfrac{x+5}{x-2}$

K. 2

Have to Know #3: Mean, Median, Mode, and Range

Mean, median, mode, and range are math vocabulary words that you have probably heard before, but the last time you really learned them as a group together was probably a long time ago. The words have probably come up in your math class, but the memory of their definitions could have, by now, seemingly melted away.

However, in my research of ACT Math tests, I was surprised at just how often the terms are used (especially the first three: mean/median/mode). Before we get to some practice problems (which, like the last lesson, feature some small ACT Math concepts that don't deserve their own lesson), let's first review the meaning of mean, median, mode, and range.

To find any of these three values, you must have a set list of numbers (often called a number set), something like this: $\{2, 3, 3, 5, 6, 8, 9, 9, 9, 9, 12, 21\}$.

Mean - this word simply means average. It's as simple as that. In our set list of numbers here, adding all the terms together is 96, then divided by the total number of items is 96/12, which gives us an average, or mean, of 8. While there are a lot of questions that ask you for the average of a set of numbers, sometimes they may replace the word with "mean" instead.

Median - this number refers to the number that is in the middle of the number line. In our list here, the middle number would be between two numbers because we have an even number (12) of items in the list. In this case, the value would fall between the sixth term in the list and the seventh term in the list. Because the 6th term is 8 and the 7th term is 9, we average the two and find that the median of this number line is 8.5. In an odd amount of numbers, like in $\{1, 3, 6\}$, the median is simply the middle term.

Mode - the mode is the number that appears in the list most often. In our example, there are four 9's, which makes 9 the mode. If two numbers are tied, they are both the mode.

Range - lastly, we have the range, which is the difference between the greatest number and the least number. In our number set, the greatest number is 21 and the least is 2. Thus, the range is 21 − 2, or 19.

Now finally for some example questions based on recent ACT's:

9. To increase the mean of 5 numbers by 5, by how much would the sum of the 5 numbers have to increase?

A. $\frac{5}{3}$

B. 1

C. $\frac{3}{5}$

D 10

E. 25

10. The product of the mean and the median of each factor of 12 listed in numerical order falls between which two whole numbers?

F. 0 and 1
G. 1 and 2
H. 8 and 9
J. 11 and 12
K. 16 and 17

11. The city of Brackton holds a dinner celebrating the achievements of local artists, and a table at the front is reserved for writers. Author A is seated first and has written 1 novel. Author B is seated second and has written 3 novels. Author C is seated third and has written 2 novels. Author D is seated fourth and has written 1 novel. After dinner begins, Author E, who has written 21 novels, arrives late and is seated in the fifth seat at the authors' table. If it can be determined, which of the following statistics was *least* changed by the arrival of Author E.

A. Mean
B. Median
C. Mode
D. Range
E. Cannot be determined from the given information

12. Dominic earns tips in the amount of \$14, \$15, \$11, \$22, and \$15 in his first five nights as a waiter. Solving which of the following equations for t gives the amount of tips he needs to earn on his sixth night working to average exactly \$16 in tips across the six nights?

F. $\frac{t+77}{6} = \frac{77}{96}$

G. $\frac{t+77}{5} = 96$

H. $\frac{77}{6} + t = 16$

J. $\frac{77}{5} + t = 96$

K. $\frac{t+77}{6} = 16$

Have to Know #4: Higher Algebra

Don't let the title of this lesson scare you! *Higher Algebra* doesn't mean it's higher than you; it simply means that it might be a tad more difficult than finding the value of one missing variable in an equation. I spoke before about how the ACT Math test can essentially be broken up into thirds: the first 20 problems are the easiest block, the middle 20 are of medium difficulty, and the last 20 (#'s 41-60) are the most difficult on the test. These are the kinds of questions that are more likely to be found among number 30 through 60. Oftentimes, like what we've discussed before, these problems are wrapped up in modeling or story problems, other times, they are more straightforward.

Let's look through a handful of examples, all of which are important, as these kinds of questions are among the most asked in the ACT Math test. Use this as an opportunity to check those *Higher Algebra* skills:

13. Which of the following inequalities is equivalent to $-3y - 9x > 3x - 6$?

A. $y > -4x + 2$
B. $y < -4x + 2$
C. $y > 4x + 2$
D. $y < 18x - 6$
E. $y > 18x + 6$

14. At Caffeine King, a local coffee shop, there are on average 4 bagels remaining in the display case by 11:00 AM. The probability, P, that exactly b bagels are still in the case by 11:00 AM can be modeled by the equation $P = \frac{4^b e^{-4}}{4!}$. Given that $e^{-4} = 0.075$, which of the following values is closest to the probability that exactly 3 bagels are in the case at 11:00 AM?

F. 0.15
G. 0.17
H. 0.20
J. 0.40
K. 0.52

15. Given that complex numbers consist of a real and imaginary dimension, and that $i^2 = -1$, then $(i + 1)(i - 4)(i + 3) = ?$

A. $14i$
B. $-6i - 6$
C. $6i + 6$
D. $-14i - 18$
E. $-14i - 12$

16. Whenever a and b are positive integers such that $16^a = (\sqrt{2})^b$, what is the value of $\frac{a}{b}$?

F. $\frac{1}{8}$

G. $\frac{1}{4}$

H. $\frac{1}{2}$

J. 4

K. 8

17. The city of Cliffside is considering the purchase of a parcel of triangle-shaped land near the edge of town. The length of one side of the parcel, as shown in the image, is 9 miles. What is the perimeter of the entire parcel of land, rounded to the nearest mile?

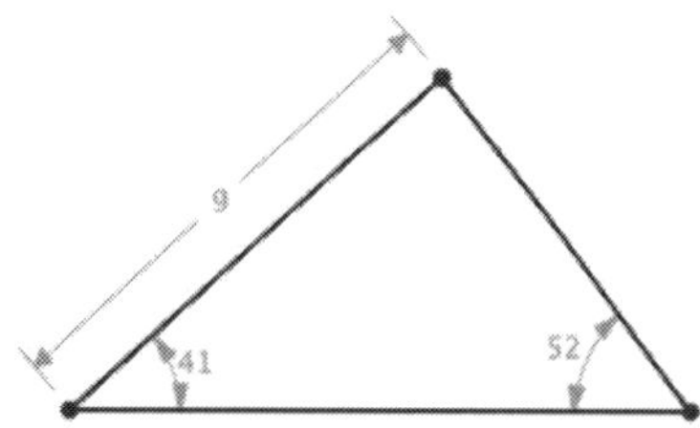

(Note: the Law of Sines states that the sine of an angle divided by its opposite side is equal to the sine of another angle divided by its opposite side. It can be expressed in the following form: $\frac{sin(a)}{A} = \frac{sin(b)}{B}$).

A. 24
B. 28
C. 29
D. 31
E. 33

18. A store displays 12 mannequin heads that can hold up to 4 items for sale (hats, scarves, sunglasses, and earmuffs). If there are 25 items displayed for sale, and none of the mannequins are empty, what is the greatest possible number of mannequins that could be displaying all 4 different products?

F. 0
G. 3
H. 4
J. 5
K. 7

Have to Know #5: Lines

There are a number of things about lines that you need to know, such as the formula for a line, finding the slope for a line, how two lines in slope-intercept formula compare to one another, the solution for two lines, and the distance and midpoint between two points when graphed. Before we get to the examples, let's summarize at least a couple of these things about lines that you need to know.

First, the formula for a line, which is $\boldsymbol{y = mx + b}$, where m represents the slope, and b represents the y-intercept, meaning where the line crosses the y-axis. Putting a line in slope-intercept form involves solving the entire equation for y (or $1y$), and setting it equal to the rest of the equation. If two lines have the same slope (the same m), then they are parallel; they never *cross*, and as such they have *no solution*. Otherwise, two lines will always have 1 solution, which is the point where they cross (if you think about it, this makes sense; that means that there is only one point or value of both x and y that will satisfy each equation). If two lines are perpendicular, then their slopes will be *negative reciprocals* of one another. What does that mean? It means you make the slope negative and flip the numerator and denominator. For example, if a line has a slope of 2, and a second line is perpendicular to the first line, the slope of this second line will be $-\frac{1}{2}$ (we made it negative and moved the 2 down to the denominator).

Second, and speaking of slope, the ACT often asks students to find **the slope of a line** that is formed by 2 points (and sometimes one that is graphed). If you're given two points and asked for the slope, remember that $slope = \frac{rise}{run}$, which just means the difference in the height (or the y values) over or divided by the difference across (or the x values). For example, let's say you're asked to find the slope between these 2 points: (0, 1) and (3, 4). The difference in the y value divided by the difference in x value looks like this: $slope = \frac{4-1}{3-0} = \frac{3}{3} = 1$. Thus, the slope is 1.

These things and more can be found in the examples below, all based on real ACT questions:

19. In the standard (x, y) coordinate plane, what is the slope of the line $5x - 2y = 7$?

A. $-\frac{7}{2}$

B. -2

C. $\frac{2}{5}$

D. $\frac{5}{2}$

E. 5

20. Which of the following (x, y) pairs is the solution for the system of equations $x - 2y = -3$ and $3x - 4y = -5$?

F. $(1, 2)$
G. $(-1, 1)$
H. $(3, 3)$
J. $(-2, -3)$
K. $(4, -4)$

21. In the standard (x, y) coordinate plane, the midpoint of segment $\overline{DE}$ is at $(1, 3)$, and D is at $(-4, -2)$. What are the x and y coordinates of E ?

A. $(4, 2)$
B. $(3, 5)$
C. $(-3, -1)$
D. $(6, 8)$
E. $(-9, -7)$

22. Line p passes through the point $(-3, 5)$ and crosses the y-axis at point $(0, 4)$. Line q is perpendicular to line p. What is the slope of line q ?

F. -3

G. $-\frac{1}{3}$

H. $-\frac{1}{9}$

J. $\frac{1}{3}$

K. 3

23. In the standard (x, y) coordinate plane, point A is at (3, 3), and point B is at (8, 15). What is the distance between point A and point B ?

A. 5
B. 12
C. 13
D. 15
E. 18

24. Walker is standing at the origin. At time $t = 0$ minutes, a cloud floats directly above his head at 22,000 feet. At time $t = 2$ minutes, the cloud has maintained an elevation of 22,000 feet, but has moved across the sky 500 feet to the south. Which of the following equations represents the line along which the cloud is floating?

F. $x = 500$
G. $x = 22{,}000$
H. $y = 1{,}000$
J. $y = 22{,}000$
K. $y = 44{,}000$

Have to Know #6: Logical Thinking with Variables

To be clear, all of mathematics is a combination of memorization and logical thinking. Usually the questions we are faced with in math class are formulaic or fall into a neat category in which there is some kind of tried and true method to resolving the problem. If you have two equations with two variables, for example, there are methods you can use to solve the problem, or if you need to find the area of a moon and see how many of them can fit into a spherical planet around which it revolves, there are formulas and methods to get you there.

However, there is a category of ACT Math question that does not fit neatly into these little methods or formula boxes, and again, in my research, I was actually surprised how often these kinds of questions are asked. There is only one way to reach true conclusions about these problems, and that is with a process that I hope you have used before: *logical thinking*. If you've ever done a Sudoku puzzle or played board or card games you have used logical thinking; it's the kind of thinking that *eliminates options that are impossible* while *testing those that are possible*.

Usually this kind of thinking is tested within little math problems that use variables, and that means that often what is needed isn't a vast library of math textbooks and formulas that you've memorized. A strategy that can be very helpful here is *Picking Numbers*. By choosing various numbers for the variables you can eliminate possibilities before narrowing in on the right answer.

Without a doubt, you will face multiple math questions on ACT day that look like the following:

25. What are the values for x that satisfy the equation $(x - a)(x - b) = 0$?

A. $-a$ and $-b$
B. a and b
C. $-a$ and b
D. a and $-b$
E. Cannot be determined from the information given

26. The sign of x is positive, the sign of y is positive, and the sign of z is negative. If it can be determined, what is the sign of the average of x, y, and z ?

F. Negative
G. Positive
H. Both negative and positive
J. Neither negative nor positive
K. Cannot be determined from the given information

27. If x and y are both integers, $x > 1$, and $y < -1$, then which of the following expressions could not possibly be true?

A. $|x| = |y|$

B. $x^2 = y^2$

C. $|x^2| = |y^2|$

D. $\frac{1}{x^2} = \frac{1}{y^2}$

E. $x^{-1} = y^{-1}$

28. For all real numbers p, q, and r, such that $r < 0 < q < 100 < p < 1000$, which of the following inequalities *must* be true ?

F. $p + q < q + r$

G. $\frac{p}{r} < \frac{q}{r}$

H. $qr < pr$

J. $p < q - r$

K. $\frac{p}{r} > \frac{q}{r}$

Have to Know #7: Probability and Expected Outcome

Calculating probability and an expected outcome fall under the math umbrella of statistics, which is as exciting as it sounds. However, most statistics questions on the ACT are not tremendously difficult, though some may fall in that final, more difficult third. You probably know what *probability* means; it's just the likelihood that something will happen. If your weather app tells you that there is a 20% chance it will rain, then the probability that it will rain is 20%, or 0.2, or 1 in 5.

Expected outcome is a bit different. Essentially, finding an expected outcome requires that you know the probability of all possible events.

Let's say I have a strange 6-sided die. On three of the sides is a 1 (thus, the odds of rolling a 1 are 50%, or 0.5, or 1 in 2), on two of the sides is a 2 (thus, the odds of rolling a 2 are 33.3%, or 0.333, or 1 in 3), and on the last side of the die is a 3 (thus, the odds of rolling a 3 are 16.7%, or 0.167, or 1 in 6). You would think that the expected outcome would be the same thing as the most likely outcome, but it is not. To find the expected outcome, multiply each possible outcome by their probabilities and add them together. In our dice example, that would be this: $1(0.5) + 2(0.333) + 3(0.167) = 1.667$. A bit strange, I know, but the expected outcome of rolling our unique dice is 1.667, even if it isn't a real possibility.

This will all perhaps be better explained in the context of a few examples! Remember to try them yourself first before getting to the explanations.

29. A couple is deciding on a name for their baby. They put their 12 favorite names in a hat and will draw one randomly to determine the baby's name. If 4 of the names begin with the letter 'J,' 3 of the names begin with the letter 'P,' 3 of the names begin with the letter 'R,' and 2 of the names begin with the letter 'C,' then what is the probability that the name picked does NOT begin with the letter 'R'?

A. $\frac{1}{4}$

B. $\frac{1}{3}$

C. $\frac{1}{2}$

D. $\frac{3}{4}$

E. $\frac{5}{6}$

30. Which of the following expressions gives the number of permutations of 3 items taken and arranged from a total set of 12 items?

F. $3 + 12$

G. $(3 + 12)!$

H. $\frac{12!}{3!}$

J. $\frac{12!}{(12-3)!}$

K. $\frac{12!}{(3!)(12-3)!}$

31. Clement must choose one elective to fill out his university schedule, and there are 30 to choose from. Each elective will take place in one of four different locations on campus. The table below lists the frequency of locations for the 30 electives to choose from. If Clement chooses an elective at random, then what is the probability that the elective will take place either at the Intramural Fields or in the Dawson Building?

Elective location	Frequency
Intramural Fields	11
Healey Center	7
Stackle Hall	5
Dawson Building	7

A. 20%
B. 30%
C. 40%
D. 50%
E. 60%

32. A certain car dealership currently has 120 cars for sale on its lot. The owner of the dealership has prepared the following table for his salesman that shows the probability of selling different numbers of cars on any given day. Based on the probability distribution in the table, what is the expected number of cars remaining in the lot after 5 working days?

Cars sold in one day	Probability
0	0.2
1	0.4
2	0.3
3	0.1

F. 119
G. 118.7
H. 115
J. 114
K. 113.5

Have to Know #8: Percentages and Ratios

One of the most common areas of frustration on ACT Math are questions that require you to calculate and work with percentages, rates, and ratios. The reason they're frustrating is because they are the kinds of questions that seem extremely simple, but it is very easy to make a small mistake that can throw you off. And, of course, the test makers know what those simple little mistakes are, and one of the wrong answer choices is going to match up with the most likely incorrect answers.

First, let's discuss the number of ways that the ACT may expect you to work with percentages:

a) **Affecting a number by a percentage** - if the ACT asked you to find 35% of 440, here is all you need to do. Simply multiply 440 by 0.35. Do NOT divide 440 by 35 or 3.5 or .35. When you multiply, here is the result: 440(0.35) = 154. In other words, 154 is 35% of 440.

b) **Decreasing/increasing a number by a percentage (or percentages)** - if a product is decreased first by 10%, then by 50%, and the final price is \$31.50, we can determine the original price. First, we need to go from the \$31.50 and determine what the cost was between the two discounts (after the 10% discount but before the 50% discount). Given that it's 50%, it is rather simple to do in the head. However, the equation for determining this middle step looks like this: $0.5(x)$ = \$31.50. In other words, 50% of our mystery price (x) is equal to \$31.50, and when you divide both sides by 0.5 you can determine that x = \$63.00. Then, we need to determine still the original price because the \$63 represents a price *after* an original discount of 10%. We can use this same equation as before, but let's call this time our original price y. Thus, $0.9(y)$ = \$63. In other words, whatever the original price was, it was decreased by 10% (which is why we are multiplying the original price by .9, which represents a result of 90% of the original price). When we divide both sides by 0.9, we see that the original price was \$63/0.9 = \$70.

c) **Comparing numbers in terms of percentage** - 22 is what percent of 81? Seems fairly straightforward, but this simple question and its variations often cause students problems. Simply divide 22 by 81 and get that 22 is (22/81) = 0.2716 = 27.16% (when rounded to the nearest hundredths place) of 81. Conversely, the ACT could also ask this: 81 is what percent of 22? Students in this situation often make the mistake of doing the math we just did and divide 22 by 81, but this question calls for the opposite. 81 is (81/22) = 3.6818 = 368.18% of 22.

Let's start out with a few percentage examples to illustrate and test proper methods, then move on to an explanation of rates and ratios.

33. What is the sum of 75% of 4 and 300% of 3?

A. 3
B. 9
C. 12
D. 13
E. 15

34. What is 1% of $\frac{1}{8}$?

F. 0.000125
G. 0.00125
H. 0.0125
J. 0.125
K. 1.25

35. Rebecca has $10 to spend on materials to create a Christmas ornament for her grandmother. She intends to purchase popsicle sticks for $2.00, glue for $1.50, yarn for $2.30, and markers for $2.70. If purchases are subject to an 8% sales tax, how much money will Rebecca have left over after purchasing all four items?

A. $0.82
B. $1.12
C. $1.44
D. $1.50
E. $1.61

36. The number of students who purchase ice cream increases by 30% between Monday and Tuesday. Then, because of a sale on ice cream, the number of students who purchase ice cream increases by an additional 40% between Tuesday and Wednesday. What is the combined percent increase in students purchasing ice cream between Monday and Wednesday?

F. 40%
G. 62%
H. 70%
J. 82%
K. 91%

Now, on to rates and ratios. A **ratio** is a fixed comparison between two things. For example: for every 3 ripe blueberries in the package, there is 1 sour one. That's a ratio of 3 to 1. With that kind of knowledge, we could calculate all sorts of things. We could be told that there are 200 blueberries in the package and asked how many are sour ($200 \times \frac{1}{4}$), or we could be told that there are 45 sour blueberries, and need to find out how many total blueberries are in the package ($\frac{45}{x} = \frac{1}{4}$, then cross multiply to solve for x), which is the kind of question that overlaps ratios and percentages.

Rates often scare students, but they essentially are ratios. For example, if we were told that a car were driving at a rate of 35 miles per hour, that simply means that for every 35 miles, 1 hour has passed, or vice versa. Often, the key to using rates and ratios is this: putting a value in the numerator, another in the denominator, and then multiplying to make a value cancel out, leaving you with the correct answer. For example: If Derek can run 12 blocks in x minutes, then how many blocks can he run in 40 minutes? Given that the rate has an unknown variable (x), the answer choices also will. If we want our answer to be in blocks, we need minutes to cancel. Thus, we would set up an equation like this:

$$\frac{x \text{ blocks}}{12 \text{ minutes}} \times 40 \text{ minutes} =$$

This equation allows minutes to cancel, giving us an answer in terms of blocks. Thus, the answer is going to end up being $\frac{40x}{12}$ blocks $= \frac{10x}{3}$ blocks. Again, remember with rates and ratios: value in numerator, value in denominator, cancel out what needs to be canceled to get answer you're looking for! Try out the following examples:

37. Chadwick is riding his skateboard at a rate of 45 inches per 2.5 seconds. At this rate, how many feet will Chadwick travel in 10 seconds?

A. 15.00
B. 11.25
C. 10.75
D. 8.00
E. 1.50

38. From the point of view of Satellite Zephyr, $\frac{1}{4}$ centimeters represents 120 kilometers. Two images that were taken from Satellite Zephyr 12 hours apart show that a cargo ship traveled $2\frac{7}{10}$ centimeters. How many kilometers did the cargo ship travel?

F. 81
G. 324
H. 342
J. 1,296
K. 1, 492

39. The ratio of the average height of Tree A to Tree B is 2:3. The ratio of the average height of Tree B to Tree C is 7:5. What is the ratio of the average height of Tree A to Tree C ?

A. 10:21
B. 11:21
C. 14:15
D. 15:14
E. 21:10

Have to Know #9: Triangles, SohCahToa, & the Pythagorean Theorem

The ACT loves triangles. It loves testing your knowledge of sine, cosine, and tangent. It loves testing your knowledge of the Pythagorean Theorem. And, it loves testing your knowledge of the angles within a triangle. It also loves questions where figuring out the side of a triangle or the angle of a triangle is just one step to solving a larger problem. Hopefully some of that sounds familiar to you, even if you don't remember exactly how to use all of it like you used to. However, before we jump into any examples, we need to discuss what all of those things are.

The first thing you need to remember is this: all of these terms we're about to define all have to do with right triangles. A **right triangle** is a triangle in which the two legs form a right, or 90 degree, angle.

Let's start with the Pythagorean Theorem, which you must memorize (if you haven't already). The ACT will never give you the **Pythagorean Theorem**, which is $a^2 + b^2 = c^2$, in which a and b are the two legs of a right triangle, and c is the hypotenuse.

What this formula allows you to do is this: if you know any two sides of a right triangle, then you can always find the third. This is helpful in all sorts of problems, like we saw in our lesson on lines: the distance between two points on the (x, y) coordinate plane form the hypotenuse of a right triangle.

Sine, cosine, and tangent are relationships between the sides of a right triangle. They can most easily be remembered by the phrase **S**OH**C**AH**T**OA, or "Some Old Hippie Caught Another Hippie Tripping On Apples." The **sine** of an angle in a right triangle is equal to the length of its opposite side over the hypotenuse (thus, **S**OH). The **cosine** of an angle in a right triangle is equal to the length of the adjacent (non-opposite leg) side of the triangle over the hypotenuse (thus, **C**AH). The **tangent** is equal to the length of the opposite side of the angle over the adjacent side (thus, **T**OA).

Look at the triangle below. All we know about this triangle is the length of one side, the fact that one angle is 90 degrees, and that another angle is 36.87 degrees. But, knowing what we know now about the angles in a triangle, the Pythagorean Theorem, sine, cosine, and tangent, we can figure out the lengths of each side and the measure of the one missing angle fairly easily (*Note: you do not need to memorize the Law of Sines or the Law of Cosines*). This is the kind of math the ACT expects you to be able to do. Let's get to some examples based on real math questions from recent ACT's:

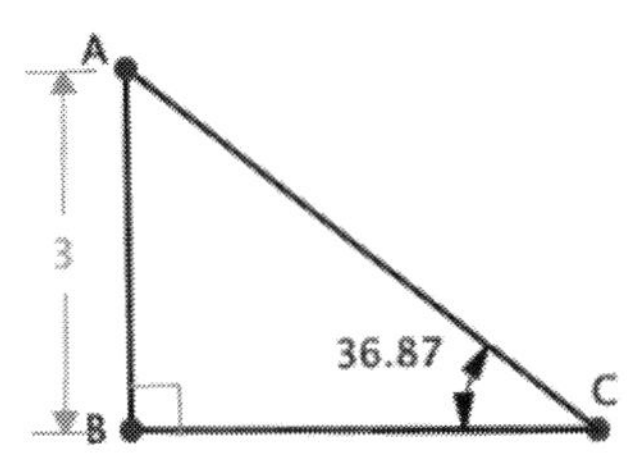

40. What is the value of tan F in right triangle △DEF below?

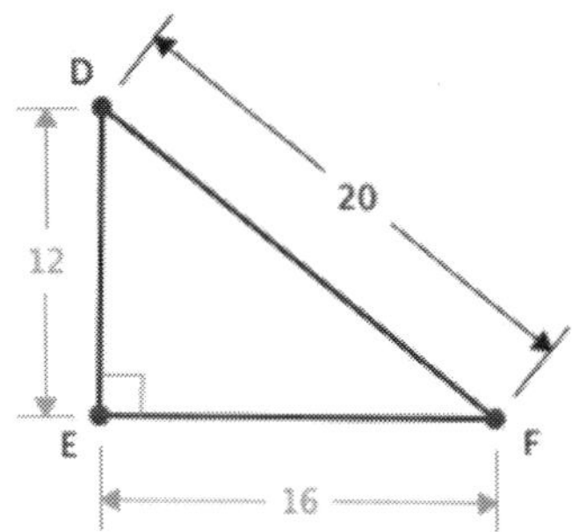

F. $\frac{3}{5}$

G. $\frac{3}{4}$

H. $\frac{4}{5}$

J. $\frac{5}{4}$

K. $\frac{5}{3}$

41. A cat is stuck at the very top of a maple tree that is 12.5 feet tall. Mr. Wilkins uses the ladder in his garage to reach the cat. If the angle between the ladder and the ground is 38.68 degrees, and if the ladder rests at the very top of the tree, then what is the length of the ladder to the nearest foot?

A. 20 feet
B. 22 feet
C. 25 feet
D. 27 feet
E. 31 feet

Numbers 42, 43, and 44 all use and refer to the following information.

The image below shows the layout for a proposed retail space. In the figure, *LMNO* is a rectangle, *LRSP* and *ROQS* are squares. Point *R* is the midpoint of $\overline{LO}$ and point *S* is the midpoint of $\overline{PQ}$. The given lengths are in meters.

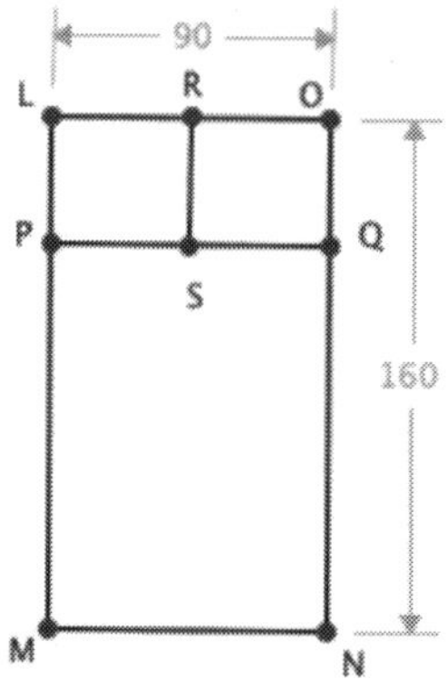

42. What is the length of $\overline{RM}$ to the nearest meter?

F. 250
G. 243
H. 212
J. 184
K. 166

43. What is the measure of $\angle RMN$ to the nearest degree?

A. 89°
B. 81°
C. 78°
D. 74°
E. 66°

44. The owner of the retail space wants to run an extension cord from point *L* to point *S*. How long must the extension cord be, to the nearest meter?

F. 45
G. 53
H. 64
J. 75
K. 90

Have to Know #10: Angles

The ACT will also test your knowledge of angles in a few different ways. The first concept that we definitely need to cover is called the **Law of Transversals**. That's a fancy name, and you don't need to remember it; it's the concept that you need to remember. Essentially, it is this: if two parallel lines are *transversed* by another line (meaning, a line goes through them), then many of the angles will have a special relationship between them. Look at this diagram:

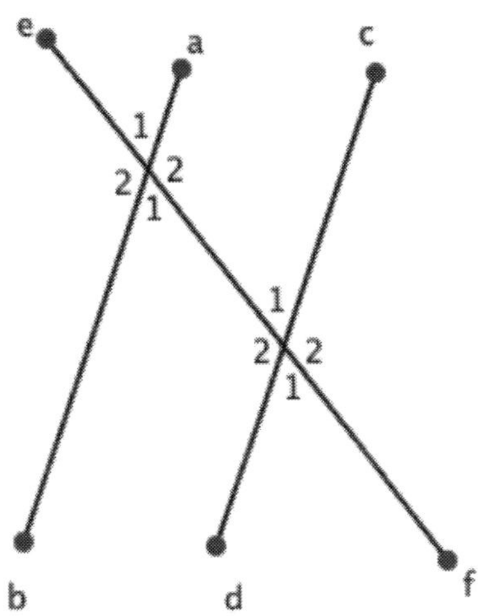

Here, lines *ab* and *cd* are parallel, and they are "cut through" or transversed by a third line, *ef*. This creates 8 angles. Let's take a closer look at where two lines cross, or where there are 4 angles. The two angles across from each other are called "opposite angles," and they are always equal. In addition, "zooming out" a bit, all four angles that are marked with a 1 are all identical; the four angles that are marked with a 2 are also identical. Without unnecessarily getting into all of the various vocabulary, this is the Law of Transversals.

The second concept that we need to know about angles is that the angles in a line add up to 180 degrees, or similarly, that the angle measure of a line is 180 degrees. When we combine those two concepts, we can do a lot with the diagram above. If we are given even just one of the 8 angles pictured, we can figure out all of the other 7 angles. For example, let's say that the topmost angle (1) is 40°. That means that every "1" is 40° and that every "2" is $180° - 40° = 140°$.

The third major concept that the above two are combined with is one we have learned about already, that being that the three angles of any triangle add up to 180 degrees. The ACT likes to combine all three of these concepts into more difficult questions, or to test one or two of them together in easier questions. Let's look at a few examples:

45. In the figure below, vertices B and D of $\triangle BCD$ lie on $\overline{AE}$, the measure of $\angle ABC$ is 155°, and the measure of $\angle CDE$ is 80°. What is the measure of $\angle BCD$?

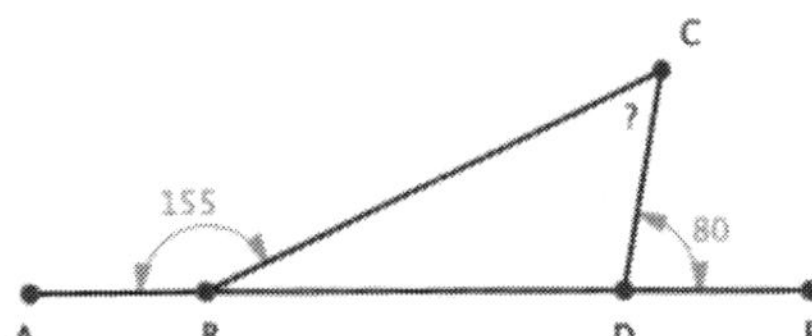

A. 25°
B. 55°
C. 70°
D. 80°
E. 100°

46. In the figure below, H and I lie on segment $\overline{AB}$, and J and K lie on segment $\overline{CD}$. In addition, segments $\overline{AB}$, $\overline{CD}$, and $\overline{EF}$ are all parallel and perpendicular to segment $\overline{ML}$. What is the measure of $\angle GIH$?

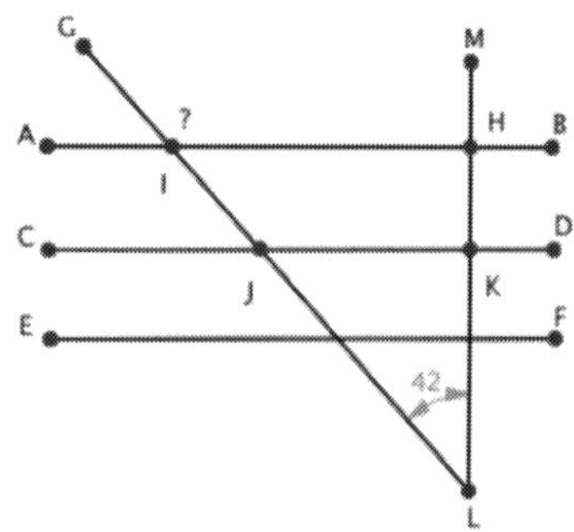

F. 21°
G. 42°
H. 48°
J. 121°
K. 132°

47. The intersection of lines c and d forms the four angles $\angle W$, $\angle X$, $\angle Y$, and $\angle Z$. The measure of $\angle Z$ is 500% larger than the measure of $\angle W$. If it can be determined, what is the value of $\angle W$?

A. 30°
B. 36°
C. 40°
D. 41°
E. Cannot be determined from the given information

48. Points U and W lie on line segment ST. What is the degree measure of $\angle VUW$?

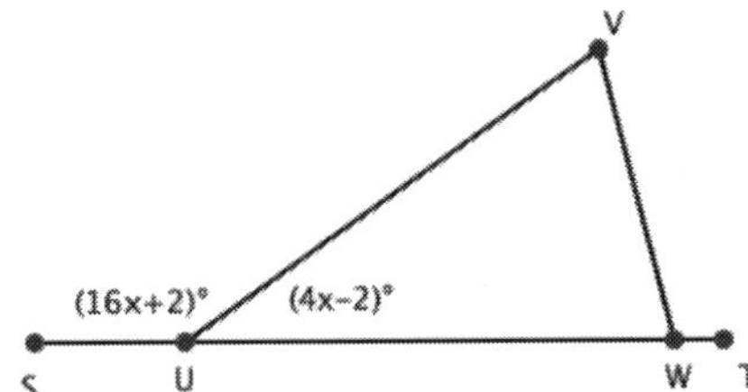

F. 9°
G. 19°
H. 34°
J. 88°
K. 146°

Have to Know #11: Perimeter, Area, and Volume

I'm guessing that you understand that the perimeter of a shape is the length of all of its sides combined, that the area of a shape is the amount of space the shape occupies (a way to measure everything within the sides of the shape), and that the volume is the amount of space a 3-d shape occupies. Before we get into how the ACT asks problems that test your knowledge of these, which isn't as straightforwardly as you might hope, let's review the kinds of formulas you need to know, and those you don't.

Area

First, you need to know how to calculate the areas of basic shapes: squares/rectangles, triangles, and circles. We'll look into circles more in our lesson exclusively on circles. The area of a square or rectangle is simply the product of two sides that form a right angle. Look at these two simple examples: The area of the rectangle on the left is simply the height, 8, times the width, 4, which is 32 units squared. The area of the square on the right is the same calculation: 5 times 5 is 25 units squared.

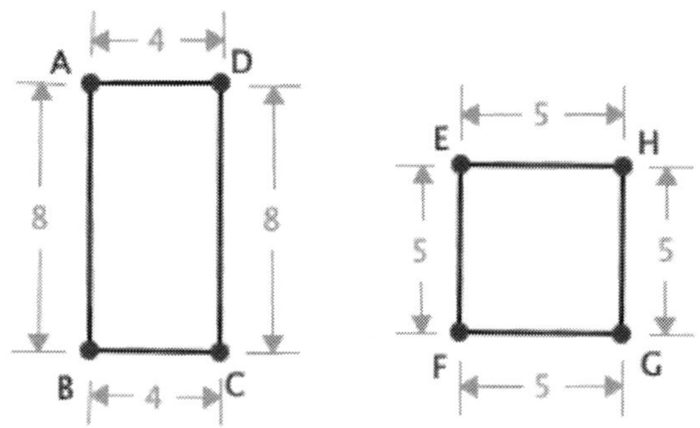

The area of a triangle you also must know. This formula works on any triangle shape, from the funkiest shape to the simplest. The formula is simply **(½)*bh***, or one half the base times the height. For example:

For both of these triangles, we apply the same formula, (½)*bh*. The area of the triangle on the left is (½)(4)(3.5), which = 7 units squared. The area of the triangle on the right is (½)(9)(3) = 13.5 units squared.

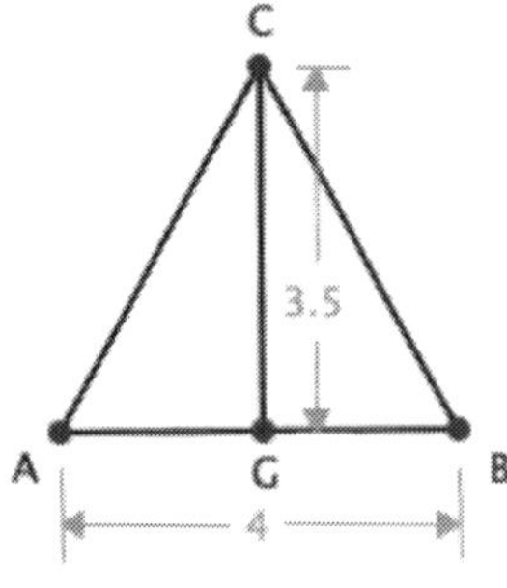

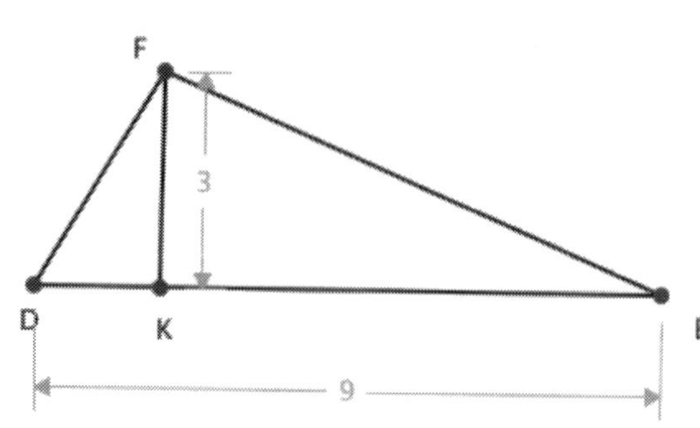

Volume

Let's talk about volume for a moment; there is a type of shape that you should know the volume of, and that is any figure that maintains the same shape uniformly up and down (a tin can as a cylinder, a block of wood for a rectangular prism, or a triangular prism of some kind). Finding the volume of these shapes is easy. You simply find the area (like we have done in plenty of example above), then multiply that area by the height. You can think of it as the same area "all of the way up".

However, there is no need to memorize the volume of more complicated shapes, like that of a cone or that of a sphere or some other 3-d shape that doesn't have uniformity along the height. I would bet that out of the last 1,000 administered ACT Math questions, not a single one requires you to know the volume of those shapes. If they want you to find the volume of shapes like those, or if finding the volume of a shape like that is required as a step to get a question right, they will give you the formula.

Draw it Out

It would be great if the ACT asked very straightforward questions about perimeter, area, and volume, but unfortunately finding any of these three things is usually one step needed in a greater problem, thus there is a greater risk for making a simple mistake. My one major piece of advice is this: if a shape or room or floor plan or anything else is described by a problem, but not given, then ***draw it out***!!!

49. Quinn wants to paint the walls of his bedroom. Each of the walls measures 12 feet wide by 10 feet tall. Two of the walls have a window that measures 3 feet wide by 5 feet tall, one of the walls has a door that measures 4 feet wide by 8 feet tall, and the final wall has no doors or windows. What is the total area that Quinn will need to paint in square feet ?

A. 120
B. 418
C. 433
D. 448
E. 480

50. If the length of a rectangle is decreased by 30%, and the width of the same rectangle is increased by 45%, the area of the resulting rectangle is larger than the area of the original rectangle by what percent?

F. 1.50%
G. 5.00%
H. 7.15%
J. 14.30%
K. 15.00%

51. Frida has a 10 oz can of soup that she wants to share with her daughter for lunch. She decides that her daughter should receive 40% of the soup, while she receives 60%. The can has a height of 98 mm and a diameter of 65 mm. Rounded to the nearest cubic millimeter, what is the volume of the portion that Frida wants to share with her daughter ?

A. 98,065
B. 130,078
C. 195,116
D. 301,104
E. 325,194

Have to Know #12: Functions

The word "function" sometimes scares students, so does the look of a function, which is something like this: $f(x) = 7x^2 - 2x$. However, the idea here is simple, think of it like this: the $f(x)$ part can be replaced with y, thus $y = 7x^2 - 2x$. They are interchangeable. Another way to think about it is this: the value of y is a *function* of x. In other words, what y is equal to depends on what x is. Typically, the ACT will ask you (using the example above) what the value of a function is ($f(x) = 7x^2 - 2x$) when x has a certain value (put like this: $f(4)$). In that case, simply plug in 4 for x and get a value of the function. Here, it looks like: $f(4) = 7(4^2) - 2(4) = 112 - 8 = 104$.

Let's look at some examples to see a bit of the various ways the ACT can ask you about functions.

52. If $f(x) = 3x^2 - 12x$, then what is $f(-2)$?

F. -24
G. -12
H. 0
J. 12
K. 36

53. A function, f , is defined by $f(a, b) = 2b^3 + 5a$. What is the value of $f(-1, 2)$?

A. 2
B. 8
C. 11
D. 15
E. 21

54. Given that $f(x) = x^2 + 3x$, and that $g(x) = 2x + 2$, what is $f(g(x))$?

F. $2(2x^2 + 7x + 5)$
G. $4x^2 + 7x + 5$
H. $4(x^2 + 3x + 3)$
J. $2x^2 + 4x + 5$
K. $x^2 + 7x + 10$

55. If $f(x) = 21$, and $g(x) = 10.5$, what is $\frac{f(x)}{g(x)}$?

A. 0.5
B. 2.0
C. 10.5
D. 31.5
E. 220.5

56. If $f(x) = \dfrac{1}{(x+3)}$, and $g(x) = \dfrac{1}{(x^2 + 2x - 3)}$, then what is $\dfrac{f(x)}{g(x)}$?

F. $x - 1$

G. $x + 1$

H. $\dfrac{1}{(x+3)^2}$

J. $\dfrac{1}{(x+3)^2(x-1)}$

K. $\dfrac{1}{(x+3)^2(x+1)}$

Have to Know #13: Circles

Although there are limitless things you could know and learn about circles, there are three things about them you MUST know for ACT Math: the formula for the area, the formula for the circumference, and what an arc is.

Area and Circumference

The formula for the area of a circle is πr^2, which is different from the formula for the perimeter or circumference of a circle, which is $2\pi r$. r, of course, represents the radius of the circle, which is half of the diameter. Look at this figure: with a simple circle like this, we can easily calculate the perimeter (circumference) and the area.

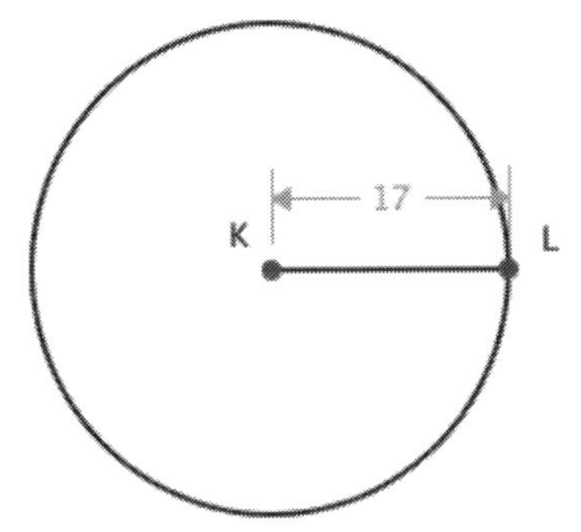

Let's start with the circumference of the circle, or the perimeter you might say, which is simply $2\pi r$. That leaves us with 2(3.14)(17), which is 34π or 106.8 rounded. As for area, we use πr^2, which is 3.14(172) = 289π, or 907.5 rounded to the first decimal place.

Knowing and mastering these two values will get you far on most ACT Math circle questions, and many of the upcoming examples will mimic the way the ACT asks you about these two values.

Arc and Interior Angles

Another circle concept, however, that is important to know is that of an arc. An arc is simply a piece of the outside of a circle, and they have both a degree measure and a distance.

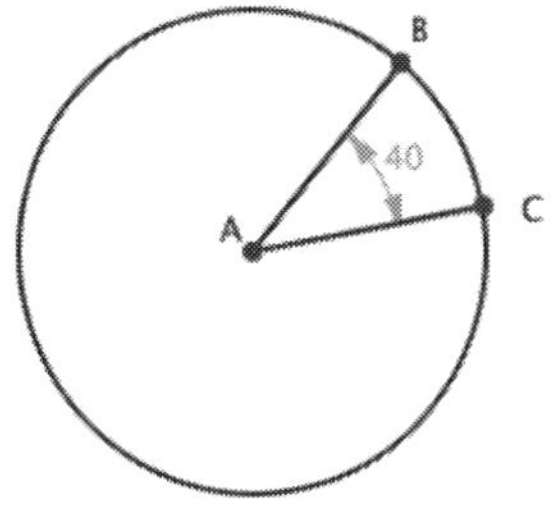

In this figure here, *BC* is an arc; by *BC* I don't mean the distance between the two that could be represented by drawing a straight line between them, but rather the length of the curve. It has a measure or angle (often called an interior angle), as you can see (40 degrees), and it also has a length or distance. Let's say that the radius of this circle is 4. That would mean that the circumference is $2\pi r$, or $2\pi 4$, or 8π. We can find the length of arc *BC* by cross multiplying; this begins with realizing that there is a ratio here: as 40 degrees is to 360 degrees (the amount of degrees in a circle), so too *BC* is to 8π. Thus, $\frac{40^o}{360^o} = \frac{BC}{8\pi}$. Working this out, we learn that $BC = 0.89\pi$.

Let's look at a few examples that mimic those found on recent ACT tests. Remember, if a shape, graph, or figure isn't drawn (as is true in all four of these), do yourself a favor and draw it out!

57. Carla purchased a round tablecloth for her outdoor table. In order to allow for the table's umbrella to be inserted into the center of the table, she must cut a circular hole out of the center of the tablecloth. If the radius of the tablecloth is 4.5 feet, and the diameter of the hole that she cuts from the center is 1 foot, then what is the total area of the tablecloth after the hole has been cut, rounded to the nearest hundredth of a foot?

A. 55.42
B. 60.48
C. 62.83
D. 63.61
E. 72.72

58. A circle has a circumference of 22 meters. What is the area of this circle, rounded to the nearest decimal?

F. 22.0 m^2
G. 31.6 m^2
H. 38.5 m^2
J. 153.9 m^2
K. 380.1 m^2

59. The radius of one circle is 5 feet long. The radius of a second circle is 40% longer than the radius of the first circle. To the nearest square foot, how much larger is the area of the second circle than the area of the first circle?

A. 2
B. 22
C. 45
D. 58
E. 75

60. Tommy attempts to cut a pizza with a diameter of 16 inches into 8 equal pieces. However, he accidentally cuts out the first piece with an interior angle of 55°. Rounded to the nearest hundredth of an inch, what is the length of the outside arc of the crust of this first slice of pizza?

F. 4.29 inches
G. 7.68 inches
H. 8.04 inches
J. 8.51 inches
K. 9.42 inches

Step 3 Correct Answers

1: B
2: G
3: B
4: K
5: A
6: K
7: A
8: H
9: E
10: K
11: C
12: K
13: B
14: H
15: E
16: F
17: B
18: H
19: D
20: F
21: D
22: K
23: C
24: J
25: B
26: K
27: E
28: G
29: D
30: J
31: E
32: K
33: C
34: G
35: A
36: J
37: A
38: J
39: C
40: G
41: A
42: K
43: D
44: H
45: B
46: K
47: A
48: H
49: B
50: F
51: B
52: K
53: C
54: F
55: B
56: F
57: C
58: H
59: E
60: G

ACT Math Step 3 *Have to Know* practice answer explanations begin on page 536.

STEP 4

ACT Math Have to Know Full-Length Practice Test

About This Unique Practice Test

If you completed all 60 problems following the 13 *Have to Know* lessons, you have completed a practice test's worth of problems. However, before moving on to *Good to Know* ACT Math (which is the next series of lessons), it is crucial that you ensure that you have a grip on all of the *Have to Know* math presented here in this test. This isn't the end, of course, of *Have to Know* material, it is prevalent in the two complete practice tests that make up Step 6 as well.

As always, explanations for each of the following 60 problems can be found in the back of the book, beginning on page 554; the answers themselves are found on page 213.

The following practice test, though it only features *Have to Know* math problems, is designed to mimic an actual ACT test. It features, for example, a gradual increase in difficulty, and is based on real-life ACT Math problems. Thus, this is a great opportunity to put into practice the *Two Pass Strategy* from Step 1 and the 4 ACT Math mini-strategies from Step 2.

Don't give up on problems, circle them and skip them, and don't use more than roughly a minute on any individual problem; circle it as well and come back if you have time; only guess if you're absolutely certain you can't get it right or give it a good guess on a second pass.

However, I have to admit something before you begin. As the creator of these questions, I was often faced with this dilemma: should I make this problem a little bit more difficult or a little bit easier? Most of the time, I leaned towards making the problems a little more difficult. This is NOT to crush your spirits or just to make me feel good for being able to make high school math questions more difficult. Instead, it's to *reinforce* what you *Have to Know* and make you *stronger* as a result.

With all of that said, remove distractions, start a 60 minute timer, and begin.

MATHEMATICS TEST

60 Minutes — 60 Questions

DIRECTIONS: Solve each problem, choose the correct answer, and then fill in the corresponding oval on your answer document.

Do not linger over problems that take too much time. Solve as many as you can; then return to the others in the time you have left for this test.

You are permitted to use a calculator on this test. You may use your calculator for any problems you choose, but some of the problems may best be done without using a calculator.

Note: Unless otherwise stated, all of the following should be assumed.

1. Illustrative figures are NOT necessarily drawn to scale.
2. Geometric figures lie in a plane.
3. The word *line* indicates a straight line.
4. The word *average* indicates arithmetic mean.

DO YOUR FIGURING HERE.

1. The product of $4x^2y^4 \cdot 3x^2y^2 \cdot 8x$ is equivalent to which of the following?

   A. $15x^5y^6$
   B. $15x^4y^8$
   C. $96x^5y^6$
   D. $96x^4y^8$
   E. $96(xy)^{11}$

2. Tabitha owns a craft store. A customer calls and orders 6 strips of ribbon with lengths of 10, 12, 9, 10, 11, and 12 inches, respectively. What is the mean of the lengths of the ribbon strips, rounded to the nearest tenth of an inch?

   F. 10.5
   G. 10.6
   H. 10.7
   J. 11.0
   K. 11.1

3. Three times the sum of x and -4 is equal to the addition of 8 and $-x$. What is the value of x ?

   A. -5
   B. -1
   C. 3
   D. 5
   E. 10

4. Chipper puts 7% of his \$66,000 annual salary into a savings account in 12 equal monthly installments. Parker, on the other hand, deposits a flat rate of \$150 a month into a savings account. Not counting for interest earned, how much more a month does Chipper put into savings than Parker?

   F. \$235
   G. \$250
   H. \$312
   J. \$322
   K. \$385

DO YOUR FIGURING HERE.

5. Bus 1 and Bus 2 are 1,000 miles apart. Bus 1 travels towards Bus 2 in a straight line at 60 miles per hour, and Bus 2 travels towards Bus 1 in a straight line at 55 miles per hour. After 4 hours of continuous driving, how far apart are the two buses?

A. 240
B. 300
C. 460
D. 540
E. 700

6. What is the median of the values of z for which $(z + 2)(z - 4)(z + 3)(z - 6) = 0$?

F. -1
G. -0.5
H. 0
J. 0.5
K. 1

7. Square $ABCD$ is shown below. If segment $\overline{BD}$ is 10 inches long, then what is the length of any side of square $ABCD$?

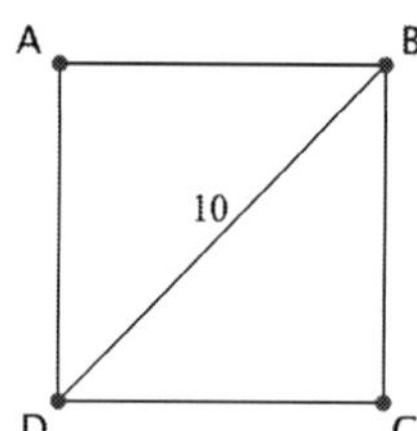

A. 5
B. $5\sqrt{2}$
C. $5\sqrt{3}$
D. 7.5
E. 10

8. If x is an integer, and $x \neq 2$, then $(2x - 4)^4 - 1$:

F. must be positive and odd.
G. must be negative and odd.
H. must be positive and even.
J. must be negative and even.
K. can be even, odd, positive, or negative.

DO YOUR FIGURING HERE.

9. In the figure below, $\overline{JI}$ is parallel to $\overline{HF}$ and $\overline{LK}$ is parallel to $\overline{HG}$. If $\angle JIF$ is 115° and $\angle LKG$ is 20°, then what is the measure of $\angle FHG$?

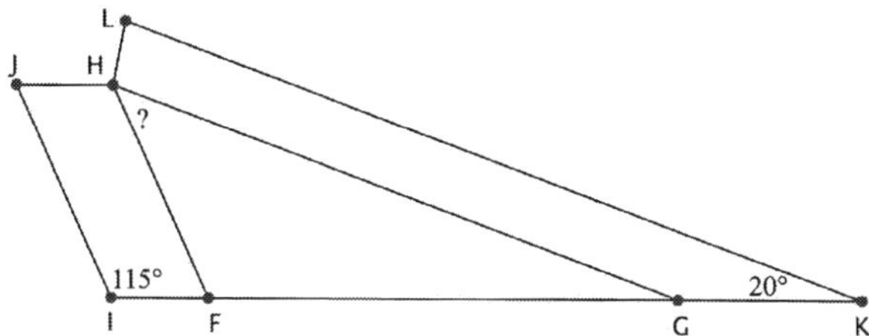

A. 45°
B. 55°
C. 65°
D. 115°
E. 120°

10. For all nonzero values of x, y, and z, $\dfrac{-15xy^3z^8}{3x^3y^2z} = ?$

F. $\dfrac{-5x^2}{yz^7}$

G. $\dfrac{-5yz^7}{x^2}$

H. $\dfrac{5y^5z^9}{x^4}$

J. $5x^4y^5z^9$

K. $-5x^2yz^7$

11. What is the slope of any line that is parallel to $6x - 5y = 10$?

A. -2

B. $-\dfrac{6}{5}$

C. $-\dfrac{5}{6}$

D. $\dfrac{5}{6}$

E. $\dfrac{6}{5}$

12. Maggie decides that she wants to install a concrete walkway around the outside of her swimming pool. Her swimming pool is 25 feet long and 20 feet wide. If the walkway will be 3 feet wide all the way around the pool, then what will be the total area of the new walkway?

F. 144 ft^2
G. 162 ft^2
H. 306 ft^2
J. 500 ft^2
K. 806 ft^2

DO YOUR FIGURING HERE.

13. Barb is trying to decide what color dress to wear to her high school dance. She has 7 red dresses, 4 black dresses, and 2 green dresses. Her sister has 3 red dresses, 6 black dresses, and 8 green dresses. If she can wear either her own dress or one of her sister's, and if she chooses a dress at random, then what is probability that the chosen dress is black?

A. $\frac{2}{15}$
B. $\frac{3}{15}$
C. $\frac{3}{10}$
D. $\frac{1}{3}$
E. $\frac{1}{2}$

14. If $f(x) = 2x^2 - x + 1$, then what is $f(2)$?

F. 3
G. 7
H. 9
J. 15
K. 17

15. Two lines intersect, creating four angles: $\angle A$, $\angle B$, $\angle C$, and $\angle D$. As a result, $\angle A \neq \angle B$ and $\angle C \neq \angle D$. If $\angle C = 40°$, then what is the value of $\angle D$?

A. 160°
B. 140°
C. 120°
D. 50°
E. 40°

16. What is the diameter of a circle with an area of 36π ?

F. 3
G. 6
H. 9
J. 12
K. 72

17. Timothy is a professional baseball player participating in a home run contest. For every home run, r, that he hits up to and including 5, he will receive \$0. After he reaches this many home runs, he will receive \$25 for each additional home run. Assuming he hits at least 5 home runs, which expression represents the total amount Timothy will earn in the home run competition?

DO YOUR FIGURING HERE.

A. $25r - 5$
B. $25(r + 5)$
C. $25(r - 5)$
D. $25r$
E. $25r + 5$

18. A car that normally sells for \$38,000 is on sale for 13% off. How much does it cost during the sale, to the nearest dollar?

F. \$29,100
G. \$29,200
H. \$32,300
J. \$33,060
K. \$42,940

19. If $g(x) = \frac{x^{\frac{1}{2}}}{x^{-1}}$, what is the value of $g(9)$?

A. $-\frac{1}{3}$

B. 0

C. $\frac{1}{3}$

D. 3

E. 27

20. Which of the following pairs of lines could have (2, – 2) as a solution?

F. $y = \frac{1}{2}x - 3 ; y = 5x - 12$

G. $y = 5x - 12 ; y = \frac{1}{3}x + 1$

H. $y = \frac{1}{3}x + 1 ; y = 11x - 3$

J. $y = \frac{1}{2}x - 3 ; y = 11x - 3$

K. $y = \frac{1}{2}x - 3 ; y = \frac{1}{3}x + 1$

Use the following information to answer questions 21-23.

DO YOUR FIGURING HERE.

Drew is a high school track athlete who specializes in three throwing events: javelin, shot put, and discus. In order to ensure he is giving roughly equal treatment to each sport, he tracks how many practice throws he makes of each across the 5 days of the week in the chart below.

	Mon.	Tues.	Wed.	Thurs.	Fri.
Javelin	12	23	11	2	19
Shot Put	18	11	0	15	18
Discus	0	0	18	15	3

On Mondays and Tuesdays, Drew throws at full strength. At full strength, Drew averages a javelin throw of 201 feet, a shot put throw of 52 feet, and a discus throw of 179 feet. However, due to arm soreness, Drew can only throw at 90% of his strength on Wednesdays, 70% of his strength on Thursdays, and 60% of his strength on Fridays.

21. What percent of Drew's throws for the week were discus throws, rounded to the nearest percent?

A. 22%
B. 33%
C. 38%
D. 41%
E. 78%

22. The track and field coach decided to observe a random throw of Drew's during Thursday practice. What was the expected outcome, rounded to the nearest foot, of the observed throw?

F. 81
G. 85
H. 116
J. 121
K. 144

23. Due to arm soreness, which of the following throws is likely to travel the farthest?

A. A shot put throw on a Wednesday
B. A shot put throw on a Thursday
C. A discus throw on a Thursday
D. A javelin throw on a Friday
E. A discus throw on a Friday

24. At her job, Gabrielle earns $\$(11h + 16.5e + 0.21s)$, where h is the number of regular time hours she worked, e is the number of overtime hours she worked, and s is the amount of her sales. What does Gabrielle earn for working 40 regular time hours and 3 overtime hours, while making \$3,234 in sales?

F. \$440.00
G. \$489.50
H. \$709.50
J. \$1,119.14
K. \$1,168.64

DO YOUR FIGURING HERE.

25. In the figure below, right angles are as marked and sides are labeled in inches. What is the area of the figure in square inches?

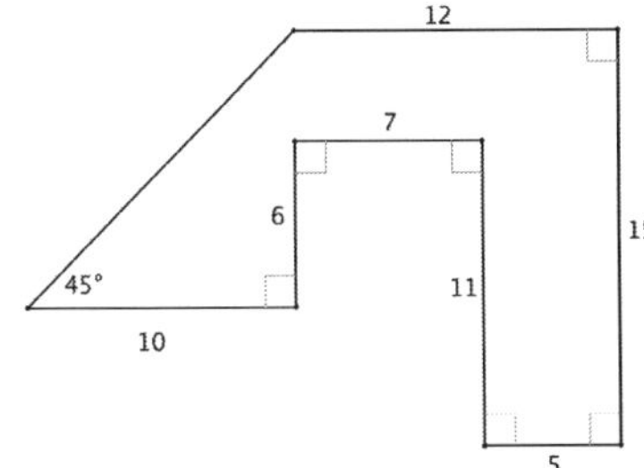

A. 151
B. 153
C. 163
D. 228
E. 230

26. In the standard (x, y) coordinate plane, point L is at $(-3, 0)$ and point M is at $(1, 3)$. What is the distance between point L and point M?

F. 3
G. $3\sqrt{3}$
H. $4\sqrt{2}$
J. 5
K. 7

27. At WaterTown Water Park, Bryan rides a slide that is 125 feet long into a swimming pool. If the slide meets the pool at an angle of 38°, then how many feet high off of the ground is the slide's starting point, rounded to the nearest tenth of a foot?

A. 47.5
B. 77.0
C. 97.7
D. 98.5
E. 203.0

28. If $-5 \leq x \leq 3$ and $|y| = 2$, then what is the greatest possible value of the product of x and y ?

DO YOUR FIGURING HERE.

F. -10
G. -6
H. 0
J. 6
K. 10

29. The table below gives values for $f(x)$ and $g(x)$ for various values of x.

x	$f(x)$	$g(x)$
-2	3	10
-1	0	5
0	-2	-4
3	6	-8
5	8	-2

What is the value of $f(g(5))$?

A. -2
B. -1
C. 0
D. 3
E. 10

30. If $i^2 = -1$, what is the value of $(i-1)(i-1)$?

F. $-2i$
G. -1
H. 0
J. i
K. $2i$

31. Missy purchased $(12x - 41)$ dollars worth of groceries at Grocery Stop. Because Grocery Stop did not have every item on her shopping list, she then went to Fancy Foods and purchased an additional $(5x + 30)$ dollars worth of groceries. If she purchased a total of \$278 worth of groceries, how much money did she spend at Grocery Stop?

A. \$55
B. \$115
C. \$163
D. \$243
E. \$245

DO YOUR FIGURING HERE.

32. Jeff has hit 0, 2, 4, 2, 1, 0, 0, 0, 3, and 2 home runs in Games 1 - 10 this season. How many home runs does he need in Game 11 and Game 12 so that the mode of his home runs will exceed the mean?

	Game 11	Game 12
F.	0	4
G.	4	0
H.	2	2
J.	3	3
K.	4	4

33. What is the value of tan A in right triangle $\triangle ABC$ shown below?

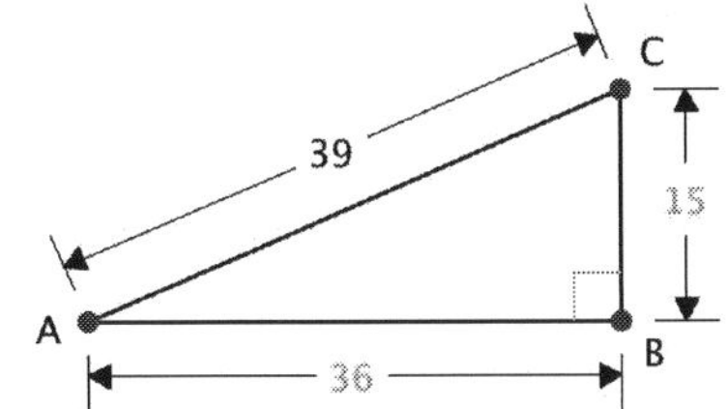

A. $\frac{5}{12}$

B. $\frac{12}{13}$

C. $\frac{13}{12}$

D. $\frac{12}{5}$

E. $\frac{13}{5}$

34. What is the equation of a line that is perpendicular to the line $y = -\frac{2}{5}x + 3$ and passes through the point (2, 3) ?

F. $y = -\frac{2}{5}x - 3$

G. $y = -\frac{2}{5}x + 5$

H. $y = \frac{2}{5}x - 4$

J. $y = \frac{5}{2}x + 3$

K. $y = \frac{5}{2}x - 2$

35. In the figure below, segments $\overline{JK}$ and $\overline{HI}$ are parallel and are transversed by segment $\overline{LM}$. If the value of angle $\angle HNO$ is 35°, then what is the value of angle $\angle LOK$?

DO YOUR FIGURING HERE.

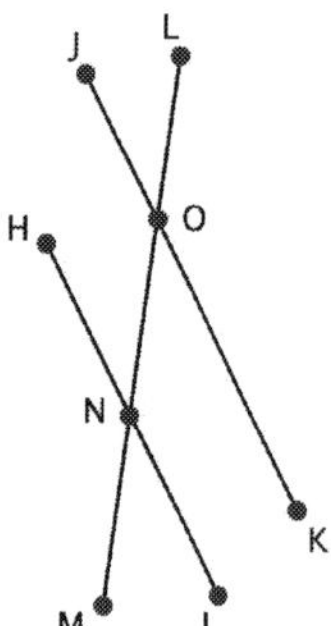

A. 35°
B. 55°
C. 115°
D. 135°
E. 145°

36. The diameter of Circle X equals the radius of Circle Y. The diameter of Circle Y equals the radius of Circle Z. If the area of Circle Z is 225π, then what is the circumference of Circle X?

F. 3.75π
G. 7.5π
H. 14.0625π
J. 15π
K. 56.25π

37. If $f(x) = \frac{2}{3}x - 14$, and $g(x) = 6x^2 + 18x + 18$, which expression represents $f(g(x))$?

A. $2(2x^2 + 6x - 1)$
B. $2x^2 + 6x + 1$
C. $2(2x^2 + 9x + 2)$
D. $9x^2 + 27x + 13$
E. $9x^2 + 27x + 41$

38. For all $x \neq 2$, the expression $\dfrac{(x+1)(x^2+x-6)}{(x-2)(x^2-5x-24)}$ is equivalent to which of the following?

F. $\dfrac{(x-1)(x+2)}{(x+8)(x-2)}$

G. $\dfrac{(x-1)}{(x+8)}$

H. $\dfrac{(x+1)}{(x-8)}$

J. $-\dfrac{1}{80}$

K. $\dfrac{1}{8}$

39. The point (0, 3) is the midpoint of the line segment in the standard (x, y) coordinate plane with endpoints $(2, -1)$ and (a, b). Which of the following is (a, b) ?

A. $(-5, 4)$
B. $(4, -5)$
C. $(6, 1)$
D. $(3, -4)$
E. $(-2, 7)$

40. The formula for converting a Celsius temperature (C) to its equivalent Fahrenheit temperature (F) is $F = \frac{9}{5}C + 32$. Which of the following is the Fahrenheit equivalent of a Celsius temperature of 31°, rounded to the nearest degree?

F. 49°
G. 50°
H. 87°
J. 88°
K. 89°

41. In the standard (x, y) coordinate plane, line A never crosses the y-axis. What is the slope of line A ?

A. 1
B. 0
C. -1
D. Undefined
E. Cannot be determined from the given information.

42. In $\triangle EFG$, $\angle E$ is a right angle, $\angle F$ measures 50°, and side EF is 14 millimeters long. What is the area of $\triangle EFG$ in square millimeters, rounded to the nearest hundredth?

F. 76.23
G. 116.79
H. 152.46
J. 196.00
K. 233.58

43. If $(x^{3z+4})^3 = x^3$ for all x, then $z = $?

A. $-\frac{4}{3}$

B. -1

C. $-\frac{3}{4}$

D. $\frac{3}{4}$

E. $\frac{4}{3}$

DO YOUR FIGURING HERE.

Use the following information to answer questions 44-46.

DO YOUR FIGURING HERE.

Island Spa and Resort is considering installing 8 new circular swimming pools around their large property to mimic the planets that revolve around the sun. The proposed diameters of the 8 swimming pools are listed below:

- Pool A (Mercury): 30 feet
- Pool B (Venus): 60 feet
- Pool C (Earth): 60 feet
- Pool D (Mars): 40 feet
- Pool E (Jupiter): 100 feet
- Pool F (Saturn): 90 feet
- Pool G (Uranus): 80 feet
- Pool H (Neptune): 75 feet

44. If all swimming pools have the same depth, then how much more water will Pool E (Jupiter) need compared to Pool C (Earth), rounded to the nearest percent?

F. 28%
G. 36%
H. 167%
J. 278%
K. 360%

45. Island Spa and Resort is considering adding a ninth pool to represent the dwarf planet Pluto. If this pool was to have a diameter of 15 feet, then which of the following measurements of the data set of the pools' diameters would change the least?

A. Mean
B. Median
C. Mode
D. Range
E. Cannot be determined from the given information.

46. Island Spa and Resort decides to allocate a section of Pool H (Neptune) for use by children only. If the interior angle of the new children's section is 120°, what is the measure of the arc of this section of Pool H (Neptune) ?

F. 5π
G. 25π
H. 37.5π
J. 75π
K. 140π

47. If $4 < \frac{1}{x^2} < 9$, then which of the following is a possible value of x ?

DO YOUR FIGURING HERE.

A. $\frac{5}{12}$

B. $\frac{1}{3}$

C. $\frac{9}{13}$

D. 4

E. 9

48. For what value of z would the following systems of equations have an infinite number of solutions?

$$2x - 7y = 4$$
$$6x - zy = 12$$

F. −5
G. 5
H. 7
J. 14
K. 21

49. What is the area in square units of a triangle formed by the points $(-1, -1)$, $(-4, -1)$, and $(-4, -5)$?

A. 5.0
B. 5.5
C. 6.0
D. 7.5
E. 10.0

50. If $7x^3y^4 < 0$, which of the following cannot possibly be true?

F. $x < 7$
G. $x > -7$
H. $y < 0$
J. $y > 7$
K. $x = 0$

51. When $x = -3$, $f(x) = -14$. When $x = -1$, $f(x) = 2$. When $x = 4$, $f(x) = -28$. Which of the following functions could be $f(x)$?

A. $f(x) = -2x^2 + 4$
B. $f(x) = 2x - 8$
C. $f(x) = x^3 + 3$
D. $f(x) = -2x - 20$
E. $f(x) = -x^2 - 5$

52. An elementary school decides to host a kickball tournament during P.E. For the randomization of teams, 8 marbles of 8 different colors are placed into a hat. Each student will draw a marble to indicate what team he or she is on. Joseph draws first, and he chooses a green marble. Maximilian draws second, and he also chooses a green marble, putting him on Joseph's team. If Jude is the third student to draw, what is the probability that he will also be on Joseph and Maximilian's team?

F. $\frac{3}{31}$

G. $\frac{7}{63}$

H. $\frac{1}{8}$

J. $\frac{4}{31}$

K. $\frac{1}{7}$

DO YOUR FIGURING HERE.

53. What is the perimeter of a right triangle with legs 10 and 15 inches long ?

A. 5
B. $5\sqrt{13}$
C. $15 + 10\sqrt{3}$
D. 40
E. $25 + 5\sqrt{13}$

54. $$\frac{\frac{1}{6} + \left(\frac{5}{2} \cdot \frac{2}{3}\right)}{\left(-\frac{11}{12} + \frac{11}{4}\right) - \left(\frac{-3 + 14}{-3 + 15}\right)} = ?$$

F. 0
G. 1
H. 2
J. 3
K. 4

55. When x is squared and added to 4 times y, the result is 13. In addition, when the product of 2 and y is added to the product of negative 2 and x, the result is negative 16. Which of the following is a solution for this system of equations?

A. $x = 8;\ y = 0$
B. $x = 0;\ y = -8$
C. $x = 10;\ y = 2$
D. $x = 5;\ y = -3$
E. $x = 3;\ y = 1$

56. Clare and MC enter a school competition to determine which student has the best handwriting. Clare writes at a pace of 22 words per minute, and MC writes at a pace of 17 words per minute. If MC starts writing at 2:00, and Clare starts writing at 2:03, then at what time will Clare pass MC in number of words written, rounded *up* to the nearest whole minute?

F. 2:14
G. 2:15
H. 2:16
J. 2:17
K. 2:18

DO YOUR FIGURING HERE.

57. In the figure below, $\overline{AB}$ is parallel to $\overline{DF}$, and $\overline{GD}$ is parallel to $\overline{EF}$. Angle $\angle AGD$ measures 150°, and $\angle ECF$ measures 90°. If segment $\overline{FC}$ is 4 meters in length, then what is the length of $\overline{EC}$, rounded to the nearest tenth of a meter?

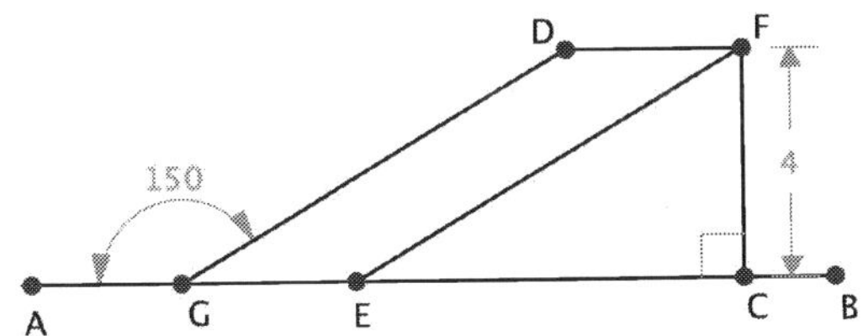

A. 4.6
B. 6.9
C. 7.1
D. 7.7
E. 8.0

58. $\left(\sqrt{x^4} - \sqrt[4]{x^8} + \frac{1}{x^{-2}}\right)^{\frac{1}{2}} = ?$

F. $-3x^2$
G. $-x^2$
H. $x - x^2$
J. x
K. x^2

59. The figure that follows shows three circles, all of which are tangent to one another. The circumference of circle L is 8π mm, the circumference of circle M is 12π mm, and the circumference of circle N is 14π mm. What is the perimeter of triangle $\triangle LMN$ in mm ?

DO YOUR FIGURING HERE.

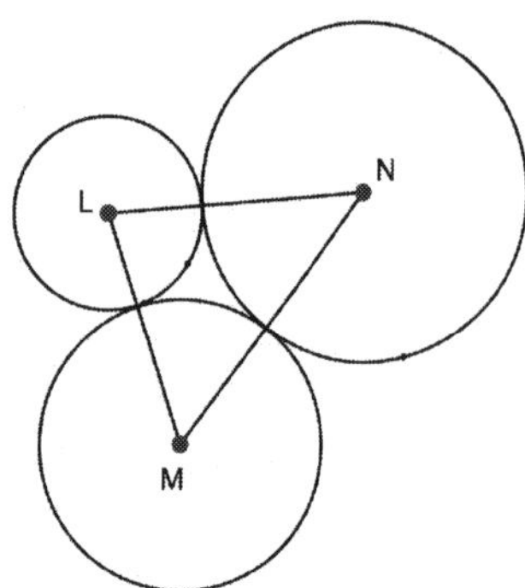

A. 8.5
B. 17
C. 25.5
D. 32
E. 34

60. Jordan decides to flip a coin 5 times in a row. What are the odds that the coin lands on heads the first, second, and third tosses, then lands on tails for both the fourth and fifth tosses?

F. $\frac{1}{128}$

G. $\frac{1}{64}$

H. $\frac{1}{32}$

J. $\frac{5}{64}$

K. $\frac{5}{32}$

Step 4 Correct Answers

1: C
2: H
3: D
4: F
5: D
6: K
7: B
8: F
9: A
10: G
11: E
12: H
13: D
14: G
15: B
16: J
17: C
18: J
19: E
20: F

21: A
22: G
23: C
24: K
25: B
26: J
27: B
28: K
29: D
30: F
31: C
32: H
33: A
34: K
35: E
36: G
37: A
38: H
39: E
40: J

41: D
42: G
43: B
44: J
45: C
46: G
47: A
48: K
49: C
50: K
51: A
52: F
53: E
54: H
55: D
56: F
57: B
58: J
59: E
60: H

ACT Math *Have to Know* Practice Test answer explanations begin on page 554.

STEP 5

ACT Math Good to Know

The material before this lesson represents the majority of ACT Math problems, covering the most asked about content and the most needed strategies. Here, we begin math that I'm calling *Good to Know*, a module that consists of 11 additional lessons. You may already know how to do many of these things, or maybe they are obscure to you. Nevertheless, you can expect about one question or less per ACT test on all of the math in this module. Between the 11 lessons here, and the multiple pieces of content within each, you can expect at least 10 or so questions on ACT day that require your knowledge of it all in one way or another. This is significant; correctly answering 10 more math questions on the ACT is roughly equivalent to an ACT Math score increase of 5 or 6 points!

Good to Know #1: Fundamental Counting Principle

We will begin with a simple idea with a too-long name: the **Fundamental Counting Principle**. It essentially says this: if there are p ways to do one thing, then q ways to do another, second thing, then there are p x q ways to do both of them. For example: if there are 8 types of ice cream, and 5 types of sprinkles, then there are $8 \times 5 = 40$ ways to combine one flavor of ice cream with one sprinkle topping. If you add in a third option, the number of possibilities increases. If there are 8 types of ice cream, 5 types of sprinkles, AND 6 different flavors of syrupy drizzle to go on top, then now there are $8 \times 5 \times 6 = 240$ different combinations.

Of course, the way in which the ACT will test your ability to think logically in this way differs and is rarely straightforward. Let's get into some examples.

1. Philip and Jenn desire to take a photograph of their five children together, and they decide that the photograph will look best if the children are lined up shoulder-to-shoulder. How many different ways can the couple line up their five children?

   A. 15
   B. 24
   C. 120
   D. 124
   E. 204

2. Delaney has x number of movies to choose from. Which of the following expressions gives the number of possible combinations of movies if Delaney desires to watch 3 movies in a row?

F. $3x$

G. x^3

H. $x(x + 1)^2$

J. x^3x^2x

K. $x(x - 1)(x - 2)$

3. The city of Doverville employs 80 police officers and 50 firefighters. The mayor will choose at random 1 police officer and 1 firefighter to represent the city during the Fourth of July Parade. How many different combinations of 1 police officer and 1 firefighter are possible?

A. 15
B. 50
C. 130
D. 131
E. 4,000

4. McGregor County issues license plates for all of its automobiles that contain 7 digits. Due to state regulations, the first two digits of the plate are fixed and cannot be changed. Due to local law, the third digit is also fixed and cannot be changed. If the remaining digits can feature either one of the 10 numbers, 0 through 9, or one of the 26 letters of the alphabet, and if the digits *can* be repeated, how many combinations of license plates are possible in McGregor County?

F. 108
G. 252
H. 1,413,720
J. 1,679,616
K. 60,466,176

Good to Know #2: Triangles Part II

We have talked a lot about triangles already in ACT Math *Have to Know* Lesson #9. We talked about the angles in a triangle, the trig functions sin, cosine, and tangent, and finding the area of a triangle. All of those things fall into the *Have to Know* math category. However, there are some other things about triangles that I would call *Good to Know*. First, there are *special triangles*, which is more of a helpful shortcut that we've briefly mentioned, and secondly there are the definitions of the various types of triangles.

Special Triangles

Let's start with so-called *special triangles*, which refers to the relationships between the sides of certain right triangles. Before I explain what they mean, and how to use them, let's learn what the two special triangles are that can be helpful on the ACT. There's the 3-4-5 triangle, and the 5-12-13 triangle.

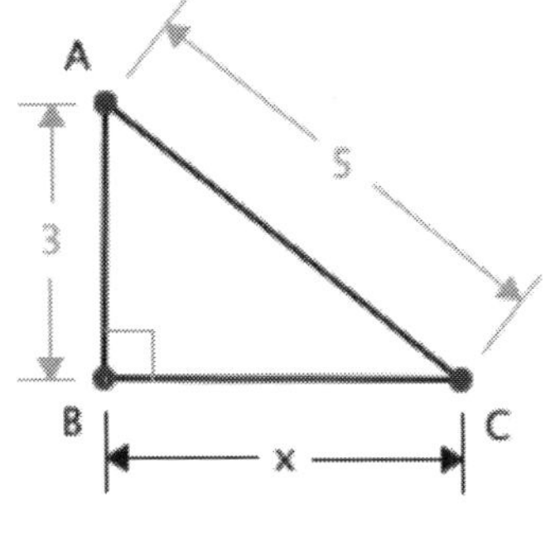

Here's what that means: when you have a right triangle with one side with a length of 3, and a hypotenuse with a length of 5, then you know automatically that the other leg is of length 4.

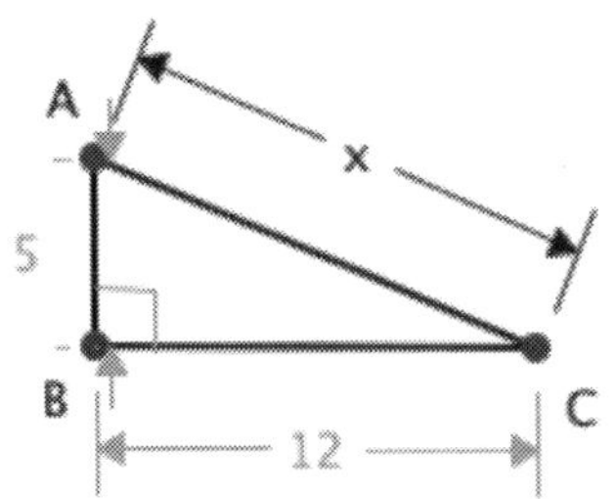

Similarly, if you have a right triangle with one leg having a length of 5, and the other leg having a length of 12, then you know for certain that the length of the hypotenuse is 13.

There is one more thing to know about these: this special relationship also works with *multiples* of each other. In other words, while there is a 3-4-5 triangle, we can multiply those numbers by 2, and learn that there is also such a thing as a 6-8-10 triangle. Like this:

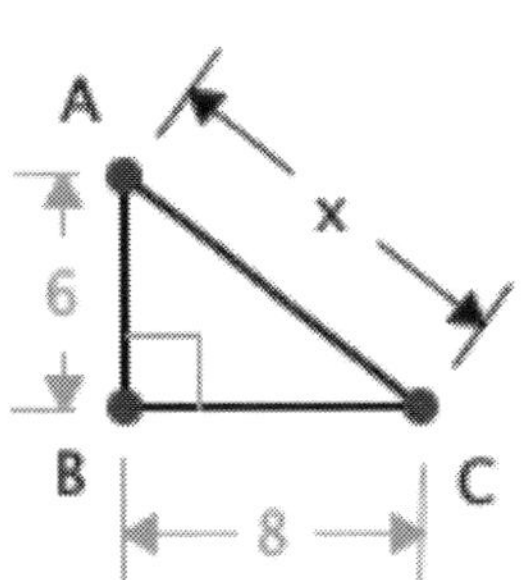

None of these special triangles fall into the *Have to Know* category, especially because you will get the same results if you use the Pythagorean Theorem, but being able to recognize these triangles can oftentimes save you precious time. Again, the ACT likes them (which just means that these kinds of triangles are used relatively often), so knowing to recognize them is only a good thing!

A second category of items that are *Good to Know* when it comes to triangles are the definitions of different triangles. The ACT occasionally likes a question that requires you to categorize a certain triangle, or a question that gives you the definition of a certain type of triangle in the question, requiring you to know what it means. Here are a few:

a) Isosceles Triangle - a triangle with exactly two sides of equal length, like these:

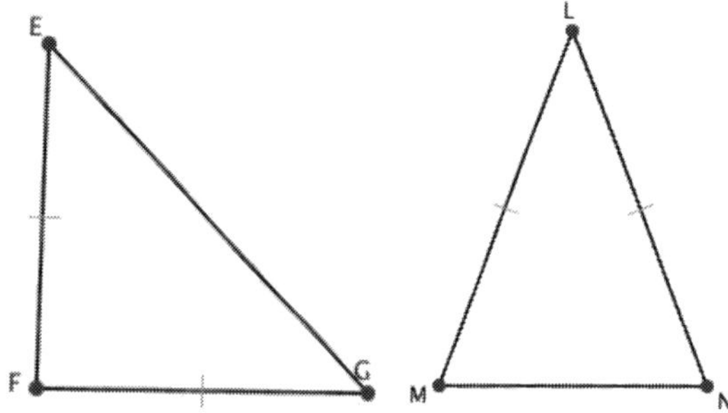

b) Equilateral triangle - a triangle with three equal sides (and also three 60° angles), like this:

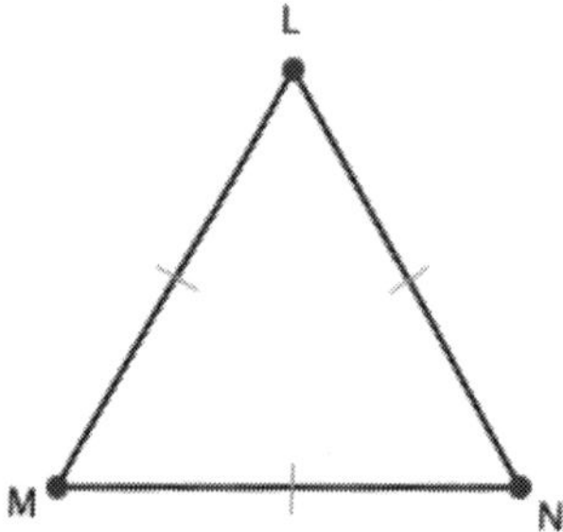

c) Scalene triangle - a triangle with three sides of unequal length. These can be right triangles, or not, like these:

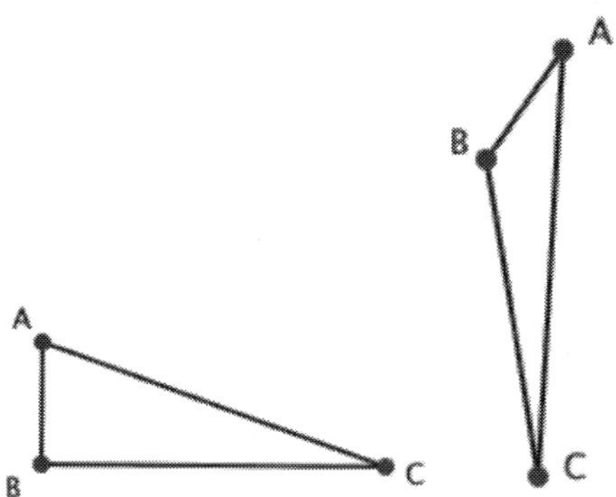

d) Acute triangle - a triangle in which all 3 angles are less than 90 degrees, like these:

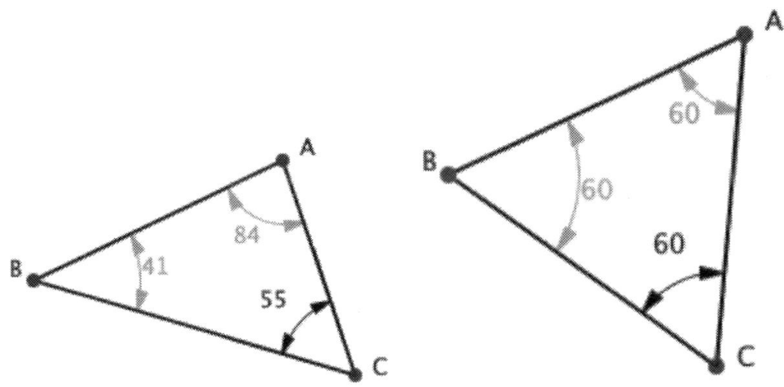

e) Obtuse triangle - a triangle in which at least one angle is greater than 90 degrees, like this:

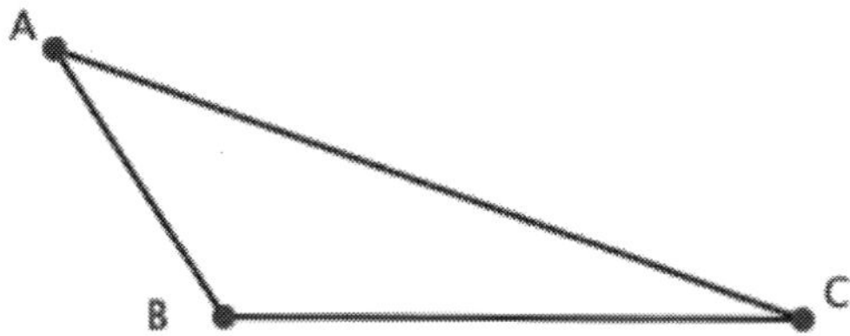

f) Similar triangles - two triangles with the same angles and equivalent sides. The two triangles below are similar; their angles are the same. On the larger triangle, let's say that the length of side AB is 10 and AC is 14. That would mean that on the smaller triangle that if DE is 5 (which is half of AB), then we know that the length of side DF is half of AC, or 7.

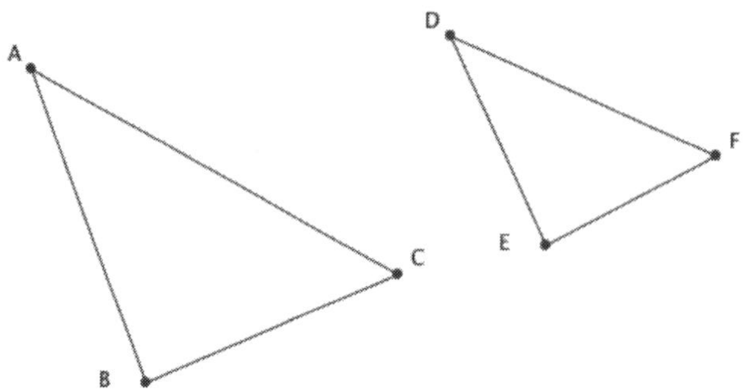

Of course, these triangle concepts overlap, and sometimes you might need to recognize that. All equilateral triangles are acute. An isosceles triangle can be obtuse. A scalene triangle can be acute or obtuse. Etc. Let's get into some examples:

5. In the standard (x, y) coordinate plane, what is the distance between the points $(-2, -2)$ and $(-7, -14)$?

A. 5
B. 9
C. 12
D. 13
E. 17

6. Triangle $\triangle LMN$ is an equilateral triangle. If angle $\angle L$ has a measure of 60°, and if side MN has a length of 12 millimeters, then which of the following statements are true ?

I. $\triangle LMN$ is an acute triangle
II. $\angle N$ is greater than 90°
III. Side LM has a length of less than 12 millimeters

F. I only
G. II only
H. III only
J. I and III only
K. I, II, and III

7. In the figure below, $\triangle MNO$ and $\triangle PQR$ are similar triangles with the given side lengths in miles. What is the perimeter, in miles, of $\triangle PQR$?

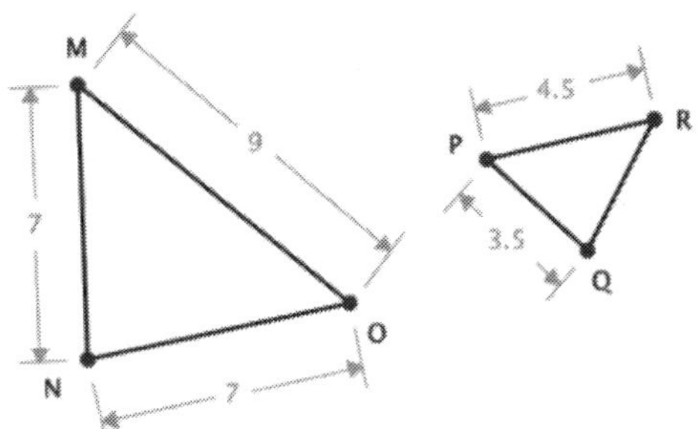

A. 3.5
B. 7.5
C. 11.5
D. 16
E. 23

Good to Know #3: Absolute Value

Absolute Value is a concept that most students have seen and worked with before, but it is time for a refresher. Absolute value is represented by two vertical lines with a numerical value or variable in between, like these:

$|-2|$ $|3|$ $|y|$

Here is the simplest explanation of this concept: whatever comes between the bars is made positive, and the bars are removed. Here's a technical, but also simple, meaning of absolute value: it simply represents the distance from 0. Thus, in the above two examples:

The value of $|-2|$ is 2, simply because -2 is 2 away from 0.

The value of $|3|$ is 3, simply because 3 is a total of 3 away from 0.

No matter what y equals, the absolute value of y will be a positive y. So, if $y = -10$ or 10, the value of the absolute value of y in that case is 10, simply because -10 is 10 units away from 0, and 10 is 10 units away from 0.

Unfortunately, it is extremely unlikely that the ACT will ask you to find the absolute value of -3 as one of its 60 questions. Here are a few examples that feature the concept that are more true to the ACT itself.

8. What is $|m - 11|$ when $m = 7$?

F. -18
G. -4
H. 4
J. 7
K. 18

9. For all nonzero values of j and k, the value of which of the following expressions is *always* negative ?

A. $\frac{|j|}{|k|}$

B. $\frac{-j}{-|k|}$

C. $\frac{-|j|}{|k|}$

D. $-\frac{|j|}{k}$

E. $-\frac{j}{k}$

10. Which of the following expressions, if any, is equivalent to $|-x|$?

F. $\frac{|x|}{|x|^2}$

G. $-\frac{|x|^2}{|x|}$

H. $-x$

J. $\frac{|-x|}{|-x|^2}$

K. $\sqrt{(-x)^2}$

Good to Know #4: Inequalities

Inequality Basics

You can expect, on average, 1 question on the ACT Math that tests or requires your understanding of inequalities. An inequality is like an algebraic equation in that it will have one or more variables, but instead of an equal sign, they are related to each other by one of four signs: greater than, less than, greater than or equal to, or less than or equal to. Look at this simple inequality:

$x > 5$

All this means is that every possible value of x must be greater than 5: it can be 100, 17, 6, or even 5.1, but it can't be 5 or less. Similarly:

$x \geq 14$

All this means, like the last one, is that x can be any number greater than 14, but it could also *be* 14; the line beneath the "greater than" symbol means "or equal to."

If you flip the signs, the explanations are the same. Look at this simple inequality:

$x < 9$

All this means is that every possible value of x must be less than 9. Its value could be 8, 0, or −418, and everything up to, but not including, 9. Lastly, here is one featuring a less than or equal to sign:

$x \leq 20$

Again, simple idea: the value of x can be anything less than 20, but can also include 20 as well.

Simplifying and Switching Signs

The only remaining thing about inequalities you might need to know is how to solve an equation or simplify an inequality, and what makes the sign "switch" from facing one side to facing another. Imagine you were asked to simplify the following inequality, solving it in terms of x:

$-x + 3 - 2x < 6$

You can treat this the exact same way you would treat an equation with an equal sign. First let's combine like terms to get $-3x + 3 < 6$. Next, we can subtract 3 from both sides and end up with $-3x < 3$. To solve for x, what comes next ought to seem pretty clear: we have to divide both sides by negative 3. However, with inequalities, there's a rule here we have to remember: if you divide or multiply both sides of an inequality by a negative number, and only a negative number, then the sign must "switch." This *doesn't* happen when adding/subtracting negative numbers to/from both sides, but *only* with multiplication or division of negative numbers. Thus, if we divide both sides by -3, we end up with the following: $x > -1$. Note that if this were $\leq$ or $\geq$, you wouldn't do anything to the "or equal to" part; it remains; just switch it from facing one way to another!

11. Which of the following inequalities orders the numbers $\frac{3}{8}$, 0.35 , and 0.04 from least to greatest?

A. $0.35 < \frac{3}{8} < 0.04$

B. $0.04 < \frac{3}{8} < 0.35$

C. $\frac{3}{8} < 0.04 < 0.35$

D. $0.04 < 0.35 < \frac{3}{8}$

E. $0.35 < 0.04 < \frac{3}{8}$

12. Which of the following inequalities is equivalent to $-2x - 4y \leq 6y + 2$?

F. $x \leq -5y - 1$
G. $x \geq -5y - 1$
H. $x \leq 5y + 1$
J. $x \geq 5y + 1$
K. $x > -5y - 1$

13. Charlotte owns a bakery on a crowded avenue in the big city. The number of cookies, c, that she sells on any given weekday relative to her largest sales day (Saturday) satisfies the inequality $|c - 30| \leq 45$. If a negative value of c denotes a decrease in sales from the previous Saturday, which of the following numbers of cookies sold on a Wednesday is NOT within the range of this inequality?

A. -40
B. -15
C. 0
D. 30
E. 70

Good to Know #5: Parabolas

Parabolas are shapes you probably learned about for the first time in Algebra I, but for many of you, that was a long time ago. On average, one ACT Math question per test requires you to be able to work with these shapes in one way or another, and it is the purpose of this small lesson to refresh you on what's most important. Before I sat down and conducted my own research over previous ACT Math tests, I used to think that parabola questions were far more common on the ACT Math test than they really are. Thus, they have landed in the *Good to Know* category instead of the *Have to Know* category.

A parabola is a shape that results from graphing a quadratic equation; a quadratic equation is a trinomial in which a variable, usually x, is raised to the second power, like this:

$y = 4x^2 + 4x - 8$

This might be bringing back bad memories of the Quadratic Formula, but don't worry, it's not necessary to memorize the Quadratic Formula to get a parabola question right on the ACT!

Here is what the quadratic we just came up with looks like when graphed:

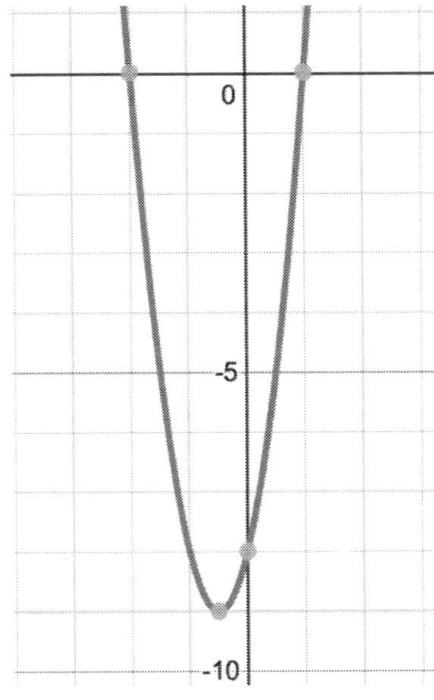

This shape is usually represented by two arrows on the lines that stretch upwards since they go on forever. There are a couple of things about this that you should know.

First are the *solutions*. Many students have no idea what that means, and are often faced with questions that ask for the solution set of a quadratic, or ask for the number of solutions for a quadratic, or something like that. Well, for any quadratic, the solutions are where the parabola crosses the x-axis. In this graph pictured, here, the parabola crosses the x-axis at -2 and 1, which are the two solutions.

It is possible, however, for a parabola to have only one solution. That would be when the "tip" of the parabola (minimum for an upwards moving parabola, maximum for a downwards moving parabola) is actually on the x-axis. Lastly, it is also possible for a parabola to have no solutions. In that case, the parabola does not cross the x-axis at all.

So, let's assume you've been given a quadratic or the formula for a parabola, like this one: $y = x^2 - 6x + 9$, and you are asked to find the solutions. One way that was probably drilled into your brain in Algebra was to use the Quadratic Formula. If you have the Quadratic Formula memorized, then go for it, but the Quadratic Formula is better used on quadratics that can't be factored easily, unlike most (or probably all) that you'll see on the ACT.

DO NOT binge study the Quadratic Formula…there are easier ways to find the solution or solutions (if there are any) for a parabola like this one, which will be best explained through our first example. First, there is graphing. On your graphing calculator, hit buttons in this order (using the trinomial from above, $y = x^2 - 6x + 9$, as an example):

1: Y= **2:** X,T,Θ,n **3:** ^ **4:** 2 **5:** - **6:** 6 **7:** X,T,Θ,n **8:** + **9:** 9 **10:** GRAPH

Anywhere the parabola crosses the x-axis, you have your solutions (in this case, the parabola never truly "crosses" the x-axis; rather, it "touches" the x-axis at $x = 3$, which is our one solution then).

The second way, which is usually my default way to solve these, is to factor the trinomial into two binomials, then set each of these equal to zero. To factor a trinomial like this one (let's remember the trinomial we're dealing with: $y = x^2 - 6x + 9$), you first identify two numbers that *multiply* to give you your third term (in this case, 9) that can also be added to equal the coefficient in front of the x in your second/middle term (in this case, -6). One thought is that $3 \times 3 = 9$, but $3 + 3 = 6$, not -6, so try again. However, notice that $(-3) \times (-3) = 9$, and $(-3) + (-3) = -6$. Thus, -3 and -3 become the second terms in our two binomials, both added to x. Factored, our trinomial now looks like:

$$y = x^2 - 6x + 9 = (x - 3)(x - 3)$$

Now that we have our two binomials $(x - 3)$ and $(x - 3)$, we should set each of them equal to 0 and solve each individually.

$(x - 3) = 0$	$(x - 3) = 0$
$x = 3$	$x = 3$

It may seem strange that our "two" solutions are the same, but there is nothing strange about it at all; all this means is that there is only 1 solution. The parabola has its vertex at $x = 3$, meaning it only has one solution. If you were to graph this on a graphing calculator, you would see a parabola with its "tip" at 3.

I think we've said enough about the parabola; let's get into a few examples based on recent ACT tests:

14. What is the mean of the 2 solutions of the equation $x^2 - 10x - 24$?

F. -12
G. -5
H. 0
J. 5
K. 7

15. What is the solution set of the equation $x(x - 1) = 2x^2 + 9x + 25$?

A. $\{-5\}$
B. $\{-5, 2.5\}$
C. $\{-2.5, 2.5\}$
D. $\{5\}$
E. The set of all real numbers

16. The 3 parabolas graphed in the standard (x, y) coordinate plane below are from a family of parabolas. A general equation that defines this family of parabolas contains the variable z in addition to x and y. For the parabola with the smallest minimum, $z = 2$; for the parabola with a minimum between the other two, $z = 4$; and for the parabola with the largest minimum, $z = 6$. Which of the following could be a general equation that defines this family of parabolas?

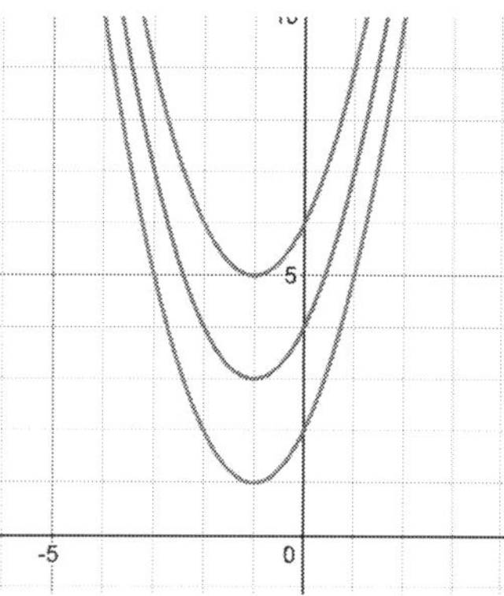

F. $y = zx^2 + 2x - 1$

G. $y = x^2 + zx + 5$

H. $y = x^2 + 2x + z$

J. $y = x^2 + 2x - z$

K. $7 = -x^2 - zx + 5$

Good to Know #6: Trig Graphs and Wave Familiarity

Usually, though not always, ACT Math questions that mention or show figures featuring waves have specifically to do with the graphs of sine and cosine, which are waves (unlike tangent, which is not a wave!). In this little lesson overall, though, we will discuss the vocabulary around waves, like wavelength and amplitude. I think the best way to teach these things is by analyzing the graph of sine, then cosine, but again, the purpose of this book is not to examine each and every possible math concept that could conceivably be asked about or required on any given ACT Math test; that kind of book would be impossibly long.

What you see here is a graph of sine and cosine. If you've never seen this, it can be intimidating. Before we talk about these trig functions in particular, we should go over basic wave vocabulary. That's a good first step because it's not uncommon for you to get an ACT Math question where you simply have to find the amplitude, period, crest, trough, or wavelength of a wave.

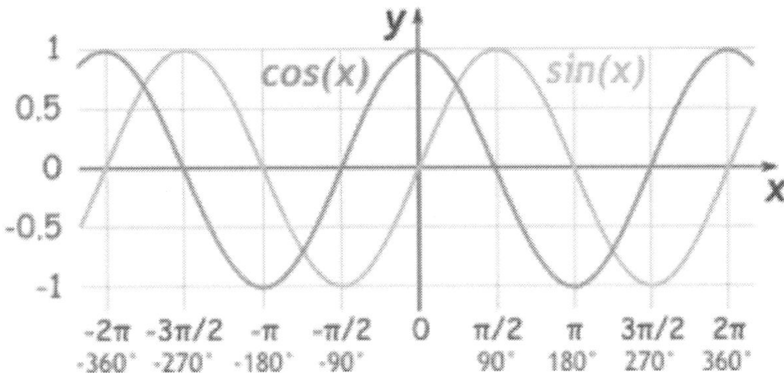

- **Crest:** the height of the tip of a wave; how far "up" it goes (for both sin(x) and cos(x), this is 1).

- **Trough:** the depth of the tip of a wave; how far "down" it goes (for both sin(x) and cos(x), this is -1).

- **Period/wavelength:** the length or width of a wave from crest to crest or trough to trough. For sin(x) and cos(x), the period/wavelength is 2π.

- **Amplitude:** the height of a wave, from the x-axis to the crest (or, the depth of a wave, from the x-axis to the trough). For both sin(x) and cos(x), this is 1.

For sine and cosine, if need be, you are able to graph these on your graphing calculator. Before you do so, hit "Mode" and make sure your calculator is set to radians, not degrees (as a side note, this would be the only conceivable situation in which your calculator would be set to radians; MAKE SURE before the test begins that your calculator is set to DEGREES, otherwise, you will be thoroughly lost on many problems).

Here is how to graph sine (once your calculator is set to radians), for example, step by step. In your calculator, hit these buttons in order:

1: Y= **2:** SIN **3:** X,T,Θ,n **4:**) **5:** GRAPH

You'll see a sine wave pop up. This would only be necessary if a question asks you what happens to the graph of a sine wave when the equation is altered with a new number in parentheses after sine (such as sin($3x$), with a number before sine (multiplied by sine, in other words, like 4sin(x)), or if a number is added to the end of the equation (such as sin(x)+2). If you've got the time, you can play with these in your calculator. In the mean time, here are a couple of examples based on how these types of wave questions have been asked in previous ACT's.

17. For four days, Olivia charts the times for high and low tide for Flint Bay. On Day 1, high tide occurred at 1:15 PM and low tide occurred at 11:45 PM; on Day 2, high tide occurred at 12:30 PM and low tide occurred at 11:00 PM; on Day 3, high tide occurred at 11:45 AM and low tide occurred at 10:15 PM; and on Day 4; high tide occurred at 11:00 AM and low tide occurred at 9:30 PM. What is the average period of the wave created by Olivia's charts?

A. 21 hours and 15 minutes
B. 21 hours and 45 minutes
C. 22 hours and 45 minutes
D. 23 hours and 15 minutes
E. 24 hours and 45 minutes

18. Consider the function $f(x) = c\sin x$, where c is a real number. As c increases, what happens to the wavelength and the amplitude of the resulting graph?

F. The period increases; the amplitude decreases.
G. The period stays the same; the amplitude increases.
H. The period decreases; the amplitude stays the same.
J. The period and the amplitude both stay the same.
K. The period and the amplitude both increase.

<u>Good to Know #7: Overlapping Line Segments and Categories</u>

I don't really know what to call this type of question besides *Overlapping Line Segments or Categories*. This represents a question that you would probably never actually have in math class, but tests your reasoning skills. The ACT likes this kind of question and, if I were to place a bet, I'd say you'd see one on your next ACT Math test.

In these kinds of questions, sometimes a line segment is either described or given, and it features usually 4 points, probably labeled A, B, C, and D (such as in #19 below). The distance between some of these points are given, and you'll need to analyze the line in the right way to determine a distance between two other points that is not yet given. While there are reasoning ways to solve these kinds of problems, for stuck students, there is always the *Drawn to Scale* mini-strategy (if you skipped that, go back and check it out in Step 2!). Because some line lengths will be given, you can use the edge of your answer sheet as a ruler, then compare to the line the length of which you are trying to find.

Another way this kind of question is asked is that some people are described as doing one thing (such as taking a Spanish class), another group of people is described as doing another (such as taking a French class), and you have determine how many do either or both. Instead of analyzing here exactly how to solve this kind of problem, let's let the examples below do the talking, one of each type described above. Try each one yourself first, reasoning your way through it, before you check answers and read the answer explanations.

19. Points B and C lie on AD. The length of AD is 45 units; $\overline{AC}$ is 27 units long; and $\overline{BD}$ is 26 units long. How many units long, if it can be determined, is $\overline{BC}$?

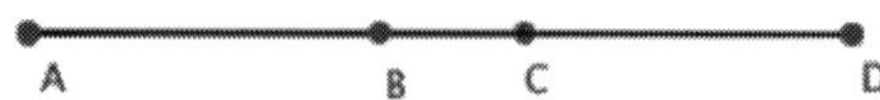

A. 8
B. 11
C. 18
D. 19
E. Cannot be determined from the given information

20. Mr. East takes a poll in his class of 25 students. He finds that 15 of them play a Spring sport and that 17 of them play a Fall sport. Given this information, what is the minimum number of students in the class who play both a Spring and a Fall sport?

F. 0
G. 2
H. 7
J. 15
K. 17

Good to Know #8: Matrices

A matrix in math is a set of numbers arranged in rows and columns, like this:

$$\begin{bmatrix} 3 & 2 & -1 \\ -4 & 2 & 1 \\ 5 & -3 & 7 \end{bmatrix}$$

For our purposes, there are two main things it's *Good to Know* about matrices: how to add/subtract them, and how to multiply them.

Let's start with a simple **addition**. We will use two matrices that have the same dimensions, which is the number of rows (rows run left to right) × the number of columns (columns run up and down), like this:

$$\begin{bmatrix} 0 & 4 \\ -3 & 7 \end{bmatrix} + \begin{bmatrix} -2 & -1 \\ 4 & -2 \end{bmatrix} = \begin{bmatrix} -2 & 3 \\ 1 & 5 \end{bmatrix}$$

The only way, in fact, to add or subtract matrices is if they have the same dimensions, otherwise, it is undefined. Above, you can see I simply added one location at a time. The top-left corner of each matrix is added together, $(0 + -2)$, which equals the top-left corner of the resulting matrix (-2).

As for **multiplication**, there is a strange rule that must be remembered: two matrices can only be multiplied if the number of columns in the first matrix equals the number of rows in the second matrix. If not, the answer is undefined. Here is an example of this:

$$\begin{bmatrix} -3 & 4 & 0 \end{bmatrix} \times \begin{bmatrix} 2 \\ 8 \\ -7 \end{bmatrix} =$$

The first of these matrices is a 1×3 (1 row and 3 columns), and the second is a 3×1 (3 rows and 1 column). Because the number of columns in the first (3) matches the number of rows in the second (also

3), they *can* be multiplied. The size of the resulting matrix will be the exact opposite; because there is one *row* in the first and one *column* in the second, respectively, the result will be a matrix that is 1×1 after finding the dot product.

$$[(-3 \times 2) + (4 \times 8) + (0 \times -7)] = [-6 + 32 + 0] = [26]$$

This would be the dot product of row 1 of the first, times column 1 of the second. In the examples below, you'll see a matrix multiplication problem that is a bit different. But remember: if the columns in the 1st match the rows in the 2nd, they can be multiplied; the result will be a matrix of size (rows in 1st) × (columns in 2nd). I remember this by the letters **crrc.** Let's make up a weird sentence to remember this by…how about, "**C**alm **R**ivers **R**eveal **C**rocs." CRRC: columns = rows, rows × columns. Hey if it works, right?

Now, let's look at some examples based on recent ACT tests:

21. Which of the following matrices is equivalent to $\begin{bmatrix} -6 & 9 \\ -8 & 4 \end{bmatrix} - \begin{bmatrix} 10 & -4 \\ -1 & 0 \end{bmatrix}$?

A. $\begin{bmatrix} 4 & 5 \\ -9 & 4 \end{bmatrix}$

B. $\begin{bmatrix} -16 & 13 \\ -7 & 4 \end{bmatrix}$

C. $\begin{bmatrix} 60 & -36 \\ 8 & 0 \end{bmatrix}$

D. $\begin{bmatrix} -16 & 5 \\ -9 & 0 \end{bmatrix}$

E. $\begin{bmatrix} 4 & 13 \\ 7 & 4 \end{bmatrix}$

22. Which of the following matrices is equal to $3\begin{bmatrix}0 & -2\\6 & 5\end{bmatrix}$?

F. $\begin{bmatrix}0 & -\frac{2}{3}\\\frac{1}{2} & \frac{3}{5}\end{bmatrix}$

G. $\begin{bmatrix}3 & 1\\9 & 8\end{bmatrix}$

H. $\begin{bmatrix}0 & -\frac{3}{2}\\2 & \frac{5}{3}\end{bmatrix}$

J. $\begin{bmatrix}0 & -6\\18 & 15\end{bmatrix}$

K. $\begin{bmatrix}18 & 9\end{bmatrix}$

23. What is the matrix product $\begin{bmatrix}-4\\x\\2x\end{bmatrix}\begin{bmatrix}x & 3 & 0\end{bmatrix}$?

A. $[-x]$

B. $\left[-x^2 + 9x - 12\right]$

C. $\begin{bmatrix}-x^2\\9x\\-12\end{bmatrix}$

D. $\begin{bmatrix}-4x & -12 & 0\\x^2 & 3x & 0\\2x^2 & 6x & 0\end{bmatrix}$

E. The product is undefined

Good to Know #9: Tricky Conversions

Another *Good to Know* ACT Math skill is the ability to convert from one unit of measure (whether it be time or distance), and perhaps even back again in the other direction (such as feet to inches, hours to minutes, etc.). One way the ACT likes to trip up students is to give them a math question in inches, then require the answer in feet, or something similar. Of course, there are 12 inches in 1 foot. But how long is 3.75 feet? Some students are too quick and say, "3 feet and 7.5 inches," but that's not the case (and, of course, one of the answer choices is going to match up well with that error). 3.75 feet, rather, is 3 feet and 3 quarters of 1 foot, or 3 feet 9 inches.

Give the following examples your best shot! Remember to take your time and don't trip up making simple mistakes.

24. A board (shown below) 7 feet 4 inches long is cut into 2 equal parts. What is the length, to the nearest inch, of each part?

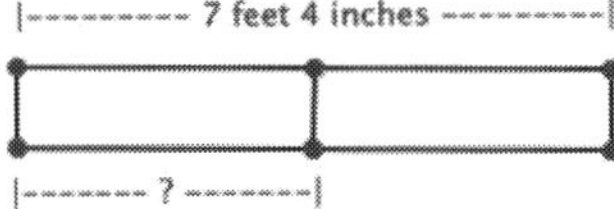

F. 3 feet 5 inches
G. 3 feet 7 inches
H. 3 feet 8 inches
J. 4 feet 0 inches
K. 4 feet 2 inches

25. Samuel is the facilities director at a high school. After measuring the floor of the cafeteria, he realizes that he will need 14,400 square feet of new tile. However, the type of tile that he needs to purchase is only sold by the square yard. How many square yards of tile will Samuel need to cover the floor of the cafeteria?

A. 240
B. 480
C. 1,600
D. 3,600
E. 4,800

26. Clarence is cruising down the highway on his motorcycle at 40 miles per hour. At that rate, how many miles will Clarence drive in 16 minutes?

F. $10\frac{2}{3}$

G. $10\frac{3}{4}$

H. 11

J. $12\frac{1}{2}$

K. 16

Good to Know #10: Logarithms and Exponents

Logarithms

Logarithms is a scary word, and the form of a logarithm usually strikes fear and confusion into the typical ACT test taker. However, if you can grasp a basic understanding of a logarithm, you will be in a great place, and getting a basic grasp is much simpler than you think. I wouldn't say that if it wasn't true. It's as simple as this: if you understand exponents, you can understand the basics of logarithms.

Take, for example, this exponent: 2^5. You know what that means: $2 \times 2 \times 2 \times 2 \times 2$, which is 32. Pretty simple, thus, we can write it like this: $2^5 = 32$.

However, what if we didn't know what the exponent was? In other words, what if we had an equation that looked like this: $2^x = 32$? Well, it is logarithms that allow you to solve this equation for x, to find a missing exponent. This is what it looks like:

$$\log_2 32 = x$$

This is simply asking: with a base of 2, what is the value of the exponent x when 2 raised to the x power equals 32?

There is a way to type logs into your calculator to figure out exponents, such as in the example above. Sometimes, however, figuring out how to properly do this on your calculator is more difficult than just writing it on paper and then using the basics of your calculator to solve. If I thought you needed to know how to type this into a calculator for the purposes of ACT Math, I would tell you, as I have before. Chances are, if you play around with your calculator and the LOG button, you will end up confused. That is because the LOG function on your calculator is automatically set to a base of 10 (as in, 10 raised to a power). You will have to go into your MATH options and find "Logbase" to change that. This is confusing and time-consuming, and unless you've already got this calculator skill mastered, keep reading.

Instead, do what I alluded to in the above paragraph. Use your calculator's basics and *Backsolving* until you get the right answer. For example, let's say you were asked to find the value of x in the following:

$\log_3 114 = x$

When written without the *log,* the equation looks like this: $3^x = 114$. Thus, 3 raised to the power of what exponent will give us 114? Well, you are going to be given 5 answer choices, right? Why not go through them and see which one fits? Let's say **C** was 3.75. Well, when I type in my calculator 3 ^ 3.75 and hit =, I get a value of 61.55; not big enough, so I need to go higher. Answer choice D is 4.31. I type in 3 ^ 4.31, and sure enough, that's the correct answer.

Recently, I saw some students in my classes working on logs for their Algebra II class. They were solving lots of complicated equations in which log functions were being multiplied by each other, divided by each other, etc. I have never seen that kind of question on the ACT Math test. It doesn't mean it can't happen, but it means that going through all of that here in preparation for ACT Math is unnecessary. If you've got the basics outlined above, you're good to go!

Exponents

While we're here, let's review some basics of exponents. We reviewed some of this a bit in previous examples in other lessons, but here is a refresher. It might have been a while since you used these, but they can certainly be helpful.

First, negative exponents. A negative exponent simply means that the term needs to be moved from the numerator into the denominator, or vice versa. For example: $3^{-3} = \frac{1}{3^3} = \frac{1}{9}$.

Second, any number except for 0 raised to the power of 0 always =1. For your sanity and mine, let's not spend 15 minutes reviewing why that is the case, but here are some examples: $(-44)^0 = 1$, $7^0 = 1$, and for all values of x that do not equal 9, $\left(\frac{x+2}{x-9}\right)^0 = 1$.

With that said, let's get into a couple of examples that test your understanding:

27. Which of the following is a value of x that satisfies $\log_x 343 = 3$?

A. 3
B. 5
C. 7
D. 9
E. 11

28. When $\log_4 x = -3$, what is x ?

F. -9

G. -3

H. $-\frac{1}{8}$

J. $\frac{1}{64}$

K. $\frac{1}{4}$

29. What is the value of $\frac{\frac{1}{3^{-3}}}{3}$?

A. -9
B. -3
C. 9
D. 27
E. 81

30. Simplify $\dfrac{a^{-3}b^{2}c^{-4}}{a^{2}b^{-2}c^{-1}}$.

F. $\dfrac{b^4}{a^5c^3}$

G. $\dfrac{b^4}{a^6c^5}$

H. $\dfrac{1}{a^6c^5}$

J. $\dfrac{1}{a^5c^3}$

K. ac^3

Good to Know #11: Formula of a Circle

Again, there are many, many additional categories or types of math questions that could be asked on ACT day, but to cover every possibility thoroughly would require a redo of every math lesson you could possibly have had from 6th to 12th grade, and then some. You can't possibly prepare anew for every one of these possibilities, but the more you practice, the more likely you are to increase your knowledge, understanding, and experience, and thus up your score. Indeed: if you can learn and master the 24 ACT Math *Have to Know* and *Good to Know* math categories and lessons as presented in this book, there is little doubt that you will succeed on test day.

The last type of math knowledge that I can put into the *Good to Know* category is that of the formula or equation of a circle. Again, being in this category simply means that there's a good chance you will have at least one question on ACT day about it, or one question that requires your knowledge of it as a step towards a right answer…it's not guaranteed. What *is* guaranteed is the material we covered on circles back in *Have to Know* Lesson 13.

Let's keep this as simple as possible. The formula for a circle is as follows:

$$(x - h)^2 + (y - k)^2 = r^2$$

The coordinate (h, k) is the center of the circle, and r is the radius.

So, if we had a circle with its center at (1, 4) and a radius of 3, its formula would look like this:

$$(x - 1)^2 + (y - 4)^2 = 9$$

With that out of the way, let's go through a few examples relative to this topic that are the kinds of questions typical of the ACT.

31. What is the formula of a circle that is centered on $(-1, 3)$ and has a radius of 5 ?

A. $(x + 1)^2 + (y - 3)^2 = 5$
B. $(x - 1)^2 + (y + 3)^2 = 5$
C. $(x + 1)^2 + (y - 3)^2 = 25$
D. $(x - 1)^2 + (y + 3)^2 = 25$
E. $(x - 1)^2 + (y - 3)^2 = 25$

32. Consider the following three circles:

I. A circle centered at $(-2, -2)$ passing through $(6, -2)$
II. A circle with a circumference of 16π
III. A circle with the equation $(x - 9)^2 + (y + 3)^2 = 64$

Which of the circles has an area of 64π ?

F. II only
G. I and II only
H. I and III only
J. II and III only
K. I, II, and III

33. In the standard (x, y) coordinate plane, Circle P is represented by the formula $(x - 2)^2 + (y - 5)^2 = 49$ and passes through which of the following points ?

A. $(2, -2)$
B. $(2, 5)$
C. $(-2, 2)$
D. $(5, -3)$
E. $(9, 12)$

Step 5 Correct Answers

1: C	12: G	23: D
2: K	13: A	24: H
3: E	14: J	25: C
4: J	15: A	26: F
5: D	16: H	27: C
6: F	17: D	28: J
7: C	18: G	29: C
8: H	19: A	30: F
9: C	20: H	31: C
10: K	21: B	32: K
11: D	22: J	33: A

ACT Math *Good to Know* practice answer explanations begin on page 570.

STEP 6

Full-Length Practice Tests

Practice Test Introduction

The two practice tests that follow below are designed to mimic real ACT Math tests as closely as possible. They include, like a real ACT Math test, a multiplicity of *Have to Know* questions, a large handful of *Good to Know* questions, and a scattering of *Possibly Might Have to Know* material. Though this book does not feature formal lessons on this last category, if you have completed the book to this point, you have encountered many in the example questions.

When I say the following tests mimic real ACT Math tests, I mean that is also true in the details. Each question has 5 answer choices; each answer choice is used exactly 6 times; the first third is the easiest third, the middle third is of middle difficulty, and the final third is the most difficult third; some problems feature given diagrams, some describe them and require the test taker to draw them; etc.

This is another opportunity to formally test your math knowledge and ACT Math capabilities. Do this test in a quiet space. Set a 60 minute timer. Utilize the 4 ACT Math mini-strategies, but most importantly, implement the *Two Pass* strategy from Step 1 by circling and skipping questions that you foresee will pose great difficulties and cost you a lot of time off the bat; bank that time for the end, ensuring you given every question a shot.

Following each test, you will find the list of correct answers, and explanations for each question can be found in the back of the book. Practice Test 1 explanations begin on page 578, and Practice Test 2 explanations begin on page 594.

Best of luck! But if you've made it this far through this book, you probably don't need luck!

PRACTICE TEST 1

60 Minutes, 60 Questions

MATHEMATICS TEST

60 Minutes — 60 Questions

DIRECTIONS: Solve each problem, choose the correct answer, and then fill in the corresponding oval on your answer document.

Do not linger over problems that take too much time. Solve as many as you can; then return to the others in the time you have left for this test.

You are permitted to use a calculator on this test. You may use your calculator for any problems you choose, but some of the problems may best be done without using a calculator.

Note: Unless otherwise stated, all of the following should be assumed.

1. Illustrative figures are NOT necessarily drawn to scale.
2. Geometric figures lie in a plane.
3. The word *line* indicates a straight line.
4. The word *average* indicates arithmetic mean.

DO YOUR FIGURING HERE.

1. Chip sold 28 candy bars for \$1.30 each. With the money from these sales, he bought 3 fishing poles and had \$13.90 left over. What was the average amount Chip paid for each fishing pole?

   A. \$3.90
   B. \$5.63
   C. \$7.50
   D. \$11.23
   E. \$22.50

2. Roberto left his home at 6:00 a.m. on Saturday and traveled 880 miles. When he arrived at his destination, it was 10:00 p.m. on the same day. Given that his home and his destination are in the same time zone, which of the following is closest to his average speed, in miles per hour, for this trip?

   F. 59
   G. 55
   H. 52
   J. 19
   K. 9

3. For her dog walking business, Sylvia charges a \$12.00 fee plus \$1.25 for each block that she walks a dog. If Sylvia is paid \$29.50 for the dog she walked today, then how many blocks did she walk the dog?

   A. 9.6
   B. 14.0
   C. 16.0
   D. 17.5
   E. 23.6

4. A point at $(4, -6)$ in the standard (x, y) coordinate plane is translated down 5 coordinate units and right 9 coordinate units. What are the coordinates of the point after the translation?

   F. $(-1, -15)$
   G. $(-1, -9)$
   H. $(-5, 9)$
   J. $(13, -5)$
   K. $(13, -11)$

5. Which of the following matrices is equal to $\begin{bmatrix} 4 & 9 \\ -3 & 7 \end{bmatrix} + \begin{bmatrix} -8 & 3 \\ 4 & 0 \end{bmatrix}$?

DO YOUR FIGURING HERE.

A. $\begin{bmatrix} -4 & 12 \\ 1 & 7 \end{bmatrix}$

B. $\begin{bmatrix} 12 & 6 \\ -7 & 7 \end{bmatrix}$

C. $\begin{bmatrix} -4 & 6 \\ 7 & 0 \end{bmatrix}$

D. $\begin{bmatrix} -2 & 3 \\ -1 & 0 \end{bmatrix}$

E. $\begin{bmatrix} -8 & 9 \\ 4 & 7 \end{bmatrix}$

6. The square root of a certain number is approximately 7.48921. The certain number is between what two integers?

F. 2 and 3
G. 3 and 4
H. 7 and 8
J. 14 and 15
K. 49 and 64

7. When points $A(2, -4)$ and B are graphed in the standard (x, y) coordinate plane, the midpoint of $\overline{AB}$ will be $(4, 1)$. What will be the coordinates of point B?

A. (6, 6)
B. (3, 6)
C. (6, − 3)
D. (−2, − 5)
E. (−2, − 7)

8. There is to be a race between 20 total cars: 12 white, 4 green, 3 red, and 1 orange. If all cars are otherwise equal, what is the probability that the winner of the race is NOT a green car?

F. $\frac{1}{10}$

G. $\frac{1}{5}$

H. $\frac{1}{2}$

J. $\frac{4}{5}$

K. $\frac{9}{10}$

DO YOUR FIGURING HERE.

9. David's bookshelves have on them 207 books, which is 30 more than 3 times the number of books he had on them last year. How many books did David have on the bookshelves last year?

A. 21
B. 39
C. 54
D. 59
E. 69

10. A function, f, is defined by $f(x, y) = -(x^3) + 3y$. What is the value of the function $f(2, -1)$?

F. -11
G. -5
H. 5
J. 7
K. 11

11. Points B and C lie on $\overline{AD}$ as shown below. The length of $\overline{AD}$ is 34 units; $\overline{AC}$ is 21 units long; and $\overline{BD}$ is 24 units long. How many units long is $\overline{BC}$?

A. 5
B. 11
C. 17
D. 19
E. 20

12. What are the values for y that satisfy the equation $(y + m)(y - n) = 0$?

F. m and n
G. m and $-n$
H. $-m$ and $-n$
J. $-m$ and n
K. mn

13. What is the solution set for x if $x^2 = 7x(x - 0) - 54$?

A. $\{-4\}$
B. $\{5\}$
C. $\{9\}$
D. $\{-2, 2\}$
E. $\{-3, 3\}$

DO YOUR FIGURING HERE.

Use the following information to answer questions 14-16.

In the figure below, E is the center of the circle, and $\overline{FG}$ is a diameter. Point H lies on the circle, I lies outside the circle on $\overleftrightarrow{FG}$, $\overleftrightarrow{IK}$ is tangent to the circle at J, and $\overline{KF}$ is perpendicular to $\overline{FG}$.

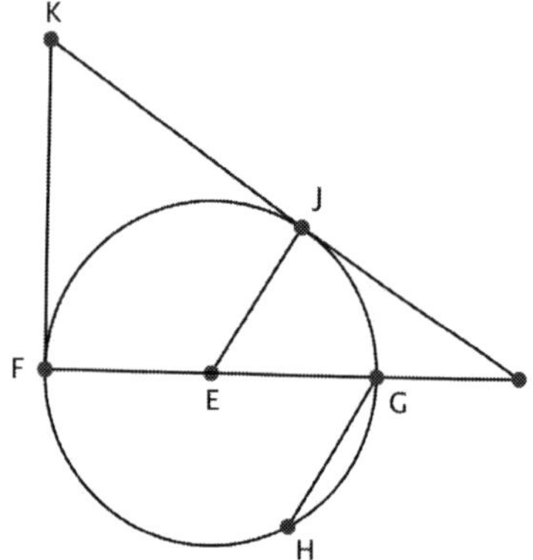

14. Which of the following angles or minor arcs has the greatest degree measure?

F. $\angle FKJ$

G. $\angle FGH$

H. $\overset{\frown}{FJ}$

J. $\overset{\frown}{JG}$

K. $\overset{\frown}{GH}$

15. If segment $\overline{EJ}$ is perpendicular to $\overline{KI}$, and if $\overline{EJ}$ has a slope of $\frac{3}{2}$, what is the slope of $\overline{KI}$?

A. $-\frac{3}{2}$

B. $-\frac{2}{3}$

C. $\frac{2}{3}$

D. $\frac{3}{2}$

E. 3

16. If segment $\overline{KF}$ is 20 units long, and the diameter of the circle centered at E is 22 units, then what is the area of the circle that lies within $\triangle KFI$?

F. 11π
G. 22π
H. 60.5π
J. 91π
K. 121π

DO YOUR FIGURING HERE.

---

17. On a map, $\frac{1}{5}$ centimeters represents 14 kilometers. Two mountains that are $3\frac{2}{5}$ centimeters apart on this map are how many actual kilometers apart?

A. 47.6
B. 119
C. 224
D. 238
E. 476

18. Candace rides her bike at a rate of 11 miles per hour. At that rate, how many miles will she ride in 11 minutes, rounded to the nearest mile?

F. 2
G. 3
H. 4
J. 22
K. 121

19. John's teacher hands him a calculator with a pre-programmed linear function, but John does not know what the function is. When 3 is entered, the calculator displays the value 7. When 12 is entered, the calculator displays the value 28. Which of the following expressions explains what the calculator will display when any number, z, is entered?

A. $\frac{3}{7}z$

B. $7z$

C. $\frac{7}{3}z$

D. $z + 4$

E. $2z + 4$

20. In the figure below, V is on $\overleftrightarrow{WX}$ and Y is on $\overleftrightarrow{WZ}$. What is the measure of $\angle VWY$?

DO YOUR FIGURING HERE.

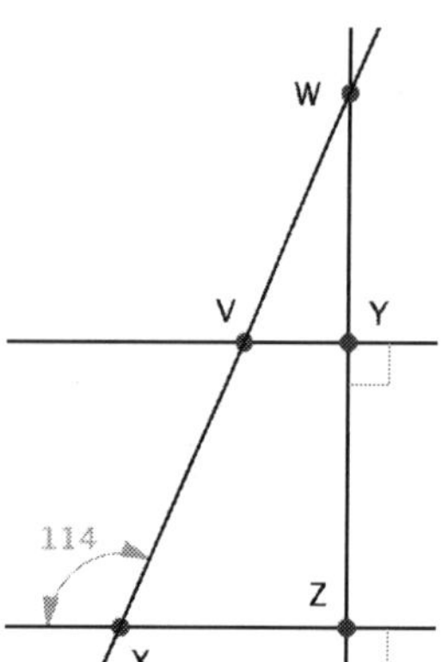

F. 12°
G. 24°
H. 66°
J. 114°
K. 156°

21. A certain stock was valued at \$500 per share at 8:00 a.m. The value of the stock dropped by 5% each hour for three straight hours before rising back to a value of \$500 by the end of the fourth hour. What percent did the stock rise in the fourth hour, rounded to the nearest percent?

A. 5
B. 10
C. 15
D. 16
E. 17

22. On a certain race track, riders are given scores based on their average times across 6 races. These scores are assigned according to the chart below.

Average (seconds)	Score
55.10 or more	Poor
51.10-55.09	Fair
46.10-51.09	Average
43.00-46.09	Good
42.99 or less	Superior

If Ethan records times of 42.50, 45.50, 45.00, 51.25, and 47.75 seconds in his first 5 races, then which of the following times in his sixth and last race would cause Ethan to receive a score of Good for the season?

F. 44.00
G. 45.00
H. 46.00
J. 48.00
K. 50.00

DO YOUR FIGURING HERE.

23. Given $x = \dfrac{y}{y-1}$ and $y < -2$, which of the following is a possible value of x ?

A. -1.71
B. -0.71
C. 0.00
D. 0.71
E. 1.71

24. The set of all possible integers divisible by both 21 and 49 is infinite. What is the least possible integer in this infinite set?

F. 7
G. 49
H. 70
J. 147
K. 294

25. Richard's caddy assures him that when he strikes the ball with his 9-iron, the ball will land within a certain area. If this area consists of 198 square feet of green, 94 square feet of fringe, 134 square feet of sand trap, and 124 square feet of rough, then which of the following is the best estimate of the probability that the ball will land in a sand trap when Richard strikes the ball?

A. 13.4%
B. 24.4%
C. 28.7%
D. 32.2%
E. 33.3%

26. A parallelogram has a perimeter of 102 inches, and 1 of its sides measures 22 inches. If it can be determined, what are the lengths, in inches, of the other 3 sides?

F. 22, 21, 21
G. 22, 22, 22
H. 22, 29, 29
J. 22, 30, 30
K. Cannot be determined from the given information

27. On a certain softball field, home plate is equivalent to the origin (0, 0) in the standard (x, y) coordinate plane, the first base line is equivalent to the positive x-axis, and the third base line is equivalent to the positive y-axis. Hitting a ball into Quadrant I is fair, and any other hit is foul. If Carla hits a fair ball from home plate that, when graphed, travels 40 feet and 96 feet down the first and third base lines, respectively, then how far did the ball travel?

A. 104 feet
B. 114 feet
C. 118 feet
D. 133 feet
E. 136 feet

28. In the isosceles triangle $\triangle ABC$ shown below, the measure of $\angle B$ is 72°. If it can be determined, what is the measure of $\angle C$?

DO YOUR FIGURING HERE.

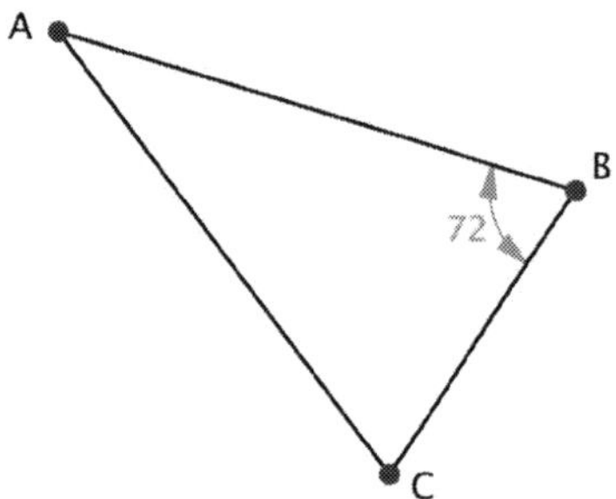

F. 36°
G. 46°
H. 72°
J. 108°
K. Cannot be determined from the given information

29. A manufacturer builds 3 different models of bicycles (X, Y, and Z). They order all of the frames, wheels, and accessories packages from a certain supplier for a fixed price. The table below gives the prices of these bicycle components for each of the three bicycle models.

Model	Frame Price	Wheel Price (for 1 wheel)	Accessories Package Price
X	\$55	\$20	\$24
Y	\$58	\$24	\$24
Z	\$70	\$33	\$24

The manufacturer gets an order for 2 X's, 7 Y's, and 5 Z's. If each bicycle needs 2 wheels, what will be the cost to the manufacturer to purchase the components necessary to build these bicycles?

A. \$1,575
B. \$1,893
C. \$1,948
D. \$2,008
E. \$2,118

30. A board 7 feet 3 inches long is cut into 3 equal parts. What is the length, to the nearest inch, of each part?

F. 2 feet 4 inches
G. 2 feet 5 inches
H. 2 feet 9 inches
J. 3 feet 1 inch
K. 5 feet 5 inches

31. In the standard (x, y) coordinate plane, H' is the image resulting from the reflection of the point $H(-4, 2)$ across the x-axis. What are the coordinates of H' ?

DO YOUR FIGURING HERE.

A. (4, 2)
B. (4, − 2)
C. (−2, 4)
D. (−4, − 2)
E. (−2, − 4)

32. Which of the following expressions is equivalent to $-\frac{1}{x^z} \times \frac{1}{21^z}$?

F. $(-x \times 21)^{-2z}$
G. $-(x \times 21)^{2z}$
H. $(-x \times 21)^{z}$
J. $-(x \times 21)^{z}$
K. $(-x \times 21)^{-z}$

33. To increase the mean of 5 numbers by 7, how much would the sum of the 5 numbers have to increase?

A. $\frac{5}{7}$
B. $\frac{7}{5}$
C. 1
D. 12
E. 35

34. Genevieve was training for a marathon. On her first practice run, she ran 11 blocks before stopping for the day. On the next day, she ran a second practice run that was $\frac{3}{5}$ farther than the distance of her practice run the previous day, then repeated the same $\frac{3}{5}$ increase in distance on her practice runs for the next two consecutive days. How many blocks did Genevieve run on her 4th day of training?

F. 28.1600 blocks
G. 30.8000 blocks
H. 45.0560 blocks
J. 70.4000 blocks
K. 72.0896 blocks

DO YOUR FIGURING HERE.

Use the following information to answer questions 35-37.

A professional baseball league is training a new umpire to replace one who is entering into retirement. When watching film, the retiring umpire is 100% accurate in properly calling pitches 'balls' or 'strikes' and 100% accurate in properly calling a player 'safe' or 'out' in close calls at first base. The umpire in training, on the other hand, is much less accurate. Both umpires were shown video of 1,000 pitches and 1,000 close calls at first base then asked to analyze them. Their conclusions are provided in the table below.

	Strikes	Balls	Safe	Out
Retiring Umpire	319	681	421	579
New Umpire	393	607	502	498

35. The new umpire is paid $35 per hour for watching and analyzing the video clips. If each clip lasts, on average, 8 seconds, then about how much money will the new umpire be paid for watching and analyzing the video clips?

A. $57.14
B. $77.78
C. $155.56
D. $187.50
E. $311.11

36. What percent of the new umpire's strike calls were inaccurate?

F. 39.3%
G. 31.9%
H. 19.1%
J. 18.8%
K. 0.0%

37. Two of the videos watched and analyzed by both the new umpire and the retiring umpire will be chosen at random. To the nearest 0.001, what is the probability that both of the chosen clips were incorrectly labeled by the new umpire?

A. 0.310
B. 0.155
C. 0.134
D. 0.012
E. 0.006

DO YOUR FIGURING HERE.

38. David is a scientist in a laboratory on a college campus and reads a sign that says that if the pressure within a certain container exceeds 255 Pascal, that he should notify the Chemistry department. David knows that the ideal gas pressure formula is given as $P = \frac{nRT}{V}$, in which V is the volume, n is the number of moles, R is a constant equal to 0.082, and T is the temperature. If the number of moles in this container is 550, the temperature is 220 K, and the volume is 42 liters, what is the gas pressure of the container, rounded to the nearest Pascal?

F. 24 Pascal
G. 110 Pascal
H. 114 Pascal
J. 236 Pascal
K. 2,362 Pascal

39. In the standard (x, y) coordinate plane, where does the graph of the equation $y = \frac{-(x+3)(x^2-x-6)}{(x+2)}$ cross the x-axis ?

A. $x = -3,\ x = 3$
B. $x = -2,\ x = 2$
C. $x = -1,\ x = 1$
D. $x = 2,\ x = 3$
E. $x = 0,\ x = 4$

40. When graphed, what is the amplitude of the function $f(x) = \frac{2}{3}\sin(2x - \pi)$?

F. $\frac{1}{3}$

G. $\frac{2}{3}$

H. $\frac{3}{2}$

J. 2

K. $2 - \pi$

41. In the standard (x, y) coordinate plane, point N lies at the origin, point M lies at point (3, 4), and point O lies at point (8, 0). What is the length, in coordinate units, of the altitude of the triangle formed by the 3 points?

A. 3
B. 4
C. 5
D. 7
E. 8

DO YOUR FIGURING HERE.

42. A car rental company has 120 cars in its lot to rent to customers. Based on over ten years of car rental data, the company created the table below showing the daily rental rates and their probabilities of occurring on any day of the year. Based on the probability distribution in the table, to the nearest whole number, what is the expected number of cars that will be rented on any given day?

Rental rate	Probability
0.25	0.10
0.50	0.20
0.75	0.40
0.90	0.20
1.00	0.10

F. 85
G. 88
H. 90
J. 94
K. 95

43. What is the degree measure of the smaller of the 2 angles formed by the 2 lines in the figure below?

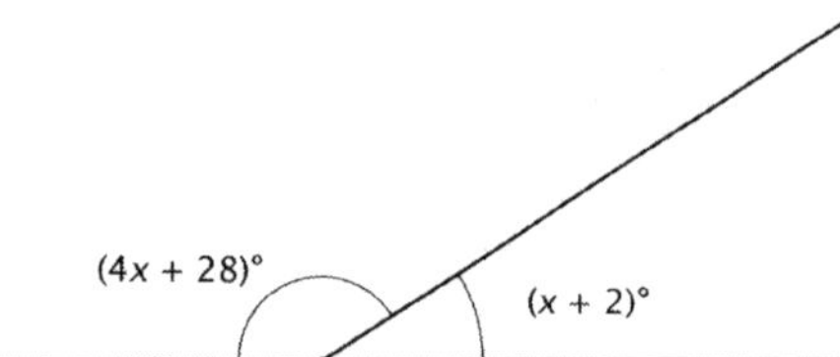

A. 30°
B. 32°
C. 55°
D. 148°
E. 150°

44. Let a equal $3b + 7 - 4c$. What happens to the value of a if the value of b decreases by 2 and the value of c increases by 1 ?

F. It increases by 11.
G. It increases by 8.
H. It is unchanged.
J. It decreases by 1.
K. It decreases by 10.

45. A retreat center has 11 rooms set aside for small groups. Each room can fit up to 12 people each. If 90 employees of a company that is using the retreat center are sent to the rooms, and each room has a minimum of 2 employees, what is the greatest possible number of rooms that can be filled with 12 people?

DO YOUR FIGURING HERE.

A. 0
B. 3
C. 4
D. 6
E. 7

46. Charlotte works for an industrial kitchen and is in charge of properly mixing ingredients for a new recipe. The recipe calls for 400 ounces of water for every 5 cups of flour. Given this ratio, how many gallons should Charlotte add for 25 liters of flour?

(Note: 1 gallon = 128 fluid ounces;
1 liter = 4.22675 cups)

F. $\frac{(400)(25)(4.22675)}{(5)(128)}$

G. $\frac{(5)(25)(4.22675)}{(400)(128)}$

H. $\frac{(400)(25)(5)}{(4.22675)(128)}$

J. $\frac{(400)(5)(4.22675)}{(25)(128)}$

K. $\frac{(5)(128)}{(400)(25)(4.22675)}$

47. For all $x > 0$, which of the following expressions, if any, are *not* always equal to x ?

I. $\frac{x^2}{x-1}$

II. $|-x|$

III. $-\sqrt{(-x)^2}$

A. I only
B. I and II only
C. I and III only
D. II and III only
E. I, II, and III

48. How many integer values of a are there that cause the fraction $\frac{3}{a}$ to lie between 0.480 and 0.205 ?

F. 3
G. 7
H. 8
J. 9
K. 10

49. Jacob is competing in a bass fishing tournament, which averages the weight of a competitor's 5 largest fish. The average weight of his first 4 fish is exactly a ounces. How many ounces higher than a must Jacob's 5th fish weigh in order to raise the average weight of the 5 fish to $a + 3$ ounces?

A. 3
B. 4
C. 12
D. 15
E. 16

50. The intersection of lines c and d forms the angles $\angle W$, $\angle X$, $\angle Y$, and $\angle Z$. The measure of $\angle Z$ is 1100% larger than the measure of $\angle W$. If it can be determined, what is the measure of $\angle W$?

F. 5°
G. 15°
H. 165°
J. 175°
K. Cannot be determined from the given information

51. A sequence is defined for all positive integers by $s_n = \frac{1}{2}s_{(n+1)} + |\, n \,| + 4$ and $s_4 = 77$. What is s_1 ?

A. 25.250
B. 23.875
C. 21.125
D. 19.750
E. 19.375

52. If x is an integer less than -2, which of the following orders the expressions $-x^3$, $-\frac{1}{x^2}$, and $|\, x \,|$?

F. $-\frac{1}{x^2} < |\, x \,| < -x^3$

G. $-\frac{1}{x^2} < -x^3 < |\, x \,|$

H. $-x^3 < -\frac{1}{x^2} < |\, x \,|$

J. $-x^3 < |\, x \,| < -\frac{1}{x^2}$

K. $|\, x \,| < -\frac{1}{x^2} < -x^3$

DO YOUR FIGURING HERE.

53. What is the 333rd digit after the decimal point in the repeating decimal $0.\overline{740231}$?

A. 0
B. 1
C. 2
D. 4
E. 7

DO YOUR FIGURING HERE.

54. A local charity is trying to determine how many t-shirts to print and sell at an upcoming event. The charity has determined, based on past events, that 15% of those on their email list will attend. If the charity also estimates that, using the same historical data, $\frac{1}{6}$ of all attendees will purchase a t-shirt, then about how many t-shirts should be printed if an invite to the event was sent to 122,000 unique emails on the charity's email list ?

F. Between 2,500 and 2,600
G. Between 3,000 and 3,100
H. Between 10,900 and 11,000
J. Between 18,250 and 18,350
K. Between 20,300 and 20,400

55. If $i = \sqrt{-1}$, then $\frac{(-3i + 1)(2i + 2)}{4} = ?$

A. 2

B. 3

C. $2 + \frac{1}{i}$

D. $-2 + i$

E. $2 - i$

56. Triangles $\triangle ABC$ and $\triangle XYZ$ are similar, right triangles. $\triangle ABC$ has a hypotenuse 10 inches long, and $\triangle XYZ$ has a hypotenuse 5 inches long. $\triangle ABC$ has one angle that is 53.13°, the opposite side of which measures 8 inches. What is the perimeter of $\triangle XYZ$, in inches ?

F. 8.5
G. 9
H. 10.5
J. 11.5
K. 12

57. If the length of the base of a triangle is increased by 10% and the height is decreased by 35%, the area of the resulting triangle is smaller than the area of the original triangle by what percent?

A. 71.5%
B. 45.0%
C. 28.5%
D. 22.5%
E. 20.0%

DO YOUR FIGURING HERE.

58. A twelve-sided dice, with sides numbered 1-12, and a six-sided dice, with sides numbered 1-6, are rolled across a table. What is the probability that the sum of the numbers on the two die is 15?

F. $\frac{1}{72}$

G. $\frac{1}{36}$

H. $\frac{1}{24}$

J. $\frac{1}{18}$

K. $\frac{5}{72}$

59. Michael calculates that he will need 5,625 square feet of wood floors in the new home he is building. However, the wood that he is looking to purchase is priced by the square *yard.* How many square yards of wood floor does he need?

A. 625
B. 735
C. 920
D. 1,750
E. 1,875

60. For all $x > 0$, which of the following expressions is NOT equivalent to $\sqrt[3]{\sqrt[3]{\sqrt[3]{x^3}}}$?

F. $\sqrt[3]{\sqrt[3]{x}}$

G. $\sqrt[18]{x^2}$

H. $\sqrt[9]{x}$

J. $x^{\frac{1}{9}}$

K. $x^{\frac{1}{6}}$

PRACTICE TEST 2

60 Minutes, 60 Questions

MATHEMATICS TEST

60 Minutes — 60 Questions

DIRECTIONS: Solve each problem, choose the correct answer, and then fill in the corresponding oval on your answer document.

Do not linger over problems that take too much time. Solve as many as you can; then return to the others in the time you have left for this test.

You are permitted to use a calculator on this test. You may use your calculator for any problems you choose, but some of the problems may best be done without using a calculator.

Note: Unless otherwise stated, all of the following should be assumed.

1. Illustrative figures are NOT necessarily drawn to scale.
2. Geometric figures lie in a plane.
3. The word *line* indicates a straight line.
4. The word *average* indicates arithmetic mean.

DO YOUR FIGURING HERE.

1. The cost for a certain town's greatest internet service is a onetime fee of \$225, plus a weekly fee of \$20. Elisa wrote a \$705 check to pay for the internet service for a number of weeks, including the onetime fee. How many weeks of membership did she pay for?

A. 6
B. 9
C. 24
D. 31
E. 35

2. A certain company prints signs for political parties. For orders of 1 to 250 signs, the company charges \$2.50 per sign, but for orders of 251 or more signs, the company charges \$2.15 per sign. A political party that ordered 425 signs was accidentally charged \$2.50 per sign. What is the total refund that the sign company owes the political party?

F. \$42.50
G. \$148.75
H. \$191.25
J. \$212.50
K. \$425.00

3. A bus is driving from Charlotte, NC to Austin, TX. Abraham and Rachel board the bus at 5:45 a.m., and the bus departs at exactly 6:00 a.m. At 7:30 a.m., Abraham checks a map and sees that the bus has traveled exactly 90 miles. At this rate, how far will the bus travel in 4 hours?

A. 150 miles
B. 180 miles
C. 220 miles
D. 240 miles
E. 360 miles

DO YOUR FIGURING HERE.

4. A local restaurant offers 17 different meal options, and 1 of them is Christopher's favorite meal. On his next visit, he decides to let his waitress choose a meal on his behalf at random, as long as it is not spicy. If the restaurant offers 5 spicy meals, what are the odds that the waitress chooses Christopher's favorite meal?

F. $\frac{1}{12}$

G. $\frac{5}{17}$

H. $\frac{5}{16}$

J. $\frac{6}{17}$

K. $\frac{5}{12}$

5. Mr. Schmidt has 21, 27, 22, 25, and 21 pupils in his first five classes of the school day. Solving which of the following equations for p gives the number of students he needs in his 6th class of the day to average exactly 24 students per class?

A. $\frac{(21+27+22+25+21)}{5} + p = 24$

B. $\frac{(21+27+22+25+21)}{6} + p = 24$

C. $\frac{(21+27+22+25+21+p)}{6} = \frac{24}{6}$

D. $\frac{(21+27+22+25+21+p)}{5} = 24$

E. $\frac{(21+27+22+25+21+p)}{6} = 24$

6. What is $x^2 - |7 - x| - (-x)$ when $x = 11$?

F. 106
G. 114
H. 125
J. 128
K. 136

7. Consider the equation $m - n = \frac{9}{4}n + 3$. For what value of n is the value of m equal to 16 ?

A. 4.00
B. 6.75
C. 10.40
D. 10.50
E. 42.25

8. After a survey, Gary made the pie chart below to show the different tastes in candy among the student body from among four options: chocolate, gummies, hard candies, or gum. After making the chart, he measures the angles of the different pieces of the pie. If more students voted for chocolate than any other option, then what percent of the student body prefers chocolate, rounded to the nearest percent?

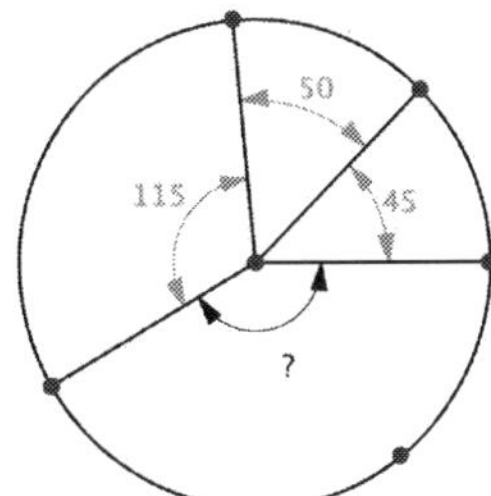

F. 25%
G. 32%
H. 38%
J. 42%
K. Cannot be determined from the given information

DO YOUR FIGURING HERE.

9. A homeowner precisely measures, in feet, the lengths and widths of an L-shaped hallway in his home. Assuming all walls meet at 90° angles, what is the square footage of the homeowner's hallway?

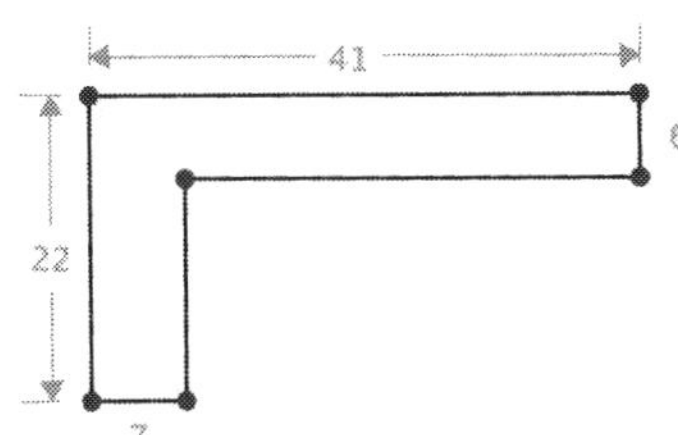

A. 76
B. 358
C. 372
D. 400
E. 902

10. Given that $f(x) = 4x - 2$ and $g(x) = \frac{x^3}{2}$, what is the value of $f(g(2))$?

F. 6
G. 14
H. 16
J. 30
K. 108

11. In the standard (x, y) coordinate plane, the point $(0, -3)$ is the midpoint of $\overline{AB}$. Point A has coordinates $(-3, 6)$. What are the coordinates of point B ?

DO YOUR FIGURING HERE.

A. $(-1.5, 1.5)$
B. $(-3, -6)$
C. $(3, -12)$
D. $(-6, 15)$
E. $(1.5, -1.5)$

12. Aaron can type 112 words per minute. What is the number of hours it takes him to type 8,400 words?

F. $1\frac{1}{15}$

G. $1\frac{1}{8}$

H. $1\frac{1}{4}$

J. $7\frac{1}{4}$

K. $7\frac{1}{2}$

13. Carlos scored 37 points in the state championship basketball game. If all of his points came from 2 and 3 point shots, and if he made a total of 15 shots, then how many 2 point shots did he make?

A. 7
B. 8
C. 9
D. 10
E. 11

14. Diana puts 30 poker chips into a hat, 13 of which are blue, 11 of which are green, and 6 of which are black. How many additional black poker chips must be put into the hat so that the probability of drawing a black poker chip is $\frac{5}{11}$?

F. 1
G. 4
H. 5
J. 13
K. 14

15. What is 4% of 6.71×10^{-3} ?

A. 0.00002684
B. 0.0002684
C. 0.0016775
D. 0.002684
E. 0.016775

DO YOUR FIGURING HERE.

16. The volume of a cone is $\pi r^2 \frac{h}{3}$, where r is the radius of the sphere and h is the height of the cone. What is the volume, in cubic feet, of a cone with a height of 1 and a *diameter* of 12 feet?

F. 12π
G. 16π
H. 38π
J. 48π
K. 151π

17. What is the product of the two solutions of the equation $x^2 - 10x + 21 = 0$?

A. -21
B. -10
C. -4
D. 10
E. 21

18. The radius of a certain circle is $3x - 2$. The diameter of the same circle is $5x + 1$. What is the area of this circle?

F. 5π
G. 13π
H. 25π
J. 169π
K. 676π

19. Imidacloprid, a neonicotinoid chemical that acts on the central nervous system of insects, is the active ingredient in many pets' flea medication. A dosage of 3.20 ml is recommended for dogs weighing 70 pounds or more, and to avoid over-dosing, the dosage decreases by 0.04 ml per pound from 3.20 ml. To the nearest 0.01 ml, what is the recommended dosage for a dog weighing 42 pounds?

A. 1.52 ml
B. 1.68 ml
C. 1.72 ml
D. 2.08 ml
E. 2.80 ml

20. In the figure below, all segments that meet do so at right angles. What is the area, in square units, of the shaded region?

F. 3
G. 4
H. 6
J. 9
K. 14

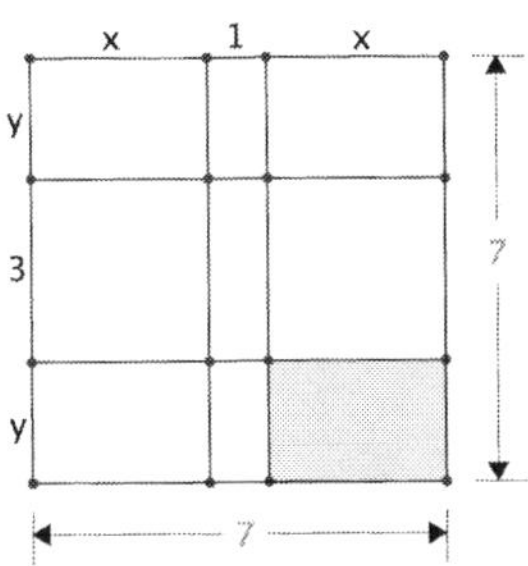

21. Which of the following is a value of x that satisfies $\log_x 125 = 3$?

DO YOUR FIGURING HERE.

A. 5
B. 15
C. 25
D. 41
E. 375

22. If a and b are positive integers, such that the greatest common factor of a^3b^2 and $a\,b^3$ is 24, then which of the following could b equal?

F. 36
G. 24
H. 8
J. 6
K. 2

23. A line contains the points F, G, H, and J. Point G lies between points F and H. Point J lies between points H and G. If segment $\overline{JH}$ is 8 units long, and if segment $\overline{FG}$ is 10 units long, then which of the following inequalities *must* be true about the lengths of these segments?

A. $\overline{GJ} < 8$
B. $8 > \overline{FG}$
C. $\overline{GH} < 10$
D. $\overline{GJ} < 10$
E. $8 < \overline{GH}$

24. One bird makes a call every 3 seconds. A second bird makes a call every 7 seconds. At a certain moment, both birds call at the same time. How many seconds elapse until the 2 birds next call at the same time?

F. 10
G. 21
H. 28
J. 41
K. 42

25. A rectangular painting is being mounted to a wall in a city museum. The painting measures 105 inches from the top left corner of the frame to the bottom right corner of the frame. If the painting is 84 inches wide, then how tall is the painting in inches?

A. 21
B. 63
C. 84
D. 85
E. 86

26. If 3 times a number n is added to -12, the result is positive. Which of the following gives the possible value(s) for n ?

DO YOUR FIGURING HERE.

F. All $n > 4$

G. All $n < -4$

H. All $n > \frac{1}{4}$

J. 4 only

K. $-\frac{1}{4}$ only

27. For all $x > 8$, $\frac{(x^2 - 10x + 16)(x + 3)}{(x^2 - 5x - 24)(x - 2)} = ?$

A. 0

B. $\frac{4}{5}$

C. 1

D. $\frac{x - 8}{x + 8}$

E. $\frac{x + 8}{x - 8}$

28. On Tuesdays at Camilla's favorite bakery, the amount of money in the cash register at any given time, m, satisfies the inequality $|m + \$25| \leq \$175$. If a negative number denotes a decrease in sales from the previous day, then which of the following dollar amounts is NOT in this range?

F. $-\$205$
G. $-\$160$
H. $-\$25$
J. $\$0$
K. $\$150$

29. Zeke wants to cook a meal consisting of one meat dish, one vegetable dish, and one dessert. While reading through cookbooks, Zeke feels comfortable cooking 80 different meat dishes, 55 different vegetable dishes, and 22 different desserts. How many meals, each consisting of one meat dish, one vegetable dish, and one dessert, is Zeke comfortable cooking?

A. 22
B. 58
C. 80
D. 157
E. 96,800

30. In the standard (x, y) coordinate plane, which of the following lines best approximates the data points (3, 5), (1, 4), (−4, 3), (−5, 2.5), (5, 6), and (2, 4.5) ?

DO YOUR FIGURING HERE.

F. $y = -\left(\frac{1}{3}\right)x + 4$

G. $y = 3x + 4$

H. $y = \left(\frac{1}{3}\right)x + 4$

J. $y = 4x - 1$

K. $y = -\left(\frac{2}{3}\right)x - 1$

31. For all x and $y \neq 0$, what is the value of $\left(\frac{\frac{x^3}{-(y^{-2})}}{(-(xy)^4}\right)^0$?

A. x^7y^5

B. $-(x^7y^5)$

C. $(xy)^2$

D. 1

E. 0

32. If $0° < \theta < 90°$ and $\cos\theta = \frac{12}{13}$, then $\sin\theta = $?

F. $-\frac{5}{12}$

G. $\frac{5}{13}$

H. $\frac{5}{12}$

J. $\frac{13}{12}$

K. $\frac{13}{5}$

33. Lila drew a picture for her mother for Valentine's Day that is 8 inches long and 10 inches wide. The picture is too large to fit in the frame, so Lila is going to cut the picture down slightly to have an area that is 70% of the area of the original drawing. The length of Lila's new picture will be 87.5% the length of the original picture. How many inches wide will the new picture be?

A. 8
B. 7.5
C. 7
D. 6.5
E. 6

Use the following information to answer questions 34-36.

DO YOUR FIGURING HERE.

Mr. Oberlee decides that he will give bonus points to any student who brings in a pie to share with the rest of math class on March 14th. Of his 25 students, only 11 of them brought in a pie to share with the class. Below are three circles that represent the three pies that were voted by the class as the most delicious.

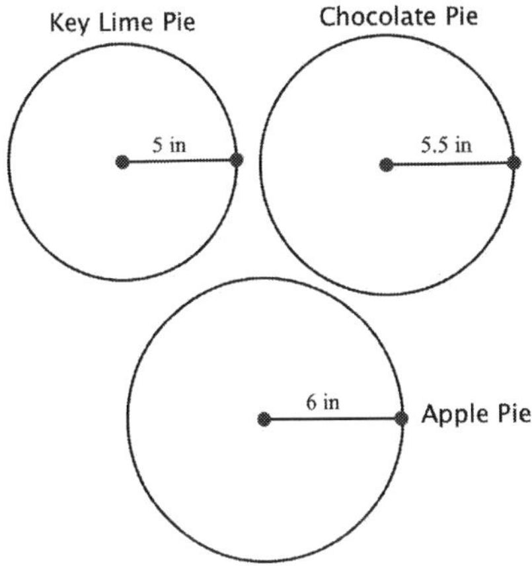

34. Mr. Oberlee traces the Chocolate Pie with its center at the origin on a poster that features the standard (x, y) coordinate plane drawn with one inch per square unit. Which of the following formulas best represents the pie's tracing?

F. $(x - 5.5)^2 + (y - 5.5)^2 = 11$
G. $(x + 5.5)^2 + (y + 5.5)^2 = 11$
H. $(x - 5.5)^2 + (y - 5.5)^2 = 30.25$
J. $x^2 + y^2 = 5.5$
K. $x^2 + y^2 = 30.25$

35. The area of the Chocolate Pie is equivalent to which of the following percentages, rounded to the nearest hundredth of a percent?

A. 84.03% of the Apple Pie
B. 121.00% of the Apple Pie
C. 69.44% of the Key Lime Pie
D. 119.01% of the Apple Pie
E. 82.64% of the Key Lime Pie

DO YOUR FIGURING HERE.

36. Which of the following inequalities or expressions properly orders the areas of these 3 pieces of pie:

Piece 1: Key Lime Pie cut with an interior angle of 25°
Piece 2: Chocolate Pie cut with an interior angle of 20°
Piece 3: Apple Pie cut with an interior angle of 25°

F. Piece 1 = Piece 2 = Piece 3
G. Piece 1 = Piece 3 < Piece 2
H. Piece 3 < Piece 1 < Piece 2
J. Piece 1 < Piece 2 < Piece 3
K. Piece 2 < Piece 1 < Piece 3

---

37. In the figure below, $\overline{AB} \parallel \overline{CD}$, and $\overline{CB}$ bisects $\angle ABD$. If the measure of $\angle ABD$ is 118°, what is the measure of $\angle BCD$?

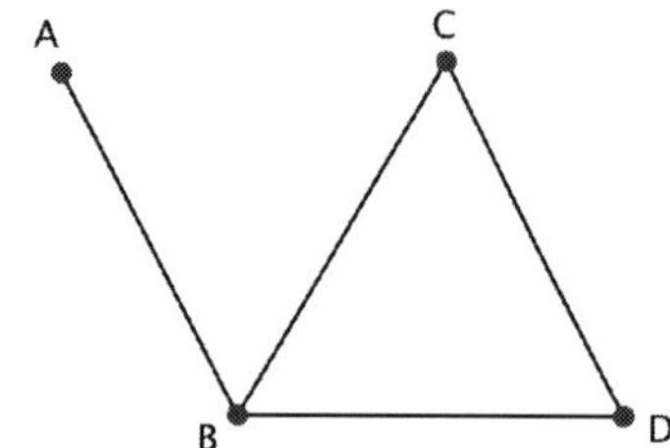

A. 49°
B. 52°
C. 59°
D. 62°
E. Cannot be determined from the given information

38. Much of the grass in Paulo's front yard has died, and he decides to replace it. The total area of grass that needs replacing is 1,350 square feet. If the local hardware store sells grass squares that are 25 inches by 25 inches, then what is the minimum number of grass squares that Paolo must purchase to replace the dead grass in his front yard?

F. 54
G. 311
H. 312
J. 195
K. 1,944

39. A group of concerned citizens tests the levels of Halo-acetic acids in a community's drinking water. Across ten testing sites, the group discovered 0.06, 0.05, 0.11, 0.10, 0.05, 0.05, 0.09, 0.06, 0.11, and 0.05 ppb (parts per billion), respectively. Given this data set, which of the following two values are equal?

A. The mean and the mode
B. The mode and the range
C. The median and the mode
D. The median and the range
E. The mean and the range

Use the following information to answer questions 40-42.

DO YOUR FIGURING HERE.

Chandra is reading a book about famous Italian landmarks and learns the following facts about the Leaning Tower of Pisa in Pisa, Italy. First, she learns that the tower is 183.25 feet tall on the lowest side and 185.92 feet tall on the highest side. Second, she learns that the tower stands at an angle of 86.03° to the ground on the low side and 93.97° on the high side. Third, she learns that the tower weighs 16,000 tons.

*Note: 1 ton = 2,000 pounds

40. Solving which of the following equations would result in the height of the tower if it were to stand perpendicular to the ground?

F. $\frac{185.92}{\cos(86.03)}$

G. $\frac{183.25}{\cos(86.03)}$

H. $\frac{185.92}{\tan(86.03)}$

J. $\frac{183.25}{\sin(86.03)}$

K. $\frac{185.92}{\sin(86.03)}$

41. If the book averages 350 words per page, and if Chandra reads at a rate of x words per minute, then how many minutes will it take her to read 15 pages?

A. $\frac{350x}{15}$

B. $\frac{x}{350(15)}$

C. $\frac{15x}{350}$

D. $\frac{350}{15x}$

E. $\frac{350(15)}{x}$

42. Suppose another city wishes to build a new tower of the exact same weight of the original Tower of Pisa. This new tower will have an average diameter of 50 feet from top to bottom and will be exactly 185 feet tall. What would be this new tower's resulting pounds per cubic foot, rounded to the nearest pound?

F. 55
G. 64
H. 88
J. 276
K. 277

43. What are the values of x and y if $3x + 2y = 14$ and $4x - y = -29$?

DO YOUR FIGURING HERE.

A. $x = 2$ and $y = 4$
B. $x = -4$ and $y = 13$
C. $x = 4$ and $y = -13$
D. $x = -2$ and $y = -4$
E. $x = -2$ and $y = -21$

44. Given $15x = 5y^5 - 25$, which of the following is an expression for y in terms of x ?

F. $y = 3x + 5$

G. $y = 3(x^{\frac{1}{5}}) - 5$

H. $y = (3x - 5)^{\frac{1}{5}}$

J. $y = (3x + 5)^{\frac{1}{5}}$

K. $y = (3x + 5)^5$

45. If an equilateral triangle has a height of 20 inches, what is its area rounded to the nearest square inch?

A. 101
B. 200
C. 231
D. 400
E. 462

46. What is the result if the mean of the first 6 prime numbers is multiplied by the mean of the factors of 10?

F. $9\frac{9}{10}$

G. $18\frac{9}{10}$

H. $21\frac{3}{4}$

J. $27\frac{3}{10}$

K. $35\frac{1}{10}$

47. Four matrices are given below.

$A = [4 \quad 5] \quad B = \begin{bmatrix} -2 \\ 8 \end{bmatrix} \quad C = \begin{bmatrix} 6 & 0 \\ 0 & 0 \end{bmatrix} \quad D = \begin{bmatrix} -4 & 4 \\ -2 & 2 \\ -3 & 3 \end{bmatrix}$

Which of the following matrix products is undefined?

A. *AB*
B. *BA*
C. *DB*
D. *BD*
E. *DC*

48. For all nonzero values of a, $\dfrac{8a^{16} - 6a^4}{2a^2} = ?$

DO YOUR FIGURING HERE.

F. $(4a^4 - 3)$

G. $\dfrac{a^2(4a^{12} - 3)}{a}$

H. $\dfrac{a^2(4a^{12} - 3)}{a^2}$

J. $a^2(4a^4 - 3)$

K. $a^2(4a^{12} - 3)$

49. Molly wants to bake chocolate chip cookies for her friends. The recipe calls for $1\frac{3}{4}$ cups of chocolate chips for every $2\frac{1}{8}$ cups of butter. If Molly uses this ratio as called for in the recipe, but decides to use all of the $2\frac{1}{3}$ cups of chocolate chips she has at hand, then how many cups of butter will Molly need?

A. $2\frac{5}{6}$

B. 3

C. $3\frac{1}{10}$

D. $3\frac{2}{3}$

E. $4\frac{1}{5}$

50. Donald is a new coach who wants to get to know his football team better. When he asks them to raise their hands if any of them play a winter sport, 29 raise their hands. When he asks them to raise their hands if any of them play a spring sport, 31 of them raise their hands. If there are 55 members of the football team, then what is the minimum number of football players who play both a winter and a spring sport?

F. 0
G. 5
H. 15
J. 29
K. 31

DO YOUR FIGURING HERE.

51. An inspector found that 193 laptops made by Chip Computers had 0 defects, 111 laptops had 1 defect, 152 laptops had 2 defects, 105 laptops had 3 defects, and 53 laptops had 4 defects. If the inspected laptops represent an accurate sample size, then which of the following fractions best approximates the likelihood that a Chip Computer has 2 or fewer defects?

A. $\frac{1}{4}$

B. $\frac{1}{2}$

C. $\frac{2}{3}$

D. $\frac{37}{50}$

E. $\frac{23}{25}$

52. In the figure below, all line segments are either horizontal or vertical, and the dimensions given are in meters. What is the perimeter, in meters, of the figure?

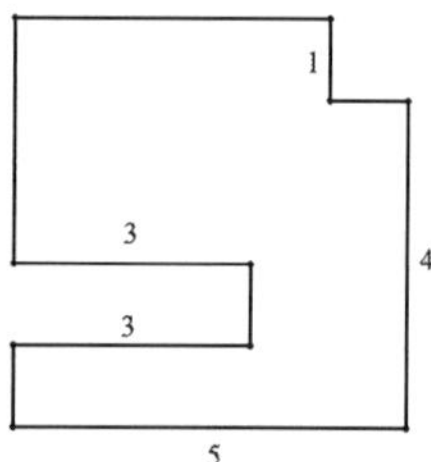

F. 19
G. 20
H. 22
J. 26
K. 27

53. Yuriy's New Year resolution is to take more steps. On his first day, he took 1,000 steps. On each successive day, he added 50 more steps than the total steps he took the day before. If Yuriy met his exact step goals for each day, then how many steps total did he take in his first 10 days?

A. 10,500
B. 12,000
C. 12,250
D. 13,600
E. 13,800

54. What is the area, in square units, of the parallelogram created by the following lines: $y = 2\frac{1}{2}x + 2$, $y = 2\frac{1}{2}x - 8$, $y = 2$, and $y = 7$?

F. 20
G. 22
H. 23
J. 26
K. 28

DO YOUR FIGURING HERE.

55. For all $y \neq 0$, which of the following expressions is equivalent to $\frac{(-\sqrt{y} - 3)(y + 5\sqrt{y} + 4)}{(\sqrt{y} + 1)(y - 4\sqrt{y} - 21}) = ?$

A. $\sqrt{y}$

B. $-\sqrt{y}$

C. $\frac{\sqrt{y}}{\sqrt{y} + 7}$

D. $\frac{\sqrt{y} + 4}{\sqrt{y} - 7}$

E. $\frac{-\sqrt{y} - 4}{\sqrt{y} - 7}$

56. When $y = \cos(x)$ is graphed on the standard (x, y) coordinate plane, the result is a wave with an amplitude of 1 and a period of 2π. How does this wave compare to that of $y = 3\cos(\frac{x}{2})$?

F. It has three times the amplitude and twice the period.
G. It has three times the amplitude and half the period.
H. It has twice the amplitude and thee times the period.
J. It has one-third the amplitude and half the period.
K. It has half the amplitude and three times the period.

57. In a standard deck of cards there are a total of 52 cards: 4 aces, 12 face cards, and 4 cards of every number 2 through 10 (4 cards with a 2, 4 cards with a 3, and so on up to 4 cards with a 10). Harriet wins a chance to draw a card at random. If she draws an ace, she will be awarded \$150, if she draws a face card, she will be awarded \$100, and if she draws any other card, she will be awarded \$10. What is the expected outcome of Harriet's award, rounded to the nearest whole dollar?

A. \$10
B. \$42
C. \$49
D. \$85
E. \$125

58. A certain rectangle's width and length are whole numbers in millimeters. In addition, the rectangle's width is greater than the rectangle's length. Lastly, the rectangle has an area of 240 square millimeters. Which of the following perimeters is *not* possible for this rectangle?

F. 482
G. 113
H. 68
J. 64
K. 62

DO YOUR FIGURING HERE.

59. Three lines with different slopes are graphed in the standard (x, y) coordinate plane. Which of the following is *not* possible?

A. Two of the lines never cross the x-axis.
B. The three lines have the same y-intercept.
C. The three lines intersect at the origin.
D. One of the lines never crosses the y-axis.
E. One of the lines is $x = 0$.

60. A new hotel is considering different dimensions for a grand ball room. Originally, the ball room was to have a length of 300 feet, a width of 150 feet, and a ceiling height of 20 feet. However, upon seeing the plans, the owner of the hotel determines that the length and width of the room should both be increased by 25%. What will be the resulting increase, to the nearest 1%, in the volume of the grand ball room?

F. 25%
G. 26%
H. 42%
J. 50%
K. 56%

Practice Test 1 Correct Answers

1: C
2: G
3: B
4: K
5: A
6: K
7: A
8: J
9: D
10: F
11: B
12: J
13: E
14: H
15: B
16: H
17: D
18: F
19: C
20: G
21: E
22: F
23: D
24: J
25: B
26: H
27: A
28: H
29: C
30: G
31: D
32: K
33: E
34: H
35: C
36: J
37: E
38: J
39: A
40: G
41: B
42: F
43: B
44: K
45: D
46: F
47: C
48: H
49: D
50: G
51: E
52: F
53: A
54: G
55: E
56: K
57: C
58: J
59: A
60: K

Practice Test 2 Correct Answers

1: C
2: G
3: D
4: F
5: E
6: J
7: A
8: J
9: B
10: G
11: C
12: H
13: B
14: K
15: B
16: F
17: E
18: J
19: D
20: H
21: A
22: K
23: E
24: G
25: B
26: F
27: C
28: F
29: E
30: H
31: D
32: G
33: A
34: K
35: A
36: K
37: C
38: H
39: D
40: J
41: E
42: H
43: B
44: J
45: C
46: H
47: D
48: K
49: A
50: G
51: D
52: J
53: C
54: F
55: E
56: F
57: B
58: G
59: A
60: K

Practice Test 1 answer explanations begin on page 578; Practice Test 2 answer explanations begin on page 594.

The ACT Reading *System*

Six Steps to ACT Reading Perfection

Introduction to ACT Reading

The ACT Reading test consists of 4 passages, each of which is followed by 10 questions; you are given 35 minutes to answer these questions, which equates to 8 minutes and 45 seconds to complete each passage. The passages themselves will always be pulled from the same 4 categories in the same order. The first passage is a bit unique relative to the other three, but all adhere to the same basic structure.

Passage I - Literary Narrative**.** The first passage on the ACT Reading test will feature an excerpt (meaning, a section/piece) from a literary source. Usually, this passage is taken from a work of fiction, but it can also come from a person's autobiography or memoir. What makes this passage unique compared to the other three is that it is literary; it will feature a character or characters who are experiencing something, and as a result this passage usually features the emotions of the characters involved.

Passage II - Social Science. The second passage on the ACT Reading test will belong to the category of Social Science (aka Social Studies). This means that the passage may feature an excerpt from a book or article that focuses on history, economics. geography, anthropology, political science, etc. You can think of this passage as being the kind of passage that you would find in a collegiate textbook; thus, it is likely to feature many, many details (more on that later).

Passage III - Humanities. The third passage on the ACT Reading test will belong to the category of Humanities. You may not be familiar with the Humanities as a category, but all this means is that the passage may feature an excerpt from a book or article that focuses on philosophy, art of all kinds, language, culture, possibly history, etc. Like Passage II, you can think of this passage as being the kind of passage that you would find in a collegiate textbook; thus, it is also likely to feature many, many details (again, more on that later).

Passage IV - Natural Science. The third passage on the ACT Reading test will belong to the category of Natural Science. This passage will feature an excerpt from a book or article that focuses on physics, chemistry, earth science, biology, geology, etc. Thus, this passage will likely be steeped in scientific terminology and many details (again, more on that later).

Timing

Perhaps more than on any other test, keeping time is key to success on the ACT Reading test. While Step 1 is dedicated to the number 1 strategy necessary to do your best on the ACT Reading test, which of course takes into account the amount of time you have, it is important to discuss time here in the introduction as well. This test should not be thought of as one 35-minute-long test, but rather as 4 tests, each taking 8 minutes and 45 seconds (or, if that's too difficult to remember, taking 9 minutes, 9 minutes, 9 minutes, then 8 minutes for the final passage).

Think of it like this: if you spend 10 minutes on Passage I, 11 minutes on Passage II, then 10 minutes on Passage III, you are leaving yourself a mere 4 minutes to complete Passage IV. Though we'll discuss what to do if you find yourself in this situation later in the book, it is to be avoided! Unfortunately, this is going to happen to many if not most students who take the ACT Reading test; they will simply run out of time. 35 minutes may seem like a lot, but not if you're trying to do your best on a really important test!

Question Breakdown

I break down ACT Reading questions into three types: micro, medium, and macro. While there will be in depth discussion on these reading questions later (Step 2 and Step 4), they are worth putting on your radar now! I define micro questions (40-45% of all questions) as those requiring you to reference 1 or 2 lines from the passage to find the correct answer. Usually these questions ask for or require reference to a specific detail. I define medium questions (40-45% of all questions) as those requiring you to reread, think over, or reason through somewhere between 3 lines to a full paragraph of information. Lastly, I define macro questions (15-18% of all questions) as those which require an understanding of or reference to the passage as a whole.

STEP 1

Active Reading and the Passage Map

As alluded to before, the ACT Reading test is a real time crunch. After all, the vast majority of students who are unprepared are going to run out of time and be left scrambling in the final minutes. Those that don't run out of time, on the other hand, have probably been left with a false feeling of accomplishment, having fallen for many good-sounding answers that are, in fact, incorrect (see "Inferring" on page 349); these students are in for a bad shock when their ACT Reading scores come back.

What can be done about this? Well, a lot, but it begins with *active reading*. First, let me sound like a pitch man for a minute: *How would YOU like to increase your ACT Reading score by as many as 3, 4, 5, 6, 7, 8, or even 9 points by implementing one simple strategy? How would it feel to be surprised by how well you can do on the ACT Reading test when your scores come in instead of feeling defeated, unprepared, or like a "bad test taker"? Well, do I have the strategy for you! Introducing Active Reading, the simple-to-implement, yet effective ACT strategy...*

OK, that's enough of that, but hopefully I sold you a little! If that beautiful pitch wasn't enough, let me tell you about Nicole. One Summer, I taught active reading to Nicole. She was looking to increase her ACT score by 4 points so that she could qualify for a big scholarship for a local school she had already been admitted into. After she got her ACT scores back (as you can see below), *voila*!

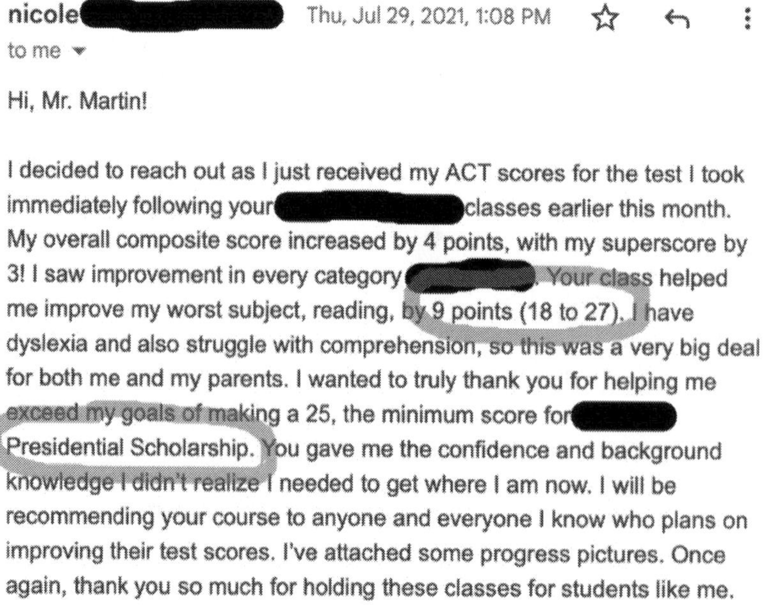

nicole [redacted] Thu, Jul 29, 2021, 1:08 PM
to me

Hi, Mr. Martin!

I decided to reach out as I just received my ACT scores for the test I took immediately following your [redacted] classes earlier this month. My overall composite score increased by 4 points, with my superscore by 3! I saw improvement in every category [redacted]. Your class helped me improve my worst subject, reading, by 9 points (18 to 27). I have dyslexia and also struggle with comprehension, so this was a very big deal for both me and my parents. I wanted to truly thank you for helping me exceed my goals of making a 25, the minimum score for [redacted] Presidential Scholarship. You gave me the confidence and background knowledge I didn't realize I needed to get where I am now. I will be recommending your course to anyone and everyone I know who plans on improving their test scores. I've attached some progress pictures. Once again, thank you so much for holding these classes for students like me.

The reason she was able to increase her ACT Reading score by 9 points is NOT because she all of a sudden learned how to read. Her reading level didn't jump up 2 grades within a one week period of taking an ACT class from me, either. Rather, she simply put into place the active reading strategy. More recently (less than a month ago as of this writing), another of my students told me in person how her ACT Reading score increased 8 points in the exact same way.

What is Active Reading?

Active reading is the opposite of **passive reading**. To do something passively means that you do it without effort, or slowly. If you are going on a simple walk to get some fresh air, you are probably walking *passively*, or at your normal pace. However, if you are going on a walk to get some exercise, you are probably walking *actively*, meaning at a bit of a faster pace to get your heart rate up. It's probably obvious, but walking at a passive rate is *way easier* than walking at an active rate, and that's the difference: *students who are most likely to see an increase in their ACT Reading scores are willing to choose to read faster than the normal person.*

Thus, **active reading** means reading at a quicker pace than normal. The active reader is NOT getting hung up on or snared by every detail; the active reader is NOT trying to memorize all of what he or she believes to be the passage's most important information; the active reader is NOT letting the passage present itself at a slow pace. Rather, the active reader IS reading the passage (in other words, the active reader is not skimming), but at a faster pace than normal. This kind of active reading means that you spend roughly 3 minutes reading the passage (give or take 30 seconds or so), allowing you to spend nearly 6 minutes actually answering the questions.

Follow my logic, if you will:

To get a good grade on the ACT Reading test, you need to get questions correct. To get questions correct, you have to spend enough time on the questions to get them correct. To have the time to spend on the questions to get them correct, you have to save time somewhere, and the only place to save time is in the reading of the passage itself.

This isn't a gimmick or a get-rich-quick scheme, but a *strategy* or *approach*. Many students of all reading abilities believe that a nice, slow reading of the passage is key because they think that they can memorize or remember most of the relevant information. This kind of student then answers the questions without bothering to find the correct answer, and instead answers based on what he or she remembers. Let's recall a couple of things, though. First, the wrong answers *are designed to sound correct* and are oftentimes *based in partial truth*. Thus, the slow-reading student is going to select answers that sound great, but are factually incorrect or not found in the passage itself. Second, this kind of student, no matter how smart, is *not* going to be able to remember all of the passage's information even if she took the full 8 minutes and 45 seconds to read it. It is generally accepted that the average adult can hold 5 to 9 pieces of information in his or her short term memory; what makes you think you can hold 150 facts about the reign of Cleopatra or the philosophy of Thomas Hobbes or the chemistry of making parmesan cheese?

Check out the following paragraph, typical of one you might see in Passage IV (the Natural Science passage):

Chlorophyll is a crucial pigment found in plants that is essential for the process of photosynthesis; its unique molecular structure and ability to absorb light make it a vital component in the process of photosynthesis, enabling plants to convert sunlight into the energy needed for growth and survival. It plays a key role in capturing sunlight and converting it into chemical energy. Structurally, chlorophyll consists of a porphyrin ring with a magnesium ion at its center and a series of double bonds. These double bonds enable chlorophyll to absorb light energy, particularly in the blue and red parts of the light spectrum. When chlorophyll absorbs light, the energy excites electrons, initiating a chain of reactions that lead to the production of ATP (adenosine triphosphate) and NADPH (nicotinamide adenine dinucleotide phosphate), which are energy-rich molecules used in the synthesis of organic compounds. Moreover, chlorophyll donates electrons during the photosynthetic electron transport chain, resulting in the creation of a proton gradient across the thylakoid membrane. This gradient powers ATP synthesis through a process called chemiosmosis.

Are you really going to slowly read this paragraph and remember all of the information, facts, and details it contains? This paragraph is roughly 170 words in length, and would be a part of a passage that is roughly 800 words long. You need to adapt a strategy that allows you to get questions correct, *not* a strategy that helps you to memorize 20 scientific and technical details about chlorophyll.

Hide and Seek

What if I told you that for each ACT Math question, the answer was hidden on the previous page? I would bet that you would spend some or most of your time going back to that previous page looking for clues that could help you pinpoint the correct answer, thus raising your ACT Math score. This is false of ACT Math, of course, but lucky for you, it is mostly *true* of ACT Reading.

More than 80% of ACT Reading questions are what I call micro or medium questions (more on that later). By in large, what that means is that you can simply go back, reread between 1 and 5 sentences, think about what you read (if necessary), and match that to the correct answer choice. Students who passively take the ACT Reading test at their own, normal, preferred pace of reading are not leaving themselves enough time to go through this process (not for all 4 passages and all 40 questions, anyway).

The Passage Map

Hopefully at this point the necessity of reading quickly (actively) has been communicated to you, and hopefully you have made the decision to maximize your time answering the questions by active reading. Great! Now, there is a technique that will help you to do this, and it is by *annotating* as you read. The word 'annotating' is usually a scary word for a high school student. This is because some teachers make you annotate while you read for class; sometimes, and depending on the teacher, this means circling any vocabulary word you do not know and defining it in the margins, and other times this means summarizing each paragraph of a textbook in one complete sentence in your notes.

However, when I say that you need to annotate while you active read on the ACT Reading test, I mean neither of those things, nor do I mean that you need to do anything near as much writing or circling or underlining as you might think.

I simply mean this: while you active read, scribble in the margin **a 1-5 word summary** of each paragraph, meaning the main idea of each paragraph.

That's it.

Notice that when you are finished with the reading itself, you will have scribbled next to each and every paragraph a small little summary of the entire essay. This is called the Passage Map. Having a Passage Map scribbled in the margins of the reading passage is extremely beneficial (meaning, it helps you get questions correct more quickly) for three particular reasons:

1) The creation of the Passage Map forces you to think "big picture" about each paragraph, moving you along; this prevents you from being "snagged" by each and every detail along the way.

2) The Passage Map serves as a map (get it?) in this way: when you need to look for a detail or a few sentences to find an answer, you can know exactly where to go look. For example, think about what you might scribble in the margins next to the paragraph 2 pages earlier about chlorophyll to sum up its main idea. For me, I might sum it up by writing something like, "What chlor. does w/ light," meaning, "What chlorophyll does with light." Thus, when number 34 (for example) on the ACT Reading test asks me for a detail about what chlorophyll does with light, I know exactly where to go hunting for the correct answer.

3) One of the most asked ACT Reading questions is about the purpose of a particular paragraph. If you already have that purpose scribbled in the margins, then precious time can be saved by referring to the Passage Map as opposed to rereading the paragraph itself.

*Also, note that I'm not leaving you in the dark on this; I have possible Passage Maps for every practice passage in this book before its answer explanations in the back of the book!

Annotating Practice

Before we get to practicing with a complete ACT Reading passage, let's practice active reading and annotating with individual paragraphs. These paragraphs are from different sources and about various topics, but each of them is the kind of paragraph you would read on the ACT Reading test as a part of a bigger passage on the same topic.

Read each of the paragraphs, paying attention to *the main idea*. When you are finished reading a paragraph, scribble in the margin a 1 to 5 word summary of this main idea, then move on to the next paragraph. Numbers 1-4 are representative of the kinds of paragraphs found in Passage I (Literary Narrative), numbers 5-8 are representative of the kinds of paragraphs found in Passage II (Social Science), numbers 9-12 are representative of the kinds of paragraphs found in Passage III (Humanities), and numbers 13-16 are representative of the kinds of paragraphs found in Passage IV (Natural Science).

When you are finished, compare your summaries with mine found on pages 305-307. However, don't be discouraged, especially if your annotations don't match mine: this is about practice, not perfection.

Passage I: Literary Narrative

1)

Mr. Woodhouse had so completely made up his mind to the visit, that in spite of the increasing coldness, he seemed to have no idea of shrinking from it, and set forward at last most punctually with his eldest daughter in his own carriage, with less apparent consciousness of the weather than either of the others; too full of the wonder of his own going, and the pleasure it was to afford at Randalls to see that it was cold, and too well wrapt up to feel it. The cold, however, was severe; and by the time the second carriage was in motion, a few flakes of snow were finding their way down, and the sky had the appearance of being so overcharged as to want only a milder air to produce a very white world in a very short time.

____

2)

Simon Wheeler backed me into a corner and blockaded me there with his chair, and then sat down and reeled off the monotonous narrative which follows this paragraph. He never smiled, he never frowned, he never changed his voice from the gentle-flowing key to which he tuned his initial sentence, he never betrayed the slightest suspicion of enthusiasm; but all through the interminable narrative there ran a vein of impressive earnestness and sincerity, which showed me plainly that, so far from his imagining that there was anything ridiculous or funny about his story, he regarded it as a really important matter, and admired its two heroes as men of transcendent genius in finesse. I let him go on in his own way, and never interrupted him once.

____

3)

No little Gradgrind had ever seen a face in the moon; it was up in the moon before it could speak distinctly. No little Gradgrind had ever learnt the silly jingle, Twinkle, twinkle, little star; how I wonder what you are! No little Gradgrind had ever known wonder on the subject, each little Gradgrind having at five years old dissected the Great Bear like a Professor Owen, and driven Charles's Wain like a locomotive engine-driver. No little Gradgrind had ever associated a cow in a field with that famous cow with the crumpled horn who tossed the dog who worried the cat who killed the rat who ate the malt, or with that yet more famous cow who swallowed Tom Thumb: it had never heard of those celebrities, and had only been introduced to a cow as a graminivorous ruminating quadruped with several stomachs.

____

4)

What could I say, my dear Jenny? This was my wonder, with each step my wonder, though I was no closer to an answer the closer I trod. Did she hear my footsteps down the hallway, or were her tears too deafening? The sound of my heels against the bathroom floor at first were purposefully soft. Then, I suppose, I wanted her to know that I was coming, that I was there, that I wanted to be of comfort. Almost everyone goes through the grief of losing a father, but at such a young age, and newly married? To be aglow with the joy of pregnancy, but shadowed by grief, that was Jenny's experience. Now, the creak of the door gave it away, but I knew from her face that whether I was there or not carried no relevance. Comfort or discomfort, silence or noise, these things were surface level, and for Jenny, irrelevant.

____

Passage II: Social Science

5)

The accuracy of polling data in presidential races prior to World War I was a topic of significant debate and skepticism. During this era, polling methods were still in their early stages of development, and the field lacked the sophisticated techniques and technologies that would emerge later. Many polls relied on limited sample sizes and often targeted specific regions or demographics, leading to biased results. Additionally, there were challenges in obtaining accurate responses due to factors such as limited access to telephones and the reluctance of some individuals to disclose their voting preferences. As a result, the reliability of pre-World War I polling data in predicting presidential outcomes was often questionable, and there were instances where the polls failed to capture the true sentiments of the electorate.

---

6)

Discovered in the 1920's by archaeologist Sir John Marshall, Mohenjo-daro offered a remarkable glimpse into the Indus Valley Civilization, one of the world's earliest urban societies. The excavations revealed a highly advanced city that thrived around 2500 BCE, with intricate urban planning, advanced drainage systems, and well-organized houses. The discovery of this ancient site shed light on the existence of a complex and sophisticated civilization that had been previously unknown. It provided valuable insights into their social structure, trade networks, writing system, and religious practices. The findings from Mohenjo-daro have significantly contributed to our understanding of early urbanization and the development of human societies in Asia.

---

7)

But what Duckworth was saying in his notes was contrary to my experience. Both of us had lived through the Great Depression, and despite his relationship with Smoot (or perhaps because of it) few journalists cared to question his economic authority; if he declared it to be true, it simply must be the case. However, many are forgetting that the protectionist policies laid out by the Smoot-Hawley Tariff Act did not live up to its promises and, in my experience, exacerbated the Depression. Simplistic economic minds will point here or there for the one root cause, the domino that launched the worst economic downturn the world has ever known. But I know, and history will prove me correct, that there is no one cause, but many causes. The fire had started by 1930, but the Smoot-Hawley bill was not the water all had hoped for but was more like, mark my words, *lighter fluid.*

---

8)

Cleopatra, the legendary queen of Egypt, possessed a captivating personality and a distinct style of rule. Known for her intelligence, charm, and charisma, Cleopatra was a skilled diplomat and a master of political intrigue. She utilized her wit and beauty to forge alliances and maintain her grip on power. Cleopatra was renowned for her eloquence and linguistic abilities, speaking several languages fluently, which allowed her to communicate with foreign dignitaries and establish strong connections. She was also a patron of the arts and embraced the luxurious lifestyle associated with her position, using grand gestures and opulent displays to reinforce her authority. Cleopatra's rule was marked by her determination to protect Egypt's independence and her unwavering commitment to the welfare of her people. Though her reign was not without controversy and conflicts, Cleopatra's unique blend of intelligence, charisma, and political acumen made her a legendary figure in history.

Passage III: Humanities

9)

While Kierkegaard admired Hegel's intellectual prowess and acknowledged his significant contributions to philosophy, he vehemently disagreed with Hegelianism and became one of its fiercest critics. Kierkegaard's philosophy focused on the individual's subjective experience, emphasizing personal choice, faith, and the importance of individual existence. In contrast, Hegel's philosophy emphasized the collective and sought to uncover universal truths through the dialectical process. Kierkegaard rejected Hegel's systematic approach, arguing that it neglected the essential aspects of human existence and the subjective experience of individuals.

---

10)

Chef Corte tells me that prior to the introduction of the tomato into Italy, the flavor profiles of Italian food leaned towards simplicity, relying on a combination of basic ingredients and traditional cooking techniques. Italian cuisine was characterized by its emphasis on fresh and seasonal ingredients, such as herbs, vegetables, legumes, grains, and meats. Flavors were often derived from aromatic herbs like basil, rosemary, and oregano, along with the use of olive oil and regional cheeses. Traditional pasta dishes, risottos, and roasted meats showcased the natural flavors of the ingredients and were enhanced by simple seasonings. While Italian cuisine had a diverse range of regional specialties, the absence of the tomato meant that the cuisine was less reliant on the sweet and tangy notes that it would later bring, resulting in a more subdued and herbaceous flavor profile. In reply, I tell him that one simple dish, his *branzino* (European sea bass pan fried in olive oil, seasoned with fresh herbs) is the reason why I recommended him for the Michelin Star.

---

11)

Jackson Pollock's most famous piece of art is undoubtedly "No. 5, 1948," an iconic painting that has become synonymous with his revolutionary style of abstract expressionism. Created in 1948, the artwork measures approximately 8 feet by 4 feet and is composed of drips, splatters, and swirls of paint on a canvas laid on the floor. "No. 5, 1948" showcases Pollock's signature "drip painting" technique, where he would energetically fling and pour paint onto the canvas using various tools, including brushes, sticks, and even syringes. The painting is dominated by a bold and dynamic composition, with a web of interlacing lines and energetic splashes of black, white, gray, brown, and vibrant hues of yellow and red. It is an embodiment of Pollock's spontaneous and intuitive approach, conveying a sense of movement and rhythm that pulls viewers into a whirlwind of emotions and sensations. "No. 5, 1948" represents Pollock's groundbreaking departure from traditional forms of painting and his exploration of the expressive potential of abstract art, leaving an indelible mark on the art world and solidifying his status as one of the most influential artists of the 20th century.

---

12)

Michelangelo signed the Pieta, his renowned sculpture depicting the Virgin Mary cradling the body of Jesus, despite it being an unusual practice for him to sign his works. The reason is believed to be connected to the mistaken attribution of the sculpture to another artist, which caused Michelangelo great frustration. According to accounts, when the Pieta was unveiled, some viewers incorrectly credited the work to another sculptor, Cristoforo Solari, who was renowned for his funerary monuments and sepulchral work. In response, Michelangelo discreetly carved his own signature on the sash running across the Virgin Mary's chest, which reads "MICHAELA[N]GELUS BONAROTUS FLORENTINUS FACIEBAT" (Michelangelo Buonarroti, Florentine, made this). By doing so, Michelangelo sought to assert his authorship and dispel any confusion regarding the true artist behind the remarkable masterpiece.

Passage IV: Natural Science

13)

The process of producing parmesan cheese begins with the addition of specific starter cultures, such as Lactobacillus and Streptococcus, to the milk. These cultures initiate the fermentation process by converting lactose, a sugar present in milk, into lactic acid. The increasing acidity helps coagulate the milk proteins, primarily casein, forming a gel-like mass known as curd. The curd is then cut into small granules, allowing the whey, a liquid portion, to separate. The curds are heated and stirred, promoting further whey expulsion. Afterwards, the curds are molded into specific forms and placed in a brine solution to enhance their flavor and texture. Following this, the cheese wheels are aged for an extended period, typically ranging from 12 to 36 months. During this maturation process, various biochemical reactions occur, including proteolysis, lipolysis, and lactose fermentation. These reactions contribute to the development of Parmesan's distinct flavor profile, as proteins are broken down into smaller peptides and amino acids, fats are metabolized, and lactose is converted into lactic acid. Ultimately, the intricate interplay of enzymes, microorganisms, and chemical reactions during the cheese making process gives rise to the characteristic taste, aroma, and texture of Parmesan cheese.

---

14)

Now class, before you pour the vinegar into the volcano, let me break it all down for you scientifically. Vinegar, which is an acidic solution containing acetic acid, reacts with baking soda, scientifically known as sodium bicarbonate. The reaction between the two involves an acid-base neutralization process. Acetic acid, as an acid, donates a proton (H+) to the bicarbonate ion (HCO3-) present in baking soda. This proton transfer results in the formation of water (H2O) and carbonic acid (H2CO3). However, carbonic acid is unstable and rapidly decomposes into carbon dioxide (CO2) and water. The effervescence you observe during this reaction is the release of carbon dioxide gas bubbles. The bubbling and fizzing are due to the rapid production of carbon dioxide gas. So, when vinegar and baking soda combine, you witness an exciting transformation involving acid-base neutralization, leading to the generation of carbon dioxide gas and water. Any questions about that before we begin?

---

15)

The systemic heart, located at the base of the octopus's body, pumps oxygenated blood to the various organs and tissues. In contrast, the gill hearts are responsible for pumping deoxygenated blood to the gills, where oxygen exchange occurs. This separation of oxygenated and deoxygenated blood within distinct circulatory pathways enhances oxygen uptake and delivery, enabling octopuses to thrive in the marine environment. The systemic heart receives oxygenated blood from the gills through the aorta, distributing it throughout the body via a network of blood vessels. The deoxygenated blood from the body is collected and further pumped to the gills for oxygenation. Meanwhile, the gill hearts facilitate the flow of blood across the delicate gill tissues, promoting efficient gas exchange. This intricate arrangement of hearts and circulatory pathways ensures a constant supply of oxygenated blood to the octopus's highly active organs, enabling them to exhibit impressive locomotion, cognitive abilities, and adaptability to diverse ecological niches.

---

16)

Tornado dissipation can occur through several mechanisms, ultimately leading to the cessation of its damaging effects. One primary factor is the disruption of the tornado's inflow of warm, moist air. As the tornado moves over cooler or drier air masses, the availability of this necessary energy source diminishes, weakening the storm. Additionally, friction between the tornado and the Earth's surface can also play a role in its demise. The roughness of the terrain can impede the inflow of air into the tornado, hindering its sustenance. Another significant factor is the interaction with larger-scale atmospheric conditions. For instance, if a tornado encounters a stable layer of air above it, known as a capping inversion, it can prevent the updraft necessary for the tornado to persist. Furthermore, wind shear, the change in wind speed and direction with height, can disrupt the rotational motion within the tornado, leading to its dissipation.

Annotating Practice - Possible Answers

Below are possible Passage Map summaries of the above paragraphs. I don't claim to have the perfect answers here; the question for you is this: did *you* write a main-idea-summary of the paragraph in the margin? It doesn't matter if it perfectly correlates to what I write here, what matters is that if you had a question that required you to find a detail about the function of the gill heart of an octopus, for example, would you know to go looking in paragraph 15, based on what you wrote in the margins? To give you an idea as to the kind of annotations that might be good for the above 16 paragraphs, here is a list:

Passage I: Literary Narrative

1) "W visits though cold" - In other words, Mr. Woodhouse makes a visit (it doesn't say in this one paragraph exactly where he is going) to see someone, but the paragraph seems to focus on the fact that he is oblivious or ignoring the cold weather and imminent snow.

2) "Serious Simon about to tell story" - This may be bordering on being a bit wordy, but you get the idea. Some man named Simon is about to tell a story to the narrator, and he is very serious and straightforward about telling the tale.

3) "Little G's only study" - This is, quite literally, the first thing that came to my mind. Is it perfect? I do not know, but it sums up the main idea of the paragraph, which is that the "little Gradgrinds" (whoever they are) study too much or are taught too much and never have child-like experiences.

4) "Wants to comfort sad Jenny" - This paragraph is told from the point of view of a man, who wants to somehow comfort his wife, Jenny, who has just lost her father. There are many other ways, I believe, to summarize the main idea of this paragraph.

Passage II: Social Science

5) "Prob's with polls" - In more detail, this paragraph speaks to the problem with collecting accurate polling data prior to World War I. Again, the purpose of this initial reading isn't for you to remember every reason why; most of those reasons will be unnecessary. The more important question is whether or not you know where to look if a question requires you to.

6) “M-d → complex civ” - In other words, I am summarizing here the idea that the Mohenjo-daro (M-d) excavation shed light on or led to (thus, the arrow) the complex Indus Valley Civilization.

7) “SHTA bad” - In other words, the Smoot-Hawley Tariff Act was bad for the economy and fueled the fire of the Great Depression. This annotation or summary may seem extremely simplistic, but that is the purpose. Again, the point is this: if I had a question on the ACT about the reality of the Smoot-Hawley Tariff Act, would I know where to look?

8) “Cleo’s ruling style +” - The main idea of this paragraph is to summarize the ruling style of Cleopatra; I added a plus-sign to the end of it to indicate that the paragraph presents her in an almost entirely positive light.

Passage III: Humanities

9) “K int. X H coll.” - In other words, Kierkegaard’s interior approach or focus on experience (“K int.”) was very much opposed or against (“X”) Hegel’s focus on the collective (“H coll.”) or greater society. Remember, these letters and abbreviations only have to make sense for a brief time (just under 9 minutes to be exact) before you simply move on to the next passage.

10) “Ital. food bef. tomato” - This one, I think, speaks for itself. The main idea of this particular paragraph is what Italian food looked like before (“bef.”) the introduction of the tomato into Italy.

11) “About No. 5 - most famous” - The main idea of this paragraph, or the main focus, is “No. 5”, which is Jackson Pollock’s most famous work of art. If you were asked a question about the making of this piece of art, or why it embodies Pollock’s style, etc., this annotation would help you know exactly where to look.

12) “Why M. signed Pieta” - In other words, the main idea of this paragraph is to explain why Michelangelo signed the Pieta, certainly one of his most famous works of art.

Passage IV: Natural Science

13) “Parm. chem. process” - The ACT Natural Science passage can get very technical and scientific. While reading these things, it is important to avoid being snared or snagged by each and every detail. Again, what is important is this: if/when you are asked about the chemical process of making parmesan cheese, do you know where to look to find the answer?

14) "Chem of vin. + b. soda" - In other words, this paragraph is about the chemistry of combining vinegar and baking soda (which are the common ingredients in the classic volcano science experiment).

15) "Octo. hearts/gills" - In other words, this passage is mainly about the octopus's three hearts and its gills, and the way these work together to help the octopus to live/thrive in its environment in unique ways.

16) "How torn's stop" - In other words, this paragraph is about the various factors that can make a tornado slow down or stop.

Again, your Passage Map annotations that you made for paragraphs 1-16 probably do not match mine, and that is OK. What is important for you is *not* to be sucked in or snared by every single detail as you read. To take paragraph 16 for example, you don't need to memorize on the first read through the passage every single factor that can slow down or stop a tornado. As has been said many times thus far, the key is this: when you are asked a question about the factors that slow down tornadoes, do you know where to look to find the correct answer AND have you given yourself enough time to do so?

This can not be stressed enough: most of the answers are *there*, in the passage, waiting to be plucked out or reasoned to. This process takes time. Active reading or quick reading with annotating guarantees that you will maximize your time on the 40 questions and thus maximize your ACT Reading score.

Practice Passage #1

Now is the time to put into practice what you have learned thus far with an actual full-length practice passage, which mimics that which you'll see on ACT day. Your instructions are to follow these steps:

1) Set a timer for 8 minutes and 45 seconds. Begin reading when you start the timer.

2) Active read each paragraph, paying attention NOT to details necessarily, but to the main idea of each individual paragraph.

3) After reading a paragraph, annotate the 1-5 word summary in the margins right next to it.

4) After reading and annotating the entire passage, you should have most of your time to answer the questions. Do so until the timer is up!

Passage II

SOCIAL SCIENCE: This is an original passage about the agrarian economy of Ancient Egypt.

Until the Persian Invasion (525 BCE) introduced a cash economy into Ancient Egypt, the economy of this kingdom was an agrarian barter system, and the Nile River was its lifeblood. The river brought water and fertile soil to the cultivated fields each year, as the seasonal floods began in September. It was during these times of growth that the kingdom carried out the construction of most temples, including the Giza pyramid complex. Quarries supplied the limestone, and foreign trade supplied slaves and other minerals, but the production and redistribution of food to laborers and overseers drove the economy and brought the massive project to completion.

From the Predynastic Period (6000 – 3150 BCE) to the end of Roman Egypt (646 CE), laborers (most of whom worked the fields, while others attended to the temples, fished, or made pottery) were paid in rations and other goods. Several historical accounts mention daily food rations of bread, beer, and sometimes fish given to laborers. This could be given to individuals, but a larger allotment was given to families. For example, ten loaves of bread and two jugs of beer were given to family units, and while the amount of daily rations given to individuals depended on their status, some received less than one loaf of bread a day. Persons of higher status, such as the heads of estates, often received meat and other goods that were not available to the lower classes. In addition to these daily rations, people also received supplemental "grain wages" weekly or monthly.

The Egyptologist Toby Wilkinson describes how food was collected and redistributed under the agrarian economy: "A certain proportion went directly to state workshops for the manufacture of secondary products—for example, tallow and leather from cattle; pork from pigs; linen from flax; bread, beer, and basketry from grain. Some of these value-added products were then traded and exchanged at a profit, producing further government income; others were redistributed as payment to state employees, thereby funding the court and its projects." Taxes were paid in the form of goods produced by laborers, but only the heads of estates delivered the revenues and the surplus food to the central administration, which was led by the pharaoh. The royal residence and provincial administration centers parsed the surplus of food out to the rest of the population.

During the times of the Old Kingdom (2686 – 2181 BCE), priests of the mortuary cults owned large tracts of land exempt from taxes. Although the king was recognized as the official steward of all lands and owned much of the land, both king and priest were allowed to trade. But for the most part, the food produced on farms along the Nile River was sent to the capital, where it was redistributed through centers or used for trading with other nations. In the funerary temples, food was redistributed to the attendants from the temple offerings. When the Middle Kingdom began, more of Egypt's land, food and tombs came under the private ownership of families and estates instead of the central administration. Despite this, workers were still paid in the same way, with daily rations and grain wages.

Despite laborers being "paid" in rations, slaves were very much a part of Ancient Egypt's economy. The construction of Egyptian pyramids powered the economy, but resulted in massive transfer of wealth to the central administration and Pharaoh in particular, and the labor power and welfare of the slaves subsidized the cost of construction. Because many of the field laborers were slaves, the masters transferred the income (i.e. goods) produced by them to the wealthy without an actual increase in income. Laborers were forced to work during a period of each year that followed the ebb and flow of the Nile River (often 10 months). Soldiers were conscripted from the same pool of slaves, and travelled outside Egypt to gather minerals not found in the kingdom (e.g. copper, hardwood), whether through trade or conquest. Aside from provisions, corvée laborers were given shelter, but received few goods other than food staples.

Although money was not used until the Persian Invasion, the kingdom of Ancient Egypt denoted the value of goods based on a unit of weight: the deben. For measuring fair exchanges, stones of a set weight were placed on one end of a balance beam, and the traded good was set on the other end. Prior to the New Kingdom (1550 – 1069 BCE), deben of various materials and weights were utilized; King Userkaf, for example, possessed a gold deben. By the dawning of the New Kingdom, a copper deben became the standard, weighing approximately 91 grams.

As more silver came to Egypt from trade with the Mediterranean region, and as more gold came from the conquered region of Nubia (modern-day Sudan), more expensive goods were known to be priced based on silver or gold deben, with proportionate changes in value. For laborers, a day's work could also be valued with deben; thus the aforementioned amount of rations to be paid out would be weighted on a scale to balance with the appropriate number of deben.

11. Which of the following statements best describes how the passage characterizes the relationship between the economies of Ancient Egypt and other nations?

    A. The passage suggests that nations and societies beyond the borders of Egypt had equal or greater influence within Egypt as the Pharaoh himself.
    B. The passage characterizes Ancient Egypt as more isolated than other societies, but still open to trade and relationship outside of its borders.
    C. The passage makes it clear that the economy of Ancient Egypt relied on a system of currency, whereas other nations were mostly agrarian.
    D. The passage implies that Ancient Egypt's economy was primarily pescatarian (its laborers mostly fished the Nile River), whereas other nations relied on an almost entirely agrarian economy.

12. The primary function of the fifth paragraph (lines 61-78) is to:

F. highlight the various roles of slaves in the ebb and flow of the economy of Ancient Egypt.
G. create feelings of sympathy in the reader regarding the plight of slaves in Ancient Egypt.
H. emphasize the military might of Ancient Egypt, powered mostly by slaves-turned-soldiers.
J. describe the circumstances leading up to the slaves' painstaking decision between shelter or food.

13. In the passage, the author mentions that one factor that could determine the amount and type of rations given to an individual might be:

A. height and weight.
B. gender.
C. status.
D. age.

14. In the context of the passage, the quote from Toby Wilkinson (lines 32-40) primarily serves to:

F. describe the numbers of laborers directly effected by food shortages year in and year out.
G. demonstrate the effects of Pharaoh's whims on the everyday lives of laboring Egyptians.
H. illustrate the cycle of food products through the Egyptian economy.
J. illustrate the role that food played in Egypt's becoming a cash economy.

15. As it is used in line 76, the word corvée most likely means:

A. overwhelmed or depressed.
B. forced or unpaid.
C. rich or sumptuous.
D. overvalued or overhyped.

16. The passage most strongly suggests that the growth of the Egyptian economy was periodic as opposed to steady because:

F. the agrarian economy depended far too much on unskilled laborers.
G. the flooding of Nile River would annually deliver fertile soil good for farming.
H. heavy snowfall in the winter killed crops and animals.
J. taxes imposed by Pharaoh ebbed and flowed and were hardly consistent.

17. Which of the following questions is most directly answered by the passage?

A. Why is the agrarian economy of Ancient Egypt ultimately traceable to the Persian Invasion in 525 BCE?
B. What were the fundamental reasons for why families were allotted greater portions in Ancient Egypt than individual laborers?
C. What is the relationship between the deben and the economy of Egypt during Roman occupation?
D. How did the economy of Ancient Egypt function if there was no currency in place within the country?

18. It can most reasonably be inferred from the passage that:

F. meat and fish were often rationed to laborers because they were less valuable and more available than grain or beer.
G. Pharaoh and his priests were allowed to trade freely in Ancient Egypt because they, unlike laborers, were trustworthy and educated.
H. soldiers were taken from the slave population because the soldier was less likely to make a temple offering than aristocrats or government employees.
J. inaccurate deben or deben scales could lead to unjust rationing for Egypt's laborers.

19. According to the passage, laborers in Ancient Egypt would receive rations consisting of:

A. bread, grain, and sometimes fish.
B. bread, meat, and sometimes beer.
C. fish, beer, and sometimes grain.
D. fish, grain, and sometimes meat.

20. The passage indicates that some laborers would receive 10 loaves of bread and 2 jugs of beer because:

F. they had an elevated status compared to the everyday, individual laborer.
G. their ancestors had courted favor from Pharaoh.
H. they had families and more mouths to feed.
J. they had, by their examples, proven effective in motivating other laborers to work harder.

Post-Passage Reflection

The answers to this practice passage can be found on the next page (and full explanations to each question as well as a possible Passage Map can be found at the back of the book beginning on page 611), but before checking your answers, think through these questions:

- Was I able to active read effectively, or did I get "snagged" on details along the way?

- Did I leave myself enough time to answer the questions well by active reading?

- Did I run out of time?

- Was I fairly confident in my answer choices?

- How many questions did I guess on because I was almost out of time?

Now, check your answers on the next page and move on to Step 2.

Step 1 Correct Answers

Passage II:
11: B
12: F
13: C
14: H
15: B
16: G
17: D
18: J
19: A
20: H

Stumped on any? You can find the explanations for this passage and a possible Passage Map beginning on page 611.

STEP 2

Micro and Medium Level Questions

In the introduction to ACT Reading, just prior to Step 1, I introduced what I call the three types of ACT Reading questions: micro, medium, and macro. If you're not familiar with the terms, 'micro' means small, and 'macro' means big (medium, of course, being between the two). These three categories or question types refer to how much information you need to reference, read over, or have a knowledge of in order to get the question correct.

Before I break down why I have a step in *The ACT Reading System* dedicated to micro and medium level questions, a word about what I *won't* be doing. Other ACT prep books break down ACT Reading questions into up to a dozen different "types," such as "Cause and Effect" and "Generalizations" and on and on and on. However, I see no value, whatsoever, in your spending time memorizing all of these categories of questions and the types of questions that can be asked within each. Here is what matters to me: *how can you get this question correct and, if possible, where can you find the correct answer?*

In my research of ACT Reading tests, I have found that the percentage of my 3 question categories can be broken down as such:

A) Macro questions - 15 to 18% of all questions on the ACT Reading test are *macro*, which means that, in order to get them correct, you will need to reference or have an understanding of the passage as a whole (or possibly almost the entirety of the passage). Questions of this type ask for the main purpose of a passage or the change in a character or place from beginning to end, etc.

These types of questions are NOT the focus of this step, so I am glossing over them now. You will learn more and practice them in a more targeted way in Step 4 (beginning on page 341).

B) Micro questions - 40 to 45% of all questions on the ACT Reading test are *micro*, which means that, in order to get them correct, you will need to reference or reread only 1 or 2 sentences in the passage itself. Sometimes, this means providing a synonym for a word, other times it means finding a specific detail, and other times it means finding a cause for a given effect.

Below is an example pair of micro questions about a paragraph you have already read and annotated in the practice from Step 1. Because this paragraph would hypothetically come from a Humanities passage (Passage III on the ACT Reading test), the questions themselves are in the 20's (#21 and #22).

Chef Corte tells me that prior to the introduction of the tomato into Italy, the flavor profiles of Italian food leaned towards simplicity, relying on a combination of basic ingredients and traditional cooking techniques. Italian cuisine was characterized by its emphasis on fresh and seasonal ingredients, such as herbs, vegetables, legumes, grains, and meats. Flavors were often derived from aromatic herbs like basil, rosemary, and oregano, along with the use of olive oil and regional cheeses. Traditional pasta dishes, risottos, and roasted meats showcased the natural flavors of the ingredients and were enhanced by simple seasonings. While Italian cuisine had a diverse range of regional specialties, the absence of the tomato meant that the cuisine was less reliant on the sweet and tangy notes that it would later bring, resulting in a more subdued and herbaceous flavor profile. In reply, I tell him that one simple dish, his *branzino* (European sea bass pan fried in olive oil, seasoned with fresh herbs) is the reason why I recommended him for the Michelin Star.

21. According to the passage, which of the following dishes would Chef Corte consider to be traditional Italian?

A. pizza topped with sardines and rosemary.
B. risotto seasoned with oregano and cheese.
C. veal smothered in herbacious tomato sauce.
D. lamb and pear, both sprinkled with cheese.

22. The author indicates that the introduction of the tomato into Italy and Italian cuisine:

F. simplified the overall flavor profile.
G. created a more subdued flavor profile.
H. resulted in a permanent loss of traditional flavors.
J. meant more reliance on sweet and tangy notes.

The correct answer for number 21 is B. Notice how, in order to get this question correct, you need to reference a couple of sentences, but no more. While it's possible to get this question correct without going back and finding the correct answer (this could be something you happen to remember when first reading the passage), it is much more likely that you will have to go hunting for the correct answer.

The correct answer for number 22 is J. Again, to get this question correct, you need to reference only a small portion of this paragraph (specifically, the second to last sentence), which says, "the absence of the tomato meant that the cuisine was less reliant on the sweet and tangy notes..."

C) Medium questions - 40 to 45% of all questions on the ACT Reading test are *medium*, which means that, in order to get them correct, you will need to reference, reread, analyze, or come to an understanding of 3 sentences to 1 full paragraph (or maybe 2) of information. Questions of this type range from asking you for the main purpose of a paragraph to understanding the role of a character or event in the overall passage to making an inference based on information given in a paragraph.

Below is an example pair of *medium* questions about a paragraph you have already read and annotated in the practice from Step 1. Because this paragraph would hypothetically come from a Natural Science passage (Passage IV on the ACT Reading test), the questions themselves are in the 30's (#33 and #34).

The systemic heart, located at the base of the octopus's body, pumps oxygenated blood to the various organs and tissues. In contrast, the gill hearts are responsible for pumping deoxygenated blood to the gills, where oxygen exchange occurs. This separation of oxygenated and deoxygenated blood within distinct circulatory pathways enhances oxygen uptake and delivery, enabling octopuses to thrive in the marine environment. The systemic heart receives oxygenated blood from the gills through the aorta, distributing it throughout the body via a network of blood vessels. The deoxygenated blood from the body is collected and further pumped to the gills for oxygenation. Meanwhile, the gill hearts facilitate the flow of blood across the delicate gill tissues, promoting efficient gas exchange. This intricate arrangement of hearts and circulatory pathways ensures a constant supply of oxygenated blood to the octopus's highly active organs, enabling them to exhibit impressive locomotion, cognitive abilities, and adaptability to diverse ecological niches.

33. The third paragraph (lines 41-60) marks a shift in the focus of the passage from:

A. the evolutionary disadvantages facing the octopus to the ways it combats such disadvantages.
B. the respiratory system of the octopus to its endocrine system.
C. the circulatory system of the octopus to the unique functions of its other organs.
D. the role of deoxygenated blood in the body of the octopus to the role of oxygenated blood.

34. Which of the following statements best summarizes the process by which the octopus delivers oxygen to its muscles and tissues for survival in the marine environment?

F. Blood travels through the aorta to the gill hearts, then to the gills, then to the systemic heart, then throughout the body.
G. Blood travels from the gill hearts to the gills, then to the systemic heart through the aorta, then throughout the body.
H. Blood travels from the systemic heart through the aorta to the gills, where blood is oxygenated and sent through gill hearts to the rest of the body.
J. Blood travels from the gill hearts through the aorta to the systemic heart, where it is sent on to the gills for oxygenization before being dispersed.

The correct answer for number 33 is C. Of course, you are a bit limited in your answer since you can't reference the paragraph immediately following this one, but you get enough from the paragraph itself, the last sentence of which ends speaking about the organs of the octopus.

The correct answer for number 34 is G. This kind of question is asking you, in essence, to summarize the paragraph as a whole (or at least more than half of the paragraph). Only choice G has the blood of the octopus traveling the correct route throughout the body based on the paragraph as a whole.

Summing Up

The reasons a focus on micro and medium level questions is featured in this step, Step 2, are these:

First, and quite simply, questions of these types together make up at least 85% of each and every ACT Reading test.

Second, the 5-step process for getting these questions correct builds off of your ability to active read. Essentially, the process is this: 1) Read the question; 2) Think about it; 3) Reference the Passage Map to figure out where to find the answer; 4) Find the correct answer by rereading; 5) Read through the answer choices and find a match.

This 5-step process, as you can tell and experienced with the practice passage at the end of Step 1, *takes time*. The more time you dedicate to this process on ACT day, the more likely you are to get the questions correct. It is that simple.

The Following Practice Passages

In the practice passages that follow, the first passage (called Passage III, in other words, a Humanities passage) features *entirely micro questions*, the second passage (called Passage IV, in other words, a Natural Science passage) features *entirely medium questions*, and finally, the final passage (called Passage I, in other words, a Literary Narrative passage) features *a mix of both*. This kind of featured practice ought to help you work on and identify areas of struggle moving forward. But, more importantly, hopefully this kind of passage trains you into the 5-step process above; after all, 85% of the ACT Reading questions depend on it!

For each test, one at a time, set a timer for 8 minutes and 45 seconds, active read and annotate, and answer the questions to the best of your ability. Answers can be found on page 329, but possible Passage Maps and explanations begin on page 614.

Micro Questions Only

The following passage (Passage III, Humanities, numbers 21-30) features only micro questions.

Set the timer to 8:45, remove distractions, take a deep breath, and begin.

Passage III

HUMANITIES: This passage is adapted from the book *Basquiat: A Tribute* (©2019 by Robert Cliff-Hayes).

Born in 1960 to a Haitian father and a Puerto Rican mother, artist Jean-Michel Basquiat grew up in the cultural melting pot of New York City. A precocious child, Basquiat showed an early interest in the art world, making frequent trips to New York's Metropolitan Museum of Art (MoMa), where he was especially enamored by Pablo Picasso's *Guernica*, a macabre cubist masterpiece that depicted the horrors of the Spanish Civil War. At seven years old, Basquiat was hospitalized after an automobile accident, and he spent hours poring over the classic medical textbook *Gray's Anatomy*, in which he saw intricate images of the human form that would play a lasting influence on his work.

In high school, Basquiat became active in New York City's burgeoning 1970's graffiti subculture, collaborating with schoolmate Al Diaz under the alias "SAMO©" (pronounced same-oh). The pair produced anti-consumerist, satirical slogans under the SAMO© moniker, like "SAMO©...4 THE SO-CALLED AVANT-GARDE" and "SAMO©...4 MASS MEDIA MINDWASH" in what art critic Jeffrey Deitch would dub "disjointed street poetry."

It was just after this period that Basquiat became acquainted with Andy Warhol, an artist who would have a long-lasting impact on his career and aesthetic vision. Warhol was already a well-known name in the art world and beyond, having established himself during the pop art movement of the 1960s. Like Basquiat, Warhol had a style that was suffused with references to popular and consumer culture.

Soon, Basquiat began frequenting one of Warhol's favorite haunts, the Mudd Club, a night club in New York's TriBeCa neighborhood that attracted the most flamboyant celebrities of the 1980's, including David Byrne and Madonna, lending him access to the figures at the forefront of pop culture and alternative art. Still, this world was at least partially alien if not entirely foreign to the young artist, who struggled with homelessness and poverty.

For money, Basquiat sold postcard-sized drawings and hand-painted sweatshirts on the streets of New York, making at most a few dollars per sale. However, on the advice of his new acquaintances from the Mudd Club, particularly up-and-coming art curator Diego Cortez, Basquiat decided to transition from graffiti to canvas-based art.

Cortez took an active role in promoting Basquiat, arranging for him to be featured in a 1981 art show called "New York/New Wave" held at the P.S.1 Contemporary Art Center, then the epicenter of New York's alternative art movement. The show marked Basquiat's first exposure to major art dealers and curators, and the artist created a sensation with childlike, cartoony renderings of car crashes, airplanes, and crowns, accompanied by nonsensical text that paid homage to SAMO©. "Jean-Michel was the person in all the huge number of artists who stood out. I hadn't seen anything like it for ten years," P.S.1 founder Alanna Heiss would later recall.

During this period, Basquiat also began working on what would become one of his most recognizable pieces, an untitled work commonly referred to as *Skull*. Inspired by the *Gray's Anatomy* textbook that had fascinated him in his childhood, the evocative, vibrant painting is at once reminiscent of the X-ray of a head and a traditional African mask, referencing Basquiat's Afro-Caribbean heritage. Towards the edges of the canvas, disjointed, incoherent lettering alludes to the artist's SAMO© period. The work became the first of Basquiat's paintings to appear inside a gallery, marking a turning point in his career.

Before long, Basquiat's canvasses began to sell for $5,000 to $10,000, and the demand surpassed his ability to keep up. The artist had found success within the alternative art scene and among commercial art dealers, but he had yet to find acceptance within the art establishment—especially among the museum curators who reigned as tastemakers. That all changed in 1983, when Basquiat, just 22, became one of the youngest artists ever to be included in the Whitney Museum of American Art's prestigious Biennial Exhibition, traditionally considered the high water mark for acceptance among the arts elite.

In the mid-1980s, Basquiat's relationship with Andy Warhol deepened, and the two collaborated on a show called *Warhol & Basquiat: Paintings*. Although the opening night was packed, critical reviews were overwhelmingly negative. Warhol had long faced criticism for being too overtly commercial in his work. Now Basquiat became a target as well. Vivien Raynor, the New York Times art critic, wrote of the exhibition: "the social comment implicit in [Basquiat's] previous work has now become obvious and rather silly."

The untimely fallout from the exhibit frayed the relationship between the two artists. Tragically, no rapprochement was forthcoming, as both faced untimely deaths in the several years that followed the exhibit. Today, however, *Warhol & Basquiat: Paintings* is considered a milestone for both, but Basquiat especially: the street artist who rose from homelessness to prestige.

21. Based on the passage, the main reason that Basquiat became a target of criticism was primarily:

A. his collaborative show with Andy Warhol.
B. the fact that he lost touch with his SAMO© roots.
C. the childlike, cartoony nature of much of his art.
D. his failure to attend the Biennial Exhibition in person.

22. In the passage, the phrase *partially alien* (line 37) most nearly refers to:

F. the feeling of inadequacy that Basquiat felt upon entering the TriBeCa neighborhood.
G. Basquiat's surprising unfamiliarity with Andy Warhol, a relatively famous artist.
H. the social and economic difference between Basquiat and other artistic celebrities.
J. the difficulty for Basquiat to transition from graffiti to canvas art.

23. Which of the following words is most nearly given a negative connotation in the passage?

A. Medical (line 11)
B. Advice (line 43)
C. Target (line 89)
D. Rose (line 99)

24. Which of the following actions referred to in the passage most clearly characterizes a significant change in the life and career of Jean-Michel Basquiat?

F. "Produced" (line 17)
G. "Transition" (line 45)
H. "Alludes" (line 67)
J. "Faced" (line 87)

25. In the passage, the author notes that an interesting aspect of Basquiat's frequent visits to the Metropolitan Museum of Art was that:

A. he did so at a young age.
B. he never painted graffiti on the outside walls.
C. he found no interest in more macabre art pieces.
D. he was in an automobile accident on one such visit to the museum.

26. The author directly refers to which of the following aspects of Basquiat's *Skull* as being a reference to his cultural heritage?

F. That it features incoherent lettering scribbled near the edges of the canvas
G. That it looks like a traditional African mask
H. That it looks like the X-ray of a human skull
J. That it was inspired by *Gray's Anatomy*

27. The author indicates that which element of Basquiat's art, present since his first days as an artist, had become too recurring and obvious to be considered new or groundbreaking by critics?

A. The incoherent scribblings
B. The social message
C. The pro-consumerist images
D. The anatomical references

28. In line 32, the word *haunts* is used to indicate:

F. the up and down nature of business in New York.
G. the way in which Andy Warhol entered a room.
H. a place of business that claimed to be haunted.
J. a location frequented by certain artistic persons.

29. The author indicates that the primary relationship between Basquiat's later artwork and his earlier, SAMO© graffiti art is:

A. dismissive: Basquiat forgot about his earlier art as it was reminiscent of his homelessness.
B. redundant: Basquiat did little but create updated pieces that merely mimicked his earlier work.
C. memorial; Basquiat would pay tribute to his earlier days in his later work.
D. inessential: if it weren't for frequent references to his graffiti days, Basquiat could have been famous.

30. Based on the passage, it can most reasonably be inferred that:

F. Diego Cortez deserves significant credit for Basquiat's public emergence as an artist.
G. Andy Warhol deserves most if not all of the credit for any fame that Basquiat achieved in his lifetime.
H. *Grey's Anatomy* was useful for Basquiat in passing the time after his automobile accident, but nothing more.
J. Basquiat deserves to be considered an artist at least as great if not greater than Pablo Picasso.

Medium Questions Only

The following passage (Passage IV, Natural Science, numbers 31-40) features only medium questions.

Set the timer to 8:45, remove distractions, take a deep breath, and begin.

Passage IV

NATURAL SCIENCE: This passage is adapted from the article "The Science of Spice" by Alexander Painter (©2018 by Food Science Quarterly).

Capsaicin ($C_{18}H_{27}NO_3$) is a crystalline compound found in the fruit of the genus *Capsicum* (peppers) that causes the well-known burning sensation in culinary dishes. The molar teeth of mammals can destroy pepper seeds, thus natural selection may have led to an increase in capsaicin, deterring mammals from eating them. Birds, which can better tolerate the sensation, disperse the plant as the seeds pass through their digestive tract intact.

Capsaicin can dissolve in fats and alcohol, but not in water. Its chemical structure has three components: an aromatic ring, a shorter lateral chain of hydrocarbons, and an organic amide bond that connects the two. The functional groups in capsaicin that cause chemical reactions are attached to the opposite sides of the double carbon bonds in the ring, making it a trans isomer. Since its extraction in 1876, researchers have studied how this colorless, odorless substance interacts with mammals. As capsaicin is an alkaloid, its unique effects on mammals give it potential as a medicine.

In various studies, capsaicin acts as an antioxidant, anticancer, and anti-inflammatory agent that can speed up metabolism and suppress the build-up of fat in our bodies. When applied to the skin, it has been shown to relieve chronic pain from different types of neuropathy and arthritis, as well as pain from rashes and psoriasis. Some of these effects are due to capsaicin's ability to bind to vanilloid receptor 1 (TRPV1), which is found in the sensory neurons. The hydroxyl (OH) group on the fourth position of the ring is especially important for its ability to bind to TRPV1. However this same binding action that results in relief can also bring pain. A heat-sensitive subunit of TRPV1 reacts to the binding by producing pain, inflammation, and a localized sense of heat. The effect is even more pronounced however when capsaicin is taken in orally because it is absorbed and reaches maximum concentration quicker than a topical cream.

Capsaicin belongs to a family of secondary metabolites known as capsaicinoids, and is the most abundant in this family, followed by dihydrocapsaicin as second most abundant. These are also the two most potent, and make up as much as 90% of the capsaicinoids found in chili peppers. There are over twenty in total. While they all share the three chemical components as described above, their chemical differences lie in the structure of the lateral chain. The compounds vary in the number of carbons in the chain (9-11), and in the number and position of double carbon bonds. For example, homocapsaicin and capsaicin have one double bond, while several others have none at all (such as nordihydrocapsaicin, homodihydrocapsaicin, and dihydrocapsaicin). Regardless of the compound, all are synthesized in peppers.

The enzyme capsaicin synthase produces capsaicin and its analogs by combining two chemicals: vanillylamine and fatty acid chains (formed from the amino acids valine or leucine). This reaction is called condensation. As the fruit matures, more capsaicinoids are produced until 40-50 days into fruit development, after which the concentration declines as the compounds degrade into secondary metabolites. The level of production is not fixed, as the concentration can vary with genetics and environmental factors. For example, water stress increases capsaicin levels. A certain fatty acid (8-methyl-noneic acid) is the limiting factor for how much of these compounds can be produced. Capsaicinoids are often produced in laboratory settings by adding the enzyme to chlorinated versions of the fatty acids and amines. Synthesis can also be achieved using traditional chemical methods, but is less effective. Using enzymes, the percent yield of capsaicinoids can be as high as 70%.

Capsaicinoids are not the only compounds in peppers that can bind to the TRPV1 receptors. Capsinoids can also do this, but do not interact with the heat-sensitive receptor subunit. Because of this, capsinoids (e.g. capsiate, dihydrocapsiate and nordihydrocapsiate) lack the pungency and sensory irritation of their analogues, but have the same beneficial effects as discussed above. Instead of an amide bond in the lateral chain, an ester bond at the same position, which lacks nitrogen and is more structurally flexible, holds these compounds. However, capsinoids are found in only a few varieties of peppers, and they exist in much lower concentrations than capsaicinoids. They are also more difficult to create in a laboratory setting because of a terminal methyl (CH_3) group in addition to the double oxygen bond found in both families of compounds.

31. According to paragraphs 2 and 3, the primary purpose of the extraction of capsaicin in 1876 and subsequent research is for:

A. veterinary purposes.
B. medical purposes.
C. culinary purposes.
D. topical purposes.

32. In the fourth paragraph (lines 38-53), the author most clearly:

F. argues for further research into the chemical differences between various capsaicinoids.
G. differentiates various capsaicinoids by the number and position of double carbon bonds.
H. lists and describes various capsaicinoids from least to most potent.
J. highlights both the differences between and similarities among various capsaicinoids.

33. In the third paragraph (lines 20-37), the reference to "the effect that is even more pronounced" (line 34) serves to distinguish:

A. the feeling of eating capsaicin while drinking water from the feeling of eating capsaicin within fatty foods.
B. the effect of capsaicin on inflamed muscles from the effect of capsaicin on the digestive tract.
C. the effect of capsaicin on cancerous cells in the skin from the effect of capsaicin on cancerous cells in the mouth.
D. the feeling of rubbing capsaicin on the skin from the feeling when capsaicin is consumed by mouth.

34. It can most reasonably be inferred from the passage that pepper plants with capsaicin-bearing seeds:

F. have been hindered in their spread and population growth by both birds and mammals.
G. have benefitted in their spread and population growth by both birds and mammals.
H. have mostly experienced a mutually beneficial relationship with birds, but not mammals.
J. have mostly experienced a mutually beneficial relationship with mammals, but not with birds.

35. In contrast to the way capsaicinoids are described in paragraph 6 (lines 73-88), capsinoids:

A. are less spicy and just as medically beneficial, but rarer and harder to create in a laboratory.
B. are just as medically beneficial, but more spicy, rarer, and harder to created in a laboratory.
C. are more common and easier to create in a laboratory, but are more spicy and not as medically beneficial.
D. are more common and less spicy, but are harder to create in a laboratory and not as medically beneficial.

36. Based on the passage, the application of capsaicin to the skin for pain relief would best be described as:

F. ineffective: it does not relieve pain.
G. counterproductive: it causes much pain and relieves none.
H. bittersweet: it both eliminates and causes pain.
J. effective: it eliminates all pain with no side effects.

37. The main purpose of the fifth paragraph (lines 54-72) is to:

A. describe in detail both the natural and artificial means of creating capsaicinoids.
B. compare and contrast the spice level of naturally-occurring and artificial capsaicinoids.
C. highlight peppers' fixed capabilities in the production of capsaicinoids.
D. describe in detail the function of the enzyme capsaicin synthase in the production of capsaicinoids.

38. The main idea of the second paragraph (lines 9-19) is to:

F. describe in detail the medical capabilities of capsaicin while simultaneously breaking down its chemical structure.
G. warn the reader about the potentially spicy effect of consuming capsaicin, even for medical purposes.
H. analyze the chemical structure of capsaicin and critique the modern understanding of its effect on the mammalian digestive system.
J. introduce the basics of capsaicin's chemic structure while transitioning into a discussion of its medical benefits.

39. It can most reasonably be inferred from the passage that capsaicin levels would be maximized:

A. by slightly underwatering pepper plants for the first 40 to 50 days of fruit development.
B. by slightly overwatering pepper plants for the first 40 to 50 days of fruit development.
C. by slightly underwatering pepper plants after the plant has first sprouted but before the first sign of fruit growth.
D. by slightly overwatering pepper plants after the plant has first sprouted but before the first sign of fruit growth.

40. Which of the following phrases best summarizes the family of secondary metabolites known as capsaicinoids?

F. There are more than twenty, all of which originate in peppers and have chemical differences.
G. Technically there are two (capsaicin and dihydrocapsaicin), but many chemical imitators.
H. Capsaicin and homocapsaicin feature multiple double bonds in their lateral chain.
J. Capsaicin is unique in that it is spicy due to its lateral chain structure.

Micro and Medium Questions

The following passage (Passage I, Literary Narrative, numbers 1-10) features a mixture of both micro and medium questions (everything, in other words, but macro questions).

Set the timer to 8:45, remove distractions, take a deep breath, and begin.

Passage I

LITERARY NARRATIVE: This passage is adapted from F. Scott Fitzgerald's *The Great Gatsby.*

Nick Carraway is at a house party in New York with his friend Jordan Baker, and they enter into conversation about driving after a near accident.

I began to like New York, the racy, adventurous feel of it at night, and the satisfaction that the constant flicker of men and women and machines gives to the restless eye. I liked to walk up Fifth Avenue and pick out romantic women from the crowd and imagine that in a few minutes I was going to enter into their lives, and no one would ever know or disapprove. Sometimes, in my mind, I followed them to their apartments on the corners of hidden streets, and they turned and smiled back at me before they faded through a door into warm darkness. At the enchanted metropolitan twilight I felt a haunting loneliness sometimes, and felt it in others—poor young clerks who loitered in front of windows waiting until it was time for a solitary restaurant dinner—young clerks in the dusk, wasting the most poignant moments of night and life.

Again at eight o'clock, when the dark lanes of the Forties were lined five deep with throbbing taxicabs, bound for the theatre district, I felt a sinking in my heart. Forms leaned together in the taxis as they waited, and voices sang, and there was laughter from unheard jokes, and lighted cigarettes made unintelligible circles inside. Imagining that I, too, was hurrying towards gaiety and sharing their intimate excitement, I wished them well.

For a while I lost sight of Jordan Baker, and then in midsummer I found her again. At first I was flattered to go places with her, because she was a golf champion, and everyone knew her name. Then it was something more. I wasn't actually in love, but I certainly felt a sort of tender curiosity. The bored haughty face that she turned to the world concealed something—most affectations conceal something eventually, even though they don't in the beginning—and one day I found what it was.

When we were on a house-party together up in Warwick, she left a borrowed car out in the rain with the top down, and then lied about it—and suddenly I remembered the story about her that had eluded me that night at Daisy's. At her first big golf tournament there was a row that nearly reached the newspapers—a suggestion that she had moved her ball from a bad lie in the semifinal round. The thing approached the proportions of a scandal—then died away. A caddy retracted his statement, and the only other witness admitted that he might have been mistaken. The incident and the name had remained together in my mind.

Jordan Baker instinctively avoided clever, shrewd men, and now I saw that this was because she felt safer on a plane where any divergence from a code would be thought impossible. She was incurably dishonest. She wasn't able to endure being at a disadvantage and, given this unwillingness, I suppose she had begun dealing in subterfuges when she was very young in order to keep that cool, insolent smile turned to the world and yet satisfy the demands of her hard, jaunty body.

It made no difference to me. Dishonesty in a woman is a thing you never blame deeply—I was casually sorry, and then I forgot. It was on that same house-party that we had a curious conversation about driving a car. It started because she passed so close to some workmen that our fender flicked a button on one man's coat.

"You're a rotten driver," I protested. "Either you ought to be more careful, or you oughtn't to drive at all."

"I am careful."

"No, you're not."

"Well, other people are," she said lightly.

"What's that got to do with it?"

"They'll keep out of my way," she insisted. "It takes two to make an accident."

"Suppose you met somebody just as careless as yourself."

"I hope I never will," she answered. "I hate careless people. That's why I like you."

Her grey, sun-strained eyes stared straight ahead, but she had deliberately shifted our relations, and for a moment I thought I loved her. But I am slow-thinking and full of interior rules that act as brakes on my desires, and I knew that first I had to get myself definitely out of that tangle back home. I'd been writing letters once a week and signing them: "Love, Nick," and all I could think of was how, when that certain girl played tennis, a faint moustache of perspiration appeared on her upper lip. Nevertheless there was a vague understanding that had to be tactfully broken off before I was free.

Everyone suspects himself of at least one of the cardinal virtues, and this is mine: I am one of the few honest people that I have ever known.

1. It can reasonably be inferred that how much time, if any, has passed between time spent "with Jordan Baker" (line 27) and the nights out described in paragraphs 1 and 2?

   A. None
   B. Three or four hours
   C. One or two days
   D. Weeks or months

2. Which of the following statements accurately contrasts the narrator's feelings for "that certain girl" (line 80) compared to Jordan Baker?

   F. He wants out of a relationship with Jordan Baker in favor of a new relationship with "that certain girl."
   G. He wants out of a relationship with "that certain girl" in favor of a new relationship with Jordan Baker.
   H. He wants a relationship with both without either woman finding out about the other.
   J. He wants a relationship with neither, despite being aggressively pursued by both.

3. The dialogue in line 65 reveals Baker's:

   A. scrupulous caution, even in mundane activities.
   B. deep suspicions of other people.
   C. arrogance or sense of self-importance.
   D. trust that her vast wealth will never fail her.

4. Given the narrator's description of Jordan Baker as "incurably dishonest" (line 49), it seems likely that the "row that nearly reached the newspapers":

   F. was based on a true event.
   G. was, at least partially, a fabrication.
   H. was a form of blackmail.
   J. was both invented and spread to the press by Jordan Baker herself.

5. Given the passage's opening remarks about New York City night life, the narrator can best be described as the kind of man:

   A. who is likely to end up handcuffed in the back of a police car.
   B. who strikes up conversations with everyone he encounters.
   C. who deeply longs to make his quiet life even quieter by settling down and starting a family.
   D. who enjoys the thrill of a night out on the town and the company of others who feel the same.

6. The passage states that the narrator does not blame Jordan Baker for her:

   F. selfishness.
   G. taste in music.
   H. dishonesty.
   J. poor driving.

7. Based on the passage, which of the following characteristics would Jordan Baker most desire in a future husband?

   A. Unpredictability and spontaneity.
   B. Steadiness and predictability.
   C. Shrewdness and cleverness.
   D. Dishonesty and a handsome face.

8. According to the description of him in the passage, the narrator has a talent for reading others' feelings and thoughts, an ability that allows him to conclude that Jordan Baker's face:

   F. meant that she was bored.
   G. meant that she was excited to see him.
   H. meant that she did not trust him.
   J. meant that she was hiding something.

9. As it it used in line 48, the prepositional phrase *on a plane* is used to refer to:

   A. a group of people.
   B. a mode of transportation.
   C. a flat surface.
   D. a higher level of thought.

10. Which of the following is a detail from the passage that is most indicative of Jordan Baker's character?

   F. The smiles of women before they disappear into their apartments.
   G. A mousatache of perspiration on the upper lip of a tennis player.
   H. Laughter from unheard jokes.
   J. A borrowed car with the top down left out in the rain.

Step 2 Correct Answers

Passage III (Micro):
21: A
22: H
23: C
24: G
25: A
26: G
27: B
28: J
29: C
30: F

Passage IV (Medium):
31: B
32: J
33: D
34: H
35: A
36: H
37: A
38: J
39: B
40: F

Passage I (Micro and Medium):
1: D
2: G
3: C
4: F
5: D
6: H
7: B
8: J
9: A
10: J

Stumped on any? You can find the explanations and possible Passage Maps for these three passages beginning on page 614.

STEP 3

The Paired Passage

What is the Paired Passage?

We have discussed that every ACT Reading test features four passages, each of which has ten questions that follow. That's true, but it isn't *technically* true; technically, there will be five passages, not four. This is because one of the four passages is called the Paired Passage, which means that it will consist of two smaller passages (called Passage A and Passage B). These two passages will be different, but similar; in other words, they will have different authors, and may even be about different topics, but there will be some overlap between the two (something they have in common).

For example, let's say that the Paired Passage was Passage III (the Humanities passage). Passage A may be about a folk blues musician who writes songs about his loneliness from his home in the Appalachian Mountains; Passage B might be about a woman who drives across the country writing blog posts about folk artists of all kinds. As you can see, the passages are different, but they have some overlap (in this case, folk art).

The Layout of the Questions

Those who prepare for the Paired Passage are at a significant advantage, and here are two reasons why. First, whereas most unprepared students will take a glimpse of this Paired Passage and have a case of shock and fear ("What is this? Why are there two? What do I do?"), I believe this passage to be the *easiest*, which puts your mind at ease. Second, you will know how the questions will be laid out, which is as such.

The first 3 or 4 questions will be exclusively about Passage A; the second 3 or 4 questions will be exclusively about Passage B; and the final 3 or 4 questions will be about both passages together. The questions about individual passages (in other words, the first 6 or 7 questions) will be exactly what you would expect from an ACT Reading passage. The final 3 or 4 questions, however, will be a bit different. When I say that they'll be about both, I mean they could require you to compare and contrast both passages, or identify a statement that only one of the authors would agree with, etc.

Approach and Strategy

This is one of those times that you need to practice to determine exactly how taking this Paired Passage works best for you. Either way, you will be active reading and annotating like normal, but there are two options:

Option 1 is to approach this passage and answer the questions like normal; active read both passages, answer the 10 questions, and move on.

Option 2 is to do things a bit differently. First, active read Passage A, then answer the questions about Passage A (again, the first 3 or 4 questions). Second, active read Passage B, then answer the questions about Passage B (again, the middle 3 or 4 questions). Third, answer the final 3 or 4 questions, which are about both passages together.

The Following Practice Passages

Because of the two approaches above, I have included 2 Paired Passages in a row following this Step. Although we haven't discussed or practiced them yet with any depth, these passages include macro questions (again, just bigger picture questions) as well as micro and medium questions because they are necessary to properly practice taking the Paired Passage.

Take these passages 1 at a time, as you've done throughout your ACT Reading practice so far. Set an 8 minute and 45 second timer. Take the first passage according to Option 1 above; take the second passage according to Option 2 above. Whatever feels better, stick with it from now on.

Again, my goal here is for you to get comfortable answering the kinds of questions that you will experience on ACT day. I want you to have an extreme level of confidence when you flip the page and see this Paired Passage. Let the unprepared others around you have anxiety about what they're looking at!

Passage I

LITERARY NARRATIVE: Passage A is adapted from the short story *The Dead* (1914) by James Joyce. Passage B is adapted from the book *Birth Night* (©2023 by Clare Josephs).

Passage A by James Joyce

She stopped, choking with sobs, and, overcome by emotion, flung herself face downward on the bed, sobbing in the quilt. Gabriel held her hand for a moment longer, irresolutely, and then, shy of intruding on her grief, let it fall gently and walked quietly to the window.

She was fast asleep.

Gabriel, leaning on his elbow, looked for a few moments unresentfully on her tangled hair and half-open mouth, listening to her deep-drawn breath. So she had had that romance in her life: a man had died for her sake. It hardly pained him now to think how poor a part he, her husband, had played in her life. He watched her while she slept, as though he and she had never lived together as man and wife. His curious eyes rested long upon her face and on her hair: and, as he thought of what she must have been then, in that time of her first girlish beauty, a strange, friendly pity for her entered his soul. He did not like to say even to himself that her face was no longer beautiful, but he knew that it was no longer the face for which Michael Furey had braved death.

The air of the room chilled his shoulders. He stretched himself cautiously along under the sheets and lay down beside his wife. One by one, they were all becoming shades. Better pass boldly into that other world, in the full glory of some passion, than fade and wither dismally with age. He thought of how she who lay beside him had locked in her heart for so many years that image of her lover's eyes when he had told her that he did not wish to live.

Generous tears filled Gabriel's eyes. He had never felt like that himself towards any woman, but he knew that such a feeling must be love. The tears gathered more thickly in his eyes and in the partial darkness he imagined he saw the form of a young man standing under a dripping tree. Other forms were near. His soul had approached that region where dwell the vast hosts of the dead. He was conscious of, but could not apprehend, their wayward and flickering existence. His own identity was fading out into a grey impalpable world: the solid world itself, which these dead had one time reared and lived in, was dissolving and dwindling.

Passage B by Clare Josephs

Given how removed Manuel had been from not only his family, but the traditions and religion of his family, it seemed unlikely that this loose "celebration" of *Dia de los Muertos*, or Day of the Dead, had any authenticity beyond the name. He recalled what he could remember about his father. There was not much there: a howling laugh, a reddened face, a farewell and a suppressed tear.

"Goodbye Manuel. Until we meet again, in this life or the next."

Had there been a crack in his voice on the words *meet again*?

Manuel trusted me with that detail, spurred in his mind in no small part from the alcohol in the cheap, canned margaritas we split 50-50. But there were more; Manuel had never spoken like this. He was quiet and reserved, observant and data driven, and smart as all get out. For all that, he was also a leaf blown by the wind; no direction, no desire, no passion to speak of, no future to fill; his compass, so to speak, was broken or missing.

Now, memories of the chocolate cake of his grandmother on his mother's side was made manifest. She refused to write down the recipe, he said. For her, that was a waste of time and a waste of ink. A little flour, an egg or two, some melted chocolate and an icing from sugar and cream cheese and more (and more and more!) chocolate. The person too helpless to bake such a simple cake would still be helpless with a detailed recipe in hand, she said.

His mother had tried to recreate the recipe for his birthday each and every year until he turned 18 and left for college. Now, for his birthday, he wasn't home.

"Today's your birthday?" I asked.

"Maybe," he replied. "Nobody knows for sure. Some say November 1st, some November 2nd. It was the stroke of midnight between the two." He paused. "'The boy who cracked open the day of the dead,' they would say."

I tried a loose "happy birthday," but Manuel did not hear me. He was lost in his thoughts. Was there something of his destiny tied up in his birthday? He, the boy who bridges the saints in heaven and those that long to get there in need of prayer. The sun was setting; birth-night was encroaching for this, my fairly new friend. It wasn't until ten or more minutes later, once the shadows of the bent and broken blinds crept up his chin and shadowed his face, that he finally broke the silence through the smile of a small child.

"Can I borrow some flour, and perhaps a few cups of sugar?"

1. In Passage A, as Gabriel is watching his wife as she sleeps, he is:

   A. contemplating her present and past relationships.
   B. lamenting the depth of their closeness.
   C. growing jealous of the man he used to be for her.
   D. deepening his love of her by truly seeing her for the first time in a long time.

2. Based on Gabriel's assertion in Passage A that "such a feeling must be love" (line 32), which of the following statements would most nearly describe his relationship to his wife?

   F. Gabriel and his wife only married for social and economic reasons.
   G. Gabriel and his wife share a love so deep that he would be willing to die for her.
   H. Gabriel and his wife may share attraction and connection, but something deeper is missing.
   J. Gabriel and his wife are in love, and that love is only deepening with the passage of time.

3. As it is used in line 39, the word *impalpable* most nearly means:

   A. bland.
   B. motionless.
   C. colorful.
   D. unintelligible.

4. In the ninth paragraph of Passage B (lines 79-88), the narrator's friend Manuel most clearly shifts from:

   F. wandering through young adult life with no clear sense of direction to embracing an immediate sense of purpose and meaning.
   G. drifting from one day to the next as his life falls apart around him to settling into a task that catches him off guard.
   H. thinking through each situation in meticulous detail to abandoning any sense of conscience, rules, or guidance.
   J. embracing the meaning in each moment of the day to letting go of himself in a semi-depressive way.

5. In Passage B, the quote, "Until we meet again, in this life or the next" (lines 49-50) can best be described as:

   A. a painful memory.
   B. a hopeful resolution.
   C. a pocket of wisdom.
   D. a challenging motivator.

6. In Passage B, it can most reasonably be inferred that Manuel's willingness to share memories of his ancestors is most directly caused by:

   F. the alcohol in cheap margaritas.
   G. the narrator's prodding questions.
   H. the day on which the discussion takes place.
   J. his talkative or outgoing disposition.

7. In Passage B, the author most directly indicates that the recreation of the grandmother's chocolate cake is:

   A. impossible, for even his grandmother only succeeded once.
   B. simple, despite the dozens of steps called for by the recipe.
   C. difficult, despite his grandmother's contrary opinion.
   D. possible, but much easier for females in his family line.

8. Compared to Passage A, Passage B features a main character who undergoes a change:

   F. for the better (from out of love to in love).
   G. for the better (from hopelessness to hope).
   H. for the worse (from in love to out of love).
   J. for the worse (from hope to hopelessness).

9. In contrast to the way the deceased ancestors are described and referenced in Passage B, the dead in Passage A are described as:

   A. memorable and loving.
   B. vengeful and angry.
   C. bright and glaring.
   D. incomprehensible and unclear.

10. Which of the following assertions about life is most strongly supported by details provided in both Passage A and Passage B?

   F. It is better to have loved and lost than never to have loved at all.
   G. A bold and reckless death is to be avoided, even if life becomes dull and simple.
   H. It is better to live life to the fullest, as evidenced by those who have passed on.
   J. Family traditions, even those that require considerable sacrifice, are worth the effort.

Passage III

HUMANITIES: Passage A is adapted from the book *The World's Dialects* (©2014 by Keegan K Smith). Passage B is adapted from the book *A Blend of Cultures* (©1999 by Dr. Jude Lawrence).

Passage A by Keegan K Smith

During the reign of the Catholic Monarchs Queen Isabel and King Ferdinand, the Castile dialect from the north-central part of modern-day Spain became the official language of the country. Since its spread to Latin America through colonialism, the language has evolved into many dialects, with differences in both vocabulary and grammar. The meanings of words, verb conjugations, and pronunciations between Latin American and Castilian Spanish are distinct, as are the dialects spoken among Latin American countries.

One of the clearest differences is the use of the plural form of 'you'. In Spain, the word 'vosotros' is used far more than 'ustedes'. In Latin America, the opposite is true. Both major dialects share the same word for the informal form (tú), as well as the singular formal form of 'you' (usted). However the word 'vos' is used instead of 'tú' in Argentina, Paraguay, and Uruguay. Outside of these nations, the word is seldom used aside for close friends or for those of certain social classes. For direct object pronouns that are male, Latin American nations use 'lo' while those in Spain use 'le', the latter of which is an indirect object pronoun in Latin America.

Verb conjugations largely follow the same linguistic patterns, with one major exception. Contrasted with the simple past tense (e.g. "I ate"), the present perfect is used to describe a past action that continues into the present, or has happened recently (e.g. "I have eaten"). Aside from Spain, Latin American nations in the Andes Mountains prefer to use the present perfect, while other Spanish-speaking nations in the Americas (e.g. México, Costa Rica) often use the former. The conjugation between the simple past and present perfect is different. For example, infinite forms of verbs that end in –ar end instead with –ado in the present perfect.

The idea of the "Spanish lisp" is rooted in differences in pronunciation. Words that contain the letter *c* followed by the letters *e* or *i* are spoken with an 's' sound in Latin America, but in Spain it is a 'th' sound. Suffixes in Spanish can carry different meanings depending on the dialect, even if the spelling of a word is exactly the same. For example, the word 'lapicero' translates to pencil in Spain, but is a ballpoint pen in the Central American and Andes regions, and a pencil holder in Argentina. The same can be said for verbs, with some having vulgar meanings in some regions but not in others. Some vocabulary differences between Castilian and Latin American dialects are blatant, with entirely different words in Spanish referring to the same object in English. For example, the word for computer in Spain is the masculine noun (el ordenador) while it is feminine in Latin America (la computadora).

Passage B by Dr Jude Lawrence

The evolution from Latin to Spanish began when the former language was introduced to the Iberian Peninsula roughly two millennia ago. The vocabulary of indigenous peoples there merged with the language to become Vulgar Latin, which was later supplemented with thousands of Arabic words spoken by the Moors. As Queen Isabel and King Ferdinand drove them out of Spain, the monarchs used the Royal Spanish Academy to establish the 'Castellano' dialect as a uniform language in both their own country and abroad as they colonized what is now Latin America.

The Spanish language itself was used as a tool of the empire. Until the 17th century, Spanish religious officials spoke and attempted conversion in local indigenous languages. From then on until the end of the 18th century, indigenous languages were suppressed and the Spanish language was used to convert the indigenous people of the Americas to Catholicism. As the Spanish Empire neared collapse in the 19th century, bilingualism throughout Latin America prevailed. When the U.S. acquired the southwestern US from Spain, they tried to eradicate both indigenous and Spanish languages through forced schooling. While some languages and cultures were lost or nearly so, ultimately they did not succeed.

From the southwestern U.S. to Chile, many indigenous peoples still speak their language while also speaking Spanish. The identity of Mestizaje, a Latin American term for the mixing of Spanish and Indigenous cultures, came into being. To a limited extent, Spanish and Native Americans combined their bloodlines, but this was limited by the social caste system. Most of the cultural fusion came from intermarrying tribes that used Spanish as their lingua franca, a language that makes it possible for speakers of two different native languages to communicate.

Many of the Spanish dialects throughout Latin America have adopted words and concepts from various indigenous languages, including Quechúa (the Andean region), Maya, and Nahuatl (Aztec language). Many Latin American names of fruits and vegetables are derived from these languages. For example, 'el chocolate' is derived from the Nahuatl word 'xocolatl', and the Spanish word for corncob (el elote) comes from the Nahuatl word 'elotl'. Conversely, those that still speak their native languages have mixed words from Spanish into their vocabulary.

21. The main purpose of the first two paragraphs of Passage A (lines 1-22) is to:

A. place the blame for differences in the Spanish language from place to place squarely on the shoulders of the Spanish monarchy.
B. initiate the reader into one theory among many as to why there has been so little change in the Spanish language from place to place throughout history.
C. introduce the history of the spread of the Spanish language from Europe and provide initial examples of differences by location.
D. highlight similarities between and differences among Castilian Spanish and the form of the language preferred by the Spanish monarchy.

22. Which of the following Spanish words referred to in Passage A would most likely be pronounced differently in Latin America and Spain?

F. lapicero
G. ordenador
H. vosotros
J. usted

23. According to Passage A, Latin American and Castilian Spanish differ in:

A. neither grammar nor vocabulary.
B. grammar and vocabulary.
C. grammar, but not vocabulary.
D. vocabulary, but not grammar.

24. The author of Passage A says that Spanish speakers in the Andes region are more likely to:

F. pronounce a 'th' sound for words containing a *c* followed by an *e* or an *i*.
G. use 'vosotros' for the second person plural.
H. use 'le' for direct object pronouns that are male.
J. end their –ar verbs with –ado.

25. According to Passage B, intermarrying indigenous tribes in the New World:

A. refused to speak Spanish.
B. only adopted Spanish nouns on occasion.
C. spoke Spanish to bridge their own language gaps.
D. only adopted Spanish verbs on occasion.

26. Based on Passage B, the Spanish language has historically been:

F. affected by the Moors, but unaffected by indigenous Americans.
G. affected by other languages with which it comes into contact.
H. affected by cultural influences, but unaffected by governmental influences.
J. unaffected by outside influences.

27. Which of the following statements best expresses the opinion the author of Passage B seems to have about forcing the use of one language upon peoples?

A. Such forcing is effective but cruel.
B. Such forcing is futile and discriminatory.
C. Such forcing is effective and necessary.
D. Such forcing is futile but necessary.

28. Based on the passages, the Castilian form of Spanish:

F. underwent change both geographically and through time.
G. was a natural, cultural development in Spain.
H. is a form of Spanish spoken to this day in the Andes region.
J. is dependent upon Moorish and Nahuatl influences.

29. Based on the passages, it can most reasonably be inferred that the authors of both Passage A and Passage B would agree:

A. that the "Spanish lisp" will inevitably make its way into the English language.
B. that future cultural overlap will be a major factor in the slow change of languages, Spanish included.
C. that the the survival of culture and the use of language are intertwined, but dependent upon both the use of and reference to original Latin.
D. that New World nations, such as Argentina and Costa Rica, need a unified front to compete with the lingering influence of Castilian Spanish.

30. Another author wrote the following about the role of language:

> *Culture and identity are downstream of language, not the other way around. To lose language is to forfeit who you are and where you are from.*

Which passage most closely echoes the view presented in this quotation?

F. Passage A, because it highlights multiple examples of the differences between the use of Spanish in both Spain and the New World.
G. Passage A, because it speaks of the spread of Spanish through colonialism.
H. Passage B, because it speaks of the success on the part of government to eradicate the use of certain languages.
J. Passage B, because it speaks often of the overlap of language and culture in the New World.

Step 3 Correct Answers

Passage I:
1: A
2: H
3: D
4: F
5: A
6: H
7: C
8: G
9: D
10: H

Passage III:
21: C
22: F
23: B
24: J
25: C
26: G
27: B
28: F
29: B
30: J

Stumped on any? You can find the explanations for these three passages and possible Passage Maps beginning on page 622.

STEP 4

Macro Questions

What are Macro Questions?

As I have now twice said, somewhere between 15 and 18% of questions on the ACT Reading test fall into the category of what I call *macro*. In other words, somewhere between 6 and 8 total questions will test your ability to have an understanding of the passage as a whole. Oftentimes, one or two of these questions are asked first (which can be a blessing, since the reading is fresh on your mind…another reason to not get snagged on details and pay attention to the bigger picture!), but they can be found anywhere among the ten questions.

Questions of this type sound like this: "Which of the following statements expresses the author's belief about (the main subject of the passage)?" or "The tone of the essay can best be described as…"

Answering these questions is a 3 step process:

Step 1: If you know the answer already, go ahead and answer it.

Step 2: If you don't know the answer right away, read over your Passage Map to determine if you can figure out the correct answer.

Step 3: Let's say steps 1 and 2 fail, what should you do? Well, you obviously don't have time to go back and reread the passage. Go ahead and make a good guess, circle the question, and if you have any time remaining within your 8 minute and 45 second timeframe, go back and give it another shot.

The Following Passage

The passage that follows features mostly macro questions (six of the ten, to be exact, which is about how many you will have on an entire ACT Reading test!). However, for the sake of reinforcement (and because, again, they make up over 80% of any ACT Reading test), I also include two micro and two medium level questions. Set a timer for 8 minutes and 45 seconds, active read, and practice doing your best on the following practice passage.

Passage IV

NATURAL SCIENCE: This passage is adapted from the video lecture titled "Into the Deep" by Dr. Mary C Maximilian (©2014 Cambridge University).

The pelagic zone, according to oceanographers, is the area of the open ocean (often called the water column) that is divided into five regions based on depth. These five regions are similar to the layers of the atmosphere (stratosphere, troposphere, etc.), but one crucial difference is that although life is scarce within the upper atmosphere, it is relatively abundant within each of the ocean's zones. As would be expected, the prevalence of life decreases as one moves downwards. However, at all levels of the ocean, life persists: a testament to the robust and resilient nature of marine lifeforms.

The epipelagic zone is the topmost of the pelagic zone's layers. Although it is the thinnest layer of the ocean (2-3% of the ocean's water volume), this zone is home to approximately 90% of all marine life. Much of this is due to the fact that the epipelagic zone is the only layer of the ocean in which photosynthesis can occur. This means that phytoplankton such as green algae can flourish, establishing the base for a wide-ranging marine food web. Yet the significance of such phytoplankton is not limited to the ocean; they are also responsible for sequestering 40% of Earth's carbon dioxide production and producing nearly half the world's oxygen.

Below the epipelagic zone lies the mesopelagic zone, defined by the level of light penetration: it begins when only 1% of surface light can be detected. In practice, this means that the mesopelagic zone stretches from approximately 650 to 3,280 feet beneath the surface. Although this zone lacks phytoplankton, it is by no means uninhabited; it is estimated to host some 10 billion tons of animal life (for comparison, that is roughly 200 times more than the yearly catch of every fishery on Earth). Moreover, this zone contains specialized creatures such as *Gonostomatidae* (also called the bristlemouth), bioluminescent finger-sized fish thought to be the Earth's most abundant vertebrates, with their numbers estimated to be in the trillions or even quadrillions.

Beneath the pelagic zone is the bathypelagic zone, which extends downwards to 13,120 feet. It is the uppermost of the zones that receive no sunlight whatsoever. Marked by extreme pressure, some 800 times that experienced on the ocean's surface, the bathypelagic zone hosts only those organisms that have adapted themselves to the unforgiving environmental conditions, with weak musculature and skeletons. Exceedingly slow metabolisms allow bathypelagic fish to remain inactive for long periods. Most of the scarce organisms in this zone feed off "marine snow," tiny particles of organic detritus—decomposing organisms, fecal matter, and silt—that sink from higher regions.

The next zone, the abyssopelagic zone, is the largest by volume. Extending to nearly 20,000 feet beneath the surface, this zone is characterized by total darkness and near-freezing temperatures. In many parts of the ocean, the abyssopelagic zone stretches all the way to the seafloor. Here too, life finds a way; this zone features examples of every primary marine invertebrate phylum and several species of fish. Intriguingly, many such species are incredibly large, in a phenomenon known as deep-sea gigantism. For example, *Architeuthis dux* (the giant squid) can reach 30 feet in length and *Macrocheira kaempferi* (the Japanese spider crab) may grow to more than 12 feet across. Scientists propose a variety of explanations for these extreme sizes, among them cold temperatures and high levels of dissolved oxygen.

Although it extends to the ocean floor, the abyssal zone is, counterintuitively, not the ocean's lowest zone. That honor belongs to the hadal zone, confined to areas with V-shaped trenches that sink deeply into the ocean floor. The deepest of these trenches, the Pacific Ocean's Mariana Trench, stretches 7 miles downward. Historically, it was thought that no life could survive in such depths. However, it is now known that various species, such as *Hirondellea gigas* (a small shrimp-like crustacean) and *Pseudoliparis swirei* (the Mariana snailfish) are at home here, where the pressure hovers at over 15,000 psi (pounds per square inch). Still, because the abyssal zone is so difficult to explore, the full range of life within this region is still uncertain.

Much the same could be said of the entire ocean, which remains a vast, unknown expanse, less than 5% of which has been explored. What is known, however, is that the oceanic ecosystem is an embodiment of life's tenacity and adaptability, even in the face of extreme conditions. From the sunlight-drenched epipelagic zone to the crushing pressures and ink-black darkness of the hadal zone, each stratum of the sea hosts a unique array of life forms, whose very presence challenges our understanding of the limits of life while underscoring the incredible diversity of Earth's biosphere.

31. Based on the passage, as one transcends the depths from the epipelagic zone to the hadal zone:

A. life, contrary to popular belief, becomes more abundant, not less.
B. life gets less abundant at first, but is inexplicably most abundant in the hadal zone.
C. life becomes less abundant, but it can be found at all layers.
D. life becomes less abundant, and the creatures that do exist get smaller closest to the hadal zone.

32. Which of the following quotes best expresses the main idea of the passage?

F. "These five regions are similar to the layers of the atmosphere" (lines 3-4)
G. "Yet the significance of such phytoplankton is not limited to the ocean (lines 20-21)
H. "the abyssal zone is, counterintuitively, not the ocean's lowest zone" (lines 66-67)
J. "the oceanic ecosystem is an embodiment of life's tenacity and adaptability" (lines 83-84)

33. According to the passage, which of the following statements is *possibly* true, not *definitively* true?

A. The mesopelagic zone is defined by light penetration; specifically, this zone begins where only 1% of of surface light is detectable.
B. Most organisms in the bathypelagic zone feed off of marine snow that sink from higher zones.
C. High levels of dissolved oxygen in the abyssopelagic zone is primarily responsible for deep-sea gigantism.
D. The Mariana Trench, despite being seven miles below the surface of the ocean, is home to various species of marine life.

34. Which of the following are consistently used throughout the passage and strengthen the credibility of the author as a scientist?

F. Self-critical statements
G. Biographical elements
H. Technical language
J. Analogies and metephors

35. The passage indicates that compared to the bathypelagic zone, the abyssopelagic zone:

A. contains a higher volume of water and less sunlight.
B. contains a higher volume of water but is just as dark.
C. contains a lower volume of water and less sunglight.
D. contains a lower volume of water but is just as dark.

36. The main purpose of the passage is to:

F. correct the most common misunderstandings of the the various levels of the pelagic zone.
G. argue for increased environmental protections for the most vulnerable species in the ocean.
H. compare and contrast the five levels of the pelagic zone to the levels of the stratosphere.
J. describe the features of and life forms present in each level of the water column.

37. The overall passage can best be described as:

A. third-person and objective.
B. first-person and objective
C. third-person and subjective.
D. second-person and subjective.

38. According to the passage, which of the following is true about the hadal zone?

F. Its floor runs more or less parallel with the surface of the ocean.
G. It is home to different classifications of animal species.
H. It is the only zone present in all of the world's oceans, seas, and lakes.
J. It only receives 1% of the sunlight that reaches the surface of the ocean.

39. What is the purpose of the second paragraph (lines 12-23)?

A. To highlight the abundant life of the ocean's topmost layer and its importance for the greater ecosystem.
B. To introduce the hypothesis that the epipelagic zone is the most fascinating layer of the water column.
C. To introduce the essay as a whole and establish the authority of the author as an oceanographer.
D. To create awareness to the consequences of the depletion of phytoplankton on a global scale.

40. The overall organization of the passage is best described as:

F. a chronological account of one scientist's descent into the hadal zone in a research submarine.
G. an ordered series of descriptions of the layers of the water column by depth.
H. a scientific explanation of both the differences and similarities between marine species at various depths.
J. an ordered account of zoological descriptions of various marine species from largest to smallest.

Step 4 Correct Answers

Passage II:
31: C
32: J
33: C
34: H
35: B
36: J
37: A
38: G
39: A
40: G

Stumped on any? You can find the explanations for this passage and a possible Passage Map beginning on page 627.

STEP 5

The Little Things

Without a doubt, if you have followed the step-by-step prescriptions and practice laid out so far in this book, you gave gained a knowledge (one might say an expertise!) in the ACT Reading test (and hopefully, along with it, a heavy dose of confidence!). However, before we move on to Step 6 (full-length practice tests), there are a few little things that need your attention.

1) Inferring

Your ability to *infer* means your ability to reach conclusions based on the evidence that you currently have. If there's construction going on on your street, your sister borrowed your car last night, and you have two flat tires when you wake up in the morning, then it's likely you will *infer* that your sister ran over some nails or screws that fell onto the road, which led to your flat tires. However, unless you are directly asked to do so by a question, *do NOT infer on the ACT Reading test!*

Why not? Isn't inferring a crucial skill in life? Isn't it akin to critical thinking, which teachers have been stressing your entire academic career???

Well, it is a good skill to have in life (and in the ACT Science test). However, for ACT Reading, inferring an answer that is not in the passage is deadly. Here's what I mean. Let's say you have a paragraph in a passage about how a major company went bankrupt because it dismissed its competitors as too small. Then, you have a question that asks for a reason why the company failed. Letter choice A says that the company failed due to money mismanagement. Now, is it *likely true* that a major company would fail and go bankrupt because of money mismanagement? Yes. Is it reasonable to *infer* that this company failed and went bankrupt in large part due to money mismanagement? Also yes. However, *does the passage say that this is what caused the company to fail*? No, which is why a large percentage of ACT test takers will bubble in A, get it wrong, follow that same way of thinking over a dozen times, and walk away feeling good about their ACT Reading score only to receive a disappointing score via email two weeks later.

You may think I took that too far, but I did not. These wrong answer choices *are designed to sound true*, which means that many reasonable, smart students will perform poorly on the ACT Reading test.
I've said it a thousand times, and I'll say it again: your ability to active read and maximize the amount of time that you get to spend going back and finding correct answers (as opposed to inferring into incorrect answers that sound great and maybe even make sense) is going to be the difference maker for your ACT Reading score.

2) Read More

Stop! Don't skip what I have to say about this!

Now that I have your attention, let's just be honest. You've heard this 1,000 times in your life, so it probably has the same effect on you as the sound of the air conditioner in your house or any other background noise might have: the amount of time that you spend on screens is killing your ability to read.

Is it true? Obviously so. Is there something you can do about it? Of course.

I remember when I was a kid, I enjoyed reading. I would bring home from the school library two books a week and read them at home. Then I remember getting made fun of for reading in the 7th grade. It killed the fun of it or any enjoyment I got out of it, and so I gave it up (except, like most students, for what my teacher made me read in school). It wasn't until I was about 20 years old that I remembered how much I enjoyed it, and ever since I've tried to read every single day.

However, this book isn't about me, but I do wish when I was in high school that there had been someone who could have encouraged me to read more (they probably did, but I wasn't listening). I'm not telling you to go check out Moby Dick at the local library and read about the details of whale hunting until your eyes bleed. But, can you find a magazine that you find interesting? If you like sports, there are sports magazines; if you like music, there are music magazines; if you like fashion, there are fashion magazines;

read the articles in the magazine for 5 to 10 minutes a day and your reading ability will absolutely skyrocket. If you read for 10 minutes a day in the Summer for example, then by the Fall, you will have read an extra 750 minutes or so, which is 12.5 hours of reading!

Think of it like this also: I bet you like movies. The reason you like movies is *not* because of the special effects or because the main character is so handsome. It's because of the story. A bad story makes for a bad movie; a good story makes for a good movie; it's that simple. You will find these same stories in good books. The hardest part about reading is like most things: starting. If you can clear that hurdle on a good book, it'll be much easier as you go. The third page will not be as difficult as the first paragraph.

If you want to increase your ACT Reading score, read more.

3) Read In Your Mind, Not With Your Lips

Let's keep this simple. Some students, when they read quietly, do so with their mouths. In other words, they mouth the words with their lips. However, doing so will slow you down significantly. Your mind can move much faster than your lips, but if you are moving your lips to the words, your mind will only move at that speed.

If this is you, close your mouth. When you take the practice passages that follow, read only with your mind!

4) Preview the Questions First?

I have only taught you one ACT Reading strategy (meaning, for the overall test), which is active reading, Passage Map making, spending most of your time on the questions, etc. However, I would be amiss if I didn't mention that some of my students in the past have benefitted from adding in an additional step.

I find that a percentage of the students benefit from previewing the ten questions *first* before reading the passage. This kind of a preview should only take 30 seconds or less, but it gives you a bit of a heads up.

If this sounds like the kind of strategy that may benefit you, then give it a shot on some of the following practice passages. Thus, your steps would look like this: 1) Quickly read over the questions themselves first (not the answer choices, just the questions); 2) Active read the passage, making a Passage Map; 3) Answer the 10 questions.

5) Still Running Out of Time?

My last little advice is this. Let's say you've practiced a lot, but you still can't manage your time well enough or read fast enough to get through each passage in 8 minutes and 45 seconds. Maybe each passage is taking you 10 minutes, leaving you only 5 minutes for the final passage. What should you do?

My advice in that case is this: save the Paired Passage for last. This is because you know that the first few questions are *only* about Passage A and that the middle few questions are *only* about Passage B. This means that, for these first 6 or 7 questions, you only have to search for answers in essentially half of a passage, not a full passage. Finding the correct answers for numbers 1, 2, and 3, in other words, only requires you to go looking in the first few paragraphs, for example. You can active read Passage A, answer the questions, then try your best on the remaining questions without reading Passage B.

If there's no time to read (3 or 4 minutes total), don't waste your time reading the passage at all then; go straight to the questions, identifying the easiest ones to answer (questions that reference specific lines or paragraphs; these are the easiest because you know exactly where to look).

In short, if you can't read fast enough, and always only have a few minutes left, save the Paired Passage for last; if you only have a few minutes, don't read at all: go straight to the questions.

STEP 6

Full-Length Practice Tests

I hope you have found *The ACT Reading System* thus far to be valuable. It sums up and represents the best of ACT Reading preparation, based off of thousands of hours of teaching about, research into, and writing about the ACT itself. If you prepared from Step 1, then you have put first-things-first, second-things-second, and so on, ordering your preparation from most to least important. You haven't wasted your time memorizing the various categorizations of ACT Reading question types, for example, but have spent your time wisely preparing through guided practice.

What follows now is two complete, full-length ACT Reading practice tests. Let's quickly review strategies and mindset before you set that timer and dive in.

1) Active Reading and the Passage Map

The ACT Reading test may seem easy when you first see that there are 35 minutes to complete it. However, you know by now not to be fooled; time is a serious factor. This is only exaggerated when you come to understand that answering the questions *takes significant time*, since you are forced to read the question, think about it, usually go find the answer, then answer it after reading through the answer choices.

Read quickly, paying attention to the greater purpose of each paragraph. Jot down that paragraph's purpose in the margins in 1-5 words. If a paragraph is especially large, then maybe do so twice (for the top half and bottom halves of paragraphs). This creates your Passage Map, which carries 3 benefits: 1) It makes you pay attention to the paragraphs' greater purpose, keeping you from being snared by every detail; 2) It gives you points of reference (which is why it's called a Passage *Map*) for finding correct answers; it helps you know where to look; and 3) It summarizes paragraphs ahead of time (good for when a question asks you for the purpose or main idea of a paragraph).

2) Time Management

The ACT Reading test is 35 minutes long, and because it is split into 4 passages of a roughly even length, you should think of this as more like 4 mini-tests. Use a clock (or even better, an old fashioned watch with the hands) to give yourself roughly even time for all four tests. This is ideal.

Of course, it is going to be extremely difficult to track the 45 seconds part, no matter what kind of clock or watch you use! However, maybe it's easier to think about it like this: 9 minutes, 9 minutes, 9 minutes, 8 minutes. That kind of thinking still gives you roughly the amount of time that you need for each test.

All of that being said, it is time to take an entire ACT Reading test! No more setting an 8 minute and 45 second timer. That was important before now to get you into the pacing. Now instead, set a 35 minute timer. Managing time across the four passages is crucial. Make sure you have the 35 minutes to dedicate to the test and won't get interrupted.

Following the tests are not only the answers themselves, but you will also find explanations for each and every question and possible Passage Maps beginning on page 630 (for Practice Test 1) and 641 (for Practice Test 2).

3) Inferring

Remember: many of the wrong answer choices on the ACT Reading test are designed to *sound true*. Answer choice A may sound terribly false, but don't just bubble in B simply because it sounds reasonable and possibly could be true. For the vast majority of questions, either the passage says it or does it (so it's true), or it doesn't. Only infer when the question requires you to (meaning, it asks you to do so!). Use active reading to give yourself the time to find the answers!

PRACTICE TEST 1

35 Minutes, 40 Questions

READING TEST

35 Minutes — 40 Questions

DIRECTIONS: There are several passages in this test. Each passage is accompanied by several questions. After reading a passage, choose the best answer to each question and fill in the corresponding oval on your answer document. You may refer to the passages as often as necessary.

Passage I

LITERARY NARRATIVE: This passage is adapted from Homer's *The Odyssey*.

Ulysses has returned home in disguise after twenty years of captivity and struggle; his estate is overrun by suitors, all of whom wish to marry his wife, Penelope.

Then the old woman took the cauldron in which she was going to wash Ulysses's feet, and poured plenty of cold water into it, adding hot till the bath was warm enough. Ulysses sat by the fire, but ere long he turned away from the light, for it occurred to him that when the old woman had hold of his leg she would recognize a certain scar which it bore, whereon the whole truth would come out. And indeed as soon as she began washing her master, she at once knew the scar as one that had been given him by a wild boar when he was hunting on Mt. Parnassus with his excellent grandfather Autolycus—who was the most accomplished thief and perjurer in the whole world—and with the sons of Autolycus.

As soon as Euryclea had got the scarred limb in her hands and had well hold of it, she recognized it and dropped the foot at once. The leg fell into the bath, which rang out and was overturned, so that all the water was spilt on the ground; Euryclea's eyes between her joy and her grief filled with tears, and she could not speak, but she caught Ulysses by the beard and said, "My dear child, I am sure you must be Ulysses himself, only I did not know you till I had actually touched and handled you."

As she spoke she looked towards Penelope, as though wanting to tell her that her dear husband was in the house, but Penelope was unable to look in that direction and observe what was going on, for Minerva had diverted her attention; so Ulysses caught Euryclea by the throat with his right hand and with his left drew her close to him, and said, "Nurse, do you wish to be the ruin of me, you who nursed me at your own breast, now that after twenty years of wandering I am at last come to my own home again? Since it has been borne in upon you by heaven to recognize me, hold your tongue, and do not say a word about it to any one else in the house, for if you do I tell you—and it shall surely be—that if heaven grants me to take the lives of these suitors, I will not spare you, though you are my own nurse, when I am killing the other women."

"My child," answered Euryclea, "what are you talking about? You know very well that nothing can either bend or break me. I will hold my tongue like a stone or a piece of iron; furthermore let me say, and lay my saying to your heart, when heaven has delivered the suitors into your hand, I will give you a list of the women in the house who have been ill-behaved, and of those who are guiltless."

And Ulysses answered, "Nurse, you ought not to speak in that way; I am well able to form my own opinion about one and all of them; hold your tongue and leave everything to heaven."

As he said this Euryclea left the cloister to fetch some more water, for the first had been all spilt; and when she had washed him and anointed him with oil, Ulysses drew his seat nearer to the fire to warm himself, and hid the scar under his rags.

Then Penelope began talking to him and said: "Listen, then, to a dream that I have had and interpret it for me if you can. I have twenty geese about the house that eat mash out of a trough, and of which I am exceedingly fond. I dreamed that a great eagle came swooping down from a mountain, and dug his curved beak into the neck of each of them till he had killed them all. Presently he soared off into the sky, and left them lying dead about the yard; whereon I wept in my dream till all my maids gathered round me, so piteously was I grieving because the eagle had killed my geese. Then he came back again, and perching on a projecting rafter spoke to me with human voice, and told me to leave off crying. 'Be of good courage,' he said, 'daughter of Icarius; this is no dream, but a vision of good omen that shall surely come to pass. The geese are the suitors, and I am no longer an eagle, but your own husband, who am come back to you, and who will bring these suitors to a disgraceful end.' On this I woke, and when I looked out I saw my geese at the trough eating their mash as usual."

"This dream, Madam," replied Ulysses, "can admit but of one interpretation, for had not Ulysses himself told you how it shall be fulfilled? The death of the suitors is portended, and not one single one of them will escape."

1. The point of view from which the passage is told is best described as that of:

A. an omniscient third-person narrator who describes the thoughts and actions of multiple characters.
B. an omniscient second-person narrator who, from within the story, addresses the reader as a character.
C. a first-person narrator who recalls an encounter with a familiar maid and a dream that was recently had.
D. a limited third-person narrator who closely recalls events from the point of view of Penelope.

2. The narrator mentions Mt. Parnassus primarily to:

F. recall the incident, remembered by Euryclea, in which Ulysses's leg becomes scarred.
G. compare Ulysses, a man of strength and other godly characters, to the gods themselves.
H. reiterate that Ulysses, even as a child, was a greater hunter than his grandfather.
J. to prefigure the triumphant return of Autolycus to his long lost home.

3. Based on the passage, Euryclea's reaction to the scarred leg of Ulysses can best be described as:

A. anger followed by cluelessness and ignorance.
B. disappointment followed by anger and despair.
C. shock followed by joy and grief.
D. astonishment followed by hatred and vengeance.

4. The sequence of events described in the third paragraph (lines 25-40) can best be characterized as:

F. Ulysses's attempt by way of threat to keep his identity a secret from Penelope.
G. a memory later shared by Euryclea to prove her innocence before Penelope.
H. a desperate attempt by Ulysses for attention after twenty years of anonymity.
J. a key exchange between two people close to Penelope that directly causes her dream.

5. According to the passage, Penelope shares her dream with Ulysses by the fire in order to:

A. reveal that she knows that he is her missing husband in disguise.
B. have Ulysses interpret the dream.
C. convince Ulysses that her suitors will soon meet their end.
D. begin to make amends for the water spilt by Euryclea when she was washing Ulysses's feet.

6. As it is used in line 78, the word *admit* most nearly means to:

F. confess to be true.
G. acknowledge a failure or fault.
H. allow someone to enter a place.
J. allow the possibility of.

7. According to the passage, it can be safely assumed that both Ulysses and Penelope share which of the following emotions about their potential reunion?

A. Anxious hopelessness
B. Doubtful terror
C. Melancholic dejection
D. Hopeful anticipation

8. Of the following characters, which one is described as being most trustworthy?

F. Ulysses
G. Penelope
H. Euryclea
J. Autolycus

9. The narrator most strongly suggests that Penelope treats visitors to her home in which of the following ways?

A. Like persons worthy of being ignored
B. In an indifferent and aloof manner
C. Like one would treat a slave or servant
D. As honored guests

10. In the passage, the narrator makes which of the following distinctions?

F. Penelope is very observant and alert, whereas Euryclea is detached from reality and naive.
G. Penelope has been content for the last twenty years, whereas Euryclea has been miserable.
H. Autolycus was a great outdoorsman, whereas Ulysses struggles mightily away from home.
J. The suitors are freeloaders, whereas Ulysses sacrifices for what is his.

Passage II

SOCIAL SCIENCE: This passage is adapted from the article "A Nation's First Leader" by J Eggers Clyburn (©2004 by Smithsonian).

Although the Revolutionary War started well for the American troops, it was not long into 1776 that things took a turn for the worse. New York City was conquered in a mere three month period between August and November after British troops commanded by General William Howe landed in Long Island. From there, Washington, who had fled the city with some 6,000 men, was chased Southwest across New Jersey by British General Cornwallis, eventually settling near McConkey's Ferry on the Pennsylvania side of the Delaware River. Though many thousands of troops made it to the encampment safely, nearly 2,000 were in need of hospital care, and a significant number of others deserted the young army out of fear that the war had already been lost.

A brutal New England winter was imminent, and as a result, military campaigns began to slow. General Cornwallis gave up further chasing of Washington into Pennsylvania, choosing instead to establish a string of outposts from northern New Jersey to as far south as Burlington. Washington, for his part, was eager to gather other split-off American forces under the command of Generals Lee and Gates.

Washington, bolstered by reports of the casual attitudes of British soldiers, began to scheme a bold plan for a surprise attack, but morale was low. However, he was given a copy of *The American Crisis*, a pamphlet published on December 19th and written by Thomas Paine (who had also authored *Common Sense*). The pamphlet begins as such:

"These are the times that try men's souls; the summer soldier and the sunshine patriot will, in this crisis, shrink from the service of his country; but he that stands it *now,* deserves the love and thanks of man and woman. Tyranny, like hell, is not easily conquered; yet we have this consolation with us, that the harder the conflict, the more glorious the triumph."

Washington, himself inspired, ordered that the pamphlet be read to all of his troops on December 20th. This raised morale among his soldiers and went a long way in giving them the courage they needed to conquer their current and difficult living conditions as well as any wounds they may have suffered in skirmishes that Fall. On the same day, and although there had been delays, the eagerly anticipated troops of both Lee and Gates arrived in camp, raising the total number of soldiers fit for duty under the orders of the Commander of the Continental Army to 6,000.

Intelligence reports that enemy troops were planning their own eventual crossing of the Delaware River temporarily disheartened Washington. More importantly, however, these reports bolstered the Colonel's ambitious plan, which was hatched December 23rd, 1776. On the following day, the secret mission was revealed at 4:00 PM to the thousands of troops who had gathered for routine reporting, and preparations began. Vessels, such as large ferries and smaller Durham boats, were brought south from Malta Island near New Hope. On Christmas Day, Washington again reiterated that the crossing would take place that evening with an attack on a garrison of German Hessian troops fighting on behalf of the British near Trenton. But first, the crossing itself had to take place, which required that not only men but dozens of horses and artillery make safe voyages to the other side of the dangerous and icy Delaware River.

At 4:00 troops were readied with ammunition, and after sunset the crossing began. Crossings were planned to take place in waves, but the weather failed to simplify the operation. Winds blew, and what began as soft rain quickly escalated to sleet and snow. This made conditions significantly more dangerous for the men, most of whom could not swim. Finally, by 3:00 AM, all men, food, horses, and artillery had made the crossing, and no less than 1 hour later the troops were ready to march into Trenton.

The troops were split. One half were put under the command of General Sullivan and the other half under General Greene. These garrisons took parallel roads into the city and, to say the least, caught the German troops off guard. The Hessian leadership assumed that there would be no attack on that wintry morning and had grown dull to surprise by numerous skirmishes with Americans evening after evening. Colonel Rall, leader of these troops, even spent most of the previous evening off his guard drinking and eating at the home of a Loyalist Patriot, Abraham Hunt.

Miraculously, only 3 American troops were killed in the fight, due in large part to the unsuspecting nature of the attack. Colonel Rall was mortally wounded, as were 22 other Hessian troops. The Americans pillaged muskets, powder, and artillery, and although the return crossing back into Pennsylvania was even more dangerous than the first, they returned to camp in a celebratory mood, which was a marked difference when compared to their first arrival earlier in the month.

11. Those soldiers who "deserted the young army" (lines 13-14) are most nearly synonymous with which of the following?

    A. "the summer soldier" (lines 31-32)
    B. "eagerly anticipated troops" (line 45)
    C. "enemy troops" (line 49)
    D. "a garrison of German Hessian troops" (lines 60-61)

12. It can be reasonably concluded that the author of the passage believes that Washington's crossing of the Delaware River:

F. was a brave and bold decision that failed to achieve the desired result.
G. was an act of heroism, and is to be praised as a strike that aided the Americans significantly.
H. ought to be remembered as a foolish enterprise that resulted in the unnecessary deaths of 3 Americans.
J. was an uncoordinated gamble that, aided by fortunate weather, was successful only by luck.

13. The main idea of the fifth paragraph (lines 38-48) is that:

A. due to his ability to sway opinion, Thomas Paine should have been recruited to a leadership position in the American army.
B. despite physical and emotional setbacks, various factors improved the morale of the American army as Washington plotted a bold move.
C. courage and strength were hopelessly fleeting for the troops under Washington's command.
D. American troops and citizens have always had the ability to embolden themselves despite failures in leadership.

14. The main purpose of the eighth paragraph (lines 76-86) is that:

F. Washington recruited everyday citizens in the days leading up to the attack to cause skirmishes.
G. Abraham Hunt might go down in history as a patriot, but he should be remembered as a traitor to the American cause.
H. a major contributor to the success of the American attack was that enemy troops were caught off guard for various reasons.
J. Hessian troops might have been willing to turn on the British if given an opportunity by Washington.

15. According to the passage, which of the following presented an imminent danger to the health and safety of American troops in December of 1776?

I. British forces that crossed the Delaware River
II. Wintery weather conditions
III. An inability to swim
IV. Skirmishes
V. Diseases, like Yellow Fever

A. I only
B. II and IV only
C. II and III only
D. I, II, III, and V only

16. The passage author most likely uses the description in lines 11-15 in order to:

F. scare the reader into believing the the Americans were likely to lose the Revolutionary War.
G. provide a detailed account of the precise number of troops that were killed between New York and Pennsylvania.
H. bolster opinion of General Lowe's military ability and might.
J. emphasize the dire straits of the American army after being driven out of New York.

17. As it is used in line 82, the phrase *grown dull* most nearly refers to the Hessian troops':

A. blunt bayonets.
B. lackadaisical attitude about the potential for danger.
C. longing for their German homeland.
D. uniforms, which had been whitened by snowfall.

18. It can most reasonably be inferred from the passage that as a general, Washington:

F. narrowly escaped with his life on dozens of occasions throughout the Revolutionary War.
G. was prone to being caught off guard, which was perhaps his one unredeemable quality.
H. knew that occasional retreat was not failure if it prolonged the war and created opportunity.
J. relied far too heavily on the generals that were under his command to shoulder responsibility.

19. As it is used in line 68, the word *waves* most nearly means:

A. successive occurrences of a specific phenomenon.
B. long bodies of water curling into an arched form.
C. moving to and fro in a swaying motion.
D. a gesture or signal made by moving one's hand back and forth.

20. According to the passage, the colonel of the Hessian troops:

F. was able to survive Washington's surprise attack, but lost troops, ammunition, and other supplies to the Americans.
G. knew of the loyalties of Abraham Hunt, but dined at his home nevertheless.
H. failed to properly station sentinels along the Delaware River.
J. had not seriously entertained the possibility of a surprise attack the day after Christmas.

Passage III

HUMANITIES: Passage A is adapted from the book *Journeys in Anthropology: To the End of the World* (©2004 by James Thomas Todd). Passage B is adapted from the book *Art: A History of Technique* (©1997 by Lauren Thomason).

Passage A by James Thomas Todd

As not only the son of an esteemed anthropologist, but being in that profession myself, I was honored to be invited to explore the *Caverne Sous la Falaise*, a limestone cave beneath a towering cliff in Southern France. It was discovered in 2006 following an earthquake that dislodged more than 400 tonnes of rock at the base of the cliff, and was subsequently closed to the public by the government. In the last few years the cave has been opened to study to scientists, archaeologists, and anthropologists like myself and my mother who obtain a special permit from the authorities.

The entrance to the cave, a gap in the rock no more than five feet in height and three feet in width, deceived me into thinking that I would be setting foot into a small cave. Upon entering and turning on my flashlight, what was lit up was an extensive cavern with seemingly unlimited depths, crevices, and avenues. A line of paracord guided our team of half a dozen scientists through the twists and turns of these depths. Whether from darkness or danger or the time it took, what was only a hike of 75 or so meters seemed to be ten times the distance. However, it was worth it.

First, we came upon charcoal sketches of animals, and the dilapidated remains of many more. Mammoths and other mammals that are since extinct stretched up and across the limestone. While many anthropologists might attempt to explain away these ancient drawings as merely a primitive attempt to try to understand the cosmos, I wonder more about the humanity of the artist. Was he or she driven by a fundamental, human passion for art itself? Perhaps, I think, this large cave was a nursery for small children, and the sitters entertained the little ones with fascinating stories of the beasts scribbled on the walls.

We then entered a "smaller" room that took my breath away. Hundreds, or perhaps thousands, of hand prints adorned the walls. Again I wonder: are our primitive, standard explanations of the motives of cave dwellers too immature, too inhuman? No one can say for sure, but I do know that whether these hands are a way to remember ancestors or something as simple as an aesthetic pleasure, we are fortunate that they have been kept in nearly pristine condition to the present day.

Passage B by Lauren Thomason

Charcoal is, perhaps, the oldest art medium in human history. In fact, charcoal cave paintings have been discovered and studied in many parts of the world and can date back as late as 30,000 years ago (or, there is debate, perhaps even further back in time). For example, Namibia can boast of a black, charcoal drawing of what appears to be a zebra that was discovered at the Apollo Cave dating to as far back as 27,500 years ago.

However, it wasn't just ancient cave dwellers who utilized the technique. In Europe, artists beginning in the 1400's were using wallow, walnut, and grape charcoal to capture their subjects. Since then, charcoal has only grown in popularity due to its striking and deep black color and the ability of the artist to take advantage of the white canvas beneath as a contrasting method. Unfortunately, over time, many of the early pieces of charcoal art were ruined due to the flaking of the medium off of the smooth canvas. By the 16th century, artists had discovered that by dipping charcoal in a gum bath, it was less likely to flake. This process was aided by the use of a rough canvas, which forces an adhesion and prevents the fading of color or flaking over time.

Today, there are many different varieties of charcoal and methods for producing them. Compressed charcoal, for example, is pressed into the shape of a block, stick, or rectangular cube. Vine charcoal, on the other hand, is longer and thinner than the compressed variety and is produced by burning grape vines in a kiln. Despite the popularity of these two types, the most popular method of applying charcoal is via a charcoal pencil. This is simply compressed charcoal that has been enclosed in wood, like a pencil. These are especially useful when an artist needs the addition of meticulous detail in his or her art.

The method of production and the ingredients put in also have an effect on the charcoal and the final result on canvas. The softer the charcoal, the longer it had been heated.

There are also a variety of application techniques, all of which produce different effects. Blending, for example, is a technique in which the artist uses either a finger or a chamois to spread charcoal; this naturalizes the transition between darker and lighter portions of a work of art. Hatching is another technique in which an artist continually applies parallel, dark lines one after another; this can have the effect of fooling the eye to believe that a work has been filled in entirely by charcoal or give texture and dimension to a piece.

21. Which of the following statements about the *Caverne Sous la Falaise* is *least* supported by Passage A?

A. There is much we do not know about our ancestors' interests and way of life.
B. The cavern might have appeal to the greater public, but is of little interest to the scientific community.
C. There is, from an archaeological perspective, likely much to be discovered yet unseen by modern eyes.
D. Artifacts that are immovable, such as cave art, are worthy of special protection.

22. Which of the following terms in Passage A best emphasizes the humanity behind the cave art of the *Caverne Sous la Falaise*?

   F. Dilapidated (line 24)
   G. Primitive (line 28)
   H. Adorned (line 37)
   J. Pristine (line 43)

23. The purpose of the quotation marks around the word *smaller* in line 35 is most likely to:

   A. state that the cave was not large enough for all of the scientists to fit in at one time.
   B. emphasize the physical size of the author's surroundings for the first time in the essay.
   C. suggest that, though the space may not be as big as the previous one, it is still rather expansive.
   D. indicate that the word is being used in a precise and scientific manner.

24. Which of the following statements best captures how Passage B characterizes the dawning of the use of charcoal in European art?

   F. The use of charcoal in this time was limited because there was only one variety for use in art.
   G. The first artists to embrace the use of untreated charcoal were ignorant of its longevity when applied to a smooth canvas.
   H. Because it was first dipped in a gum bath, it was unlikely to flake off of a canvas.
   J. It was a flawless process that only began as recently as the 1600's.

25. The statement in lines 78-81 is typical of Passage B in the way it:

   A. stresses the dignity of black and white art over that in color.
   B. further expands upon the vast varieties of charcoal and their potential for different uses by artists.
   C. conveys the necessity of the reader to be open minded to different mediums on the market besides charcoal.
   D. narrows the expectations of the reader from complex to simpler artistic possibilities.

26. Which of the following methods of charcoal application is *not* mentioned in the passage?

   F. Swiping from the corner of a soft charcoal block
   G. Applying parallel, dark lines one after another
   H. Using a finger to spread charcoal across a canvas
   J. Utilizing charcoal in a pencil casing for detail

27. As it is used in the passage, the term *capture* (line 55) primarily serves to:

   A. refer to the process by which an artist would replicate a subject on canvas.
   B. compare and contrast black and white photographs to the art produced by charcoal.
   C. indicate the difference between the use of charcoal in the 1400's compared to the 1600's.
   D. stress the temporary nature of art produced by charcoal that had not been dipped in gum.

28. With which of the following statements would the authors of both Passage A and Passage B most agree?

   F. Cave dwellers discovered early on that dipping charcoal in gum was an effective deterrent to flaking.
   G. Limestone is an ideal canvas for charcoal.
   H. Modern art is more beautiful and valuable than cave art due to an unfolding of charcoal techniques over time.
   J. Charcoal art has the potential to degrade over time if not properly treated and applied.

29. An element of Passage A that is not present in Passage B are rhetorical questions intended to:

   A. awaken the potential of charcoal art.
   B. condemn the cave dweller as incapable of art worthy of note.
   C. simplify the process of charcoal art, given the immense variety available to the modern artist.
   D. cast doubt upon typical stereotypes of cave dwellers.

30. If the author of Passage B had visited the *Caverne Sous la Falaise* and was asked to assist the author of Passage A in describing the experience, it is likely that she would have contributed which of the following to Passage A?

   F. The type of charcoal used to paint the animals and the method of application to the cave wall.
   G. A paragraph comparing and contrasting the animals of the *Caverne Sous la Falaise* to the zebra of the Apollo cave.
   H. A more European and anthropological perspective on the size, scope, and importance of the hands on the wall.
   J. A more experienced point of view on the origins and history of cave art the world over.

Passage IV

NATURAL SCIENCE: This passage is adapted from the article "Unyielding Havoc: The History and Devastating Effects of the Invasive Red Ant" by Whitney Culver (©2009 by Southeastern Science Quarterly).

The red imported fire ant, *Solenopsis invicta*, is a polymorphic species of ant native to central South America but considered an invasive species in the United States, Australia, parts of Asia, and other locations across the globe. Historically, *S. invicta* has often been confused with the black imported fire ant, *Solenopsis richteri*, a species native to southeastern South America but similarly invasive to the United States. Genetic and phenotypic research suggests a close genetic relationship between the two, so much so that hybridization or an intermixing of species occurs in areas where the two overlap (northern Mississippi, United States).

Worker ants within *S. invicta* measure between 2.4 and 6.0 mm, but larger workers or major workers are distinguishable from smaller workers by head size (0.66 to 1.41 mm in height for smaller workers, 1.35 to 1.40 mm for major workers). This difference in size, which makes them polymorphic, is indistinguishable in larvae until the fourth and final larval instar, or stage of development. The larval stages begin with an oval-shaped egg that assumes the shape of an embryo, becoming a true larva with the shedding of the shell within a week. Larvae measure approximately 3 mm in length. Upon pupation, the differences in head size between the different castes of workers becomes apparent, though both feature antennae with two or three sensilla, or sensory organs, each. In many colonies, major workers can make up as many as 35% of the total population, the function of which is to leave the colony and forage. Smaller workers care for the brood. Though worker ants can be female, only the queens, a third caste of *S. invicta*, can lay eggs.

Worker ants communicate using pheromones and semiochemicals, secreted chemical factors that trigger a social response. One example of semiochemical communication occurs when a major worker ant discovers a food source that is too heavy to carry individually. In such a situation, a worker will secrete trail pheromones alerting other ants, who synthesize the pheromones by the Dufour's gland, to the presence of the food. Similarly, when a mound is under attack, *S. invicta* will release alarm pheromones alerting the colony to the presence of a threat. Some scientists speculate the presence of a brood pheromone designed to aid workers in the segregation of brood by age and caste, resulting in care for eggs that includes antennation, licking, and grooming.

S. invicta has a natural predator in its native Brazil, a species of phorid fly of the genus *Apocephalus* also known as the ant-decapitator fly, which lays eggs in the ant's severed head. Due to the invasive nature of the ant and the havoc it can wreak on local ecosystems, scientists are studying whether or not to import a population of the phorid fly into the United States to help control the ant's spread. However, a number of insects, birds, and arachnids have learned to feed on the invasive species across the globe. The *S. invicta* that tends to be most vulnerable is the queen, which is in flight before the establishment of a new colony. In such a situation, she is particularly susceptible to being consumed by *Anax junius*, *Somatochlora provocans*, and *Tramea carolina*, all species of dragonfly native to North America, and various birds, such as the chimney swift (*Chaetura pelagica*) and the eastern kingbird (*Tyrannus tyrannus*). As many as 16 unique species of arachnid are also known to prey on *S. invicta*, including the southern black widow spider (*Lycosa timuga*) and the wolf spider (*Lycosa timuga*), the latter of which is documented to eat all three castes of the red invasive fire ant for a total of roughly 75% of its total diet.

One reason the *S. invicta* is a problematic invasive species is the effect it has on the diversity and abundance of native species, particularly arthropods and vertebrates. The Stock Island tree snail (*Orthalicus reses*), for example, is now extinct in the wild due mostly to the presence and predation of the red imported fire ant. Though interactions with mammals are rare, human beings are stung (not bitten, contrary to popular belief) by the venomous ant roughly 14 million times per year. The complex venom, fueled by the primary lipophilic alkaloid toxin *solenopsin*, usually results in mild discomfort, swelling, and itching for humans. However, because of the threat the ants pose to more susceptible populations of humans, it is important for scientists and the greater population to continue to find methods of containing this invasive species.

31. The third paragraph (lines 33-47) marks a shift in the passage from a focus on:

- **A.** the invasive range of *S. invicta* to the physical characteristics of *S. invicta*.
- **B.** the invasive range of *S. invicta* to the types of sociochemical communication among *S. invicta*.
- **C.** the physical characteristics of *S. invicta* to the types of sociochemical communication among *S. invicta*.
- **D.** the types of sociochemical communication among *S. invicta* to the physical characteristics of *S. invicta*.

32. Based on the passage, the author's use of the word "assumes" (line 21) most nearly describes the way an *S. invicta* egg:

- **F.** makes a characteristic decision about which of three castes of ant to permanently become.
- **G.** changes or takes on a new form prior to later larval growth stages.
- **H.** can sometimes be mistaken by worker ants for the similar-looking eggs of *S. richteri*.
- **J.** responds to alarm pheromones when there is an eternal threat to the colony.

33. Which of the following statements best summarizes the effect that *S. invicta* has had on ecosystems into which it has been introduced?

A. Though the red fire ant is technically categorized as an *invasive* species, it has proven to overall be beneficial to these ecosystems.
B. Though the red fire ant is technically categorized as an *invasive* species, it has shown hybridization potential with many native species.
C. Though the red fire ant has been utilized as food by many native species, it has proven more harmful to the flourishing of many non-native species.
D. Though the red fire ant has been utilized as food by many native species, it has proven more harmful to the flourishing of many native species.

34. Based on the passage, which of the following are physical differences between the worker and major worker castes of *S. invicta*?

F. Head size only
G. Head size and physical appearance at the fourth and final instar stages of larval development
H. The number of sensilla on their antennae upon pupation only
J. Head size and the number of sensilla on their antennae upon pupation

35. The passage most strongly suggests that compared to the red fire ant *S. invicta*, the black fire ant *S. richteri* is unique in that it:

A. is confined in the United States to northern Mississippi.
B. can enter into hybridization with other ant species.
C. is not considered invasive to the United States.
D. is native to southeastern South America.

36. Which of the following provides the best paraphrase of lines 51-55?

F. Introduction of *Apocephalus* might slow *S. invicta*, but scientists are cautious about unintended ecological effects.
G. *Apocephalus* are known to decapitate *S. invicta* in South America, but it it unlikely they will do so in invasive environments.
H. Because *S. invicta* are known to decapitate *Apocephalus*, the fly's introduction into the United States will further the spread of the red fire ant.
J. *Apocephalus*, being the only known creature to kill *S. invicta*, is the only solution to slow the invasive spread of the red fire ant.

37. Based on the passage, it can most reasonably be inferred that *S. invicta* populations:

A. have naturally migrated into Australia and parts of Asia, but were mistakenly introduced into the United States.
B. are consumed by native mammalian species at least as often as they are by native arachnid species.
C. are made up of mostly smaller workers.
D. are likely to be brought to extinction as dragonfly populations increase.

38. As it is used in line 20, the word *stages* most nearly means:

F. ages or periods of time.
G. steps in a process of development.
H. raised platforms on which to be seen.
J. arrangements or styles.

39. According to the passage, when a major worker ant of *S. invicta* encounters a food source too heavy to individually lift, it will do which of the following?

A. Release trail pheromones
B. Release alarm pheromones
C. Leave it until smaller food sources are proven to be unavailable
D. Remain with the food source until found by others

40. Based on the passage, the venom of the invasive red fire ant:

F. is not considered a threat to any human being.
G. is the main reason why *S. invicta* is so rarely consumed by birds.
H. is injected through a sting, not a bite.
J. is non-toxic, unlike that of the black fire ant.

PRACTICE TEST 2

35 Minutes, 40 Questions

READING TEST

35 Minutes — 40 Questions

DIRECTIONS: There are several passages in this test. Each passage is accompanied by several questions. After reading a passage, choose the best answer to each question and fill in the corresponding oval on your answer document. You may refer to the passages as often as necessary.

Passage I

LITERARY NARRATIVE: This passage is adapted from the story "The Grove" by Martin J. Phillips.

That night the three returned to the property. Joey's knees bobbed up and down against the back of the driver's seat. Once deep into the grove Dillon let them take off the blindfolds. A full moon illuminated the night, and its rays pierced a few of the thick branches like silver spears.

"We have got to make this quick," Dillon said. "Janie is coming over to the house tonight when the band starts."

"I thought you said she hated fraternities," Joey said. "Why would she want to come over to our house, and while we're at it, why are we even here right now, why did I agree to this? Let's get out of here while we got the chance."

Red punched him in the shoulder and called him a wimp. "Dillon let's get on with it! It's a little bright for my liking, and besides, we do not want to keep Janie waiting."

The truck roared like a lion when Dillon slammed the accelerator. They weaved in and out and all around the arching giants and left deep tracks in the wet earth. Mud and grass were thrown into the air behind them. Joey buried his face in his hands and Red screamed with excitement. Dillon had never done anything like this, but it gave him a thrill he had rarely felt. What Janie might think, what his parents might say if they heard, was irrelevant. They drew near to the path to the creek and turned around; at least two of them had their minds set on doing more damage. After a couple of more minutes they neared the end of the cornfield on what was to them the left side of the property.

"What's that?" Dillon asked. When they were fifty feet away, they could see it more clearly. A vacant tractor was parked in the middle of their path. Dillon pressed the brake with a soft foot. Red stretched his eyes and leaned over to Joey to get a better look, whispering with concerned confidence that it had indeed been there on the way in.

Dillon adjusted his posture, easing his foot off of the brake. Like a postman he rolled down the window and reached his hand out towards the tractor, placing his hand upon the hood. He gasped and turned to his friends. "It's warm," he said. "How could it be warm?"

From behind an aged pecan tree, a shotgun's barrel emerged, followed by the limping body of the man who held it. Like an old dog he shuffled to a spot directly in front of the truck. Joey ducked and covered his head with his arms and screamed something about having told them so. Red said to run him over because they had a right to if their lives were threatened. Dillon shifted into reverse and hit the gas, but the tires only spun on their axles in the churned up mud like fireworks.

"Stop trying to be nice and go!" Red screamed.

The wheels spun. Cordia raised the gun. Red ducked beside Joey as Dillon put up his hands as if to surrender, remembering what the old man had said about being shot at in his youth. Before he closed his eyes Dillon saw a wry smile come across the old face as the gun settled on his shoulder. The moment after the weapon was fired felt like an eternity. However, no glass shattered. No one screamed or bled. Dillon cracked open his eyes like peanuts.

Pecans and branches rained down like hail, rattling the truck with a chorus of cracks and thuds. The antenna was snapped by an arm-width limb. Cordia let out a jackal's cackle and fired into the tree again with the same enthusiasm as the truck's spinning wheels. Through the open window he shouted at Dillon, "Son, just like I told you just this afternoon, turn around!" He reloaded. "Your truck's in the way of my harvest! Can't you see I'm out to farm? Turn around!" He fired into the tree twice more.

Now that Cordia had walked to one side of the path Dillon thrust the truck into drive and accelerated steadily to dislodge the tires. He drove around the old farmer as another shot was fired. More pecans landed like buckshot and a thick branch slammed into the bed and shattered a brake light. Dillon hit the gas and swiped a tree with his side mirror, which broke off and rolled to the feet of Cordia. Dillon accelerated as a final blast from the gun trumpeted a closing onslaught of pecans and branches that fell silently into the churned up tracks of mud that the college student's once prized possession had left behind. He clenched his fists, and no one spoke as the bruised and battered vehicle rumbled down the unpaved red clay and turned onto a long stretch of highway.

1. The passage can most reasonably be described as a series of actions that, taken together, reveal:

A. the reluctance of a trio of college-age friends to engage in risk-taking activities.
B. deep levels of tension between a trio of college-age friends and a rural property owner they have wronged.
C. the natural camaraderie between a trio of college-age friends and the converging of their opinions in matters small and large.
D. a natural hierarchical structure of companionship between a trio of college-age friends mature enough to survive a frightening encounter.

2. Which of the following quotes is most revelatory of Dillon's personality and best explains his disobedience of Red, who insists, upon seeing the emergence of "a shotgun's barrel" (line 44) from behind a tree, that Dillon run over the shotgun's owner?

F. "Dillon let them take off the blindfolds" (lines 3-4).
G. "Dillon had never done anything like this" (line 24).
H. "Dillon pressed the brake with a soft foot" (lines 34-35).
J. "Dillon hit the gas and swiped a tree" (line 77).

3. As it is used in line 83, the phrase "He clenched his fists" most clearly reveals:

A. Dillon's fear that Janie would be angry that he was late to meet her at the fraternity party.
B. Dillon's fear that the old farmer in the pecan grove would use his shotgun to injure one or all of the boys in the truck.
C. Dillon's anger over Red's prodding insistence to commit daring, immoral acts.
D. Dillon's anger at the damage to his truck, his most valuable possession.

4. Based on the passage, it is clear that Dillon's decision to drive his truck through the pecan grove can best be described as:

F. well thought out and carefully crafted.
G. uninfluenced by others around him.
H. originating with Janie, who takes advantage of her influence over Dillon.
J. heavily dependent upon social pressures from friends.

5. The passage seems to imply that when the trio of friends return to the fraternity house, that Janie, upon learning the truth of their experience in the pecan grove, will be:

A. unfazed by the damage done to the truck and Dillon's decision to drive through the grove.
B. disappointed in Dillon's decision, since she holds him to a higher standard than his friends do.
C. delighted that a bit of revenge, however small, has been dealt out to the old farmer.
D. surprised, given the reputation of the old farmer, that they made it out alive.

6. The main function of the sixth paragraph (lines 32-38) in the overall narrative of the story is to:

F. justify the friends' decision to trespass on Cordia's property by revealing his hidden motives.
G. provide key information related to the layout, shape, and acreage of the pecan grove.
H. create and heighten a feeling of both suspense and intrigue in the reader.
J. anticipate the destruction of Cordia's property at a later point in the story.

7. The interaction between Joey and Red in the backseat of the truck, particularly Red's punching of Joey in the shoulder, serves to reveal that Red:

A. does not tolerate Joey's fearful and contradicting statements.
B. is aggressive primarily because he is frightened.
C. anticipates that they will need to be tough to survive the altercation that is to come.
D. is afraid, but does not intend to tolerate Joey's teasing and jokes about Red's impatience.

8. In the passage, Cordia is metaphorically referred to as:

F. a smoking gun.
G. pecans and branches.
H. buckshot.
J. a jackal.

9. The passage indicates that the trio of friends:

A. have stolen pecans from Cordia in the past.
B. do not care to have Janie visit them at the fraternity house.
C. plotted revenge on Cordia as they fled the scene.
D. have trespassed on Cordia's property before.

10. It can most reasonably be inferred from the passage that Cordia limps and shuffles as he walks mainly because:

F. the churned up mud makes it difficult to take steps.
G. he had been injured in war when he was younger.
H. he is elderly.
J. it is pitch dark and he cannot see where he is stepping.

Passage II

SOCIAL SCIENCE: Passage A is adapted from the book *England and America: A Critical Comparison* (©2012 by Edward P. Block). Passage B is adapted from the book *Richard's Brother* (©1998 by Lee W. Painter).

Passage A by Edward P. Block

The American Constitution, written in 1787 and ratified in 1788, is the founding legal document of the United States, securing rights for citizens and dictating the movements of government and its system of checks and balances, among many other things. Change of this document in the form of amendments is a very strict and legal process, thus there are only 27 such amendments to the US Constitution. In the United Kingdom, such a document and process do not strictly exist.

Enacted in 1215 by King John of England, Magna Carta (originally *Magna Carta Libertatum*, meaning "Great Charter of Freedoms" in Medieval Latin) consisted of 63 clauses, most of which dealt with issues specific to King John himself. Over the next 10 years, the vast majority of these clauses would be rewritten or redacted; thus, many of the most significant changes to Magna Carta happened in the infancy of the document's influence, beginning in 1216 when Henry III, son of John, ascended to the throne. He would reissue Magna Carta more than once, most significantly in 1225 in exchange for new taxes. For a considerable time, Magna Carta was reissued by each monarch in turn and eventually solidified itself as an immovable stone in the construction of the English judicial system.

However, one clause in the original has served as a sort of bedrock of British law and an understanding of human rights the world over, most notably the Bill of Rights in the aforementioned US Constitution. It reads as such:

No free man shall be seized or imprisoned, or stripped of his rights or possessions, or outlawed or exiled, or deprived of his standing in any other way, nor will we proceed with force against him, or send others to do so, except by the lawful judgement of his equals or by the law of the land. To no one will we sell, to no one deny or delay right or justice.

This clause, number 39 in the 1215 Magna Carta, is one of only three clauses original to the document to be considered law in the United Kingdom in the present day. Much of this has to do with the organic development of British law, the courts of which may reinterpret a statute of a document such as Magna Carta from one generation to the next. On occasion, a new law may be passed by Parliament that overrules any previous legal documents, especially those issued by monarchs long ago. In modern times, the constitution of the United Kingdom, also known as the British Constitution, consists of both written and unwritten arrangements. Though uncodified into a singular body of written text or law, the piecemeal constitution of the UK does not preserve a vigilante system of justice but, quite the opposite, steadily governs the courts of Great Britain and Northern Ireland.

Passage B by Lee W. Painter

King John, the youngest of four surviving sons of King Henry II, ascended to the throne in 1199 after the death of his brother Richard, often called Richard the Lionhearted. As a young man, and being the youngest of 4 sons, he was given the nickname John Lackland because he was unlikely to inherit any land. However, John inherited at the death of his brother not only all of England and Ireland (over which he had been considered Lord for 22 years), but English-occupied France as well (including Normandy, Aquitaine, and Anjou).

Despite the signing of the Treaty of Le Goulet by both King John and Philip II, King of France, which recognized John's ownership over certain French lands, war broke in 1202 between the two sides. Though he secured early victories, John too quickly diminished funds and other military resources, and by 1204 his geographic presence on the continent was swallowed by the advances of the French King. For a decade or so and with military motives, John imposed high taxes on the citizens of England, who turned against their barons, who in turn grew increasingly angry at their king. Despite the influx in tax revenue and continental alliances, John was once and for all defeated by Philip II in 1214, permanently leaving behind the French land he had once inherited.

When John returned to England, circumstances were not much better, and his relationships with the barons continued to spoil. Despite the mutual acceptance of Magna Carta in 1215, both sides failed to live up to the document's obligations. These barons, forever known as Rebel Barons, were led by Robert Fitzwalter and others in a rebellion that led to a civil war. Louis of France, new King of France and son of Philip II, was solicited by the barons and sailed against his father's wishes to England to assist them in the war against the British King. So successful was the French army that half of England fell under French control, and Louis was proclaimed "King of England" in London by the barons themselves. After John's death, the barons softened on Louis, who was forced to sign the Treaty of Lambeth, retreat to France, and surrender any English lands and castles he claimed to be his own.

11. The author of Passage A mentions the "very strict and legal process" (lines 6-7) of amending the US Constitution primarily to:

- **A.** solidify an argument that the American Constitution is extremely applicable in the daily lives of citizens.
- **B.** reinforce the claim that the American Constitution is greater than that of other nations.
- **C.** shed light on the difficulty of passing needed laws in the American legal system.
- **D.** establish a legal system familiar to American readers so as to more easily contrast that found in the UK.

12. It can reasonably be inferred that the author of Passage A thinks that the dictates of King John of England have had what effect on modern British law?

F. No significant effect whatsoever
G. A delayed effect, only perceivable in modern times
H. An infallible, unchangeable effect
J. A moderate effect

13. The author of Passage A most directly indicates that he attributes most early changes to Magna Carta to which of the following?

A. King John of England
B. American influence from the outside
C. British Parliament
D. King Henry III

14. The author of Passage B most strongly indicates that the greatest single factor in the rebellion of the Rebel Barons upon King John's return to England was:

F. the loss of lands on the European continent.
G. the breaking of the Treaty of Le Goulet.
H. King John's overtaxing of citizens.
J. the aggression of Philip II, King of France.

15. The author of Passage B describes the circumstances leading up to and including the declaration of Louis as "King of England" (lines 84-90) primarily to:

A. downplay the lasting effect of ongoing warfare between two nations.
B. emphasize the depth of the failures traced to John's poor decision making.
C. establish Louis as superior in battle to both Richard the Lionhearted and John.
D. suggest that English leadership should rely more on documents such as Magna Carta than military whims.

16. According to Passage B, which of the following was true about the Rebel Barons?

F. They were unfailingly obedient to their king, no matter the cost.
G. They were easily swayed by foreign influences, especially those from France.
H. Their loyalties could be easily swayed, especially by changing circumstances.
J. They were reluctant to obey legal documents, Magna Carta being a rare exception.

17. As he is presented in Passage B, Philip II believes that English territory under the rule of John and any other English monarch:

A. is up for grabs when militarily susceptible due to domestic political turmoil.
B. is up for grabs when militarily susceptible due to domestic economic issues.
C. should be restricted to, and in some sense naturally includes, the English island itself.
D. should be expanded onto the European continent when economically beneficial for French citizens.

18. Which of the following statements best captures a main difference in the focus of the two passages?

F. Passage A focuses on the apparent contradictions in the British Constitution, while Passage B focuses on the motivations of the 13th century Rebel Barons.
G. Passage A focuses on the lasting nature of the majority of the clauses of Magna Carta, while Passage B focuses on the ramifications of the untimely death of Richard the Lionhearted.
H. Passage A focuses on the role of monarchs in creating a foundation for the modern British Constitution, while Passage B focuses on the military victories of the French in the 13th century.
J. Passage A focuses on the history of Magna Carta and its relationship to the British Constitution, while Passage B focuses on the domestic and foreign failures of King John of England.

19. As it is described in both Passage A and Passage B, Magna Carta in the years following its enactment in 1215 is characterized as being:

A. universal and immutable.
B. difficult to interpret and applicable to few.
C. largely ignored and subject to change.
D. over-the-top and unnecessarily lengthy.

20. Both passages support the idea that England in the early 13th-century was a time:

F. marked by turmoil, upheaval, and change.
G. in which Henry III made few legal changes.
H. for laying the groundwork for the eventual writing of Magna Carta.
J. uninfluenced by foreign interference.

Passage III

HUMANITIES: This passage is adapted from the book *A History of The Philosophical Contributions of Central and Eastern Europe* (©2020 by J. A. McAleer).

Though some have identified phenomenology as a school or a minor branch of philosophy, it is rather something quite different, perhaps best defined as a style of thought or a method of some kind concerned primarily with the objective study of subjective experiences. This differentiates it from other fields in philosophy, such as ethics, metaphysics, logic, and epistemology. Though scientific, phenomenology is not to be confused with other subjective sciences, such as psychology or neurology, though these fields have much to say and contribute to one another.

The founding of this philosophical style can be traced back to a professor and author named Edmund Husserl (1859-1938), an Austrian-German who taught and wrote in the late nineteenth and early twentieth centuries. Interestingly, his first published work (1891) was titled *Philosophy of Arithmetic*, a treatise on the philosophy of mathematics, the focus of which is the concept of *number* as a psychological one (thus, of subjective origin). As he grew as a philosopher, his phenomenological approach also grew, in which he noticed that in any interaction (such as one's viewing of a beautiful piece of art, the sound of far off sirens, or the witnessing of a crime or heroic achievement, for example), there are two factors to consider. First, there is the object itself (the art, the siren, the crime or achievement, etc.), which is the focus of most of philosophical inquiry. Second, there is the subject, the one doing the experiencing; this was the focus of Husserl. Using the Kantian distinction between *noumenon* and *phenomenon*, Husserl necessitated a process called bracketing or *epoché* in which the object itself (*noumenon*) is separated off or lost from focus entirely so as to unpack or gather the experience (*phenomenon*) of the subject.

Edith Stein (1891-1942), perhaps one of Husserl's most famous students and disciples, studied under the phenomenologist at the University of Göttingen. Her focus was primarily empathy, in particular the empathetic subject and his or her experience of empathy as such. For Stein, the empathetic experience does not require a conscious or logical process, but is a result of the sense-forward or empirical experience of the other person (however unconsciously). This experience transcends a mere emotional response to another's difficulties but, as it were, puts the subject in the place of the object, as if the former were also experiencing the latter's experience. Stein, due to her Jewish background, unfortunately became a target of the Nazis, and she lost her life at Auschwitz at the age of 50.

Another famous phenomenologist of this era was Max Scheler (1874-1928), who was nicknamed the "Adam of the philosophical paradise." Martin Heidegger, one of the most influential philosophers of the 20th century, called Scheler "the strongest philosophical force in modern Germany, nay, in contemporary Europe and in contemporary philosophy as such." Scheler first met Husserl at the Martin Luther University of Halle-Wittenberg in 1901, but was never his student. In fact, throughout their careers, Husserl and Scheler were known to disagree on minor issues, such as the method and purpose of phenomenology itself. Nevertheless, Scheler joined the Phenomenology Circle of Munich as a professor at the University of Munich. However, he only taught there from 1907 to 1910 because he became caught up in local and university politics and subsequently lost his job. After spending time as a writer, Scheler found another teaching position at the University of Cologne, where he taught from 1919-1928.

For Scheler, philosophy at large and phenomenology in particular is not to be reduced to a sterile and value-free enterprise. Rather, participation in either requires a movement or decision of love. One can not properly gain the truth, whether metaphysical conclusions about the human person or logical conclusions about mathematics, without the precondition of love for the subject of inquiry. This definition or understanding of love served to differentiate it from the mere emotional responses or reactions to that which one loves/likes and hates. Love, as an encompassing act of the will, brings out and deepens the reality and beauty of the other, whether that be a person or, for phenomenological purposes, the object of study. Sadly, Scheler developed the habit of smoking 60 to 80 cigarettes a day near the end of his life and died of complications from a heart attack on May 19, 1928.

Phenomenology has also had its critics. Some, such as Daniel Dennett (1942 –) argue that phenomenology as a method, and thus all of its conclusions and theories, should be discarded wholesale. According to Dennett, the subject of study of phenomenology (the phenomena of the individual) is reducible entirely to *qualia*, defined as instances of subjective experience and criticized for differing from person to person. For example, the sight experience of the color red is *qualia*, but different subjects will pinpoint varied shades as the true, objective red. Thus, says Dennett, if *qualia* differ from person to person, then gathering subjective experiences of multiple individuals taints a pool of data, making it incapable of objective philosophical or scientific study.

21. The structure of the passage can best be described as an overview of phenomenology primarily focusing on:

A. contradictions in the philosophical movement that have lead to division from within.
B. the surging popularity of the method throughout various European universities, but particularly those in Austria and Germany.
C. the downfall of the movement early on, but its resurgence near the end of the twentieth century.
D. its origins and major contributors spanning the late nineteenth and twentieth centuries.

22. In the passage, Daniel Dennett argues that *qualia* can be problematic from an objective, philosophical point of view because:

F. *qualia*, as a concept, predates Edmund Husserl.
G. *qualia* is not a subjective experience.
H. *qualia* can differ from person to person.
J. *qualia* is limited to visual experience of colors.

23. Based on the passage, what would Max Scheler argue is necessary for one to "properly gain the truth" (lines 72-73) in, not only philosophy, but any field of study?

A. The precondition of love, which deepens the reality and beauty of the other
B. An openness to the metaphysical, particularly the difference between the *noumenon* and *phenomenon*
C. The reduction of phenomenology to a sterile and value-free enterprise
D. Emotional responses or reactions to that which one loves, likes, or hates.

24. In the passage, it is strongly suggested that advancements in fields such as psychology and neurology:

F. will benefit phenomenology as a method.
G. will hinder the growth of phenomenology.
H. will threaten the existence of phenomenology.
J. will have no effect on phenomenology.

25. As it is used in line 62, the word *Circle* most nearly refers to:

A. a shape more properly called an *oval*.
B. a group of people with shared interests.
C. the movement of one object around another.
D. a perfectly round shape.

26. In the passage, the reference to "the sound of far off sirens" (lines 22-23) provides an example of:

F. a *phenomenon* of a subject.
G. the subjective origin of all experiences.
H. an empathetic experience.
J. a precondition for the use of *epoché*.

27. The passage makes it clear that, for Daniel Dennett, the varied responses or reactions to the same sense experience by different persons:

A. is evidence for the discrediting of phenomenology.
B. proves the efficacy of phenomenology.
C. is the starting point of philosophical inquiry.
D. is an opportunity to distinguish *phenomenon* and *noumenon*.

28. The passage most strongly suggests that Edith Stein used a phenomenological approach to reach which of the following conclusions?

F. Empathy is something to be avoided, as it causes a subject to focus too deeply on another.
G. An empathetic response transcends a mere emotional response.
H. Empathy can and should be detached from the object of empathy: the other person.
J. Empathy, by its nature, always requires both a conscious and a logical process.

29. The author most directly describes the philosophical practice of phenomenology as which of the following?

A. A minor branch of philosophy
B. A major branch of philosophy
C. A style of thought or a type of method
D. A school of thought

30. In the passage, the author makes clear that Edmund Husserl had what kind of an effect on Max Scheler?

F. Scheler learned of Husserl's phenomenology and rejected it wholesale.
G. Husserl, as Scheler's professor, taught Scheler about love as a precondition in philosophy.
H. Though they disagree on minor issues, Scheler was dependent on the thought of Husserl in his professional life.
J. Because the two never met, if Husserl had any effect on Scheler, it was minor at best.

Passage IV

NATURAL SCIENCE: This passage is adapted from the article "The Rocks of Space: From Shooting Star to Museum Display" by Caitlin Richards (©2008 by Nevada Astronomical Annual Magazine).

A meteorite is a solid object originating outside of the atmosphere of earth that survives its descent to the planet's surface. More than 90% of verified meteorites are rocky, but a small percentage contain iron or nickel. Although it is estimated that as much as 120 tons of space matter (consisting mostly of space dust, or finite particles) enter the atmosphere of earth each and every day, a relatively small amount will survive the 62 mile descent from the Van Karmen line at the edge of space to the surface of the planet. This is due to the burning up of meteors in the atmosphere at temperatures as high as 2,000 degrees Kelvin (over 3,000 degrees Fahrenheit). Those that survive the descent will retain a fusion crust, a telltale meteorite sign that is often confused with desert varnish, hematite coatings, and spheroidal weathering (the process in which concentric outer layers of rock break away in pieces).

Since the early 19th century, less than 1,900 meteorites have been discovered and verified in the United States. Despite the rarity of having discovered a meteorite, thousands of persons each year seek expert classification to determine the nature of a stone they have stumbled upon. A test by a professional can help to reveal if the mineral in question is a meteorwrong (such as hematite and magnetite, both dense iron-oxides, or slag, the metallic byproduct of smelting) or one of three varieties of meteorite: stony-type, iron-type, or stony/iron-type.

While some stony-type meteorites may contain small traces of metal, they are mostly composed of minerals that contain silicates (materials made of Silicon and Oxygen). Of these stony-type meteorites, the most common is the chondrite, representing roughly 86% of all meteorite types and 88% of all stony-type meteorite samples. Chondrites originate from asteroids and are estimated to be over 4.5 billion years old (in other words, material from which the solar system formed). What separates a chondrite from an achondrite (a second, rarer variety of stony-type meteorite) is that the former has never undergone an igneous or melting phase. Almost all chondrites are composed of 33-43% SiO_2 (Silicon Dioxide), which is slightly less than most lunar (43-48%) or Martian (44-53%, with outliers on either side) rocks. Most terrestrial meteorwrongs (sandstone, quartzite, basalt, and rhyolite, among others) possess much higher concentrations of Silicon Dioxide because they contain quartz, a mineral never found in meteorites. In addition, most chondrites contain higher levels of Magnesium Oxide (MgO) than terrestrial meteorwrongs or lunar meteorites. While the percentage of MgO in Martian rocks varies greatly, that of the chondrite will likely fall between 21 and 26%, with very few outliers.

Iron-type meteorites (also known as ferrous meteorites or siderites) consist overwhelmingly of meteoric iron, an iron-nickel alloy. Typically, meteoric iron consists of two phases. The first, kamacite, typically features an isometric-hexoctahedral crystalline structure, and is composed of an iron:nickel ratio between 90%:10% and 95%:5%. Occasionally, kamacite may contain traces of cobalt or carbon, and it is not uncommon for it to intermix with the second siderite phase (taenite) in the same meteorite, forming Widmanstätten patterns, or fine interleaving of the two phases in ribbons or bands called *lamellae*. Taenite differs from kamacite primarily in iron:nickel ratio, which can vary from 80%:20% to 35%:65%. Ataxites, iron-type meteorites in which taenite is the dominant constituent, best show the opaque nature and metallic grayish color of taenite; this is a second characteristic that distinguishes taenite from kamacite, as the latter is not opaque and features a metallic luster. Most iron meteorites are believed to have originated in the cores of asteroids that melted long ago, early in their individual histories; as the asteroids melted over time, the densest elements sank to the center to form a metallic core.

Stony/iron-type meteorites, as the name suggests, are meteorites made up of nearly equal parts silicates and meteoric iron. Also known as siderolites, these meteorites are achondrites, meaning they do not contain the round grains known as chondrules that typically form as molten droplets in space before accretion into parent asteroids. Of the two types of stony/iron-type meteorites, the pallasite contains a beautiful olive-green crystal called *olivine* (a form of magnesium-iron silicate), which can also be found in the earth's mantle. Many scientists believe that the pallasite comes from the boundary between an asteroid's metallic core and silicate-rich mantle, but others maintain that the number of olivine-rich asteroids in the solar system is few, and these thus hypothesize that impact melting (when a meteorite strikes the earth) plays a direct role in the formation of olivine in pallasites.

A second stony-iron meteorite is the mesosiderite, which, as a breccia, consists of a variety of rocks (in this case, silicates and metal) cemented together by a finer material. Mesosiderites form when debris from an asteroid collision mixes together; specifically, molten metal from an asteroid core intermixes with solid fragments of silicate rocks.

31. One of the main ideas presented in the passage is that a a meteorwrong, of which there are many types:

A. is easily mistaken for a meteorite, and scientific study is mostly unable to pinpoint a difference.
B. is easily mistaken for a meteorite, but scientific study can differentiate the two.
C. can never be made up of or possess a significant amount of quartz.
D. is rarely discovered, let alone submitted for a scientific analysis.

32. Based on the passage, which of the following is most likely to be true about an authentic meteorite?

F. The meteorite is a chondrite.
G. The meteorite contains both kamacite and taenite.
H. The meteorite comes from the metallic core of an asteroid.
J. The meteorite is cemented together by a finer material.

33. The passage indicates that the main difference between stony-type and iron-type meteorites is:

A. stony-type meteorites are exclusively lunar, but iron-type originate in an asteroid's core.
B. iron-type meteorites are exclusively lunar, but stony-type originate in an asteroid's core.
C. stony-type meteorites originate in an asteroid's core, but iron-type originate in an asteroid's mantle.
D. iron-type meteorites originate in an asteroid's core, but stony-type originate in an asteroid's mantle.

34. It can be reasonably inferred that the passage author considers which of the following topics to be an area of needed scientific research in the field of meteorology?

F. The chemical difference between lunar and Martian rocks
G. The root cause of olivine in pallasites
H. The time it takes for mesosiderites to form
J. The chemical makeup of the chondrite

35. The passage indicates that a meteorite composed of at least 90% iron is likely to possess what characteristic?

A. An opaque look
B. A metallic, grayish color
C. A metallic luster
D. Bands of *lamellae*

36. In the passage, the primary purpose of the second paragraph (lines 18-28) is to:

F. highlight the rarity of a meteorite find and introduce the three meteorite types.
G. transition the passage from a detailed overview of a meteorite's chemical makeup to a more broad discussion of meteorite origins.
H. pinpoint the most likely locations across the United States to discover authentic meteorites.
J. raise awareness of the often faulty process of meteorite verification by scientists.

37. According to the passage, which of the following might be an example of a meteorwrong?

A. A basalt sample showing signs of spheroidal weathering
B. A siderite sample with a fusion crust
C. A pallasite sample containing olivine
D. A majority-kamacite sample with Widmanstätten patterns

38. Based on the passage, the author's assertion that "as much as 120 tons of space matter…enter the atmosphere of earth each and every day" (lines 5-8) is best described as:

F. a sobering statistic about the effect of man-made space debris on meteorites.
G. a frightening statistic meant to awaken the reader to the likelihood of being struck by a meteorite.
H. a surprising statistic meant to set the stage for additional information about the rarity of meteorites.
J. a jolting statistic means to arouse the reader's curiosity about the ever-increasing likelihood or making a meteorite find.

39. The author references the igneous or melting phase of many asteroids in the third paragraph (line 40) primarily in order to:

A. differentiate chondrites from achondrites.
B. highlight the formation of quartz in most meteorites.
C. shed light on the origins of most meteorwrongs.
D. contrast lunar and Martian rocks.

40. As it is used in line 22, the word *nature* most nearly means:

F. essence.
G. creation.
H. appearance.
J. landscape.

Step 6 Correct Answers

Practice Test 1

Passage I	Passage II	Passage III	Passage IV
1: A	11: A	21: B	31: C
2: F	12: G	22: H	32: G
3: C	13: B	23: C	33: D
4: F	14: H	24: G	34: G
5: B	15: C	25: B	35: D
6: J	16: J	26: F	36: F
7: D	17: B	27: A	37: C
8: H	18: H	28: J	38: G
9: D	19: A	29: D	39: A
10: J	20: J	30: F	40: H

Practice Test 2

Passage I	Passage II	Passage III	Passage IV
1: B	11: D	21: D	31: B
2: G	12: J	22: H	32: F
3: D	13: D	23: A	33: D
4: J	14: H	24: F	34: G
5: B	15: B	25: B	35: C
6: H	16: H	26: J	36: F
7: A	17: C	27: A	37: A
8: J	18: J	28: G	38: H
9: D	19: C	29: C	39: A
10: H	20: F	30: H	40: F

Stumped on any? You will find the explanations and possible Passage Maps for each answer beginning on page 630 (Practice Test 1) and 641 (Practice Test 2).

The ACT Science *System*

Six Steps to ACT Science Perfection

Introduction to ACT Science

The ACT Science test consists of 6 passages, each of which is followed by 6 or 7 questions; you are given 35 minutes to answer these 40 questions to the best of your ability, which equates to 5 minutes and 50 seconds per passage (that may sound like a lot, but anyone who has taken the test knows the truth that the time will fly by!). The passages themselves are drawn from a diverse array of science topics, including physics, chemistry, geology, biology, astronomy, etc., but in no particular order.

There are three types or categories of ACT Science passages that will be discussed in this book, and they are as follows:

1) Data Representation - two of the six passages will be in the category of Data Representation; each of these passages is followed by 6 questions. Essentially, these passages present lots of data in the form of graphs, charts, tables, diagrams, etc., and it will mostly be your responsibility to read, find, and interpret that data. What's also important about this type of passage is what it is missing, which is multiple experiments or studies to compare and contrast. In that sense, these two passages are *simpler* in structure.

2) Research Summary - three of the six passages will be in the category of Research Summary; each of these passages is followed by 7 questions (thus, 21 total questions or over half of all ACT Science questions follow these passages). Essentially, these passages also present lots of data in the form of graphs, charts, tables, diagrams, etc., but they also include descriptions and results from multiple experiments or studies.

In general, I will not make a big fuss in this book in distinguishing the two types of passages presented above, though there will be some discussion in the matter. More on this in Step 1.

3) Conflicting Viewpoints - one of the six passages will be in the category of Conflicting Viewpoints; this passage is followed by 7 questions. This passage is unique in that it rarely features any data presented in

graphs and tables; rather, it focuses on a disagreement between two or more scientists about a particular topic. Typically, this passage features only written words in the form of paragraphs. While many students are caught off guard by this passage and do not know how to hit this curveball, you, on the other hand, will be prepared; Step 4 of *The ACT Science System* is dedicated to this kind of passage.

What This Test Isn't

There are many students who excel in science class in high school and perform poorly on the ACT Science test. If this is you, you are not alone. In high school, there are lots of ways to boost your grade, including doing homework, studying for tests and quizzes, participating in class, cleaning your lab station well, presenting results effectively as a group, doing that random extra credit assignment that your teacher offered at the end of the quarter, and the list goes on and on. Unfortunately, the ACT Science test is really none of those things; it is not really like any test you have ever taken before. Think about it: when was the last time your teacher gave you a *timed* test requiring you to analyze material you had never seen?

Even the name of this test is a bit deceiving in that you will not really be *doing* any science (which is really what science *is*, since science is a method to acquiring knowledge). For example, I remember in my sophomore year of high school that I was the class pro at balancing chemical equations. Students from around the class would bring me equations they were stumped on and I would be able to piece together the atoms in a matter of seconds (using mols, on the other hand, was quite a chemistry struggle for me!). This is a *skill* in science; but the ACT Science Test is not about testing these kinds of scientific skills. It's not really about how much science you know, either, as *very few* of the questions require any kind of previous science knowledge at all (and even these questions rely on basic scientific ideas, like the difference between a meter and a millimeter).

Instead, this test is more true to its old name: *Science Reasoning*. This means that the subject matter is scientific, and you have to reason your way through it given the information before you. 'Reasoning' might sound like a scary word, but it isn't. It simply means that you have to think your way to correct answers sometimes, which can often mean eliminating answers you know to be wrong one at a time until you're left with just one. And even then, most of this reasoning involves reading data off of a chart or table and then taking one additional step (like comparing it to another piece of data or reaching a conclusion about all of the data, etc.).

Strategy

Strategy for taking the ACT Science test in the most effective and efficient way comes down to reading through the passage as fast as you can remembering a couple of things to do and avoid. This kind of "fast reading" is called *active reading*. For the purposes of ACT Science, this means that you have your pencil in hand and are *willing* or *choosing* to read over everything quickly and well. If you are familiar with what I say about active reading in The ACT Reading System, then you might be surprised that I am not making as big of a deal here as I did there. In fact, the ability to active read is Step 1 in The ACT Reading System. With ACT Science, however, there's typically *not* a lot to read. This means that what you do with the information before you is more critical, and is summed up by the following list of things to do and to avoid:

Do:

- <u>Read quickly</u> - as has been said, you don't want to be sitting there tired with your head leaning on your arm as if you're about to fall asleep. This is going to cause you to read very slowly and without any kind of comprehension. Those who choose (using their will power!) to read quickly and alertly are at a significant advantage over the student half asleep yawning and sighing his way through the test.

- <u>Underline/circle key words and ideas</u> - when you come to a seemingly key word being defined in the passage, circle it or underline it or both. This draws the attention of your mind to that information.

- <u>Annotate or doodle to extract trends/relationships</u> - make use of the margins. Next to written paragraphs, if you are told that as a certain chemical is burned at higher and higher temperatures, the color changes from purple to red to pink to white, jot in the margins something like this: **temp ↑ purp. to white**. This takes an idea and concretizes it into something manageable.

- Notice data trends along *x* and *y* axes - though you don't have time to analyze each piece of data or information in every table and graph, you can notice trends. In a graph, you may notice that a trend goes up, then decreases (for example). In a table, notice that as one data set decreases, another also decreases. In other words, a brief overview of the data is called for, though not a thorough review.

Avoid:

- "Sticker shock" - this is a phrase that refers to the shock of seeing the higher-than-expected price of something you want to buy. Although you don't want to buy anything during the ACT Science test, you can still be left with a terrible shock each time you turn the page. When you do so, what you'll likely see with most of the passages is diagrams, charts, data, and scientific words and terms that you've never heard, don't recognize, and that just plain look scary. However: *no student taking the ACT Science test has ever seen this stuff either*. You are on the same level as everyone in the room. Again, *the ACT is expecting you to have little to no previous science knowledge; the fact that you don't know what is before you is absolutely irrelevant!* It doesn't matter if it's physics or chemistry or about animals or outer space: you will not be familiar with any of what you see before you, and that's the point.

But, here's the silver lining: *it all makes sense*. What you see in front you in that ACT Science passage is something that is ordered, organized, and the result of a science experiment or experiments. It is well thought out. It is, by its nature, *sensical*, not nonsensical. Your reaction to what you see initially is confusion, but what you're looking at *isn't* confusion. That's why you have to read it!

- Pronouncing scientific terms - during the ACT Science test, you are going to come across lots of scientific terms that, again, you've probably never heard and could barely pronounce. For example: *Azeotropic distillation*, or *Klebsiella pneumoniae*, or *Coma Berenices*. You don't need to correctly pronounce these words; just call them "Az" and "Kleb" and "Coma B" in your mind.

- Memorizing data - during your first read through the passage, you don't have to memorize data presented to you in tables, graphs, charts, etc. Instead, simply glance over these means of presenting data to come to a basic understanding of the data itself. Look for what is along the x-axis, what is along the y-axis, and what trends may be obvious in the data.

- Getting hung up on very difficult questions - let's face it: some of the ACT Science questions are going to be purposefully at a higher level of difficulty. You can expect roughly 2-3 of these types of questions on your next ACT Science test; they require an understanding of the passage, an understanding of data, and some deep reasoning skills (more on these in Step 5). Give them your best shot, of course, but remember that if you spend 2 minutes on 2 of these questions, that's 4 minutes gone, almost guaranteeing that you will not give yourself sufficient time on easier questions at the end of the test in the final passage. Have the wisdom to circle these questions after making a guess so you can return to them if you have spare time at the end of the test.

Another "Strategy"

The ACT exam will begin at 8:00 AM (unless you're in some kind of situation that is an exception). This means that sometime around 11:00 AM the ACT Science exam will begin. This means that you've already taken a 45 minute long ACT English test (with 75 questions), a 60 minute long ACT Math test (with 60 questions), and a 35 minute long ACT Reading test (with 40 questions). Needless to say, you are worn out. You need a nap or an energy drink or a day at the beach or a nice long hug or all of the above.

However, what this means is that *most students make the major mistake of not choosing to stick it out through the ACT Science test*! The vast majority of ACT students in the room aren't aware that they are tired and fading. This leads not only to careless mistakes which sometimes can't be avoided, but one major mistake that can be avoided: *guessing just because they're tired.* You know the feeling. You're on number 22 of the ACT Science test and it's asking about some molecule you've never heard of and what it does when exposed to some chemical and you just don't *feel like* figuring it out so you glance over the answers and put C.

You've been there, right? It's the effect of being overtired and just plain over it.

However, think of it like this: even if you do that only 8 times, chances are that you will get 6 of those 8 questions incorrect. That doesn't sound like a big deal. However, getting those six questions wrong… *could drop your ACT Science score as many as SEVEN POINTS!*

Did you hear that? As many as SEVEN POINTS, and a minimum of FOUR POINTS! A drop of 4 points on the ACT Science test will mean a 1 point decrease in your overall ACT score, but a drop of 7 points will mean a 2 point decrease in your overall ACT score.

Now, reverse your thinking: if you can stick with it and try on these questions and get most of them correct, you are raising your ACT score by a point or two. So, how to avoid this over-exhausted-guessing-spree?

a) - the basics. Get a good sleep the night before, wake up early enough to eat a good, balanced breakfast before the ACT (NOT a bowl of sugary cereal and an energy drink, but eggs, bacon, and fruit), and a good snack on the break. Between ACT Math and Reading, you will get a break of 10 minutes. That's not very long, but it's long enough to get a bit of a recharge. Don't eat a bag of salty chips; eat a protein bar or an apple or something like that.

b) - take a good, deep, long breath between each of the ACT Science passages while committing yourself to do your best on this one passage before you. This five-second investment will take you far and help eliminate the temptation to guess all the time out of exhaustion.

Timing

Keeping time on the ACT Science test is relatively straightforward. As has been said, each test requires you to use an average of 5 minutes and 50 seconds per passage. That's difficult to do, since keeping track of whether or not 5 minutes and 50 seconds or 6 minutes has gone by. It is easier to remember that you have 6 minutes for each passage except for one; in other words, one of the Data Representation passages (the ones with only data that have only 6 questions after them) should only take you 5 minutes.

Unfortunately, one mistake that many students make is that they start guessing when they hear "Five minutes remaining!" However, this call isn't a signal to the end of the test, but rather simply a five minute warning; this is not the time to start guessing, seeing as it will take you about 5 minutes to complete an entire passage!

STEP 1

Reading, Analyzing, and Interpreting Data

As has been said, the ACT Science test does not require that you have much previous scientific knowledge. Instead, it is testing your reasoning skills. However, even those reasoning skills are built upon a more basic scientific or mathematic skill: reading, analyzing, and comparing information off of charts, tables, and graphs. This skill is *the most necessary skill* on the ACT Science test.

It's All About the Data

There is often a lot going on in any given ACT Science passage. Sometimes, you have a diagram of some process or scientific object, like a cell or animal. Sometimes there might be a very complicated-looking equation shoved in there somewhere (but don't worry: any math required on the ACT is so basic that you are not allowed to use a calculator; usually these equations, if present, are designed to scare the student). Sometimes you have paragraphs of information that feature multiple definitions of very scientific words you may have never heard before.

The *good news* is that the number one thing that will move the needle on your ACT Science score the most involves none of these things. Instead, it involves your ability to look at the graphs, charts, and tables and read them properly, pulling out the correct information and perhaps inferring to a correct answer or comparing the data to another piece of data. In fact, about 60% of all ACT Science questions require this skill in one way or another…so it's important!

Passage Types and Data

In the introduction to ACT Science, I differentiated between three "types" of ACT Science Passages: Data Representation, Research Summaries, and Conflicting Viewpoints. Most of the time, the Conflicting Viewpoints passage (again, more discussion on this in Step 4) features no data, charts, tables, or graphs, making it mostly irrelevant for our current discussion under Step 1. It is the former two that need a bit more discussion.

Data Representation passages do just that: they represent a bunch of data from one kind of experiment or topic. Often, data in this passage is presented in different ways. For example, you might have a pie chart called "Figure 1," a table of data called "Table 1," and a graph of other data called "Figure 2." These types of passages are *typically* the "easiest," and because they only have 6 questions that follow them as opposed to 7, they should usually take a bit less time too.

Research Summaries passages, like Data Representation Passages, feature lots of data presented in charts, graphs, and tables. However, these passages feature multiple trials, experiments, or studies that have overlapping variables. For example, you may have a Trial 1 that tests the rate of growth of various plants watered with a sports drink, a Trial 2 that tests the rate of growth of these same plants watered with an energy drink, and a Trial 3 that tests the rate of growth of these same plants watered with coffee (and all three trials will be compared to a control group grown with water). What's happening here is that the **independent variable** (meaning, what the scientists control, in this case, what is being used to water the plants) is changing from trial to trial. This is resulting in new data, or values for the **dependent variable** (in this case, the rate of growth of the various plants). Some of the questions will require you to compare these one to the other.

The Practice That Follows

Now, it is time to put into practice this number 1 skill. You will be presented with 6 ACT Science passages (called Passage I, II, III, IV, V, and VI) in a row, just like on the real ACT. Each and every question associated with these passages in Step 1 have to do exclusively with this skill. In other words, other elements of the passage (most especially what is defined, given, or described in the written portion) are unnecessary for getting these questions correct. Importantly, I will be using *these same passages* to ask new, different types of questions in Step 2, Step 3, and Step 5 as well.

So, without further ado, let's practice this skill. Remember: each question is exclusively about the data!

Passage I

Most of the water consumption within the United States is used by the agricultural industry for food production. This heavily contributes to the overuse of groundwater aquifers. Therefore, finding alternative resources of water for agricultural production is necessary to lessen the looming threat of food and water scarcity. One issue is that alternative water sources in certain regions often contain a higher concentration of salt compared to groundwater aquifers, and many food crops are not selected for traits like tolerance to salt. In recent years, new varieties, also called *variants*, of crops have been selected mostly for commercial benefit, with little regard for producing varieties that can withstand changes in salt concentrations. As a result, a group of researchers sought to determine plant variants that are resilient to waters with higher salt concentrations.

Researchers first tested the salt tolerance in variants of two regularly consumed crops, tomato and pepper, by testing the consumable yields of each plant when grown in the same soil. The control for the experiment was freshwater from a ground water aquifer, while the experimental condition was done with water containing a higher salt content. The results are recorded in Table 1 (tomato) and Table 2 (pepper) below.

	Fruit yield (grams)	
Tomato variant	Control	Experimental
Bloody Butcher	2785	1719
Juane Flamme	2317	1355
Quarter Century	1415	928

Table 1

	Fruit yield (grams)	
Pepper variant	Control	Experimental
California Wonder	2591	1993
Thai Hot	295	291
Ancho	1514	1489

Table 2

The researchers next tested the concentration of sodium within the plant tissue of the different variants for both the control and saltwater (experimental) groups. Their findings are recorded in Figure 1 (tomato) and Figure 2 (pepper) below in millimoles per kilogram.

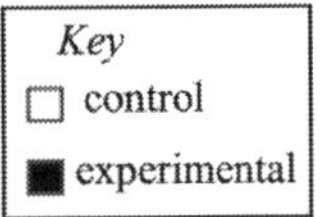

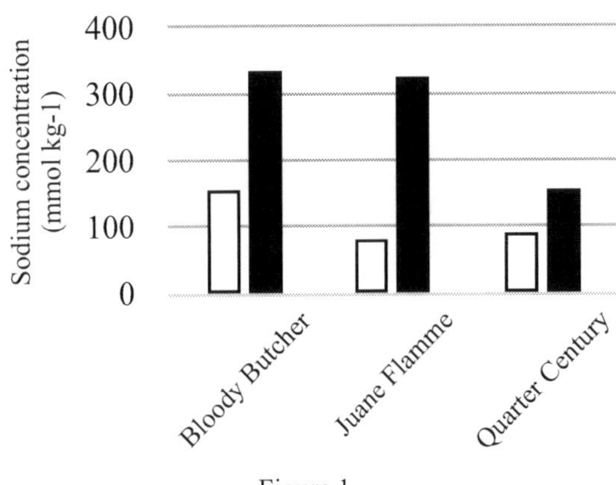

Figure 1

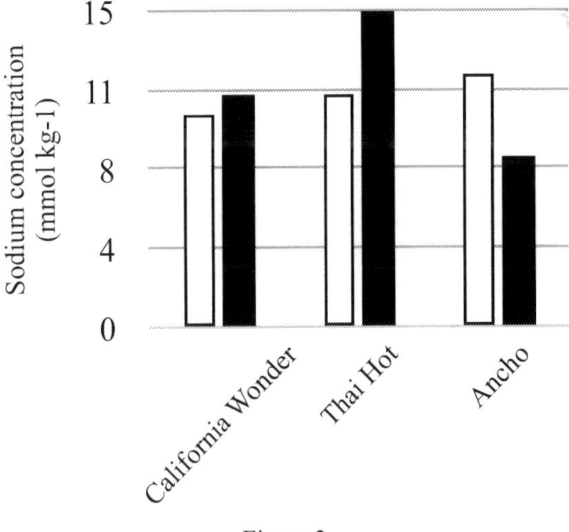

Figure 2

1. Based on Figures 1 and 2, which variety of fruit saw the greatest difference in sodium concentration between the control and experimental groups?

   A. Bloody Butcher
   B. Juane Flamme
   C. Thai Hot
   D. Ancho

2. According to Tables 1 and 2, which plant variety yielded the most fruit with experimental watering relative to the control?

F. Bloody Butcher
G. Juane Flamme
H. California Wonder
J. Thai Hot

3. If a higher sodium concentration results in a saltier taste, then which variety of fruit's experimental yield will taste less salty than the control?

A. Bloody Butcher
B. Juane Flamme
C. California Wonder
D. Ancho

4. Based on Figures 1 and 2, which variety of fruit contains the highest sodium concentration in mmol/kg-1?

F. Bloody Butcher
G. Juane Flamme
H. Thai Hot
J. Ancho

Passage II

A group of high school students investigated the momentum of carts rolling down an inclined plane across a designated finish line. The students used three carts, labeled Cart A, Cart B, and Cart C. Cart A had a mass of 12.5 kg, Cart B had a mass of 21.8 kg, and Cart C had a mass of 34.7 kg. They conducted five trials, progressively increasing the release height of the carts. The purpose of the experiment was to explore how changes in release height affect the velocity and momentum of the carts.

Velocity is a fundamental concept in physics that represents the speed of an object in a specific direction. In this experiment, velocity was measured as each cart crossed the finish line, but can also be determined using the equation $v = \sqrt{2gh}$, where v is the velocity, g is the acceleration due to gravity (approximately 9.8 m/s²), and h is the release height of the cart.

Momentum is a property of a moving object that depends on its mass and velocity. It describes the quantity of motion possessed by an object and is calculated by multiplying the mass of the object by its velocity. The equation for momentum is given as $p = mv$, where p represents the momentum, m is the mass of the object, and v denotes the velocity.

After collecting data, the students calculated the momentum for each cart and trial. Figure 1 shows the recorded velocity for each cart as it crossed the finish line, and Figure 2 shows the calculated momentum for each cart as it crossed the finish line.

Figure 1

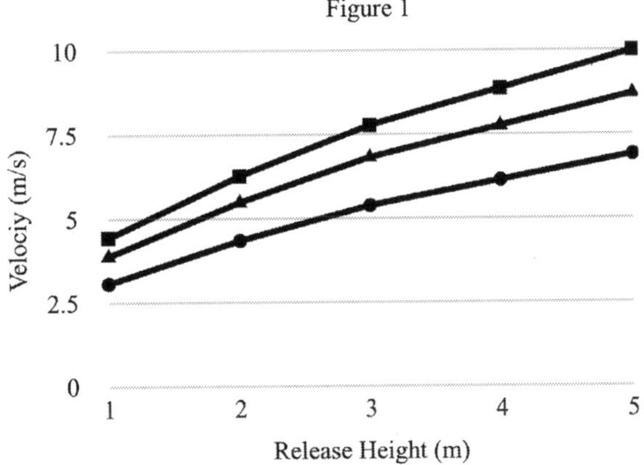

Figure 2

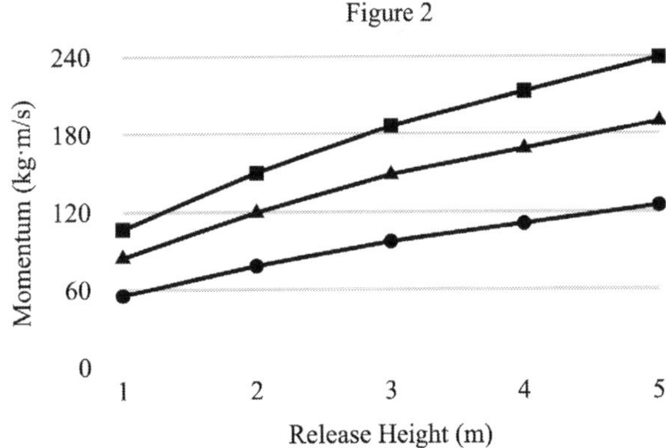

5. If Cart B were to be released from a height of 4.5 meters, it would be expected to cross the finish line with an expected momentum of:

   A. 8.5 kg·m/s
   B. 160 kg·m/s
   C. 180 kg·m/s
   D. 200 kg·m/s

6. According to Figure 1, the smallest difference in velocity recorded between the three carts resulted from a release height of:

   F. 1 meter
   G. 2 meters
   H. 3 meters
   J. 5 meters

7. One of the students decides to conduct a sixth trial in which Cart C is released from a height of 8 meters. Is it likely that it will record a velocity greater than 7.5 m/s as it crosses the finish line?

   A. Yes: an increase of 1 or more m/s is expected, enough to reach the milestone.
   B. Yes: the cart has already reached this milestone, and a drop in velocity is unexpected.
   C. No: based on its current trajectory, it is unlikely that the cart will reach the milestone.
   D. No: the mass of the cart would have to be significantly increased to mathematically have a chance to reach the milestone.

8. Which of the following carts had the highest velocity as it crossed the finish line?

   F. Cart A released at a height of 1 meter
   G. Cart A released at a height of 2 meters
   H. Cart B released at a height of 3 meters
   J. Cart C released at a height of 4 meters

Passage III

The *Mpemba Effect* refers to a curious phenomenon in which hot water freezes faster than cold water under certain circumstances. Several proposed explanations have been put forth to shed light on the Mpemba Effect. One possibility relates to the evaporation of the hot water during the cooling process. As hot water is exposed to lower temperatures, it undergoes rapid evaporation, resulting in a reduction in its volume. This reduction in volume leads to an increase in the concentration of dissolved solids in the remaining water. Consequently, the higher concentration of dissolved solids may lower the freezing point of the hot water, allowing it to freeze more rapidly.

A group of students designed an experiment to test the Mpemba Effect. They collected four beakers and labeled them A, B, C, and D. *Thermocouples*, or thermoelectric devices for measuring temperature, were placed in the bottom of each beaker. Beakers A and B were filled with distilled (purified) water, and beakers C and D were filled with tap water. The water in beakers A and C was heated to 50 degrees Celsius, and the water in beakers B and D was left at room temperature (around 30 degrees Celsius).

The students recorded the temperature of each beaker after placing it in a freezer with a temperature of -18° Celsius until it had reached 0° Celsius, the freezing point of water. The observations of the students are given below. Table 1 corresponds to beaker A, Table 2 to beaker B, Table 3 to beaker C, and Table 4 to beaker D.

Table 1 (Beaker A)	
Time Elapsed (minutes)	Temperature (°C)
0	50
5	42
10	36
15	30
20	25
25	21
30	17
35	13
40	10
45	8
50	5
55	2
60	0

Table 2 (Beaker B)	
Time Elapsed (minutes)	Temperature (°C)
0	30
5	26
10	23
15	20
20	18
25	17
30	14
35	12
40	10
45	8
50	6
55	5
60	4
65	3
70	0

Table 3 (Beaker C)	
Time Elapsed (minutes)	Temperature (°C)
0	50
5	44
10	38
15	33
20	28
25	24
30	20
35	17
40	14
45	11
50	8
55	5
60	3
65	0

Table 4 (Beaker D)	
Time Elapsed (minutes)	Temperature (°C)
0	30
5	26
10	22
15	19
20	18
25	17
30	15
35	13
40	11
45	10
50	8
55	6
60	4
65	2
70	1
75	0

9. If all four beakers had been placed in the freezer at the exact same time, and the temperatures were checked after 70 minuted had elapsed, what percent of the beakers would read a temperature of 0° Celsius or colder?

A. 0%
B. 25%
C. 75%
D. 100%

10. If the beakers' temperatures had been checked in 1 minute intervals instead of 5 minute intervals, then the temperature of Beaker C after 37 minutes had elapsed would be expected to be about:

F. 11° Celsius
G. 16° Celsius
H. 18° Celsius
J. 21° Celsius

11. Which beaker saw the greatest drop in temperature between 10 minutes having elapsed and 45 minutes having elapsed?

A. Beaker A
B. Beaker B
C. Beaker C
D. Beaker D

12. Which beaker held water that took the most amount of time to drop from 20° Celsius to 0° Celsius?

F. Beaker A
G. Beaker B
H. Beaker C
J. Beaker D

Passage IV

Real-time polymerase chain reaction (PCR) *analysis* is a laboratory technique that can be used to help determine if a specific type of DNA is present in a sample. This technique works by increasing the total amount of DNA present in a sample, a step called *amplification*, and then detecting if the DNA matches the target DNA.

Detection of the target DNA is determined by the *cycle threshold* (CT) value. The CT value is the number of cycles of amplification that is needed for a specific DNA sequence to be detected in a sample. The lower the CT value, the more likely it is that the sample contains the DNA of interest. Most real-time PCR analyses undergo a total of 40 cycles of amplification.

While this technique is often used for medical purposes, it also has applications in food safety. Due to the safety concerns regarding food allergens, scientists will use real-time PCR to search for the DNA of common allergen causing ingredients in commercial products to ensure that the package label is accurate. One common and often dangerous food allergy is an allergy to peanuts. If a person is severely allergic to peanuts and unknowingly ingests even a small amount, it could be deadly. Therefore, scientists completed real-time PCR analysis to test commercial food products for DNA that matches the peanut.

Table 1 shows commercial food products, their current package labels for allergens, and the CT values discovered by a researcher for each following real-time PCR analysis to detect peanut DNA. An N.D. value means that there was no detection of the target DNA after 40 cycles of amplification.

Table 1

Food	Food Packaging Allergen Declaration	Peanut CT Value
Cereal bar I	Peanut, hazelnut	17.97
Cereal bar II	Almond and tree nuts	32.40
Cereal bar III	Hazelnut, almond and peanut traces	33.74
Cereal bar IV	May contain tree nut traces	35.90
Chocolate with pistachio	Pistachio, almond, hazelnut, tree nut traces	36.80
Sausage with walnut	Walnuts	N.D.
Chocolate	Almond and hazelnut traces	37.99
Cookies with fiber	Not declared	32.25

Table 2 displays example CT values and the likelihood of the values causing an allergic reaction in an individual with peanut allergy (if testing for peanut DNA).

Table 2

Example CT Value	Likelihood of Causing Peanut Allergic Reaction
≤ 29	High
30-35	High to moderate
36-40	Low to none

13. A scientist finds that a new type of energy bar contains a CT value of 39.7. Should the manufacturer label the bar as likely to cause a peanut-triggered allergic reaction?

A. Yes: the higher the CT value, the more likely the bar will trigger an allergic reaction.
B. Yes: a CT value that ends in a decimal is more likely to cause a reaction than those that are whole numbers.
C. No: a CT value between 36 and 40 is extremely unlikely to cause such an allergic reaction.
D. No: any CT value less than 50 has a 0% likelihood in triggering such an allergic reaction.

14. How many of the foods tested by the researcher possesses a high likelihood to trigger an allergic reaction if consumed by someone with a severe peanut allergy?

F. 1
G. 2
H. 6
J. 7

15. What percent of the foods tested by the researcher that have a high to moderate likelihood of causing a peanut allergic reaction state the presence of peanuts in their food packaging?

A. 0%
B. 33%
C. 50%
D. 67%

16. A food company creates a new cereal bar and declares on the food packaging that it may contain traces of tree nuts and walnuts. It would be expected that such a cereal bar, if tested by the researcher, would generate a CT value of:

F. 0-15
G. 15-25
H. 25-30
J. 30-40

Passage V

Enzymes are substances that act as a catalyst to speed up biochemical reactions. When a *substrate* binds to the active site of an enzyme, a reaction can occur in which the substrate is converted into one or more products. The digestive enzyme, Trypsin, catalyzes the process of breaking down proteins in the small intestine into amino acids, which can then be absorbed into the blood stream. Importantly, any physical or chemical changes to an enzyme's environment, such as changes in temperature, pH, and salt concentration, can alter its ability to function by denaturing or inactivating the enzyme.

Two experiments sought to compare the ability of Trypsin to generate products (amino acids) at two different pH levels. For each experiment, four vials were made to contain 1mM of Trypsin and differing concentrations of substrate. The values of light absorbance for each sample were recorded every 30 seconds for 2.5 minutes using a *spectrophotometer*, an apparatus for measuring the intensity of light. The measured absorbance values were collected at a wavelength that corresponds to the relative amount of product that was generated in the samples. In other words, a higher absorbance value at the indicated wavelength would mean more product was made by the Trypsin.

Experiment 1

Four vials were made to contain 1mM of Trypsin and differing levels of substrate concentration maintained at a pH of 8. The absorbance values after each 30 second time period for each substrate level is recorded in Table 1.

	Absorbance value				
Substrate level (mM)	0.5 min	1 min	1.5 min	2 min	2.5 min
0.04	0.023	0.035	0.053	0.069	0.082
0.09	0.039	0.082	0.125	0.154	0.184
0.15	0.067	0.137	0.199	0.261	0.310
0.24	0.115	0.239	0.340	0.431	0.511

Table 1

Experiment 2

Four vials were made to contain 1mM of Trypsin and differing levels of substrate concentration maintained at a pH of 6. The absorbance values after each 30 second time period for each substrate level is recorded in Table 2.

	Absorbance value				
Substrate level (mM)	0.5 min	1 min	1.5 min	2 min	2.5 min
0.04	0.006	0.011	0.017	0.023	0.027
0.09	0.014	0.028	0.042	0.055	0.068
0.15	0.027	0.053	0.078	0.102	0.149
0.24	0.060	0.090	0.145	0.190	0.233

Table 2

17. After 2 minutes of interaction, a vial with a pH of 8 containing 1mM of Trypsin and a substrate level of 0.09mM will result in an absorbance level of:

A. 0.068
B. 0.055
C. 0.154
D. 0.184

18. A vial containing 1mM of Trypsin and a substrate level of 0.15 with a pH value of 6 would result in an absorbance level of 0.040 after roughly:

F. 30 seconds of interaction.
G. 45 seconds of interaction.
H. 60 seconds of interaction.
J. 75 seconds of interaction.

19. Which of the following substrate levels resulted in the highest average absorbance value across the five time measurements?

A. 0.04mM interacting with 1mM of Trypsin at a pH level of 6
B. 0.24mM interacting with 1mM of Trypsin at a pH level of 6
C. 0.15mM interacting with 1mM of Trypsin at a pH level of 8
D. 0.24mM interacting with 1mM of Trypsin at a pH level of 8

20. If measurements were taken every 15 seconds, then it would be expected that an absorbance value of 0.062 would be measured:

F. after a substrate level of 0.04 interacted with 1mM of Trypsin at a pH of 8 for 1.25 minutes.
G. after a substrate level of 0.09 interacted with 1mM of Trypsin at a pH of 8 for 1.25 minutes.
H. after a substrate level of 0.04 interacted with 1mM of Trypsin at a pH of 6 for 2.25 minutes.
J. after a substrate level of 0.09 interacted with 1mM of Trypsin at a pH of 6 for 2.25 minutes.

Passage VI

With the traditional *optical microscope*, the user looks into the eyepieces to view a sample or specimen. The objective lens focuses light from the sample into the eyepieces. The eyepiece lens and the objective lens both provide magnification, but the latter more so. The condenser lens helps to concentrate light on the sample for easy viewing. Figure 1 displays the visual path of an optical microscope.

While the more advanced *fluorescent microscope* shares some similarities to the optical microscope, one key difference is that fluorescent microscopes utilize a process called *photoluminescence*. This is where molecules in a sample can be put into an excited state and absorb energy from a high intensity light, causing the molecules to emit light at a longer wavelength. The filter then works by separating any surrounding light, so only the fluorescence emitted by the molecules in a sample can be visualized. The detector can be used to display the fluorescent sample on a digital screen for easy viewing. Figure 2 displays the visual path of a fluorescent microscope.

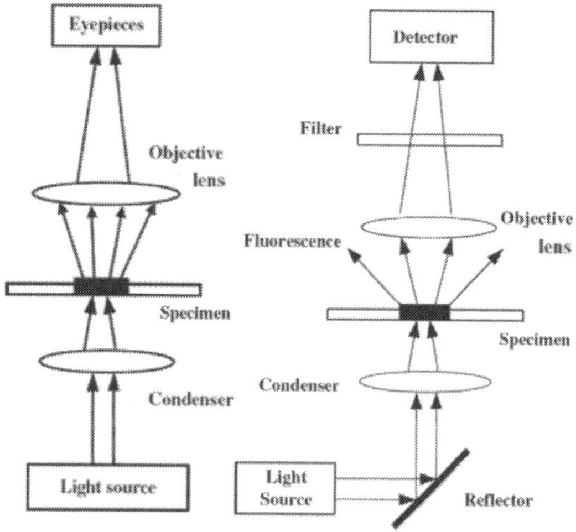

Figure 1 Figure 2

A teacher sought to test a group of students' ability to distinguish neutrophil white blood cells within a blood sample using both optical (Study 1) and fluorescent (Study 2) microscopes. To distinguish a neutrophil under the optical microscope, the students were to look for a round cell body with a multi-lobed nucleus that is around 12-14 μm in diameter. For the fluorescent microscope, the blood sample was treated with an antibody that causes only neutrophil cells to fluoresce green.

Table 1 displays the results of Study 1, consisting of each student's answer for the number of neutrophils found in a blood sample and the percentage of correct cells that were identified using the optical microscope. Table 2 displays the results of Study 2, consisting of each student's answer for the number of neutrophils found in a blood sample and the percentage of correct cells that were identified using the fluorescent microscope.

Optical Microscope	Neutrophil count	Percent correct
Student 1	5	33%
Student 2	8	53%
Student 3	10	67%
Student 4	4	27%

Table 1

Fluorescent Microscope	Neutrophil count	Percent correct
Student 1	13	76%
Student 2	16	94%
Student 3	17	100%
Student 4	13	76%

Table 2

21. Suppose the teacher will present an award to the student who is most proficient at finding neutrophils under both microscopes. Which student is most likely to receive the award based on the results of Study 1 and Study 2?

A. Student 1
B. Student 2
C. Student 3
D. Student 4

22. How many neutrophils were present in the blood samples in Study 1 and Study 2 combined?

F. 17
G. 28
H. 30
J. 32

23. If a fifth student counts neutrophils under the optical microscope and finds 47% of the total, then the amount of neutrophils found by her would be:

A. 6
B. 7
C. 8
D. 9

24. Which of the students, if any, displayed an ability to better identify neutrophils under an optical microscope compared to a fluorescent microscope?

F. Student 1
G. Student 3
H. Student 4
J. None of the students displayed this ability.

Step 1 Correct Answers

Passage I:	Passage II:	Passage III:	Passage IV:	Passage V:	Passage VI:
1: B	5: C	9: C	13: C	17: C	21: C
2: J	6: F	10: G	14: F	18: G	22: J
3: D	7: A	11: A	15: B	19: D	23: B
4: F	8: H	12: J	16: J	20: J	24: J

Stumped on any? You can find the explanations for each of these questions beginning on page 653.

STEP 2

Reading and Applying Written Descriptions

A lot (and I really do mean *a lot*) of ACT tutors and instructors (or high school science teachers who don't know any better) often tell students that all they need to do is what we did in Step 1: read data and answer questions about it. I wish, so badly, that that were true; it would make this test a whole lot easier and your preparation a lot simpler. However, it simply isn't true (I know: I've researched the ACT more than anyone): you will need the written information if you want to do your best on the ACT Science test. And, because I want you to do your best, I have included a step dedicated to your ability to do just that.

As has been noted (and as you've seen from the previous passages), there can often be a good bit of reading to get through in order to properly understand an ACT Science passage. Though we haven't discussed it in any in depth, there is also usually 1 passage that is exclusively written words (the Conflicting Viewpoints passage; more on the in Step 4). Because of this, the second most important skill in the ACT Science test is your ability to read, understand, and apply what is described in the written descriptions. In fact, about 25% of ACT Science questions require that you *merely* reference the written descriptions (in other words, the percentage of questions that require an understanding of written material is far greater than 25%).

Diagrams

On occasion, an ACT Science passage will feature a diagram of some kind. These diagrams do not give data, of course. Rather, they show the layout of an experiment, how some kind of apparatus works, etc. I consider these diagrams to be a part of the written material that we are discussing here in Step 2 since there is no data within them to study as we did in Step 1. You will notice (if you haven't already) that one of the practice passages that follows contains a couple of diagrams.

Sticker Shock

In the introduction to *The ACT Science System* I spoke briefly about "sticker shock." What I meant was this: often, when students take the ACT Science test, they are shocked/scared/etc. about what they initially see when they flip the page to a new science passage: graphs, diagrams, charts, figures, and scientific terminology that they have never come across in all their years studying science. However, *no one* taking the ACT has seen this stuff. Just because you aren't familiar with a word that comes up in the written portion of the passage doesn't mean you're stupid or the only one; I guarantee the student to your left and your right are thinking the exact same thing.

Active Reading

To get through the written information properly, follow these steps. First, take a deep breath, which gets much-needed oxygen flowing to the brain. Second, take a good posture and have your pencil in hand. Third, read quickly, but for general understanding; don't get caught up on every single word or detail that comes up. If a particular passage needs you to know or understand a word and its meaning, the test makers usually do two things: 1) italicize the word, and 2) define the word. These are clues that this is important and need to be underlined or circled. Other items in the written passage may or may not be important. For example, a scary looking equation is probably not important and certainly won't be solved (remember: no calculator on the ACT Science test, so no difficult math either).

The Purpose of this Step and the Practice that Follows

The purpose of this step is simple: to get you used to reading and understanding the written descriptions that are a part of each ACT Science passage. Each of the questions that follow ask exclusively about the written portion of each passage and DO NOT require a reference to the data that is presented in charts/tables/graphs (as was the case in Step 1). Of course, there is overlap between these two portions of the passage; there are many questions that will require you to find data and also understand something from the passage. However, due to the importance of that skill, it has its own step: Step 3.

So, let's practice this skill or reading, interpreting, and applying information from the written portions of these passages. Remember: each question is *exclusively* about the *written* material (not the data)!

Passage I

Most of the water consumption within the United States is used by the agricultural industry for food production. This heavily contributes to the overuse of groundwater aquifers. Therefore, finding alternative resources of water for agricultural production is necessary to lessen the looming threat of food and water scarcity. One issue is that alternative water sources in certain regions often contain a higher concentration of salt compared to groundwater aquifers, and many food crops are not selected for traits like tolerance to salt. In recent years, new varieties, also called *variants*, of crops have been selected mostly for commercial benefit, with little regard for producing varieties that can withstand changes in salt concentrations. As a result, a group of researchers sought to determine plant variants that are resilient to waters with higher salt concentrations.

Researchers first tested the salt tolerance in variants of two regularly consumed crops, tomato and pepper, by testing the consumable yields of each plant when grown in the same soil. The control for the experiment was freshwater from a ground water aquifer, while the experimental condition was done with water containing a higher salt content. The results are recorded in Table 1 (tomato) and Table 2 (pepper) below.

	Fruit yield (grams)	
Tomato variant	Control	Experimental
Bloody Butcher	2785	1719
Juane Flamme	2317	1355
Quarter Century	1415	928

Table 1

	Fruit yield (grams)	
Pepper variant	Control	Experimental
California Wonder	2591	1993
Thai Hot	295	291
Ancho	1514	1489

Table 2

The researchers next tested the concentration of sodium within the plant tissue of the different variants for both the control and saltwater (experimental) groups. Their findings are recorded in Figure 1 (tomato) and Figure 2 (pepper) below in millimoles per kilogram.

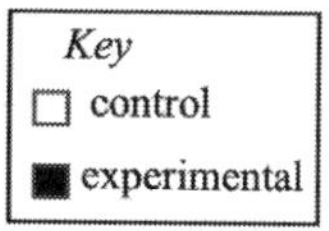

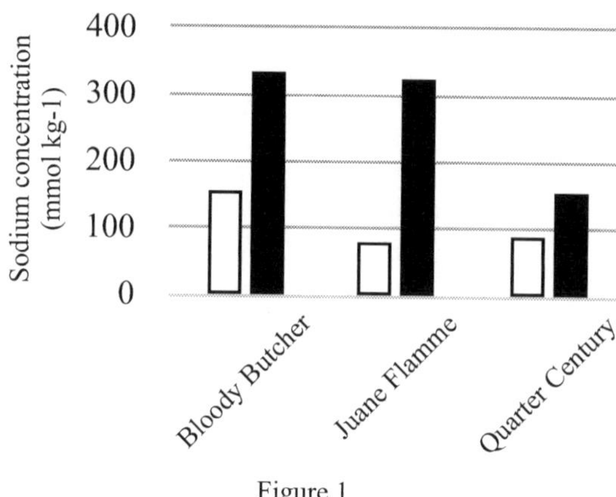

Figure 1

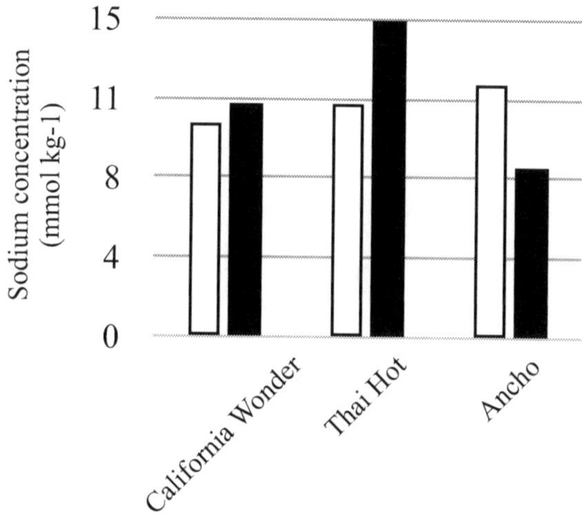

Figure 2

1. Why did the experimental group of tomatoes and peppers test for a higher concentration of salt than the control group?

   A. Because the groundwater aquifers from which they were watered typically contain a heavy concentration of salt.
   B. Because the alternative water sources from which they were watered typically contain a heavy concentration of salt.
   C. Because the soil in which they were grown featured a high concentration of sodium and sodium-containing minerals.
   D. Because tomatoes and peppers are more likely to absorb salt when watered from groundwater aquifers.

2. Which of the following is, agriculturally speaking, an example of a *variant*?

F. A groundwater aquifer
G. The California Wonder
H. Salt
J. The pepper

3. Which of the factors listed below were the same for both the control and experimental groups?

I. The variants of crops tested
II. The source of the water
III. The soil in which the plants were grown

A. I only
B. I and III only
C. II and III only
D. I, II, and III

Passage II

A group of high school students investigated the momentum of carts rolling down an inclined plane across a designated finish line. The students used three carts, labeled Cart A, Cart B, and Cart C. Cart A had a mass of 12.5 kg, Cart B had a mass of 21.8 kg, and Cart C had a mass of 34.7 kg. They conducted five trials, progressively increasing the release height of the carts. The purpose of the experiment was to explore how changes in release height affect the velocity and momentum of the carts.

Velocity is a fundamental concept in physics that represents the speed of an object in a specific direction. In this experiment, velocity was measured as each cart crossed the finish line, but can also be determined using the equation $v = \sqrt{2gh}$, where v is the velocity, g is the acceleration due to gravity (approximately 9.8 m/s^2), and h is the release height of the cart.

Momentum is a property of a moving object that depends on its mass and velocity. It describes the quantity of motion possessed by an object and is calculated by multiplying the mass of the object by its velocity. The equation for momentum is given as $p = mv$, where p represents the momentum, m is the mass of the object, and v denotes the velocity.

After collecting data, the students calculated the momentum for each cart and trial. Figure 1 shows the recorded velocity for each cart as it crossed the finish line, and Figure 2 shows the calculated momentum for each cart as it crossed the finish line.

Key:

Figure 1

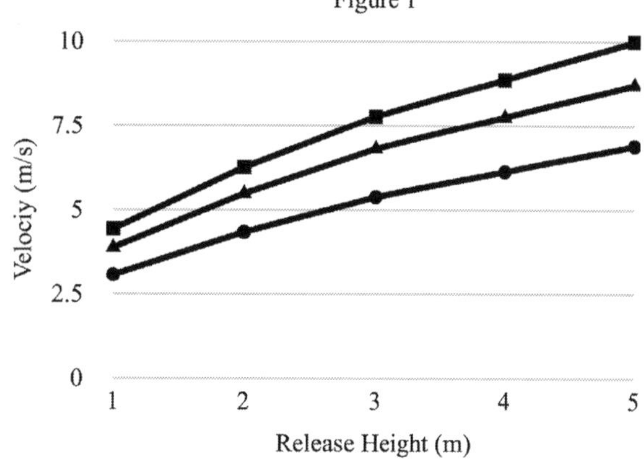

Figure 2

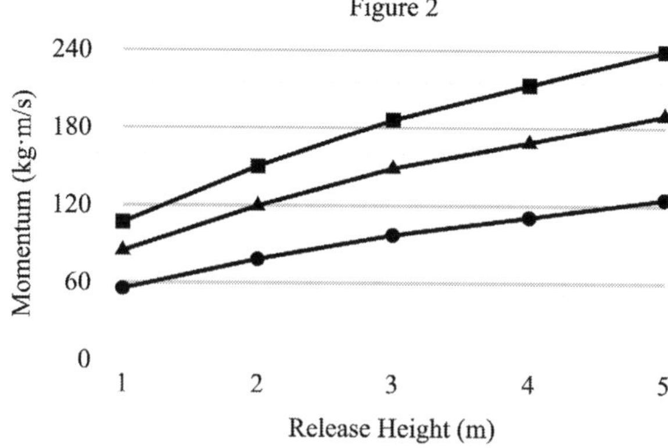

4. Which of the following correctly orders the events in the experiment?

   F. Students took data, then calculated the momentum, then calculated the velocity.
   G. Students released a cart, then measured the velocity, then calculated the momentum.
   H. Students made a hypothesis about each cart's velocity and momentum, then measured each as the cart crossed the finish line.
   J. Students calculated momentum, then made a hypothesis about the velocity, then calculated the velocity.

5. What action was taken in the experiment to ensure that both the velocity and momentum of each cart as it crossed the finish line would differ from the other two carts when released from the same height?

   A. The carts' wheels featured different tread patterns.
   B. The carts' wheels were different widths.
   C. The carts differed in volume.
   D. The carts differed in mass.

6. Which of the following is dependent upon the value of the acceleration due to gravity (approximately 9.8 m/s^2)?

   I. Mass
   II. Velocity
   III. Momentum

   F. II only
   G. III only
   H. II and III only
   J. I, II, and III

Passage III

The *Mpemba Effect* refers to a curious phenomenon in which hot water freezes faster than cold water under certain circumstances. Several proposed explanations have been put forth to shed light on the Mpemba Effect. One possibility relates to the evaporation of the hot water during the cooling process. As hot water is exposed to lower temperatures, it undergoes rapid evaporation, resulting in a reduction in its volume. This reduction in volume leads to an increase in the concentration of dissolved solids in the remaining water. Consequently, the higher concentration of dissolved solids may lower the freezing point of the hot water, allowing it to freeze more rapidly.

A group of students designed an experiment to test the Mpemba Effect. They collected four beakers and labeled them A, B, C, and D. *Thermocouples*, or thermoelectric devices for measuring temperature, were placed in the bottom of each beaker. Beakers A and B were filled with distilled (purified) water, and beakers C and D were filled with tap water. The water in beakers A and C was heated to 50 degrees Celsius, and the water in beakers B and D was left at room temperature (around 30 degrees Celsius).

The students recorded the temperature of each beaker after placing it in a freezer with a temperature of -18° Celsius until it had reached 0° Celsius, the freezing point of water. The observations of the students are given below. Table 1 corresponds to beaker A, Table 2 to beaker B, Table 3 to beaker C, and Table 4 to beaker D.

Table 1 (Beaker A)	
Time Elapsed (minutes)	Temperature (°C)
0	50
5	42
10	36
15	30
20	25
25	21
30	17
35	13
40	10
45	8
50	5
55	2
60	0

Table 2 (Beaker B)	
Time Elapsed (minutes)	Temperature (°C)
0	30
5	26
10	23
15	20
20	18
25	17
30	14
35	12
40	10
45	8
50	6
55	5
60	4
65	3
70	0

Table 3 (Beaker C)	
Time Elapsed (minutes)	Temperature (°C)
0	50
5	44
10	38
15	33
20	28
25	24
30	20
35	17
40	14
45	11
50	8
55	5
60	3
65	0

Table 4 (Beaker D)	
Time Elapsed (minutes)	Temperature (°C)
0	30
5	26
10	22
15	19
20	18
25	17
30	15
35	13
40	11
45	10
50	8
55	6
60	4
65	2
70	1
75	0

7. One factor that may cause hot water to freeze faster than cold water is:

A. a lower presence of dissolved solids before undergoing rapid evaporation.
B. a higher presence of dissolved solids before undergoing rapid evaporation.
C. a lower presence of dissolved solids after undergoing rapid evaporation.
D. a higher presence of dissolved solids after undergoing rapid evaporation.

8. Given the definition of the Mpemba Effect in the passage, which of the following is an assumption made by the students conducting the experiment?

F. That boiling water is "hot" water.
G. That water measuring a temperature of 30° Celsius is "hot" water.
H. That room temperature water is "cold" water.
J. That water measuring a temperature of 50° Celsius is "cold" water.

9. Which of the following was not one of the water varieties tested in the study?

A. A beaker of tap water heated to 50° Celsius then placed in a freezer set to -18° Celsius.
B. A beaker of purified water kept at 30° Celsius then placed in a freezer set to -18° Celsius.
C. A beaker of salt water heated to 50° Celsius then placed in a freezer set to -18° Celsius.
D. A beaker of tap water kept at 30° Celsius then placed in a freezer set to -18° Celsius.

Passage IV

Real-time polymerase chain reaction (PCR) *analysis* is a laboratory technique that can be used to help determine if a specific type of DNA is present in a sample. This technique works by increasing the total amount of DNA present in a sample, a step called *amplification*, and then detecting if the DNA matches the target DNA.

Detection of the target DNA is determined by the *cycle threshold* (CT) value. The CT value is the number of cycles of amplification that is needed for a specific DNA sequence to be detected in a sample. The lower the CT value, the more likely it is that the sample contains the DNA of interest. Most real-time PCR analyses undergo a total of 40 cycles of amplification.

While this technique is often used for medical purposes, it also has applications in food safety. Due to the safety concerns regarding food allergens, scientists will use real-time PCR to search for the DNA of common allergen causing ingredients in commercial products to ensure that the package label is accurate. One common and often dangerous food allergy is an allergy to peanuts. If a person is severely allergic to peanuts and unknowingly ingests even a small amount, it could be deadly. Therefore, scientists completed real-time PCR analysis to test commercial food products for DNA that matches the peanut.

Table 1 shows commercial food products, their current package labels for allergens, and the CT values discovered for each following real-time PCR analysis to detect peanut DNA. An N.D. value means that there was no detection of the target DNA after 40 cycles of amplification.

Table 1

Food	Food Packaging Allergen Declaration	Peanut CT Value
Cereal bar I	Peanut, hazelnut	17.97
Cereal bar II	Almond and tree nuts	32.40
Cereal bar III	Hazelnut, almond and peanut traces	33.74
Cereal bar IV	May contain tree nut traces	35.90
Chocolate with pistachio	Pistachio, almond, hazelnut, tree nut traces	36.80
Sausage with walnut	Walnuts	N.D.
Chocolate	Almond and hazelnut traces	37.99
Cookies with fiber	Not declared	32.25

Table 2 displays example CT values and the likelihood of the values causing an allergic reaction in an individual with peanut allergy (if testing for peanut DNA).

Table 2

Example CT Value	Likelihood of Causing Peanut Allergic Reaction
≤ 29	High
30-35	High to moderate
36-40	Low to none

10. In PCR analysis and application, scientists assume:

F. that 40 cycles of amplification is sufficient to determine the presence of a certain DNA in a sample.
G. that ingesting even a small amount of peanut DNA can be deadly for a person with a severe peanut allergy.
H. that the technique can be used to determine the presence of certain DNA in a sample.
J. that all commercially available products contain at least a small trace of peanut DNA.

11. Imagine a laboratory can perform real-time polymerase chain reaction analysis via amplification of DNA once per day and only on weekdays. How many weeks maximum would the lab need to determine the cycle threshold value of a sample?

A. 5
B. 7
C. 8
D. 10

12. Food producers who desire that those with a severe peanut allergy to be able to consume their product would like a CT value that is:

F. low: a low CT score means that few iterations of PCR analysis were necessary to detect potentially harmful DNA.
G. low: a low CT score means that many iterations of PCR analysis were necessary to detect potentially harmful DNA.
H. high: a high CT score means that few iterations of PCR analysis were necessary to detect potentially harmful DNA.
J. high: a high CT score means that many iterations of PCR analysis were necessary to detect potentially harmful DNA.

Passage V

Enzymes are substances that act as a catalyst to speed up biochemical reactions. When a *substrate* binds to the active site of an enzyme, a reaction can occur in which the substrate is converted into one or more products. The digestive enzyme, Trypsin, catalyzes the process of breaking down proteins in the small intestine into amino acids, which can then be absorbed into the blood stream. Importantly, any physical or chemical changes to an enzyme's environment, such as changes in temperature, pH, and salt concentration, can alter its ability to function by denaturing or inactivating the enzyme.

Two experiments sought to compare the ability of Trypsin to generate products (amino acids) at two different pH levels. For each experiment, four vials were made to contain 1mM of Trypsin and differing concentrations of substrate. The values of light absorbance for each sample were recorded every 30 seconds for 2.5 minutes using a *spectrophotometer*, an apparatus for measuring the intensity of light. The measured absorbance values were collected at a wavelength that corresponds to the relative amount of product that was generated in the samples. In other words, a higher absorbance value at the indicated wavelength would mean more product was made by the Trypsin.

Experiment 1

Four vials were made to contain 1mM of Trypsin and differing levels of substrate concentration maintained at a pH of 8. The absorbance values after each 30 second time period for each substrate level is recorded in Table 1.

	Absorbance value				
Substrate level (mM)	0.5 min	1 min	1.5 min	2 min	2.5 min
0.04	0.023	0.035	0.053	0.069	0.082
0.09	0.039	0.082	0.125	0.154	0.184
0.15	0.067	0.137	0.199	0.261	0.310
0.24	0.115	0.239	0.340	0.431	0.511

Table 1

Experiment 2

Four vials were made to contain 1mM of Trypsin and differing levels of substrate concentration maintained at a pH of 6. The absorbance values after each 30 second time period for each substrate level is recorded in Table 2.

	Absorbance value				
Substrate level (mM)	0.5 min	1 min	1.5 min	2 min	2.5 min
0.04	0.006	0.011	0.017	0.023	0.027
0.09	0.014	0.028	0.042	0.055	0.068
0.15	0.027	0.053	0.078	0.102	0.149
0.24	0.060	0.090	0.145	0.190	0.233

Table 2

13. What did each vial in the experiment have in common?

A. The Trypsin level
B. The substrate level
C. The pH
D. The absorbance value

14. In the experiments, a higher absorbance value at the indicated wavelength means:

F. less product was made by the Trypsin.
G. less enzymes were present in the vial.
H. more substrates were catalyzed by Trypsin enzymes.
J. more substrates had failed to react with an enzyme.

15. If the scientists wanted to conduct further experiments testing how Trypsin responds to chemical or physical changes to its environment besides pH, then one additional change that could be made to the vials might include:

A. a change in temperature.
B. a change in substrate levels.
C. a change in enzyme.
D. a change in Trypsin levels.

Passage VI

With the traditional *optical microscope*, the user looks into the eyepieces to view a sample or specimen. The objective lens focuses light from the sample into the eyepieces. The eyepiece lens and the objective lens both provide magnification, but the latter more so. The condenser lens helps to concentrate light on the sample for easy viewing. Figure 1 displays the visual path of an optical microscope.

While the more advanced *fluorescent microscope* shares some similarities to the optical microscope, one key difference is that fluorescent microscopes utilize a process called *photoluminescence*. This is where molecules in a sample can be put into an excited state and absorb energy from a high intensity light, causing the molecules to emit light at a longer wavelength. The filter then works by separating any surrounding light, so only the fluorescence emitted by the molecules in a sample can be visualized. The detector can be used to display the fluorescent sample on a digital screen for easy viewing. Figure 2 displays the visual path of a fluorescent microscope.

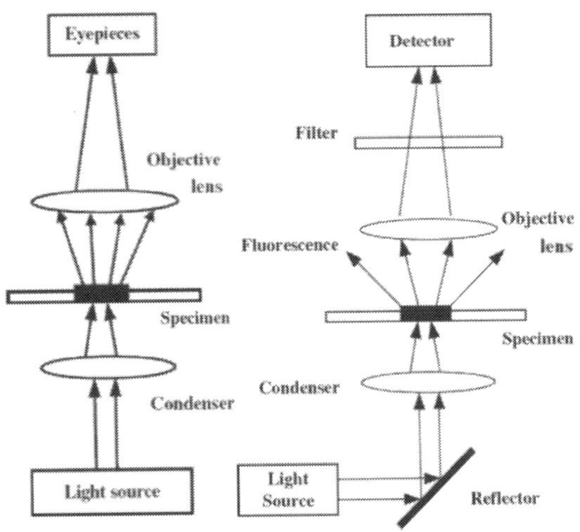

Figure 1

Figure 2

A teacher sought to test a group of students' ability to distinguish neutrophil white blood cells within a blood sample using both optical (Study 1) and fluorescent (Study 2) microscopes. To distinguish a neutrophil under the optical microscope, the students were to look for a round cell body with a multi-lobed nucleus that is around 12-14 μm in diameter. For the fluorescent microscope, the blood sample was treated with an antibody that causes only neutrophil cells to fluoresce green.

Table 1 displays the results of Study 1, consisting of each student's answer for the number of neutrophils found in a blood sample and the percentage of correct cells that were identified using the optical microscope. Table 2 displays the results of Study 2, consisting of each student's answer for the number of neutrophils found in a blood sample and the percentage of correct cells that were identified using the fluorescent microscope.

Optical Microscope	Neutrophil count	Percent correct
Student 1	5	33%
Student 2	8	53%
Student 3	10	67%
Student 4	4	27%

Table 1

Fluorescent Microscope	Neutrophil count	Percent correct
Student 1	13	76%
Student 2	16	94%
Student 3	17	100%
Student 4	13	76%

Table 2

16. According to their descriptions, which of the following is a difference between optical and fluorescent microscopes?

F. The optical microscope utilizes a process called photoluminescence.
G. The fluorescent microscope makes use of less lenses to focus on a specimen than does the optical microscope.
H. Under an optical microscope, molecules in a sample are put into an excited state.
J. The eyepiece of the fluorescent microscope provides additional magnification.

17. According to Figure 2, the part of the fluorescent microscope responsible for separating out unnecessary light is placed relative to the path of light:

A. immediately prior to the objective lens.
B. immediately prior to the detector.
C. immediately after the condenser.
D. immediately after the reflector.

18. One precondition for the obtaining of accurate results from the studies was that:

F. the antibody in Study 1 would cause all blood cells but neutrophil cells to fluoresce green.
G. five minutes per student per microscope is sufficient time to count neutrophil cells.
H. the antibody in Study 2 would only cause neutrophil cells to fluoresce green.
J. square neutrophil cells with a single-lobed nucleus were not to be considered in either study.

Step 2 Correct Answers

Passage I:	Passage II:	Passage III:	Passage IV:	Passage V:	Passage VI:
1: B	4: G	7: D	10: F	13: A	16: G
2: G	5: D	8: H	11: C	14: H	17: B
3: B	6: H	9: C	12: J	15: A	18: H

Stumped on any? You can find the explanations for each of these questions beginning on page 656.

STEP 3

Pairing a Passage's Written Descriptions and Data

In Step 1, you practiced simply reading charts, tables, graphs, etc. in order to find data and apply it in a relevant way to determine an answer. In Step 2, you practiced reading through and thinking about the passage's written information in order to answer questions correctly. Here, we combine these two skills to take your preparation to the next level.

Putting It Together

One of the reasons for active reading on your initial read through of the passage, as has been said, is so that you can have the time to find proper information (either data from charts/tables/graphs or information in the written section, including a diagram on occasion). Here, it is time to realize that you may have to do both of those things. While, strictly speaking, only 12% to 15% of the questions require this two step process, the reason the ability to reference both is Step 3 instead of 4 or 5 is that it reinforces the two main skills associated with the ACT Science test from Steps 1 and 2.

The Following Practice

I think you are used to this by now. The following practice passages are the same as those featured in Step 1 and Step 2. Notice how they may require more of you than simply reading data or finding information in the passage, but rather both.

So, without further ado, let's practice putting these two skills together!

Passage I

Most of the water consumption within the United States is used by the agricultural industry for food production. This heavily contributes to the overuse of groundwater aquifers. Therefore, finding alternative resources of water for agricultural production is necessary to lessen the looming threat of food and water scarcity. One issue is that alternative water sources in certain regions often contain a higher concentration of salt compared to groundwater aquifers, and many food crops are not selected for traits like tolerance to salt. In recent years, new varieties, also called *variants*, of crops have been selected mostly for commercial benefit, with little regard for producing varieties that can withstand changes in salt concentrations. As a result, a group of researchers sought to determine plant variants that are resilient to waters with higher salt concentrations.

Researchers first tested the salt tolerance in variants of two regularly consumed crops, tomato and pepper, by testing the consumable yields of each plant when grown in the same soil. The control for the experiment was freshwater from a ground water aquifer, while the experimental condition was done with water containing a higher salt content. The results are recorded in Table 1 (tomato) and Table 2 (pepper) below.

Fruit yield (grams)		
Tomato variant	Control	Experimental
Bloody Butcher	2785	1719
Juane Flamme	2317	1355
Quarter Century	1415	928

Table 1

Fruit yield (grams)		
Pepper variant	Control	Experimental
California Wonder	2591	1993
Thai Hot	295	291
Ancho	1514	1489

Table 2

The researchers next tested the concentration of sodium within the plant tissue of the different variants for both the control and saltwater (experimental) groups. Their findings are recorded in Figure 1 (tomato) and Figure 2 (pepper) below in millimoles per kilogram.

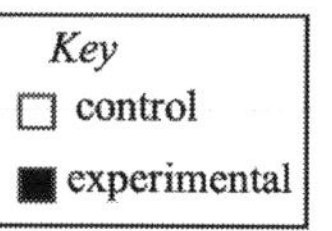

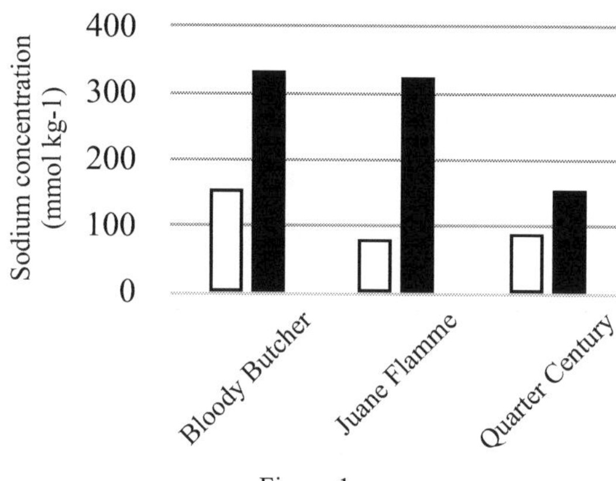

Figure 1

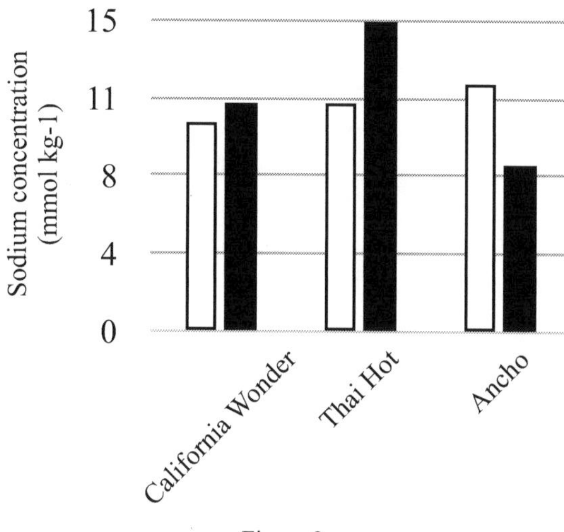

Figure 2

1. Based on sodium concentration alone, which variety of crop shows the most potential in helping to decrease agricultural dependence on groundwater aquifers?

A. Bloody Butcher
B. Juane Flamme
C. Thai Hot
D. Ancho

2. Which variety of fruit most likely has the most natural salty taste?

F. Thai Hot
G. Bloody Butcher
H. California Wonder
J. Juane Flamme

3. Which of the following varieties of fruit, based on Tables 1 and 2, demonstrates the greatest tolerance to salt in its water supply?

A. Thai Hot
B. Bloody Butcher
C. California Wonder
D. Juane Flamme

Passage II

A group of high school students investigated the momentum of carts rolling down an inclined plane across a designated finish line. The students used three carts, labeled Cart A, Cart B, and Cart C. Cart A had a mass of 12.5 kg, Cart B had a mass of 21.8 kg, and Cart C had a mass of 34.7 kg. They conducted five trials, progressively increasing the release height of the carts. The purpose of the experiment was to explore how changes in release height affect the velocity and momentum of the carts.

Velocity is a fundamental concept in physics that represents the speed of an object in a specific direction. In this experiment, velocity was measured as each cart crossed the finish line, but can also be determined using the equation $v = \sqrt{2gh}$, where v is the velocity, g is the acceleration due to gravity (approximately 9.8 m/s^2), and h is the release height of the cart.

Momentum is a property of a moving object that depends on its mass and velocity. It describes the quantity of motion possessed by an object and is calculated by multiplying the mass of the object by its velocity. The equation for momentum is given as $p = mv$, where p represents the momentum, m is the mass of the object, and v denotes the velocity.

After collecting data, the students calculated the momentum for each cart and trial. Figure 1 shows the recorded velocity for each cart as it crossed the finish line, and Figure 2 shows the calculated momentum for each cart as it crossed the finish line.

Key:

Figure 1

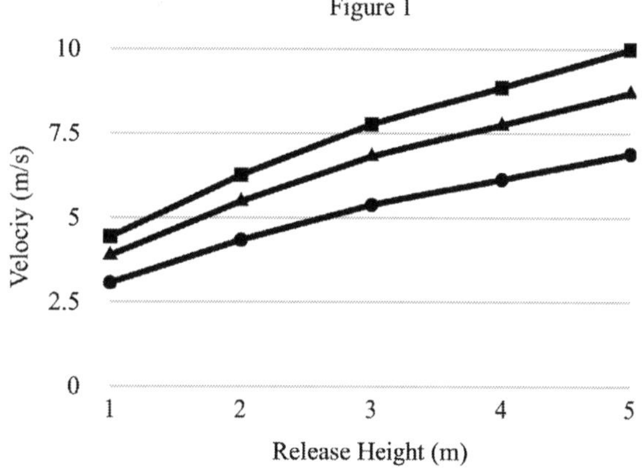

Figure 2

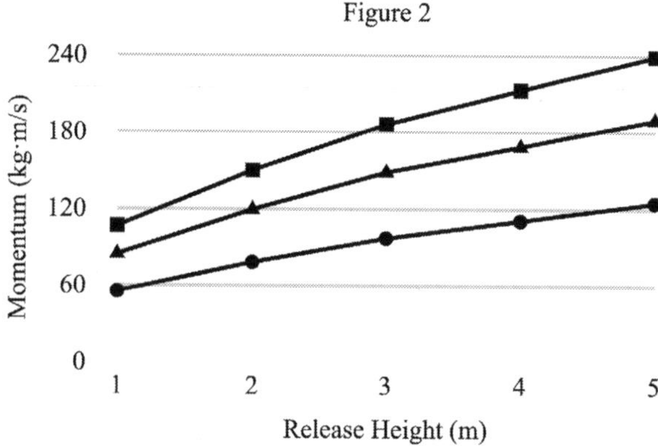

4. In this same experiment, a cart with a mass of 17 kg released from a height of 4 meters would be expected to have momentum as it crossed the finish line that measured approximately:

   F. 80 kg·m/s
   G. 140 kg·m/s
   H. 195 kg·m/s
   J. 245 kg·m/s

5. At a height of 2 meters, the value of p for a cart weighing 12.5 kg is approximately how much greater than the value of p for a cart weighing 34.7 kg?

   A. 30 kg·m/s
   B. 45 kg·m/s
   C. 55 kg·m/s
   D. 75 kg·m/s

6. Which of the following carts would have the least velocity as it crossed the finish line?

   F. A cart weighing 10 kg released from a height of 5 meters
   G. A cart weighing 10 kg released from a height of 2 meters
   H. A cart weighing 15 kg released from a height of 4 meters
   J. A cart weighing 35 kg released at a height of 3 meters

Passage III

The *Mpemba Effect* refers to a curious phenomenon in which hot water freezes faster than cold water under certain circumstances. Several proposed explanations have been put forth to shed light on the Mpemba Effect. One possibility relates to the evaporation of the hot water during the cooling process. As hot water is exposed to lower temperatures, it undergoes rapid evaporation, resulting in a reduction in its volume. This reduction in volume leads to an increase in the concentration of dissolved solids in the remaining water. Consequently, the higher concentration of dissolved solids may lower the freezing point of the hot water, allowing it to freeze more rapidly.

A group of students designed an experiment to test the Mpemba Effect. They collected four beakers and labeled them A, B, C, and D. *Thermocouples*, or thermoelectric devices for measuring temperature, were placed in the bottom of each beaker. Beakers A and B were filled with distilled (purified) water, and beakers C and D were filled with tap water. The water in beakers A and C was heated to 50 degrees Celsius, and the water in beakers B and D was left at room temperature (around 30 degrees Celsius).

The students recorded the temperature of each beaker after placing it in a freezer with a temperature of -18° Celsius until it had reached 0° Celsius, the freezing point of water. The observations of the students are given below. Table 1 corresponds to beaker A, Table 2 to beaker B, Table 3 to beaker C, and Table 4 to beaker D.

Table 1 (Beaker A)	
Time Elapsed (minutes)	Temperature (°C)
0	50
5	42
10	36
15	30
20	25
25	21
30	17
35	13
40	10
45	8
50	5
55	2
60	0

Table 2 (Beaker B)	
Time Elapsed (minutes)	Temperature (°C)
0	30
5	26
10	23
15	20
20	18
25	17
30	14
35	12
40	10
45	8
50	6
55	5
60	4
65	3
70	0

Table 3 (Beaker C)	
Time Elapsed (minutes)	Temperature (°C)
0	50
5	44
10	38
15	33
20	28
25	24
30	20
35	17
40	14
45	11
50	8
55	5
60	3
65	0

Table 4 (Beaker D)	
Time Elapsed (minutes)	Temperature (°C)
0	30
5	26
10	22
15	19
20	18
25	17
30	15
35	13
40	11
45	10
50	8
55	6
60	4
65	2
70	1
75	0

7. Based on the results of the experiment, which of the following would most likely be the last to reach a temperature of 0° Celsius?

A. A gallon of tap water at room temperature placed in a freezer set at a temperature of -18° Celsius
B. A gallon of purified water at room temperature placed in a freezer set at a temperature of -18° Celsius
C. A gallon of tap water heated to 50° Celsius placed in a freezer set at a temperature of -18° Celsius
D. A gallon of purified water heated to 50° Celsius placed in a freezer set at a temperature of -18° Celsius

8. Which of the beakers most likely underwent rapid evaporation?

F. Beaker A
G. Beaker B
H. Beaker C
J. Beaker D

9. Suppose a student repeated the experiment and put into Beaker E a mixture of tap and purified water. If the water was placed into the freezer at room temperature, it would be expected that the water would reach a temperature of 10° Celsius after:

A. 40 minutes
B. 42.5 minutes
C. 45 minutes
D. 47.5 minutes

Passage IV

Real-time polymerase chain reaction (PCR) *analysis* is a laboratory technique that can be used to help determine if a specific type of DNA is present in a sample. This technique works by increasing the total amount of DNA present in a sample, a step called *amplification*, and then detecting if the DNA matches the target DNA.

Detection of the target DNA is determined by the *cycle threshold* (CT) value. The CT value is the number of cycles of amplification that is needed for a specific DNA sequence to be detected in a sample. The lower the CT value, the more likely it is that the sample contains the DNA of interest. Most real-time PCR analyses undergo a total of 40 cycles of amplification.

While this technique is often used for medical purposes, it also has applications in food safety. Due to the safety concerns regarding food allergens, scientists will use real-time PCR to search for the DNA of common allergen causing ingredients in commercial products to ensure that the package label is accurate. One common and often dangerous food allergy is an allergy to peanuts. If a person is severely allergic to peanuts and unknowingly ingests even a small amount, it could be deadly. Therefore, scientists completed real-time PCR analysis to test commercial food products for DNA that matches the peanut.

Table 1 shows commercial food products, their current package labels for allergens, and the CT values discovered for each following real-time PCR analysis to detect peanut DNA. An N.D. value means that there was no detection of the target DNA after 40 cycles of amplification.

Table 1

Food	Food Packaging Allergen Declaration	Peanut CT Value
Cereal bar I	Peanut, hazelnut	17.97
Cereal bar II	Almond and tree nuts	32.40
Cereal bar III	Hazelnut, almond and peanut traces	33.74
Cereal bar IV	May contain tree nut traces	35.90
Chocolate with pistachio	Pistachio, almond, hazelnut, tree nut traces	36.80
Sausage with walnut	Walnuts	N.D.
Chocolate	Almond and hazelnut traces	37.99
Cookies with fiber	Not declared	32.25

Table 2 displays example CT values and the likelihood of the values causing an allergic reaction in an individual with peanut allergy (if testing for peanut DNA).

Table 2

Example CT Value	Likelihood of Causing Peanut Allergic Reaction
≤ 29	High
30-35	High to moderate
36-40	Low to none

10. Which of the following is *true* about the Cookies with fiber?

F. Their likelihood of causing a peanut allergic reaction is low to none.
G. They contain traces of DNA that can cause a peanut allergic reaction.
H. There is a 0% chance that they will cause a peanut allergic reaction.
J. Their cycle threshold value is not declared.

11. On average, how many cycles of amplification were needed to discover the presence of peanut DNA in the tested foods declared to contain peanuts and not just peanut traces?

A. 4.1
B. 12.03
C. 17.97
D. 35.90

12. According to the results of the analysis of the various foods, which is least likely to cause a peanut allergic reaction?

F. Sausage with walnut
G. Cereal bar I
H. Chocolate
J. Cookies with fiber

Passage V

Enzymes are substances that act as a catalyst to speed up biochemical reactions. When a *substrate* binds to the active site of an enzyme, a reaction can occur in which the substrate is converted into one or more products. The digestive enzyme, Trypsin, catalyzes the process of breaking down proteins in the small intestine into amino acids, which can then be absorbed into the blood stream. Importantly, any physical or chemical changes to an enzyme's environment, such as changes in temperature, pH, and salt concentration, can alter its ability to function by denaturing or inactivating the enzyme.

Two experiments sought to compare the ability of Trypsin to generate products (amino acids) at two different pH levels. For each experiment, four vials were made to contain 1mM of Trypsin and differing concentrations of substrate. The values of light absorbance for each sample were recorded every 30 seconds for 2.5 minutes using a *spectrophotometer*, an apparatus for measuring the intensity of light. The measured absorbance values were collected at a wavelength that corresponds to the relative amount of product that was generated in the samples. In other words, a higher absorbance value at the indicated wavelength would mean more product was made by the Trypsin.

Experiment 1

Four vials were made to contain 1mM of Trypsin and differing levels of substrate concentration maintained at a pH of 8. The absorbance values after each 30 second time period for each substrate level is recorded in Table 1.

Absorbance value					
Substrate level (mM)	0.5 min	1 min	1.5 min	2 min	2.5 min
0.04	0.023	0.035	0.053	0.069	0.082
0.09	0.039	0.082	0.125	0.154	0.184
0.15	0.067	0.137	0.199	0.261	0.310
0.24	0.115	0.239	0.340	0.431	0.511

Table 1

Experiment 2

Four vials were made to contain 1mM of Trypsin and differing levels of substrate concentration maintained at a pH of 6. The absorbance values after each 30 second time period for each substrate level is recorded in Table 2.

Absorbance value					
Substrate level (mM)	0.5 min	1 min	1.5 min	2 min	2.5 min
0.04	0.006	0.011	0.017	0.023	0.027
0.09	0.014	0.028	0.042	0.055	0.068
0.15	0.027	0.053	0.078	0.102	0.149
0.24	0.060	0.090	0.145	0.190	0.233

Table 2

13. Compared to the same vial at a pH of 6, a vial at a pH of 8 containing a substrate level of 0.15mM and 1mM of Trypsin:

A. is experiencing more instances of the breaking down of amino acids into proteins.
B. is experiencing more instances of the breaking down of proteins into amino acids.
C. is experiencing less instances of the breaking down of amino acids into proteins.
D. is experiencing less instances of the breaking down of proteins into amino acids.

14. Among the results of the experiments, the best conditions for maximizing the amount of product catalyzed by the enzyme Trypsin regardless of substrate level are:

F. a pH of 6 for 0.5 minutes.
G. a pH of 6 for 2.5 minutes.
H. a pH of 8 for 0.5 minutes.
J. a pH of 8 for 2.5 minutes.

15. If a spectrophotometer measured an absorbance value of 0.011 after 1 minute in a vial containing 0.24mM of substrate and 1mM of Trypsin, the pH of that same vial would be expected to be closest to:

A. 4
B. 6
C. 7
D. 9

Passage VI

With the traditional *optical microscope*, the user looks into the eyepieces to view a sample or specimen. The objective lens focuses light from the sample into the eyepieces. The eyepiece lens and the objective lens both provide magnification, but the latter more so. The condenser lens helps to concentrate light on the sample for easy viewing. Figure 1 displays the visual path of an optical microscope.

While the more advanced *fluorescent microscope* shares some similarities to the optical microscope, one key difference is that fluorescent microscopes utilize a process called *photoluminescence*. This is where molecules in a sample can be put into an excited state and absorb energy from a high intensity light, causing the molecules to emit light at a longer wavelength. The filter then works by separating any surrounding light, so only the fluorescence emitted by the molecules in a sample can be visualized. The detector can be used to display the fluorescent sample on a digital screen for easy viewing. Figure 2 displays the visual path of a fluorescent microscope.

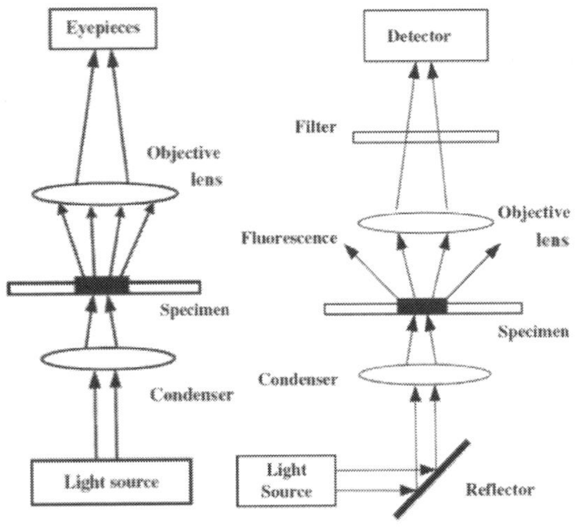

Figure 1　　Figure 2

A teacher sought to test a group of students' ability to distinguish neutrophil white blood cells within a blood sample using both optical (Study 1) and fluorescent (Study 2) microscopes. To distinguish a neutrophil under the optical microscope, the students were to look for a round cell body with a multi-lobed nucleus that is around 12-14 μm in diameter. For the fluorescent microscope, the blood sample was treated with an antibody that causes only neutrophil cells to fluoresce green.

Table 1 displays the results of Study 1, consisting of each student's answer for the number of neutrophils found in a blood sample and the percentage of correct cells that were identified using the optical microscope. Table 2 displays the results of Study 2, consisting of each student's answer for the number of neutrophils found in a blood sample and the percentage of correct cells that were identified using the fluorescent microscope.

Optical Microscope	Neutrophil count	Percent correct
Student 1	5	33%
Student 2	8	53%
Student 3	10	67%
Student 4	4	27%

Table 1

Fluorescent Microscope	Neutrophil count	Percent correct
Student 1	13	76%
Student 2	16	94%
Student 3	17	100%
Student 4	13	76%

Table 2

16. In one of the studies, Student 4 did not count 4 oval cell bodies that had the proper nucleus sizes, even though they were true neutrophils. If she had done so, her percent correct would have been:

F. 33%
G. 53%
H. 93%
J. 100%

17. The utilization of photoluminescence had what effect on the results of the two studies?

A. It more than quartered some students' abilities to discover neutrophils.
B. It more than halved some students' abilities to discover neutrophils.
C. It more than doubled some students' abilities to discover neutrophils.
D. It more than quadrupled some students' abilities to discover neutrophils.

18. A student guessed before the studies that the more a microscope alters or affects light with additional steps and parts, the less accurate the results would be. Was this student correct in her guess?

F. No: the fluorescent microscope, which affects light more than the optical microscope, yielded better results.
G. No: the optical microscope, which affects light more than the fluorescent microscope, yielded better results.
H. Yes: the fluorescent microscope, which affects light more than the optical microscope, yielded better results.
J. Yes: the optical microscope, which affects light more than the fluorescent microscope, yielded better results.

Step 3 Correct Answers

Passage I:	Passage II:	Passage III:	Passage IV:	Passage V:	Passage VI:
1: D	4: H	7: A	10: G	13: B	16: G
2: G	5: D	8: F	11: C	14: J	17: C
3: A	6: J	9: B	12: F	15: A	18: F

Stumped on any? You can find the explanations for each of these questions beginning on page 659.

STEP 4

Conflicting Viewpoints

What Is Conflicting Viewpoints?

In the introduction to *The ACT Science System*, I briefly mentioned that there are three types of passages in every ACT Science test. The first two have been discussed a bit more since then, but it is time to return to the third type, which is so different that it requires its own step in this book: Conflicting Viewpoints.

The Conflicting Viewpoints passage is something closer to an ACT Reading passage than it is the other ACT Science passages. I say that a bit tongue-in-cheek, but there's truth in it. The Conflicting Viewpoints passage almost never features any charts, diagrams, or data (though it could, and has in the past, so that's not a guarantee). Instead, it is much more likely to feature *only* words. There will be an opening paragraph (sometimes as short as a sentence, sometimes much longer) that introduces a broad topic on which there may be varying points of view in the scientific community (for example, if Pluto is a planet or not). Then, some number of scientists (as little as 2 and as many as 4) will present a contrary thesis with their reasons why they are correct in 1 or 2 paragraphs.

For example, Scientist 1 might believe that Pluto is a planet. He will then give all the reasons why he is correct on that. Scientist 2 might believe that Pluto is an exoplanet. She will then give all the reasons why she is correct on that. It may stop there, but as I said, there could be 3 or 4 scientists' ideas that are presented here. Scientist 3 then might believe that Pluto is a meteor, and Scientist 4 that it is a Dwarf Planet. I'm no expert on Pluto, so forgive me if I misrepresent what was once a planet in my childhood, but these kinds of differences is what you can expect to find in the Conflicting Viewpoints passage.

How to Read It

I have stressed the necessity of active (quick) reading to this point in *The ACT Science System*, and it is now worth stressing once again. You don't need to read this passage *s l o w l y* in an attempt to memorize every reason, evidence, or statistic presented by any of the scientists. Instead, with your pencil in hand, quickly read through the passage. Underline each scientists' main idea or thesis statement; maybe even double-underline it or put a star next to it so it stands out. If something jumps out to you as important, underline it as well or circle what you think may be key words, especially if you think it's a key reason why this scientist believes what she does (aka, underline the main pieces of evidence). Avoid underlining everything: only what seems to be key.

Major ideas are more important than minor details. The major thesis of each scientist, the major similarities, and the major difference are much more important to focus on during your initial read. Remember: your first read through is designed to give you the time to go and find details if necessary.

The Questions

As there is rarely any data given as a part of these passages, the questions are not similar to those of Step 1 or 3 that require reference to charts/tables/graphs. Instead, it is much more likely that you will have a variety of questions (7 total) that test your understanding of each scientist's position. For example, one question will probably give you a piece of evidence or a discovery and ask which scientist's position it helps. Another question might give you a statement and ask which scientist most agrees with it. Another question will simply restate an idea from the passage and ask which scientist agrees. In other words, the questions focus mostly on the similarities and differences between the points of view.

The Following Passages

What follows here is two Conflicting Viewpoints passages. The questions are designed to mimic as accurately as possible the types of questions that you will see on ACT day. As has been said, more than likely the Conflicting Viewpoints passage that you encounter will present the points of view of two scientists. However, because it is possible that there may be more, each of the following passages presents three points of view on different topics to get you used to this kind of thinking. So, set a timer for 6 minutes (5 minutes 50 seconds if you're being precise!) for each passage, take a deep breath, and do your best on the following passages one at a time; doing so will give you a serious advantage!

Passage I

Fast radio bursts (FRBs) are intense bursts of radio waves originating from deep space. These bursts last for a very short duration, typically just a few milliseconds, but within that brief time, they release an enormous amount of energy. FRBs are detected as sudden and powerful spikes in radio signals across a range of frequencies. These signals are typically observed by radio telescopes and analyzed by astronomers. FRBs are challenging to study because they occur throughout the universe at unpredictable times and locations, making it difficult to anticipate sources. Three scientists discuss their theories regarding the origin of FRBs.

Scientist 1

FRBs are generated by highly magnetized, rapidly rotating neutron stars called magnetars. Neutron stars are extremely dense remnants of massive stars that have undergone a supernova explosion. Magnetars are a specific type of neutron star with an exceptionally strong magnetic field. An FRB occurs when the intense magnetic field of a magnetar becomes disrupted, leading to a burst of radio waves. The disruption occurs because the magnetic field lines of the magnetar become twisted and rearranged due to various instabilities, or starquakes, within the star. FRB 121102 for example, one of the only FRBs known to repeat, has been discovered to originate from a source surrounded by an intense magnetic field. This type of magnetic field is only otherwise found around a Milky Way magnetar.

Scientist 2

FRBs are caused by the merger of compact objects, such as when a neutron star merges with another neutron star, or a black hole and neutron star merge. Compact object mergers are cataclysmic events that can release enormous amounts of energy of all wavelengths. During such a merger, the intense gravitational forces and tidal interactions can cause the objects involved to collide violently, producing powerful electromagnetic emissions, including the radio waves characteristic of an FRB. This explains why the vast majority of FRBs (FRBs 121102 and 181906 excluded) do not repeat, but are rather one-time events containing the energy output of hundreds of millions of stars.

Scientist 3

FRBs have multiple origins, not merely one. This is due to the fact that there are a multitude of large-scale and hyper-energy-producing events across the universe. One of the multitude of sources of FRBs is certainly neutron stars, one of which has been detected as the probable source of FRB 121102 three billion light years away (well outside the Milky Way galaxy). On the other hand, it seems equally probable that other cataclysmic events (such as black hole and neutron star collisions, for example) produce waves of multiple wavelengths simultaneously. One such FRB known as FRB 171209 is also thought to be the source of a gamma ray burst known as GRB 110715A.

1. According to Scientist 2, FRB 181906:

A. is the only example of an FRB that repeats.
B. originates approximately 3 billion light years away.
C. is caused by the violent collisions of cosmic objects.
D. does not contain the energy output of multiple stars.

2. Which of the scientists rely on the existence of internal disruptions of neutron stars to explain the origins of all FRBs?

F. Scientist 1 only
G. Scientist 2 only
H. Scientists 1 and 3 only
J. Scientists 2 and 3 only

3. Suppose it were definitely discovered that the source of FRB 121102 was the collision of two black holes. This discovery would support the position of:

A. Scientist 1 only.
B. Scientist 2 only.
C. Scientists 1 and 3 only.
D. Scientists 2 and 3 only.

4. Which of the following discoveries would bolster the position of Scientist 1 relative to that of Scientist 2?

F. That magnetars also release gamma rays
G. That the merger of celestial objects can produce gamma rays but not radio waves
H. An FRB that lasts more than a few milliseconds
J. An FRB that repeats once every few years

5. Detailed surveys of star clusters in and near the Milky Way galaxy reveal that there is no direct evidence of any major merger of compact objects in its history. These results are *inconsistent* with the argument of which scientist?

A. Scientist 1
B. Scientist 2
C. Scientist 3
D. It is inconsistent with the positions of none of the 3 scientists.

6. All three scientists agree that which of the following plays a role in the generation of many FRBs?

F. The extreme gravitational pull of black holes and superstars
G. Instabilities, or starquakes, that take place within a neutron star
H. The relatively small size of the Milky Way relative to the Andromeda galaxy
J. The dense remnants of stars that have experienced supernova

7. If gravitational forces play a role in the intensity of starquakes, then which of the three scientists would agree that gravitational forces play a role in the origins of FRBs?

A. Scientists 1, 2, and 3
B. Scientists 1 and 3 only
C. Scientists 2 and 3 only
D. Scientist 1 only

Passage II

Humans, along with all other species, experience biological aging. Biological aging refers to the gradual deterioration of biological systems and functions over time. It is distinct from other types of aging, such as psychological aging and social aging. Biological aging is a natural process that occurs in living organisms, including humans. Biological aging is characterized by a progressive decline in various physiological processes, such as cellular metabolism, tissue repair, immune function, and organ functionality. Although it has been studied extensively, the reasons why the decline associated with aging occurs is still unknown. Three scientists debate competing theories that explain biological aging.

Scientist 1

Biological aging is a result of genetic programming and evolutionary mechanisms. Organisms have an inherent biological clock or aging "program" that influences the rate of aging. Aging is an adaptive trait coded into DNA that has evolved over time to optimize the allocation of resources and enhance the survival of the species. It is likely that various physiological factors, such as hormonal changes and the decline of repair mechanisms, are orchestrated by the aging program to regulate the aging process.

Scientist 2

Aging is primarily caused by the gradual accumulation of cellular damage over time. A multitude of factors contribute to the progressive decline in cellular and tissue function, such as oxidative stress, DNA mutations, and the accumulation of cellular waste products. As cells throughout the body are exposed to environmental stressors and waste from internal metabolic processes, damage occurs at the molecular level. Over time, this accumulated damage overwhelms the cellular repair mechanisms, leading to a decline in organ function and the onset of age-related diseases.

Scientist 3

The progressive shortening of telomeres, protective structures located at the ends of chromosomes, plays the most significant role in the aging process. Telomeres naturally shorten with each cell division due to the incomplete replication of DNA ends. As telomeres become critically short, cells can no longer divide and function properly, known as cellular senescence. This leads to a gradual decline in tissue regeneration and function. Telomere shortening acts as a "molecular clock" that contributes to the overall aging of organisms.

8. Which of the following scientists, if any, state(s) that DNA plays a role in the aging process?

F. None of the 3 scientists
G. Scientists 1 and 3 only
H. Scientists 2 and 3 only
J. All 3 of the scientists

9. Suppose it is discovered that those with thyroiditis, a condition that affects hormonal output, tend to age faster than those without the condition. This finding would most bolster the position(s) of:

A. Scientist 1
B. Scientist 2
C. Scientist 3
D. Scientists 2 and 3

10. If the shortening of telomeres over time were classified as "cellular damage," then which two scientists could both be correct in their assessment as to the cause of aging?

F. Scientists 1 and 2
G. Scientists 1 and 3
H. Scientists 2 and 3
J. Scientists 1, 2, and 3

11. According to the theory of Scientist 2, a medication that might slow the aging process would be one that:

A. helps regulate and support proper hormonal production.
B. slows the shortening of telomeres.
C. helps cells to dispose of waste more permanently.
D. increases the accumulation of cellular damage over time.

12. According to at least one scientist, cellular senescence:

F. is necessary to slow aging and relies on environmental stressors and DNA mutations.
G. is necessary to slow aging and relies on the proper functioning of telomeres.
H. furthers the aging process and is rooted in the gradual shortening of telomeres.
J. furthers the aging process and relies on the proper functioning of telomeres.

13. *Cellular stress response* (CRS) is a reaction to the changes or fluctuations of extracellular conditions that damage the structure and function of molecules. Exposure to harmful chemicals is known to trigger CRS. Which scientist(s) would recommend avoiding exposure to harmful chemicals to keep the aging process in check?

A. Scientist 1
B. Scientist 2
C. Scientist 3
D. Scientists 2 and 3

14. Suppose a fourth scientist claims that the aging process is the gradual effect of the normal functioning of the body at the cellular or chromosomal level as opposed to a genetically predetermined outcome. Which of the scientists would agree with this claim?

F. Scientist 2 only
G. Scientists 1 and 3
H. Scientists 2 and 3
J. Scientists 1, 2, and 3

Step 4 Correct Answers

Passage I:
1: C
2: F
3: D
4: G
5: D
6: J
7: A

Passage II:
8: J
9: A
10: H
11: C
12: H
13: B
14: H

Stumped on any? You can find the explanations for each of these questions beginning on page 662.

STEP 5

The More Complex Questions

While it is of course true that most of the questions on the ACT Science test mimic those taught and practiced thus far in this book, it is also true that each ACT Science test will feature a handful of "other" or you may think "more difficult" questions. These questions vary in their types and number on any given test. Some of these questions require you to convert that data before you into some new kind of chart or graph. Some of these questions require you to reach bigger conclusions from lots of data. Some of these questions require previous science knowledge. Some of these questions require complex or deep reasoning. Some of them require an unexpected step of some kind. Some of them require inference (reaching the most likely conclusion based on the data).

Although the percentage of any of these questions individually on any ACT Science test is low (as low as 0%; for any of the types in the above paragraph, you may have 0 total questions, or you may have 5), together they make up a substantial block of more difficult or rare questions that are worth preparing for. While some of that preparation may come from the practice tests featured in Step 6, they are worth isolating into their own step for practice as well.

The Following Practice Passages

The following practice passages are the same as you have seen thus far in Steps 1, 2, and 3. You might think it a bit strange that I didn't just make this current information into Step 4 to keep them all in a row. However, remember that the purpose of *The ACT Science System* is to prepare you for the ACT Science test in order of importance. If these questions were more important than a step on the Conflicting Viewpoints passage, then the order of steps would have reflected that.

Take a deep breath, and give the following variety of questions your best shot!

Passage I

Most of the water consumption within the United States is used by the agricultural industry for food production. This heavily contributes to the overuse of groundwater aquifers. Therefore, finding alternative resources of water for agricultural production is necessary to lessen the looming threat of food and water scarcity. One issue is that alternative water sources in certain regions often contain a higher concentration of salt compared to groundwater aquifers, and many food crops are not selected for traits like tolerance to salt. In recent years, new varieties, also called *variants*, of crops have been selected mostly for commercial benefit, with little regard for producing varieties that can withstand changes in salt concentrations. As a result, a group of researchers sought to determine plant variants that are resilient to waters with higher salt concentrations.

Researchers first tested the salt tolerance in variants of two regularly consumed crops, tomato and pepper, by testing the consumable yields of each plant when grown in the same soil. The control for the experiment was freshwater from a ground water aquifer, while the experimental condition was done with water containing a higher salt content. The results are recorded in Table 1 (tomato) and Table 2 (pepper) below.

Fruit yield (grams)		
Tomato variant	Control	Experimental
Bloody Butcher	2785	1719
Juane Flamme	2317	1355
Quarter Century	1415	928

Table 1

Fruit yield (grams)		
Pepper variant	Control	Experimental
California Wonder	2591	1993
Thai Hot	295	291
Ancho	1514	1489

Table 2

The researchers next tested the concentration of sodium within the plant tissue of the different variants for both the control and saltwater (experimental) groups. Their findings are recorded in Figure 1 (tomato) and Figure 2 (pepper) below in millimoles per kilogram.

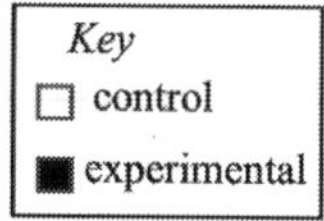

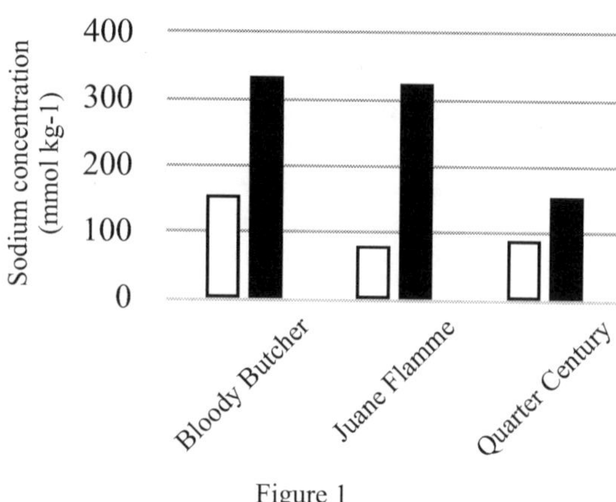

Figure 1

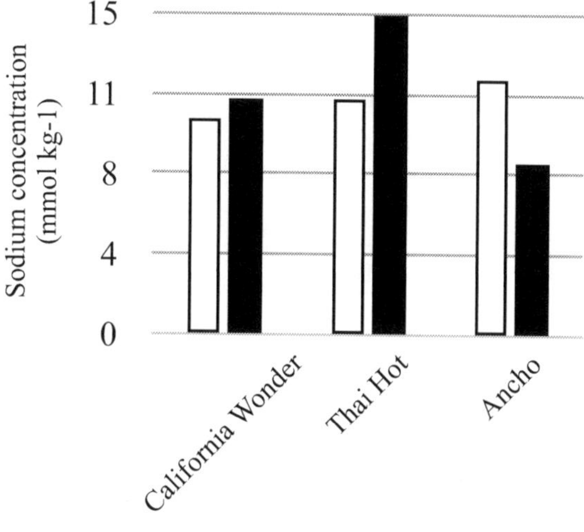

Figure 2

1. Better Boy is a variety of tomato that, when watered from a source low in salt, typically features a sodium concentration of 27.5 mmol/kg-1. What would be the expected sodium concentration of Better Boy if it were to be watered from an alternative source with a high concentration of salt?

   A. 0 mmol/kg-1
   B. 5 mmol/kg-1
   C. 75 mmol/kg-1
   D. 950 mmol/kg-1

2. Which of the following pie charts most accurately represents the total yield of the three tomato variants when watered from an underground aquifer?

F.

G.

H.

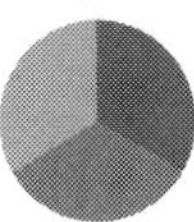

J.

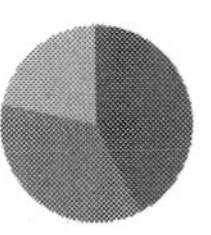

3. A scientist breeds a tomato containing 50% of the DNA of both Bloody Butcher and Juane Flamme. If this new tomato were subjected to the same experiment, the amount of fruit it would yield if watered with a groundwater aquifer would most likely be closest to:

A. 1,525 grams
B. 2,525 grams
C. 2,785 grams
D. 5,000 grams

Passage II

A group of high school students investigated the momentum of carts rolling down an inclined plane across a designated finish line. The students used three carts, labeled Cart A, Cart B, and Cart C. Cart A had a mass of 12.5 kg, Cart B had a mass of 21.8 kg, and Cart C had a mass of 34.7 kg. They conducted five trials, progressively increasing the release height of the carts. The purpose of the experiment was to explore how changes in release height affect the velocity and momentum of the carts.

Velocity is a fundamental concept in physics that represents the speed of an object in a specific direction. In this experiment, velocity was measured as each cart crossed the finish line, but can also be determined using the equation $v = \sqrt{2gh}$, where v is the velocity, g is the acceleration due to gravity (approximately 9.8 m/s^2), and h is the release height of the cart.

Momentum is a property of a moving object that depends on its mass and velocity. It describes the quantity of motion possessed by an object and is calculated by multiplying the mass of the object by its velocity. The equation for momentum is given as $p = mv$, where p represents the momentum, m is the mass of the object, and v denotes the velocity.

After collecting data, the students calculated the momentum for each cart and trial. Figure 1 shows the recorded velocity for each cart as it crossed the finish line, and Figure 2 shows the calculated momentum for each cart as it crossed the finish line.

Key:
- ■ Cart A
- ▲ Cart B
- ● Cart C

Figure 1

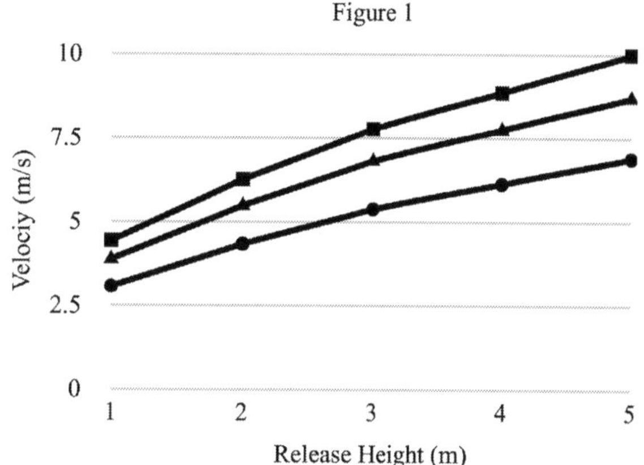

Figure 2

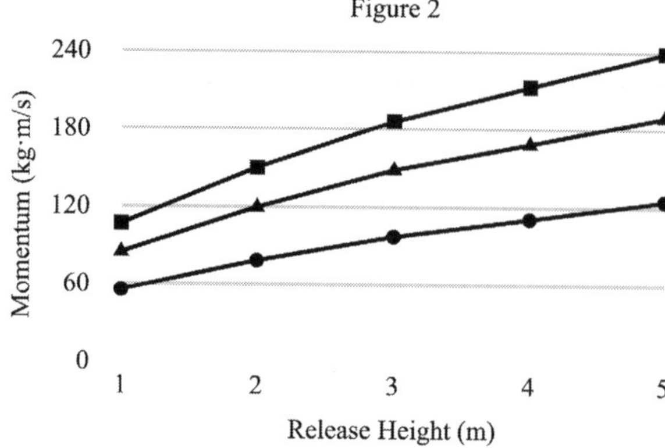

4. On the moon, the acceleration due to gravity is approximately 1.625 m/s^2, or 17% of that of earth. If students were to repeat the experiment on the moon with Cart B, what would be its approximate expected velocity when released from a height of 3 meters?

   F. 1.15 m/s
   G. 5.05 m/s
   H. 8.35 m/s
   J. 33.75 m/s

5. What was the velocity of Cart B as it crossed the finish line after being released from a height of 2 meters when expressed in *centimeters* per second?

   A. 5.48 cm/s
   B. 54.8 cm/s
   C. 548 cm/s
   D. 5,480 cm/s

6. Acceleration is defined as an object's change in velocity divided by the change in time over which this took place. If it took Cart A 1.5 seconds to reach the finish line from a release height of 5 meters, and assuming it was released from rest, then what was Cart A's acceleration when it crossed the finish line?

   F. −6.67 m/s^2
   G. −3.33 m/s^2
   H. 3.33 m/s^2
   J. 6.67 m/s^2

Passage III

The *Mpemba Effect* refers to a curious phenomenon in which hot water freezes faster than cold water under certain circumstances. Several proposed explanations have been put forth to shed light on the Mpemba Effect. One possibility relates to the evaporation of the hot water during the cooling process. As hot water is exposed to lower temperatures, it undergoes rapid evaporation, resulting in a reduction in its volume. This reduction in volume leads to an increase in the concentration of dissolved solids in the remaining water. Consequently, the higher concentration of dissolved solids may lower the freezing point of the hot water, allowing it to freeze more rapidly.

A group of students designed an experiment to test the Mpemba Effect. They collected four beakers and labeled them A, B, C, and D. *Thermocouples*, or thermoelectric devices for measuring temperature, were placed in the bottom of each beaker. Beakers A and B were filled with distilled (purified) water, and beakers C and D were filled with tap water. The water in beakers A and C was heated to 50 degrees Celsius, and the water in beakers B and D was left at room temperature (around 30 degrees Celsius).

The students recorded the temperature of each beaker after placing it in a freezer with a temperature of -18° Celsius until it had reached 0° Celsius, the freezing point of water. The observations of the students are given below. Table 1 corresponds to beaker A, Table 2 to beaker B, Table 3 to beaker C, and Table 4 to beaker D.

Table 1 (Beaker A)	
Time Elapsed (minutes)	Temperature (°C)
0	50
5	42
10	36
15	30
20	25
25	21
30	17
35	13
40	10
45	8
50	5
55	2
60	0

Table 2 (Beaker B)	
Time Elapsed (minutes)	Temperature (°C)
0	30
5	26
10	23
15	20
20	18
25	17
30	14
35	12
40	10
45	8
50	6
55	5
60	4
65	3
70	0

Table 3 (Beaker C)	
Time Elapsed (minutes)	Temperature (°C)
0	50
5	44
10	38
15	33
20	28
25	24
30	20
35	17
40	14
45	11
50	8
55	5
60	3
65	0

Table 4 (Beaker D)	
Time Elapsed (minutes)	Temperature (°C)
0	30
5	26
10	22
15	19
20	18
25	17
30	15
35	13
40	11
45	10
50	8
55	6
60	4
65	2
70	1
75	0

7. Suppose the students began with the hypothesis that the Mpemba Effect would *not* be seen in water that had been purified. Was the students' hypothesis falsified?

A. Yes: the beaker of heated and purified water was the first to freeze.
B. Yes: the beaker of room temperature purified water was the first to freeze.
C. No: the beaker of heated and purified water was the first to freeze.
D. No: the beaker of room temperature purified water was the first to freeze.

8. After the experiment is over, a student filled Beaker E with water and put it in the same freezer as Beakers A, B, C, and D. If it took the water 85 minutes to reach a temperature of 0° Celsius, which of the following could be true of the water prior to being put in the freezer?

F. It was sourced from a freshwater spring and heated to a temperature of 50° Celsius.
G. It was sourced from a freshwater spring and kept at room temperature.
H. It was sourced from the ocean and heated to a temperature of 50° Celsius.
J. It was sourced from the ocean and kept at room temperature.

9. Below is the formula for converting °Celsius into °Fahrenheit:

$$°F = (°C \cdot 1.8) + 32$$

Which of the following temperatures in Fahrenheit was the temperature after 30 minutes had elapsed of the purified water that had been put into the freezer with an initial temperature of 50° Celsius?

A. −30.1° F
B. 1° F
C. 62.6° F
D. 100.1° F

Passage IV

Real-time polymerase chain reaction (PCR) *analysis* is a laboratory technique that can be used to help determine if a specific type of DNA is present in a sample. This technique works by increasing the total amount of DNA present in a sample, a step called *amplification*, and then detecting if the DNA matches the target DNA.

Detection of the target DNA is determined by the *cycle threshold* (CT) value. The CT value is the number of cycles of amplification that is needed for a specific DNA sequence to be detected in a sample. The lower the CT value, the more likely it is that the sample contains the DNA of interest. Most real-time PCR analyses undergo a total of 40 cycles of amplification.

While this technique is often used for medical purposes, it also has applications in food safety. Due to the safety concerns regarding food allergens, scientists will use real-time PCR to search for the DNA of common allergen causing ingredients in commercial products to ensure that the package label is accurate. One common and often dangerous food allergy is an allergy to peanuts. If a person is severely allergic to peanuts and unknowingly ingests even a small amount, it could be deadly. Therefore, scientists completed real-time PCR analysis to test commercial food products for DNA that matches the peanut.

Table 1 shows commercial food products, their current package labels for allergens, and the CT values discovered for each following real-time PCR analysis to detect peanut DNA. An N.D. value means that there was no detection of the target DNA after 40 cycles of amplification.

Table 1

Food	Food Packaging Allergen Declaration	Peanut CT Value
Cereal bar I	Peanut, hazelnut	17.97
Cereal bar II	Almond and tree nuts	32.40
Cereal bar III	Hazelnut, almond and peanut traces	33.74
Cereal bar IV	May contain tree nut traces	35.90
Chocolate with pistachio	Pistachio, almond, hazelnut, tree nut traces	36.80
Sausage with walnut	Walnuts	N.D.
Chocolate	Almond and hazelnut traces	37.99
Cookies with fiber	Not declared	32.25

Table 2 displays example CT values and the likelihood of the values causing an allergic reaction in an individual with peanut allergy (if testing for peanut DNA).

Table 2

Example CT Value	Likelihood of Causing Peanut Allergic Reaction
≤ 29	High
30-35	High to moderate
36-40	Low to none

10. Which of the following graphs best represents the relationship between the number of cycles of amplification needed for detection of a certain DNA sequence and the likelihood that that same DNA will cause an allergic reaction?

F.

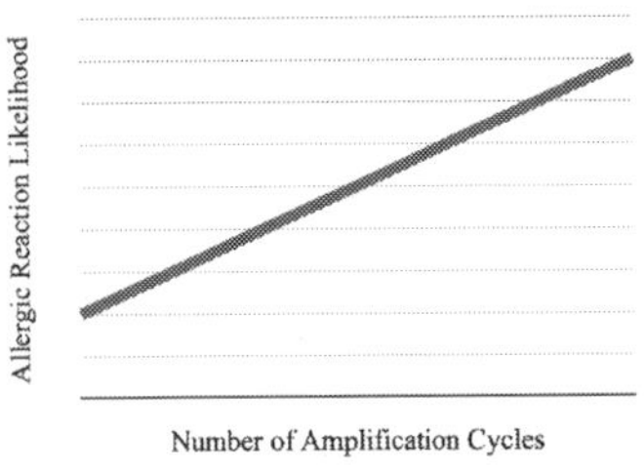

Allergic Reaction Likelihood

Number of Amplification Cycles

G.

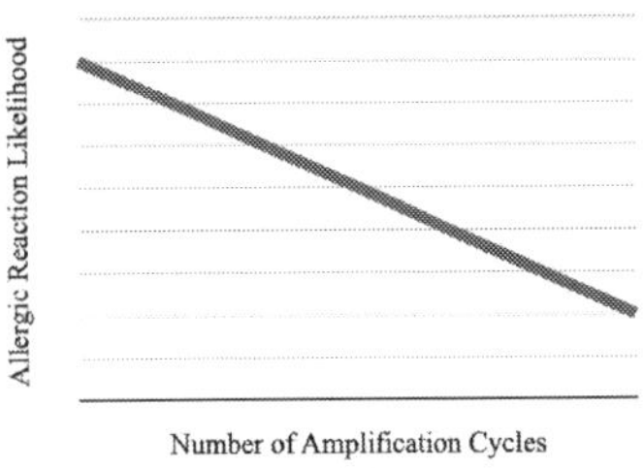

Allergic Reaction Likelihood

Number of Amplification Cycles

H.

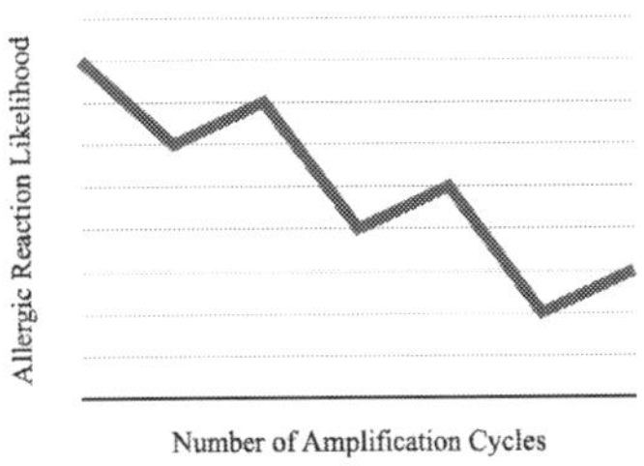

Allergic Reaction Likelihood

Number of Amplification Cycles

J.

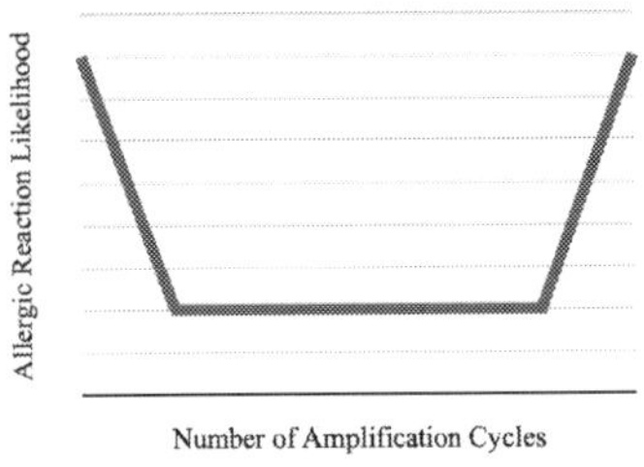

Allergic Reaction Likelihood

Number of Amplification Cycles

11. A lawmaker is proposing a fine of $100,000 per product on any company that manufactures a food with a High to Moderate likelihood of causing a peanut allergy that does not declare peanuts or peanut traces on their packaging. If the same company manufactured all of the products tested in Table 1, then how much money would the company owe in fines if the new law were to be passed?

A. $100,000
B. $200,000
C. $300,000
D. $400,000

12. It has been discovered that DNA has a half-life (the amount of time it takes for half of a substance to dissolve) of 521 years. Thus, in 1,042 years, it is likely that the CT value of a material with a current CT value of 40:

F. would then have a CT value of 10.
G. would then have a CT value of 20.
H. would then have a CT value of 30.
J. would then have a CT value greater than 40.

Passage V

Enzymes are substances that act as a catalyst to speed up biochemical reactions. When a *substrate* binds to the active site of an enzyme, a reaction can occur in which the substrate is converted into one or more products. The digestive enzyme, Trypsin, catalyzes the process of breaking down proteins in the small intestine into amino acids, which can then be absorbed into the blood stream. Importantly, any physical or chemical changes to an enzyme's environment, such as changes in temperature, pH, and salt concentration, can alter its ability to function by denaturing or inactivating the enzyme.

Two experiments sought to compare the ability of Trypsin to generate products (amino acids) at two different pH levels. For each experiment, four vials were made to contain 1mM of Trypsin and differing concentrations of substrate. The values of light absorbance for each sample were recorded every 30 seconds for 2.5 minutes using a *spectrophotometer*, an apparatus for measuring the intensity of light. The measured absorbance values were collected at a wavelength that corresponds to the relative amount of product that was generated in the samples. In other words, a higher absorbance value at the indicated wavelength would mean more product was made by the Trypsin.

Experiment 1

Four vials were made to contain 1mM of Trypsin and differing levels of substrate concentration maintained at a pH of 8. The absorbance values after each 30 second time period for each substrate level is recorded in Table 1.

	Absorbance value				
Substrate level (mM)	0.5 min	1 min	1.5 min	2 min	2.5 min
0.04	0.023	0.035	0.053	0.069	0.082
0.09	0.039	0.082	0.125	0.154	0.184
0.15	0.067	0.137	0.199	0.261	0.310
0.24	0.115	0.239	0.340	0.431	0.511

Table 1

Experiment 2

Four vials were made to contain 1mM of Trypsin and differing levels of substrate concentration maintained at a pH of 6. The absorbance values after each 30 second time period for each substrate level is recorded in Table 2.

	Absorbance value				
Substrate level (mM)	0.5 min	1 min	1.5 min	2 min	2.5 min
0.04	0.006	0.011	0.017	0.023	0.027
0.09	0.014	0.028	0.042	0.055	0.068
0.15	0.027	0.053	0.078	0.102	0.149
0.24	0.060	0.090	0.145	0.190	0.233

Table 2

13. Does the enzyme Trypsin function more effectively in a more basic or more acidic environment?

A. Basic: the absorbance levels of the more basic vials are higher than the more acidic vials.
B. Basic: the absorbance levels of the more basic vials are lower than the more acidic vials.
C. Acidic: the absorbance levels of the more acidic vials are higher than the more basic vials.
D. Acidic: the absorbance levels of the more acidic vials are lower than the more basic vials.

14. A scientist hypothesizes that persons whose liquid diet consists of mostly acidic drinks (orange juice, coffee, wine, etc.) will have a lesser concentration of amino acids in the blood stream than the person who mostly drinks water. Is the null hypothesis rejected by the findings of Experiments 1 and 2?

F. No: the more basic vials had more substrate catalyzed into product than the acidic vials.
G. No: the more acidic vials had more substrate catalyzed into product than the basic vials.
H. Yes: the more basic vials had more substrate catalyzed into product than the acidic vials.
J. Yes: the more acidic vials had more substrate catalyzed into product than the basic vials.

15. Which of the following is the dependent variable across both experiments?

A. The substrate level
B. The amount of Trypsin in each vial
C. The absorbance value
D. The pH levels of the vials

Passage VI

With the traditional *optical microscope*, the user looks into the eyepieces to view a sample or specimen. The objective lens focuses light from the sample into the eyepieces. The eyepiece lens and the objective lens both provide magnification, but the latter more so. The condenser lens helps to concentrate light on the sample for easy viewing. Figure 1 displays the visual path of an optical microscope.

While the more advanced *fluorescent microscope* shares some similarities to the optical microscope, one key difference is that fluorescent microscopes utilize a process called *photoluminescence*. This is where molecules in a sample can be put into an excited state and absorb energy from a high intensity light, causing the molecules to emit light at a longer wavelength. The filter then works by separating any surrounding light, so only the fluorescence emitted by the molecules in a sample can be visualized. The detector can be used to display the fluorescent sample on a digital screen for easy viewing. Figure 2 displays the visual path of a fluorescent microscope.

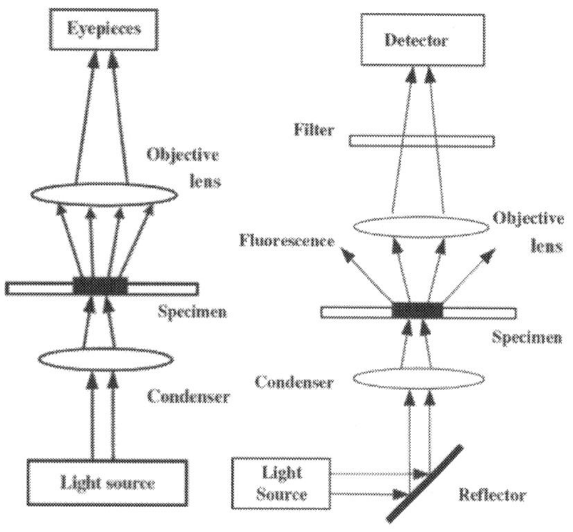

Figure 1 Figure 2

A teacher sought to test a group of students' ability to distinguish neutrophil white blood cells within a blood sample using both optical (Study 1) and fluorescent (Study 2) microscopes. To distinguish a neutrophil under the optical microscope, the students were to look for a round cell body with a multi-lobed nucleus that is around 12-14 μm in diameter. For the fluorescent microscope, the blood sample was treated with an antibody that causes only neutrophil cells to fluoresce green.

Table 1 displays the results of Study 1, consisting of each student's answer for the number of neutrophils found in a blood sample and the percentage of correct cells that were identified using the optical microscope. Table 2 displays the results of Study 2, consisting of each student's answer for the number of neutrophils found in a blood sample and the percentage of correct cells that were identified using the fluorescent microscope.

Optical Microscope	Neutrophil count	Percent correct
Student 1	5	33%
Student 2	8	53%
Student 3	10	67%
Student 4	4	27%

Table 1

Fluorescent Microscope	Neutrophil count	Percent correct
Student 1	13	76%
Student 2	16	94%
Student 3	17	100%
Student 4	13	76%

Table 2

16. Suppose Student 5 comes into class late and sits at his station to work without carefully reading the directions. If he identifies 45 neutrophil white blood cells when looking at the sample through the optical microscope, it is likely that he:

    F. mistakenly adjusted the reflector of the light source.
    G. ignored neutrophils that fluoresced green and counted dark-grey or black neutrophils instead.
    H. mistook each cell, no matter the shape or diameter of the nucleus, for a neutrophil cell.
    J. severely undercounted neutrophil cells due to a malfunction of the microscope itself.

17. For an additional study the following day, the teacher treats the blood sample with an antibody that turns multiple white blood cells blue. The student most likely to identify the most neutrophil cells correctly is the one who uses the fluorescent microscope and:

    A. searches for cells with a multi-lobed nucleus that have a diameter of around 12-14 μm.
    B. searches for cells with a multi-lobed nucleus that have a radius of around 12-14 μm.
    C. searches for cells that fluoresce closest to the blue-green side of the light spectrum.
    D. searches for cells that fluoresce closest to the blue-indigo side of the light spectrum.

18. If one μm is equal to one millionth of a meter, then about how large is the diameter of the nucleus of a neutrophil in meters?

A. 0.0000013
B. 0.000013
C. 0.00013
D. 0.0013

Step 5 Correct Answers

Passage I:	Passage II:	Passage III:	Passage IV:	Passage V:	Passage VI:
1: C	4: F	7: A	10: G	13: A	16: H
2: G	5: C	8: J	11: B	14: F	17: A
3: B	6: J	9: C	12: J	15: C	18: B

Stumped on any? You can find the explanations for each of these questions beginning on page 664.

STEP 6

Full-Length Practice Tests

I hope you have found *The ACT Science System* to be valuable thus far. It sums up and represents the best of ACT Science preparation, based off of thousands of hours of teaching, research into, and writing about the ACT itself. If you prepared from Step 1, then you have put first-things-first, second-things-second, and so on, ordering your preparation from most to least important based on the kinds of questions actually asked by the ACT. You haven't wasted your time memorizing the various categorizations of ACT Science question types or letting YouTube's algorithm throw endless videos at you over and over. Instead, you have spent your time wisely preparing through guided practice.

What follows now is two complete, full-length ACT Science practice tests. Let's quickly review strategies and what has been discussed before you set that timer and dive in.

1) Overall and Secondary Strategy

The ACT Science test will require that you use your time well and effectively. Taking "as much time as you need" on Passages I, II, III, and IV will all but guarantee that you will hear "Five minutes remaining!" when you're only halfway through Passage V, leaving you to guess entirely on Passage VI's questions. Instead, do your best to spend 5 minutes and 50 seconds (or, for the sake of simplicity, 6 minutes) on each passage. This means: 1) actively (quickly) reading the written portion of each passage as you circle/underline key terms and definitions and jot in the margins summaries of main ideas, and 2) glancing over data in charts/tables/graphs to get the main idea. This approach will guarantee you maximize the time you spend on the questions themselves, which is necessary: it takes *time* to get ACT Science questions correct because most (if not all) of them require you to look back into the passage for answers.

Secondarily, remember that this is the ACT's 4th quarter. That's cheesy, I know, but the idea works: you are tired, and if you give up, you very well may lose. Guessing can sometimes be acceptable on the ACT Science test (if a question is just too difficult and will require minutes you don't have, or if you are of course running out of time), but *never* just because you're tired and over it and want to go home and get back in bed for the rest of the day. Think about it like this: just about every time you guess, your ACT Science score is going down a point. Instead, take a deep breath prior to each individual passage and begin again.

2) It's All (Well, Mostly) About the Data

Except for the Conflicting Viewpoints passage (as discussed in Step 4), the ACT Science test's questions require you to read charts/tables/graphs properly more than anything else. Practice is the best way to get better at this skill. Again, on your first read through the passage, don't try to memorize this data: just glance over the x and y axes (in other words, see what's being measured) and look for any patterns in the data.

3) Questions that Require Previous Science Knowledge

It's not the time to go back and reread all of your previous science textbooks. You may go home and memorize the layer's of the earth's crust or the number of endangered lizard species in the United States, but questions that require you to have previous scientific knowledge are very rare. For most students, the few (or less) questions that require a foundation of science knowledge are not *too* difficult since, most often, it tests the basics. However, if you come to such a question, and have no idea, it's good to guess and save the time. If something clicks in you later, you can always come back.

That's it! For each of the following two practice tests, it is best to mimic the actual ACT as closely as possible. Set a 35 minute timer on your phone, put it on loud, then throw it in the hallway. Don't get up to get it, though you'll be tempted. Practice active reading and maximizing the time you spend on the actual questions (which is where ACT Science scores go up or down). Remember: practice really doesn't make perfect; instead, perfect practice *perfects*, meaning makes you better. So, practice as perfectly as you can!

Following each test, you'll find not only the correct answers on page 484, but also explanations for each question beginning on page 667 (Practice Test 1) and page 672 (Practice Test 2).

PRACTICE TEST 1

35 Minutes, 40 Questions

SCIENCE TEST

35 Minutes — 40 Questions

DIRECTIONS: There are several passages in this test. Each passage is followed by several questions. After reading a passage, choose the best answer to each question and fill in the corresponding oval on your answer document. You may refer to the passages as often as necessary.

You are NOT permitted to use a calculator on this test.

Passage I

Escherichia coli (*E. coli*) is a coliform bacterium that is commonly found in the lower intestine of warm-blooded organisms. Though most strains are harmless, some serotypes can cause food poisoning in their hosts. In humans, the bacterium is often transmitted through food items, such as undercooked hamburgers and unpasteurized milk. Scientists recently tested methods for minimizing the likelihood of ground beef becoming contaminated with *E. coli*.

Experiment 1

Scientists first studied the effects of radiation on ground beef. After taking an initial count of colony forming units (cfu/gm) of *E. coli*, ground beef was exposed to radiation for 15 minutes. Every 5 minutes, the ground beef was sampled to determine the death rate of *E. coli*, if any. Table 1 shows the results.

Table 1

Time of exposure (minutes)	*E. coli* count
0	20,000 cfu/gm
5	15,000 cfu/gm
10	10,000 cfu/gm
15	5,000 cfu/gm

Experiment 2

Scientists also tested the effects of acid on *E. coli*. In this experiment, an initial count was done on a contaminated ground beef specimen, then 3 additional samples from the same specimen of beef were placed in a 10% vinegar-acidic solution for 5, 10, and 15 minutes, respectively. The results of the measured death rate of the *E. coli* are shown in Table 2.

Table 2

Time of exposure (minutes)	*E. coli* count
0	25,000 cfu/gm
5	15,000 cfu/gm
10	10,000 cfu/gm
15	15,000 cfu/gm

Experiment 3

In the third experiment, four samples with 20,000 cfu/gm count *E. coli* were soaked in a vinegar-acidic solution for 5 minutes, then stored for 24 hours at varying temperatures before undergoing a final *E. coli* count. The results are shown below in Table 3.

Table 3

Temperature of exposure (24 hours)	*E. coli* count
4°F	15,000 cfu/gm
20°F	30,000 cfu/gm
40°F	60,000 cfu/gm
50°F	70,000 cfu/gm

1. If another trial had been performed in Experiment 2 in which additional ground beef had been exposed to the vinegar-acidic solution for 20 minutes, the *E. coli* count most likely would have been:

   A. less than 5,000 cfu/gm.
   B. between 5,000 cfu/gm and 10,000 cfu/gm.
   C. between 10,000 cfu/gm and 15,000 cfu/gm.
   D. greater than 15,000 cfu/gm.

2. Suppose Experiment 3 had been repeated, but the 4 ground beef samples had been soaked in the vinegar-acidic solution for 10 minutes before a 24 hour storage. Would the *E. coli* count after 24 hours of storage at 50°F likely be greater or less than 70,000 cfu/gm?

   F. Greater, because the *E. coli* count after soaking would be lessened at the beginning of storage.
   G. Greater, because the *E. coli* count after soaking would be increased at the beginning of storage.
   H. Less, because the *E. coli* count after soaking would be lessened at the beginning of storage.
   J. Less, because the *E. coli* count after soaking would be increased at the beginning of storage.

3. An international beef distributor has decided to label any ground beef with a cfu/gm count of over 60,000 as *critical* and unfit for consumption. How many of the results of the 3 experiments are *critical*?

   A. 0
   B. 1
   C. 2
   D. 4

4. Which of the experiments exposed ground beef to radiation, if any?

   F. Experiment 1 only
   G. Experiment 2 only
   H. Experiments 1 and 2 only
   J. Experiments 1, 2, and 3

5. Is the relationship between the time of exposure to radiation and the *E. coli* count in ground beef a direct relationship or an inverse relationship?

   A. Direct; as the time of exposure to radiation increased, the *E. coli* count in the ground beef increased.
   B. Direct; as the time of exposure to radiation increased, the *E. coli* count in the ground beef decreased.
   C. Inverse; as the time of exposure to radiation increased, the *E. coli* count in the ground beef increased.
   D. Inverse; as the time of exposure to radiation increased, the *E. coli* count in the ground beef decreased.

6. Which of the following sequence of events is most likely to result in the lowest cfu/gm count of *E. coli* in a sample of ground beef?

   F. Expose it to radiation for 10 minutes, soak it in a vinegar-acidic solution for 10 minutes, then store it at 4°F for 24 hours.
   G. Expose it to radiation for 10 minutes, soak it in a vinegar-acidic solution for 15 minutes, then store it at 4°F for 24 hours.
   H. Expose it to radiation for 15 minutes, soak it in a vinegar-acidic solution for 15 minutes, then store it at 4°F for 24 hours.
   J. Expose it to radiation for 15 minutes, soak it in a vinegar-acidic solution for 10 minutes, then store it at 4°F for 24 hours.

7. Assume that an exposure to a vinegar-acidic solution for *greater than* 5 minutes creates an undesirable taste in ground beef. What percent of the results in Tables 1, 2, and 3 are undesirable?

   A. 16.67%
   B. 25%
   C. 33.33%
   D. 58.33%

Passage II

Glycene max is a soybean and species of legume native to East Asia. *G. max* usually undergoes *self-pollination* (in which both the egg and pollen are from the same *G. max* plant), but it is believed *cross-pollination* (in which the egg and pollen are from different *G. max* plants) could increase soybean yield. A study was conducted to examine the results of several pollination methods on bean yield and bean mass in a *G. max* population.

Before pollination could occur, 720 *G. max* flowering plants were separated into 3 equal groups of 240 each (Groups 1-3). The groups of *G. max* plants were then isolated from each other and placed into pollination cages to protect them from insects. Each group was then exposed to a different pollination method (see Table 1). The percent of plants that produced beans and the average mass per bean for each of the three groups were determined 4 weeks after the pollination occurred (see Figures 1 and 2, respectively).

Table 1

Group	Pollination method
1	cross-pollination using wild bees
2	cross-pollination using honey bees
3	self-pollination*

*No pollinators were allowed to interact with the plants

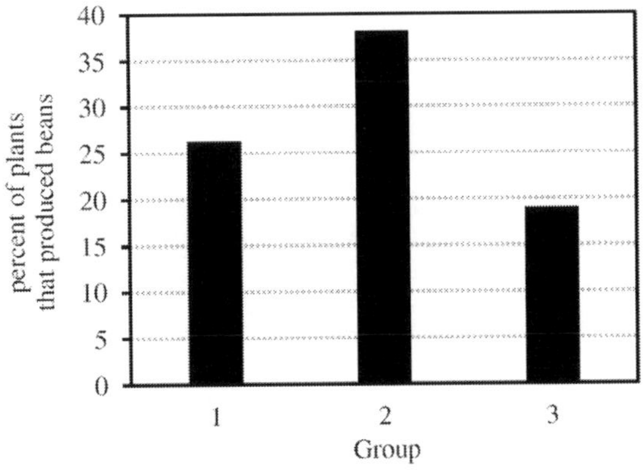

Figure 1

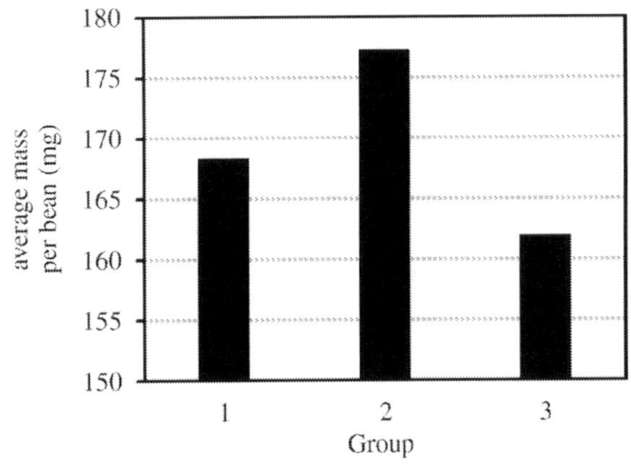

Figure 2

8. According to Figure 1, as bees are introduced into a population of *G. max* plants, the percent of plants that produces beans:

F. increases.
G. decreases.
H. decreases, then increases.
J. increases, then decreases.

9. When pollinators are not allowed to interact with *G. max* plants, which of the following occurs?

I. Self-pollination
II. The percent of plants producing beans is maximized
III. The egg and pollen come from the same *G. max* plant

A. I only
B. I and II only
C. I and III only
D. II and III only

10. According to Figure 1, the number of bean-producing plants that resulted from cross-pollination using honey bees is approximately how many?

F. 19
G. 26
H. 38
J. 91

11. Based on the information in the passage, it can be reasonably expected that both the percent of plants producing beans and the average mass per bean could be lessened in the wild due to which of the following factors?

A. The presence of honey bees.
B. The presence of wild bees.
C. A decrease in bees due to inclement weather.
D. An increase in pollinators due to inclement weather.

12. Which of the following can be reasonably inferred from the passage?

F. The bigger the plant, the bigger the bean.
G. The smaller the plant, the bigger the bean.
H. A healthy population of bees is good for *G. max* farmers.
J. Self-pollinating plants are always poor investments for farmers.

13. A *G. max* soybean is chosen at random from the experiment and is found to weigh 179 mg. It is most likely that this soybean:

A. is from Group 1 because self-pollinating *G. max* plants produce the largest soybeans.
B. is from Group 2 because *G. max* plants pollinated using honey bees produce the largest soybeans.
C. is from Group 2 because self-pollinating *G. max* plants produce the largest soybeans.
D. is from Group 3 because *G. max* plants pollinated using honey bees produce the largest soybeans.

Passage III

There is debate about the genetic origins of human life on earth. It is widely agreed that the earliest fossil evidence of modern humans (*Homo sapiens*) first appeared in Africa 130,000 years ago and also that there is evidence of modern humans from the Near East dating to 90,000 years ago. However, there is disagreement about the process that led to the evolution of modern humans. During the process of evolution, mutations of DNA appear in offspring. While many mutations are harmful and detrimental to the individual, a few may be helpful in the survival of an individual. DNA coding for useful traits is passed onto offspring and over long periods of time enough of these genetic changes accumulates for the group of organisms to have evolved into a different species. Two scientists provided explanations as to how these DNA changes came about in the development of *Homo sapiens*.

Scientist 1

The evolution of *Homo sapiens* was a result of parallel evolution involving *Homo erectus* (a species preceding that of *Homo sapiens*) and an intermediary species of some sort, such as Neanderthals and/or Denisovans. This process occurred in Africa, Europe, and Asia with some genetic intermixing among some members of these various populations occurring before *Homo sapiens* killed off these populations. There is clear anatomical evidence for this theory seen when comparing certain minor anatomical features, such as skull shape and structure, of *Homo erectus* populations with modern humans from these areas. The anatomical differences are so minor as to be negligible, thus proving the Multi-Regional Hypothesis that modern humans evolved separately in populations of Africa, Europe, and Asia.

Scientist 2

The evolution of *Homo sapiens* occurred within one fairly small and isolated population of people, most likely in Africa. It is this population of people that would eventually spread across Asia, Africa, and Europe. As this spread took place, they displaced and replaced other humanoid populations, such as Neanderthals and Denisovans. When one looks at DNA evidence of living humans, especially that of mitochondrial DNA and the mutation rate of DNA, one can calculate with astonishing accuracy when modern humans diverged from a common ancestor. Most such calculations conclude that this divergence occurred approximately 200,000 years ago, which is far too recent to support the Multi-Regional Hypothesis. In addition, molecular biology also suggests that the Out of Africa Hypothesis, that the first modern humans evolved exclusively in Africa, is the truth of our origin as a species.

14. According to Scientist 2, the presence of *Homo sapiens* in the Near East 90,000 years ago is the result of:

F. the migration of Neanderthals and Denisovans from a central point.
G. the migration of *Homo sapiens* from a central point.
H. the intermixing of Neanderthal and *Homo sapiens* populations in the Near East.
J. genetic mutations of a *Homo erectus* population that already lived in the Near East.

15. Suppose an archaeologist discovered the remains of a *Homo erectus* individual from the Near East with a femur bone essentially identical to the femur bones of modern humans in the same area. This discovery provides support for the hypothesis of which scientist?

A. Scientist 1 only
B. Scientist 2 only
C. Scientists 1 and 2
D. This discovery supports the hypothesis of neither scientist

16. Suppose it were discovered that the earliest *Homo sapiens* bone fragments discovered in Africa featured as many anatomic similarities to modern Europeans as the earliest European *Homo sapiens* fragments. Would this discovery support Scientist 1's hypothesis?

F. Yes; Scientist 1 accounts for such anatomic similarities, unlike Scientist 2.
G. Yes; Scientist 1 believes that all *Homo sapiens* originated in Africa before spreading across the globe.
H. No; Scientist 1 relies upon anatomic similarities being tied to individual locations and populations.
J. No; Scientist 1 does not rely upon anatomical similarities to reach his hypothesis.

17. Suppose that the remains of a *Homo sapiens* individual were discovered in Europe dating to 215,000 years ago. This discovery would *weaken* which of the scientists' explanations?

A. Scientist 1 only
B. Scientist 2 only
C. Scientists 1 and 2
D. The discovery weakens the explanation of neither scientist

18. With which of the following statements would Scientists 1 and 2 both agree?

F. At one point, *Homo sapiens* lived in the same area as other pre-modern humanoid species.
G. All pre-modern humanoid species were killed off intentionally by early *Homo sapiens*.
H. *Homo sapiens* resulted from the intermixing of pre-modern humanoid populations.
J. *Homo sapiens* fossils are almost always indistinguishable from the fossils of pre-modern humanoid species.

19. Suppose the bones of a previously unknown humanoid species were discovered to have been living in the same time and place as some of the earliest *Homo sapiens*. With which of the following statements would both Scientists agree?

A. There must be an earlier community of *Homo sapiens* undiscovered in Africa.
B. *Homo sapiens* evolved from this species.
C. *Homo sapiens* was most likely responsible for the killing off of this species.
D. *Homo sapiens* migrated to this location from elsewhere.

20. Which of the following is a key difference between Scientist 1 and 2?

F. Scientist 1 emphasizes anatomical data, while Scientist 2 emphasizes DNA analysis.
G. Scientist 1 emphasizes DNA analysis, while Scientist 2 emphasizes anatomical data.
H. Scientist 1 believes that *Homo sapiens* evolved from humanoid populations, while Scientist 2 does not.
J. Scientist 2 believes that *Homo sapiens* evolved from humanoid populations, while Scientist 1 does not.

Passage IV

P. aurelia and *P. caudatum* are two species of *paramecium*, unicellular organisms that primarily occupy stagnant pools of fresh water. Paramecium are covered in *cilia*, hairlike extensions that act as flippers to push the organism through the water. When paramecium encounter negative or predatory stimuli, they use their cilia to rotate 180 degrees and flee. *P. aurelia* and *P. caudatum* have very similar food requirements and compete for survival when kept under similar conditions.

Experiment 1

In Experiment 1, a scientist measured the populations, *P*, of *P. aurelia* and *P. caudatum* when isolated in an unfiltered jar of fresh water kept at room temperature. At Day 0, 20 of each species were introduced to the environment. Population levels were measured every 5 days (P_5, P_{10}, P_{15}, etc.). The results are shown in Figure 1.

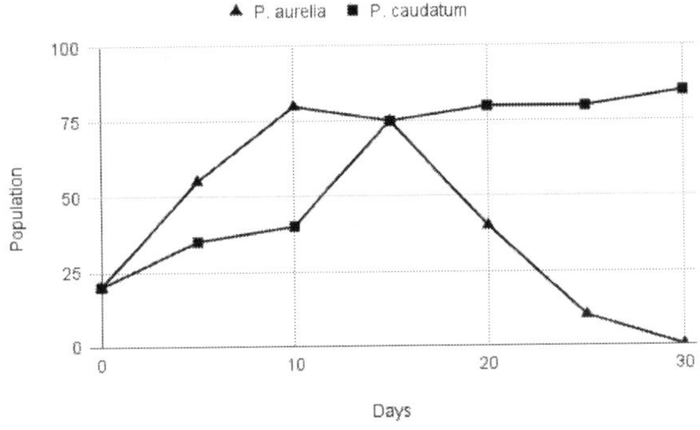

Figure 1

Experiment 2

In Experiment 2, a scientist measured the populations, *P*, of *P. aurelia* and *P. caudatum* when isolated in a room-temperature, unfiltered jar of fresh water that had been first given a bottom layer of 4 ounces of green algae. Population levels were measured every 5 days (P_5, P_{10}, P_{15}, etc.). The results are shown in Figure 2.

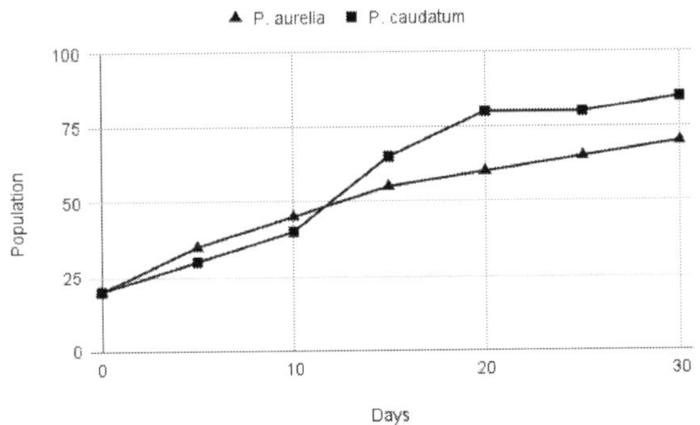

Figure 2

Experiment 3

In Experiment 3, the conditions of Experiment 2 were repeated with the addition of *Didinium nasutum*, a carnivorous unicellular ciliate that preys on paramecium. Aided by its toxicysts, *D. nasutum* paralyzes paramecium before consuming them through its expandable cytosome. Population levels for the three unicellular organisms were measured every 5 days (P_5, P_{10}, P_{15}, etc.). The results are shown in Figure 3.

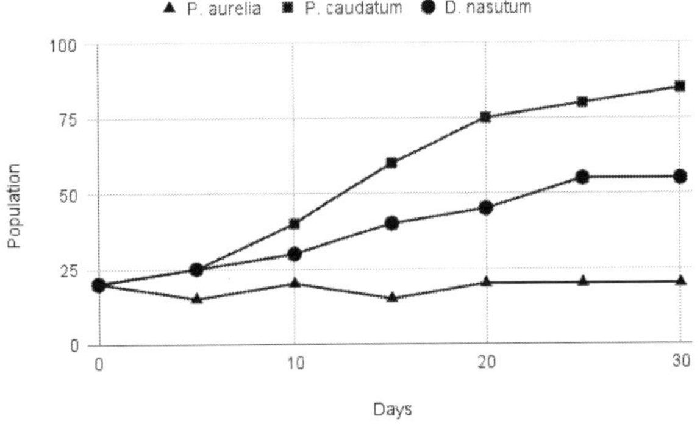

Figure 3

21. In the results of which experiment, if any, is there direct evidence that *P. aurelia* and *P. caudatum* are willing to consume other paramecium?

A. Experiment 1
B. Experiment 2
C. Experiment 3
D. None of the experiments has direct evidence that *P. aurelia* and *P caudatum* are willing to consume other paramecium.

22. Which of the following statements regarding *P* best describes a difference between Experiment 2 and Experiment 3?

F. The presence of *D. nasutum* affects the P_0 through P_{30} of *P. caudatum* more than the P_0 through P_{30} of *P. aurelia*.
G. The presence of *D. nasutum* affects the P_0 through P_{30} of *P. aurelia* more than the P_0 through P_{30} of *P. caudatum*.
H. The presence of green algae affects the P_0 through P_{30} of *P. caudatum* more than the P_0 through P_{30} of *D. nasatum*.
J. The presence of green algae affects the P_0 through P_{30} of *P. aurelia* more than the P_0 through P_{30} of *D. nasatum*.

23. If Experiment 3 were repeated with the addition of *Tetrahymena pyriformis*, which preys on *D. nasutum*, with a $P_0 = 20$, then it could be reasonably expected that the P_{25} of *P. aurelia* would be:

A. Greater than the P_{25} of *P. aurelia* in Experiment 3.
B. Less than the P_{25} of *P. aurelia* in Experiment 3.
C. Greater than the P_{25} of *P. caudatum* in Experiment 3.
D. Greater than the P_{25} of *D. nasutum* in Experiment 3.

24. Compared to Experiment 1, was the P_{20} of *P. aurelia* and *P. caudatum* greater than, less than, or equal to the P_{20} of both species in Experiment 2?

	P. aurelia	*P. caudatum*
F.	Greater than	Less than
G.	Less than	Equal to
H.	Greater than	Equal to
J.	Equal to	Greater than

25. Between all three experiments, the value of which of the following represents the lowest total number of paramecium after at least 20 days of population growth or decrease?

A. P_{20} of Experiment 1
B. P_{30} of Experiment 1
C. P_{20} of Experiment 2
D. P_{30} of Experiment 3

26. If it can be inferred, which of the following values is most likely the greatest?

F. The number of *P. aurelia* paralyzed by toxicysts in Experiment 3
G. The number of *P. caudatum* paralyzed by toxicysts in Experiment 3
H. The P_{30} of *P. aurelia* in Experiment 3
J. The P_{25} of *P. aurelia* in Experiment 3

27. Suppose green algae is rendered nutrient free after 50 days of isolation in room-temperature water. If Experiment 2 were carried out through 80 days, then which of the following could *not* be reasonably inferred?

A. At P_{80}, the population of *P. aurelia* would be approaching 0.
B. At P_{65}, the population of *P. aurelia* would begin to decline sharply.
C. At P_{60}, the population of *P. caudatum* would begin to level off.
D. At P_{70}, the population of *P. caudatum* would begin to decline sharply.

Passage V

A *solute* is any substance that is dissolved into another substance, which is called the *solvent*. A scientist tested the *solubility* (a measure of how much solute will dissolve into the solvent) of seven different substances. The solubility of a substance is defined as the concentration of dissolved solute that is in equilibrium with the solvent. Table 1 records the concentration in grams of dissolved substances in 100 grams (g) of water at various temperatures. The concentrations are expressed in grams of solute per 100 grams of water (H_2O).

When the mass of solvent (m_{sv}) is divided by the mass of solute (m_{su}), the result is the amount of solvent necessary to dissolve one unit mass of solute at 20°C. This measurement, m_{sv}/m_{su}, is used for descriptive purposes. Table 2 lists these terms and their accompanying measurements. Table 3 lists the m_{sv}/m_{su} values for the seven substances listed in Table 1.

Temp (°C)	$Na_2C_2O_4$	$NaNO_3$	HCl	$CaSO_4 \cdot 2H_2O$	$FeSO_4$	NaCl	NH_3
0	2.69	72	83	0.223	16	37	90
20	3.41	86	72	0.255	29	37	55
40	4.18	105	63	0.265	40	38	36
60	4.93	125	55	0.244	60	38	23
80	5.71	145	48	0.234	87	39	14
100	6.5	165	43	0.205	80	40	8

Table 1

Descriptive Term	m_{sv}/m_{su} Range
Very soluble	< 1
Freely soluble	1 to 10
Soluble	10 to 30
Sparingly soluble	30 to 100
Slightly soluble	100 to 1,000
Very slightly soluble	1,000 to 10,000
Practically insoluble	> 10,000

Table 2

Substance	m_{sv}/m_{su}
$Na_2C_2O_4$	29.3
$NaNO_3$	1.16
HCl	1.39
$CaSO_4 \cdot 2H_2O$	392.16
$FeSO_4$	3.45
NaCl	2.70
NH_3	1.82

Table 3

28. Before testing the solubility, the scientist hypothesized that exactly one of the seven substances would be considered *very soluble*. Was this hypothesis consistent with the results of the experiment?

F. No; more than one of the seven substances is to be considered very soluble.
G. No; none of the seven substances is to be considered very soluble.
H. No; there is not enough data available to reach a conclusion about the appropriate descriptive term for any of the seven substances.
J. Yes; exactly one of the seven substances is to be considered very soluble.

29. How many grams of Hydrogen Chloride (HCl) will dissolve into 100 grams of water at 60°C?

A. 43
B. 48
C. 55
D. 63

30. Based on Tables 2 and 3, what fraction of the seven substances deserves to be described as *freely soluble*?

F. $\frac{6}{7}$

G. $\frac{5}{7}$

H. $\frac{2}{7}$

J. $\frac{1}{7}$

31. If *solubility equipollence* is reached when 100 grams of a solute dissolve into 100 grams of a solvent, then it could be reasonably inferred that Sodium Nitrate ($NaNO_3$) reaches *solubility equipollence* in water at approximately what temperature?

A. 15°C
B. 35°C
C. 60°C
D. 140°C

32. Before testing the solubility, the scientist hypothesized that any substance containing sodium (Na) was *freely soluble*. What this hypothesis consistent with the results of the experiment?

F. Yes; both substances tested that contain sodium yielded a m_{sv}/m_{su} between 1 and 10.
G. Yes; both substances tested that contain sodium yielded a m_{sv}/m_{su} between 1 and 10.
H. No; none of the three substances tested that contain sodium yielded a m_{sv}/m_{su} between 1 and 10.
J. No; only two of the three substances tested that contain sodium yielded a m_{sv}/m_{su} between 1 and 10.

33. The scientist creates the following line chart from some of the data gathered in Table 1:

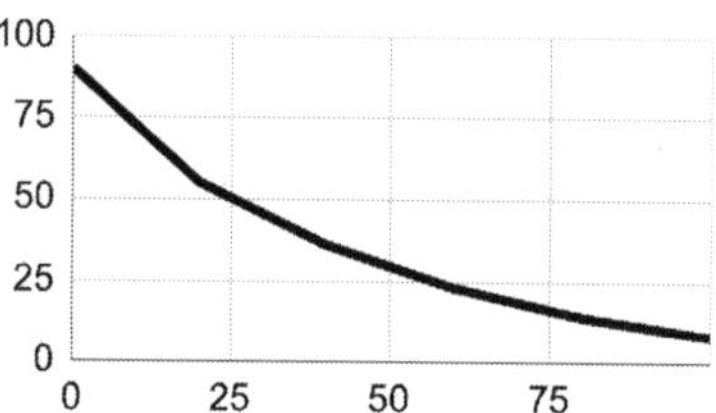

If the *x*-axis measures °C and the *y*-axis measures dissolved g of the solute/100 g H_2O, the line chart represents the data of which solute?

A. Ammonia (NH_3)
B. Iron (II) sulfate ($FeSO_4$)
C. Sodium nitrate ($NaNO_3$)
D. Sodium oxalate ($Na_2C_2SO_4$)

Passage VI

Due to their rapid reproduction rates, two species of fly were used by students at a local university to study genetics. For each study, both the *genotype*, the genetic makeup of an organism, and the *phenotype*, the observable characteristics of a genotype, were observed and recorded across three generations.

Study 1

Drosophila melanogaster, the common fruit fly, was first studied. *D. melanogaster* most commonly inherits and passes on a red eye color. However, there are many other eye color possibilities due to loss of one or more of the pigments normally synthesized and combined to produce red. Students were interested in understanding what effect a breeding of *D. melanogaster* with *homozygous* (identical) *alleles* (genetic variations) of a red and brown phenotype would have on descendants after two subsequent generations.

All specimens in the parental (P) generation possess homozygous alleles, a breeding of which results in a population (F_1) consisting entirely of *heterozygous* (a mix of dominant and recessive) alleles. A third generation (F_2) was then observed and compared to the students' expected outcomes. Students expected that 3/4 of F_2 would be of phenotype red and that 1/4 of F_2 would be of phenotype brown. Their findings are recorded in Table 1.

Table 1*

	Phenotype	Genotype		Phenotype	Genotype
P	Red eye	BB	x	Brown eye	bb
F_1	Red eye	Bb	x	Red eye	Bb
			Observed numbers		Expected numbers
F_2	Red eye	B__	63		61.5
	Brown Eye	bb	19		20.5
	Total		82		82

**B* is dominant; *b* is recessive; a blank means *undetermined*

Study 2

Musca domestica, the common housefly, were also studied in a *dihybrid experiment*, one in which specimens containing two pairs of homozygous alleles are crossed. Dihybrid experiments can yield surprising results after two subsequent generations.

All specimens in the parental (P) generation possess two pairs of homozygous alleles, a breeding of which results in a population (F_1) consisting entirely of heterozygous alleles. This population consists entirely of genotypes with two gene pairs, both with a dominant and recessive allele, resulting in a dominant phenotype. A third generation (F_2) was then observed and compared to the students' expected outcomes. Students expected that 9/16 of F_2 would be of phenotype red, 3/16 would be of phenotype brown, 3/16 would be of phenotype sepia (dark brown), and 1/16 would be of a fourth phenotype resulting from a doubly homozygous recessive genotype. Their findings are recorded in Table 2.

Table 2*

	Phenotype	Genotype		Phenotype	Genotype
P	Sepia eye	ddBB	x	Brown eye	DDbb
F_1	Red eye	DdBb	x	Red eye	DdBb
			Observed numbers		Expected numbers
F_2	Red eye	D__B__	67		64.7
	Sepia eye	ddB__	18		21.6
	Brown eye	D__bb	30		21.6
	____ eye	ddbb	____		7.2
	Total		115		115

**B* or *D* is dominant; *b* or *d* is recessive; a blank means *undetermined*

34. How many generations, on average, were studied and utilized across the two studies?

    F. 2
    G. 3
    H. 82
    J. 197

35. Based on the tables, which of the following phenotype/genotype observations most deviated from the students' expected outcomes?

    A. Brown eye/bb
    B. Red eye/B__
    C. Sepia eye/ddB__
    D. Brown eye/D__bb

36. Based on the data, what is the most likely explanation for zero observed doubly homozygous recessive genotypes in Study 2?

F. Based on the conclusions of Study 1, it is reasonable to infer that a doubly homozygous genotype ddbb is not a genetic possibility.
G. Based on the students' expectations, it is unlikely that a sample size of 115 *Musca domestica* specimens would result in 1 or more doubly homozygous genotypes.
H. The doubly homozygous genotype ddbb in the *Musca domestica* manifests as a brown eye phenotype.
J. The doubly homozygous genotype ddbb in the *Musca domestica* has a direct relationship with the numbers of larvae that die prior to hatching.

37. The primary reason that each study required three generations of flies was to:

A. ensure an intermixing of alleles sufficient enough to diversify the eye color phenotype.
B. allow the fly populations to multiply to a large enough sample size to avoid a margin of error greater than +−4%.
C. create a population of flies at F_2 comprised entirely of homozygous alleles.
D. create a population of flies at F_2 with at least 10% sepia eye phenotype.

38. Suppose a farmer purchased two white sheep, the offspring of which had offspring with other white sheep. If a lamb in this third generation were born with black wool, and if the genotype in sheep determining wool color consisted of two alleles, this would mean that:

F. this lamb inherited a recessive black wool gene from its father and mother, resulting in a recessive heterozygous genotype.
G. this lamb inherited a dominant black wool gene from its father and mother, resulting in a recessive heterozygous genotype.
H. this lamb inherited a dominant black wool gene from its father and mother, resulting in a recessive homozygous genotype.
J. this lamb inherited a recessive black wool gene from its father and mother, resulting in a recessive homozygous genotype.

39. Suppose a student argues that more research must be done on the second allele of F_2 fruit flies with a red phenotype eye color to ensure accuracy when comparing observed to expected numbers. Is this student correct?

A. Yes; the field of genetics is almost unpredictable without accurate allele counts.
B. Yes; determining if the second allele is dominant (B) or recessive (b) is necessary in distinguishing dominant or recessive phenotypes.
C. No; one dominant allele (B) is enough to ensure accurate numbers in *D. melanogaster*.
D. No; if the second allele is found to be recessive (b), it would be assumed that the phenotype is also recessive.

40. Which of the following pairs of pie charts accurately displays the observed numbers compared to the expected numbers for Study 2?

	Observed	Expected
F.		
G.		
H.		
J.		

PRACTICE TEST 2

35 Minutes, 40 Questions

SCIENCE TEST

35 Minutes — 40 Questions

DIRECTIONS: There are several passages in this test. Each passage is followed by several questions. After reading a passage, choose the best answer to each question and fill in the corresponding oval on your answer document. You may refer to the passages as often as necessary.

You are NOT permitted to use a calculator on this test.

Passage I

Although the probability of life currently existing on Mars is low (as low as 0), many scientists are convinced that the Red Planet once sustained life. While current conditions on Mars include freezing temperatures and high radiation levels, there is evidence to suggest that ancient Mars had a climate that could support life.

One main factor in determining the potential for life on a planet includes the existence of water. Due to the global presence of sulfate and chloride salts on Mars today, it is thought that the planet once had *hypersaline*, or extremely salty, bodies of water. Interestingly, there are bodies of water currently existing on Earth that are comparable to those that are thought to have been present on ancient Mars. This type of environment is not suitable for the majority of living microorganisms, as extremely high salinity levels are often toxic to cells. Nevertheless scientists have been able to discover microorganisms on earth that are able to withstand these types of harsh conditions.

In the study below, scientists sought to determine the biological diversity present in a hypersaline lake that is thought to be analogous to those found on ancient Mars. Table 1 highlights the geochemical properties in the hypersaline lake.

Table 1	
Properties	
pH	~ 8.0 to 8.3
Salinity (%)	37.1
Organic carbon (%)	~ 1 to 3

Figure 1 illustrates the estimated organism diversity in the hypersaline lake.

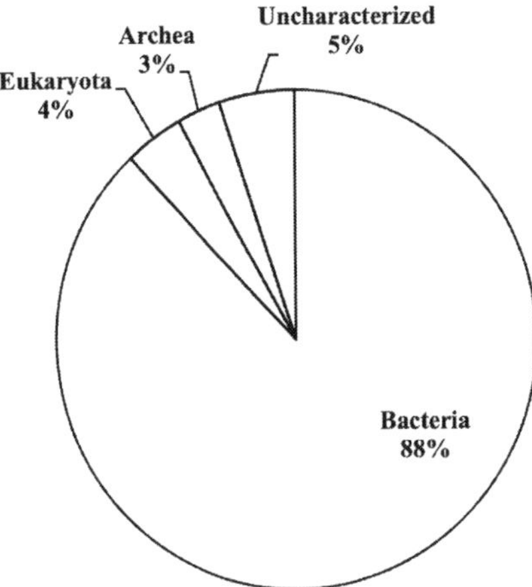

Figure 1

Figure 2 illustrates the estimated bacteria phyla diversity in the hypersaline lake.

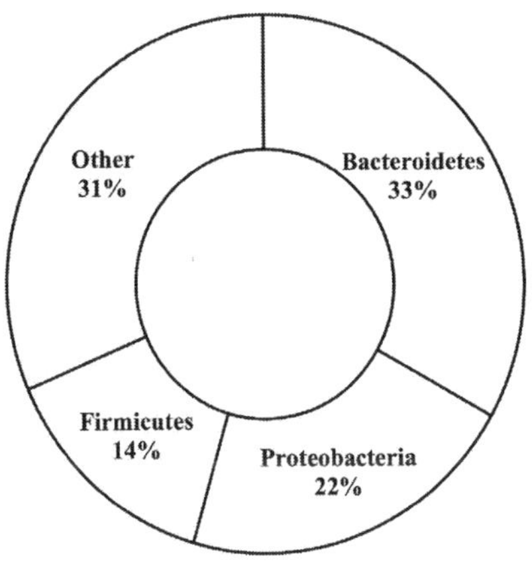

Figure 2

1. Based on the data in Figure 1 and Figure 2, about what percent of the estimated organism diversity in the hypersaline lake is made up of bacteroidetes?

   A. 12%
   B. 29%
   C. 33%
   D. 88%

2. According to the passage, if the salt levels of the lake were to be reduced over time, the overall percent of organism diversity in the lake occupied by bacteria would:

   F. decrease, because other types of life would be more likely to survive in the lake.
   G. decrease, because other types of life would be less likely to survive in the lake.
   H. increase, because other types of life would be more likely to survive in the lake.
   J. increase, because other types of life would be less likely to survive in the lake.

3. Consider the estimated organism and bacteria diversity in the hypersaline lake. Which of the following properly orders species based on percentage from lowest to highest occupation levels?

   A. Archea, Eukaryota, Proteobacteria, Firmicutes
   B. Eukaryota, Firmicutes, Proteobacteria, Bacteroidetes
   C. Firmicutes, Proteobacteria, Bacteroidetes, Archea
   D. Bacteroidetes, Proteobacteria, Eukaryota, Archea

4. The passage makes clear that one reason why current life on Mars is extremely improbable is due to:

   F. low radiation and high temperatures.
   G. high radiation and low temperatures.
   H. low levels of salinity in its lakes.
   J. high levels of salinity in its lakes.

5. A scientist reexamined the diversity of the life in the hypersaline lake and discovered the presence of the fungus *Wallemia ichthyophaga*. At most, *Wallemia i.* makes up what percent of the total diversity?

   A. 1%
   B. 2%
   C. 4%
   D. 5%

6. According to the passage, if it were discovered that life had once existed on Mars, it would most likely be:

   F. a bacteroidete that had grown and lived in a lake with little to no salt.
   G. a bacteroidete that had grown and lived in a hypersaline lake.
   H. a proteobacteria that had grown and lived in a lake with little to no salt.
   J. a proteobacteria that had grown and lived in a hypersaline lake.

Passage II

Athene cunicularia is a species of burrowing owl found throughout the open landscapes of both South and North America. Researchers hypothesized that *A. cunicularia* would favor prey of certain colors over others. This hypothesis was tested with three experiments using *Eublepharis macularius*, a species of gecko, which were purposefully bred with yellow, white, grey, purple, and brown skin. For each experiment, two geckos of each color were held in a large, open owl habitat that mimicked a forest, and the color of each gecko eaten by the owl was documented over a period of 24 hours. Every time the owl ate a gecko, another of the same color was added back into the habitat.

Experiment 1

In Experiment 1, ten wild-caught *A. cunicularia* were monitored one at a time in the habitat, having been placed there the same day as their capture. Figure 1 shows the average number of geckos of each color eaten over the 24 hour period.

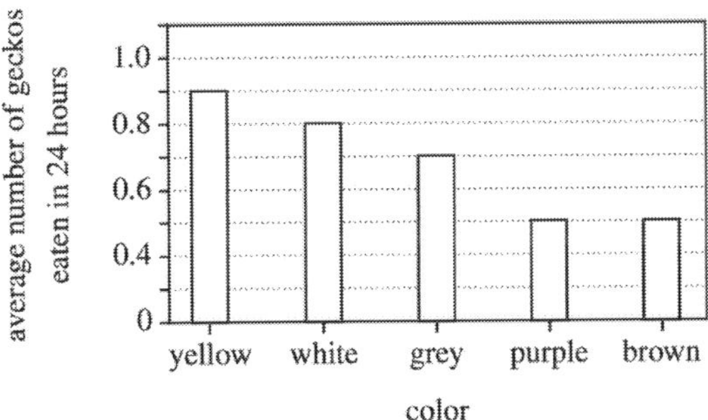

Figure 1

Experiment 2

In Experiment 2, ten wild-caught *A. cunicularia* were kept in the owl habitat for one month. Then, Experiment 1 was repeated. Figure 2 shows the average number of geckos of each color eaten over the 24 hour period.

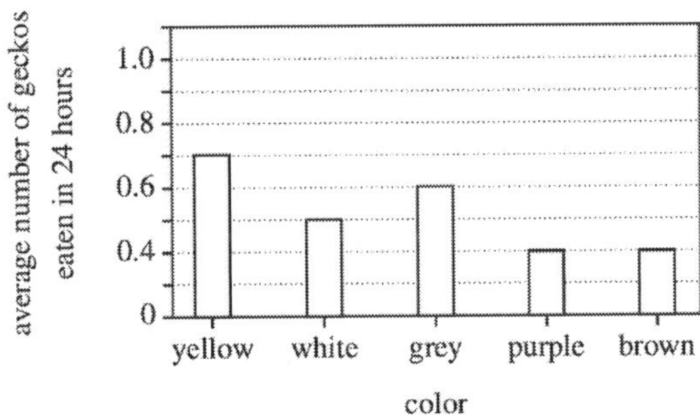

Figure 2

Experiment 3

In Experiment 3, ten *A. cunicularia* were hatched, raised, and bred in the laboratory. When they reached adulthood, Experiment 1 was repeated. Figure 3 shows the average number of geckos of each color eaten over the 24 hour period.

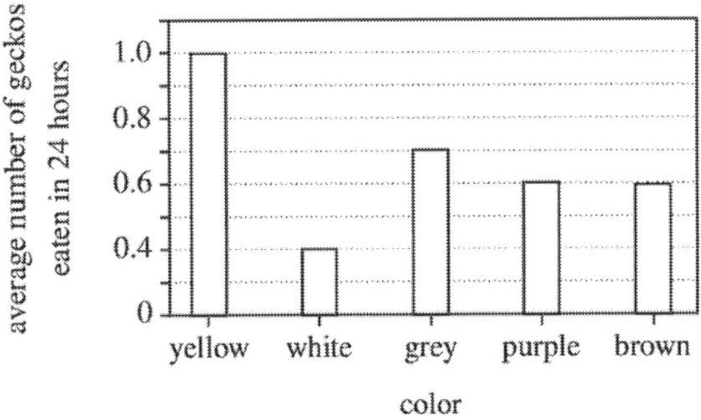

Figure 3

7. If the researchers had repeated the experiment with ten wild-caught owls that were kept in the habitat for two weeks, then the average number of yellow geckos eaten would have most likely been closest to:

A. 0.5
B. 0.6
C. 0.7
D. 0.8

8. As the time that the owls were held in captivity increased, the total number of geckos consumed:

F. increased only.
G. decreased only.
H. increased then decreased.
J. decreased then increased.

9. Given that wild geckos are not perfectly bred with pure colors, which of the following colors is least likely to be found thriving in the natural habitat of the *A. cunicularia*?

A. Grayish-purple
B. Brownish-purple
C. Yellowish-white
D. Grayish-white

10. If Experiment 3 were repeated, but *Eublepharis macularius* were not replaced as they were consumed, then the last gecko in the habitat would most likely be of what color?

F. Yellow
G. White
H. Grey
J. Purple

11. Based on the information in the passage, which of the following is likely to be true about *A. cunicularia*?

 A. The longer *A. cunicularia* is kept in captivity, the less it will tend to eat.
 B. There is no difference in the amount that wild and captive *A. cunicularia* tend to eat.
 C. Captive *A. cunicularia* tend to eat more than wild *A. cunicularia.*
 D. Wild *A. cunicularia* tend to eat more than captive *A. cunicularia.*

12. Which of the following is an assumption made by the researchers across all three experiments?

 F. That *A. cunicularia* prey upon a variety of animal types, including mammals, reptiles, and amphibians
 G. That *Eublepharis macularius* can only be bred into five color varieties
 H. That *A. cunicularia* are less likely to hunt for food in environments with little to no competition for the same prey
 J. That 24 hours is enough time to gather sufficient data on the eating preferences of *A. cunicularia*

13. If the owls used in Experiment 3 were released into the wild, and assuming *Eublepharis macularius* of each color were present in their new habitat, then which of the following changes to their preferences would be most likely?

 A. They would greatly increase their preference for white *Eublepharis macularius.*
 B. They would greatly decrease their preference for white *Eublepharis macularius.*
 C. They would greatly increase their preference for yellow *Eublepharis macularius.*
 D. They would greatly increase their preference for purple and brown *Eublepharis macularius.*

Passage III

Endocrine-disrupting chemicals (EDC's) have the potential to be detrimental to the reproductive health of aquatic organisms, as they have the ability to interfere with sex hormone production and secretion. Previous research has discovered that the minimum EDC concentration required to alter sex hormone levels (i.e. testosterone and estradiol) in aquatic animals is 1,000 ng/L. In addition to the concentration levels, the *half-life*, or the time required for the concentration of a chemical to be reduced by half, is also of concern. The longer the half-life of a chemical, the longer it takes for a chemical to be cleared from a sample.

In this study, scientists aimed to determine if significant amounts of EDC's could be found in the water and marine sediment of several bodies of water, all of which are found in the same greater habitat (within a 50 mile radius).

Table 1 shows the physical and chemical parameters of the sampled bodies of water in this study.

Table 1

Sampling site #	Depth (m)*	Temperature (°C)	pH
1	-1.30	15.5	7.97
2	-0.50	15.9	7.99
3	-1.30	15.5	7.97
4	-0.30	15.6	8.08
5	-1.32	15.2	7.94
6	-2.10	15.4	7.92

*note: the deeper the stream, the lower the concentration of EDC's in water

Table 2 displays common EDC's and their corresponding concentration ranges found in the bodies of water (both water and marine sediment) over a 7-month period.

Table 2

EDC	Concentration range in water (ng/L)	Concentration range in sediment (ng/L)
BPA	298-3,620	1,140-50,000
BADGE	2,140-28,000	4,290-61,000
BPAF	132-1,070	730-155,000
BPB	47-3,660	820-9,420

Table 3 displays the EDC's and their corresponding half-lives in both water and marine sediments.

Table 3

EDC	Half-life in water (days)	Half-life in sediment (days)
BPA	37.5	337.5
BADGE	60.0	540.0
BPAF	180.0	1,600.0
BPB	38.0	340.0

14. According to Table 1, which body of water is most similar to sampling site #1?

F. Sampling site #6
G. Sampling site #5
H. Sampling site #3
J. Sampling site #2

15. According to Table 1, there is a direct relationship between:

A. water depth and temperature.
B. temperature and pH levels.
C. sampling site and temperature.
D. water depth and pH levels.

16. Tables 2 and 3 indicate that:

F. it is more difficult to remove EDC's from marine sediment than from water.
G. it is more difficult to remove EDC's from water than from marine sediment.
H. there is no overlap between the concentration ranges of various EDC's in water.
J. there is no overlap between the concentration ranges of various EDC's in marine sediment.

17. Suppose scientists also tested the streams for the EDC *polychlorinated biphenyls* and discovered a concentration range in water of 550-4,459 ng/L. A possible concentration range in sediment could be:

A. 61-383 ng/L
B. 202-28,704 ng/L
C. 3,355-49,049 ng/L
D. 4,459-172,390 ng/L

18. About how long would it take to reduce 75% of the amount of ng/L of BADGE from Sampling site #5?

F. 60 days
G. 120 days
H. 540 days
J. 1,080 days

19. Consider a hypothetical stream in the same greater habitat as the study. If this stream had a depth of -0.15 m, then what would be its likely concentration range of BPA in water?

A. 200 ng/L
B. 4,200 ng/L
C. 32,000 ng/L
D. 55,000 ng/L

Passage IV

The mission of the Voyager probes (Voyager 1 and 2) when they launched in 1977 was to explore Jupiter and its surrounding moons. Scientists could not begin to anticipate the discoveries they would make as they traveled through the solar system. As Voyager 2 approached Jupiter in the summer of 1979, images of Io (one of Jupiter's moons) revealed what appeared to be an erupting volcano on a celestial body otherwise devoid of an atmosphere or any form of liquid. As it revealed the only known active volcano beyond earth, the discovery was quite remarkable. Additional photographs revealed Io to be an incredibly geologically active world with extensive sulfur deposits on its surface. Two scientists document their disagreements about the fundamental reasons for and chemical compositions of the volcanoes of Io.

Scientist 1

Io is Jupiter's innermost Galilean moon, meaning it was large enough to be one of the four moons visible to Galileo through his early telescope. It is, however, a relatively small celestial body with a diameter approximately one-quarter that of Earth. Despite its small size, it has become quite a geologic phenomenon. As a consequence of its proximity to Jupiter, it is caught in a gravitational tug-of-war between Jupiter and the other Galilean moons. This gravitational action is the core reason for Io's extreme volcanic activity, which is characterized by extensive flows of molten sulfur (which flows at a much lower temperature than molten lava) and other sulfur-rich compounds on the surface. This makes Io's volcanic activity quite different from the volcanic activity observed on Earth in that there is no molten rock flowing on Io, unlike our own planet.

Scientist 2

The volcanoes of Io are more similar to those found on Earth than may be thought possible by other scientists. Based upon the Voyager photographs, the existence of mountains 10km (or 6.2 miles) in height cannot be explained solely by the presence of sulfur, which liquifies at a relatively low temperature. Instead, mountains of that height require, geologically speaking, the presence of silica rocks, which means that these volcanoes must be similar in composition to those found on Earth. Though Io is far from the sun relative to Earth, the friction created beneath the surface of the moon caused by the extreme competitive gravitational pulls of Jupiter and the other Galilean moons is enough to melt rock into lava that would at least partially resemble that found on Earth. Though sulfur is undeniably present on the planet, both in volcanic flows and plumes, it is intermixed with molten silica rock.

20. Which of the scientists, if either, claimed that Io is subject to gravitational pulls in multiple directions?

F. Scientist 1 only
G. Scientist 2 only
H. Both Scientist 1 and Scientist 2
J. Neither Scientist 1 nor Scientist 2

21. Suppose it were discovered that high levels of friction have the ability to melt rock into a molten state. This finding would be most consistent with the explanation given by:

A. Scientist 1 only
B. Scientist 2 only
C. Both Scientist 1 and Scientist 2
D. Neither Scientist 1 nor Scientist 2

22. Based on Scientist 1's explanation, one factor that does *not* contribute to Io's extreme volcanic activity is:

F. its size relative to Earth.
G. the heavy presence of sulfur.
H. the gravitational pull of Jupiter.
J. the gravitational pull of other Galilean moons.

23. Given that sulfur is a lighter substance than silica rock, which of the following inequalities properly orders the expected height of the volcanic plumes from similarly sized volcanoes as described in the passage?

A. Scientist 1's Theory = Scientist 2's Theory < Earth's
B. Scientist 1's Theory < Scientist 2's Theory = Earth's
C. Scientist 1's Theory > Scientist 2's Theory > Earth's
D. Scientist 1's Theory > Scientist 2's Theory = Earth's

24. Which of the scientists claimed that the active volcanoes of Io most likely contain sulfur, which liquefies at a lower temperature than silica rock?

F. Scientist 1 only
G. Scientist 2 only
H. Both Scientist 1 and Scientist 2
J. Neither Scientist 1 nor Scientist 2

25. Scientist 2's explanation would be most strongly weakened relative to Scientist 1's if which of the following observations were made?

A. That silica rock melts at a much lower point than previously thought.
B. That sulfur has the ability to build upon itself in such a way that it does not break or crack under significant pressure.
C. That Jupiter's mass is significantly larger than previously thought.
D. That Jupiter's mass is significantly smaller than previously thought.

26. If sulfur is yellow, and magma is red, then what color plume would each scientist expect to see in a high definition image of one of Io's volcanic eruptions?

F. Scientist 1 = yellow, Scientist 2 = orange
G. Scientist 1 = yellow, Scientist 2 = red
H. Scientist 1 = orange, Scientist 2 = red
J. Scientist 1 = red, Scientist 2 = yellow

Passage V

A *voltage divider* is a series of resistors that can be tapped at intermediate points to produce a specific fraction of the voltage applied between its ends. A *voltage tap* allows an observer to measure the voltage at the specified junction between resistors.

Voltage dividers follow the principle of *Kirchoff's Law*, which states that the sum of all voltages in a circuit must equal zero. In an ideal circuit, the output of each voltage tap is directly proportional to the resistance of the circuit at the point of measurement. Each resistor reduces the voltage by an amount proportional to their resistance, known as a resistor's *voltage drop*.

Figure 1 is a diagram of a voltage divider in a circuit that is powered by a 12 volt supply. The circuit contains three resistors in series: R1, R2, and R3. The circuit in Figure 1 also contains 3 voltage taps which measure the currents V_1, V_2, and V_3. These voltage taps are located between R1 and R2, between R2 and R3, and after R3, respectively.

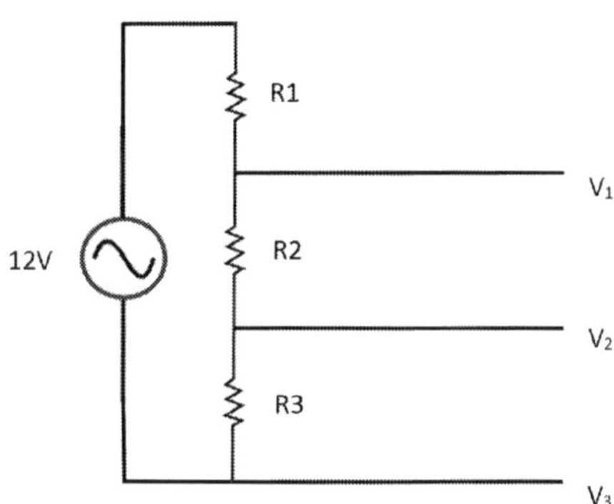

*Note: since V*in* is 12V, then $V_1 = \frac{R2 + R3}{R1 + R2 + R3} \times 12V$

Figure 1

An electrical engineering student conducted four trials in which he altered the resistance (measured in *ohms*) of resistors R1, R2, and R3 and measured the voltage drop at each voltage tap. The results of the four trials are recorded in Tables 1–4.

Table 1

Resistance (ohms)		Voltage Drop	
R1	100	V1	4.0
R2	100	V2	4.0
R3	100	V3	4.0

Table 2

Resistance (ohms)		Voltage Drop	
R1	100	V1	2.0
R2	200	V2	4.0
R3	300	V3	6.0

Table 3

Resistance (ohms)		Voltage Drop	
R1	300	V1	2.25
R2	900	V2	6.75
R3	400	V3	3

Table 4

Resistance (ohms)		Voltage Drop	
R1	10	V1	0.108
R2	100	V2	1.081
R3	1000	V3	10.81

27. According to the results of Trials 2–4, from which of the following resistors was the greatest percent of voltage drop observed following R1, R2, and R3, respectively?

	Trial 2	Trial 3	Trial 4
A.	R2	R3	R2
B.	R1	R1	R1
C.	R3	R2	R3
D.	R3	R3	R3

28. According to the results of Trial 4, the percent of voltage drop recorded by the second resistor in the series is closest to which of the following?

F. 9%
G. 33%
H. 91%
J. 100%

29. Is the statement, "When the resistance of a resistor is doubled, the recorded voltage drop is doubled" supported by the results of Trials 1-4?

A. No; the voltage drop will also depend upon the resistance of the other resistors in the voltage divider.
B. No; there is no direct relationship between the resistance and the voltage drop.
C. Yes; Trials 1 and 2 provide evidence enough to prove this claim.
D. Yes; Trials 2 and 3 provide evidence enough to prove this claim.

30. What were the independent (manipulated) and dependent variables in each of the 4 trials?

	Independent	Dependent
F.	Voltage drop	Resistance
G.	12V power supply	Voltage drop
H.	Resistance	Voltage drop
J.	Resistance	12V power supply

31. According to the results of the trials, which of the 3 resistors, if any, reduced the voltage proportional to their resistance by more than 50% of the entire circuit?

A. R3 of Trial 2 and R3 of Trial 4
B. R2 of Trial 3 and R3 of Trial 4
C. R3 of Trial 2 and R2 of Trial 4
D. None of the resistors

32. Is it possible to manipulate the voltage divider in such a way as to produce an exception to *Kirchoff's Law*?

F. Yes; the user can alter the voltage current to do so.
G. Yes; the user can change the number of resistors to do so.
H. No; without voltage taps, the circuit can not be considered a voltage divider.
J. No; no matter the voltage or number of resistors, the voltage divider will always follow *Kirchoff's Law*.

33. Imagine that a fourth resistor (R4) were to be added to the voltage divider after R3, which was then followed by a corresponding voltage tap (V4). If the resistance of each resistor were set at 100 ohms, the expected reading at V4 would be:

A. 1.5 volts
B. 2.0 volts
C. 3.0 volts
D. 4.0 volts

Passage VI

Caffeine is a central nervous system stimulant found in coffee that is commonly used by individuals to increase alertness and focus. Because of this, a group of scientists wanted to test if caffeine administration could increase brain function in rats. To do so, rats were given an assessment called the Morris Water Maze test in which rats are placed one at a time in a pool of opaque water and must search for a hidden platform by swimming. The faster a rat can reach the platform, the better the brain function is thought to be. Once a rat has reached the platform, it is removed from the maze, the timer is reset, and the next rat is placed in the water.

In Trial 1, 8 rats (Rats 1-8) were administered a dose of caffeine before being subject to the Morris Water Maze test. The results are recorded in Figure 1 below.

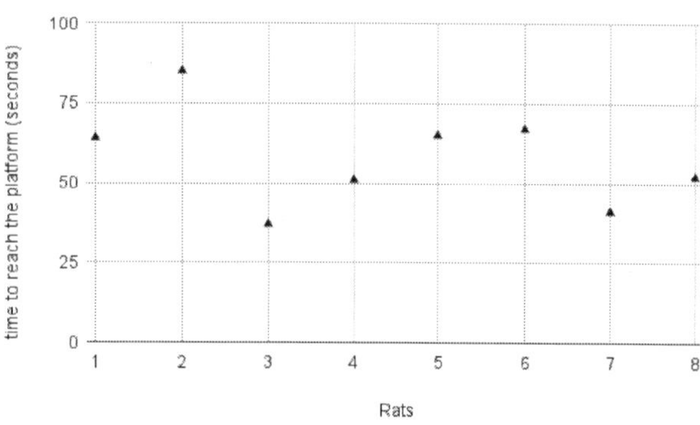

Figure 1

In Trial 2, 8 new rats (Rats 9-16), which were *not* given caffeine, were subject to the Morris Water Maze test. The results are recorded in Figure 2 below.

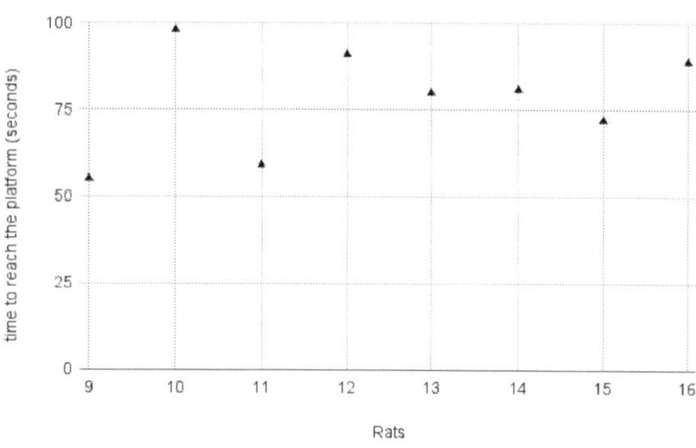

Figure 2

In Trial 3, the same 8 rats from Trial 1 (Rats 1-8) were again administered the Morris Water Maze test (with the platform in a new location) exactly 1 hour after Trial 1. The results are recorded in Figure 3 below.

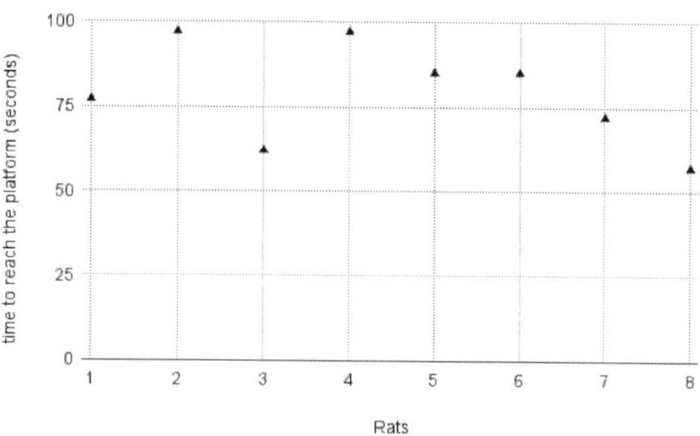

Figure 3

34. Which of the following factors did *not* directly contribute to the amount of time it took rats to complete the Morris Water Maze test, thus accounting for discrepancy among the 24 results?

F. Whether or not a rat was administered caffeine
G. The platform's new location in Trial 3
H. That rats are better swimmers than mice
J. The opaque nature of the water itself

35. Given that rats are not worn to significant exhaustion of energy by a swim of less than 100 seconds, which of the following conclusions can be reached by the scientists based on the results of the three trials?

A. That, once caffeine wears off, there is a withdrawal in the user that inhibits performance
B. That, once caffeine wears off, there is an improvement in the user in terms of performance
C. That, once caffeine is administered, there will be an immediate, negative effect on performance
D. That, despite the administration of caffeine, performance is impacted neither negatively nor positively

36. According to the study, which of the following rats exhibited the greatest drop in performance after an hour of rest following the administration of caffeine?

F. Rat 4
G. Rat 5
H. Rat 6
J. Rat 8

37. Suppose scientists repeated Trial 3, but retested the rats after a rest of 15 minutes as opposed to 1 hour. Assuming that 15 minutes rest is enough time for a rat to recover from physical activity, it would be expected that Rat 3 would perform the Morris Water Maze test in a time:

A. Between 40 and 60 seconds
B. Between 60 and 70 seconds
C. Between 70 and 90 seconds
D. Between 90 and 100 seconds

38. The average time it takes a rat that has not been administered caffeine to complete the Morris Water Maze test is roughly:

F. 0.50 minutes
G. 0.75 minutes
H. 1 minute
J. 1.25 minutes

39. Suppose Rat 1 and Rat 9 were placed in the Morris Water Maze test at the same time and the winner recorded. Suppose then that this was repeated for Rat 2 and Rat 10, and so on 8 times until Rat 8 and Rat 16 also competed. How many of the competitions would have been won by rats who did not consume caffeine?

A. 1 of 8
B. 2 of 8
C. 7 of 8
D. 8 of 8

40. Based on the results of the 3 trials, which of the following rats finished with the fastest average time to complete the Morris Water Maze test?

F. Rat 11
G. Rat 9
H. Rat 4
J. Rat 2

Step 6 Correct Answers

Practice Test 1

Passage I	Passage II	Passage III	Passage IV	Passage V	Passage VI
1: D	8: F	14: G	21: D	28: G	34: G
2: H	9: C	15: A	22: G	29: C	35: D
3: B	10: J	16: H	23: A	30: G	36: H
4: F	11: C	17: B	24: H	31: B	37: A
5: D	12: H	18: F	25: B	32: J	38: J
6: J	13: B	19: C	26: F	33: A	39: C
7: A		20: F	27: D		40: J

Practice Test 2

Passage I	Passage II	Passage III	Passage IV	Passage V	Passage VI
1: B	7: D	14: H	20: H	27: C	34: H
2: F	8: J	15: D	21: B	28: F	35: A
3: B	9: C	16: F	22: F	29: A	36: F
4: G	10: G	17: C	23: C	30: H	37: A
5: D	11: D	18: J	24: H	31: B	38: J
6: G	12: J	19: B	25: B	32: J	39: A
	13: A		26: F	33: C	40: G

Stumped on any? You will find the explanations for each answer beginning on page 667 (Practice Test 1) and 672 (Practice Test 2).

In Conclusion

Congratulations! If you have completed this entire book, I must say, I am impressed. Rest assured that you have not wasted your time with out of order prep. You have systematized your preparation for the ACT English, Math, Reading, and Science tests, and in doing so you've put first-things-first, and I hope you have seen which areas of practice and skill need more work while also growing in confidence, knowledge, and skill.

If you are still in need of practice, I recommend doing an internet search for the terms "Preparing for the ACT" followed by the current year (like: "Preparing for the ACT 2023"). This will bring up a PDF document of an authentic, recent, and publicly available ACT test that you are free to use and practice with. There are, of course, also dozens of ACT prep books of all kinds.

The ACT also has a program called **Test Information Release** (or TIR). If you take the ACT exam in December, April, or June, you are eligible. Essentially, you can pay an extra fee to get back from the ACT your original answers to the test, the correct answers, and the questions themselves. This can help you see what is actually bringing your score down or up from the ACT's point of view.

What follows is the explanations to every practice question in this book beginning with The ACT English System then moving into The ACT Math, Reading, and Science Systems, respectively.

Thanks for using The ACT System!

ACT English Explanations

Answer Explanations - Step 1

Correct Answers:

Passage I
1: C
2: J
3: A
4: G
5: B
6: J
7: A
8: J

Passage II
9: B
10: G
11: D
12: F
13: A
14: H
15: C
16: F

Passage I: Flannery's Childhood Home

#1 The correct answer is **C**. It might seem like the answer should be "Yes,..." because the previous sentence mentions peacocks. However, stay focused: the **subject** of the paragraph is the writer Flannery O'Connor, not the peacocks. Thus, an additional sentence about them derails from the focus, which is why **A** and **B** are incorrect. **D** is incorrect because the information has not already been provided.

#2 The correct answer is **J**. These types of questions are among the most missed on ACT English. I believe this is true because the question itself is simply kind of *l o n g*. However, the question says we need a sentence that tells us two things: a) The house is still standing, and b) The house is open to the public. **J** tells us that the home is "preserved to this day" (still standing) and has been converted into "a museum" (open to the public). **F** may be about homes, **G** may be about Flannery O'Connor, and **H** may be a bout Savannah, GA, but none of those three options fulfill the basic two requirements of the question itself.

#3 The correct answer is **A**. The remainder of this paragraph is about Flannery as a child, thus **A** works as it says it "gives us a window into the everyday childhood environment" of her. In addition, only **A** makes sense when you read the next sentence, which says, "Flannery was **one of these children**." Without the sentence in question, that phrase makes no sense, and should leave you asking, "What children?" **B**, though it says the sentence should be kept, has a subject matter that is irrelevant; this essay and this paragraph are not about trees and their value. **C** and **D** of course are incorrect because they say the sentence should be deleted.

#4 The correct answer is **G**. There are clues in the sentence that tell us where it should be located. One of these clues is "all girls." All of a sudden, we are talking about multiple girls, not just Flannery O'Connor, thus a sentence before must change the subject matter to a multiple girls; this is what the first sentence of the paragraph does. As written, the second sentence in the paragraph mentions "these activities." That is another clue as to the location; the sentence to be added mentions activities: drawing and playing make-believe. This is why the sentence belongs at point B sandwiched between the sentence that mentions her "friends" and the sentence that mentions "these activities." Thus, answer choices **F, H,** and **J** make no logical sense.

#5 First of all, the question asks you which phrase introduces the subject of a paragraph. Thus, you need to read the paragraph first to understand the subject of it (how else is there to do it?). Well, after a reading, hopefully you see that the subject of the paragraph is a physical space where the family raised chickens and where Flannery trained a chicken. **A** fails to define a space, so it is incorrect. The answer can't be **C** because chickens aren't raised in a car. **D** is a tempting wrong choice because the word "coop" is a space where chickens are raised, but later in the paragraph it speaks of the space being a place to grow plants, which is of course more fitting for a garden than a coop. That's why the answer is **B**; that is a space where chickens can be raised, that borders an alley, where plants are grown, and where a girl can spend time.

#6 This question is extremely similar to #1. It seems like a relevant sentence. It's about the O'Connor family, and it's about chickens, so what's not to like? Well, there is something about it that is unlikeable: *it's obviously true*. Is there some other reason that a family would raise chickens? Additionally, it shifts the subject matter away from Flannery and the garden to the family as a whole. This is why the answer can't be **F** or **G**. The answer can't be **H** either; this is because we do need more information about her childhood home because that is the subject of the essay as a whole. Thus, the correct answer is **J**; we should assume that information to be true.

#7 Oh boy...if you see those sentences numbered as they are in this paragraph, you know what's coming! Either you're going to be asked about the location of a sentence or their proper order. In this case, it's the former. You might be surprised at a reread of the paragraph because all seems well. The first sentence mentions that there was no air conditioning, and then the second sentence (the sentence in question) mentions a reprieve from the heat, and then the third sentence mentions hearing voices below the home (presumably, while the windows are open). Well, if this was your thinking, your instincts were correct. The answer for those reasons is **A**; no other ordering of the sentences makes logical sense.

#8 This "Yes or No" question represents the mini-lesson I slipped in. This question (a classic ACT example) asks about the author's **main purpose**. In this case, is the main purpose of the essay Flannery O'Connor's characters? You should think, "No, that's not the main purpose, though I do remember some mention or mentions of her characters." If you don't know whether or not at this point the answer is yes or no, circle the question and move on; you shouldn't waste valuable time and reread the essay at this point. In other words, come back to it at the end of the test if you have time. Now, the purpose of the essay is to speak on her childhood home, not her characters. That eliminates **F** and **G**. Of our two "No" options, **H** is incorrect because the history of Savannah, though mentioned in the essay, is not its primary purpose. Thus, the answer must again be **J** because, as it says, the purpose of the essay is to describe her home.

Passage II: The Texas State Fair

#9 Context is key. Context is key. If you haven't learned this by now let me say it again: context is key. Sentences belong (or don't) in paragraphs if they move it along from one sentence to the next. Imagine this paragraph without the sentence: how could we understand what the last sentence says ("what he meant") without the sentence being kept there? Who is "he" and what did he say? Thus, the sentence should be kept, so that eliminates **C** and **D**. However, reading the other answer choices don't make immediate sense. Do we need to know the father's desires (Answer **A**)? If this is an essay about the father's desires, then yes. Do we need anticipation to be built (Answer **B**). Well, the writer of the essay (the daughter) and her little brothers don't understand what he's talking about. Then, in paragraph 2, they begin to get excited. All of this points to two things: first, this is not an essay about the father's desires, and second, this essay is building anticipation. Thus, the answer is **B**.

#10 We need a phrase that explains their excitement (the first part of the sentence) and makes it clear that they are going to the fair (following sentence). Thus, **H** does not work because it doesn't explain their excitement (how can you begin to get excited while you sleep?). **J** is simply a redundancy; we already know excitement is building. **F** fails because the father's rumbling stomach could not possibly cause the children to believe they are going to the fair. This is why the answer is **G**; the giant carousel explains the excitement and causes them to understand that they are going to the fair.

#11 Smell that funnel cake (also called an "elephant ear" in some places)? It evokes lots of feelings of being at a fair or carnival of some kind. This feeling may be enough for some people to choose **A** or **B**. However, this sentence is a complete disruption. Without it, we have a good connection between "packs of little tickets" mentioned in the first sentence and "almost all of theirs" in the third. "Almost all of theirs" makes little or no sense if the sentence is inserted. It's not **C** because people are mostly familiar with that food, but even if not, that's not the main reason why it doesn't belong. This is why **D** is the correct answer: the details interrupt the paragraph's logical flow.

#12 This time, the question isn't asking you outright if the sentence belongs. Rather, we need to ask the following: what does the sentence do for the paragraph? We go from spotting the ride (sentence 1) to paying tickets (sentence 3). This is why **F** is correct. Let's eliminate the other choices as well. **G** is probably the most tempting option of the four because "an eternity" is an exaggeration, but it is a necessary or fitting one. This is because the sentence provides context for our understanding of the word "finally" in the third sentence. **H** doesn't work because there's no mention anywhere else of the fear that is referred to in this option. **J** doesn't work because the time waiting in line isn't mentioned to let the reader know that it takes time to count tickets, but rather is mentioned to bridge sentences, continue the logical flow the paragraph, and build anticipation.

#13 One clue to getting this question correct is the pronoun "it" after the colon that refers to something spinning. That pronoun doesn't work with choice **D** because "stars" is plural, so that option is out. It doesn't work with **C** either because you would never refer to the father as "it." Lastly, **B** does not work either because, while the stomach could be "it," it isn't the stomach that is spinning so as to pin the father and daughter to the walls. Thus, **A** makes sense: when the room ("it") spins, they are pinned to the walls.

#14 The clue here is that we need a choice that not only works, but refers back to the opening paragraph. Let's go one option at a time. **F** has a consistent tone with the rest of the essay, but it: a) Doesn't refer back to the opening paragraph, and b) Contradicts the father's smiling in the sentence before. Thus, A is out. **G** does not work because the books of tickets aren't mentioned in the first paragraph. **J** doesn't work for the same reason; no mention of dragon coasters in paragraph 1! Thus, the answer is **H**; it mentions the father, who is grinning in the previous sentence. Most importantly however, it mentions the turkey leg that is referenced in the first paragraph.

#15 In a way, you may have known this sentence was coming because of the letters A, B, C, and D sprinkled throughout the essay. We need a location in the essay that gives the reader an understanding of "them" and references a ride that goes at high speeds. This is why **C** has to be the correct answer. **A, B,** and **D** do not make any sense in context.

#16 Again, you want to know if the answer is "Yes" or "No" before we get to the answer choices. If you don't know, then don't reread the essay at this point; circle this question, skip it in your answer booklet, and then come back with time at the end. The idea that this is a gift for her father is a bit irrelevant, the main question is this: is this essay a fun family memory? I hope it is pretty clear that the answer is "yes." That eliminates **H** and **J**. Answer choice **G** correctly says "yes," but it proposes that the essay is all about different kinds of family activities, but that isn't true: the essay focuses on one activity, which is going to the fair. That is why **F** is the correct answer: the essay focuses on the fun she shared with her father at the fair.

Answer Explanations - Step 2

Correct Answers:

Passage I
1: D
2: G
3: D
4: J
5: C
6: G
7: A
8: H
9: B
10: F
11: D
12: H
13: B
14: J
15: B

Passage II
16: F
17: B
18: H
19: A
20: G
21: C
22: J
23: D
24: J
25: A
26: F
27: C
28: H
29: B
30: H

Passage I: Uluru

#1 As written, it is redundant; we already know this took place in July. Thus, **A** is out. This also eliminates answer choices **B** and **C**. These options also are redundant. You may be tempted by **C** because it provides the most information, but don't be fooled: we already know all of it. That is why the correct answer is **D.**

#2 Another classic "Kept" or "Deleted" question. In this case, the preceding sentence is about Gosse discovering the rock, and the sentence after the one in question is about the rock already having a name. This fact, "the rock already possessed a name," is contrasting. That contrast is highlighted if the sentence is included here. Thus, that eliminates **H** and **J**. Speaking of choice **H**, it was just shown that the details about Ayers are fitting, but the details are also in line with the paragraph's purpose, thus **H** is eliminated. As for **J**, it raises no questions. **F** is incorrect because Ayers is not the one who discovered the rock; that was Gosse. Thus, **G** must be correct. **G** also says exactly what we want the sentence to do: contrast with the rock's other name.

#3 At first glance, the commas in the answer choices are distracting. Are we setting off these phrases correctly with the commas? Well, it turns out, this isn't a question of comma usage. The first three words of the sentence are "This latter name," referring to *Uluru*; thus we don't need to again state that the name that is the subject of the paragraph that "was given to it by the Pitjantjatjara." This is why **A, B,** and **C** are all incorrect: they're all redundant (comma problems with B and C besides). Thus, the answer is **D**. When we delete the phrase altogether and the commas with it the sentence flows on perfectly well and links "This latter name" with the verb "was."

#4 Here we have our third question out of the first four that tested your ability to spot redundancy. Were you able to see why the phrase "like a mountain" does not belong at the end of this sentence, which provides a definition of an inselberg? We already heard that it is "a hill or mountain." **G** says "that surrounds it," referring to the landscape; however, before the word "landscape" is the word "surrounding," thus this option is incorrect as well. **H** mentions that an inselberg is made of rock; however this is information we already know as well (earlier it says an inselberg is "composed of rock"). That leaves **J**, which is, of course, correct. That an inselberg is isolated is a detail that has not yet been mentioned.

#5 Hopefully you see now if you didn't at first that "closest" and "nearest" are synonyms; we don't need to say the same thing twice. This already eliminates **A** and **B.** As for **D**, "most in proximity" is overly wordy compared to **C**. You may think, "that's not fair, they mean the same thing!" That's correct, they do, but the "tie" so to speak goes to the answer choice that is less wordy; it is *best*. This is why **C** is the correct answer; it communicates that a formation is near without being redundant or too wordy.

#6 While this question does not test redundancy or verbosity recognition, it harkens back to Step 1; one of these phrases is the *best*. However, in this case, you are given very specific instructions for the purpose of the phrase: you need one that illustrates a "precise distance." As written, "which is pretty close by" is not specific enough, so **F** is out. Letter choice **H** has the same problem; it is too vague. Letter choice **J** starts to be more specific by mentioning a mode of transportation, but it never says how long it would take to get there by car (or, while we're on it, how far away it is *precisely*). Thus, **G** is correct; it gives a precise distance: "16 miles to the West."

#7 The word "remnant" means something leftover or remaining. Thus, **B** and **D** are redundant. As for **C**, it basically defines the word "remnant" in the place of the word itself, which means it is too wordy. This is why **A** is the correct answer.

#8 In this case, **G** may be tempting at first glance. This is because it is a little less wordy than the phrase as written, choice **F**, and still makes sense. However, the phrase "the test of time" implies that time has gone by; we don't need, then, to say that time "has passed" or that it is "still passing." This is why **H** is correct. **F, G,** and **J** all redundantly and unnecessarily say that the time "has passed" or "is passing."

#9 Notice a theme to these questions? "Species" and "types" of bats mean the same thing. This is why **A** can't be the correct or *best* answer. **D** adds the adjective "categorical" to "types," but even that is redundant; different types are by definition different categories of things. That leaves **B** and **C**; each of these choices is one simple word. In this case, although we haven't discussed the uses of colons, you might see that inserting one here is at a minimum disruptive to the sentence. **B** is correct for these reasons.

#10 We are looking for an option that tells us that 70 or more species of reptiles have been found around Uluru. Well, all of the answer choices do that. This is a classic question of verbosity; which option gives us what we are looking for that is the least wordy? That is clearly not **G, H,** or **J**; all of them are too wordy. **F** is correct for this reason.

#11 Here, we have a sentence giving an example of a reptile, and the question is whether or not it belongs. Notice that after bats are mentioned, we aren't given a type of bat. If the sentence said something like, "For example, the Black Fanged Slitherer was previously thought to be extinct until it was caught just off of Uluru," then we'd be on to something more relevant. In addition, a historic or scientific essay of this type isn't going to deal in categories that are, for the most part, presumed to be true: most people know that snakes are reptiles. These are all reasons why the sentence doesn't belong. If we examine the "Yes" options one by one, they also fall apart for other reasons. **A** can't be correct because it presupposes a question asked earlier in the essay, but no such question exists. **B** can't be correct because it does not deepen our understanding of the animal life because it is not specific enough. Examining the "No" answers, we see that **C** can't be correct because this information about snakes is not given elsewhere in the paragraph. That leaves **D**, which hits the nail on the head. The sentence adds nothing to our understanding about Uluru, as it says, which is why it is the correct answer.

#12 This question combines your ability to see if sentences belong in context and to recognize redundancy. In this case, the sentence is about how bats make their home around Uluru. No big deal, except that has already been said in the second sentence of the paragraph. For this reason, it doesn't belong, and thus **F** and **G** are incorrect. **J** can not be correct because the sentence is on topic; this paragraph is about animal species in and around Uluru, and so is the sentence. **H** correctly recognizes that the information given in the sentence is redundant and doesn't belong, and thus it it the correct answer.

#13 While the colon used in choice **D** is appropriate, the answer is incorrect for the same reason that **A** and **C** are incorrect: they are all too wordy! This is a classic question of verbosity, and thus the correct answer is **B**; it communicates the present name of the rock in the least amount of words possible, and thus it is *best*.

#14 The sentence in question gives us a clear context clue. It says "This episode took place…" That is just about all we need to correctly place it; it will come after a sentence that mentions an event or episode. The details about the millions of years or technical names of the periods this episode took place in might look scary, but are really not necessary to perfectly comprehend to get this question correct. Starting with answer choice **F**, the sentence before Point A is about the name of the inselberg being Uluru; no event is mentioned. **F** therefore is incorrect. **G** does not work for the same reason; the sentence before point B is the definition of an inselberg, and there is no mention of an event in it. Now let's turn our attention to choice **H**. However, point C comes after a sentence about the rock being composed of arkose; putting a sentence here also would separate two sentences that logically flow from one to the other. That leaves **J**, which is correct; point D in paragraph 3 comes immediately after mention of "the Peterman Orogeny," an event that fits the description of the sentence!

#15 This question asks whether or not the essay as a whole is about the history of an important Australian landmark. Because the entire essay is about one, Uluru, then yes, this essay certainly does just that. This eliminates answer choices **C** and **D**, both of which say "No." Let's look now at choice **A**. While this option begins with "Yes," it says that the essay is about the author's firsthand experience visiting the landmark. However, there is no evidence that the author has been there, and the entire essay is in the third person (as opposed to the first person, which would be written with the word "I", like "When *I* visited Uluru, it was really hot…"). This is why **B** is correct; this option syncs with the requirements of the question and accurately says that all of these requirements have been met by the essay.

Passage II: The Palace of Versailles

#16 All four of these answer choices, essentially, say the same thing. However, three of them are overly wordy (verbose). These wrong answers are **G, H,** and **J**. As it is written, it is less wordy and communicates what needs to be. Thus, **F** is the correct answer.

#17 As it is written, it seems like nothing is wrong. However, at a closer glance, you may notice that "wealth" and "money" are the same thing. That is redundant, so **A** has to be incorrect. **C** is also incorrect because "power" and "control" are the same thing. Lastly, choice **D** had a redundancy built in ("gold" and "money"); the wording is also strange and irregular. **B** is correct; the two words are not synonyms and communicate different ideas.

#18 This is an example of a classic ACT question that tests your ability to recognize the proper ordering of words as well as when an option is too wordy. Here, what needs to be communicated is that some of the structures are still standing. The best and fastest way to get this question correct is to let your "ear" pick up on which choices sound wrong. By "ear," I simply mean your ability to read and hear in your head that something is off. This kind of intuition should eliminate choices **F** and **G**; in these examples, the ordering of words is out of whack. The remaining two choices are almost identical, and the ordering of their words is on par. Because they mean the same thing, and because both make sense, there must be a tiebreaker: verbosity. So, which has fewer words? That would be **H**, making it the correct answer, and making **J** incorrect.

#19 We need a sentence that transitions. A good transition sentence will build on the topic of the first paragraph and tease or introduce the topic of the second paragraph. The first paragraph was about European palaces and their general history and importance. The second paragraph is about the Palace of Versailles in particular. That is why the correct answer is **A**; the first, dependent clause of the sentence mentions the homes of Paragraph 1, and the second, independent clause of the sentence references the Palace of Versailles in particular. **B** references the plural homes or palaces of Paragraph 1, but Paragraph 2 has nothing to do with homes being destroyed. **C** references plural landmarks, which probably fulfills our first requirement about Paragraph 1, but although Paragraph 2 mentions gardens, that is certainly not the topic of the paragraph as a whole. Lastly, **D** also references plural homes, but Paragraph 2 has nothing to do with groups raising funds.

#20 Here, "uniquely" and "stands apart" are synonymous; they both indicate that there is something special about the Palace of Versailles relative to other palaces. As written, it is redundant, so **A** is incorrect. **H** is problematic because it places the adverb "uniquely" behind the verb "stands", which in the context of this particular sentence does not work. Based on everything that we've said, it would be most tempting to conclude that the least wordy choice would be correct. However, in this case, **J** is also incorrect because it does not indicate that the Palace of Versailles is unique or special; the use of the word "stands" here makes it sound like the Palace has political or moral views that it will never abandon. This is why **G** is correct; it says what the sentence requires without the redundancy.

#21 We already know that the Hall of Mirrors is large ("...a massive mirror-filled room..."), so **A** is incorrect because it is redundant. **D** is incorrect for the same reason; it is redundant. Like #20, it may be tempting to choose **B** because it is less wordy, but that changes the meaning of the sentence completely; the Hall of Mirrors isn't the Palace, but in it. This is why **C** is correct; we want to know that the Hall of Mirrors is the best-known feature within the Palace.

#22 Here you are asked what would happen if the preceding sentence about a couple of the Palace's other features was deleted. **F** is incorrect because the sentence has nothing to do with visitors and their ability to enter the Palace. **G** may be tempting because you may think, "If the Palace and these features were lost, that would be tragic". That's true, but there is nothing in the previous sentence that mentions what would happen if the Palace were destroyed. As for **H**, for all you know, visitors may very well be going East to West when they go from the Garden to the Royal Opera, but there is no indication of that in the sentence (or anywhere else in the essay for that matter). **J** then is correct because the sentence does just what choice **J** indicates: it continues a paragraph that was designed to point out some of its more beautiful and historic features.

#23 The dependent clause at the beginning of this sentence ("With ornate statues...") ends with the comma. It is called a *modifying clause* (more on that in a later Step). All you need to know for now is that it modifies or describes the noun after the comma. In this case, that's "the Palace." Thus, we do not need the word "Palace" in the clause itself. That would be like saying, "As I took a bite of my delicious hamburger, my hamburger tasted good!" So, we can eliminate answer choices **A** and **C**. Choice **B** can also be eliminated because: a) "each and every" is redundant, and b) the word "decorated" is redundant because the clause itself is saying there are decorations in every corner. For these reasons, **D** is correct; it is not verbose or redundant and tells simply where the statues and decorations are.

#24 This is a case of both verbosity and redundancy. Choice **F** is redundant; if something is aesthetically pleasing (at least in this case) it is beautiful. Same with **H**; we do not need the adverb "attractively" to describe "pretty" because that is redundant. As for the other two choices, **G** is not *wrong*, but it is certainly not the best choice between the two. A four-word three-hyphened word is, well, *wordy*. In addition, "easy-on-the-eye" has a connotation of slang, which makes it a bit informal for this kind of essay; it is also simply wordier than the correct answer. That is why the *best* answer, and the correct answer, is **J**; it says what is needed without verbosity or redundancy.

#25 This question is very similar to that of #18 in this same Step. The ACT is fond of this kind of question; what is the best ordering of words? Well, again, your best guide is your "ear" or instinct; which one sounds correct, and says what needs to be said in the fewest words possible? **B, C,** and **D** are all problematic; they jumble words and should sound "off." Only choice **A**, as it is written, says that the Palace is still popular without a jumbled mix of incorrectly ordered or oddly used words.

#26 To get this question correct, we need to first read the sentence before, then the proposed sentence, and then the sentence after to determine if the proposed sentence fits the paragraph well. In this case, it does! It helps to transition from the idea that the palace has historical significance and gives context for the phrase "After the Revolution" in the following sentence. Thus, it does belong, so we can eliminate **H** and **J**. Letter choice **G** makes no sense at all because the Palace was not destroyed and is talked about as still standing in the present day. This is why **F** is correct, and in fact, this choice says what we concluded at the beginning of this explanation in that it gives evidence of the Palace's historical significance.

#27 **A** might be a very tempting choice here because it is a great way to start a sentence and tells us how long the Palace was used as a home for French royalty. However, we already know that based on the end of the sentence ("for about 100 years"). Thus, **A** is incorrect. The same is true for choice **B**; we know later in the sentence that the home was used for monarchs. That leaves **C** and **D**. **D** is incorrect because "Palace Versailles" is not the correct title of the palace. Thus, **C** is correct because it correctly titles the palace and adds no redundancies.

#28 This is an example of the kind of question I proposed in mini-lesson 2. What you need to do is to re-read the sentence with the underlined portion in the various proposed places. We need a place that stresses that the Palace's condition has gotten better and gotten worse. Let's try **F**, "Where it is now." This position rightly says that the Palace was restored in many phases, but it fails to stress that the Palace also went through various spouts of disrepair or worsening. Choice **G** is incorrect because it then makes the sentence say, "In the many phases of years," which is a phrase with no meaning. Choice **H** makes the sentence say, "… the Palace went through many phases of disrepair and restoration." This is the correct answer; it correctly describes the many phases of ups and downs the Palace has had. **J** is incorrect because "many phases of Palace" is also a phrase that makes no sense.

#29 Let's start with choice **D** this time. Ending the sentence with a period might not be grammatically incorrect, but it is certainly incomplete, meaning it creates an incomplete thought ("took place…" where?). That leaves **A, B,** and **C**. All three of these choices essentially say the same thing, so now we are in the territory of trying to identify the *best* answer. **C** is simply odd; who says that? No one. That leaves us with **B** and **A**. While **A** is acceptable, and is even heard of or said often, **B** says the same thing in a less-wordy way. This is why **B** is the *best* answer, and thus is correct.

#30 It is one of the goals of these lesson plans to have you be able to answer these questions "Yes" or "No" before you read the answer choices. We are being asked if this essay compares and contrasts different buildings. However, almost the entirety of the essay is about the Palace of Versailles, and it is never compared to other European buildings. That is why the answer the to initial question is "No." Thus, **F** and **G** are incorrect. **H** says that the essay is only about the Palace of Versailles, which is true, which is why choice **H** is correct. Looking over choice **J**, it says that the essay has nothing to say about other buildings. That is not true; the first paragraph is a general overview of historic European palaces. Thus, **J** is incorrect.

Answer Explanations - Step 3

Correct Answers:

Passage I	Passage II	Passage III
1: B	16: H	31: B
2: F	17: D	32: J
3: C	18: J	33: A
4: J	19: A	34: G
5: C	20: F	35: B
6: J	21: D	36: H
7: B	22: H	37: A
8: H	23: D	38: J
9: A	24: F	39: C
10: G	25: C	40: G
11: D	26: G	41: C
12: G	27: B	42: F
13: A	28: J	43: D
14: H	29: C	44: G
15: D	30: F	45: A

Passage I: Unity Through Tragedy

#1 Here, "Like many Americans" is a dependent clause; it introduces the sentence. The independent clause, "I remember where I was on September 11, 2001" can stand alone as a sentence, but the dependent clause can't. As an introductory phrase, it must be set off by a comma. If it were at the end of the sentence, we wouldn't need a comma, but because it's at the beginning, it must be. Answer choice **A** and **C** can be eliminated because they do not have a comma after "Americans." Choice **D** can also be rejected because it isolates "Americans" by commas as if the word were a nonessential phrase; in this sentence, that is not the case. That is why the answer is **B**; it separates the introductory phrase from the rest of the sentence by a comma.

#2 Here we have a question of wordiness and context. "Awoke up" is not a grammatically proper phrase, so **H** is incorrect. **G** has the problem of being overly wordy; why say "rose up from my mattress" when there is a less-wordy option available? While **J** is not grammatically incorrect, it is something that is never said and makes no sense. Thus, **F** is the correct answer because it makes sense in context in the least words possible.

#3 This question is one of those in which the words are jumbled up; we need the answer choice that simply makes the most sense. What is a "down the street good friend"? Don't try to convince yourself that this is a thing or somehow makes sense, just recognize that it is a meaningless phrase designed to distract you. Thus, we can eliminate answer choices **A** and **B**. **D** is incorrect because deleting the underlined portion makes the sentence a fragment and incomplete. **C** is the correct option because it correctly characterizes the friend as "good" (the adjective is placed before the noun) and then puts the propositional phrase after in a place that makes sense.

#4 We said that the number one most tested comma rule is the ability to recognize when nonessential phrases should be set off by commas. Think about the sentence when the phrase "unaware of what was happening in New York" is removed. Now we have, "I attended my high-school classes through mid-morning." That is a sentence that works, and that's why the phrase in the middle is nonessential. Choices **G** and **H** place commas in incorrect places, isolating the wrong phrases, and that's why they do not work. Choice **F** has no commas at all, thus is incorrect. Thus, choice **J** is correct because it sets off the nonessential phrase.

#5 Here we are revisiting our Step 1 skill: does this sentence belong? Is it relevant and does it move the paragraph along, or is it a detour, shifting the topic of the paragraph? In this case, it is a distraction. It may seem relevant since the sentence previous mentioned English class and so does the sentence in question, but that is not good enough. The paragraph is about what happened that day; the sentence in question is about English class, and that's a distraction. Thus, we can eliminate **A** and **B**, which both say yes. Letter **D** says that it doesn't belong because the paragraph is about Math class; that's not true, so it is incorrect. The correct answer is **C** because it says that the proposed sentence "shifts the focus;" that is true.

#6 As written, we have a comma followed by a FANBOYS conjunction, in this case "and." That would be correct if the clauses before and after were both independent clauses. "Horrifyingly, I watched as the second tower was struck" is such a clause, but "as the Twin Towers then collapsed one after another" is not; that can't stand alone as a sentence. So, **F** and **G** are both out for this reason. **H** removes the "and," but then that makes the sentence sound like all of the events happen at the exact same time (the second tower is struck as the Towers fall). Only **J** maintains the integrity of the sentence and proposes the events in the correct order as taking place one after another.

#7 Of course, there is no nation called "United America." That eliminates **A**. For that matter, it also eliminates **D**, which also has the problem of putting a comma after the adjective "United." As for **C**, there is nothing grammatically wrong with it, but it is overly wordy. That is why the answer is **B**: America.

#8 Here we have a nonessential clause ("but also those from a generation before me") inserted into the greater sentence. We learned that you can set off such a clause with commas, and that seems to be what is at play here, but **F** has a problem: the clause is finished with an em dash. That means it has to be started with an em dash as well, just like you would with parentheses. **J** and **F** properly set off the phrase in some way, but neither are an em dash, and thus are incorrect. **G** does not work because it does nothing to set off the nonessential clause, not to mention that it has no em dash. That is why the answer of course is **H**; it provides the first em dash that pairs with the other already in the sentence.

#9 Let's assume that we are unsure as to whether or not this is a proper way to use a colon. Where does that leave us? We know the answer can't be **B** because it puts a semicolon in its place, but we know a semicolon can only be used to separate independent clauses. **D** is the kind of option that makes you second guess what you know or recognize commas. The question is, if it kind of sounds like a "pause" works, can we throw a comma in there? No, remember, we can't just throw in commas to make pauses; commas are used deliberately. For a comma to belong here, we would need a complete, dependent clause to follow (something like, "forget, which is unity"). So **D** is incorrect. If you can get that far, you can know that the colon is being used correctly. As a reminder, a colon has many uses, but it always follows a complete clause/sentence. Here, the tiebreaker is wordiness. **C** is incorrect because it says what is needed but in too many words. Thus, the correct answer is **A**, no change.

#10 Here we have multiple adjectives in a series in front of a noun. Before we review the rule, let's eliminate choice **J** since it puts two adjectives between commas without any context and thus it is meaningless. The question is whether or not a comma is needed after the word "simpler." Or, looking at choice **H**, whether or not we need to reverse the adjectives. We would need to reverse the adjectives only if one of them absolutely belonged prior to the noun (in this case "identity"). Like we said in the lesson, there are lots of combinations like that; even with the word "identity" you could have a combination like "stolen identity." However, there's no reason to have the word "simpler" or "truer" tied to "identity" in any specific order. Not only does this mean that **H** is incorrect, but it also means that we need a comma after "simpler." Thus, **F** is also incorrect because there is no comma. Only choice **G** puts the comma, and this is why it is correct.

#11 All of the choices are grammatically correct, thus there is something else to look out for here. Because all of the answer choices have different meaning, we must have a question of redundancy here. Let's start with **A**, which says "at retail locations…" This is incorrect though because the sentence already says "at stores." Moving to **B**, this too is redundant; the sentence begins by letting us know that it is American flags that were in short supply, so it is redundant to put it at the end of the sentence again. Looking at **C**, we have a similar problem; **C** tells us that the flags were once easy to purchase, but this is also something we already know ("once readily available at stores"). Thus the answer is **D**; it is the only choice that is not redundant.

#12 Here again we have adjectives in a series. This time, there is something else at play: do we need a comma after the introductory clause? Let's start with the adjectives rule. Can we reverse the adjectives "awful" and "terrorist" and still get the same meaning? "Because more than twenty years have passed since these terrorist, awful attacks…" Um, no, that changes the meaning; a "terrorist attack" is a particular kind of attack; this is an adjective/noun combo that can't be separated. This means that we DO NOT need the comma after "awful." That eliminates **F** and **H**. The question then becomes whether or not we need a comma after "attacks." In this case, the answer is yes. This is clearly an opening dependent clause, thus we need a comma to separate it from the main clause. That is why **J** is incorrect and why **G** is the correct answer.

#13 The student who thinks that commas exist to create artificial pauses that sound good is likely to get this question wrong. Some answers have a comma after "pride." Let's examine that first. Letter **C** does this, and it makes "I've noticed that the pride" a dependent clause to open the sentence. But that's not a dependent clause, and it makes a mess of the rest of the sentence. So **C** is incorrect. **D** does a similar thing, but this time making the clause extend to after the word "unity." But look at what would then come after the comma: "that strengthened in the months following has slowly faded away." That is a sentence nothing short of interrupted by something! Turning our attention to **B**, we see that this option makes "and unity" into a nonessential clause. However, that is not a nonessential clause. "Unity," along with "pride" are what are strengthened; just because it kind of sounds nice to put in commas, that doesn't mean they belong. The answer then is **A** because the sentence is fine the way it is written.

#14 We need to go back and simply insert this sentence into the different places and see where it fits; it's as simple as that. The correct answer on these kinds of questions is never going to kind of be an OK place for a sentence; rather, it is going to deliberately belong in that paragraph for a reason. **F** is incorrect because inserting the sentence as the last sentence of the first paragraph disrupts the flow of event's for the author's morning. **G** is an example of a place where you might be tempted to say, "Well that kind of sounds OK." But it is not. The sentence following is "This is particularly true…." What is particularly true? That changes if we insert the sentence there. Because the sentence is a positive statement about people coming together, **H** would work (and yes it is the correct answer). This works because it begins a list in the paragraph of all of the positive things Americans did after 9/11. **J** for what it's worth is not a good fit; the sentence before stresses a negative, thus to throw in a sentence about people coming together is contrary to the sentence before it.

#15 Again, we need to know if the answer is "Yes" or "No" before diving in. The question asks if the essay is a history of the

USA. Although it is an event from American history, it is certainly not a history of America. We can eliminate then **A** and **B. C** says that it's not a history of America because the essay says nothing about any event within American history. Well that's not true; the entire essay is about an event from American history. **D** says that the answer is no because the essay is not only about only 1 event, but it is also more of a personal perspective (as opposed to a historical text that is usually less personal). That is why **D** is the correct answer.

Passage II: The Colosseum

#16 As written, I hope you can see that the sentence needs to offset some kind of introductory phrase with a comma. We need to think: what is the independent clause of this sentence, the piece that could stand alone as a sentence? Is it: "history the Colosseum was first constructed nearly 2000 years ago"? No; that doesn't make sense. This is why **G** is incorrect. Letter **F** has this same problem of failing to separate the dependent clause from the independent. The independent clause of the sentence is "the Colosseum was first constructed nearly 2,000 years ago," so we need an answer that separates that off. That's why the answer is **H** because it properly does this. **J** is incorrect because it incorrectly makes "history" a nonessential word or phrase, which it is not.

#17 Here we have underlined a bridge between two clauses. What we need to know is if these two clauses are independent (can stand alone as a sentence) or if one is dependent. In this case, what comes before and after the semicolon are both independent clauses. The question itself is worded a bit differently; it asks for which option is unacceptable. In other words, there will be three correct answer and one wrong one, which must be identified. Here, you are being tested as to whether or not you know the ways to combine these clauses. **A** is acceptable; it treats the clauses as independent sentences. **B** is also acceptable; we discussed that an em dash (—) is a way to combine independent clauses. **C** is also acceptable; it uses a comma and appropriately adds a FANBOYS (for, and, nor, but, or, yet, so) conjunction to bridge them. **D**, then, is not acceptable; you can't add a FANBOYS conjunction after a semicolon, only after a comma. Thus **D** is our correct answer because it is the only incorrect option.

#18 Nothing grammatically incorrect here with any of the options. What we need is the *best* option. All of them say essentially the same thing, but one of them says it in the most succinct or you might say "regular" way. That is why the answer is **J**. Other choices (**F, G, H**) are all incorrect because they are simply too wordy.

#19 Let's eliminate choice **D** simply because it is too wordy. There has to be a way to line up these words properly. Hopefully your "ear" (your ability to "hear" that things are right or wrong) can tell you that **C** is also incorrect; not only because the words are out of order but because it artificially inserts commas between them. We said before that adjectives in front of nouns act like one big noun. "Terrorist attack" was an example from the previous test. Other examples are things like "bowling ball" or "sports car." In this case "Roman emperor Vespasian" acts like one big noun; we don't need commas to separate off any of those words. **B** then is also incorrect for this reason. **A** is correct because it rightly adds no commas and orders the words properly.

#20 This is an example of a jumbled words kind of question. Read the sentence with each option in place. **H** doesn't work because it makes the sentence an incomplete sentence or dependent clause. **G** is also incorrect; it confuses various verb tenses into nonsense. **J** would be correct if what comes before or after "generated" were a dependent clause, but that is not the case; the comma artificially splits the sentence open. **F** is the correct answer then; the verb tense is correct and treats the sentence for what it is: one sentence or independent clause.

#21 Word to the wise: unless it is used in a question, the word "which" usually comes after a comma. "Which" is one way to begin a dependent clause. Here you can see that "The Colosseum was fully constructed after ten years" is the independent clause. **B** is incorrect because we aren't linking two independent clauses. **C** is also incorrect because it artificially makes "ten years" into a nonessential series of words, but that is incorrect. **A** is incorrect because it fails to segregate off the dependent clause that starts with "which." This is why **D** is correct.

#22 These kinds of questions are among the most missed in ACT English. The reason for this is that there's a lot to read, not because it is too difficult. The question tells you what the sentence must do: talk about "consecutive emperors." **F** speaks about Vespasian and his rise to power, but nothing about consecutive emperors. **G** speaks of the Roman Empire, but nothing about emperors or even the Colosseum for that matter. **J** speaks of the time it would take to build large structures, not emperors. **H** correctly speaks of Vespasian's death and his son's opening of the Colosseum as emperor. That is why **H** is correct.

#23 Parts, pieces, sections, and segments are all synonyms. That is why **A, B,** and **C** are all incorrect; they are redundant. **D** is the correct answer because it says what the sentence requires without the redundancy.

#24 Here we are dealing with the question of nonessential words and phrases, our #1 comma ability based on recent ACT's. Already let's eliminate **J** because it uses a colon, which must follow an independent clause, and in this case it does not. Let's also eliminate **G** because it sets off "The amphitheater" from the rest of the sentence, but that fractures the independent clause (there is no dependent clause in this sentence to set off at all; from start to finish it is independent). The question is whether or not "overall" is nonessential. The test for this is to remove it from the sentence and see if what is left works as an independent clause: "The amphitheater covers about 300,000 square feet." Yes, that clearly works. The word "overall" then is added for emphasis and is thus nonessential. That is why **H** is incorrect; it fails to set off "overall" with commas. The correct answer is **F** because it does separate "overall" off with commas.

#25 This is a question again of linking clauses, or not. Are these two independent clauses? A quick check tells us no. The second clause in the sentence "remarkably could hold as many as 50,000 spectators at one time" looks like an independent clause, but it is missing a subject, like the word "it" or even "the Colosseum" or "the building." This is why **A, B,** and **D** are all incorrect; each would work if we were combining independent clauses. **C** is correct because what follows "world" isn't a dependent clause at all; remove the punctuation from the middle of the sentence and it flows from start to finish as one independent clause or complete thought.

#26 At first read, the sentence in question does not seem irrelevant. Throughout the paragraph we have phrases like "For centuries" and "It once," which implies that at one day the Colosseum was bustling, and now it is not. The sentence in question begins to wind down, so to speak, the Colosseum as a center of bustling activity to an abandoned building. In fact, reading on to the second paragraph, we see this is what is happening. Thus, the sentence must be kept, which is why **H** and **J** are incorrect. As for why it should be kept, notice that **G** says what we just inferred: that the activity of the Colosseum was halted. That is why **G** is correct. As for **F**, getting "deeper insight into world events" is too broad; there are millions of sentences we could throw in here that would give us that kind of insight, but that wouldn't mean they would belong.

#27 As written, we have one comma after the word "projects," which would turn something into a dependent clause. However, we are dealing here with combining independent clauses. Separate the two and ask, "Can these stand alone as sentences?" Let's look at them: "Large parts were removed to provide stone for other construction projects" and "Much of the ornate construction —such as marble statues—was taken away or destroyed." Those are both independent clauses; we need something more than a comma (a comma could work, but we'd also need a FANBOYS conjunction, but that's not here). Thus, **A** is incorrect. For that matter, **C** is out as well; it inserts a comma without purpose after "much." **D** uses a colon to separate the clauses; this is OK to do of course. The problem is that it puts a comma after "much," which disrupts the sentence; again, we can't just put in commas for no reason. That's why the answer is **B**; it properly unites the independent clauses with a semicolon.

#28 If you read the last answer explanation, I already gave this one away! One use for em dashes (—) is to set off clauses or words like parentheses. The phrase "such as marble statues" is set off in the beginning with an em dash, so it must be fully set off in the end with the same punctuation (this would also apply if it were commas or parentheses). That is why **J** is the correct answer. **F, G,** and **H** fail to finish the "setting off" with an em dash, and are thus incorrect. As a reminder, we could have a single em dash in a sentence if it is used to set off independent clauses, but that's not what is happening before the word "such."

#29 Here, the phrase "While conservation of the Colosseum began in the 18th century" is the dependent clause, and "actual restoration did not begin until the mid-1990's" is the independent clause. To combine them into one complex sentence, all we need is one thing: a comma. Using a period implies two independent clauses, but we don't have that, so **A** and **B** are both incorrect. The preposition "in the 18th century" is not nonessential; prepositions generally "flow" with a sentence. Thus it does not need to be set off, which is why **D** is incorrect. **C** correctly sets off the opening phrase with a comma and is the right answer.

#30 Here we have a clue: "by referring back to the opening paragraph." Starting with **F**, you may notice that not only does it close the preceding paragraph well ("Although repair is ongoing"), but also refers back to the opening paragraph by referring to how recognizable the Colosseum is (the first sentence of the essay says, "Few archetypes of ancient civilization are better known…"). That is why **F** is correct. **G** would work if the essay was about the effect of weather on landmarks worldwide, but it isn't. **H** fails because the purpose of the essay isn't the Roman Empire or its fall. **J** is the longest option, and it is probably good here to reject the myth that the longest option is always correct. That isn't true. Here, the sentence sounds really nice, but there is nothing in the opening paragraph about how landmarks around the world need help, so it too is incorrect.

Passage III: Stunt Kite

#31 Here, there is nothing grammatically incorrect about any of the options, thus, this is a question of verbosity (overly wordy) reminiscent of Step 2. Thus, we need the least wordy option. Well, **A, C,** and **D** are all incorrect for that very reason; they all say what is needed for the sentence, but in too many words. That is why the answer is **B**. The word "kind" works because we know what that represents: a kind of kite, because "kites" is used in the first clause of the sentence.

#32 This question is testing two things from Step 3. The first is how to set off a dependent clause with a comma. In other words, "When he set it up" is that clause, and must be set off from the rest of the sentence with a comma. This eliminates choices **F** and **H**. Every option (including **F** and **H**) uses a colon. Thus, we need to remember the colon rule: *it must follow a complete thought.* Of our remaining options, we can eliminate option **G** because, although "When he set it up, I noticed something" is a complete thought when set apart from the sentence, in this case, we can't separate "something" from "odd." What comes after the colon in that case is, well, also odd; the word "odd" being set off by a comma. That makes something that, hopefully, looks and "sounds" too off. Technically speaking, what must follow a colon is a list, a quote, a complete/independent clause, or a noun/noun phrase that emphasizes, completes, or dramatizes the first clause. None of these things occurs in this case. That's why the answer is **J**; we have a complete clause before and after the colon.

#33 D is always a tantalizing option for questions like this. At first when you delete the underlined portion, the sentence kind of flows and works. But doesn't it sound odd? It starts the sentence off with two dependent clauses back to back. Not only that, but we have ", but" (a comma followed by a FANBOYS) after "kite," which would work if what came before it were an independent clause. That's not the case; by deleting the underlined portion, we're left with "As a heavy wind launched the kite;" that's not independent, so **D** is incorrect. As we said, the ", but" means that what comes before is a complete thought that could stand alone, so let's deal with that. There we have "As a heavy wind blew over the field" and "We launched the kite." The first part is an introductory phrase that must be set off by a comma, the second is the complete thought it must be set off from. This is why **A** is correct. **B** and **C** have too many commas and are incorrect.

#34 Since **J** is formatted a bit differently than the other options, let's start there. The adverb "quickly" is misplaced; if we were going to use that word, we would need to use it like this: "...this kite quickly shot into the air..." It simply makes no sense to end a sentence with an adverb set off by a comma. **J** is thus incorrect. The comma used in choice **F** is correct, so it may look tempting. But **F** and **H** are both incorrect for the same reason: they are redundant. **G** is right because it communicates that the kite went off quickly in only one word. We already know that bullets are fast and rapid; that's why the simile "like a bullet" works in the first place.

#35 Here the question is asking for the best phrase. In this case, the best phrase is the one that attributes to the uncle the ability to control more than just the height. However, **A** and **D** both speak of the height, so they are wrong. **C** speaks nothing of the uncle's control (another necessity based on the question itself), so it is incorrect too. **B** speaks of the uncle's ability to direct the kite to a certain spot in which direction, and thus it is correct.

#36 We are trying here to join two independent clauses. As written, there is no punctuation to denote the distinction between the two independent clauses, so **F** is incorrect. Same goes for **G**; although there's a FANBOYS (for, and, nor, but, or, yet, so) conjunction, there is no comma. **J** is wrong for the opposite reason: there's a comma, but no FANBOYS conjunction. Only choice **H** correctly separates the independent clauses with a comma and a FANBOYS conjunction, so it is correct.

#37 After the word "for," the sentence's second independent clause begins. We don't need to separate off the subject of the sentence, "my uncle," which is why **C** is incorrect. **B** has the problem of putting a comma after the conjunction, which is purposeless; **B** is incorrect. **D** is grammatically correct, but we already know who the pronoun "he" refers to, so we don't need to restate that (it is redundant, in other words). That is why the answer is **A**; it allows the second independent clause to proceed as normal.

#38 At first this seems like a straightforward question of how to use a comma: do we have an introductory phrase that is straightforward, or do we have a nonessential phrase in there that has to be set off by commas? However, the phrase "as I was watching" is redundant! The entire essay is from the author's point of view; of course he is watching! That is why the answer is **J**; it is the only option that deletes that phrase. **F, G,** and **H** are all redundant. You may think, "but that's not fair!" Well, the ACT mixes and matches question types; it isn't all straightforward.

#39 This is a lot of commas to sort through, but let's do that by first identifying the independent clause here. It is: "I shouted to my uncle." That is enough for us to know that we will need a comma after the word "uncle." That eliminates **A** and **B** as incorrect. After that, the question is whether or not "for a moment" is a nonessential phrase. If we remove it, we are still left with a dependent clause: "thinking he had lost control." That signals that, indeed, "for a moment" is nonessential and must be set off by commas. That means we need three commas total: after "uncle," after "thinking," and after "moment." That is why **D** is incorrect; it sets off the wrong phrase ("a moment"). This is why **C** is correct. It has all three commas in the correct places.

#40 The way the paragraph is written, without the proposed sentence, it ends on kind of a cliffhanger: what happened to the kite when he pulled back hard? The sentence that is being proposed answers that question: it rockets into the sky and disaster was avoided. So, yes, we want the sentence. That eliminates **H** and **J** as incorrect. **F** says "Yes," which is correct so far, but it mentions something about the word "rocketed" linking with a rocket mentioned earlier. However, there is no rocket mentioned earlier, so it is incorrect. **G,** then, is correct because it rightly says that the proposed sentence tells the reader that the kite did not crash, which is what we need to know (it is a fitting end to the sentence).

#41 We have here four options all essentially saying the same thing in different words and very tenses. We need to read them all in the context of the sentence and find the shortest one that is also grammatically correct. Hopefully you noticed off the bat that "how it is to fly" is correct, but could be said in a shorter way: *how to fly*. That is why **C** is the correct answer; it says what is needed in the fewest words possible. Like we just said, as written is too wordy, which is why **A** is incorrect. **B** has a similar problem and is incorrect; "it were" is an unnecessary addition to the phrase. **D** simply makes no sense and is incorrect.

#42 Here we have two adjectives describing the word "eights." But, we can't rearrange these adjectives; it makes no sense to say, "I could do figure amazing eights." So, "figure eights" is more like the noun with only one adjective, "amazing," describing it. We don't need a comma between them, in other words. For these reasons, we can eliminate **G** and **H** as incorrect. **J** is incorrect because it puts a hyphen between "amazing" and "figure-eights"; we don't do that with adjectives. That is why the answer is **F**; as written, it correctly describes the figure eights as "amazing."

#43 There is an em dash later in the sentence, which can only mean two things. First, there are two independent clauses being linked, or second, em dashes are being used as parentheses. What comes before the em dash later in the sentence is NOT an independent clause, so it must be parentheses. Only **D** correctly opens the phrase with an em dash, so it is correct! **A, B,** and **C** fail to do so, so they are all incorrect.

#44 This one is tricky, but common on the ACT. First, let's recognize that "Since that day" is an opening phrase and will need a comma to come after it to set it off. That eliminates **F**, which is an incorrect option. Looking at the rest, let's identify the independent clause: "I have gotten my own stunt kite…" So, "though still a bit of an amateur" is the nonessential phrase and must be set off by commas. **H** fails to include the pronoun "I," so it is incorrect. **J** fails to begin to set off the nonessential phrase by eliminating a comma, so it is out. That is why **G** is correct; it correctly sets off both the introductory phrase and the nonessential phrase.

#45 Again, we want to know: is the answer Yes or No? Here, the question asks if the essay is about the author acquiring a new hobby, which it indeed is. So that eliminates **C** and **D**. **B** says that the answer is "Yes" because the essay compares and contrasts different hobbies. But that isn't true; the only hobby mentioned is flying stunt kites. So **B** is incorrect. **A** correctly says that the essay is about how the author came to acquire the hobby of flying stunt kites.

Answer Explanations - Step 4

Correct Answers:

Passage I	Passage II	Passage III
1: D	16: G	31: B
2: H	17: B	32: J
3: C	18: J	33: B
4: G	19: A	34: F
5: A	20: F	35: D
6: J	21: D	36: J
7: A	22: G	37: D
8: J	23: C	38: G
9: C	24: G	39: A
10: F	25: C	40: G
11: B	26: H	41: C
12: H	27: A	42: F
13: D	28: H	43: A
14: F	29: C	44: J
15: D	30: H	45: B

Passage I: Norman Rockwell, American Artist

#1 Here we have an introductory phrase that must be set off by a comma. We know this because if we remove the word "Rather" from the beginning, what comes after is a complete, independent clause. That is why the correct answer here is **D**. Choice **A** has the problem of no comma. **B** and **C** both have a different problem: they introduce a pronoun ("He") into the sentence when it is not justified to do so; a pronoun isn't needed there because the name "Rockwell" immediately follows, thus we know who "acquired fame" apart from the pronoun.

#2 The verb tense of this sentence is past tense; we want a choice that matches up with "acquired fame." This would be **H**, which is the correct answer and continues the past tense. As written, it is nonsensical; nobody says "as to depicting." **G** doesn't work because the sentence has no use for the word "then" because the sentence isn't describing something chronological. **J** is also nonsensical; "of depicting" would have to follow a very specific noun, like: "I am conscious of depicting my brother as crazy in my new book," or something like that. That's not what this sentence does though.

#3 Although the sentence prior to the one in question mentions fame, that doesn't mean that a sentence about fame can be inserted here. In this case, the sentence quotes another text altogether to give us information about fame and how artists have achieved it. This can't work here; it shifts the focus away from Rockwell dramatically, and moves from specific to broad without any justification; that is why **A** and **B** are incorrect. **C** says exactly what we are looking for, that the focus of the paragraph and essay shift into something irrelevant if this sentence is inserted. **D**, while correct that the answer is "No," incorrectly says that Rockwell was not famous after his death. We may be able to guess that he was famous at death, but the last part ("which has been stated") makes us sure: so far in this little paragraph, there's been no mention that Rockwell is not famous after death.

#4 As far as commas go, the way it is written seems correct because we have two commas identifying one noun, and the comma comes after the first adjective. However, this is a case in which the adjectives ("paying" and "first") can't be reversed, which is why **F** is incorrect. A "paying job" is a noun all its own and is used often in plain speech to distinguish it from volunteer work or school work. And if that's the case, and "first" comes before "paying," we will not need a comma. That is why **G** is the correct answer. **H** seems the shortest, and it is, but it makes no sense when read in context. This is also true for **J**; when inserted, it makes the sentence into something else, as in not a sentence any more!

#5 Three of these options are redundant. Choice **D** is one of these redundant options; it has already been stated that this work was done for the Boy Scouts. Moving to **C**, we see this is incorrect as well; it was stated earlier in the sentence that this was done for $50, so this option is incorrect. Then there's **B**, which is also redundant; the opening sentence of the paragraph says he was 18. That is why **A** is the correct answer; it tells us something relevant that has not been stated.

#6 The word "remains" implies that something from the past is still true or relevant in the present time. This is why **F, G,** and **H** are all incorrect. Each of them is redundant; if his cover *remains* as one of his most valuable works, we already know that it is that way today. "Today," "still," and "to this day" are all redundant when combined with the word "remains." This is why **J** is the correct answer; all we need is the word "remains" to communicate the necessary idea that today this cover is still valuable.

#7 First, let us eliminate answer choice **C**. This option is in the present tense, but the paragraph is in the past tense. When put into the sentence, **A, B,** and **D** all seem to fit in a way. Let's look at **B** and **D**. You could easily say a person "was being promoted" or "was receiving a promotion" but the sentence itself doesn't call for this wording (called the *past progressive tense*). That wording would make more sense if: a) The rest of the paragraph was in this tense, or b) The use of it is a setup for another past event taking place (such as like this: "he was being promoted when his life took an unexpected turn…" or "he was receiving a promotion when he received a letter from his mother…"). For those reasons, let's eliminate answer choices **B** and **D**. As written, the sentence works, is not wordy, and is in the proper verb tense. That is why the correct answer is **A**.

#8 This kind of question is indicative of the way in which the ACT pairs verbs with subjects. The verb (as underlined, "was featured") comes after a nonessential clause is set off by commas. If we eliminate that nonessential clause, and only read the independent clause that comes after the comma, we have a sentence that says this: "The Boy Scouts was often featured in his work." That kind of splicing is what makes sense of the sentence if you fail to see it the first time. As written, "was" (singular) does not fit with "Scouts" (plural). That is why **F** is incorrect. **H** has the same problem, so it is out. As for **G**, it is incorrect because it creates a sentence fragment ("The Scouts to be…"?); the verb "to be" needs to be conjugated here. That is why the answer is **J**; it has a plural verb ("were") with a plural subject ("Scouts"). As for the ordering of "often" and "featured," it doesn't really matter which comes first.

#9 Here we have a comma and a FANBOYS conjunction (as a reminder: for, and, nor, but, or, yet, so) underlined. Again, this is only going to work if what comes after the "and" is an independent clause, so let's put that to the test: ", and *was frequently hired to do the same for various publications throughout his career.*" That's not a complete thought…what or who *was* frequently hired? There's no subject within the clause to fit with the verb *was*. thus, **A** is incorrect. **D** is incorrect for the completely opposite reason; in this option, the subject "he" is put before the verb "was," creating an independent clause. However, this clause needs to be set off with a comma, and it is not. **B** would work if it had a FANBOYS conjunction; just like **D**, choice **B** puts a subject to the verb, but it is missing the necessary conjunction to set it off properly. Only **C** works because it recognizes that what comes after *Post* is not an independent clause, but rather a continuation of the clause already at play (which begins with "Rockwell"). That is why **C** is correct.

#10 Here we have four options that all look similar. This was our mini-lesson in part 4. We need the one that means "to join." This is why **F** is correct; "enlist" means "to join." **G, H,** and **J**, though they look like "enlist" and are spelled similarly, are incorrect from a vocabulary point of view, which is why those three are incorrect.

#11 As written, we have a contradiction. If Rockwell tried to join the army, why would he turn away? In other words, when someone "turns away" they are *choosing* to turn away, to not be a part of something anymore. The context of the sentence, that he is underweight and that he wants to join the Navy, implies that the Navy turned him away, not that he did so voluntarily. Thus, **A** is out and is incorrect. **C** has the same problem; it implies that Rockwell somehow turned the Navy away, so it is incorrect. **D** creates a sentence fragment; it has no verb to fit with the subject "they." These are all reasons why **B** is correct; it rightly identifies that Rockwell was the one who was turned away from the Navy, the reason being that he was underweight.

#12 Grammatically speaking, there is no problem with the way this is written. However, remember, the ACT expects sometimes the *best* answer, not any given grammatically correct one. It is redundant to add the description of him as an artist who draws; that is implied in the word "artist." **F, G,** and **J** all have this flaw. **H** is correct because it is the only choice that is not redundant.

#13 This question is a good example of verbosity in that you need to identify which of the options is the least wordy while giving the sentence what it needs. Here, all four choices say the exact same thing and imply that Rockwell was inspired to paint the *Four Freedoms* because of a Roosevelt speech. **A, B,** and **C** all grammatically work, but are too wordy when compared to the correct answer: **D**.

#14 First of all, the verb "intends" needs the word "to" if we are being told what is actually intended. "I intend to go to the store today" is an example. Because that is the case in this sentence, we can eliminate **G** and **J** because neither have the word "to" following it. This question reminds me of the *listen* rule. You don't need to memorize what I have said in this paragraph…doesn't it just sound funny to say, "I intend go to the store today"? It sounds like a caveman talking. Now, back to the question. We need proper subject/verb agreement. Thus which is correct: "Some intend to awaken…" or "Some intends to awaken…"? Of course, it is the first option; "Some" is plural, and needs the plural conjugation of the verb "to intend." That is why **F** is correct and why **H** (which conjugates the verb as if the subject were singular, as in "He intends to") is incorrect.

#15 It is your goal to know if the answer is "Yes" or "No" before reading through the answer choices. The question asks if the essay is about the history of American art. While Rockwell is an American artist, the essay is only about him, so the answer is No. This eliminates **A** and **B**. Answer choice **C** (which is incorrect) says that Rockwell was born in Toronto. The essay never says if that is true or false (by the way, it is false), but even if it is true that's not the reason why the answer is no. **D** correctly says that the essay is only about one artist.

Passage II: The Challenger Deep

#16 This sentence is in the present tense, but the underlined verb "were" is in the past tense, so **F** is incorrect. **H** and **J** could work if they came immediately after the comma and not after the word "and," but they don't, which is why they are incorrect. **G** is correct because it pairs the singular, present tense verb "is" to the subject, which is "one place."

#17 "Deepest" and "farthest down" are synonyms. In other words, as written, this question is redundant. For this reason alone we can eliminate choices **A** and **C** as incorrect. In questions of redundancy the correct or *best* answer is usually the shortest, but in this case that is not right. If we simply put the word "area" into the sentence (which is what answer choice **D** suggests), we have a new problem: the sentence no longer expresses a complete thought. You wouldn't say, "This is certainly true of the area of the ocean: the Mariana Trench" because there are many areas of the ocean; it would be more proper to say "an area," but it doesn't. **B** is correct because it identifies the Mariana Trench as the *deepest* area of the ocean, not just an area.

#18 As written, the underlined portion has a semicolon, which is fine. However, that semicolon is followed by a FANBOYS (for, and, nor, but, or, yet, so) conjunction, which is not fine. That is why **F** is incorrect. The same is true for **H**; you can't put a FANBOYS after a semicolon. **G** has the problem of failing to put a FANBOYS after the comma, which is necessary because this part of the sentence is bridging two independent clauses. That is why the correct answer is **J**; it properly uses a semicolon to combine two independent clauses without adding in a FANBOYS conjunction.

#19 If you read the entire sentence before looking to all of the answer choices, the underlined portion should strike you as working just fine. That's because it does! **A** is correct; it is past tense and fits with the subject "visit" well. You are allowed to be confident about an answer, circle it, and move on. This sentence is one independent clause, containing no dependent clauses or nonessential words or phrases. This is why **B** is incorrect because it shows that a nonessential phrase is beginning, but that phrase is never set off later. **C** has the problem of being in the future tense; **D** is incorrect because it is in the present tense (and is too wordy and awkward) but somehow hopes that something will happen in the year 1960.

#20 Here you are asked for a phrase that serves a dual purpose: a) It tells that the voyage was dangerous, and b) It shows the explorers were courageous. Let's start with **J** and go backwards. Although this choice talks about the two explorers, it neither reveals the danger nor speaks of their courage, so it is incorrect. **H** speaks of danger, but that probably isn't the kind of danger that two men in a submarine are worried about (not to mention, the phrase says nothing of their courage). **G** says how deep they had to go; just speaking of the depth might be enough for a reader to assume it was dangerous, but again, there is nothing here about their courage. **F** is the correct answer; the *crack* they hear on the way down reveals the danger, and their decision to carry on reveals their courage.

#21 Here, "have observed" (choice **B**) is incorrect because that is the present perfect tense; we need something in past tense. **C** is incorrect because it creates an incomplete sentence by never fitting a verb with "Walsh and Piccard," the subject of the sentence. The only difference between **A** and **D** is that the last word is either "observe" or "observed." Think about this sentence: "They have observe a fish," or this one: "I have observe a shooting star." Do either of those make sense? No, which is why **A** is incorrect and why **D** is correct.

#22 The problem with choice **F**, the way this is written (which is also one of the problems with choice **H** as well), is that it turns the word "short" into an adverb: "shortly." It makes no sense to perform the act of cutting in a "short" way, which is how the adverb "shortly" modifies the verb "cut." For those reasons alone, F and H are incorrect. To "cut something short" means to end something prematurely, and just because "low" and "short" are synonyms, that doesn't mean they are interchangeable. For this reason, **J** is incorrect and **G** is the correct answer.

#23 B might have you wondering: who is Cameron? This may prompt you to read on and see that James Cameron was the next to reach the *Challenger Deep*. However, he is introduced in the next sentence, and thus it is inappropriate to throw out his name here. Even so, **B** is also incorrect because it would need to be set off by a comma and then later would need a verb to create an independent clause. This question is merely a question of setting off introductory words or phrases. **D** is an introductory phrase, but is not set off by a comma. So then the question is: if a sentence is begun with an adverb like "Incredibly" does it need a comma? The answer is yes. *But wait!* you think, *I read articles and books all the time in which this isn't done!* That is true, but guess what? This isn't an article on some website, but ACT English. It's what *they want* that matters, and they want you to see when commas ought to have deliberate use. In this case, you need to set off the word with a comma. **A** is thus incorrect, and **C** is correct due to its comma.

#24 When you are alone, you are by yourself. As written, then, this is redundant. **F** is thus incorrect. **J** has the same problem; "solitarily" and "companionless" are synonymous and thus redundant, so it is incorrect as well. The tiebreaker between **H** and **G** is verbosity, meaning (because neither is redundant, they are both grammatically correct, and they both mean the same thing) the less wordy one is *best*. This is of course **G**, the correct answer.

#25 An em dash can be used to set off two independent clauses, so that's what we need to check here. Before the em dash we have, "Despite the failure of a few instruments on the way down due to extreme pressure." That is not an independent clause; it is a dependent one. Any option that tries to link this clause with the one that comes later ("The dive was a success") as if they are independent clauses will be incorrect. This is why **A** is incorrect. **D** does the same thing in that it tries to link the clauses using a comma and a FANBOYS conjunction. **B** uses a colon, but you have to remember the colon's number one rule: it always follows a complete thought, which is not the case here, so **B** is also incorrect. **C** correctly sets off the opening/dependent clause with a comma from the independent clause that follows.

#26 Here, the prepositional phrase "on the ocean floor" is set off from the rest of the sentence. Although prepositional phrases come up in the next Step, here it is important to know that they don't need to be set off by commas in the flow of a sentence. Think about this sentence: I went to the store on the hill in the rain under an umbrella next to my daughter. Lots of prepositional phrases there, but they don't need to be set off by commas. For this reason, both **F** and **G** are incorrect. **G** has the additional problem that "on the ocean floor" is not an independent clause, which is what is needed if only one em dash is going to be used in a sentence. **J**, grammatically speaking, is fine. However, it leaves the reader wondering...three "what" down there? Three days? Hours? Minutes? That is why **H** is the correct answer; it defines what "three" refers to and doesn't arbitrarily set off the prepositional phrase.

#27 This sentence moves back into the present tense, which you can tell by the phrase "these are" at the beginning. This question is entirely a question of verb tense because that is the only difference between all of the answer choices. **B** and **C** are incorrect because they are past and future tenses, respectively. **D** says it "was to be." This kind of wording would only make sense if the sentence went on to say something like, "which was to be the total number **until** three more people dove down there for fun." This is why **A** is correct; it simply keeps the verb tense present.

#28 The sentence that is being proposed is tricky and indicative of the kinds of sentences or phrases the ACT will propose to you on test day. It is tricky because the sentence *mentions* Walsh and Piccard, who you already know were two of the men to descend into the *Challenger Deep*. However, the subject of the sentence is not the *Challenger Deep* or the men who descended into it, but rather the two men to have landed on the moon. Just because the sentence prior mentions the moon landing, that does not mean any sentence about the moon is appropriate. This sentence is like a detour or pit stop and interrupts the flow of the paragraph, so it does not belong. **F** and **G** are thus incorrect. **H** is correct because it rightly identifies the sentence as a distraction from the focus of the essay. **J**, although it correctly says "No," is incorrect because the reason for that No (that the essay makes no mention of the explorers being inspired by the men who landed on the moon) is not correct; that's not *why* the sentence doesn't belong.

#29 As written, you might be tempted to put "NO CHANGE" because most of the essay was in the past tense; "waited" makes it sound like the explorers were going to the bottom and there waited new creatures to be discovered. But, we are out of that part of the essay and are now on to a new paragraph in the present tense. **A** and **B** are both incorrect for reasons of verb tense. **D**, while it is in the present tense, is singular, but we need a plural conjugation to fit with "creatures and other wonders." This is why **C** is the correct answer; the creatures are as of yet undiscovered, so they "are waiting."

#30 The question asks if the essay's purpose was to describe the instruments on board submarines. The answer to that question is "No"; the essay was about *The Challenger Deep*. That eliminates **F** and **G**. Choice **H** correctly says "No," but says the instruments are mentioned somewhere but not described. If you can't remember if they were mentioned or not, it is OK to go back and look. Spoiler alert: they are mentioned (remember a few of Cameron's failed?). This is why **H** is correct. However, if you can't figure that out, ask yourself if **J** is definitely true or false. **J** says that these instruments are unnecessary and a burden. Even if you don't remember reading anything about instruments, you can probably assume that instruments on board a protective submarine are important! Thus, **J** is incorrect.

Passage III: The Pont du Gard

#31 A prepositional phrase (like "to France") is not something that needs to be set off by commas, which is why **A** is incorrect. Because it is "visitors to France" who "are," we don't need to separate the former subject from the latter verb. In other words, "Visitors to France" isn't an introductory phrase, but is essential to the independent clause of the sentence. **C** incorrectly sets off the word "visitors" and **D** incorrectly sets off the whole phrase as some kind of introductory phrase. This is why **B** is the correct answer; it does not separate an essential part of the independent clause (the subject that pairs with the verb "are") from the rest of the sentence.

#32 Are we trying to say that the Pont du Gard *has to be* an aqueduct bridge? No, we are simply trying to say that the Pont du Gard is an example of an aqueduct bridge. This is why **F** is incorrect. The other options test your ability to recognize verb tenses. Because the rest of the paragraph is in the present tense, we need an option in the present tense. This is option **J**, which is the correct answer. **G** is in the future tense, which is incorrect. **H** is in the past tense, which is also incorrect.

#33 Again, what you need to be able to identify is the nature of the clauses that come before and after the comma. Before we have this: "The bridge crosses the Gardon River," which is an independent clause (it can stand alone as a sentence). After we have this: "today is listed as a UNESCO World Heritage Site," which is NOT an independent clause (it begs the question: *what* is listed as a UNESCO Site?). So, **A** is incorrect for this reason, **D** is incorrect for this reason, and **C** is also incorrect for this reason! All three of those options are ways of combining independent clauses into one sentence. That is why **B** is correct; it smoothly maintains the sentence as one long independent clause or thought uninterrupted by punctuation.

#34 This is a question of verbosity, meaning wordiness. **G, H,** and **J** are all incorrect because, though they say the same thing and do so in a grammatically correct way, they are all too wordy. **F** is correct because the word "empire" is shortest and what the sentence is intending to communicate.

#35 These kinds of questions are more often than not missed on ACT day. The reason? Many students read "the delivery of" (choice A) in the context of the sentence, see that it works, bubble it in, and move on. However, the question asks for a choice that does NOT work. **A**, then, is incorrect because it *is* an appropriate alternative. The same is true for both **B** and **C**; all three of those options work when substituted into the sentence. **D**, however, does *not* work, which in this instance actually makes it the correct answer. "Having delivered" is the kind of phrase that would begin a dependent clause, like in this sentence: "The delivery driver, having delivered all of the packages, went home."

#36 The way this is written makes it sound like the steepness of the bridge is the bridge's decision, or that there are circumstances that change whether or not the bridge goes down by one inch from one side to the other. That isn't the case, which is why **F** is incorrect. The previous sentence shifts the verb tense from past tense to present tense (notice how the sentence says, "The Pont du Gard aqueduct *is*..." However, although choice **H** uses the word "is," this tense (called the present progressive) makes it sound like the bridge is in motion, descending an inch like someone "is descending" down a mountain. That is why **H** is incorrect. The difference between **G** and **J** is a matter of subject/verb agreement. "The bridge" is singular, so we need a singular conjugation, which is provided by choice **J**, which is why it is correct. "The bridge descend" does not have subject/verb agreement, which is why **G** is incorrect.

#37 Choices **A** and **B** make it seem like this question is testing the ordering of adjectives before a noun. Sometimes that is important of course. Between those two options, **B** would be better, however, **A** and **B** are incorrect for a different reason: they have the word "noteworthy" in them. For that matter, **C** is incorrect for the same reason. If you keep reading, it says that the feature of the bridge is "worthy of note." Thus, **A, B,** and **C** are all incorrect because they are redundant! **D** is correct because it leaves out the word "noteworthy." Remember: *read all answer choices in the context of an entire sentence!!!*

#38 This is another example of a vocabulary in context question. All of these options look similar, but we need an option that means "layers" or "rows" (which are words used in the next couple of sentences). The only answer then is **G**, because "tiers" means "layers," like the seven tiers on a wedding cake. **F, H,** and **J** are all words with incorrect meanings for this context.

#39 The question here is one of nonessential words and phrases. Does the word "respectively" detour the sentence, or is it a part of the flow? Well, I'll just tell you: it is a detour; it must be set off by commas. Think of the sentence without it: "The lowest and middle rows contain 6 and 11 arches, all of which are over 65 feet in height." Clearly, when you throw the word "respectively" in there, it is a bit of a pit stop or detour. That is why **A** is the correct answer. **D** has no commas at all, even to set off the final dependent clause, which is why it is incorrect. **C** makes it seem like "respectively all of which" is its own nonessential phrase, but that disrupts the final clause of the sentence, which is why it is incorrect. **B** is probably the most tempting incorrect option, but it fails to completely set off the nonessential word "respectively." You may disagree and think, "but a pause isn't necessary there." It isn't about pauses in your mind, it's about a comma's deliberate use. That is why **B** is incorrect.

#40 This is the second time you've seen such a question in the practice passages. Here, it is about the proper placement of the adverb "undoubtedly." Try out each of the choices. Because it is presented as a fact that arches distribute weight and force, the adverb "undoubtedly" before "distribute" is over the top, which is why **F** is incorrect. **H** is incorrect for the exact same reason; it simply places the adverb after distribute instead of before, but it has the same effect on the verb distribute and the sentence as a whole. **J** is incorrect for a bit of a different reason. Putting the adverb "undoubtedly" after "longevity" sounds OK, but it would have to be set off by commas. Thus, **J** is incorrect. **G** is correct because it places the adverb in a place that makes sense for the sentence ("undoubtedly contributed") and doesn't need to be set off by commas.

#41 Here again you have to read the question precisely: which option gives evidence that Roman engineering was brilliant? **A** does not display the brilliance of Roman engineering; stacking blocks up on top of each other is not brilliant engineering. **B** says that the blocks fit together imprecisely; but if blocks are placed imprecisely, that is the opposite of brilliant engineering. **D** starts off well, saying that the blocks could withstand wind and rain "but not the test of time." How can the engineering be brilliant if it can't withstand the test of time? **C** is thus the correct answer; it says that the blocks did not need mortar, which displays a brilliance in engineering.

#42 We need a verb here that is past tense because the action of the sentence is in the past (and the sentence says, "came the end," which is past tense. **G** is present tense, so it is incorrect. **H** is also present tense, so also incorrect. **J** is future tense, so it is incorrect. **F** is correct because it rightly uses the verb "to prove" in the past tense.

#43 What is needed here is an option that helps the reader understand that the Pont du Gard has lasted because it was used as a toll bridge. **B** is incorrect because it implies that the bridge is being used as a toll bridge now; but that is not the case. **C** is incorrect because it does not create even a complete sentence; there is no subject/verb agreement. **D** has the exact same problem; if you read the sentence with "to guarantee" in place, the sentence will make no sense and will be begging for another clause to finish it out. Only choice **A** makes sense; it implies that the bridge was used as a toll bridge and from then to the present day the funds from that use has guaranteed that the bridge was maintained.

#44 **F** is incorrect because, though it is about toll bridges, which are mentioned in the previous sentence, the essay isn't about toll bridges. **G** is incorrect for similar reasons; skilled engineers and maintaining bridges are mentioned in the essay, but that is not a fitting conclusion because that is not what the essay is about. **H** has the problem of shifting to the first person: it uses the pronoun "us," which is not used elsewhere in the entire essay. Not only that, but it posits that the point of the essay was to discuss the Fall of Rome, which it was not. **J** is the only sentence that is explicitly about the Pont du Gard, which is the focus of the essay; this is why **J** is correct.

#45 Here we need to read the sentence and bring its general purpose to the 4 proposed points. The sentence is about the running of water on an aqueduct. Thus, it needs to be placed in a paragraph or among sentences that would be fitting. Choice **A** doesn't work; you might think it would be fine there, but the sentences around it are not about the function of an aqueduct generally. **B** is the correct answer because the sentence before is about how aqueducts carry water. **C** does not work because the sentence prior is about the function of the arch, which is the purpose of that paragraph as a whole. Lastly, **D** is incorrect as well because the paragraph it is in is about stacking blocks; this is also the focus of the sentence before and the sentence after as well.

Answer Explanations - Step 5

Correct Answers:

Passage I	Passage II	Passage III
1: C	**16: G**	**31: B**
2: G	**17: C**	**32: H**
3: A	**18: F**	**33: B**
4: H	**19: A**	**34: J**
5: D	**20: J**	**35: A**
6: F	**21: B**	**36: H**
7: B	**22: J**	**37: D**
8: J	**23: D**	**38: G**
9: B	**24: H**	**39: D**
10: F	**25: B**	**40: H**
11: C	**26: G**	**41: C**
12: G	**27: C**	**42: F**
13: D	**28: G**	**43: B**
14: J	**29: A**	**44: J**
15: A	**30: F**	**45: D**

Passage I: Steve Irwin, Crocodile Hunter

#1 As written, there is nothing grammatically incorrect. However, the sentence is directed to "you"; this is called "Second Person," and thus the pronoun "he" is wrong. This means that **A** and **B** are both incorrect. **D** is incorrect because "does you" does not have subject/verb agreement. This is why **C** is the correct answer; the pronoun is appropriate, and there is subject/verb agreement with "do you."

#2 This is an example of "sentence structure" that was taught in Step 5. As written, there is no problem with the sentence ending with "*Hunter*." But, what comes next is a sentence fragment, in other words, not a sentence that can stand alone. In fact, "Which" is only going to begin a sentence that is a question. This is why **F** is incorrect. **J** is incorrect for the same reason; the semicolon proposes that there are two complete thoughts (independent clauses) being combined, but the second one begins with "which" and is a fragment. **H** is tempting, but this creates two independent clauses, and we can't combine them into one complex sentence with only a comma; we would need a FANBOYS conjunction as well. This is why **G** is the correct answer; it correctly combines an independent clause with a dependent clause via a comma.

#3 Here, you must choose the correct prepositional phrase as was taught in Step 5. This is also an idiom (as was mentioned in Step 4). Do you keep the attention...in the world? No, that is why **B** is incorrect. Do you keep the attention...at the entire world? No, that isn't a phrase either; that is why **C** is also incorrect. **D** works; you keep the attention *of* the world, but it is a bit wordier than choice **A**, which says the same thing. This is why **A** is correct.

#4 Hopefully you can see that "attention from other people" is very wordy compared to "attention." So, let's go ahead and eliminate choice **F** as incorrect for this reason. **G** has a different problem: what is "them"? There is nothing plural in the sentence (or even the sentence prior) that could reasonably be referred to by the pronoun "them," thus **G** is incorrect. That leaves us with two choices: "attention" or "it." What could "it" possibly refer to? It would refer to "the spotlight," which is a synonym for "attention." Tricky? Yes. Subtle? Yes. However, this is why **H** is correct and **J** is incorrect; **J** is technically redundant.

#5 As written, we have a colon after "His philosophy was", but that is not a complete thought. That is our #1 colon rule, so **A** is incorrect. **B** as the exact same problem; what comes before the semicolon is not an independent clause, so it can't have semicolon after it. This is why **B** is incorrect. **C** has the problem of failing to combine two independent clauses in a proper way; if there's a comma, a FANBOYS (for, and, nor, but, or, yet, so) is needed. **D** is the correct answer because there is an independent clause before, thus the colon is appropriate.

#6 Here we need the correct transitional phrase (or "connector word/words") that bridges the two sentences. Actually, according to the question (which is NOT acceptable), we need to identify either three correct ones or the one incorrect one. We know that "Thus" works, because getting rid of it is not an option. "Thus" implies cause and effect, like this: "I'm old. Thus, my hair is turning grey." My hair is turning grey *because of* (cause and effect) being old. **G, H,** and **J** all do this, and are all synonymous with "Thus." This is why **F** is the correct answer (because it is incorrect); "Rather" implies contradiction, but that is not the relationship between the two sentences.

#7 Isolating the word "because" with a comma makes it seem like an introductory word; this is tempting because "his parents were the owners of the Australia Zoo" is an independent clause. However, so is "he had access to them all" later in the sentence. So, we can't keep this sentence as is, and **A** is wrong. **D** turns the sentence into nonsense; "Because they owned of..." makes no sense, so **D** is incorrect. **C** separates the subject ("his parents") from the verb ("were"), and thus it is incorrect. **B** correctly has no commas, ensuring that "Because his parents were the owners of the Australia Zoo" is left as a dependent clause.

#8 Like many sentences proposed by the ACT, this one detracts from the purpose of the paragraph by shifting the focus of the paragraph from Steve Irwin to crocodiles. That is why the answer is "No," and thus **F** and **G** are incorrect. **H** says that "the Australia Zoo never held crocodiles" was "stated earlier in the essay", but that is not true; it never said that. This is why **J** is correct; it rightly notes that the proposed sentence is redundant (it already said that he dealt with crocodiles in the zoo) and, like we said, it notes that the proposed sentence detracts from the paragraph's purpose.

#9 This is a question of verb tense, as was taught in Step 4. It says that Steve "gained," so we need a past tense verb to match to that subject. This is why **B** is the correct answer. **A** is wrong because it is present tense; **C** is wrong because it is the plural conjugation (like, "They share"). **D** is incorrect because "Steve...and to share" is nonsensical.

#10 Here you have to choose the correct prepositional phrase. Do you commit to, at, for, or from a cause? You commit *to* something, and even though the other answers have problems beyond this first word, that is why **G, H,** and **J** are all incorrect. **F** is correct because you commit *to* something.

#11 First, let's deal with **D**. This is why underlined portions must be read in the context of the entire sentence. "...that generated..." is a phrase that could occur in many sentences. However, in this circumstance, if the underlined portion were eliminated, we would have no subject to link with the verb "generated"; in other words, we'd be left wondering, "What was generated?" Thus, **D** is incorrect. As for the other options, they are all grammatically correct and synonymous; the tiebreaker is the *best* answer, and the best answer here is the least wordy one: that is why **C** is the correct answer and by **B** and **A** are incorrect.

#12 The sentence is in the past tense, so eliminate options that are not. This includes option **H** (incorrect since it is in the present tense) and option **J** (incorrect because it is in the future tense). Does it make sense to say, "The funds funneled were they?" Unless you are Yoda, that doesn't make any sense; the ordering of the words is backwards (and the pronoun "they" is thrown in there). That is why **F** is incorrect. **G** is correct because it has subject/verb agreement in the proper tense (and it makes sense!).

#13 As written, what is *trying* to be communicated is clear, which is why many will put **A** as the correct answer. However, remember the teaching about modifying clauses from Step 5: whatever comes after the comma is what is being modified. In this case (as written), the sentence says that "the search" (after the comma) is the one who heard "a message come through the radio." Searches can't hear messages, which is why **A** is incorrect. **B** is also incorrect; "A message hearing come through the radio" is nonsensical and ought to sound funny. **C** is tempting, but notice that the first two clauses in the sentence ("The crew heard a message" and "it came through the radio") are both independent clauses; the fact that they are separated by a comma makes the sentence grammatically incorrect; thus **C** is incorrect. That leaves **D**, which is correct because it properly combines two independent clauses (comma and "and," one of the FANBOYS conjunctions) and communicates the proper message as well.

#14 If we strip away the punctuation, we are left with two independent clauses in this long sentence. They are: "Steve lost his life at the young age of 54" and "he was pierced by a stingray barb." As written, the punctuation does not account for this (there is no comma/FANBOYS, semicolon, colon, em dash), so **F** is incorrect. While we are thinking like that, **G** is incorrect for the exact same reason. **H** and **J** both make two sentences of the material, but which is best? Choice **H** puts a comma after "filming," which makes "In 2006 filming" into an introductory phrase, but that doesn't work because it unnecessarily separates those three words from the prepositional phrase "around the Great Barrier Reef." That is why **J** is correct; this option actually creates two independent clauses in the second sentence, which works because there is a ", and" after "Barrier Reef."

#15 At first, **A** seems like it could not be the correct answer because it begins with the word "You." However, that isn't a disqualifier because the entire essay is written to "You." In fact, the first paragraph proves this and contains "You" statements. The sentence for **A** mention's Steve's legacy and the Australia Zoo. This is the correct answer! **B** is about conservation, but that's not really the focus of the essay even though is it mentioned as important to Steve Irwin. **C** is incorrect because the essay isn't about crocodiles and their appeal to children. **D** is incorrect because, like the other choices, just because the sentence mentions something that is also mentioned in the essay (in this case, the Great Barrier Reef), that doesn't mean it is the best sentence.

Passage II: The Theory of Beauty

#16 In the preceding sentence, the author mentions seeing sunsets in a unique way. She is trying to make the same point about "the forest, a stream, or the night sky" too. The choice that effectively makes this point is **G**, making the previous sentence "true of" those things as well. The other choices might not have grammatical problems all, but should *sound* strange. Is she seeing sunsets "within the forest", etc.? No, which is why **F** is incorrect. When she sees sunsets, does she "become the forest", etc.? No, which is why **H** is incorrect. Saying that this is "only about" the forest, etc. is a contradiction; we just said it's true about sunsets in the first sentence; that is shy **J** is incorrect.

#17 Here, "on the other hand" is a nonessential phrase. If it was to be removed, the sentence would flow perfectly well: "I have trained myself...". This is why it has to be set off with commas. Only answer choice **C** does this. **B** ignores that it is nonessential by failing to have any commas. **A** makes "I on the other hand" into an introductory phrase, but that is problematic because it separates the subject "I" from "have" as part of its own dependent clause; that doesn't work here. **D** either makes "I" into an introductory phrase or begins to set off the entire middle of the sentence as nonessential; neither works.

#18 This is a question of subject/verb agreement. In this case, the subject is "it", which is singular. **J** is incorrect because "have" is the plural conjugation. **H** is incorrect because it is in the future tense. This means that you have to determine if the correct spelling is "has led" or "has lead." "To lead" is a verb, but also "lead" is a heavy mineral. When conjugated in the past singular, you would say "led," like, "I led the team to victory." That is why the correct answer is **F**. **G** misspells the word "led."

#19 In this case, you must have a grip on the general topic of the paragraph to ensure that you get the question correct. Reading on, you should see some sentences about colors intermixing and things like that (as a side note, it is also appropriate to leave this question for now and return after reading through the paragraph and answering any questions you encounter). This is why **A** is the correct answer; the phrase as written brings up the ideas of beauty and color. **B** is incorrect because the paragraph is not about recognizing beauty in other people; **C** is incorrect because the paragraph is not about the history of film or light use in those films; **D** is incorrect because the paragraph is not about how different people like herself have come to be interested in the topic of art (besides, we already learned that in the first paragraph, which makes this choice a bit redundant as well).

#20 Here we have another instance of setting off nonessential words or phrases which, again, is the #1 tested comma usage on recent ACT's. Here, we have an independent clause that is ended with a comma, then a FANBOYS conjunction is present ("but"). This signals the beginning of another independent clause. Looking, we see that "Others appear ugly or detestable" is also an independent clause. Off the bat we can thus eliminate **H** as incorrect because there is no comma before the "but," which would be necessary since we are combining multiple independent clauses. The key to the question is recognizing that the word "however" is nonessential. **F** fails to set off this word with commas, so it is incorrect. **G** sets off "however," but it also sets off the word "others," but "others" is not a nonessential word. That is why **J** is correct; it sets off "however" as nonessential and has the comma+FANBOYS to separate the two independent clauses.

#21 **C** is incorrect because the word "which" must be set off by a comma. Even if you couldn't see that, however, there is another reason why **C, D,** and **A** are all incorrect: they are redundant. The sentence just said that grey and black are in a *swirl*, which means already that the two colors are intermixing or mixed up. This is why the correct answer is **B**.

#22 This is a question that tests your ability to use the correct pronoun and conjugate the verb correctly. Because the sentence is in the present tense ("if one adds" and "inclinations change"), we need a verb in the present tense. This eliminates choices **G** and **H**; they are in the past tense, so are both incorrect. Now it comes down to pronoun use. Most students will get this question incorrect because they will quickly bubble in **F**, but that is incorrect. The reason for this is because of the correct pronoun that is needed. Remember, a pronoun refers to something or someone that is established in the greater context. The question is: what should the pronoun refer to? Not "inclinations", but *beholder*. That is singular, and "they" is plural, which is why **F** is wrong. **J** correctly uses the singular "he or she" to refer to the singular "beholder."

#23 We need the correct combination of words that will perfectly communicate that it is interesting that "preferences in aesthetics go beyond colors." **A** is incorrect because the colon does not follow a complete thought, which is our #1 colon rule. **B** is incorrect because it artificially inserts a comma after "preferences," which in the sentence creates an introductory phrase that turns the rest of the sentence into nonsense ("in aesthetics go far beyond colors and appear to be universal" is not an independent clause or complete thought). **C** has the problem of failing to set off the word "interestingly." It could go here, but it is nonessential in that case, and would need to be set off by commas. **D** is thus the correct answer; it properly sets off "Interestingly" as an introductory word, separated from the independent clause that is the rest of the sentence.

#24 This is a matter of choosing the correct prepositional phrase. Is a building built "of right angles"? Unless right angles are the same thing as bricks and mortar, no. Thus, **G** is incorrect. Is a building built "in right angles"? Unless it is literally built inside of right angles somehow, then no, that is not what is trying to be said; thus, **F** is incorrect. Is a building built "for right angles"? Unless the right angles are paying for the buildings and are the new owners, then no; thus, **J** is incorrect. That leaves **H**, which correctly says that the buildings are built at 90 degree angles, meaning their shapes are rectangles and squares.

#25 Here, a FANBOYS conjunction is underlined, and it just so happens that this conjunction comes after a comma. That means that what comes next must be an independent clause. **A** and **C** can both be eliminated on this ground; what comes after the comma is not a complete thought. As for **B** and **D**, the difference between them is what we called in Step 5 a transition; the question is which of the two is better in this context: "for" or "but." "For" implies cause and effect, but that is not the relationship between the two clauses. This is why **D** is incorrect. **B** is thus correct because it adds the pronoun "they" to create an independent clause and correctly uses the conjunction "but."

#26 As written, what comes after "art." is an incomplete thought or, you might say, a sentence fragment. That is why **F** is incorrect. **J** is also incorrect; it isn't the art that is intense, but the way in which the art was studied. **H** has the problem of separating the prepositional phrases that are a part of the flow of the sentence away from the rest of the sentence. If the phrase "with intensity and interest over the course of a lifetime" came at the beginning of the sentence, that could work if it were set off by a comma. This is why **G** is the correct answer; it is the only choice that does not interrupt the sentence or change the author's intention.

#27 Again, which prepositional phrase is proper in context? "Under construction" is a phrase to describe a building, not how someone consults; this is why **D** is incorrect. **B** is silly; did she consult "on top of" all of the construction (as if there's a bunch of rubble and rebar sticking from concrete and she is standing on top of it all wearing a hardhat)? No. **A** is similar; it makes it sound like she is over it all in a helicopter. This is why **C** is correct; it rightly identifies that she was a consultant in (of you could say "for") the construction.

#28 This is a question of verbosity; all of the answer choices say the same thing, but **F, H,** and **J** are too wordy. This is why the correct answer is **G**; it says what the sentence needs in the fewest words possible.

#29 This is a question of not only pronoun use, but you might say "sentence structure," or identifying that some words or phrases create nonsense. **B** and **D** are not grammatically incorrect, but they oddly shift the point of view of the essay to third person (he, she, them, they); but the entirety of the essay so far is in the first person. **C** creates nonsense; what must follow "although every" has to be singular (like, "although every apple..."), but here "human beings" is plural. This is why **A** is the correct answer; it uses a pronoun that is in the first person ("we") and maintains the structure of the sentence (it doesn't create nonsense).

#30 Hopefully you can identify if the answer here is "Yes" or "No" before reading through the choices. If not, it is OK to circle a question of this type and come back to it when you are finished with the entire English test. Here, the question asks if the essay is a personal account of the theories of art and beauty and how they are fascinating. Well, yep, that is exactly what the essay is about. We can thus eliminate **H** and **J** as incorrect. **G** says that the essay is not an essay, but a letter. However, the ACT will never give you a letter, but always an essay. Even if you flip back, you'll see no "Dear Sally" to begin the essay. That is why the answer is **F**; it correctly says that the essay is in the first person (thus it is a personal account) and has examples of why art and beauty are fascinating topics of study.

Passage III: An Inventor's Childhood

#31 The proposed sentence, it seems, can't be immediately dismissed. It mentions "him", which references Alexander Graham Bell (who was brought up in the first sentence), and it mentions the "triumphant invention", which references the invention of the telephone. The question is: does the rest of the paragraph have to do with his upbringing? That is the shift that is taking place in the sentence. Looking ahead, the next sentence mentions "three aspects of his childhood," so we can conclude rightfully that the answer is "Yes," this sentence belongs. That eliminates **C** and **D** as incorrect. **A** says that Alexander invented the telephone as a child, and that this fact is stated later in the paragraph. Reading ahead, there is no mention of this in the paragraph; this is why **A** is incorrect. **B** rightfully said that the subject of the essay is shifted from Bell to his childhood.

#32 This is an example of a transition or transitional phrase; we need the best choice to bridge thoughts between sentences based on context. As written, it proposes no such transition is needed. That could be best, but we have to keep reading ahead a bit to figure it out. The next sentence begins with "Second." That is the only clue you need to determine that **H** is the correct answer. **G** and **J** unnecessarily use a transition that creates contrast, but that is not what the context calls for. **F** would work if the following sentence (instead of saying, "Second,") said, "Then, his parents..." or "Not to mention, his parents...", but it doesn't. That is why **F** is incorrect.

#33 As written, there is something nonsensical about this. Shouldn't it say, "...his curiosities and *the* inventing spirit inside of him"? Yes, it should; that is why we can eliminate choice **A** as incorrect. The rest of the answer choices all say the same thing. The problem is that **C** and **D** are not only too wordy, but also redundant (can his "inventing spirit" be somewhere besides inside him or in his spirit?). That is why the answer is **B**: it is the least wordy and has no redundancies.

#34 This, as written, is a run-on sentence. We're trying here to combine two independent clauses, so **F** is incorrect because it fails to do so correctly. The other options contain punctuation that permits combining these clauses: the semicolon, the colon, and the em dash. The correct answer hinges on this word "rather." First, that word makes no sense as a concluding word to the first independent clause ("...he had a natural genius that he refused to squander rather"); this is why we can go ahead and eliminate **G** as incorrect. Let's isolate the second clause and begin it with that word: "Rather, he used it for good." That word must be set off by a comma; it is nonessential and as a transition or "connector word" needs the comma. That is why **H** is incorrect; there is no comma. **J** is correct because it uses a semicolon properly and correctly sets off the introductory word "rather" with a comma.

#35 This is a classic question of verbosity (too many words). All of the options mean the same thing, but **B, C,** and **D** are all incorrect because they are too wordy compared to the less-wordy correct answer: **A**.

#36 "Even so" implies contradiction between two sentences. For example, I might say, "I hate cartoons. Even so, I am willing to watch them with my children." While we're at it, "On the other hand" and "Be that as it may" are transitional phrases that do this exact same thing to a pair of sentences: imply contradiction. "I hate cartoons. On the other hand (or Be that as it may), I'm willing to watch them with my children" works. That is why **F, G,** and **J** are all incorrect. The sentence needs to begin with a transitional phrase that implies cause and effect (he was curious about human speaking (cause) and he developed voice talents (effect)). This is why **H** is correct; it rightly unites the two sentences.

#37 If you read the two sentences that are being united here, which begin a few lines before with #36, it is clearly two independent clauses (complete sentences or complete thoughts, in other words). Punctuation has to be used here to correctly combine them. **B** and **C** fail to do this; these two options simply let the sentence run on and on with commas (and no FANBOYS conjunctions), so they are incorrect. The problem with **A**, which is why it is incorrect, is that it misplaces the phrase "in addition;" that phrase is supposed to be a transitional phrase between the two sentences. In its current location, it is not only awkward, but redundant (it has the same effect on the sentence that the word "and" does earlier in the sentence). That is why **D** is correct; it rightly deals with two independent clauses by ending one with a period and beginning the second, and it rightly places the transitional phrase "In addition" at the beginning of the second sentence.

#38 Here, you must identify the proper prepositional phrase. You must rely on your *listening skills*, and by that I mean this: don't some of these simply sound awkward or nonsensical? If so, you have good instincts because you have been (presumably, though not true for everyone) listening to English your entire life. **J** is incorrect; it could be an option if the word "all" was not a part of it, but it is. **H** is a jumble of nonsense; it's incorrect. **F** is incorrect as well; have you ever heard someone say, "I'm destined of working over a hospital to help save lives." No, and for good reason; it makes no sense. That is why the correct answer is **G**; it rightly uses the verb "to work" and correctly uses the proposition "within" before "the realm."

#39 As written, the verb is conjugated in the present tense, but the rest of the sentence is in the past tense ("encouraged"). So **A** is incorrect for this reason. If the phrase "to tinker" wasn't squeezed in there, we could identify this as the combination of two independent clauses. But, that's not what his happening here; the phrase "to tinker" *is* there, and it follows "to invent." Those two verbs are part of a sequence, and the underlined portion is the third verb to be listed in this sequence. That is why **D** is correct. **B** and **C** are incorrect because we don't need to begin a new independent clause here; doing so fails to complete the sequence of verbs set off by commas.

#40 As written, this sentence is nonsense; you can't say "by gathering and use"; it would have to say, "by gathering and using." **F** and **G** both use "gathering," so they can be eliminated as incorrect. As for **J**, it is equally nonsensical. "...for to be commonly gather" is not a phrase you will ever hear because it simply makes no sense. For starters, if it were to make sense, it would have to say "for to be commonly gathered." Only answer choice **H** correctly ends the first independent clause with a semicolon, then properly begins the second independent clause.

#41 Step 5 taught you about modifying clauses and that they modify (change, alter, identify, describe) the word, noun, or subject that immediately follows the comma. As written, it makes it sound like "a flour mill" (it immediately follows the comma) grew up in Scotland...um, no. This is why **A** is incorrect. The other wrong answers are all wrong for this same reason: the modifying clause modifies the wrong subject. **B**, for example, makes it sound like Alexander ran the flour mill, but that is not true, which is why **B** is incorrect. **D** is also incorrect; this choice makes it sound like the flour mill was Alexander's neighbor, but the sentence is clearly trying to say that the Herdman family were the neighbors, and that they ran the mill. Only choice **C** has a modifying clause that works properly: it correctly says that Alexander was growing up in Scotland.

#42 The subject that should agree with the verb here is "a dehusking device," which is singular. This makes **G** incorrect because it uses the verb "were," which is plural. **H** is incorrect because it doesn't even conjugate the verb "to be," thus it is nonsensical and overly wordy. **J** is singular ("was"), but says that the deshusking device was using the family. Besides sounding like something out of a cheaply made horror movie, it is not what the sentence is trying to imply. Only choice **F** correctly conjugates the verb and states that the family used Alexander's dehusking invention.

#43 In this sentence, the independent clause is "he mastered the piano when he was a child." Everything else is nonessential or, according to the analogy used earlier in the book, a pitstop that slows the car. That is how we know that **A** is incorrect. Maybe you think to yourself, "I don't need to pause as I read this sentence," but remember that commas in ACT English have *deliberate use*, to set off nonessential and introductory words and phrases (among other things). **C** is also incorrect: it can be eliminated because there is not a complete thought before the colon. **D** is incorrect because of the location of the phrase "in fact." In this context, this phrase is a transition; it unites the previous sentence to the present one by helping the reader see the cause and effect nature of the two sentences. That is why **B** is correct; it positions the transitional phrase "In fact" in the proper place, and it correctly sets off "with no training" as a nonessential clause.

#44 Whose genius? As written, the pronoun "her" makes it sound like Alexander applies his mother's genius. His mother might have been a genius, who knows, but the sentence is clearly trying to imply that Alexander's genius is that which is being applied. This is why **F** is incorrect. **H** is wrong for the same reason. **G** has the problem of being plural, but we need a singular pronoun. This is why **J** is correct; the pronoun "his" matches with Alexander and is singular.

#45 The opening paragraph is about Alexander being the inventor of the telephone and about his childhood. **A** is about children, but not Alexander Graham Bell, so it is incorrect. **B** is about families and Alexander's ability to play the piano, but that in no way links to the first paragraph (and isn't a good way to end the essay as whole anyway). **C** links with a story earlier in the essay, but makes a claim that is not supported by the essay: Alexander's invention of the dehusking device didn't *cause* him to invent the telephone, so **C** is also incorrect. If there way any doubt about **C**, then **D** should help you get through the weeds. **D** is correct because it straightforwardly mentions Alexander's invention of the telephone. It also uses the transition "As a consequence," which fittingly ends the essay because the previous sentence is a summary of one of the essay's main points.

Answer Explanations - Step 6

Correct Answers:

Passage I
1: C
2: F
3: D
4: H
5: A
6: H
7: D
8: G
9: C
10: J
11: A
12: J
13: C
14: G
15: B

Passage II
16: H
17: D
18: F
19: B
20: J
21: A
22: G
23: B
24: F
25: D
26: H
27: A
28: G
29: A
30: J

Passage I: Mammoth Cave

#1 In this sentence, "located in Kentucky" is a nonessential phrase. It is sandwiched in there between the subject, "Mammoth Cave," and the verb, "is." Thus, it must be set off by commas. Only answer **C** does this, which is why it is correct. **A** has no commas setting it off, which is why it is incorrect. **B** creates a new nonessential phrase ("where it is located"), but that isn't set off by commas either, which is why it is incorrect. Lastly, **D** sets off the preposition "in Kentucky," but the clause as a whole begins with "located," which also must be set off as a part of it; that is why **D** is incorrect.

#2 First, we can eliminate **J** because what must follow "is able" must be "to match," not "to matches;" that's nonsense, so **J** is incorrect. **G** and **H** make the same mistake: they use "it's." Remember, "it's" is a contraction meaning "it is," but that doesn't make sense in either answer choice. That is why **F** is correct; it rightly uses "its", which is possessive: the cave *possesses* a massive size, which is what the sentence is trying to communicate.

#3 This is a question of subject/verb agreement. What is it that "estimate" or "estimates"? It is "Researchers," which is plural. That eliminates **A** and **C**, both of which conjugate the verb to match a singular subject (you can't say, "Researchers estimates..."). **B** inserts two commas, setting off "the total length" as a nonessential clause or phrase. But that is not the case; the commas are unnecessary. You can tell this because take out "the total length" from the sentence and see what happens: it turns into nonsense. The phrase is necessary, and thus the correct answer is **D**: it treats "the total length" as an essential phrase and has subject/verb agreement.

#4 This question is a combination of Step 6 subjects! First, because we are dealing with a distance, we need *farther*, not *further*. This eliminates **F** and **G**. Second, because we are dealing with a comparison (and not a matter of time), we need *than*, not *then*. That eliminates **J**. That is why the correct answer is **H**; it correctly uses "farther" and "than."

#5 First, because we are dealing with only one distance, we can eliminate any option that uses the plural "distances." This is why **B** and **D** are incorrect. Remember, *between* is used when referencing two objects/spaces/things, and *among* when referencing more than two. This is why *between* is correct here: Boston and Atlanta are *two* cities. Thus, **C** is incorrect because it uses "among," and **A** is correct because it uses the word "between."

#6 Although Mammoth Cave is probably made up of multiple *caves*, it is the singular "Mammoth Cave" that the word "cave" is referencing. This is why **F** and **G** are incorrect; they put the apostrophe after the letter "s," which indicates that the passages are the possession of multiple caves. Option **J** artificially adds a comma after the word "cave's", which is incorrect; that does not need to be set off. This is why **H** is correct; it rightly denotes possession by the singular "cave" and only sets off the word "However" with a comma to start the sentence.

#7 First, we are dealing with the past tense, so we can eliminate any option that uses the present tense "become"; thus, **A** and **B** are incorrect. That leaves a question of less vs fewer. Remember that *fewer* is used when what it references can be numbered or counted (or you might say, exist as individuals). What is being referenced in this case is "cracks," which *can* be numbered or counted, or which do exist individually. This is why **D** is correct; it rightly uses "fewer." **C** uses "less," which is reserved to refer to something that can't be numbered, or which can't exist individually (like "air," "water," "love," etc.).

#8 This is a question of sentence structure. Remember to read the entirety of both sentences that this line overlaps. If you read only the underlined portion, "as the water moved through" might sound like a fine phrase to end a sentence with (like, "During the hurricane, I got scared in the house as the water moved through."). However, in this case, the water is moving through *the limestone*, so we can't separate the two. This eliminates **F** and **J** as they both insert periods after "through". As for **H**, it separates off "the limestone" from the preposition "through." This is unnecessary and disruptive, so **H** is incorrect. That leaves **G**, the correct answer, which rightly sets off "as the water moved through the limestone" from the independent clause "it actively dissolved minerals in the rock" with a comma.

#9 As written, this is redundant. We don't need to say "they were now big enough" because the sentence already states that they were "large enough." That is why **A** is incorrect. **D** has a similar problem; it says "over time," but that idea is already implied by the first word in the sentence: "Eventually". Thus, **D** is incorrect because it is redundant. **B** has a couple of problems; first, it again says that these are something "large," which is redundant; second, it is overly wordy when compared to **C**. **C** is correct because if the sentence is ended with the word "into," it is already implied that what is being entered into is the cracks that are now large enough.

#10 This is a question of who vs whom, to start. Remember the rule: rephrase the clause with "he" or "him". Here, we could say, "Was *he* the first to discover the cave?" or "Was *him* the first to discover the cave?" Putting "him" there makes no sense; it would be "he." That means that the sentence calls for *who*, not *whom*. This eliminates **F** and **H** as incorrect. The other thing to consider in this question is verb tense. In this case, we are dealing in the past tense. That means that the correct answer is **J**, which uses the past tense "were." **G** is incorrect because it uses the present tense "are."

#11 Here, the subject of the sentence is "tribes," so the verb "to use" will need a plural conjugation. This eliminates **B** and **D**, both of which have subject/verb agreement problems. **C** has a pronoun error; it says "them", but the pronoun that follows "used" is referring to something singular ("the cave" from the previous sentence), not something plural (even though "the elements" is in the previous sentence, that is not what is being referenced here; that is not what is being "used" in the sentence). That is why **A** is correct; it rightly has subject/verb agreement and uses the singular pronoun "it" to refer to "the cave."

#12 "They're" is a contraction representing "they are." Because "some of they are possessions" makes no sense, we can eliminate **F** as incorrect. Similar nonsense is the result when you consider choice **G**: "some of them possessions" makes no sense. What the sentence is trying to say is that the possessions were, well, *possessed* by the Native Americans; that is why the correct answer is **J**, because "their" is possessive. As for **H**, it is incorrect because "there" as reference to a place makes no sense coming before the word "possessions."

#13 First we can eliminate choices **A** and **B** because they are in the future tense and the sentence calls for past tense. Now it is simply a question of lie vs lay. Remember, "lie" is something a subject does *to itself* ("My dog will lie down (you could say, *lie itself down*) in its crate when it is tired"). Here, the body is being put down *by something/someone else*. That is why "lay" is needed (as in "I lay the dog down in the crate at night"). This means **D** is incorrect because it uses "lie;" **C** is correct because it rightly uses "lay."

#14 If you read the following sentence (the one about how surveyors have made huge leaps in understanding), it becomes clear that the sentence being referenced by the question belongs. This is because the next sentence has a little word in it: "however." This word contrasts with something, but it's not Mammoth Cave becoming a national park (sentence 1) that it contrasts with. When the sentence is inserted, it suddenly makes sense that the "huge leaps in understanding" contrasts with "only 40 miles of passageway" that at the time had been mapped out. This eliminates choices **H** and **J**. **F** says that the sentence should be kept because it is necessary to know that Mammoth Cave is the world's largest; however, that's not true, we already know that with or without the proposed sentence (see the first sentence of the essay!). This is why **G** is correct; it rightly notes that research has come a long way since 1941 by giving a number of miles that had, at the time, been mapped: 40.

#15 The proposed sentence has to do with water flowing through cracks. Hopefully that rings a bell: wasn't there a paragraph about water flowing through limestone? Even if you can't remember that, placing the sentence one at a time should help you. Choice **A** makes no sense because paragraph 1 is entirely about the large size of Mammoth Cave and mentions nothing about water. Choice **C** also makes no sense because paragraph 3 is about the use of the cave by Native Americans and also mentions nothing about water. **D** is also incorrect because the last paragraph, paragraph 4, mentions nothing about water flowing over rocks and is more about the cave's overall recent history. This is why **B** is the correct answer: paragraph 2 is all about how the caves were formed when water flowed through the cracks in the limestone.

Passage II: Nikola Tesla

#16 This kind of jumble of words and verb tenses is exactly what the ACT English section likes to throw at you. Try one at a time and trust your *listening judgment*; some should, hopefully, *sound* like nonsense. **F** says, "as if Nikola Tesla," but when read in the context of the sentence, it makes you want to ask, "as if Nikola Tesla...what?" It feels incomplete because the phrase "as if" is always followed by a complete thought, like "as if Nikola Tesla really cared." **G** should sound funny because the verb "have" is a plural conjugation, so there is no subject/verb agreement; we need singular because "Nikola Tesla" is singular. **H** is correct because it rightly does this. **J** is a nonsense jumble of words; it makes it sound like other inventors tried to be like Nikola Tesla, but that is not the purpose of the sentence.

#17 You should recognize that the phrase "overall more work" makes no sense. Maybe in some contexts you could have it look like this: "Overall, more work...", or like this: "Overall, work...". This is why **A** is incorrect. **B** is also incorrect because the sentence calls for the word "work" to be used as a noun (it is the object of the verb "indicates"), not as a verb, but **B** turns it into a verb (that, even still, doesn't make sense). This leaves you to discern if we need "good" or "well" to describe "work." "Well," though, is an adverb, and would be proper if we needed to describe the verb "to work" (as in, "I worked well on the yard today"). But, as we said, "work" here is a noun, so what is needed is an adjective: "good." This is why **D** is correct and **C** is incorrect.

#18 All four of these choices have modifying clauses. **G** says that "science and technological pursuits" were dedicated, but it is Tesla who is supposed to be described that way, so **G** is incorrect. **H** says that "technological pursuits" are "a scientist" (because they follow the comma), so it is incorrect. **J** says that "pursuits" had a career in science, so it is incorrect. **F** is the only option that correctly uses a modifying clause; it rightly modifies "Tesla" (after the comma) with the clause "Throughout his life".

#19 At first, it seems like nothing is wrong with the way this is written. But, to be technical, the FANBOYS conjunction "so" is not the *best choice* here. Why? Because "so" implies cause and effect. Did Tesla's humble beginnings cause his mother to run the farm? No; both of them probably have the same cause. This is why **B** is correct; it combines these two independent clauses in the *best* way. **C** is incorrect for a couple of reasons, but the primary reason is because it uses the pronoun "she," but there is no woman yet identified that the pronoun can refer to (who is "she"?). **D** is incorrect because, although it uses the FANBOYS conjunction "and," there is no comma after the word "beginnings."

#20 In Step 6, I introduced you to the idea that, actually, semicolons technically have a second use. The odds of you needing to know that semicolons are used to combine independent clauses on ACT English? 100%. The odds of you needing to know that semicolons can be used like commas in a series? Closer to 0% than 1%, which is why this is the only question in this book that tests your knowledge of it. All you need to remember, though, is that if semicolons are being used in a series, you can't replace one of them with a comma or some other punctuation; you have to be consistent. This is why **J** is the correct answer; the series already uses semicolons, so it must be finished that way. **F, G,** and **H** all use commas after "Graz," but like we said, it must be a semicolon because a semicolon is used to begin the setting off of the list of three clauses earlier in the sentence (after the word "student").

#21 The paragraph that precedes this possible sentence placement begins to tell a story about how Edison undervalued Tesla. Then, it says that Edison offered Tesla $50,000...doesn't sound like he's being undervalued to me! This is why the sentence does, indeed, belong. Choices **C** and **D** can be eliminated for this reason. Of the other two options, **B** is incorrect because it seems to say that the essay (or maybe the paragraph) is about American humor, but that's not true. **A** is correct because, without the sentence, there is no way to understand how Tesla was undervalued.

#22 This is strictly a question of apostrophe use. Two people are possessing something, but the thing that is possessed (in this case, "rivalry") is possessed by the both of them. If we were to leave the sentence as it's written, it means that Tesla had a rivalry, and then Edison had a rivalry as well that he didn't share with Tesla. But that's not the case, which is why **F** is incorrect. **J** can be eliminated because there are no apostrophes to denote possession. **H** is incorrect because it pluralizes "Tesla" and "Edison" as if there were multiple of both, like a family feud. That is why the answer is **G**; because only "Edison" contains the apostrophe and then the s, what is signified is that the pair shared a rivalry, which is what the sentence is attempting to say.

#23 Is there a kind of rivalry that two people can have that's not "against each other"? No, which means that **A** is redundant and incorrect. **C** is incorrect for the same reason; the clause in the commas simply restates what is already stated about the pair being rivals. **D** replaces the word "rivalry" with a definition of rivalry; of course this isn't grammatically incorrect, nor is it redundant, but it is *verbose* (too wordy). That is why the answer is **B**; everything that is needed be said is summed up in the word "rivalry."

#24 Even if you don't know what a "magnate" is, hopefully you can eliminate the other answer choices. **G** is incorrect because I don't think Tesla is partnering with a magnet. **H** and **J** are incorrect for the same reason: Tesla wouldn't be partnering with a "manage" or the color magenta either. Because a magnate is a wealthy business person, that is the word that fits; thus, **F** is the correct answer.

#25 Remember our who vs whom rule (restate the clause with *he* or *him*): did *he* see Tesla's potential, or did *him* see Tesla's potential? *He* makes sense there, so "who" is the word we are looking for. That eliminates **A** and **B**, both of which use "whom." **C** puts the pronoun "he" before "saw," but we don't need that pronoun; we already know that it is Westinghouse "who saw" the potential. That is why **D** is correct: it correctly uses "who" in place of "whom" and does not unnecessarily insert a pronoun.

#26 The question says that the correct phrase will show that the inventions have "had a lasting effect." This is why **H** is correct; it is the only option that says that derivatives of his inventions are still being used today. **F, G,** and **J** make no mention of this, which is why they are all incorrect. **G** makes mention of the inventions being used for a time, but then they were "phased out," which contradicts the requirement that the inventions have a *lasting effect*.

#27 If **C** were to be correct, there would need to be some kind of clause after the comma; either that or the sentence would need an overall change to make it make sense. **B** is incorrect because it wrongly replaces the preposition "to" with "too." As I just said, "to" here is being used to start a prepositional phrase. **D**, though still a prepositional phrase, strangely puts in the word "the" before homes; this has the effect of *specifying* certain homes and businesses, but this is meant to be a general statement. For that reason, **A** is correct in that "to" is used as a preposition and creates a phrase that remains general.

#28 Each of these four options has the pronoun "he" or "they." The first thing to do is to figure out which of those is proper. What, exactly, is this pronoun supposed to refer to? Though it may be tempting, the answer to that question is not *eccentricities*, but rather "Tesla"; *he* is the one having a difficult time finding funding. This eliminates **F** and **H** as incorrect. **J** would only work if "having found it..." were the beginning of a nonessential phrase set off by commas, but neither of those things is true here. That is why **G** is correct; it uses the correct pronoun "he" to replace "Tesla" and it uses the correct verb tense.

#29 "One thing is for sure" is an independent clause, and so is the clause that comes next: "Nikola Tesla was one of the foremost brilliant people of his day and age." What is needed is a proper way to combine two independent clauses. We can thus eliminate choices **C** and **D** as neither does so. Although **B** has a comma plus a FANBOYS conjunction, there is another problem: have you ever heard anyone say, "One thing is to be for sure"? While there is nothing incorrect here grammatically speaking, it changes the *idiom* (remember, a group of words that always goes together?) "On thing is for sure." Thus, **B** is incorrect. **A** is correct because it keeps the idiom correct (and less wordy) and it properly combines independent clauses.

#30 All four of these options are synonyms; they all say the exact same thing. None of them is *grammatically* superior to any other. Simply, **F, G,** and **J** are too wordy. That is why **J** is the correct answer.

Answer Explanations - Step 7 - Practice Test #1

Correct Answers:

Passage I	Passage II	Passage III	Passage IV	Passage V
1: C	16: F	31: A	46: G	61: B
2: F	17: B	32: J	47: A	62: F
3: D	18: J	33: C	48: G	63: A
4: J	19: C	34: J	49: B	64: F
5: A	20: F	35: A	50: G	65: D
6: H	21: A	36: H	51: B	66: H
7: D	22: H	37: A	52: J	67: D
8: J	23: A	38: F	53: D	68: G
9: B	24: F	39: B	54: H	69: A
10: H	25: C	40: J	55: B	70: G
11: B	26: G	41: C	56: F	71: C
12: J	27: C	42: H	57: C	72: J
13: C	28: H	43: C	58: H	73: D
14: G	29: D	44: G	59: B	74: F
15: D	30: G	45: A	60: G	75: C

Passage I: Fallingwater

#1 This is a question of verb tense and subject verb agreement. Because the sentence is in the present tense ("Most would agree"), we need a verb in the present that fits with the subject ("boulder," singular). **B** can be eliminated because it is in the past tense. **A** and **D** can also both be eliminated because they are conjugated to fit with a plural subject; in other words, they would work if "boulders" were bulging through the floor, but not "boulder." That is why the correct answer is **C**; "is" is both singular and present tense.

#2 This is a comma question of setting off a nonessential clause. Remember that a nonessential clause can be spied by it being lifted from the sentence. Here, we can see that the main clause of the sentence (or independent clause or main thought you might say) is this: "there is very little practical use for a large rock." The large nonessential clause in the middle is just that: one (not two) large clause. That is why it must be set off by commas, and why **F** is the correct answer. **G** is incorrect because it never sets off the phrase with a comma. **H** is incorrect because it wrongly creates a nonessential clause within a nonessential clause. **J** is incorrect because it it also fails to set off the nonessential clause at the correct place.

#3 Due to the wordiness of the words underlined and before this, it seems like commas would be a good idea, but they are not. I know that "famous American architect Frank Lloyd Wright" is pretty wordy. However, there is no need for commas here. "Famous American architect" is essentially one large adjective describing the one person "Frank Lloyd Wright." Thus, **D** is the correct answer. **B** sets off Wright's name as if it is a nonessential phrase, but that is incorrect. **C** is incorrect because it artificially inserts a semicolon into the sentence, but that would only work if we were linking two independent clauses. **A** separates "for the famous American architect Frank Lloyd Wright" off as its own nonessential clause, which would be OK if it weren't for "and his client Edgar Kauffman" that follows, because those 5 words are also a part of the same clause. In other words, they can't be set off. That is why **A** is incorrect.

#4 Based on the context of the sentence, it is clear that a noun is needed here. **F, G,** and **H** are all verbs of some kind. This is why the correct answer is **J**; "effect" is a noun and properly works.

#5 Answer choices **B, C,** and **D** all create a new independent clause that ends with the word "Pennsylvania." However, all that comes after "Pennsylvania" is a comma; there is no FANBOYS conjunction after it. That means that **B, C,** and **D** are all incorrect; only **A** rightly creates an introductory phrase that can be set off with a comma.

#6 What is needed is an option that stresses Fallingwater's *importance.* **F** is incorrect because having a nice view doesn't stress the importance of the home. **G** and **J** are wrong for the same reasons; those are all nice things about the home, but they don't stress or highlight the home's importance. That is why **H** is correct; having "historic and cultural significance" stresses the home's importance.

#7 Here you are asked for the order of sentences in the paragraph. Look at sentence 2: "Fallingwater is the name of this home" is a phrase that introduces the name *for the first time.* It makes no sense coming after sentence 1, which is written assuming that you already know that the name of the home is Fallingwater ("Fallingwater draws over 100,000…"). So we know for sure that sentence 2 comes before sentence 1. Out of all four options, only one has this: **D**, which is the correct answer. **A, B,** and **C** are all incorrect because they put sentence 2 after sentence 1.

#8 We already know that the plans called for a home above the falls. We learned that the home is over the waterfall in the last paragraph. That means **F** is incorrect because it is redundant. **G** is also redundant; it says Kauffman wasn't thrilled with the plans, and then later in the sentence it says the plans didn't suit his desires. **H** is wrong for the exact same reason; it says Kauffman lost the view he wanted, which is what is stated later in the same sentence. That is why **J** is correct; it is the only choice without a redundancy.

#9 Here, we need the correct transition linking the two sentences. The sentence previous states that Kauffman did not like the initial plans. The sentence following says that Kauffman "came around" to the idea. That's contrasting, which is why **B** is correct; "However" properly contrasts the two sentences because a change has taken place. **A** and **C** would both imply cause and effect, but that's not the case. **D** does not work either; "Otherwise" is used to mean something like "Or else," like this: "It's a good thing my dog is cute. Otherwise, I would have gotten rid of it long ago."

#10 Here, "At one point" is an introductory phrase, so it must be set off with a comma. That is why **H** is correct. **G** is incorrect because it is nonsensical to switch the words "Kauffman" and "point." **F** is incorrect because, as written, there is a comma after Kauffman, which separates him from the word "thought." **J** is incorrect because it sets off "At one point" with an em dash (—); that would only be acceptable in this circumstance if that was the beginning of a nonessential clause also closed off later in the sentence with an em dash, but that never happens.

#11 The easiest way to think about the correct answer here is to reimagine the independent clause without the very long nonessential or dependent clause in the middle. That would mean this: "Kauffman thought the space set out for his personal desk <u>that was</u> too small." **A** would only work if the beginning of the clause said something like, "Kauffman had a desk that was too small." But that's not the case, and hopefully you can *listen* and hear that this makes no sense as written. **C** is incorrect because it creates a new independent clause, and the sentence and its punctuation do not account for that. **D** is incorrect; "Kauffman thought the space set out for his personal desk too small" is missing something: what did he think? That is why **B** is correct; it rightly says that he thought the space "to be too small."

#12 There's nothing grammatically incorrect here, but it is contradictory. How can he read the plans that he had sealed up in the wall? This is why **F** is incorrect. Other problems besides, **G** and **H** imply the same thing. That is why **J** is correct; it is the only choice that rightly concludes that the plans put into the wall were not read again (which is why they were put into the wall in the first place).

#13 This should strike you as only loosely connected to the previous paragraph. In other words, it's not a fitting conclusion to a paragraph about the disagreements between Kauffman and Wright. Thus, it does not belong, and that is why **A** and **B** are incorrect. As for **D**, it correctly says "No," but it implies that the sentence contradicts earlier statements, but there have been no statements so far about the sturdiness of the home. That is why **C** is correct; it rightly says "No," giving a true reason: the information is not relevant.

#14 Starting the sentence with "Having been used" implies that the sentence is being lead off with an introductory phrase. However, if you read the entire sentence this way, you will notice that never happens; what should be an introductory phrase is ended with a period as opposed to set off by a comma before an independent clause. This is why **F, H,** and **J** are all incorrect; any of these three options creates an incomplete sentence for the same reason. **G** is the correct answer because it is the only option that creates an independent clause that can be ended with a period.

#15 As always, there are clues in this sentence that can help place it correctly. The sentence is about writing a check. Unless you remember exactly where the sentence may go (which is certainly great!), then we need to go back and check this idea in the context of all four choices (or at least enough possibilities until we can be sure of the correct answer). **A** is not a good fit; the previous sentence is about a boulder, and the sentence following references this boulder as "such a feature," so inserting a sentence about writing a check would be disruptive. **B** is also not a good fit; the first paragraph already has a fitting sentence to end it, and inserting a random sentence here about writing a check would be irrelevant. **C** is probably the most tempting wrong answer; the sentence before is about Kauffman's dislike of the plans, and so the idea of inserting a sentence that implies that Kauffman wouldn't pay Wright seems fitting. However, the sentence is about the *space* needed to write a check, not about how Kauffman was angry with Wright. This is why **D** is the correct answer; it rightly follows a sentence about Kauffman's desk being "too small," meaning there might not be enough space on it to write a check.

Passage II: Turn Out the Lights!

#16 What we have here is two independent clauses, and what is underlined is the link between them. There are only a handful of ways to properly join independent clauses into a single sentence (comma+FANBOYS conjunction, semicolon, — (em dash), or colon). Letters **G, H,** and **J** do none of these things, and thus they are all incorrect. **F** rightly separates the two independent clauses into their own sentences.

#17 This is a great time to illustrate again our main comma rule: commas in English are *deliberate*; they don't belong just because a pause "sounds" good. If you're reading this, I'm guessing that you most likely put **A** because a pause kind of sounds nice after "operate." However, the comma does not belong; it interrupts the flow of the sentence, which is also why options **D** and **C** are incorrect. Only **B** correctly leaves out any commas and allows the sentence to flow as it is intended.

#18 As written, the word "clarify" is in the present tense. The paragraph however is written in the past tense, describing an event that already happened. This is why **F** and **H** are incorrect. "Were to clarify" implies a time the clarifying should be done, like "They were to clarify where they had been when they got home." This is why **G** is incorrect. That is why the answer is **J**; it rightly conjugates the verb in the past tense.

#19 Here, the verb tense has shifted to the present to describe the hatching of sea turtle eggs. This is one reason why **A** and **D** are both incorrect. **B** would only be correct if a new nonessential clause was being introduced, but if you keep reading, the sentence would then end abruptly. That is why **C** is correct; it rightly begins the nonessential clause with "which" after a comma and uses the verb "has," which is present tense.

#20 After the word "change" there is a comma, and then an independent clause (but not FANBOYS conjunction). This means that whatever comes before the comma can't be an independent clause. However, when you insert options **G, H,** or **J**, that is what you get, which is why they are all incorrect. Only **F** leaves the opening clause as a dependent clause or introductory phrase.

#21 Every one of these options says the same thing: that the beach is dark. As you can see, **B, C,** and **D** are all very wordy, which is why **A** is the correct answer: it says what the sentence needs without being overly wordy.

#22 This is a question of "further" vs "farther." "Further" refers to something growing or extending that isn't distance, like "Further research is necessary." "Farther" refers to distance, and that is what we have here. Thus, we can eliminate **F** and **G** because both use "further." **J** is too wordy, and it also says that the lights "went" farther inland as if they can walk themselves farther. That is why **H** is the correct answer; it rightly uses "farther" to refer to distance in the least wordy way possible.

#23 All four of these options essentially say the exact same thing, and none of them contains grammar errors. You know what that means: you need the option that is the least wordy. That is why **B, C,** and **D** are all incorrect; they are all too wordy. That leaves **A**, which is correct because it says what the sentence needs without being overly wordy.

#24 Remember: "lie" is something I do to myself (or a subject does to itself): "I lie down for a nap," or, "The cat lied down in the middle of the road" (I had a cat that used to do that...RIP Mittens!). "Lay" is something a subject does to something else, like "I laid the book on the shelf." Here, cash is being put on the table by someone else: that's what we need "laid." That eliminates **G** and **J** because they say "lied." **H** has the problem of being in the present tense when the greater context is in the past tense...so it's out. That is why the correct answer is **F**.

#25 The key to this question is to leave off the sentence and reread at least the previous sentence. In this case, if we did that, the paragraph would leave off with the people telling the story leaving money on the tabletop. You could probably fill in the blank and guess that the next thing they did was rush to the beach, but the sentence that is there gives you that detail. **A** says something about people all over the world taking care of animals, but there is none of that in the sentence, so it is incorrect. **B** says that there's a restating of a fact about sea turtle eggs, but that isn't in the sentence, so it's out. **D** says that the sentence helps humans love animals more, but that is not in the sentence either. That is why **C** is correct: the sentence simply provides a detail in the flow of the story.

#26 This is an example of an idiom: a group of words that always goes together in English. We say that people arrive "just in time." It's as simple as that. That's why **G** is correct. It's not that there's grammar issues with **F, H,** and **J**, but rather, in English, those things don't have any meaning whatsoever.

#27 We need to try the phrase in question in all of the locations to see which fits. **A** is tempting because the current placement isn't terrible, but there is something a bit off about it (the question asks for the *best* placement, not any placement that works). **B** is incorrect because "Some to darken bait lights" makes no sense. **C** fits well; it puts the preposition "to darken bait lights" immediately behind the action of using black garbage bags, and this is why it is correct. **D** is incorrect because "nearby to darken bait lights piers" is also nonsensical.

#28 Here, "like the baby turtles" is a nonessential phrase that has to be set off by commas, so we definitely need a comma after "turtles." This eliminates **G** and **J** as incorrect. **F** has the problem of artificially placing a comma after "drawn," which separates the prepositional phrase "to it myself" apart from the rest of the clause. This is why **H** is correct: it properly sets off the nonessential phrase and uses no other commas that do not belong.

#29 This sentence ought not be too difficult to place because it is a simple sentence in the narrative about the turtles hatching. We just need to look back at the proposed locations and ask, "Does a sentence about turtles walking to the ocean belong here?" **A** can't work; the detail of the turtles is too soon and disrupts the paragraph. **B** is probably the most tempting wrong answer because this paragraph is about turtles hatching. However, this paragraph is more scientific and is in the present tense; the sentence we are trying to place is a part of the story and is in the past tense. **C** is also tempting because at this point we are back into the story. However, placing the sentence here is premature; the person telling the story hasn't made it down to the beach yet and would have no perspective as to how many turtles there are or if they've hatched or what they're doing. That is why the correct answer is **D**; only at this point does the perspective of the hundreds of baby turtles walking make sense because the previous sentence says that they arrived to the beach just in time.

#30 Again, we want to know if the answer is "Yes" or "No" before reading the answer choices. The question asks if the essay gives the scientific background to a personal experience, and yes, that is exactly what this essay does. It is a personal story, but it also tells us scientifically about the hatching of sea turtle eggs. That eliminates **H** and **J**. **F** states that the essay is about the author's interest in marine biology, however, that is never mentioned in the essay, so it is incorrect. **G** rightly says that a personal story is bolstered or supported by the science of turtle eggs hatching.

Passage III: Jefferson and Lewis

#31 Here, **C** is nonsensical when read in the context of the entire sentence, so it is incorrect. **B** does not work because "which" is a word applied to non-human things, but here we are dealing with a person; thus, "who" would be more appropriate. **D** is also nonsensical; you wouldn't say he's a "president knowing for." You say he is "known for" something if he is famous for something. That is why **A** is correct.

#32 There are a lot of words here, but again, that does not mean that a comma is necessarily required. In ACT English, commas are used *deliberately*, not to create artificial pauses to break up long stretches of words. In this sentence, there are no nonessential clauses that sidetrack the sentence; there are also no introductory phrases to begin the sentence or any dependent clauses of any kind. That is why **J** is the correct answer. **H** is probably the most tempting wrong answer because it "seems" like a pause would be good where a comma is, but that is unnecessary, so it is incorrect. **F** and **G** have the same problem; they put commas in places they don't belong.

#33 Here, notice what comes before and after the comma: independent clauses. Again, there are a handful of ways to unite these clauses. One way is to simply create two separate sentences, but that is not an option. The other options are to use a comma and a FANBOYS conjunction, an em dash (—), a colon, or a semicolon. Here, though there is a comma, there is no FANBOYS conjunction, so **A** is incorrect. **B** has no punctuation at all, so it is incorrect as well. **D** is very tempting; it rightly uses a semicolon. However, the second clause is started with the word "because," which would then turn the second half into an introductory phrase that would need to be set off from more information with a comma (in other words, what comes after the semicolon is no longer an independent clause). That is why **C** is correct; it rightly uses a colon to separate two independent clauses.

#34 We need a sentence that introduces us to the idea that Jefferson chose Lewis to go to the Pacific Ocean. **F** talks of the West Coast, but that has nothing to do with choosing a person to lead the expedition, so it is incorrect. The same can be said for **H**. Choice **G** mentions Thomas Jefferson, but it is about Jefferson being busy, not about Jefferson choosing a person to go West. That is why **J** is the correct answer: Jefferson needed to choose "the right man for the job" (as the question says, we need a sentence that transitions to Jefferson choosing Lewis).

#35 Again, check what comes before and after what is underlined (read in the context of the entire sentence!). What we have is two independent clauses, from "Jefferson" to "expedition" is one, and "he" to "leader" is another. There are a few ways to join these together. We could make them two sentences, use a comma and a FANBOYS conjunction, use an em-dash (—), use a colon, or use a semicolon. There is only one answer choice that does any of these, and that is answer choice **A**; it rightly has a FANBOYS conjunction ("and") after the comma between the two clauses. **B, C,** and **D** not only fail to properly combine these two independent clauses, but they are all nonsensical as well for various reasons.

#36 Although there are multiple words underlined here, this is a question of choosing the proper transition. "Because" implies cause and effect, but there is no cause and effect between him having qualities necessary and him not knowing much; what is needed is a transition that creates contrast. This is why **F** is incorrect. **G** makes the least sense; why would he have to explain his qualities? That is why **G** is incorrect. As for **J**, it creates one long sentence with two independent clauses, but there is no proper punctuation to join them. **H** is correct because it creates the proper contrast between the two clauses in the sentence.

#37 There is nothing grammatically incorrect with any of the answer choices, which must mean that there is a *best* answer. In this case, three of these answer choices are redundant. **B** says "experts were needed," but the sentence says later that he was sent to experts (thus, it's redundant). **C** has a redundancy within it; "because of this" and "having been caused by this" mean the same thing. **D** says "there were many things Lewis did not know", but the sentence before said that already. **A** is the shortest, but more importantly, it contains no redundancies.

#38 The question asks for the answer that stresses the seriousness of the training. As written, choice **F**, it says that the skills could prove "life-saving." That's pretty serious. Is **G**, proving he's a Renaissance man, more important than that? No, so **G** is incorrect. Is **H**, proving his critics wrong, more important than saving lives? No, so **H** is incorrect. Is **J**, proving a fun entry into knowledge, more important than saving lives? No, so **J** is incorrect. That is why the correct answer is **F**, it is the choice that makes his training with experts the most important.

#39 As written, there is something very short about the sentence; it ends very abruptly, especially compared to the rest of the essay. Because it is an opening sentence, it establishes the tone of the rest of the paragraph, and it's hard to imagine the paragraph continuing with short abrupt sentences like these. Those are some reasons why the answer is "Yes," but even if you're unsure and read the answer choices **C** and **D**, their reasons why the answer is "No" aren't good enough. Now, as for **A**, it says that we need to know that Lewis studied medicine, but we already know that. This is why **B** is correct. Yes, it gives credibility to his study, but if you read on in the paragraph, all of the other people that Lewis studied under are named, which is what the proposed phrase does here.

#40 We are trying to place the word "under," so we must try them out one at a time. Thinking of **F**, there's nothing grammatically incorrect, but there is something funny about the sentence as written; for starters, it says that Lewis is tutoring Andrew Ellicot, but shouldn't it be the other way around? That is why the answer is **J**, it rightly places "under" after "tutored," which makes it clear that Lewis is the one being tutored. The other answer choices, **F, G,** and **H** do not solve the problems that exist with the sentence as written.

#41 The introductory clause in this sentence ("Though capable of learning such a vast array of knowledge") is a *modifying clause*. That means that it is going to describe or modify or refer to whatever comes after the comma. In this case, the question is, what is "capable of learning"? **A** says that "Lewis's intellect" is capable of learning. However, that doesn't sound exactly right… isn't an intellect the result of learning? **B** says that "Lewis's willingness" is capable of learning, but that's not what we're looking for either. **D** says that "multiple subjects" are capable of learning; again, close but no cigar. **C** rightly says that "Lewis" was capable of learning, and thus that is the correct answer.

#42 This is an example of an idiom. There's nothing wrong grammatically with any of these answers, but only one of them is *best*. What do we do with time? We *spend* it. That is why **H** is correct. **F, G,** and **J** are fine, but not better than saying that Lewis "spent" hours in the library.

#43 The previous sentence said that Lewis was willing and eager to learn, and then the sentence in question highlights that by saying that Lewis spent time in Jefferson's library. What this sentence does is it gives evidence for the sentence before it, or proves it, you might say. Let's look for an option that says something like that. **A** talks about Jefferson's jealousy, but there is no indication of that, so it is incorrect. **B** says that libraries should be in all homes, but there's no indication of that not only in the sentence, but the paragraph or even the essay, so it too is incorrect. **D** says that the library demonstrates Jefferson's love of learning. Now, while that is *probably true*, the question isn't asking for any statement that might be true, but for what the sentence does to this particular paragraph. **C** rightly says that Lewis went above and beyond in his learning, which is exactly what the sentence shows.

#44 The sentence before this one mentions how dangerous the journey is, and then the sentence of which the underlined is a part is about how an explorer lost his life. **F**, or "conversely," implies contradiction between two sentences, but we don't have that here, so it is incorrect. **H**, or "suspiciously," implies mystery, and would introduce a mysterious element to the paragraph, but that is not what the paragraph needs, so it is incorrect. **J**, or "uniquely," implies that something is unique, but a person dying on an expedition that is dangerous is not unique. **G**, which says "Miraculously," works because it implies that there could have been many more deaths on an expedition as dangerous as that one (it also links well with the word "only" that is in the sentence).

#45 If we are looking for a phrase to end a paragraph, it needs to wrap up the paragraph, but if we are looking for a phrase to end an essay, it needs to wrap up the essay as a whole quite nicely. Was the essay as a whole about the Louisiana Purchase? Although this purchase of land is mentioned, that is not the topic of the essay, so **B** is incorrect. Is the essay about Jefferson's library (choice **C**) or learning (choice **D**)? No and no. Rather, the essay is about the Lewis and Clark expedition, which is why **A** is correct. Another way to get at the proper answer here is to read before the colon: "Jefferson got his wish." And what was that? To get to the Pacific Ocean, which is what choice **A** says.

Passage IV: The Eastern Indigo Snake

#46 We need a phrase that most contrasts the author with her friends. As for the author, it says she finds "them fascinating." Looking over the answer choices, **D** says that the friends are "enamored by" snakes, which essentially means the same thing as finding them fascinating. This is why **D** is incorrect. As for the other choices, all of them communicate the same idea, which is that her friends do not like snakes. That being said, **F** and **H** are incorrect because they are not as strongly worded as **G**, which is the correct answer.

#47 Here what is needed is a phrase that, according to the question, sets up the next question. In this case, the next sentence is about "visiting him in his office." **B** is incorrect because it is about camping, and I doubt that her father has an office at a campsite. **D** is incorrect because it mentions stories her father told, but the next sentence mentions nothing about stories. **C** is the most tempting incorrect choice. However, if **C** ("my father had a book of snakes that he kept on the bookshelf…") were to be correct, then we would expect the following sentence to say something like this: "One of those books showed pictures of snakes from around the world." But, **A** is correct because it communicates the the father was a professor at a university, and this links perfectly well with the fact that she visited him in his office (not to mention that the sentence after the phrase in question also mentions "campus").

#48 Because a semicolon is underlined, the essential thing to look for here is whether or not two independent clauses are being linked in this sentence. After the semicolon we have "I was honored...", which is an independent clause. However, before the semicolon, we have "This is why, when finally allowed as a teenager to be his intern," which is not an independent clause (it can't stand on its own as a sentence). For this reason, **F** is incorrect; a semicolon can only be used to link two independent clauses. **H** is wrong for the exact same reason. As for **J**, apart from other problems, "then" does the same thing for the sentence as the word "when" earlier in the sentence; both of them specify a time that something happened or was done. That is why the answer is **G**; this answer rightly finishes setting off the nonessential clause ("when finally allowed as a teenager to be his intern") with a comma without any additional awkward phrasing or redundancies.

#49 "I'm eager" is present tense, but the story being told is in the past tense; this is why **A** is incorrect. Let's simplify this sentence by wiping away prepositional phrases; which of these is correct? "I was honored... and eagerly to help" or "I was honored...and eager to help"? It is the second, which is why **C** is incorrect. Now, both **B** and **D** rightly say "eager," but **D** adds "in my desire." However, that's redundant: if you're eager to do something, you have the desire to do it. That is why **B** is the correct answer.

#50 Commas in ACT English, again, are used *deliberately*. In this case, the introductory clause "The Eastern Indigo Snake is not only the longest species of snake native to the United States" is one long clause, and within it there is no derailing nonessential clause. Thus, **F, H,** and **J** are all incorrect because they all wrongly insert commas into places they don't belong. **G** is correct because it rightly leaves out the commas and lets the phrase flow uninterrupted.

#51 "Those" is a plural pronoun that has to refer to something that has already been established as plural. However, there is nothing in the sentence or the previous sentence for that, or any other pronoun, to reasonably refer to. In other words, we're left asking, "The snake plays a role in the balance of life in...what?" **B** is the correct answer because it rightly answers this question; **A, C,** and **D** all use a pronoun in the aforementioned way, and thus they are all incorrect.

#52 The question asks for a relevant phrase, which means one that fits into the flow of the paragraph in a deliberate way.The previous sentence is about the states the snake is found in; the sentence after is about how rarely they have been spotted. **F** is incorrect because we don't need to know they have never been found in Arkansas; we already know that by deduction based on where they *are* found in the previous sentence. **G** seems OK because it is a fact that points to how they help the balance of life in forests. However, that does not, in a deliberate way, connect the previous and following sentences. **H** is a fact we already know, so it too is incorrect. **J** says the species is endangered; this phrase fits well with the transition "However" that begins the sentence and explains why the next sentence discusses how rarely the snake has been seen.

#53 As written, there is a comma after "endeavor," which signals that what is being begun is a nonessential phrase. However, there is no comma to finish such a phrase and we are left with an incomplete sentence (The new endeavor...what? We need a verb to have a complete thought or independent clause). That is why **A** and **B** are incorrect; neither of them creates a complete sentence. The only difference between **C** and **D** is verb tense. The verb "had been" implies that something existed and then changed. This seems tempting because the next sentence even has the phrase "had been" in it. However, it is incorrect. It would only be correct if the author were trying to say, "The new endeavor had been a collaborative effort, but we ended up going solo." That's not the case, which is why **C** is incorrect. **D** correctly puts the effort in the past with "was" without implying change of the project.

#54 Let's eliminate **G** as nonsensical; plug it in, and the sentence becomes nonsense. As for **J**, the word "which" at this point in a sentence is always going to come after a comma; besides, the word that goes here refers to people ("biologists"), which means we need who or whom; this is why **J** is incorrect. Remember our who/whom rule: *who* goes where *he* goes, and *whom* goes where *him* goes. Does it make more sense to say that *he* shared the urgency or that *him* shared the urgency? Of course, it is *he*; "him shared" makes no sense. That is why **F** is incorrect and why **H** is correct.

#55 This is obviously a question of commas...do we need commas or not in the underlined portion? No, we don't; remember, commas in ACT English are *deliberate*, not just thrown in to make artificial pauses. Because **A, C**, and **D** use a comma, they are all incorrect. **B** is correct because it has no commas to interrupt it.

#56 These questions always are the trickiest; you've got to read the question, understand it, and then choose the correct answer in context. Here, the question is asking for a shift in focus from research to actual release of the snake, which is implied by the next sentence. **G** is too broad; it doesn't transition the paragraph to something specific; besides, it is redundant, so incorrect. **H** delays getting to the specific release; it implies that there is more looking to do. **J** shifts the focus of the essay to to the Longleaf Pine, as if the next sentence is going to tell us more about that kind of tree. This is why the correct answer is **F**; the forest is selected, thus things are getting specific. Having a forest in which to let the snakes go shifts the focus, as the question requires, to the "actual release" of the snakes.

#57 I hope that the sentence preceding this one seems like the kind of one to end a paragraph; the one being proposed is random, and unfitting for this point in the essay. Besides, it says something we already know about the father. That is why the answer is "No," it doesn't belong. Thus, **A** and **B** are incorrect. **D** says that the sentence doesn't belong because it suggests the writer was a part of the project, but that is true. Thus, **C** is correct because it rightly says that the information has already been said.

#58 All four of these say the same thing, that the snake got away. This is an example of a question that needs the *best* answer. That is why the answer is **H**. As for **F, G,** and **J**, they are all grammatically fine, but too wordy compared to "escaped."

#59 This sentence is a factual sentence about the look of the snake; take a look back at all four choices and see which fits. **A** is incorrect because it is premature; it's not yet time to physically describe the snake. **B** is in a spot in which the snake has begun to be described, which is why it is the correct answer. **C** is incorrect because it is too late; same with **D**. By this point in the essay, the snake is no longer being physically described.

#60 Does this essay talk about an author's meaningful participation in a project? Yes, it sure does. That is why **H** and **J** are incorrect. As for **F**, it indicates that the author herself organized the project, but that's not true. **G** is correct because it rightly says that she helped in the project to release the endangered snake.

Passage V: Fred "Nall" Hollis

#61 If there is no comma after "Hollis," the sentence sounds like Fred Hollis gives a nickname to a person named "Nall." However, it is clear that "Nall" is Hollis's nickname. Thus, **A** and **C** are incorrect on those grounds alone. However, "When Fred Hollis" is not an introductory phrase (which is why **D** is incorrect); the phrase here that needs to be set off by commas is "nicknamed Nall," which is a nonessential phrase. We know it is nonessential because, if eliminated from the sentence, the sentence carries on just fine. This is why **B** is the correct answer.

#62 The word "foresee" means to see into the future. **G** then is redundant. **J** has a problem as well; this option says "back then," but we already know this is in the past, meaning the "back then" is unnecessary. **H** is also redundant; we already know that Fred Hollis came from a small town. Thus the correct answer is **F**; all we need is the word "foresee" because the other options are all redundant.

#63 The question states that all options are accurate, so again we need the *best* answer. In this case, which option states that Nall's art is both unique and beautiful? **B** is incorrect because the generic word "area" does not portray his art in any kind of positive light. **C** and **D**, as a matter of fact, both have this same problem: they are both bland and boring. **A** is the correct answer because calling someone's work a piece of "artistic genius" means it is unique and beautiful.

#64 Choice **J** can be quickly eliminated; "they are" makes no sense in the context of the paragraph. **H** is not a word in the English language, so it is out. **G** is incorrect because the underlined portion is not meant to claim possession (remember, "its" is possessive, like, "Its name is Fluffy"). That is why **F** is correct; "it's" is a contraction that means "it is," which is appropriate for the sentence.

#65 The sentence is communicating that most people have to stop to contemplate a work of Nall because there is beauty and purpose in it. If the phrase were eliminated, it would make it simply say, "It's almost impossible to pass by one of Nall's pieces…."**A** says that the underlined portion gives people a reason not to stop for one of Nall's pieces, but that is the opposite of what the sentence already says. **B** says something we already know and in simpler terms: that Nall's work is beautiful, which is why it is incorrect. **C** wrongly says that the detail adds irony, but that is incorrect. That leaves **D**, which is correct because it rightly says that the underlined portion gives a reason why people stop to contemplate his work. The first part of the sentence implies we want to stop for Nall's work, and the underlined portion tells us why.

#66 Before the comma, there is an independent clause (again, that means that the clause could stand alone as a sentence): "Nall was admitted to the School of Fine Arts in Paris." This is also true for what comes after the comma; it too is an independent clause: "Here he learned to further harness his artistic ability." Thus, we have to join the two in a proper way. **F** is incorrect because, though there is a comma, it is missing a FANBOYS (for, and, nor, but, or, yet, so) conjunction to link the two independent clauses. **G** has the opposite problem; there is a FANBOYS conjunction, but no comma, so it too is incorrect. **J** makes no attempt to link the two independent clauses with punctuation, so it is incorrect. **H** is correct because it is the only one to link the two independent clauses properly; in this case, it is with a semicolon.

#67 When read in the context of the sentence, the only way that "being" or "those being" could ever fit in this sentence is if it were to begin some kind of nonessential clause set off by a comma. However, there is no comma here to set off such a dependent clause, so **A** and **B** are incorrect. That leaves us with two words that rhyme, but only one of them fits. "much as" is a combination of words that works if you were to say "as much as," but that is not the case here. That is why **C** is incorrect. **D** is correct because "such as" properly introduces the examples of cultures that follow.

#68 This is an example of choosing the proper vocabulary word; the ACT is trusting that you can recognize which word is proper, like much else on the ACT, based on context. If something is "incorporated," it becomes a part of something else; but this sentence isn't trying to say that Nall's pieces became a part of America and Europe, so **F** is incorrect. **G** is incorrect because, to me at least, "seasoned" sounds like Nall brought some art to American and Europe and then the Americans and Europeans seasoned them with salt, pepper, etc. **J** sounds like Nall's pieces didn't do well ("underwhelmed"), meaning people weren't attracted to them or found them boring. However, based on the context of the essay as a whole, that would be strange; the essay is a praise of Nall and his work. That is why **G** is correct; "featured" means that they were shown in America and Europe.

#69 What is needed here is something like a transition, but in the form of a sentence. The sentence before speaks of Dalí's influence on Nall's work. The sentence following describes a human character in his art as being in black/white with hints of lovely color. **B** implies that Dalí did some of Nall's art; that does not transition to the example in the next sentence, so it is incorrect. **C** speaks of Nall's art going to Europe, but that would only make sense if the rest of the paragraph were about the various art galleries or locations in Europe his art was featured, so it too is incorrect. **D** simply contradicts the previous sentence, which, if it were put in the paragraph, would derail the paragraph that had been already introduced. **A** is the correct answer because it begins to transition from Dalí's influence to what Nall himself was capable of in his own art; it also makes sense of the phrase "For example" that begins the following sentence.

#70 As written, there is an em-dash (—) uniting two words. Em dashes can work in two situations: to link independent clauses or in a pair to act as parentheses. However, though what comes before the em dash is an independent clause, what follows is not; there is also not another dash anywhere. This is why **F** is incorrect. **H** inserts a colon and removes the word "with." Though what comes before the colon is an independent clause, what follows after the colon puts emphasis on "black and white," thus making it sound like "black and white" are "lovely hints of color." But that is contradictory and makes no sense, which is why **H** is incorrect. **J** artificially inserts a comma, which awkwardly separates "with" from the words that "with" is trying to connect to. This is why **G** is the correct answer; only **G** allows the sentence to flow properly without interruption from punctuation.

#71 If you read through the options, it becomes clear that all four of these sentences are attempting to say the same thing. That simply means that three of them will have errors, and one won't. **A** seems fine, but it is problematic because it says that the person looking at the art is a "distorted observer." **B** looks pretty good as well until you get to the end: is the observer's sense of wonder "out of proportion"? That's not right, which is why **B** is also incorrect. **D** also makes the mistake of saying that the observer is "out of proportion and distorted." This is why **C** is correct; it is the only option that rightly says the art is out of proportion and that the observer has a sense of wonder.

#72 The underlined portion of this sentence is an independent clause, but so is the clause that comes after the comma ("Nall has not forgotten his small town roots"). But a comma isn't sufficient to link the two independent clauses, which is why **F** is incorrect. **G** and **H** do the exact same thing: introduce an independent clause that isn't properly linked to the independent clause that follows the comma. This is why **J** is correct; it is the only option to insert an introductory phrase (dependent clause) that can properly be set off by a comma from the main independent clause of the sentence.

#73 What is needed here is the proper pronoun to agree with the verb "owns." **B** is not a pronoun and makes no sense, and is incorrect. Clearly, the sentence is trying to say that Nall still owns and operates a studio. This is why the correct answer is **D**; it replaces Nall with the correct pronoun "he." **C** has "he" in it, but "he or she" is used to refer to a singular person whose sex is unknown (like this: "A person robbed the bank. He or she stole a billion dollars."). Of course, Nall is not a "they," which is why **A** is incorrect.

#74 All of these options essentially say the exact same thing: that Nall still makes art. This means we are looking for the best answer. In this case, that would be the least wordy option. **G, H,** and **J** are all too wordy when compared to **F**, which is the correct answer.

#75 Again, give it your best shot to know if the answer is "Yes" or "No" before reading the answer choices. If that is a struggle, you could usually circle this kind of question and return to it if you have time at the end; that way, you can give yourself a chance to read over the essay to find the right answer. With this being #75 though, this *is* the end, so do what you need to do to get the question correct, and balance that against any other questions you wanted to go back to. Here, the question asks if the essay is about the circumstances of Nall's art being displayed in museums around the world. That is not the central purpose of the essay, so the answer is "No." This eliminates **A** and **B** as incorrect. **D** says that the answer is "No" because the essay never mentions that Nall's work gained international attention. But the essay *does* mention that he had work shown in Europe (particularly Italy) in the first paragraph. This is why **C** is the correct answer; it rightly says that though Nall is mentioned as receiving international attention, that isn't the focus of the essay as a whole.

Answer Explanations - Step 7 - Practice Test #2

Correct Answers:

Passage I	Passage II	Passage III	Passage IV	Passage V
1: A	16: F	31: C	46: J	61: B
2: J	17: C	32: J	47: C	62: J
3: B	18: H	33: A	48: H	63: B
4: G	19: A	34: F	49: C	64: H
5: D	20: H	35: C	50: G	65: C
6: G	21: A	36: H	51: D	66: G
7: D	22: H	37: D	52: F	67: D
8: G	23: C	38: F	53: A	68: F
9: D	24: J	39: D	54: J	69: A
10: F	25: A	40: J	55: D	70: G
11: D	26: J	41: B	56: G	71: C
12: F	27: A	42: J	57: B	72: H
13: B	28: G	43: C	58: F	73: D
14: H	29: A	44: H	59: B	74: F
15: A	30: H	45: B	60: G	75: B

Passage I: Goodall and the Chimps

#1 **C** and **D** are both redundant (they both say things already stated in the sentence) and can both be eliminated. **B** is not only too wordy, but "and that she did earn a spot in history" is not a functioning dependent clause. **A** is correct because the word "did" is not only grammatically correct, but implies that she earned a spot in history as she intended.

#2 There is a semicolon in the underlined portion. This should prompt you to check if the sentence is attempting to combine two independent clauses. However, the first clause ("While she is known…mostly by men") is not an independent clause, but rather a dependent, introductory clause. This means that it simply needs to be set off from the rest of the sentence (or the independent clause you could say) by only a comma. Thus, **F** is incorrect. **H** uses a comma and a FANBOYS conjunction ("but" in this case), and for the same reason as the semicolon (comma+FANBOYS is used to combine independent clauses just like a semicolon) is incorrect. **G** is incorrect because beginning this clause with the word "preferring" creates another dependent or nonessential clause, and that would leave the sentence without an independent clause at all, which is impossible in English. This is why the answer is **J**; it rightly sets off the introductory clause with a comma and creates an independent clause after the comma.

#3 The question asks for a choice that stresses her difficulty and strife. While the reader be able to imply that there was difficulty and strife involved if the answer choices were **A, C,** or **D**, none of those three is as strongly worded as choice **B**, which is the correct answer.

#4 As written, what could "it" possibly refer to? There is no obvious answer, so choice **F** incorrect. It seems pretty clear that the "groundbreaking observation" is trying to be attributed to Goodall, who is a singular female. Choices **H** and **J** are incorrect because they are plural pronouns. That is why the correct answer is **G**: "hers" is singular and refers to Goodall herself.

#5 A look over the four options makes it pretty clear that they are all attempting to say the same thing. Thus, three of them will have some kind of error. **A** has such a problem: beginning with "inserting" turns the underlined part into a dependent clause, making an incomplete sentence. **B** begins with "over and over insert," but isn't the more common phrasing "insert over and over"? Besides, the ending of the sentence, "into where the termites lived" is a little wordy compared to other options. For these reasons, **B** is incorrect. **C** also creates an incomplete sentence; in addition, it uses the designation "there" and then attempts to say where "there" is instead of simply saying "termite mounds" in the first place. **D** rightly creates a complete sentence that is not overly wordy.

#6 Letter **J** insinuates that the underlined portion shifts the focus of the paragraph, but that isn't the case; the focus is still on the chimpanzees eating termites, so it is incorrect. **H** says that the underlined portion is repetitive, but it has not yet been said that the next step in the process is for the chimpanzee to remove the stalk, so **H** is also incorrect. **F** says that the phrase is necessary for us to know what kind of ape is being observed, but that's not true; we already know that it is chimpanzees with or without the phrase, so **F** is incorrect. That leaves **G**, which rightly says that it simply provides a step in the chimpanzee's process of eating termites; thus it is the correct answer.

#7 We need a choice that emphasizes that the chimpanzee is a *hunter*. **A** doesn't emphasize that at all; it just says that the termites were eaten. This is also true for **B** and **C**; neither emphasizes the chimp as a hunter. **D**, however, uses the word "predator" to describe the chimpanzee, thus stating strongly that the chimp is a hunter; this is why it is the correct answer.

#8 This is one of those unique questions where the correct answer is the only choice that is wrong. "Consumption" of course means "eating." Because **F** and **H** are synonyms of "consumption," they would both work in the sentence, so they are (as far as the question is concerned) incorrect. **J** is an interesting option and needs exploring. What happens when the underlined portion is deleted? Well, the sentence then says this: "…it was believed that chimps ate a mostly vegetarian diet supplemented by some insects." This implies that the insects were eaten along with a vegetarian diet, which means that **J** would work in the sentence. Thus, **J** (because it works) is incorrect. This is why **G** is the right answer; "combustion" means explosion, and I don't think the chimps are blowing up termites.

#9 A comma would only be needed after "tree" if we were setting off items or actions in a list or setting off a nonessential clause. While this happens elsewhere in the sentence, it does not need to happen here. Because **A, B,** and **C** all use this comma, they are all incorrect. **D** is correct because it rightly leaves out this comma and keeps the compound verb (climb and surround) together.

#10 We simply need a past tense verb that indicates that the chimps shared the carcass with each other. Well, "shared" happens to perfectly do this, which is why the correct answer is **F**. **G** is grammatically incorrect and does not work in the sentence; this is also true of **H**; both of those are thus incorrect. **J** is present tense, which is why it is incorrect.

#11 Read the sentence at a normal pace. Does anything stick out to you as unnecessary or nonessential? Any introductory phrases or dependent clauses? Don't try to convince yourself that the prepositional phrase "with the chimpanzees" is some kind of nonessential phrase that sounds good when set off by commas. That is not the case. There is no need for the *deliberate* use of a comma in this sentence. For this reason, **A, B,** and **C** are all incorrect because they insert commas where none belong. **D** is correct because it lets the sentence flow as it is intended to do.

#12 All of these four options mean essentially the same thing, and they all grammatically fit within the sentence. That means what is needed is the *best* answer. In this case, **G, H,** and **J** are all too wordy, and are thus incorrect, when compared to the short and simple **F**, which is correct.

#13 "Goliath" is not the chimp's title, which is why **A** is incorrect. It also isn't his "designation;" that word is too informal and not applied to names, which is why **D** is correct. **C**, or "known by," may be tempting, but when referring to someone's name, it would be more proper to say "known as." This is why **C** is incorrect. **B** is correct because it rightly says that the chimp is "named" Goliath because, well, that's his name.

#14 "Mike" refers to a chimp, and this chimp takes over some other chimp's job. This is what can be gleamed from the sentence that needs placing. Simply apply that idea to all four options. **F** does not work because that would insert the sentence about Mike in the middle of the story about the chimps hunting another monkey. **G** doesn't work either; though the sentence before mentions the names of apes, it doesn't set up the paragraph to state that one of these apes had a job that could be taken over by another named Mike. **H**, on the other hand, is the correct answer; this is because the preceding sentence says that a chimp named "Goliath" was the alpha male: this is the position that Mike takes over. **J** also does not work, of course; this is because it would be the concluding sentence of the essay, but the essay is already concluded nicely with a reference to Goodall, not the chimps.

#15 Again, give it your best shot to know if the answer is "Yes" or "No" before reading the answer choices. If that is a struggle, circle this question and return to it if you have time at the end; that way, you can give yourself a chance to read over the essay to find the right answer. In this case, the answer is "Yes," the essay does highlight one scientist (Jane Goodall) and her contribution to the knowledge of animals (chimpanzees). Thus, **C** and **D** are incorrect since they both say "No." **B** says that the essay compares and contrasts scientists, but the essay is only about one scientist, which is why **B** is incorrect. **A** rightly says "Yes," giving the true reason that the essay centers on the work of one scientist: Jane Goodall.

Passage II: A Fishing Memory

#16 Remove the "yet urgent" and what do you get? A sentence that flows smoothly, uniting the adjective "gentle" with the noun "fashion." That means that the phrase "yet urgent" is nonessential and must be set off by commas. **G, H,** and **J** all fail to fully set off the phrase with commas. This is why **F** is the correct answer.

#17 Here we need the correct prepositional phrase. If he were to stare "from" the dark morning he would have to be *in* the dark morning. But, he's not; he is inside the bedroom looking outside the window. This is why **A** is incorrect. If he were to stare "behind" the dark morning, he would have to see to the other side of it, or something like that; this is why **B** is incorrect. **D** has the same problem; how could he possibly see "above" the dark morning? That makes little sense. That is why the correct answer is **C**: he stares from his room *into* the dark morning that is outside the window.

#18 All of the choices are grammatically correct and true, and the question asks for the one that best transitions into the next paragraph. **F, G, H** and **J** could all end this paragraph fairly well, so the question is, what is the next paragraph about? Reading ahead, it's about rigging the fishing poles the evening prior. Because **F, G,** and **J** all fail to mention this, they are all incorrect. **H** is correct because it rightly mentions that the tackle and poles were already prepared.

#19 "“Can I help, Grandpa?” I’d ask” is an independent clause, and so is “even though he never needed it, he’d let me be his assistant.” We have to join these in a proper way: a comma+FANBOYS, a semicolon, a colon, an em-dash, or separate them into two separate sentences. Only one of them does that, and that’s **A**, which is the correct answer because it uses a comma and a FANBOYS conjunction. As for **B, C,** and **D**, they all fail to properly link independent clauses.

#20 The opening paragraph is about the boy waking up while it’s still dark to go fishing. **H** mentions “before first light,” which means it is the correct answer. **F** and **J** both mention the previous paragraph, but don’t refer back to the opening paragraph. **G** says something about weather, but there is no mention of bad weather in the first paragraph.

#21 There are a couple of things going on here, so let’s address them one at a time. First question: is a comma necessary after the word “large”? Technically, there are two adjectives describing the word “rig”: “large” and “oil.” However, the rule is this: if the adjectives can be reversed, use a comma to set them off. Does “oil, large rig” make any sense? No, because an “oil rig” is its own noun. So, we do not need a comma after the word “large,” which means that choice **D** is incorrect. I think it’s also safe to eliminate **C** because it separates “oil” from “rig” with an unnecessary comma. The next question is this: do we need to set off “about a mile off the coast of the island” from the rest of the sentence? No, it is not a dependent or nonessential clause; it fits perfectly well in the flow of the sentence. This is why we can now eliminate **B**. Only **A** leaves out all commas, which makes it the correct answer.

#22 “he was simply tying” would only work if the sentence went on to say, “he was simply tying a rope *when* a shark came….”. In other words, the “when” is missing to properly continue the flow of the story, which is why **F** is incorrect. **G** is strange because it seems to want to say, “to tie simply he would do this or that.” But it never does so; this is why **G** is incorrect. **J** is an example of nonsense; it should recognized as too strangely worded to be correct. **H** is correct because it uses words in their proper order to put the tying of the rope in the past tense.

#23 The question says we need a choice that shows the grandfather’s delight. **A** says “Carefully,” but there is no joy or delight implied in that word, which means it is incorrect. The exact same thing can be said for **B** (“Unexpectedly”) and **D** (“Dutifully”). **C** uses an adverb that implies delight and joy: “Excitedly,” which is why **C** is the correct answer.

#24 The topic of the paragraph is how the pair would get their boat to the rig, tie it up, and start fishing. The sentence proposed is about the thousands of species of shrimp. Does that fit in? No, which is why **F** and **G** are incorrect. **H** wrongly says that the sentence implies that they will catch fish (because the sentence says that shrimp are eaten by a variety of fish), but that is not *why* it is wrong. **J** correctly says “No,” giving a valid reason: the proposed sentence detracts from the purpose of the story and interrupts its progress.

#25 Let’s start with **D**, and let’s rule it out as incorrect because it is nonsensical. **B** can also be ruled out because it uses the pronoun “they”…but who are “they”, the fish? I don’t think the fish will fill up ice chests with themselves, thus **B** is incorrect. **C** is too strange to be correct…who would say “we were to be filling” an ice chest when there is a simpler way to communicate the idea that the ice chest became filled up with fish? That is why **A** is correct: it says in the most simple way that the ice chest became filled with fish.

#26 As written (choice **F**) should sound a little odd; the sentence makes it sound like they can name every kind of fish they caught except for one; this is also true of choice **H**. Their strange nature makes them both incorrect because we are looking for a good or normal fit at this point in the sentence. **G** has a problem because it sort of contradicts the rest of the sentence; it sounds like they caught a lot of different kinds of delicious fish, not a “lack” of them. This option is also incorrect. **J** is correct because it simply fits the best in the sentence; you might say it is normal or not-strange like the other options.

#27 Here is yet another example of a nonessential clause. Again, the test as to whether or not it actually is a nonessential clause is to remove it from the sentence and see if the sentence flows well without it. In this case, removing “quality time not included” results in the sentence saying this: “…my favorite part was never knowing what we would pull from the water.” Clearly, the “quality time not included” is a nonessential phrase and must be set off by commas from the rest of the sentence. **A** is the correct answer because it is the only choice to do this. **B, C,** and **D** are all incorrect because they are missing at least one comma (or two, as in choice **D**) to completely set off the nonessential phrase.

#28 If you are struggling putting these three sentences in order, there are some clues to follow. As always, look for references to other sentences that serve as signposts, allowing you to see that a certain sentence comes before or after another. Sentence 1 begins with “In other words.” That is a strange way to begin a paragraph because it is a clarifying phrase, and what it attempts to clarify usually comes in the sentence before. This would mean that **F** and **H** are both incorrect because they put sentence 1 first. Another clue can be found in sentence 3, which includes the phrase “any one of these.” The question is: any one of what? Well, it is clear from the paragraph that this means “any one of these fish,” as in the list of fish listed off in sentence 2. This means that sentence 3 must follow sentence 2, but sentence 1 can’t come before sentence 2. That leaves only one possible order: 2, 3, 1. This is why **G** is correct. **J** wrongly puts sentence 3 before sentence 2; this would make the phrase “any one of these” have no point of reference.

#29 The word “battle” certainly doesn’t fail to transition the sentence to the next one; this is why **D** is incorrect. It is clear as well that **C** is also incorrect; this is because the word "battle" doesn't *understate* how tiresome the fight with the fish was. **B** is also incorrect because the theme of battling is nowhere to be found in the first paragraph. This is why **A** is correct; the word "battle" puts emphasis on the fact that the angler had to fight the fish long and hard.

#30 We already know that the kid had the fish on the line for a long time; look at the first sentence of the paragraph: "...for what seemed like hours..." That means the underlined portion is redundant and does not belong. This means of course that **F** and **G** are both incorrect. **H** rightly says that the idea has already been stated, and is thus redundant, making it the correct answer. **J,** though it says the phrase should be deleted, gives an incorrect reason for its being deleted: who cares about the reaction of the workers in the last sentence of an essay about a grandfather taking his grandson fishing?

Passage III: The Sailing Stones

#31 What comes before the comma (from "Visitors" to "visit") is an independent clause, and so is that which comes after the comma (from "from lively cities" to "too short"). This means we need punctuation that accounts for that. **A** is incorrect because, though there is a comma, there is no FANBOYS conjunction to go with it. **B** is incorrect for this same reason, but it also has the comma in a strange place. **D** is also incorrect because it has no punctuation at all. **C** is correct because it separates the two independent clauses into two sentences.

#32 What we have here are four options that all grammatically work. Because we need the best answer, one thing to do would be to try out the shortest answer of them all, which is choice **J**. Because this option works, let's think about if the other choices add anything we need. **F** says "as one may experience," but that is unnecessary to say; if a person is on vacation to this area, or course he or she might experience it. **G** is also redundant; if it is "sure" to be too short, we don't need to also say "most definitely." **H** adds a phrase that adds nothing to the sentence at all; it is simply too wordy.

#33 This is an example of an idiom: a group of words in the English language that always go together. The "receiving end" means the "recipient of," which is exactly the context that the sentence calls for. This is why **A** is the correct answer. **B, C,** and **D** do not create a series of words that is purposefully used in the English language, and are thus incorrect.

#34 The question asks for a phrase that suggests two things about the sailing stones: a) not man-made, and b) difficult to explain. **G** is lacking in both of these, and is thus incorrect. **H** is contradictory; if something happens "logically" it is probably pretty easy to explain. **J** calls them an "event," but still it falls short in both categories. This is why the answer is **F**; if the stones are "natural" then they are not "man-made," and if the stones are a "phenomenon" then they are not easy to explain.

#35 As written, we have an incomplete sentence, which is why **A** is incorrect. **B** seems to work OK until you get to the verb "cut" (plural) which would have to attach to the subject "movement" (singular), which is grammatically incorrect, so **B** is incorrect. **D** is problematic because the verb "to create" could only come after "movement" if it were the beginning of a new nonessential clause, but because there is no comma, this is not happening, which is why **D** is incorrect. **C** correctly says that the movement "creates trails", and that the trails "cut." In other words, **C** creates subject-verb agreement to the extent that what it creates is a functioning sentence.

#36 Each of the four choices has "giving the" at the beginning of it, so this is merely a question of correct vocabulary. An image that deceives is an "illusion," which is why **H** is the correct answer. **F, G,** and **J** are incorrect because they simply use the incorrect words.

#37 Choice **A** has to be incorrect because the previous sentence said this exact same thing already: that the stones appear to have been moving of their own accord. Choice **B** has the same problem; the last sentence of the previous paragraph says that the stones have been "on the receiving end of growing interest." **C** is also redundant; the first sentence of this paragraph says that this is "natural." That is why the answer is **D**: there should be none of these other sentences here because they are all redundant, repeating facts that have already been stated.

#38 "The stones are" means that a verb ending in "ing" must follow "are." This eliminates **H** and **J** as incorrect. As for **G**, it is wrong because when the word "across" is removed, it makes it sound like the stones have the ability to move the desert itself, which isn't possible. This is why the answer is **F**; it rightly uses a verb ending in "ing" after "are" and says that the stones are moving across the desert, not moving the desert itself.

#39 Well, it is pretty clear that this previous sentence doesn't describe every detail in the water cycle, and this is why **A** is incorrect. Since the previous sentence is the beginning of a scientific explanation as to how the stones move across the desert, it isn't a distraction and shouldn't be deleted, which is why **B** is incorrect. **C** is a tempting answer, but still it is incorrect because it says nothing about "hot days." This is why **D** is the correct answer; this choice says that the sentence explains how ice could end up in the desert, which is exactly what the sentence does when it says that the ice forms during "cold nights."

#40 When something is "accompanied," it is usually "accompanied *by*"; we have to know what accompanies that certain thing. This is why **J** is the correct answer; it is the only choice that puts the preposition "by" behind "accompanied." The other choices, **F, G,** and **H** are all incorrect because none of them does this. Specifically, **F** doesn't work because it is, as written, nonsensical. **G**

makes no sense: how could the stones be accompanied *through* the wind? **H** is incorrect because it creates a nonsensical sentence ("When this breakup is accompanied with the ice is pushed...").

#41 Again, em dashes (these things: —) can be used to either combined independent clauses or take the place of parentheses. Notice that, a few words later, there is another em dash, which has to be serving one of these two purposes. It just so happens that between the underlined portion and the next em dash is a nonessential phrase, which must mean that the em dashes are being used like parentheses. This is why **B** is the correct answer; it rightly opens the nonessential phrase with an em dash. **A, C,** and **D** all fail to do so: if an em dash is used to "close" a phrase later, it must be used to begin a phrase at some point. It can't be that the later em dash is used for separating independent clauses because what comes before is a dependent or introductory clause.

#42 If the word "though" were to be put in before the word "technically" here, it would need to be set off somehow as a nonessential clause. That is not the case, which is why **F** is incorrect. As for the other choices, it is clear that **G** and **H** are incorrect because they are too wordy. **J** is correct because it is less wordy and gives what the sentence needs.

#43 "movement of mud was to blame the others"? This makes it sound like mud, while moving, tried to blame people for something. This is why **A** is incorrect. **B** puts a comma and adds, "and though others"; the problem with this is that this begins a new nonessential clause, and because the sentence ends shortly thereafter with a period, we are left with an incomplete sentence. **D** is wrong because it is nonsensical; "was to blame theorized that something..." makes no sense at all and is missing words, punctuation, or both to form a complete thought. This is why **C** is the correct answer; it correctly adds a dependent clause to the end of an independent clause.

#44 Let's eliminate **J** as incorrect because the pronoun "they" is in a place that makes the sentence nonsensical. **G** can also be eliminated because it is strangely worded. Now we are left with a simple who vs whom distinction. The rule is this: put *who* where *he* goes, and put *whom* where *him* goes. Is it better to say "he travels far to catch a glimpse" or "him travels far to catch a glimpse"? It is the former, *he*, which is why **H** is correct and **F** is incorrect.

#45 As written, there is no clear reason why it ought to be deleted. The sentence preceding it about the scientists seeking explanation isn't as good a fit to end a paragraph or the essay as a whole compared to the one present here. **C** is incorrect because it says that the sentence shifts the focus, but that is not true; the focus is supposed to be on the stones, not on the tourists. **D** falsely claims that the sentence assumes that everyone will get to see the stones, but that is not implied in the sentence, and thus this option is incorrect. **A** rightly says that the sentence should be kept, but the reason is strange: because it stresses that scientists should do research? That's not the purpose of the sentence. **B** is the correct answer because it rightly says that the sentence should be kept for a good reason: that it links with the first paragraph (because the first paragraph is about visitors to the stones, which is mentioned in this sentence as well).

Passage IV: The Moai of Easter Island

#46 The underlined portion here contains a semicolon. Again, the main purpose of a semicolon is to link independent clauses. In this case, what comes before the semicolon is an independent clause, but what comes after is a dependent clause. This means that **F** is incorrect. Such a clause must simply set off from the independent clause of the sentence by a comma, which eliminates answer choice **G** as incorrect. As for **H**, because there is a comma and a FANBOYS conjunction, the only way this could work (like the semicolon) is if what comes after is independent. However, this is not the case. This is why **J** is the correct answer: it rightly sets off the dependent clause "of which it is a special territory" from the independent clause of the sentence with a comma.

#47 This question is extremely similar to the one that precedes it. There is an independent clause to begin the sentence, followed by a dependent clause that must be set off with a simple comma. This is why **C** is the correct answer. Choices **A** and **B** are incorrect because they wrongly insert commas into the dependent clause without deliberate purpose. **D** is incorrect because it fails to set off the dependent clause ("which occurred on Easter Sunday") with a comma.

#48 Remember the #1 colon rule: a colon must always follow a complete thought. Although there are lots of words before the colon, there is no complete thought (which is why **F** is incorrect). The sentence begins with a long introductory phrase, then begins the independent clause ("the most academically appealing aspect of the island") without ever attaching a verb to the subject within it. This is because a nonessential phrase is inserted. This phrase is this: "not to mention its most mysterious." As a nonessential phrase, it must be set off by commas. This is why **H** is correct. **J** is incorrect because it fails to close off the nonessential phrase with a comma. **G** is incorrect because it unnecessarily inserts a comma after the word "its."

#49 We only need one noun to possess "height and weight." As written, there are two: "stone" and "it," which are linked with an "and" and are both shown to possess the height and weight. But both of these refer to the same thing: a stone. This is why **A** and **B** are both incorrect (though **B** also has the added problem of putting the apostrophe after the 's', which means that multiple stones possess it). **D** neglects to insert an apostrophe, but the apostrophe is necessary because the sentence is attempting to denote possession. This is why **C** is the correct answer: it rightly uses an apostrophe before the 's' to denote that the stone possesses height and weight.

#50 Because a semicolon is present in the underlined portion, the first question is whether or not two independent clauses are being linked. Here, the answer is no, and thus **F** is incorrect. **J** does something similar: it uses a comma and a FANBOYS conjunction, but again, this is incorrect because independent clauses are not being linked. **H** is incorrect because it fails to close off the word "respectively" with a comma. **G** is the correct answer because it rightly closes off the word "respectively" (technically a nonessential phrase; you can tell this because if the word is removed from the sentence, the sentence flows freely) with a comma.

#51 "They carve" (choice **A**) can be eliminated because it is in the present tense. As a matter of fact, this is also true of **B** and **C**: both of these choices are also in the present tense. **D** then is correct because, consistent with the essay, it is in the past tense.

#52 When multiple adjectives are describing a noun, as is the case here, the question is this: can the adjectives be reversed? If so, a comma will be needed after the first adjective. If not, no such comma is needed. It makes sense to talk of an "inactive volcanic crater," but does it make sense to talk of a "volcanic inactive crater"? No, because the word "volcanic" must come immediately before "crater." This means that no comma is necessary after "inactive," which is why **G** and **H** are incorrect. As for **J**, it makes the mistake of unnecessarily putting a comma after "crater," which separates the prepositional phrase beginning with "on" from the rest of the sentence when it ought to flow smoothly. This is why **F** is the correct answer: it inserts no commas because none are needed.

#53 Choices **B** and **C** can't be correct because both assume that two independent clauses are being linked. But, that is not the case; the first clause (beginning with "While"), is not independent. **D** is incorrect because it fails to set off the introductory clause from the independent clause of the sentence with a comma. This is why **A** is correct; as written, this choice properly sets off the opening clause from the independent clause beginning with "hundreds of statues."

#54 This essay has the tone of formality; it sounds like something out of a history textbook. This is why **F** is incorrect; "pillow talk" is not only informal, but it is more synonymous with "gossip." There's nothing grammatically incorrect about it; there must simply be a *better* answer. Of the remaining choices, **G** and **H** are too wordy. This is why **J** is correct; it provides the idea needed by the sentence with the fewest words possible.

#55 This question is tricky because you must read the question stem first: we need a choice that is NOT acceptable. Of the answers, all of the following are more or less synonymous with "arrived", and are thus incorrect: "landed" (choice **A**), "came" (choice **B**), and "reached the shore" (choice **C**). This is why choice **D** is the correct answer: "glanced" is not a synonym of "arrived."

#56 This is a great example of a question that requires you to read the entire sentence to get the question correct. The sentence is saying that there is teamwork involved in this process of moving the stones, and that they are happening at the same time: some men lift logs from the back of the line to the front **while** men pull on the stones by rope. This is why **G** is the correct answer; it uses "while" to indicate that the two actions are happening at the same time. **F** can't be correct because it implies contrast, but that isn't the relationship between the two actions. **J** simply does not belong, and besides, it would probably need to be set off from the rest of the sentence by a comma. **H** uses "However" to begin the sentence, but that changes the meaning of the opening clause; instead of it being an action that men are doing, it creates a phrase that fails to link with the clause that comes after about the men lifting logs from the back of the line.

#57 Without the information being added, the sentence sounds like a random scientific fact about the island. This eliminates **C** and **D** as incorrect. **A** correctly says that the sentence belongs, but wrongly says the reason that this is so is because the new information tells the reader that the island is wooded. This is wrong because that is the purpose of the sentence already there, not of the information being proposed. This is why **B** is the correct answer: it links the fact to the theory being proposed.

#58 Choices **G** and **H** do not work because they are plural conjugations of a verb, but we need a singular option ("A second hypothesis" is singular). Because the sentence is trying to say that a hypothesis has been growing in popularity, **J** is incorrect. Only choice **F** rightly denotes that the hypothesis continues to get more and more popular by conjugating the verb to match the singular subject.

#59 Choices **A, C,** and **D** are all not only saying that the "ropes were tied to" statues, but that the statues had been previously carved. However, this is redundant: if a statue is made of stone, isn't it already carved (otherwise, it's not a statue but just a big piece of rock)? Thus all three of those options are incorrect. **B** is correct because it is not redundant.

#60 Hopefully it "sounds" strange for the pronoun "them" to be put in this situation (this is why **F** is incorrect). It would be good instincts if you thought to yourself, "not *them* but *they*." Unfortunately, "they" is not one of our choices. While **J** ("all they") may be tempting for this reason, don't be fooled: "all of them" would be appropriate here, not "all they." **H** uses a singular pronoun, "it," but we are attempting to describe a plural subject: the "statues." This is why **G** is the only acceptable answer; instead of a pronoun, the title of the stone statues can fit in this place just fine.

Passage V: John Hart, Unsung Hero

#61 Reading through the four options, they are all attempting to say the same thing. However, **A, C,** and **D** are all too wordy and don't quite hit the mark, which is why they are all incorrect. **B** is correct because it is the *best* answer, and it is best because it is the least wordy.

#62 Three of these options (**F, G,** and **H**) all begin the sentence with some kind of transition, meaning it creates a special or specific relationship with the sentence that came before. **F** is incorrect because "On the contrary" implies contrast or a stark difference between the two sentences, but the second sentence doesn't have this relationship with the first. **G** and **H** are synonymous; both of them imply that the second sentence is a conclusion or flows in logical order from the first; but that is not the case (the fact that they are exact synonyms is a clue that they are both incorrect as well). All of this means that the sentence doesn't need a transition, or at least any of these three. Beginning the sentence with "Most" works perfectly well, especially if you read the entire sentence (as you should). This is why **J** is the correct answer.

#63 First, let's eliminate **D** because "rather" on its own here is nonsensical because the word "than" needs to follow it to make any sense. Clearly the sentence is trying to say that Jefferson, Washington, etc. took risks *for* the USA. **A** and **C** both mean something different than that, and they are both incorrect. Because choice **B** is synonymous with "for" ("...they are not the only ones who took risks on behalf of/for so great a nation."), it is the correct answer.

#64 The first requirement of the question is that the correct answer "fit the tone" of the essay. This is enough to eliminate **F** as the incorrect answer; "some person" is too informal. The second requirement of the question is that the right answer emphasize that the subject of the essay (meaning the person who the essay is about) have a story worth telling. **G** can be eliminated as incorrect because "a man" is too bland. **J** is much closer to what the question requires, but what is required is the *best* answer. This is why **H** is correct. The story of "an unsung hero" is a story more worthy of telling than that of "a great citizen."

#65 The paragraph already ended on a good note with a sentence that makes you want to ask: "Who is this unsung hero?" That is why a random fact about George Washington, though neat and historically important, does not belong here. This eliminates options **A** and **B**, which for this reason are both incorrect. **D** claims that the first paragraph never mentions George Washington, but that's not true; his name comes up in the second sentence of the opening paragraph. This is why **C** is correct; it rightly says "No" and says that the information is only loosely tied to the first paragraph, which is true.

#66 Because a semicolon is underlined, the first question must be whether or not two independent clauses are being linked. However, the first clause ("As a politician...American colonies") is not independent; in other words, it couldn't stand alone as a sentence. This is why **F** is incorrect; a semicolon is used to link two independent clauses. Looking at the rest of the answer choices, **H** and **J** both make attempts at linking independent clauses (comma+FANBOYS and a period, respectively), which is why they are both incorrect as well. This is why **G** is the correct answer; it rightly separates the introductory phrase (or dependent clause) from the rest of the sentence with a simple comma.

#67 None of these four answer choices contains grammar errors, and all of them mean the same thing. That means, of course, that what is required is the *best* answer. None of them are redundant (meaning none of them are repeating information already stated or implied), but one of them is less wordy than the others. This is why **D** is the correct answer; it says what the sentence requires in the least words possible. As for **A, B,** and **C**, they are all simply unnecessarily wordy.

#68 For **G** to work, it would have to say something like, "where he *was* to hide," but as it is written it is nonsensical, and thus it is incorrect. **H** sounds like some kind of slang, but grammatically speaking, "he be hiding" is incorrect and nonsensical. **J** is incorrect because "were" is a plural conjugation, but we need a singular conjugation to link with "he." This is why **F** is correct: it is singular and grammatically sound.

#69 The question asks for the choice that gives the most drama. Thus, you need to compare and contrast the options and see which is the most dramatic. Each of the options has an element of drama. **B** mentions that "the troops searched." **C** speaks of "enemy forces." **D** mentions "soldiers in red uniforms." However, all of these are incorrect because they are not as dramatic as choice **A**. "...the British hunted him like an animal" is the best answer.

#70 "after living in terrible conditions for such a long time" is a modifying clause, which means it describes or it will modify what comes immediately after the comma. Did "the relief of returning home" live in terrible conditions? No, which is why **F** is incorrect. Did "home" live in terrible conditions? No, which is why **H** is incorrect. Did "the caves" live in terrible conditions? No, which is why **J** is incorrect. Did "Hart" live in terrible conditions? Yes, which is why **G** is the correct answer.

#71 Who are "they"? The only people this pronoun could refer to is Washington's patriot army, but it's not them that said that about Washington, which is why **B** is incorrect. **D** ("its'") is not a word in the English language, and thus is incorrect. **A** is possessive, which is incorrect in this context. This is why **C** is correct; *it's* is a contraction meaning "it is," which is proper in this context.

#72 There are clues to help you place sentence 4. The biggest of them is that sentence 2 begins with "For example." If this sentence were in the right place, based on the content of sentence 1, you would expect sentence 2 to give an example of how relieved John Hart was when he returned home. Instead, the sentence is about how Hart's land was used during the war. This is why **H** is the correct answer; by inserting the sentence there, it gives sentence 2 an example of Hart "doing his part." **F, G,** and **J** all fail to properly transition the paragraph.

#73 As written, what does "there" refer to? There is nothing in this or the previous sentence that designates a place for him to have passed away. This is why **A** is incorrect. **B** creates a second independent clause, but gives no punctuation to combine the clause that would have to end with "1779" and the clause that would now begin with "there," so **B** is also incorrect. As for **C**, it is incorrect simply because it is too wordy; there is a simpler way to word what is needed here. This is why **D** is the correct answer; not only is it grammatically correct, but it is less wordy compared to other options.

#74 After "the land" there is the verb "to build" and then the prepositional phrase "in the first place." It makes no sense to set off any of it with a comma, which is why **F** is the correct answer. Remember: commas aren't thrown into sentences to create a pause because it kind of sounds nice to create a pause there. Rather, they are deliberate, and in this sentence, the clause from "Since" to "place" is one long introductory clause. **G, H,** and **J** are all incorrect because they insert commas in places where they do not belong.

#75 This is a biographical fact about John Hart's life. Simply look at the four options and determine if a biographical fact is appropriate or not. Choice **A** is incorrect because the first paragraph is not yet about John Hart, but the country as a whole. Choice **C** is incorrect because, by this point, the story has shifted to be that of his hiding out in the mountains. Choice **D** is incorrect because a biographical fact about John Hart's wife is not an appropriate way to end the paragraph about his hiding in the mountains. Choice **B** is correct because this paragraph, the second paragraph in the essay, is primarily focused on biographical details.

ACT Math Explanations

Answer Explanations - Step 2

Correct answers:

Backsolving:	**Picking Numbers:**	**Drawn to Scale:**	**The Calculator:**
1: D	**4: G**	**8: H**	**9: D**
2: F	**5: E**		**10: G**
3: D	**6: J**		
	7: A		

1. Correct answer: **D**. The typical way to solve this problem would be to set up an equation and solve for your missing variable. Since this question is looking for an average, then we need to add up all relevant terms, divide by the number of terms, and set it equal to the average that is desired. In this case, such an equation would look like this:

$$\frac{(19 + 27 + 34 + 27 + x)}{5} = 30$$

After multiplying both sides by 5 so that the 5's cancel on the left hand side, we are left with this:

$$(19 + 27 + 34 + 27 + x) = 150\,.$$

Then, of course, subtracting 19, 27, 34, and 27 from both sides, we are left with this:

$$x = 150 - 19 - 27 - 34 - 27 = 43$$

However, there is a reason that this example is under the *Backsolving* section; we can also solve by trying out answers one at a time and seeing if it is correct. Let's start in the middle with C: 34. When we do the math to determine the average, it looks like this:

$$\frac{(19 + 27 + 34 + 27 + 34)}{5} = \frac{141}{5} = 28.2$$

Thus, we see by *Backsolving* that answer choice C (34) is too low, and when we go higher to answer choice D (43), we do the math to find that it is the correct answer:

$$\frac{(19 + 27 + 34 + 27 + 43)}{5} = \frac{150}{5} = 30$$

2. Correct answer: **F.** Of course, this early into our book, we haven't yet discussed lines, the formula of a line, what it means for a line to have solutions, or for two lines to have a solution, etc. For our purposes here, we simply need to understand this: each of these five answer choices is an $(x,\ y)$ coordinate, thus an x and a y value. When we plug in the answers one at a time (aka *Backsolving*), which of them satisfies the equation we've been given? Let's try them one at a time until we find the correct answer. Start with F:

$$5 + \frac{1}{2}(-4) = 5 - 2 = 3$$

...that's it! In other words, when we plug in $x = -4$ and $y = 5$ into the given equation, it *satisfies*, or also equals 3.

3. Correct answer: **D.** Here, to solve this problem without *Backsolving*, we need to begin with the number we know and work backwards. We know that 3,150 baseball bats are permanently damaged. We know also that these permanently damaged bats are 3 out of 4 damaged bats, and that then 1 out of 60 bats produced. First, let's figure out how many bats per year are are damaged. If 3,150 bats are permanently damaged, and this is 3 out of 4 damaged bats, then we can set up an equation like this to determine the number of damaged bats:

$$3{,}150 = (\frac{3}{4})(x)$$

In this equation, x represents the number of damaged bats, When solved, we get that there are 4,200 damaged bats every year. This isn't yet the correct answer. We also know that the 4,200 damaged bats are only $\frac{1}{60}$ of all bats produced. Thus, if we multiply the number of damaged bats by 60, we will learn the number of bats produced in the manufacturing facility each week:

$$4{,}200 \times 60 = 252{,}000$$

However, of course *Backsolving* is another means to solve the problem. If you're stuck and can't quite figure out the forwards math one step at a time, why not simply try out the answer choices one at a time? Let's start with answer choice C (141,750) and pretend that this is how many bats are produced each week. First, we reduce it to $\frac{1}{60}$ of its size to find how many damaged bats there are, then multiply this new number by 0.75 (or multiply by $\frac{3}{4}$) to find the permanently damaged ones:

$$141{,}750 \times \frac{1}{60} = 2362.5, \text{ then... } 2362.5 \times \frac{3}{4} = 1771.875$$

This number is far lower than our given 3,150 permanently damaged bats. Thus, going higher to answer choice D (252,000) will yield the correct answer.

4. Correct answer: **G**. This problem would normally require us to simplify, add like terms, and simplify some more. However, let's use the *Picking Numbers* strategy first to solve, then we'll look at a more traditional way. Because the correct answer choice is equivalent to the polynomial in the question stem (that just means the question itself), and because both have the variable x, then let's choose a number for x, plug it into the question to get a value, then see which answer choice also gives us the same value when we plug in the same number for x. When choosing a value for x, you want to avoid numbers like -1, 0, and 1; go a little bit bigger. Let's pretend that $x = 4$. Plugging that into the question looks like this:

$$\frac{(4^2 - (5 \times 4) - 6)}{(4 + 1)} + 4 + 1 = \frac{(16 - 20 - 6)}{5} + 5 = \frac{-10}{5} + 5 = -2 + 5 = 3$$

So, if the polynomial in the question itself $= 3$ when $x = 4$, then all we have to do is plug $x = 4$ into each answer choice one at a time until we get a value of 4. Starting with F, we get $4 - 5 = -1$, not 3. Try again. Moving onto G, we get $2(4) - 5 = 8 - 5 = 3$. That's it!

The more traditional way to solve this problem involves simplifying, which would require us to factor first. I say that because in the numerator of the question, we have a trinomial: $x^2 - 5x - 6$. A trinomial will factor into two binomials, to look something like this (I'm making up these numbers): $(x - 4)(x + 7)$. Does that look familiar? That is the kind of form we have to get this trinomial into. So that we can (more than likely) cancel out the term in the denominator (the $x + 1$).

To factor a trinomial into two binomials, we need to find two numbers that *multiply* to give us the last number in the trinomial (in our case, -6) that also *add together* to give us our middle number (in our case, -5). There are four pairs of numbers that multiply to give us -6: -3×2, -2×3, 6×-1, and -6×1. But, which pair of them also add up together to equal -5 ? That would be the last pair in the sequence: -6×1. These two numbers are going to be added to an x term in each of our two binomials that result from the factoring of a trinomial.

Thus, here is how our trinomial breaks down when factored: $x^2 - 5x - 6 = (x - 6)(x + 1)$. Having accomplished this step, we can now write out our entire equation, replacing the trinomial with the two resulting binomials so as to cancel them out. Once they are canceled, we can then simplify and add like terms, like so:

$$(\frac{x^2 - 5x - 6}{x + 1}) + x + 1 = \frac{(x - 6)(x + 1)}{x + 1} + x + 1 = (x - 6) + x + 1 = 2x - 5.$$

5. Correct answer: **E**. Because this problem, again, is in the *Picking Numbers* section, let's use that strategy first to solve. Then, we will solve it in the more traditional way. If we're looking for an average, that means adding all terms together and then dividing by the number of terms. Here, we have 4 terms, all of which contain the variable a. Let's pick a number for a, then find the average, then apply that same value for a into the answer choices until we find the same average.

When utilizing *Picking Numbers*, avoid really small numbers for variables, like -1, 0, and 1. Let's pretend in this case that $a = 5$ and go from there. If $a = 5$, then our four terms become actual values, like this:

First: $3a^2 - 7 = 3(5)^2 - 7 = 75 - 7 = 68$

Second:	$2a^2 + 1 = 2(5)^2 + 1 = 50 + 1 = 51$
Third:	$-4a^2 + 12 = -4(5)^2 + 12 = -100 + 12 = -88$
Fourth:	$3a^2 - 2 = 3(5)^2 - 2 = 75 - 2 = 73$

So, when $a = 5$, our terms become 68, 51, −88, and 73. Let's add them together and divide by 4 to find the average:

$$\frac{68 + 51 - 88 + 73}{4} = \frac{104}{4} = 26$$

Now, we need to simply plug in $a = 5$ into our answer choices one at a time and see which of them is equal to 26. Starting with A, we get the following: $-a^2 + 1 = -25 + 1 = -24$, so this choice is incorrect. Now move on to B: $\frac{1}{2}a^2 + 1 = 12.5 + 1 = 13.5$, also incorrect. Now let's try C: $a^2 + \frac{1}{2} = 25 + \frac{1}{2} = 25.5$, also wrong. Now try D: $-a^2 + \frac{1}{2} = -25 + \frac{1}{2} = -24.5$, still wrong! That leaves us with only one choice, E: $a^2 + 1 = 25 + 1 = 26$, that's it!

Hopefully, you'll be able to do some of this math in your head and see more quickly than it took you to read this paragraph that the correct answer is E!

Now for a more traditional solving. If you don't want to pick numbers in this particular problem, then don't worry, you don't have to. All you have to do is treat these four terms just like numbers, meaning: add the four terms together and divide by 4, like this:

$$\frac{(3a^2 - 7) + (2a^2 + 1) + (-4a^2 + 12) + (3a^2 - 2)}{4}$$

You must be careful now to add like terms without making a simple mistake. Start with the a^2 terms, then the whole numbers:

$$\frac{(3a^2 - 7) + (2a^2 + 1) + (-4a^2 + 12) + (3a^2 - 2)}{4} = \frac{(3a^2 + 2a^2 - 4a^2 + 3a^2) + (-7 + 1 + 12 - 2)}{4} = \frac{4a^2 + 4}{4} = a^2 + 1$$

6. Correct answer: **J**. The absolute best way to solve this particular problem is to invent a certain number of people in line to buy ice cream (aka, *Picking Numbers*), apply the percentage changes to this number of people one day at a time, and then figure out the percent increase at the end. Many students on a problem like this simply attempt to add the percentages together (in this case, 35% + 40% = 75%), but that will be incorrect since the 40% "step" in this problem is applied *after* an initial 35% change has happened.

Step 1: Let's assume that the number of people in line to buy ice cream is initially 100. Why 100? Not only is it easy to apply percent changes to 100 (since, after all, 100 is the baseline for all percentages), but it is also easy to see a percent change when compared to an initial number of 100 in the very end of the problem.

Step 2: Increase our starting point by 35%. To increase a number by 35%, we must multiply it by 1.35. Thus, a 35% increase of our initial 100 people in line looks like this: 100(1.35) = 135.

Step 3: Increase this new number of people in line by another 40%. Using the same math as the previous step, this increase looks like this: 135(1.4) = 189.

Step 4: We began with 100 people in line, then after our two subsequent percent increases, went up to 189 people in line. Thus, it is easy to see that the combined percent increase over the two increases is 89%.

7. Correct answer: **A**. This question requires some logical thinking, some *Picking Numbers*, and some math skill as well. Before we do any of that, let's wrap our minds around what is actually being asked: which variable, *a, b, c,* or *d* is the smallest; not the variable manipulated or changed in any way, but the actual variable itself. First, let's put the math skill to the test by rewriting the inequality in a form that makes more sense; in other words, we need to get rid of the negative exponents. To do so, the exponents need to be moved (if they're in the numerator they go to the denominator, or vice versa) as they are made positive. Like this:

$$a^{-2} > b^{-2} > c^{-2} > d^{-2} = \frac{1}{a^2} > \frac{1}{b^2} > \frac{1}{c^2} > \frac{1}{d^2}$$

Some with excellent thinking skills may be able to solve the problem by clear and concise thinking at this point, and if that is you, then that is good. However, most of us need to turn this into something more concrete, something more real, and to do that, we should pick numbers. In other words, let's choose values for *a, b, c,* and *d* that make the above inequality real. Let's just start with *b* and *c* and go from there. Let's choose that $b = 4$ and $c = 5$ and see if the inequality holds true. If not, we can reverse the terms.

$$\frac{1}{b^2} > \frac{1}{c^2} = \frac{1}{4^2} > \frac{1}{5^2} = \frac{1}{16} > \frac{1}{25}$$

Now the question is this: is it true that $\frac{1}{16}$ is greater than $\frac{1}{25}$? Yes, it is true. We chose correctly the first time for *b* and *c*. Now, let's pick numbers for *a* and *d* that also make the inequality true. How about $a = 3$ and $b = 6$. When we do that, our inequality now looks like this:

$$\frac{1}{a^2} > \frac{1}{b^2} > \frac{1}{c^2} > \frac{1}{d^2} = \frac{1}{3^2} > \frac{1}{4^2} > \frac{1}{5^2} > \frac{1}{6^2} = \frac{1}{9} > \frac{1}{16} > \frac{1}{25} > \frac{1}{36}$$

Now, let's recall the actual question: "which of the following numbers has the least value"? A lot of students here will see, and correctly, that $\frac{1}{36}$ is the smallest of the values in our hypothetical inequality, and because $\frac{1}{36} = \frac{1}{d^2}$, students will then say that the correct answer to the question is *d*. However, that would be wrong. The question asks for which *variable* is the smallest of the four, not which manipulated variable is the smallest. Remember the numbers we picked to make the inequality true: $a = 3$, $b = 4$, $c = 5$, $d = 6$. Thus, *d* is actually the largest variable, and *a* is the smallest. This is why *a* is the correct answer. To make the inequality true, it must be the smallest of the 4 options.

8. Correct answer: **H**. Before we use any kind of knowledge of angles to accurately solve this problem, let's use the strategy that is being taught here: the *Drawn to Scale* strategy. The angle that is being asked about is $\angle ACB$. Tilt your paper so that segment *CB* is flat, or the bottom of a triangle. Now...what angle does it simply *look like*? It should look pretty close to a 90° angle, maybe slightly smaller. There is only one angle that is close to 90°, which is H: 85°. That is all you need to get this particular question correct.

Mathematically speaking, what is at play here is a law called the Law of Transversals; more information about this law is found in the lesson Math *Have to Know* #10 on angles. Simply put, because this shape is a parallelogram, that means that segments *AD* and *BC* are parallel, as are segments *AB* and *DC*. Because we know that $\angle FDA$ is 115°, we also know that $\angle DAB$ is 115°. If $\angle DAB$ is 115°, and $\angle CAB$ is 30°, then we also know that $\angle DAC$ is $(115° - 30°) = 85°$. Without getting into every detail of how the Law of Transversals works (again, see Math *Have to Know* Strategy #10), $\angle DAC$, which we have just learned is 85°, is the exact same as $\angle ACB$. Thus, $\angle ACB$ must also equal 85°.

9. Correct answer: **D**. Again, you may have been taught to find a common denominator between these three fractions, then edit the fraction so that it is equivalent to the original, then add the fractions, then simplify the new fraction to find your answer. There's nothing wrong with that at all, except that it is time consuming. And guess what you don't have a lot of on the ACT Math test? Time. Instead, use the calculator to your advantage and save yourself precious seconds. When I type these terms into the calculator and add them, here's what I get:

$$\frac{4}{17} + \frac{1}{2} + \frac{1}{68} = 0.2353 + 0.5 + 0.0147 = 0.75$$

Of course, converting 0.75 into a fraction isn't too terribly difficult. If you were given a difficult decimal, say something like 0.4358, then work your way through the answer choices one at a time, dividing the fractions in your calculator until you find a match.

10. Correct answer: **G**. In the correct ordering of this inequality, the danger is in students attempting to do the work all in the head and making a simple mistake. Here, we are given a fraction (⅓) to put in correct order with decimals. Simply type the fraction, whatever it is, into the calculator to also make it a decimal before comparing. Of course, this fraction is the equivalent of 0.33, so now we have 3 fractions that we simply need to order correctly: 0.33, 0.3, and 0.04. Because the inequalities in the answers start with the largest and move to the smallest, let's identify them from greatest to least. Well, it just so happens that I just did that when I listed them a moment ago: 0.33 is the largest, then 0.3, then 0.04. So, our inequality needs to begin with (⅓) as the largest. Only G does this, and double checking, it lists the others in proper order as well.

Answer Explanations - Step 3

Correct answers:

1: B	**11: C**	**21: D**	**31: E**	**41: A**	**51: B**
2: G	**12: K**	**22: K**	**32: K**	**42: K**	**52: K**
3: B	**13: B**	**23: C**	**33: C**	**43: D**	**53: C**
4: K	**14: H**	**24: J**	**34: G**	**44: H**	**54: F**
5: A	**15: E**	**25: B**	**35: A**	**45: B**	**55: B**
6: K	**16: F**	**26: K**	**36: J**	**46: K**	**56: F**
7: A	**17: B**	**27: E**	**37: A**	**47: A**	**57: C**
8: H	**18: H**	**28: G**	**38: J**	**48: H**	**58: H**
9: E	**19: D**	**29: D**	**39: C**	**49: B**	**59: E**
10: K	**20: F**	**30: J**	**40: G**	**50: F**	**60: G**

1. Correct answer: **B**. The estimate for the total job was $1,950, which includes the fee that is charged no matter how much fence is installed. Thus, ($1,950 – $600) = $1,350 represents the amount of money that is actually spent on fence installation. Because Cliff wants 150 feet of fence, then determining the cost per foot of fence for the installation is now a simple division problem: ($1,350 ÷ 150) = 9. Thus, Baldwin Fence, Inc. charges $9 per foot of fence.

2. Correct answer: **G**. A significant-enough number of ACT Math questions describe a shape or a diagram; sometimes it's a triangle, other times a sphere, etc. The rule is this: if a shape is being described, then *draw it out*. This prevents simple mistakes and ensures that you get the answer correct (or at least maximizes your chances). Here, you simply need to draw a small rectangle and a larger rectangle around it, labeling it with the appropriate sizes.

Because this question is asking for the part of the wall *not* covered by the white board, we need to find the area of the larger board and subtract the area of the smaller white board from that. The area of the wall as a whole is this: $(10\text{ft} \times 9\text{ft}) = 90\text{ft}^2$. The area of the white board is $(4\text{ft} \times 7\text{ft}) = 28\text{ft}^2$. Thus, $90\text{ft}^2 - 28\text{ft}^2 = 62\text{ft}^2$.

3. Correct answer: **B**. This question is a good example of a *ratio* question (more on that in *Have to Know* Lesson #8). A ratio or rate consists of two values that are in a relationship, like miles-per-hour, as in driving, or cups-of-flour-per-cups-of-sugar, as in a recipe. Although the question itself, especially in a modeling situation as we have here, is extremely unlikely to frame it this way, it is necessary for you to rewrite the ratios as fractions, which will set up a cross-multiplying situation that is much easier to solve. Here, we are working with water-per-tablespoons-of-coffee to make a strong coffee. Here is the recipe he reads about online, rewritten as water-per-tablespoons-of-coffee (water in the numerator, tablespoons of coffee in the denominator:

$$\frac{\frac{2}{3}}{1\frac{1}{4}} \text{ cups of water/tablespoons of coffee grounds}$$

As a reminder, the question is asking us to find how many coffee grounds would be needed if he has $2\frac{1}{2}$ cups of water. Thus, we can set up a cross-multiplying equation to solve for our missing amount of coffee grounds (let's call it x) that looks like this:

$$\frac{\frac{2}{3}}{1\frac{1}{4}} = \frac{2\frac{1}{2}}{x}$$

Cross multiplying, as a reminder, means multiplying the numerator of one term by the denominator of the other, then vice versa, and setting them equal to each other. For us, that would result in this:

$$\frac{2}{3}x = (2\frac{1}{2})(1\frac{1}{4})$$

Personally, whenever I'm dealing with multiplying or dividing fractions on the ACT, I almost always convert them to decimals. Otherwise, we have to change the values of the two terms on the right to get rid of the leading coefficients of 2 and 1. Solve from here however you like, but I'm going to change to decimals, like this, and solve for x:

$$0.667x = (2.5)(1.25)\ldots x = \frac{(2.5)(1.25)}{0.667}\ldots x = 4.685 \text{ tablespoons of coffee needed.}$$

Because the answer choices are in fractions, I simply need to go one at a time and determine which is equivalent to 4.685. It must be B or C since the two of them begin with a 4. When I type $4\frac{11}{16}$ into the calculator, I get something very close to 4.685 (there's bound to be fractional error since I rounded $\frac{2}{3}$ to 0.667). Thus, B is correct.

4. Correct answer: **K**. In this example, the starting values of the two stocks is irrelevant; what is relevant is the difference between them, which is $30. The question can be simplified perhaps by first realizing this: how long, then, will it take for Stock A to gain $30 on Stock B? If Stock A is going to increase by $1 a day, and Stock B is going to increase by $0.50 a day, then that means that Stock A is going to gain $0.50 a day on Stock B. So, if Stock A, relatively speaking, increases by $0.50 a day, then how long will it then take it to gain the $30 necessary? The result of this simple division will be our answer:

$$\frac{\$30}{\$0.50} = 60, \text{ thus, 60 total days for the two stocks to reach the same value.}$$

5. Correct answer: **A**. The biggest danger in this problem is making a simple mistake (as in many ACT Math problems). The mistake to be made is this: see that minus sign straight in the middle, between the two terms? That minus sign means that *everything* to the right of it must be subtracted, one term at a time. Let's take this one step at a time:

Step 1: Distribute each y term to look like this:

$$y(6-y)-y(y+9)=(6y-y^2)-(y^2+9y)$$

Step 2: Add like terms. Again, the two terms in the rightmost parentheses (y^2 and $9y$) must *both* be subtracted, like this:

$$(6y-y^2)-(y^2+9y)=(6y-9y)+(-y^2-y^2)=-3y-2y^2$$

This corresponds, meaning is the same thing as, choice A: $-2y^2-3y$.

If you're scared of making a simple mistake, recognize that this question is a strong candidate for the *Picking Numbers* strategy, since the question and answer both have a variable. Choose a value for y, something like $y = 3$, plug it into the question and answers, and look for a match!

6. Correct answer: **K**. There are two ways to solve this problem. First, you can use *Picking Numbers*, choose a value for both x and y, then plug those values into the question and answers and find a match. Another way is to simply simplify the complicated expression one step at a time. This is what we'll do here. The first thing to do is to work on the term in the numerator, since you have multiple terms being raised together to the 4th power, like this: $(3x^{-2}\sqrt{y})^4$. To get rid of that 4th power, it must be applied to each term one at a time, like this:

$$(3x^{-2}\sqrt{y})^4=3^4(x^{-2})^4(\sqrt{y})^4=3^4(x^{-2})^4(y^{\frac{1}{2}})^4$$

Notice that I changed the last term, the $\sqrt{y}$ to a y raised to the power of $\frac{1}{2}$. These two terms are equivalent, and for our purposes it will be easier to work with. Now, the first term is simple enough. $3^4 = 81$. This is enough for us to go ahead and eliminate answer options G and J, since there are no numbers in the denominator and the two of them do not have the number 81 in them. It is the next two terms where students make mistakes. If you have a value with an exponent being raised to *another* exponent, you multiply the exponents together, like this:

$$3^4(x^{-2})^4(y^{\frac{1}{2}})^4=81(x^{-2\cdot4})(y^{\frac{1}{2}\cdot4})=81x^{-8}y^2$$

Because the term in the numerator in the original question was already in this kind of form, let's put the two together now: our newer, simplified numerator over the original denominator:

$$\frac{81x^{-8}y^2}{x^2y^{-5}}$$

From here, you next need to know what to do with negative exponents. It is simple enough: make the exponent positive and reciprocate it (if it's in the numerator, move it to the denominator, and vice versa). Thus, our expression gets simplified to this:

$$\frac{81x^{-8}y^2}{x^2y^{-5}} = \frac{81y^5y^2}{x^2x^8}$$

Lastly, you need to know what to do with like terms with exponents that are multiplied together. Here, you *add* the exponents together, like this:

$$\frac{81y^5y^2}{x^2x^8} = \frac{81y^{5+2}}{x^{2+8}} = \frac{81y^7}{x^{10}}, \text{ which is choice K.}$$

7. Correct answer: **A**. There are two ways to solve this problem. The first is to use *Picking Numbers* and choose a value for a, then plug that into both the question and the answers. The second way is to find common denominators for the fractions in both the numerator and denominator, then properly divide. Let's solve it both ways.

First, *Picking Numbers*. Let's pretend that $a = 4$ so that the fraction of which is a part will simply equal 1. Now, I'm also going to convert all of these fractions to decimals, that way I can solve the entire thing in my calculator, like this:

$$\frac{\frac{a}{4}+\frac{1}{3}}{\frac{1}{2}-\frac{1}{3}} = \frac{1+0.333}{0.5-0.333} = \frac{1.333}{0.167} = 7.982$$

Now the question is this: which of the five answer choices equals approximately 7.982 when a has a value of 4? You can tell that when I say "approximately 7.982" that that really is probably going to mean 8; there is a bit off error when you round off fractions to the nearest decimal (which we did twice in the equation above). When you plug in $a = 4$ into answer choice A, you get $\frac{3(4)+4}{2} = \frac{16}{2} = 8$...that's it!

Second, we can solve the "proper" way. The first step here is to find common denominators and rewrite the fractions equivalently with their new denominators, like this:

$$\frac{\frac{a}{4}+\frac{1}{3}}{\frac{1}{2}-\frac{1}{3}} = \frac{\frac{3a}{12}+\frac{4}{12}}{\frac{3}{6}-\frac{2}{6}} = \frac{\frac{3a+4}{12}}{\frac{1}{6}}$$

The second step is to divide the fraction in the numerator by the fraction in the denominator. This is one of those tricky little steps that many students forget how to do, but it is fairly simple. Take the fraction in the denominator, reciprocate it (aka flip it), and then multiply it by the fraction in the numerator, like this:

$$\frac{\frac{3a+4}{12}}{\frac{1}{6}} = \left(\frac{3a+4}{12}\right)\left(\frac{6}{1}\right)$$

From there, simply multiply, and then simplify:

$$\left(\frac{3a+4}{12}\right)\left(\frac{6}{1}\right) = \frac{18a+24}{12} = \frac{3a+4}{2}$$

8. Correct answer: **H**. Again, there are two ways to solve this problem. You can use *Picking Numbers*, which would mean choosing a value for x and applying it to the question and finding a match in the answers. In fact, unless you are fast at simplifying trinomials (which is a necessary step in solving this problem the "proper" way), then this is what you should do. The second way to solve it, as I said, is to factor the trinomials in the numerator and denominator and then cancel out like terms (you can learn more about factoring trinomials in *Good to Know* Lesson #5: Parabolas). Let's solve it both ways.

First, *Picking Numbers*. Let's assume that $x = 3$ and see what value we get. Plugging in $x = 3$, our expression is reduced like this:

$$\frac{(x^2+5x+4)(x-8)}{(x^2-7x-8)(x+2)} = \frac{(3^2+5(3)+4)(3-8)}{(3^2-7(3)-8)(3+2)} = \frac{(9+15+4)(-5)}{(9-21-8)(5)} = \frac{28(-5)}{-20(5)} = \frac{-140}{-100} = \frac{7}{5}$$

Then, we must plug in $x = 3$ into each answer choice until we get an answer that also equals seven fifths. Because the math here is simple enough, I can look ahead and see that H is going to give me what I'm looking for, like this:

$$\frac{x+4}{x+2} = \frac{3+4}{3+2} = \frac{7}{5}$$

Second, we can factor the trinomials in both the numerator and denominator and simplify by canceling out like terms. The trinomials I am talking about are the expressions in the numerator and denominator that feature an x^2 term. Let's simplify each trinomial one at a time, starting with ($x^2 + 5x + 4$). A simplified trinomial will result in two binomials (x plus or minus some number) times (x plus or minus some number). To figure out those "some number"s, we need to ask ourselves this question about this trinomial in particular: what are two numbers that *multiply* to equal the last term in the trinomial (4), but also *add* to equal the middle number in the trinomial (5)? Well, $(4 \times 1) = 4$, and $(4 + 1) = 5$, so we've found our two "some number"s, which are 4 and 1. Thus, our factored trinomial looks like this:

$$(x^2 + 5x + 4) = (x + 4)(x + 1)$$

We have to do the same thing to the trinomial in the denominator: ($x^2 - 7x - 8$). We need two numbers that *multiply* to give us -8 and add together to give us -7. There are lots of numbers that multiply to give us -8 (like 4 times -2, and -1 times 8), but only one pair that also adds up to -7: -8 and 1. Thus, our factored trinomial looks like this:

$$(x^2 - 7x - 8) = (x - 8)(x + 1)$$

Let's rewrite the entire expression with our trinomials factored, then cancel out like terms. In other words, if a binomial appears in the numerator and in the denominator (like you're about to see with (x +1)), then they simply cancel out. Our work now looks like this:

$$\frac{(x^2 + 5x + 4)(x - 8)}{(x^2 - 7x - 8)(x + 2)} = \frac{(x + 4)(x + 1))(x - 8)}{(x - 8)(x + 1)(x + 2)} = \frac{(x + 4)}{(x + 2)},$$ which is answer choice H.

9. Correct answer: **E**. The easiest way to conceptualize this problem is to invent your own number set (*Picking Numbers*, essentially) and do the math that the question is asking. The question presupposes that we have a number set consisting of 5 numbers, and it doesn't really matter what those five numbers are. How about we use this set for our purposes: {1, 1, 1, 1, 1}. Right now, the mean or average is 1. The question asks us this: if we increase the mean by 5, how much would the sum of the numbers increase? Well, our current mean is 1, and to increase it by 5 would mean we'd have to have a number set with a mean of 6, something that now looks like this: {6, 6, 6, 6, 6}. The sum of our previous number set was (1+1+1+1+1) = 5, and now the sum of our new number set is (6+6+6+6+6) = 30. Thus, the sum of the 5 numbers in our number set would have to increase by 25.

10. Correct answer: **K.** Here, we are asked for the product of the mean and the median of a number set. Before we get to that, we have to figure out what the number set even is! We are told that the number set is each factor of 12 listed in numerical order.

A factor of a number is simply a number that evenly divides into that bigger number. The easiest way to figure out the factors of a given number is to determine all of the pairs that multiply to equal the bigger number. For 12, there are a few pairs that multiply to give us that number: (1 x 12 = 12), (2 x 6 = 12), and (3 x 4 = 12). Thus, the factors of 12 in numerical order, and our number set, is this: {1, 2, 3, 4, 6, 12}.

Next, the question requires us to determine the mean and the median. First, the mean of course is the average, which can be found as such: Mean = (1+2+3+4+6+12)/6 = 4.667. The median is the term in the middle, which falls between 3 and 4 in our number set. Thus we need the average of 3 and 4, which is 3.5.

Lastly, the problem asks for the *product* of the mean and the median. The product of two numbers is simply the result if you multiply them. So, our answer is going to result from multiplying the mean and the median that we just determined: (4.667 x 3.5) = 16.3345, which falls between 16 and 17, which is answer choice K.

11. Correct answer: **C**. The difficulty of this problem really lies in the fact that it is a modeling problem; you have to get through the long story, plucking out the math you need along the way. The question requires us to compare the values of the mean, median, mode, and range of two separate number sets: before Author E arrives, and after Author E arrives, and then find which value is *least* changed.
I think the best way to visualize the changes, and see which changes the least, is to create two columns, one for before and one for after.

	Before	After
Number set:	{1, 1, 2, 3}	{1, 1, 2, 3, 21}

Mean (average):	$\frac{1+1+2+3}{4} = 1\frac{3}{4}$	$\frac{1+1+2+3+21}{5} = 5\frac{3}{5}$
Median (middle term):	1.5	2
Mode (appears most):	1	1
Range (difference):	$(3-1) = 2$	$(21-1) = 20$

Thus, the number that is changed the least is the mode, because it does not change at all. This is answer choice C.

12. Correct answer: **K.** This question is difficult because it isn't the first step in an equation, and it isn't the last step either. By that I mean that each answer choice is written in a form that has assumed that step or two has been done in the equation to determine the value of t. Let's do the math from the very beginning one step at a time until we get an equation that looks like the answers (featuring numbers like 77 and/or 96 and/or 16, etc.)

Because t represents an amount of tips, our initial equation can and should be written as such:

$$\frac{14+15+11+22+15+t}{6} = 16$$

The 6 in the denominator represents the number of tips received, or the number of nights in a row he receives tips. Because it is an average, we need the equation on the left (the total tips received divided by the number of tips) to equal the average we want, in this case 16. Now, there's just one step left to do to simplify:

$$\frac{(14+15+11+22+15)+t}{6} = 16 \quad \ldots \quad \frac{77+t}{6} = 16\text{, which is answer choice K.}$$

13. Correct answer: **B.** Working an inequality is almost the same as working any other equation (as a side note, for more on Inequalities, see *Good to Know* Lesson #4). You can add the same term to both sides, you can divide or multiply both sides by the same term, etc. The only exception is when multiplying or dividing both sides by a negative number. In that case, the inequality symbol will switch from facing one side to another.

In this problem, each answer choice features an isolated y on the left side of the inequality. Thus, we need to work the actual given inequality in the same fashion and solve for y. First, let's add $9x$ to both sides to isolate the y term on the left side, like this:

$$-3y - 9x > 3x - 6 \quad \ldots \quad -3y > 12x - 6$$

At this point, we need to divide both sides by -3 so that the y is isolated by itself on the left side. However, as I said a moment ago, when an inequality is affected by a negative on both sides (NOT addition or subtraction of a negative number, but multiplication or division) then the inequality will switch from $>$ to $<$ or from $<$ to $>$ (or, for that matter, from $\geq$ to $\leq$ and $\leq$ to $\geq$). That is what is about to happen here:

$$-3y > 12x - 6 \quad \ldots \quad y < -4x + 2$$

14. Correct answer: **H**. This kind of problem is extremely common on the ACT Math test. By "this kind of problem" I mean a problem in which a complicated-looking equation is presented with 3 or more missing variables. The *look* of it is intimidating, but this kind of problem is always (always, always, always) way simpler than it seems. The ACT is counting on many students looking at this equation and saying to themselves, "I have no idea what this means, and it is scary." However, don't be so hasty! The ACT on these kinds of problems will always give you the value of all but 1 of the missing variables and ask you to solve for that one missing variable. In this particular equation, there are 3 missing variables as written: P, b, and e. b is the number of bagels, which they give us in the final line of the question (3). e^{-4} is also given to us (0.075). That means that the only missing variable is P, which fortunately is already isolated on the left side of the equation.

I will admit that there is another math concept in this equation that might throw you off, which is that of *factorial.* This is what the ! means after the 4 (it is pronounced "4 factorial"). When you have a number "factorial" you simply multiply the number by each number as it is decreased by 1. For example, 4! is the same thing as $4 \times 3 \times 2 \times 1$.

All we have to do now is plug in the missing variables and put the entire thing into the calculator to find the missing probability of 3 bagels remaining in the display case. Let's rewrite the equation for P, replacing known variables and the 4! with numbers along the way:

$$P = \frac{4^b e^{-4}}{4!} = \frac{4^3(0.075)}{4(3)(2)(1)} = \frac{64(0.075)}{24} = \frac{4.8}{24} = 0.2$$

Thus, H (0.2) is the correct probability.

15. Correct answer: **E**. You don't need to have any concept of the use of the imaginary number i in higher mathematics to get this question correct, or any other question in ACT Math for that matter. Here, simply FOIL the terms one at a time, and any time you get an i^2, simply change it to a -1. As a reminder, FOIL is an acronym that stands for "first, outside, inside, last," and simply refers to an order in which you could multiply terms when two binomials are being multiplied one by another. This particular problem has you multiplying not 2, but 3 binomials all by each other. Let's simply start with the first 2 binomials, then when we've simplified it as best we can, let's add in the third binomial.

Here's what I mean; let's do this math first (and bring in the final $(i + 3)$ when we've simplified this):

$$(i + 1)(i - 4) = i^2 - 4i + i - 4 = i^2 - 3i - 4$$

This is what we get when we multiply the first two binomials together. However, we can't quite bring back and multiply by that third binomial quite yet. Remember: each i^2 is equivalent to -1, so we need to replace the i^2 term first with -1 and add like terms:

$$i^2 - 3i - 4 = -1 - 3i - 4 = -3i - 5$$

Thus, our first two binomials $((i + 1)(i - 4))$ is equivalent to $(-3i - 5)$. Now, let's bring back that third binomial and multiply it by our new, simplified binomial:

$$(-3i - 5)(i + 3) = -3i^2 - 5i - 9i - 15 = -3i^2 - 14i - 15$$

Now, we need to replace the i^2 term with a -1 as we did before and add any like terms to get our final answer:

$$-3i^2 - 14i - 15 = -3(-1) - 14i - 15 = 3 - 14i - 15 = -14i - 12$$

Thus, our three binomials multiplied by each other can be simplified down to $-14i - 12$, or answer choice E.

16. Correct answer: **F**. In order to find the value of $\frac{a}{b}$, we have to, of course, determine the value of a and b. The difficulty is that a and b are both exponents. The trick here is in realizing that when $a = 1$, we get this: $16^1 = 16$. Because that number is much larger than $\sqrt{2}$, we need to figure out what value of b will raise $\sqrt{2}$ to a value of 16. Well, let's try out some different values (all of which you can simply do in your calculator if not in your head):

$$\sqrt{2}^2 = 2\text{, and then } \sqrt{2}^4 = 4\text{, and then } \sqrt{2}^6 = 8\text{, and then } \sqrt{2}^8 = 16.$$

Thus, when $a = 1$, then b has to equal 8 for the two sides of the equation to be equal to each other.

So, $\frac{a}{b} = \frac{1}{8}$, which is answer choice F.

17. Correct answer: **B.** You might think that this problem really belongs in a lesson exclusively on triangles, and that would be true if there wasn't an equation given and you had to find the lengths of the sides of the triangle independently. However, we are in luck, because the ACT here has given us the Law of Sines to help us quickly identify the missing sides of the triangle. Essentially, if we know an angle and its opposite side, we can set that relationship equal to another angle and its opposite side and solve for whatever variable may be missing (thus, Algebra).

First, let's solve for the side opposite that of 41°:

$$\frac{sin(a)}{A} = \frac{sin(b)}{B} \quad \dots \quad \frac{sin(52)}{9} = \frac{sin(41)}{B} \quad \dots \quad B = \frac{sin(41)(9)}{sin(52)} = 7.49$$

Next, we need to solve for the final side. This can be done in innumerable ways (see ACT Math *Have to Know* #9 on triangles for all of the ways). Let's keep using the Law of Sines, since it has been given to us. Let's call the final missing, bottom side C. However, we need the other, third angle that isn't given. But finding the missing angle is simple since the 3 angles in a triangle always add up to 180°. Thus our missing angle can be found by simple subtraction: 180° – 41° – 52° = 87°. So, since we know the angle opposite our final missing side, let's do the same math as before using the Law of Sines:

$$\frac{sin(a)}{A} = \frac{sin(b)}{B} \quad \ldots \quad \frac{sin(52)}{9} = \frac{sin(87)}{C} \quad \ldots. \quad C = \frac{sin(87)(9)}{sin(52)} = 11.41$$

Now that we have found the approximate lengths of the other two sides of the given triangle, we can answer the question, which asks for the perimeter to the nearest mile: 9 + 7.49 + 11.41 = 27.9, or very near 28 miles.

18. Correct answer: **H.** Although this question is appearing under the *Higher Algebra* section of this ACT book, it would be unnecessary to create an equation to solve this problem. The first step in solving it is in actually understanding what the problem is asking. There are 12 mannequins, and each has at least 1 item on it. How many mannequins can display 4 items if each mannequin has at least one item on it?

I think the more efficient way to answer this question is to do some kind of visual representation of the 12 mannequins. Here, each capital 'M' represents a mannequin. Next to each 'M' you'll notice one lowercase 'i', which represents an item.

M: i	M: i	M: i	M: i
M: i	M: i	M: i	M: i
M: i	M: i	M: i	M: i

Now, I've made sure that each of the 12 mannequins has at least 1 item. Since the question states that I only have 25 items to put on the mannequins in the first place, that means I only have 13 items left to distribute. At this point, I need to distribute the 13 items so that mannequins now get full with 4 items:

M: iiii	M: iiii	M: i	M: i
M: iiii	M: ii	M: i	M: i
M: iiii	M: i	M: i	M: i

Although I was able to add extra items to 5 more mannequins before I ran out, I was only able to fill up 4 of the mannequins with all 4 items. Thus, the answer is H.

19. Correct answer: **D.** We simply need to rewrite this line into slope-intercept form, which would mean isolating the y on the left side of the equation. When this is done, whatever coefficient is in front of the x on the right side of the equation is the slope. As a reminder, slope intercept form looks like this: $y = mx + b$, in which m is the slope and b is the y-intercept (where the line crosses the y-axis, though that isn't relevant for this particular problem). Simplifying the problem into this form looks like this:

$$5x - 2y = 7 \quad \ldots \quad -2y = -5x + 7 \quad \ldots \quad y = \frac{5}{2}x - \frac{7}{2}$$

Thus, now in slope-intercept form, we can see that the value of m, or the slope, is $\frac{5}{2}$.

20. Correct answer: **F.** Any point that a line touches is a solution for that line. Thus, for any line, there are an infinite number of solutions. However, if two lines cross one another, there is only going to be 1 solution for the two lines: the point where they cross. There are two ways to solve this particular problem. The more visual way would be to put both of these lines into slope-intercept form, graph them one at a time based on the y-intercept and slope, and try to manually see where they cross one another.

Another way to solve this problem would be to use *Backsolving* (which is what I would do), to simply try out the points one at a time. Plug each point's x and y values into each equation and see if it works or satisfies. Fair warning: to be sure, some of the wrong answer points (if not all of the wrong answers) are going to satisfy or be solutions for one line or another, but not both; only one of them is going to satisfy *both* lines' equations. Let's simply try them out one at a time and see which one satisfies both equations.

F. (1, 2): $x - 2y = -3$ ... $1 - 2(2) = -3$ ... $-3 = -3$ ... so far so good; now the other

$3x - 4y = -5$ ... $3(1) - 4(2) = -5$ ... $-5 = -5$ ... that's it!!!

Letter F, or point (1, 2), satisfies both equations, making it the correct answer. If you try any of the other points like we did above, it will satisfy one or neither, but not both. Just to give you an idea of what that looks like, take point G for example:

G. (–1, 1): $x - 2y = -3$ ... $-1 - 2(1) = -3$ ... $-3 = -3$ ... so far so good; now the other

$3x - 4y = -5$ ... $3(-1) - 4(1) = -5$ ... $-7 = -5$ ... no, doesn't satisfy!

21. Correct answer: **D.** I don't have the Midpoint Formula memorized, and even if I did, I wouldn't be using it to set up equations to answer questions involving midpoints. In this particular question, you are being asked to find the coordinates of E. You can think of the problem like this: the line segment DE starts at D $(-4, -2)$, then goes to the halfway point at the midpoint $(1, 3)$, and then continues on the same distance and direction to point E, which is what we need to find.

Well, let's just think about it. On the x-axis, we go from a point of -4 (the x coordinate of D) to a point of 1 (the x-coordinate of the midpoint), which is an increase of 5. Well, we simply need to go 5 more to find the x-coordinate of E, which takes us up to 6. This is already enough to get the question correct, since there is only one answer that has an x-coordinate of 6.
To be thorough, let's find the y-coordinate of E using the same logic. On the y-axis, we go from a point of -2 (the y coordinate of D) to a point of 3 (the y-coordinate of the midpoint), which is an increase of 5. Well, we simply need to go 5 more to find the y-coordinate of E, which takes us up to 8.

If the x-coordinate of E is 6, and the y-coordinate of E is 8, then that makes our final answer D: (6, 8).

22. Correct answer: **K.** First, the questions is asking for the slope of line q, which is *perpendicular* to line p; this means that the two lines cross forming four 90° angles. Before we get into how to compare the slopes of two lines that are perpendicular, let's start here: we have to find the slope of line p.

Slope can simply be remembered as RISE over RUN; in other words, the change between 2 points on the y-axis over the change between the same 2 points on the x-axis. We are given 2 points for line p, which is enough to find its slope. Let's denote $(-3, 5)$ as point 1 and $(0, 4)$ as point 2.

$$slope = \frac{rise}{run} = \frac{(y2 - y1)}{(x2 - x1)} = \frac{4-5}{0--3} = \frac{-1}{3} = -\frac{1}{3}$$

You'll notice that the slope of line p, or $-\frac{1}{3}$, is one of the answer choices. However, we have to remember that we're looking for the slope of line q, which is *perpendicular* to line p. This doesn't mean that they have the same slope, but quite the opposite. The slope of line q is going to be the *negative reciprocal* of the slope of line p, which means this: make the slope negative, and flip it upside down (moving the numerator to the denominator and moving the denominator to the numerator). Thus the negative reciprocal of $-\frac{1}{3}$ is $--\frac{3}{1}$, or just 3. This is the answer we are looking for.

23. Correct answer: **C.** You do NOT need to have memorized the distance formula to get this question correct. I, the man typing out this ACT Math book, don't have the distance formula memorized. You don't need it. There is an easier way (which, mathematically, is what the distance formula is based upon in the first place). The easier way is this: simply draw a graph and plot the two points (as I've done below), then make out of them a triangle (as I've beautifully done below). You will notice that the distance between the two points (what the question is requiring us to find) is simply the hypotenuse of a triangle. Then, because we know the lengths of the other 2 sides of our triangle (labeled below), we can use the Pythagorean Theorem ($a^2 + b^2 = c^2$) to find our missing side.

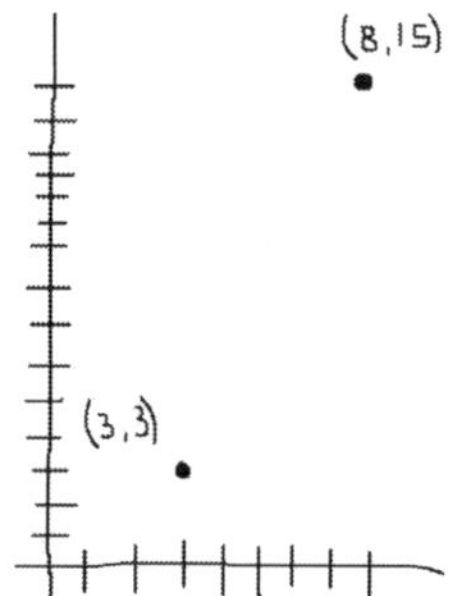

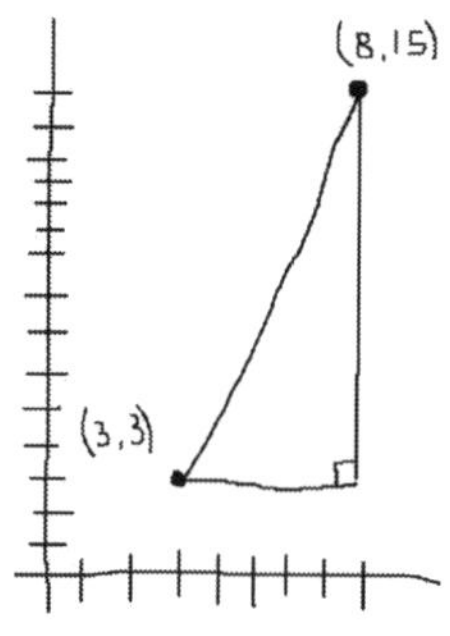

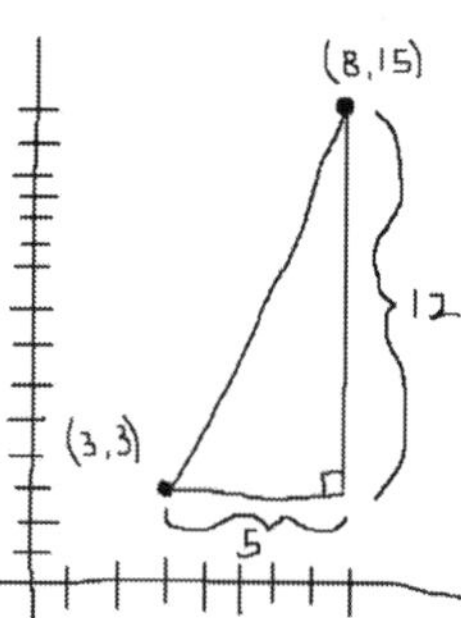

As you see in the last image above, I have labeled the length of the bottom side of the triangle 5. I know this length because it is simply the difference in x values between our two points; aka, $(8 - 3) = 5$. Similarly, I know the length of the right side of the triangle to be 12 because the difference in y values between our two points is $(15 - 3) = 12$.

You may be able to recognize this triangle as a *special triangle* (more on that in ACT Math *Good to Know* Lesson #2: Triangles Part II). This kind of special triangle is called a 5-12-13 triangle, meaning that we can know automatically that the length of the hypotenuse (aka the distance between the two points) is 13. However, let's use the Pythagorean Theorem as well to confirm:

$$a^2 + b^2 = c^2 \quad \ldots \quad (5)^2 + (12)^2 = c^2 \quad \ldots \quad 25 + 144 = c^2 \quad \ldots \quad 169 = c^2 \quad \ldots \quad 13 = c$$

24. Correct answer: **J.** This question is much easier than it seems. What makes it seem difficult is that there's a t variable monitoring time (which ends up being irrelevant) as well as a cloud moving across two-dimensional space (aka, on the (x, y) coordinate plane). Let's draw out what is happening here:

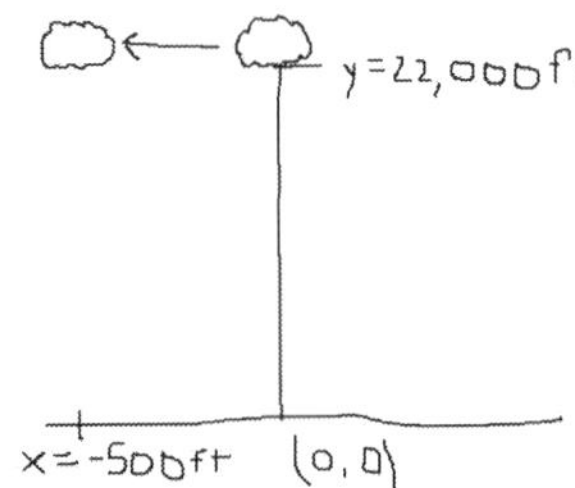

As you can see based on this expert drawing, the cloud is floating at a constant height of 22,000 feet. For our purposes, the path of the cloud floats along a straight line at 22,000 feet. In other words, at $y = 22{,}000$. If you go into your graphing calculator, hit the Y= button, type in any number (5, for example), then hit GRAPH, you're going to see a horizontal line across the screen from left to right. This is what is happening with this cloud; it is floating along the line $y = 22{,}000$.

25. Correct answer: **B.** In this problem, we are looking for values of x that can satisfy the equation $(x - a)(x - b) = 0$. Notice that both of the binomials are being multiplied by one another. This means that if either of them equals 0, then no matter what number the other may equal, the equation as a whole will equal 0. Thus, we simply need to find two values: one that will make the binomial on the left (aka $(x - a)$) equal 0, and another that will make the binomial on the right (aka $(x - b)$) also equal 0.

Well, if $x = a$, then in the binomial on the left, you will end up with this: $(a - a)$, which is equal to 0. In addition, if $x = b$, then in the binomial on the right, you will end up with this: $(b - b)$, which is also equal to 0. Thus, the two values of x that satisfy the equation are a and b, since these two values make the two binomials equal to 0.

26. Correct answer: **K.** In this question, all we know is that x is positive, y is positive, and z is negative, but we don't know how large or small they are. If we choose numbers for these three variables of all sizes, we will see that it is not possible to know what the sign of their average is. If x and y are small (let's say, 2 and 3), and z is a relatively large negative number (let's say -100), we could end up with an equation like this:

$$\text{Average} = \frac{2 + 3 - 100}{3} = -\frac{95}{3}, \text{ which of course has a negative sign.}$$

On the other hand, if we choose relatively large values for x and y (let's say 100 and 200) and a relatively small value for z (say, -2), then we could end up with an equation like this:

$$\text{Average} = \frac{100 + 200 - 2}{3} = \frac{298}{3}, \text{ which of course has a positive sign.}$$

Thus, because there are no constraints or limits on the size of x, y, and z, then it is not possible to determine.

27. Correct answer: **E.** Again, the key to these *Logical Thinking with Variables* problems is to choose values, eliminate possibilities, and repeat if necessary. As for this problem, let's pick numbers for x and y that are equivalent. For example, let's assume that $x = 2$ and $y = -2$. I want to do this because the answer choices set some versions of x and y equal to each other.

Answer choice A puts their absolute values equal to each other. Absolute value simply means the distance a value is from 0, and because 2 and -2 are both 2 spots from 0, it is true that the absolute value of x and y can be the same. As for options B, C, and D, each of them features some variation in which the values of x and y are squared, which is going to make them equal. If $y = -2$, then squaring it will make it $= 4$, which of course is the same as 2 squared. Thus, B, C, and D are all possible.

Answer choice E, on the other hand, is not possible. A negative exponent simply means that the value is flipped from the numerator to the denominator, like this:

$$x^{-1} = y^{-1} \quad \ldots \quad \frac{1}{x} = \frac{1}{y} \quad \ldots \quad (\text{plug in } x = 2 \text{ and } y = -2) \quad \ldots \quad \frac{1}{2} = \frac{1}{-2} \quad \ldots \quad \text{can't be equal!}$$

28. Correct answer: **G.** In this problem, we are given very clear parameters as to the value of three variables: r, q, and p. Let's pick numbers for each of these based on the inequality constraint and see which we can eliminate. Remember: we can eliminate an option if it isn't true or can't be true (since we're looking for the option that *must* be true).

Let's assume that $r = -5$, $q = 60$, and $p = 700$.

F. $p + q < q + r$ ... $700 + 60 < 60 + (-5)$ ... this does not work; on to the next answer.

G. $\frac{p}{r} < \frac{q}{r}$ ... $\frac{700}{-5} < \frac{60}{-5}$ ... $-140 < -12$ ... this works! Let's try the rest:

H. $qr < pr$ ... $60(-5) < 700(-5)$ ... $-300 < -3{,}500$ ... this does not work...next!

J. $p < q - r$ ... $700 < 60 - (-5)$ ... $700 < 65$ ... this does not work...next!

K. $\frac{p}{r} < \frac{q}{r}$ ... This is the opposite of choice G, which gives us an option that does *not* work.

Thus, we can definitively say that G is the only option that *must* work!

29. Correct answer: **D**. You may think that this is a strange name to decide the name for your baby, and you'd be correct...but don't get distracted! We are looking for the probability that the name does *not* begin with the letter 'R', which means we need two numbers: the total number of names in the hat (which, we are told, is 12) and the number of names that do not begin with 'R', which is 4 (letter 'J') + 3 (letter 'P') + 2 (letter 'C'). Thus, our probability can be determined as follows:

$$\frac{4+3+2}{12} = \frac{9}{12} = \frac{3}{4}$$

30. Correct answer: **J.** The formula for the number of permutations n objects taken r at a time is as follows:

$$_nP_r = \frac{n!}{(n-r)!}$$

Thus, for our purposes here, 12 objects or items taken and arranged 3 at a time is equivalent to:

$$_nP_r = \frac{n!}{(n-r)!} = \frac{12!}{(12-3)!}\text{, or answer choice J.}$$

However, I'm guessing you don't have that formula memorized, and I don't think it will benefit you in the slightest if you do memorize it. What *could* be of great benefit to you, on the other hand, is if you use your noggin to figure out how to solve this problem in an alternative way. Simplify the problem a bit; instead of trying to figure out how to determine the number of ways to take and arrange 3 items from a total of 12 items, let's assume we want to take and arrange 1 item from a total of 5 items. In that case, there are exactly 5 ways to take 1 object out of a group of 5. Thus, plugging in 5 and 1 into the answer choices instead of 12 and 3, we will see that only one of them actually equals 5, which is choice J, like this:

$$\frac{5!}{(5-1)!} = \frac{5 \cdot 4 \cdot 3 \cdot 2 \cdot 1}{4 \cdot 3 \cdot 2 \cdot 1} = 5$$

It's been mentioned elsewhere in this book, but if you are confused about the exclamation point after these numbers, don't be; learning what this means is rather simple. The exclamation point is called "factorial", thus 5! is pronounced "5 factorial." Above you can see what it means; simply multiply 5 by each integer below it down to and including 1. Thus, $5! = 5 \cdot 4 \cdot 3 \cdot 2 \cdot 1 = 120$.

31. Correct answer: **E.** Here, we simply need to do a division problem by forming a fraction to determine the percent likelihood that the answer choices call for. There are 30 electives to choose from, so we know that is the total amount that will go in the denominator. As for the numerator, we are looking for the likelihood that the elective will take place at either the Intramural Fields (11 options) or the Dawson Building (7 options). Thus, our math looks like this:

$$\frac{11+7}{30} = \frac{18}{30} = 0.6\text{, or }60\%$$

32. Correct answer: **K.** The table of cars sold represents the number of cars that are likely to be sold on one day, but the question asks for how many cars are remaining on the lot after 5 days. Let's take this problem in steps.

Step 1: We need to find the expected outcome of the number of cars sold in a single day. To do that, we must add the multiplication of the number of cars sold by its probability. Here is how to calculate the expected outcome, aka, how many cars are expected to sell on the lot in a single day:

Expected cars sold in a day = $0(0.2) + 1(0.4) + 2(0.3) + 3(0.1) = 0 + 0.4 + 0.6 + 0.3 = 1.3$

Now that we know that it is expected to sell 1.3 cars in a day, we can move on to step 2.

Step 2: We need now to find how many cars are expected to sell across 5 days. This is simple enough; we just need to take our expected outcome and multiply it by 5, like so: $(5 \cdot 1.3) = 6.5$. However, the problem asks us for how many cars are expected to be remaining in the lot after 5 working days. This means we need to subtract our 6.5 expected cars sold from the 120 that are in the lot at the beginning of the week, like so: $(120 - 6.5) = 113.5$, or answer choice K.

33. Correct answer: **C**. First, let's find 75% of 4. That is simply 4(0.75) = 3. Next, let's find 300% of 3. This is simply 3(3.00) = 9. As for their sum, that simply means that we add them together. In this case, the sum of 75% of 4 and 300% of 3 = 3 + 9 = 12, or answer C.

34. Correct answer: **G**. To solve this problem effectively, let's first convert the fraction $\frac{1}{8}$ into a decimal, which is 0.125. Thus, we are now looking for 1% of 0.125. Now, if I wanted to find 100% of 0.125, I would multiply it by 1.00. If I wanted to find 10% of 0.125, I would multiply it by 0.10. However, the question is asking for just 1% of 0.125, which means we need to multiply it by 0.01, like so:

0.125(0.01) = 0.00125, which is answer choice G.

35. Correct answer: **A**. To answer this question correctly, we need to first add up the cost of the items. The total cost (pre-tax) of the items needed to create the ornament is \$2.00 + \$1.50 + \$2.30 + \$2.70 = \$8.50. Now, this \$8.50 is subject to an 8% sales tax, which means that the \$8.50 needs to go up by 8%. There are two ways to do the math on this, which are exactly the same. Either:

\$8.50 (1.08) = \$9.18 ... or ... \$8.50 + \$8.50(0.08) = \$9.18

The question asks how much money she will have leftover after spending \$10. Thus, the correct answer can be found in this way: \$10.00 – \$9.18 = \$0.82, or 82 cents, option A.

36. Correct answer: **J**. It may seem like the way to solve this problem is to simply add 30% + 40% and get that the answer is 70%, but that isn't how it works. Mathematically speaking, because the number goes up by 30% before being affected by another 40%, the answer has to be *greater* than 70% of the original number, which already narrows down our answer choices.

However, to do the math effectively, let's use some *Picking Numbers*, and assume that there are 100 students who purchase ice cream on Monday. 100 is a good starting point because it will be easy to find the percent increase after the two iterations. If we get an answer in the end that 182 students purchased ice cream on Wednesday (an 82% increase over 100), we know the answer is J. If we get an answer in the end that 191 students purchased ice cream on Wednesday, we know the answer is K.

Monday to Tuesday there is a 30% increase, thus if we start with 100, we get this:

100(1.30) = 130, meaning that 130 students purchased ice cream on Tuesday.

Tuesday to Wednesday, there is a 40% increase, thus if we start with 130, we get this:

130(1.40) = 182, meaning that 182 students purchased ice cream on Wednesday.

As we said before, 182, when compared to our starting point of 100, represents an increase of 82%, or answer choice J.

37. Correct answer: **A**. An added difficulty to this question is that the question gives you a rate of inches, but asks for an answer in terms of feet. Don't let that confuse you; let's find the answer in inches that we're looking for, then simply divide by 12 to find the answer in feet.

Remember, we need to set up our ratio so that a metric will cancel out, leaving the metric we want in the numerator. In this case, we want inches in the numerator in our answer (let's call it x inches), so we need to set up an equation in which seconds cancels, leaving us a value in inches, that looks like this:

$$\frac{45 \text{ inches}}{2.5 \text{ seconds}} \cdot 10 \text{ seconds} = \frac{450 \text{ inches}}{2.5} = 180 \text{ inches}$$

Now, to find our final answer, we simply divide the 180 inches by 12 inches per foot and get a final answer of 15 feet, which is answer choice A.

38. Correct answer: **J.** Just like the above question, we are solving for kilometers, so we want centimeters to cancel. If we multiply our given ratio by the $2\frac{7}{10}$ centimeters, we need to structure the ratio so that kilometers is in the numerator and centimeters in the denominator. Also, don't let the fractions scare you. Simply rewrite them as decimals to make the math easier for the calculator. Our equation to solve will now look like this:

$$\frac{120 \text{ kilometers}}{0.25 \text{ centimeters}} \cdot 2.7 \text{ centimeters} = \frac{324 \text{ kilometers}}{0.25} = 1{,}296 \text{ kilometers}$$

Thus, the answer is J: 1,296 kilometers.

39. Correct answer: **C.** To solve this problem, play with the ratios until the number representing Tree B is the same in both ratios. Like this: if the ratio of Tree A to Tree B is 2:3, then it is also 4:6, 6:9, 8:12, 10:15, 12:18, and 14:21.

I stopped at 14:21 purposefully, since I can see that in the next ratio of Tree B to Tree C, it begins with the number 7, which divides into 21 (which is the value of Tree B where we left off). If the ratio of Tree B to Tree C is 7:5, then it is also 14:10, and then 21:15.

Here is what we now have:

The ratio of Tree A to Tree B is 14:21, and the ratio of Tree B to Tree C is 21:15. Because the Tree B's match, we can see that the ratio of Tree A to Tree C is 14:15, which is answer choice C.

40. Correct answer: **G.** The tangent of any angle, if you remember, is the opposite side over the adjacent side. The angle we are evaluating from is that of F, which just refers to the angle that touches the point F. Opposite point F is a side with length 12, and the adjacent side is the other side that isn't the hypotenuse, which has a length of 16. Thus, our equation looks like this:

$$\tan F = \frac{\text{opposite}}{\text{adjacent}} = \frac{12}{16} = \frac{3}{4}$$

Thus, the answer is G.

41. Correct answer: **A.** The first thing to note about this question is that it is *describing* a triangle, and not giving you a triangle. What that means is that it is important for you to draw it as it is being described in your answer booklet so that you can actually visualize what is happening. Does this mean that you've got to draw an actual tree with leaves and a man named Mr. Wilkins climbing a ladder? No, just a triangle, using the information we've got. I've done this below, and I've marked the missing side of the triangle that the question is asking for (which is the length of the ladder) as x:

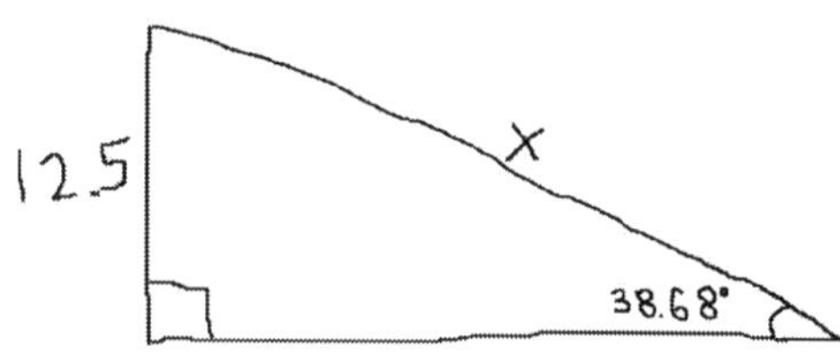

What we need now is an equation that uses the angle we know and the side we know in order to find our missing hypotenuse. Recall our acronym: SOHCAHTOA. Out of the S (sin), the C (cosine), and the T (tangent), one of them is of perfect use to us since it requires the use of the known and the missing sides. This would be sine, since the sine of any angle is defined as the opposite side over the hypotenuse.

Thus we can set up an equation like this, which is how we will solve for x:

$$\sin(38.68) = \frac{12.5}{x}$$

So far so good. Next, we need to solve for x by manipulating the equation so that x is isolated on one side. To do this, we need to first multiply both sides by x to remove it from the denominator, then divide both sides by the sin(38.68) to get the x all by itself, like this:

$$\sin(38.68)(x) = \frac{12.5}{x}(x) \quad \ldots \quad \sin(38.68)(x) = 12.5 \quad \ldots \quad \frac{\sin(38.68)(x)}{\sin(38.68)} = \frac{12.5}{\sin(38.68)}$$

After canceling out the sin(38.68) on the left side of the equation, we are left with a value for x that can easily be put in the calculator, like this:

$x = \frac{12.5}{\sin(38.68)} = 20.00$, meaning that the ladder height (the hypotenuse) is closest to 20 feet.

42. Correct answer: **K.** You may notice that the length of segment *RM*, which we must find to answer the question, is not actually drawn on this diagram. That means that it is up to you to draw a new diagram or shape to help visualize what you need to do to find this length. Below is such a drawing.

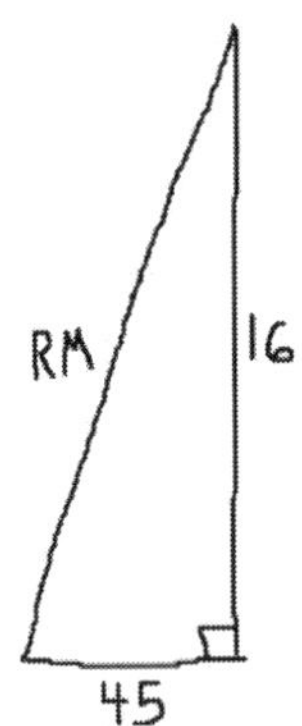

You'll notice, too, that the length of segment *RM* is the hypotenuse of a triangle. Because we know that the length top to bottom of the retail space is 160 meters, we know that the length of the right side of the triangle is also 160 meters. Lastly, because we know that point *R* is the midpoint of segment *LO* at the top, which is 90 meters, we know that half of the segment *MN* at the bottom is 45 meters. Thus, here is our triangle with our one missing side.

Because it is a right triangle, and because there is only 1 missing side, we can of course use the Pythagorean Theorem to find that missing side. As a reminder, the Pythagorean Theorem says that $a^2 + b^2 = c^2$, in which c is the hypotenuse and a and b are the two legs. In the equation below, I'm going to use c, but just recognize that c and *RM* are the same thing.

$$(45)^2 + (160)^2 = c^2 \quad \ldots \quad 27{,}625 = c^2 \quad \ldots \quad \sqrt{27{,}625} = \sqrt{c^2} \quad \ldots \quad c = 166.21$$

Because the question asks for the length to the nearest meter, we round down to 166, which is answer choice K.

43. Correct answer: **D.** Fortunately, this question requires the same "triangle" we used in the above question. I'm going to redraw this triangle with information that we know, including the points on the diagram, and simply mark the angle we are looking for as $x°$.

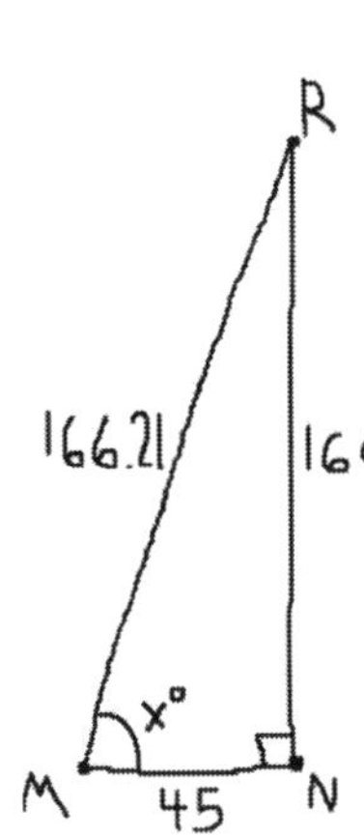

Hopefully, when you first answered this problem, you either drew a brand new triangle like I have done here, or you at least made markings on the original diagram. This is how to avoid simple mistakes. Now, because we know that one angle is 90°, we would be able to easily find our required missing angle (again, called $x°$ on the diagram to the left) if we knew the uppermost angle, or angle *MRN*. But, we don't, so we have to fall back onto another way, which is using the trig functions represented by the acronym SOHCAHTOA.

My default is to use sine if possible, and it is possible here. The difficulty in this problem however is that it isn't a side that is missing, but an *angle*, which means that we are going to have to get into a concept called arcsin (on your calculator it looks like this, $\sin^{-1}$ and is probably a 2nd function above the sin button). This function is used to find a missing angle when the value of sin (aka, the opposite side over the hypotenuse) is known.

Before we actually use arcsin, let's set up what this equation looks like in its original form:

$$\sin(x) = \frac{\text{opposite}}{\text{hypotenuse}} = \frac{160}{166.21} = 0.9626\text{, or in short, } \sin(x) = 0.9626$$

Now that we have the value of sin, which is 0.9626, the time has come to use arcsin. When done properly, this will give us the missing angle value, and thus our correct answer. To do this, type arcsin (again, you probably on your calculator hit 2nd, then sin), then input the 0.9626 in parentheses following, then hit Enter, like so:

$$\sin(x) = 0.9626 \quad \ldots \quad \sin^{-1}(0.9626) = x° \quad \ldots \quad x° = 74.28°$$

If you need practice on this, try using arccos and arctan from the exact same angle, and see if you can get the same value for $x°$.

44. Correct answer: **H.** This problem is similar to the last couple of them in that you are asked to find the distance between two points that ends up being the hypotenuse of a triangle. Here, we are running a point diagonal across a square made up of 4 sides, each with a length of 45 meters. Below I have drawn the triangle we are working with.

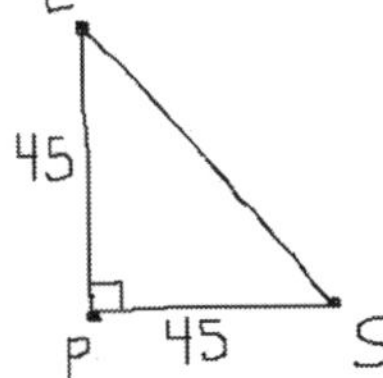

Again, the length we are looking for is the hypotenuse of this little triangle. A too-quick student might guess that the correct answer is 45 because this is part of a square. However, this is the diagonal of the square, not a side, which is longer than any of the sides. A simple use of the Pythagorean Theorem is enough to help us find the missing side. Because the Theorem is $a^2 + b^2 = c^2$, I'm going to call the missing side of our triangle here c.

$$a^2 + b^2 = c^2 \quad \ldots \quad (45)^2 + (45)^2 = c^2 \quad \ldots \quad 4{,}050 = c^2 \quad \ldots \quad \sqrt{4050} = \sqrt{c^2} \quad \ldots \quad c = 63.64$$

The question asks for the length of the extension cord that runs from *L* to *S* to the nearest meter; rounding up, that would be 64 meters, or answer choice H.

45. Correct answer: **B.** First of all, before we get into the actual mathematics of this particular question, remember our ACT Math mini-strategy #3: *Drawn to Scale*. Every figure on the ACT *is* drawn to scale. In other words, if a line *looks* like it is twice the length of another line, that's because it *is* twice the length of another line, and if an angle *looks* like it is about 135°, that's because it *is* about 135°. If you turn your paper sideways and put line segment *CD* horizontal, doesn't our missing angle *look* like it is about 45° or so? How many answer choices, given the look of the angle, actually *look* like they could be correct answers?

Before definitively answering that question, on to the math. There are two concepts that we need to remember to get this question right. First, that the angles in a line add up to 180°, and second that the angles in a triangle also add up to 180°. With that in mind, let's break this problem down into two steps:

Step 1: If angle *ABC* is 155°, then that means that angle *CBD* (the smallest angle inside the triangle) is 180° – 155° = 25°. Similarly, if angle *CDE* is 80°, then that means that angle *CDB* (the other angle inside the triangle) is 180° – 80° = 100°.

Step 2: We now know two out of three angle values within the triangle *BCD*. This means that we simply need to subtract the two angles that we've figured out from 180° to determine our missing angle, like so: 180° – 25° – 100° = 55°, which is the correct answer.

In closing, back to the *Drawn to Scale* strategy we discussed at the beginning of this answer explanation. Do you see it now? Angle *CDB* is very, very close (just by looks!) to a 45° angle, making the only conceivable answer B: 55°.

46. Correct answer: **K**. Don't let the look of this figure scare you away. If we use our knowledge of angles from the lesson, we can reason our way to a correct answer. The reason we are given the angle at the bottom of 42° is because once we have the value of the other acute angle in the triangle, we can determine angle *GIH*. Here, I've redrawn the smaller triangle to show you what I mean:

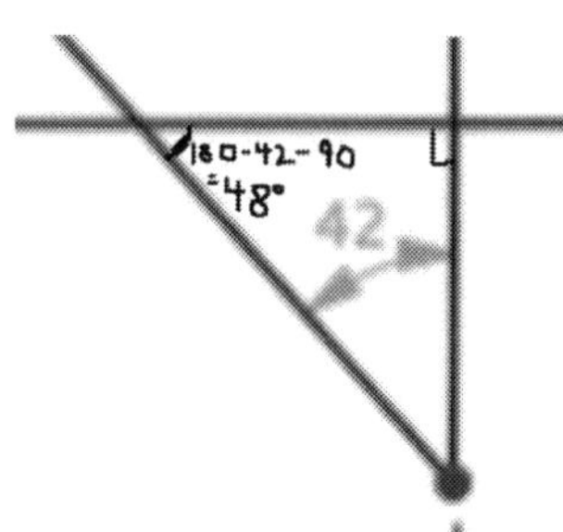

Sorry if that is a little blurry or small, but I've written in there that the value of the angle in the top-left corner is 180° – 42° – 90° = 48°.

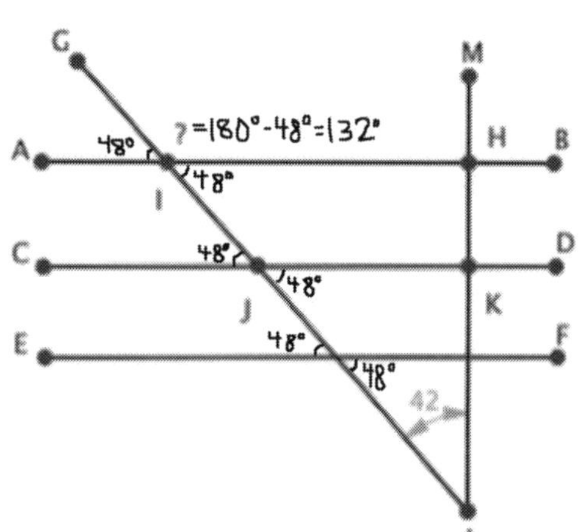

Because of the Law of Transversals, we can be sure that this is the value of many other angles in our figure, as you can see from the image here.

As you can see, we can use the Law of Transversals to determine pairs of opposite angles that also equal 48° (6 in total in our diagram) all the way up to angles *GIA* and *HIJ*. Knowing either one is enough to solve for our missing angle, marked with a question mark.

To find our missing angle (the math of which I've also drawn into the diagram), we simply need to use the fact that the angles in a line add up to 180°.

Thus, 180° – 48° = 132°, which is answer choice K.

Lastly, hopefully you can see by now (with our *Drawn to Scale* strategy in mind) that the angle itself is very obtuse, meaning that the answer must be either J or K. If you can't figure out the math, let this be a bit of a guide in making a smart guess, at the very least!

47. Correct answer: **A.** The best thing to do here is to draw a crude image of what is being described, two lines crossing each other. Here is what you do know. First, it is impossible that these two lines are perpendicular, which would form four 90° angles.

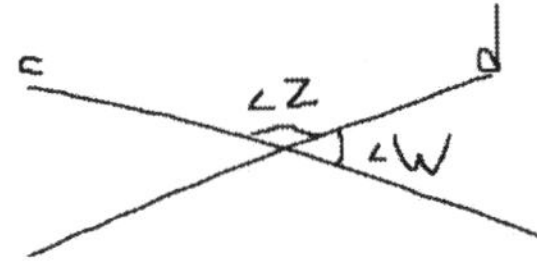

We know this because if all angles were the same, it would be impossible for one of the angles to be bigger than another, let alone 500% bigger. This is also why angles Z and W can't be opposite angles, because that would mean they have the same value. These two angles must, combined, form a line. The lines and angles must look something like the image I've drawn to the left.

Second, we know that two angles in a line add up to 180°. If we call the value of angle W $x°$, then angle Z must be $5x°$, since it is 500% (5 times) bigger. This is enough for us to set up an equation and solve for angle W.

$$x° + 5x° = 180° \quad \ldots \quad 6x° = 180 \quad \ldots \quad x° = \frac{180}{6} \quad \ldots \quad x° = 30°$$

48. Correct answer: **H**. Again, before we get into how to solve this problem mathematically, let's think about the *Drawn to Scale* mini-strategy. Angle VUW is a very acute angle. Just by the *look* of it, I would guess it is somewhere around 40°, and there's only one answer choice that's in the ballpark of 40°....on to the math of it!

The fact that there are extra line segments that form a triangle is completely irrelevant to this question. What is relevant is that we have two angles that add up to a line. Let's solve this in two steps:

Step 1: We simply need to set up an equation in which these two angles add up to 180°; this will help us to solve for x, which is necessary in solving this problem. Here is what we need:

$$(16x + 2)° + (4x - 2)° = 180° \quad \ldots \quad 20x = 180° \quad \ldots \quad x = 9$$

At this point, some students will quickly put that F: 9° is the correct answer. However, at this point all you have done is solve for x, not the angle VUW. Again...does that *look* like a 9° angle to you? Hopefully not.

Step 2: Now that we know the value of x, we simply need to plug that in to our missing angle's equation and solve, like this:

$\angle VUW = (4x - 2)° = (4(9) - 2)° = (36 - 2)° = 34°$, or answer choice H.

49. Correct answer: **B.** Again, it would be helpful if you drew out the four walls: one with a door, one with a window, another with a window, and one with no window or door at all. However, let's now solve it in three steps. First, let's calculate the amount of wall space there is. Second, let's calculate the amount of space is occupied by doors and windows. Third, let's subtract to find how much space is being painted.

Step 1: Each wall is 12 feet by 10 feet. To find the area, simply multiply the two. However, let's remember that there are 4 walls. This is why in the equations below, I am multiplying the area by four:

$$\text{Wall Space} = (10\text{ft} \cdot 12\text{ft}) \cdot 4 = 120\text{ft}^2 \cdot 4 = 480\text{ft}^2$$

Step 2: There are three spaces that are not being painted. In the equations below, I begin with the area of the door, then add in each window:

$$\text{Unpainted Space} = (4\text{ft} \cdot 8\text{ft}) + (3\text{ft} \cdot 5\text{ft}) + (3\text{ft} \cdot 5\text{ft}) = 32\text{ft}^2 + 15\text{ft}^2 + 15\text{ft}^2 = 62\text{ft}^2$$

Step 3: Lastly, simply subtract the unpainted area from the total wall area:

$\text{Total Painted Area} = 480\text{ft}^2 - 62\text{ft}^2 = 418\text{ft}^2$, which is answer choice B.

50. Correct answer: **F.** What we need to do is to create a rectangle, then create a second one with decreased/increased side lengths, then compare their areas. Just like we saw in previous questions, if we are trying to find percent increases or decreases, it is helpful to begin with the number 100. In our case, 100ft^2 (assuming it is in feet; it doesn't say). Thus, our baseline rectangle is going to be one with a length of 10 and a height of 10 (but, you might object, isn't that a square? Yes, but every square is a rectangle because it has 4 90 degree angles, so it works!).

Second, we need to create a fictional rectangle that meets the decrease/increase requirements. Well, since we chose as a baseline a rectangle with a length of 10 and a width of 10, making percent changes to these sides will not be too difficult.

The length of our new rectangle is 30% smaller than 10, or (1.00 – 0.30)(10), or 7.
The width of our new rectangle is 45% larger than 10, or (1.00 + 0.45)(10), or 14.5.

The area of this new rectangle is (7 x 14.5), or 101.5ft^2 .

If our baseline rectangle had an area of 100ft^2, and our updated rectangle has an area of 101.5ft^2, then clearly the area increase is $(101.5\text{ft}^2 - 100\text{ft}^2)$, or 1.5ft^2. Well, though the percent increase is obvious based on the numbers that we chose, to find the percent increase we simply need to do a little math:

$$\text{Percent Increase} = \frac{\text{Area Increase}}{\text{Original Area}} = \frac{1.5\text{ft}^2}{100\text{ft}^2} = 0.015 \text{, or } 1.5\%, \text{ which is answer choice F.}$$

51. Correct answer: **B**. To find the correct answer to this question, we need to solve it in two steps. First, we need to determine the volume of the can of soup. Second, we need to find Frida's daughter's portion, or 40%.

Step 1: The volume of a three dimensional shape that is uniform from top to bottom can be found by calculating first the area of the top or bottom, then multiplying by the height. In this case, since it is a can of soup, it has a circular top. For more on circles, see ACT Math *Have to Know* Lesson #13. For now, let's simply recall that the area of a circle is πr^2, in which r is the radius. However, we aren't given the radius of the can, but the diameter; the radius is simply half of the diameter, or for us (65mm/2), or 32.5mm. For our purposes, the formula for the volume of this can is $\pi r^2 h$, in which h is the height of the can (98mm), r is the radius (32.5mm), and π is a constant with a value of 3.14159 (or just hit the π button on your calculator!).

$$\text{Can Volume} = \pi r^2 h = \pi(32.5)^2(98) = (3.14159)(1056.25)(98) = 325{,}193.8\text{mm}3$$

Step 2: Now that we have the volume of the can, it is time to determine Frida's daughter's portion, which is 40%. All we need to do is multiply the volume of the can by 0.4, which will give us the 40%:

$$325{,}193.8\text{mm}3(0.4) = 130{,}077.5\text{mm}3 \text{, or rounded, } 130{,}078, \text{ which is answer choice B.}$$

52. Correct answer: **K**. When we are asked for $f(-2)$, that simply means this: what is the value of the function when $x = -2$? So, all we need to do is plug in $x = -2$ into the function wherever there is an x, and that will spit out a value, which is our answer. If $f(x) = 3x^2 - 12x$, then $f(-2)$ can be worked out like this:

$$f(-2) = 3x^2 - 12x = 3(-2)^2 - 12(-2) = 3(4) - (-24) = 12 + 24 = 36 \text{, which is answer choice K.}$$

53. Correct answer: **C.** This question may have the added layer of featuring two variables (a and b), but it works the exact same way as any function problem. The function is defined as $f(a, b)$, and we are asked to find the value of $f(-1, 2)$, so we should plug in $a = -1$ and $b = 2$ into the function and see what value results. If $f(a, b) = 2b^3 + 5a$, then $f(-1, 2)$ can be worked out like this:

$$f(-1{,}2) = 2b^3 + 5a = 2(2)^3 + 5(-1) = 2(8) + (-5) = 16 - 5 = 11 \text{, which is answer choice C.}$$

54. Correct answer: **F.** This may look complex, like the kind of problem that only someone who is very good at math would be able to get correct, but that is not true at all. The exact same principle applies in this function problem as in any other function problem. If we were looking for $f(2)$, we would plug in 2 anywhere there were an x in the function. Here, we are looking for $f(g(x))$, which means that we will plug in $g(x)$ anywhere there is an x in $f(x)$. Because $g(x) = 2x + 2$, we will have to plug in $(2x + 2)$ anywhere there is an x in $f(x) = x^2 + 3x$, like this:

$$f(g(x)) = x^2 + 3x = (2x + 2)^2 + 3(2x + 2) = (2x + 2)(2x + 2) + 3(2x + 2) =$$

$$(4x^2 + 4x + 4x + 4) + (6x + 6) = 4x^2 + 14x + 10$$

Now, $4x^2 + 14x + 10$ is a fine answer, but it can be factored a bit further (which is how the first three answer choices are presented). Though there's a leading coefficient of 4 in front of that first term, not all terms (4, 14, and 10) are divisible by 4, but they are are divisible by 2. Thus, if we factor out a 2 from each term, we get:

$$f(g(x)) = 4x^2 + 14x + 10 = 2(2x^2 + 7x + 5) \text{, which is answer choice F.}$$

55. Correct answer: **B**. I'm guessing that, if you're reading this explanation, then you're a bit thrown off by the division of one function by another. However, do not be thrown; the problem is as simple as it seems. We are given a value for $f(x)$, which is 21, and we are given a value for $g(x)$, which is 10.5, and we are asked to divide the former by the latter. Like this:

$$\frac{f(x)}{g(x)} = \frac{21}{10.5} = 2 \text{, which is answer choice B.}$$

56. Correct answer: **F**. This problem is the exact same as number 55 above, the difference being that now there are added elements, like variables, trinomials and binomials, and how to divide fractions.

Let's solve this problem in two different ways to help you learn to see these multiple ways as well. The first way we'll solve it is by *Picking Numbers*, and the second is the more traditional way.

Method 1: *Picking Numbers*

We need to choose a value for x, plug it in, divide, and see what number we get. Then, we can do the same in the answer choices and match them up. Let's assume that $x = 3$. However, it doesn't matter what you choose. So, when $x = 3$...

$$f(x) = \frac{1}{(x+3)} = \frac{1}{(3+3)} = \frac{1}{6} \quad \text{and} \quad g(x) = \frac{1}{(x^2+2x-3)} = \frac{1}{(3^2+2(3)-3)} = \frac{1}{(9+6-3)} = \frac{1}{12}$$

Now, I need to divide $f(x)$ by $g(x)$. As a reminder, to divide a fraction into another, take the fraction in the denominator, flip it upside down, and now multiply it by the fraction in the numerator. You'll see that happen here:

$$\frac{f(x)}{g(x)} = \frac{\frac{1}{6}}{\frac{1}{12}} = \frac{1}{6} \cdot \frac{12}{1} = \frac{12}{6} = 2$$, so now, which answer = 2 when we plug in a value of 3 for x?

F: $x - 1 = 3 - 1 = 2$...that's it!

Method 2: Traditional Simplification of Polynomials

Before we put these terms over one another, we need to factor the trinomial $(x^2 + 2x - 3)$ in the denominator of $g(x)$ into 2 binomials. To do this, we need two numbers that multiply to give us a value of -3, but which add together to give us 2. These two numbers are -1 and 3, which are the two values added to x in each binomial, like this:

$$x^2 + 2x - 3 = (x-1)(x+3), \quad \text{thus} \quad g(x) = \frac{1}{(x-1)(x+3)}$$

Now that we have that simplified, it is time to divide. Again, to divide fraction into another, take the fraction in the denominator, flip it upside down, and now multiply it by the fraction in the numerator. You'll see that happen here:

$$\frac{f(x)}{g(x)} = \frac{\frac{1}{(x+3)}}{\frac{1}{(x-1)(x+3)}} = \frac{1}{(x+3)} \cdot \frac{(x-1)(x+3)}{1} = \frac{(x-1)(x+3)}{(x+3)} = x - 1$$, which again, is choice F.

57. Correct answer: **C.** You might think, "Isn't 1 foot a little wide for the diameter of a skinny umbrella?" Well, you'd be right; Carla needs to take it easy.

However, that kind of thinking is a distraction...stay focused!

We need to find the area of the larger circle, then find the area of the smaller circle, then subtract the latter from the former, which will give us the total area of the tablecloth after the (unnecessarily big) hole has been cut. Let's recall that the formula for the area of a circle is this: Area = πr^2. There is a simple mistake to be made in this problem, however, which needs to be noticed before we get started. We are given the *radius* of the larger circle, which is what we need, but we are given the *diameter* of the smaller circle, which is 1 foot. We need to make sure we're working with the *radius* of the smaller circle, which is 0.5 feet.

$$\text{Larger Circle Area} = \pi r^2 = \pi(4.5)^2 = \pi(20.25) = 63.62\text{ft}^2$$

$$\text{Smaller Circle Area} = \pi r^2 = \pi(0.5)^2 = \pi(0.25) = 0.79\text{ft}^2$$

Now, subtracting the area of the smaller from the larger: $63.62 - 0.79 = 62.83$, which is choice C.

58. Correct answer: **H.** This is a two step problem. First, we need to use the circumference given to find the radius of the circle, then second, we need to use that radius to find the area of the circle.

Step 1: recall that the formula for the circumference of a circle is this: $2\pi r$. Thus, to find the radius, we need to set the circumference that we are given equal to this formula, and solve for r, like so:

$$\text{Circumference} = 2\pi r \quad \ldots \quad 22 = 2\pi r \quad \ldots \quad \frac{22}{2\pi} = r \quad \ldots \quad r = 3.50$$

Step 2: now that we know that the radius of this circle is 3.50, we can use that information to find the area. Recall that the formula for the area of a circle is this: Area = πr^2. Now we just need to plug and solve:

$$\text{Area} = \pi r^2 = \pi(3.5)^2 = \pi 12.25 = 38.48, \text{ which rounds to 38.5, or choice H.}$$

59. Correct answer: **E**. In this problem, we are comparing the areas of two circles. We need to solve it in two steps. The first step will be to find the area of each circle (we will call one "smaller circle" and the other "larger circle"), and then the second step will be to subtract.

Step 1: Let's begin with the smaller circle. We know that the radius of this circle is 5 feet, which is enough for us to find the area. Recall that the formula for the area of a circle is this: πr^2 .

$$\text{Smaller Cirlce Area} = \pi r^2 = \pi(5)^2 = \pi(25) = 78.54 \text{ ft}^2$$

As for the second, bigger circle, all we know is that the radius of this circle is 40% longer than that of the smaller circle. To increase the radius of the first circle by 40%, simply multiply it by 1.4, like this: 5(1.4) = 7. Thus, the radius of the larger circle is 7, which means that we can now find its area:

$$\text{Larger Cirlce Area} = \pi r^2 = \pi(7)^2 = \pi(49) = 153.94 \text{ ft}^2$$

Step 2: We are asked how much larger is the area of the second, larger circle than the first, smaller circle, so now all that's left for us to do is subtract:

$$\text{Larger Circle Area} - \text{Smaller Circle Area} = 153.94 \text{ ft}^2 - 78.54 \text{ ft}^2 = 75.40 \text{ ft}^2$$

Because the answer requires us to round to the nearest square foot, we round down from 75.40 to 75, which is answer choice E.

60. Correct answer: **G.** Recall that the arc of a circle is simply a piece of the circumference, and that there is a ratio at play here: as the arc of a circle is to the circumference, so too the interior angle of the arc is to all the angles in a circle. Let's lay these 4 things out one at a time and see what we know:

1) The arc of the circle: this is what we're trying to find; let's call it x.

2) The circumference: we don't yet know this, but we can find it. We are told that the pizza has a diameter of 16, which means a radius of 8. If the formula for the circumference of a circle is $2\pi r$, then the circumference of this pizza is $2\pi r = 2\pi(8) = 50.27$ inches.

3) The interior angle: we are told this: 55°.

4) The total degree of a circle: this is 360°.

Now that we know 3 of the 4 values, we can set up an equation in which we cross multiply. First, let's actually set up the ratio:

$$\frac{\text{arc}}{\text{circumference}} = \frac{\text{interior angle}}{\text{sum of all angles}} \quad \ldots \quad \frac{x}{50.27} = \frac{55}{360}$$

As a reminder, to cross multiply, you set up a new equation in which the numerator of one side is multiplied by the denominator of the other side, and vice versa, and the two values are set equal to each other. Or, similarly, in this equation, you can just multiply both sides by 50.27 to isolate the x. Either way, you will end up with the same thing.

$$\frac{x}{50.27} = \frac{55}{360} \quad \ldots \quad x = \frac{55(50.27)}{360} = 7.68 \text{ inches.}$$

Thus, back to the original question. The length of the outside arc of this crust of pizza is 7.68 inches, or answer choice G.

Answer Explanations - Step 4

Correct answers:

1: C	**11: E**	**21: A**	**31: C**	**41: D**	**51: A**
2: H	**12: H**	**22: G**	**32: H**	**42: G**	**52: F**
3: D	**13: D**	**23: C**	**33: A**	**43: B**	**53: E**
4: F	**14: G**	**24: K**	**34: K**	**44: J**	**54: H**
5: D	**15: B**	**25: B**	**35: E**	**45: C**	**55: D**
6: K	**16: J**	**26: J**	**36: G**	**46: G**	**56: F**
7: B	**17: C**	**27: B**	**37: A**	**47: A**	**57: B**
8: F	**18: J**	**28: K**	**38: H**	**48: K**	**58: J**
9: A	**19: E**	**29: D**	**39: E**	**49: C**	**59: E**
10: G	**20: F**	**30: F**	**40: J**	**50: K**	**60: H**

1. Correct answer: **C**. One by one, multiply like terms. First, we know that $4 \times 3 \times 8 = 96$, eliminating answer choices A and B. Next, multiply the x terms. What needs to be remembered here is that when multiplying variables, you do not *multiply* their exponents, but rather, you *add* their exponents. Thus:

$$x^2 \times x^2 \times x = x^{2+2+1} = x^5$$

This is already enough to get the question correct, since only choice C begins with $96x^5$. To be thorough, we will multiply the y terms. If the y terms multiply to equal y^6, which is also attached to answer C, we can definitively say we've found the correct answer:

$$y^4 \times y^2 = y^{4+2} = y^6$$

Thus, after this very thorough look, the correct answer is C.

2. Correct answer: **H**. Because the question asks for the mean, there is no need to order the numbers in numerical order. Simply add the lengths of the ribbons and divide by the total number of ribbons:

$$\frac{10 + 12 + 9 + 10 + 11 + 12}{6} = 10.667$$

Because the question asks you to round to the nearest tenth of an inch, we round up to 10.7, which matches with answer choice H.

3. Correct answer: **D**. This problem requires you to convert the words into an Algebra problem. Before the equal sign, it says, "Three times the sum of x and -4," which looks like this: $3(x - 4)$. After the equal sign, it says, "the addition of 8 and $-x$," which looks like $8 - x$. Thus, our Algebra problem looks like this:

$$3(x - 4) = 8 - x \quad \ldots \quad 3x - 12 = 8 - x \quad \ldots \quad 4x = 20 \quad \ldots \quad x = 5$$

This matches answer choice D.

4. Correct answer: **F**. First, determine how much money per month Chipper puts away. If he puts away 7% of his \$66,000 salary per year, that means he puts away \$66,000(.07) = \$4,620 each year. Now, divide that by 12 to determine how much is put away per month: \$4,620/12 = \$385.

To find how much more Chipper puts away per month than Parker, subtract Parker's monthly savings from Chipper's: \$385 – \$150 = \$235, which is answer choice F.

5. Correct answer: **D**. Because both buses are traveling towards each other, find the distance traveled by each bus in 4 hours, then subtract those distances from the 1,000 miles they start apart from each other. Bus 1 travels at 60 miles per hour. Over four hours, that's:

$$60\frac{\text{miles}}{\text{hour}} \times 4 \text{ hours} = 240 \text{ miles}$$

Similarly, Bus 2 travels at 55 miles per hour. Over four hours, that's:

$$55\frac{\text{miles}}{\text{hour}} \times 4 \text{ hours} = 220 \text{ miles}$$

Subtract both distances from the original 1,000 miles they started apart: 1,000 – 240 – 220 = 540 miles apart after four hours of driving towards each other, which is answer choice D.

6. Correct answer: **K**. This is one of those problems that looks far more complicated than it is. You have 4 binomials (an expression with two terms, like z and 2) that are all being multiplied by one another and set equal to 0. If any of the four binomials actually equals 0, then no matter what the other terms equal, the entire expression will equal 0. For example, let's say that $z = -2$. In that case, the first binomial, $(z + 2)$, would look like this: $(z + 2) = (-2 + 2) = 0$, which would make the entire thing equal to 0. Thus, –2 is one value of z that makes the expression = 0. Move on to the other three binomials and determine what values of z make each one equal 0.

For $(z - 4)$, if $z = 4$, it will be equal to 0. For $(z + 3)$, if $z = -3$, it will be equal to 0. Lastly, for $(z - 6)$, if $z = 6$, it will be equal to 0.

This means our four z values that make the expression equal 0 are: –2, 4, –3, and 6. The questions asks for us to find the median of these terms, which is the middle term in an odd number set or the average of the 2 middle terms in an even number set. We do have an even number set (there are 4 numbers to work with), but first we have to order them in numerical order, like this: {–3, –2, 4, 6}. The median will be the average of the middle terms, which are –2 and 4. Thus, our median is: $(-2 + 4)/2 = 1$, which is answer choice K.

7. Correct answer: **B**. This question requires use of the Pythagorean Theorem (since the two sides and segment BD form a right triangle), which is written as $a^2 + b^2 = c^2$, in which a and b are the two legs of a right triangle and c is the hypotenuse. In this case, the hypotenuse is segment BD with length 10. The reason we can solve it is because the two legs are the same. In essence, we can rewrite the Pythagorean Theorem to look like this: $a^2 + a^2 = c^2$, since a and b in this triangle are identical. This gives us then $2a^2 = c^2$, which we can then solve for a since we know $c = 10$, like this:

$$2a^2 = 10^2 \quad \ldots \quad 2a^2 = 100 \quad \ldots \quad a^2 = 50 \quad \ldots \quad a = \sqrt{50} \quad \ldots \quad a = 5\sqrt{2}, \text{ or answer B.}$$

8. Correct answer: **F**. Here, try integers of various kinds (if necessary) to eliminate wrong answers, which is the main strategy for these logical thinking with variables questions. Let's try first $x = 1$ and see what happens:

$$(2(1) - 4)^4 - 1 = (-2)^4 - 1 = 16 - 1 = 15$$

Because the result, 15, is an odd number and a positive number, we can then eliminate G, H, and J as correct answers. Let's choose a number this time that's a little bit different than 1, maybe an even negative number, like $x = -6$, to see if there is a variety of possible outcomes (which is necessary for K to be correct):

$$(2(-6) - 4)^4 - 1 = (-12 - 4)^4 - 1 = (-16)^4 - 1 = 65325$$

Another positive, odd number. Looking closely, the only way for this expression to be negative is if $x = 2$, since then you would have 0 in parentheses being raised to the 4th power, which is 0, then subtracting 1 would make the expression equal –1. Thus, for all $x \neq 2$, the expression will always be positive and odd, which is answer choice F.

9. Correct answer: **A**. Because segment JI is parallel to segment HF, angle $\angle JIF$ will be equal to angle $\angle HFG$; thus, $\angle HFG = 115°$. Similarly, because segment LK is parallel to segment HG, angle $\angle LKG$ will be equal to angle $\angle HGF$; thus, $\angle HGF = 20°$. At this point, we now have 2 of the 3 angles of triangle $\triangle HFG$, which means we can subtract the 2 angles we know from 180° to find the missing angle $\angle FHG$. Like this: 180° – 20° – 115° = 45°, which matches answer choice A.

10. Correct answer: **G**. For questions requiring the simplification of an expression involving multiple variables, like this one, simplify like terms one at a time until you settle on the correct answer.

First, there is a –15 term in the numerator, which is being divided by a 3 term in the denominator. The result must be –5, and because there are no other negative terms in the entire expression to make it positive, we can eliminate answers H and J, since they make the expression as a whole positive.

Next, move on to the x term. In the numerator, there is an x, and in the denominator, there is an x^3 term. When variables raised to an exponent are being divided or multiplied, you subtract or add the exponents, respectively. In this particular case, the math with the x variable looks like this:

$$\frac{x}{x^3} = \frac{1}{x^{3-1}} = \frac{1}{x^2}$$

So far, then, we know that the final answer must begin with -5 and must have an x^2 term in the denominator. This is already enough for us to get the question correct! Only answer choice G features this combination. To be thorough, you can follow the same step above with each other variable, but below is the entire expression simplified one step at a time so you can see each point in the process:

$$\frac{-15xy^3z^8}{3x^3y^2z} = \frac{-5y^{(3-2)}z^{(8-1)}}{x^{(3-1)}} = \frac{-5yz^7}{x^2}\text{, which matches answer choice G.}$$

11. Correct answer: **E**. First, put the line in slope-intercept form ($y = mx + b$), like this:

$$6x - 5y = 10 \quad \ldots \quad -5y = -6x + 10 \quad \ldots \quad y = \frac{6}{5}x - 2$$

Because the question asks for a line parallel to this one, we simply need to identify the slope, which in the original equation is m and right before the x, which above is $\frac{6}{5}$. Thus, the correct answer is E.

12. Correct answer: **H**. Because the pool is contained within the walkway, the area of the walkway will be determined by finding the area of the rectangle made by the walkway, then subtract the area of the pool.

If the pool is 25 feet long, and the walkway extends 3 feet on both sides, then the larger rectangle made by the walkway is $25 + 3 + 3 = 31$ feet long.

If the pool is 20 feet wide, and the walkway extends 3 feet on both sides, then the larger rectangle made by the walkway is $20 + 3 + 3 = 26$ feet wide.

The area of the larger rectangle made by the walkway is $26 \times 31 = 806$ ft^2.

The area of the pool within the walkway is $25 \times 20 = 500$ ft^2.

Now that we have our measurements, all that is left to do is subtract the area of the pool from the larger rectangle made by the walkway, like this: 806 ft^2 $- 500$ ft^2 $= 306$ ft^2. This is answer choice H.

13. Correct answer: **D**. To find the probability, divide the total number of black dresses by the total number of dresses, like this:

$$\frac{4+6}{7+4+2+3+6+8} = \frac{10}{30} = \frac{1}{3}\text{, which matches answer choice D.}$$

14. Correct answer: **G**. To solve this function, plug in $x = 2$ into the function and find the resulting value, like this:

$$f(x) = 2x^2 - x + 1 = 2(2)^2 - 2 + 1 = 8 - 2 + 1 = 7\text{, which matches answer choice G.}$$

15. Correct answer: **B**. Because two lines are crossing, four angles will be formed. If one of them measures 40°, then the angle opposite of that one will also measure 40°. We know that $\angle C$ is the one that measures 40°, but we are told that $\angle C$ does not equal $\angle D$, so the value of $\angle D$ can't be 40°.

The other two angles, on the other hand, will form a line with the 40° angle. That means that the other two angles (one of which is $\angle D$) must have a value of $180° - 40° = 140°$, which is answer choice B.

16. Correct answer: **J**. First, use the circle's area to find the radius. Recall that the formula for the area of a circle is πr^2. So, if the circle has an area of 36π, then $r^2 = 36$, and $r = 6$. The question asks for the diameter of this circle, not the radius. Since the diameter is $2r$, then the diameter of the circle is $2 \times 6 = 12$, which is answer choice J.

17. Correct answer: **C**. First, recognize that the question requires that Timothy hit at least 5 home runs, so trying out options using $r = 4$ or some lower number will not work. However, the *Picking Numbers* strategy is great for this question. He receives \$25 for each home run that he hits over 5. So, let's start by pretending that $r = 6$, which would result in him making \$25, and try it out one question at a time.

A: If $r = 6$, then $25r - 5 = 25(6) - 5 = 145$, not 25. Try again.

B: If $r = 6$, then $25(r + 5) = 25(6 + 5) = 25(11) = 275$, not 25. Try again.

C: If $r = 6$, then $25(r - 5) = 25(6 - 5) = 25(1) = 25$, that's it! This is why C is correct.

If you wanted to try another value of r to be thorough, or if you wanted to go through D and E quickly to certainly discount them, that would be fine. But, not if it is going to cost you any real time. Be confident and move on!

18. Correct answer: **J**. Notice that this car is not on sale for 13% of the original price, but for 13% *off*. This means that the sale cost of the car is 87% of the original cost. Thus, if we multiply the original cost by 0.87, we will get the 13% off sale price, like this:

$38,000(0.87) = $33,060, which matches with answer choice J.

19. Correct answer: **E**. Here, plug in $x = 9$ into the equation, and solve. Before doing so, let's discuss the two strange variables in the question. When x (or any other number for that reason) is raised to the ½ power, this is the same thing as finding the square root of that number. Secondly, in the denominator, the variable is raised to a negative power. To fix this, make it positive and move it to the numerator. With these two things in mind, and to show what I am talking about, we can rewrite the function to look like this:

$$g(x) = \frac{x^{\frac{1}{2}}}{x^{-1}} = \sqrt{x} \cdot x^1$$

Thus, when $x = 9$, we can solve it like so:

$\sqrt{x} \cdot x^1 = \sqrt{x} \cdot x = \sqrt{9} \cdot 9 = 3 \cdot 9 = 27$, which matches answer choice E.

20. Correct answer: **F**. Remember that the solution of two lines is the point where they cross. The fastest way to solve for this problem is to plug in (2, – 2) (in other words, plug in $x = 2$ and $y = -2$) into each equation one at a time and see if it is *satisfied*.

Start with F, plugging in (2, – 2) into each of the two lines:

First line: $y = \frac{1}{2}x - 3$ ... $-2 = \frac{1}{2}(2) - 3$ ... $-2 = 1 - 3$ ... $-2 = -2$, which works!

Second line: $y = 5x - 12$ ... $-2 = 5(2) - 12$ ... $-2 = 10 - 12$ ... $-2 = -2$, which works!

Because the point (2, – 2) satisfies the equations of both lines, it is the point where they cross. If you try out this point on any of the other answer choices, it is very likely that (2, – 2) will satisfy 1 but not both lines. This is why the answer is F.

21. Correct answer: **A**. To find the percent of his throws that were discus, simply add the discus throws and divide it by the total number of throws. To make the addition simpler, let's first add up the amount of throws he took across the week with each:

Javelin throws = $12 + 23 + 11 + 2 + 19 = 67$
Shot put throws = $18 + 11 + 0 + 15 + 18 = 62$
Discus throws = $0 + 0 + 18 + 15 + 3 = 36$

Now, to find the percent, divide the discus throws by all throws, and then multiply by 100:

$$\frac{36}{67 + 62 + 36} = \frac{36}{165} = 0.218$$

When multiplied by 100, we get 21.8%, which rounds to 22%, which matches answer choice A.

22. Correct answer: **G**. Expected outcome, remember, is not the same thing as *most likely*. Expected outcome relies on knowing the probabilities of all outcomes, and multiplying all of the outcomes by those probabilities. First, let's determine the probability of each throw on Thursday:

$$\text{Javelin} = \frac{2}{2 + 15 + 15} = \frac{2}{32} = 0.0625$$

$$\text{Shot Put} = \frac{15}{2 + 15 + 15} = \frac{15}{32} = 0.46875$$

$$\text{Discus} = \frac{15}{2 + 15 + 15} = \frac{15}{32} = 0.46875$$

Now, we have to determine the most likely distance for each throw. Remember that on Thursday, Drew only throws at 70% of his strength. Thus, we have to multiply each "full strength" throw by 0.7. Let's do that by each throw type:

Javelin = 201(0.7) = 140.7 feet
Shot put = 52(0.7) = 36.4 feet
Discus = 179(0.7) = 125.3 feet

This is all of the data that we need to solve the problem. To find the expected outcome, we need to multiply each throw distance by each probability, and add them together:

$$\text{Expected outcome} = 0.0625(140.7) + 0.46875(36.4) + 0.46875(125.3) = 8.79 + 17.06 + 58.73 = 84.58$$

This rounds up to 85 feet, which matches with answer choice G.

23. Correct answer: **C**. Because shot put throws do not travel very far at all relative to javelin and discus, they can be easily eliminated; even a shot put throw at full strength isn't going to match either of the other throws, even with arm soreness playing a role. In addition, Friday's throws are weaker than any other day of the week, which is a way to know that E will also be impossible (since letter C is about the same throw, discus, on an earlier day in the week).

That leaves C and D. Finding these distances was part of the analysis needed in the last problem, so just do the same thing: simply find the distance of each throw and compare. To find the distance, take the "full strength" distance and multiply by either 0.9 (a Wednesday throw of 90%), 0.7 (a Thursday throw of 70%), or 0.6 (a Friday throw of 60%).

C: A discus throw on Thursday = 179(0.7) = 125.3 feet
D: A javelin throw on a Friday = 201(0.6) = 120.6 feet

Thus, a discus throw on Thursday will travel the farthest out of the five options, which is why answer C is correct.

24. Correct answer: **K**. To answer this question correctly, simply plug the correct values in for the proper variables, and solve. She works 40 regular time hours, so $h = 40$; she works 3 overtime hours, so $e = 3$; she makes $3,234 in sales, so $s = 3{,}234$. Plugging them in and solving looks like this:

$$\$(11h + 16.5e + 0.21s) = \$(11(40) + 16.5(3) + 0.21(3234)) = \$(440 + 49.5 + 679.14) = \$1{,}168.64$$

Thus, the answer is K.

25. Correct answer: **B**. Obviously, there is no formula for the area of a weird shaped figure with two rectangles attached to a triangle; simply divide the figure into as many shapes as necessary, find the areas of the smaller shapes, and add them together. Below I have drawn on the figure some to show how I divided up the figure, which is into two rectangles and a triangle:

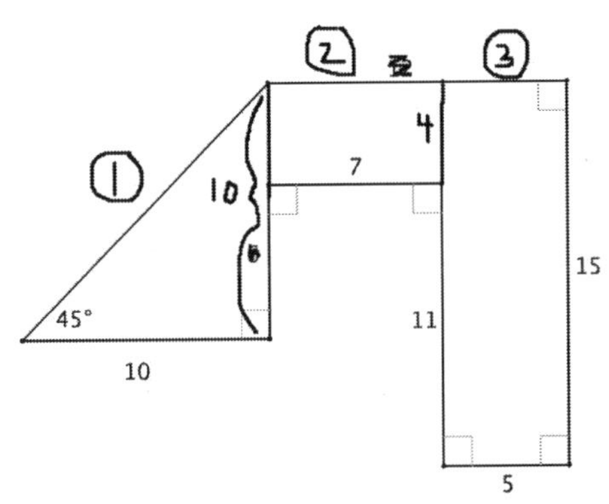

Start with what I've called shape number one. Of course, the area of a triangle is $\frac{1}{2}bh$, where b is the base and h is the height. The tricky thing is that the height is not given to us. However, we know it is 10. Because the angle in the lower left hand corner is 45 degrees, and it is a 90 degree triangle, the other angle must also be 45. Because its opposite side is 10, then the opposite side of the 45 degree angle that is given is 10. With that in mind, $\frac{1}{2}bh = \frac{1}{2}(10)(10) = 50$. So, the area of shape 1 is 50.

Shape 2 is a simple rectangle; multiply the length by the width to get the area, which in this case is $7 \times 4 = 28$.

Shape 3 is also a simple rectangle; multiply the length by the width to get the area, which in this case is $5 \times 15 = 75$.

Now, add the areas together: $50 + 28 + 75 = 153$, or answer choice B.

26. Correct answer: **J**. Again, there is no need to memorize the distance formula. Instead, draw out the two points (as I've done below), then treat the distance between the two as the hypotenuse in a right triangle.

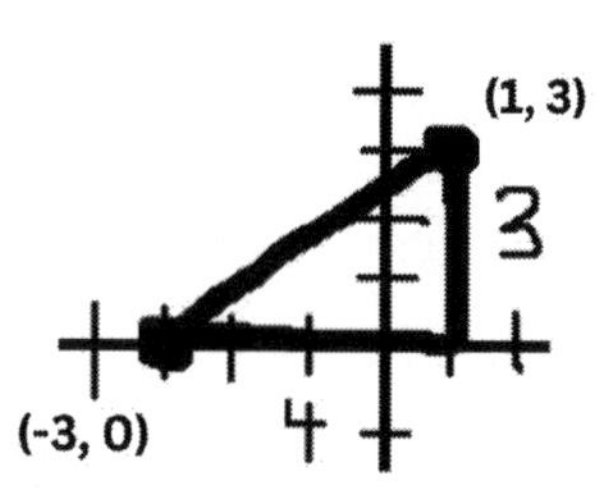

Sorry for the poor drawing, but it gives you the right idea. The distance between the two points is a hypotenuse, and because we know the lengths of the other two sides (just simply counting by tick marks on the coordinate plane, or by finding the difference between each x point and each y point), we can use the Pythagorean Theorem to find the hypotenuse.

The Pythagorean Theorem is $a^2 + b^2 = c^2$, in which a and b are the two legs of the triangle and c is the hypotenuse. Let's plug in our values and solve for c:

$$a^2 + b^2 = c^2 \quad \ldots \quad 3^2 + 4^2 = c^2 \quad \ldots \quad 9 + 16 = c^2 \quad \ldots \quad \sqrt{25} = \sqrt{c^2} \quad \ldots \quad 5 = c$$

Thus, the distance between the two points is J: 5.

Another method for solving this triangle more quickly is realizing that it is what is called a *special triangle*; we'll learn more about that in *Good to Know* Lesson #2.

27. Correct answer: **B**. Because this problem describes a triangle, but doesn't actually draw it out for you, be sure to actually draw the triangle being described as you solve it. I have done that below:

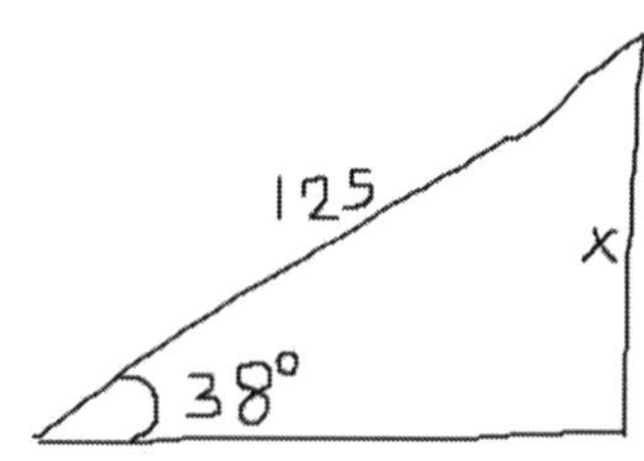

Drawing this triangle allows me to solve the problem without making a simple mistake, because guaranteed the most likely simple mistakes will result in a wrong answer choice. We are looking for the *opposite* side of the 38°, which I have marked with an x. So, we need a trig function (sin, cos, or tan) that uses what we know (the angle and the hypotenuse) and what we need to know (the opposite); this is sin, which is the opposite side over the hypotenuse. Our original equation will look like this:

$$\sin(38) = \frac{x}{125}$$

When I multiply both sides by 125, the x is isolated, then we can solve for x:

$$\sin(38) = \frac{x}{125} \quad \ldots \quad (125)\sin(38) = x \quad \ldots \quad 125(0.616) = x \quad \ldots \quad x = 76.96$$

Because the question asks us to round to the nearest tenth of a foot, we round up to 77.0, which is answer choice B.

28. Correct answer: **K**. Because x must be a negative number by definition (somewhere between, yet including, -3 and -5), then the value of y that would result in the greatest value of the product of x and y would also be negative, since multiplying two negative numbers results in a positive number. Looking at y, there are only two possible values for y: either 2 or -2, since the absolute value of either of those numbers is 2. Thus, the greatest possible product of x and y is $xy = (-5)(-2) = 10$, which is answer choice K.

29. Correct answer: **D**. To find $f(g(5))$, first find $g(5)$; this will result in a number that can then be plugged into $f(x)$. According to the chart, $g(5) = -2$. In other words, when $x = 5$ (bottom of the chart), $g(x) = -2$.

Now, plug -2 into $f(x)$. If we begin in the column on the left that features various values of x, the top line uses the value of $x = -2$. Look over from there to the middle column, the $f(x)$ column, and see that when $x = -2$, the function $f(x) = 3$, which is answer choice D.

30. Correct answer: **F**. Using i is one of the ACT Math test's favorite tricks. I think that the ACT is hoping that some of the students will be familiar with its usage in some sort of math class, but maybe they themselves have never covered it. However, you don't have to have any knowledge of the origin, usage, or purpose of the variable i. The process for solving this ACT Math problem is simple: FOIL (meaning, properly multiply) the two binomials; then, wherever there is an i^2 term, just replace it with a -1 and simplify/solve from there. First, let's multiply the two binomials together without changing the i^2 terms:

$$(i - 1)(i - 1) = i^2 - i - i + 1 = i^2 - 2i + 1$$

Next, replace any i^2 term with a -1 and simplify, like this:

$$i^2 - 2i + 1 = -1 - 2i + 1 = -2i$$, which matches answer choice F.

31. Correct answer: **C**. The first expression, $(12x - 41)$, represents the money spent at Grocery Stop. The second expression, $(5x + 30)$, represents the money spent at Fancy Foods. Because we know that she spent \$278 total, we can simply add the two expressions together and set them equal to \$278. This will allow us to solve for x, then we can plug that number back into Grocery Stop's expression.

Step 1: Solve for x:

$$(12x - 41) + (5x + 30) = 278 \quad \ldots \quad 17x - 11 = 278 \quad \ldots \quad 17x = 289 \quad \ldots \quad x = 17$$

Now that we know the value of x, we can plug it in to Grocery Stop's expression.

Step 2: Plug $x = 17$ into Grocery Stop's expression:

$$12x - 41 = 12(17) - 41 = 204 - 41 = 163$$

Thus, Missy spent \$163 at Grocery Stop, which matches answer choice C.

32. Correct answer: **H**. Though you technically do not need to order a set of numbers to find the mode or the mean, it will help avoid simple mistakes to do so. Written in ascending order, the home runs Jeff has in his first 10 games looks like this:

$$\{0, 0, 0, 0, 1, 2, 2, 2, 3, 4\}$$

The mode, remember, is the number that occurs the most, which at the moment is 0.

The mean is the average, which is $\dfrac{(0+0+0+0+1+2+2+2+2+3+4)}{10} = \dfrac{16}{10} = 1.6$

Now, the question asks how many home runs Jeff needs to hit so that the *mode* of the home runs will then exceed the mean. So, the mode must then either be 2, 3, or 4. However, notice that even if he hits 4 home runs in both games, the mode will still be 0, since then there would still be less games with 4 home runs than 0. The same thing can be said if he hits 3 home runs in these back to back games.

Because there are already 3 games in which Jeff hit 2 home runs, adding 2 more games with 2 home runs brings the mode up to 2. This is because with back to back games of 2 home runs, the number of 2 home run games goes from 3 up to 5, which is more than the 4 games that have 0 home runs.

Now that the mode is 2, test the mean. When you add 2 more games of 2 home runs, the mean does increase, but only slightly, up to 1.67 from 1.6.

Thus, if Jeff hits 2 home runs in Game 11 and then 2 home runs in Game 12, the mode (2) will then exceed the mean (1.67). This is why H is the right answer.

33. Correct answer: **A**. Remember the acronym SOHCAHTOA to remember the values of the functions sin, cos, and tan. The last three letters (the TOA) refers to the tangent of an angle, which is equal to the opposite side over the adjacent side. From the point of view of angle A, the opposite side is side CB, which has a length of 15. The adjacent side is the AB side (not the AC side; that's the hypotenuse), which has a length of 36. Thus:

The value of the tan $A = \dfrac{15}{36}$,

which can be simplified when the numerator and denominator are divided by 3, like this:

$$\frac{15}{36} = \frac{5}{12}$$, which matches answer choice A.

34. Correct answer: **K**. First, if a line is perpendicular to another line that means they have opposite slopes. The opposite of a slope is its negative inverse (meaning make it negative, then move the numerator to the denominator and the denominator to the numerator). The line in the question has a form of $y = -\frac{2}{5}x + 3$, in which $-\frac{2}{5}$ is the slope. The negative inverse or opposite of this slope is $\frac{5}{2}$.

This eliminates answer choices F, G, and H, since those three options do not have the correct slope. However, now it seems like there is a problem: how to choose which of the remaining two lines? Well, according to the question, the line that is correct must pass through point (2, 3). By definition, any point on a line will satisfy the equation if plugged in. So, we must plug in $x = 2$ and $y = 3$ into each line and see which satisfies.

Start with J: $y = \frac{5}{2}x + 3$ ... $3 = \frac{5}{2}(2) + 3$ ... $3 = \frac{15}{2} + 3$ ... $3 = \frac{21}{2}$? No, doesn't satisfy!

Now try K: $y = \frac{5}{2}x - 2$ ... $3 = \frac{5}{2}(2) - 2$ ... $3 = \frac{10}{2} - 2$ ... $3 = 5 - 2$ ... $3 = 3$, that's it!

35. Correct answer: **E**. If you remember, the Law of Transversals, in layman's terms, basically means that if two parallel lines are transversed or cut through by another line, then 4 of the 8 angles will have the same value, and so will the other 4; if you know even 1 of 8 angles, you can find them all. Because we are told that the value of $\angle HNO$ is 35°, we now have enough information to find all 8 angles formed by these three lines.

Because $\angle HNO$ is 35°, we also know (according to the Law of Transversals) that $\angle JOL$ also has a measure of 35°. The angle we are looking for, angle $\angle LOK$, shares a line (segment JK) with angle $\angle JOL$; in other words, these two angles must add up to equal 180°. Thus, we can find our missing angle like this:

$$\angle JOL + \angle LOK = 180° \quad ... \quad \angle LOK = 180° - \angle JOL \quad ... \quad \angle LOK = 180° - 35° \quad ... \quad \angle LOK = 145°$$

This is why the answer is E: 145°.

36. Correct answer: **G**. Begin with Circle *Z*. We are told that Circle *Z*'s area is 225π; recall that the formula for the area of a circle is πr^2. If $225\pi = \pi r^2$, then $r^2 = 225$. So, the square root of 225 is the radius of Circle *Z*: $r = \sqrt{225} = 15$.

Now that we know that the radius of Circle *Z* is 15, we can use that to figure out the radius of Circle *Y*. We are told that the diameter of Circle *Y* is the radius of Circle *Z*, which means that the diameter of Circle *Y* is 15, meaning the radius of Circle *Y* is half of 15, or 7.5

Lastly, we are told that the diameter of Circle *X* is equal to the radius of Circle *Y*. Because we now know that the radius of Circle *Y* is 7.5, this means we now know that the diameter of Circle *X* is 7.5, and thus that the radius of Circle *X* is 3.75.

Recall that the formula for the circumference of a circle is $2\pi r$. Because we are looking for the circumference of Circle *X*, plug in the *r* of Circle *X* into this equation to solve, like this:

Circumference of Circle $X = 2\pi r = 2\pi(3.75) = 7.5\pi$, which matches answer choice G.

37. Correct answer: **A**. Because we are asked for $f(g(x))$, we must plug $g(x)$ into the function $f(x)$ anywhere that there is an x. In $f(x)$, there is one x right after the $\frac{2}{3}$, so this is where we must put the entire expression $g(x)$, like this:

$$f(x) = \frac{2}{3}x - 14 = \frac{2}{3}(6x^2 + 18x + 18) - 14 = 4x^2 + 12x + 12 - 14 = 4x^2 + 12x - 2$$

So far, this is good, but it can be simplified further (which is necessary; if you look at the answer choices none of them match $4x^2 + 12x - 2$). The terms are all divisible by 2, which we can factor to the outside of the parentheses, like this:

$4x^2 + 12x - 2 = 2(2x^2 + 6x - 1)$, which matches answer choice A.

38. Correct answer: **H**. There are two ways of solving this problem, and it doesn't matter which of them you choose. Let's solve it both ways so you can learn both:

<u>First method: factoring the trinomials and simplifying</u>

A trinomial is a polynomial with three terms. In both the numerator and the denominator of this particular problem, there is a trinomial, but also a binomial (a polynomial with two terms). Each of the trinomials can be factored into two binomials being multiplied by one another. One way to do this is to use the Quadratic Formula, but here's the thing: I don't even know the Quadratic Formula, and you don't need it on the ACT (contrary to popular belief). If you know it, and can do it quickly, then yes it could help you during a problem like this one, but I have never encountered an ACT Math problem in which it is necessary.

To factor a trinomial into two binomials, you have to find a special pair of numbers. These numbers are these: what are the two numbers that can be multiplied to result in the last term in the trinomial, but add together to equal the term/coefficient in the middle term? That may sound complicated, but let's follow this process with the trinomial in the numerator, then the one in the denominator.

The trinomial in the numerator is $(x^2 + x - 6)$. We need two numbers that multiply to give us -6, but add together to give us 1 (which is the number, though hidden, in front of the middle x term). If you multiply 3 and -2, you get -6, and if you add 3 and -2, you get 1. Our two binomials, then, will be $x +$ each of these two numbers. Thus, this trinomial can be factored into two binomials that look like this:

$$(x^2 + x - 6) = (x + 3)(x - 2)$$

The trinomial in the denominator is $(x^2 - 5x - 24)$. We need two numbers that multiply to give us -24, but add together to give us -5. If you multiply -8 and 3, you get -24, and if you add -8 and 3, you get -5. Our two binomials, then, will be $x +$ each of these two numbers. Thus, this trinomial can be factored into two binomials that look like this:

$$(x^2 - 5x - 24) = (x - 8)(x + 3)$$

Now that we have done that, we can rewrite the original equation and replace the trinomials with binomials, and then cancel out any binomials that are the same:

$$\frac{(x+1)(x^2+x-6)}{(x-2)(x^2-5x-24)} = \frac{(x+1)(x+3)(x-2)}{(x-2)(x-8)(x+3)} = \frac{(x+1)}{(x-8)}, \text{ which matches answer choice H.}$$

<u>Second method: *Picking Numbers*</u>

A second strategy for solving this problem is by using the strategy *Picking Numbers*, which means pretending that x equals a certain number, then plugging that into the equation and answer choices to find a match. The question says that we can't use $x = 2$, so let's use $x = 3$. Below, I rewrite the problem, putting a 3 anywhere there is an x:

$$\frac{(x+1)(x^2+x-6)}{(x-2)(x^2-5x-24)} = \frac{(3+1)(3^2+3-6)}{(3-2)(3^2-5(3)-24)} = \frac{(4)(9+3-6)}{(1)(9-15-24)} = \frac{(4)(6)}{(1)(-30)} = \frac{24}{-30} = -\frac{4}{5}$$

Next, plug in $x = 3$ into each of the answer choices to determine which also equals $-\frac{4}{5}$.

Answer F: $\frac{(x-1)(x+2)}{(x+8)(x-2)} = \frac{(3-1)(3+2)}{(3+8)(3-2)} = \frac{(2)(5)}{(11)(1)} = \frac{10}{11}$, which is not correct.

Answer G: $\frac{(x-1)}{(x+8)} = \frac{(3-1)}{(3+8)} = \frac{2}{11}$, which is not correct.

Answer H: $\frac{(x+1)}{(x-8)} = \frac{(3+1)}{(3-8)} = \frac{4}{-5} = -\frac{4}{5}$, that's it!

39. Correct answer: **E**. There is a midpoint formula that you may have used in math class. I hesitate pulling it out and using it here because it is not necessary to know this formula to solve the little midpoint questions you are likely to find on the ACT. Let's simply think this through first.

A line segment starts at point (2, – 1), then moves on to a midpoint at (0, 3). To find the other endpoint, what the question calls (a, b), find the change that was made in the x and y values between these two points, then make the same changes starting from the midpoint.

The line segment starts with an x value of 2, then moves to a midpoint with an x value of 0. That is a change of –2. So, this same change needs to be made starting with the midpoint to find the x value of the other endpoint. So, starting with an x value of 0 (the midpoint), make a change of –2. The result is that the other endpoint, or (a, b), has an x value of –2. Since E is the only answer choice with an x value of –2, this would already be enough to get the question correct.

However, we can apply the same reasoning to the y values of the points. The first endpoint has a y value of – 1, then moved to an endpoint with a y value of 3. This is a change in y value of +4. So, starting at the midpoint, make the same change to find the y value of (a, b). If the midpoint has a y value of 3, we add 4 to find that the missing endpoint has a y value of $3 + 4 = 7$.

Thus, $(a, b) = (-2, 7)$, which matches answer choice E.

40. Correct answer: **J**. You don't need to have any knowledge about temperatures or the relationship between Celsius and Fahrenheit to get this question correct. The equation given has two variables (F and C), and you are given 1 of the 2 (that $C = 31$), leaving just 1 that you need to find using Algebra, like this:

$$F = \frac{9}{5}C + 32 \quad \ldots \quad F = \frac{9}{5}(31) + 32 \quad \ldots \quad F = 55.8 + 32 \quad \ldots \quad F = 87.8$$

The question requires that you round up to the nearest degree, which is up to 88, which matches answer choice J.

41. Correct answer: **D**. If a line never crosses the y-axis, that means it goes straight up and down. This question asks for the slope of such a line. Remember, the slope of a line can be described as "rise over run," or $\frac{\text{rise}}{\text{run}}$, or can be thought of as the change on the y-axis divided by the change on the x-axis.

If you think about a line that goes straight up and down, but never goes side to side at all along the x axis, then the "rise" will be infinite, and the "run" will be 0. Such a slope would look like this: $\frac{\infty}{0}$, or infinity divided by 0. It isn't possible to divide any number, let alone infinity, by 0; any such attempt or number is undefined, which is why the correct answer is D: undefined.

42. Correct answer: **G**. First, draw the triangle being described so that it can be visualized and to avoid simple mistakes (which I have done below). The question asks for the *area* of this triangle; recall that the formula for the area of a triangle is $\frac{1}{2}bh$, in which b is the base and h is the height. Fortunately, we know the base (though you could have drawn this triangle with side GE on the bottom, in which case you'd know the height), which is 14, which means that we need to find the height, which is side GE. To do so, we will need one of or trig functions (sin, cos, or tan). We know the angle to go from (angle F, which is 50), but we need one that uses what we know (side EF) and what we don't (side GE). This needed function is tangent, which is equivalent to the opposite side (GE, which we'll call x in the equation below) over the adjacent side (EF, or 14).

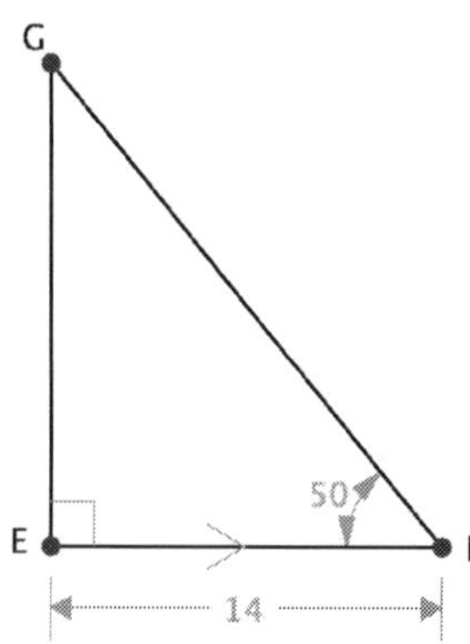

$$\tan(50) = \frac{\text{opposite}}{\text{adjacent}} \quad \ldots \quad \tan(50) = \frac{x}{14} \quad \ldots \quad (14)\tan(50) = x \quad \ldots \quad x = 16.68$$

Side GE, which we called x above, is the height of the triangle. Now, we can plug the base (14) and the height (16.68) into the formula for the area of a triangle, like this:

$$\frac{1}{2}bh = \frac{1}{2}(14)(16.68) = 116.79, \text{ which is answer choice G.}$$

43. Correct answer: **B**. First, let's simplify the exponents on the left side of the equation. When an exponent is raised to an exponent, you *multiply* the exponents. Take this smaller example: x^{3^3}. Some would try to *add* these exponents, but that would be what you would do if the same variables, each raised to an exponent, were being multiplied by one another. Here, we multiply these exponents, like this:

$$x^{3^3} = x^{3 \cdot 3} = x^9$$

If you try out a number for x, like $x = 3$, you will see that this is the case. Now, let's apply the same way of thinking to simplify the term on the left side of the equation in the original problem:

$$(x^{3z+4})^3 = x^{(3z+4) \cdot 3} = x^{9z+12}$$

Now that we have simplified, let's rewrite the original equation: $x^{9z+12} = x^3$.

The key to getting this question correct from here is to recognize that if the base is the same (which is what we have here; both sides of the equation feature a base of x), the exponents can be set equal to each other in a new equation. Then, we can solve for z to get the question correct:

$x^{9z+12} = x^3$ ... $9z + 12 = 3$ ... $9z = -9$ ... $z = -1$, which matches answer choice B.

44. Correct answer: **J**. Because the swimming pools have the same depth, it is unnecessary to know the volume of these pools (which would be the volume of a cylinder). Instead, find the area of both Pool C (which has a diameter of 60) and Pool E (which has a diameter of 100), then make the correct comparison. Recall that the formula for the area of a circle is πr^2.

$$\text{Area of Pool C} = \pi r^2 = \pi(30)^2 = 2{,}827.43$$

$$\text{Area of Pool E} = \pi r^2 = \pi(50)^2 = 7{,}853.98$$

To find how much more water Pool E needs compared to Pool C, divide the area of Pool E by the area of Pool C, then multiply by 100 (because the answers are in percents), like this:

$\frac{\text{Area of Pool E}}{\text{Area of Pool C}} \times 100 = \frac{7{,}853.98}{2{,}827.43} \times 100 = 277.78\,\%$, which rounds up to answer choice J: 278%

45. Correct answer: **C**. First, create a number set of the first 8 pools (before the addition of Pluto), then find the mean, median, mode, and range:

Number set: {30, 40, 60, 60, 75, 80, 90, 100}

$$\text{Mean (average)} = \frac{(30 + 40 + 60 + 60 + 75 + 80 + 90 + 100)}{8} = \frac{535}{8} = 66.875$$

$$\text{Median (middle term)} = \frac{(60 + 75)}{2} = \frac{135}{2} = 67.5$$

Mode (number that occurs the most) $= 60$

Range (difference between greatest and smallest) $= 100 - 30 = 70$

Now, what you *could* do is spend the time finding all of these values for the same number set, but with the addition of a pool with a diameter of 15 feet. *However*, that is completely unnecessary. The only way that the mode can change is if Pluto's pool had the same diameter as one of the other pools, but it does not. As every other value (mean, median, range) changes, the mode will stay the same. Because the question asks for which value changes the *least*, we can be confident that the correct answer is C: the mode.

46. Correct answer: **G**. To find the measure of the arc of a circle, find the ratio or percent the section occupies by dividing the interior angle (120) by the total angle measures in a circle (360), then set that equal to the arc itself (which we'll call x) divided by the circumference of the entire circle. From there, you can cross multiply to solve for x. As a reminder, the formula for the circumference of a circle is $2\pi r$, or πd, in which d is the diameter; the circumference we need, which is the circumference of Pool H, is $\pi d = 75\pi$.

$\frac{120}{360} = \frac{x}{75\pi}$ ... $360x = 120(75\pi)$ ... $x = \frac{(120)(75\pi)}{360} = 25\pi$, which matches answer choice G.

47. Correct answer: **A**. The simplest way to solve this problem is to use *Backsolving*, the mini-strategy in which you plug in the answer choices one at a time to determine if it fits in the inequality.

Let's go through the answer choices one at a time to determine if they fit the inequality.

$$\text{Choice A:} \quad \frac{1}{x^2} = \frac{1}{(\frac{5}{12})^2} = \frac{1}{(.4167)^2} = \frac{1}{0.174} = 5.74$$

Fortunately, this is as far as we need to go! 5.74 is between 4 and 9. I doubt on the real ACT that you'd have time to go through and check every single answer; that's the kind of step you might need to take if you have spare time at the end (which hardly ever happens, if ever, on ACT Math!). Be confident and move on: the correct answer is A.

48. Correct answer: **K**. Usually, two lines have only 1 solution (the point where they cross). Sometimes, two lines have 0 solutions (they are parallel). For two lines to have an infinite number of solutions, they have to be *the same line*, stacked one on top of another.

Before we get to that, notice how these two lines are separated off from the question, literally stacked one on top of another? That is because there is a way in Algebra to add lines and subtract lines, which is done by adding or subtracting each similar term one at a time; this trick can also be combined with the fact that lines or entire equations can be changed (for example, multiplied by 10 or divided by -7) so long as each term is equally affected. As far as this particular question is concerned, if you can subtract one line from another, and you are left with all 0's, then you know that they are the same line.

As they are written, the $2x$ term from one line sits directly above the $6x$ term in the other line. Because $6x$ is $3 \times 2x$, and these terms are unchangeable, then for these two lines to be the same, each other term in the second line must also be $3 \times$ as large as the first line. If you look at the final term, the number in the top line is 4, and wouldn't you know it, the number in the bottom line is $3 \times 4 = 12$.

That brings us to the middle term. In the top line, we have 7. Sticking with the pattern of multiplying the bottom term by 3 to make it the same line as the one in the top, we need $3 \times 7 = 21$ where there is a z in that second line. This is why the answer is K: 21.

If you still do not understand, think of it like this: Making the z a 21 would mean that if the top line were multiplied by 3 throughout, it would be identical to the bottom line, which simply shows that they are the same; you could then subtract the bottom line from the top line to get all 0's.

49. Correct answer: **C**. First, of course, draw the triangle to get an idea of what it looks like before trying to find the area. I have done that below. Recall of course that the area of a triangle is $\frac{1}{2}bh$, in which b is the base and h is the height.

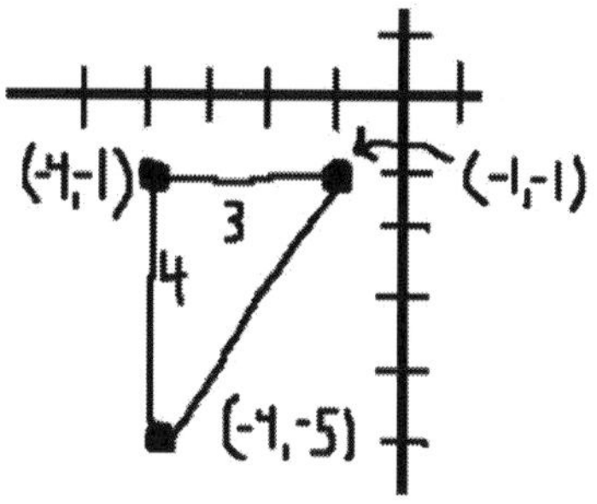

As you can see, I have plotted the three points, drawn lines between them to make a triangle, and labeled the lengths of the two sides that are necessary to find the area (3 and 4, respectively). It may throw some students off that the triangle is "upside down," but that doesn't affect the math at all; the height is still 4 and the "base" is still 3.

Now for the math:

$\frac{1}{2}bh = \frac{1}{2}(3)(4) = 6$, which matches answer choice C.

50. Correct answer: **K**. To answer this question, which is a kind of *Logical Thinking with Variables* question, use a combination of the *Picking Numbers* and *Backsolving* strategies in which you go one by one down the answer choices, eliminating wrong answers one at a time.

Just looking at the inequality, which again says that $7x^3y^4 < 0$, I can see a couple of things about it. First, no matter what y equals (whether a negative number like -3 or a positive number like 5), the y^4 term will *always be positive*. This means that, for the expression $7x^3y^4$ to be negative, the x^3 term must always be negative. The only way for a cubed number to be negative is if the original number, in this case x, is negative.

Lastly, you are not looking for something that is true. The question asks for an answer that can't possibly be true.

Answer F ($x < 7$): because we already determined that x must be a negative number, then this inequality *can* be true, which means it is not correct.

Answer G ($x > -7$): again, we determined that x has to be a negative number, which means it could possibly be any value greater than -7, like -5 for example. This answer therefore is not correct.

Answer H ($y < 0$): we also determined that y could be any value and that, no matter what, the result would be positive. Thus, it *is* possible for y to be less than 0, making this answer choice also incorrect.

Answer J ($y > 7$): we already determined that y can equal any number negative or positive, including anything greater than 7. Because this choice *is* possible, it is also incorrect.

Answer K ($x = 0$): finally, we've found it! When x is equal to 0, the entire equation is now equal to 0. The inequality is $<$ (less than), not $\leq$ (less than or equal to). For that reason, it is *not possible* for x to equal 0, making choice K the correct answer.

51. Correct answer: **A**. This question is pure *Backsolving*. Simply plug in the values for x into the functions in the answer choices and find which of them results in the numbers stated by the question.

Let's start with A. First, we'll plug in an x value of -3 and see if the result of the function is -14:

$$f(x) = -2x^2 + 4 = -2(-3^2) + 4 = -18 + 4 = -14$$

So far so good. Try at least one more, if not both, to determine if A is truly the correct answer. You know that some of these functions are going to work for some of the values for x, maybe even two out of three. Below, I'll try $x = -1$ and $x = 4$ back to back to determine if they also result in values of 2 and -28, respectively:

$$f(x) = -2x^2 + 4 = -2(-1^2) + 4 = -2 + 4 = 2$$

$$f(x) = -2x^2 + 4 = -2(4^2) + 4 = -32 + 4 = -28$$

Thus, the correct answer is A; the function $f(x) = -2x^2 + 4$ is the function with the values stated in the question.

52. Correct answer: **F**. First, recognize that there are a total of $8 \times 8 = 64$ marbles in the hat. Because there are 8 green marbles, the odds that the first player (Joseph) draws a green is $\frac{8}{64}$. Next, we are told that Maximilian draws a green marble. Because there are now only 63 marbles in the hat (Joseph drew one already) and only 7 green marbles in the hat (again, because Joseph drew one), the odds of him also drawing a green marble is $\frac{(8-1)}{(64-1)} = \frac{7}{63}$. Now, Jude is going to draw a marble, and the question asks for the probability that he also draws a green marble. To find this probability, use the same thinking: when Jude draws, there are now only 6 green marbles left (because the previous 2 boys drew green marbles) and only 62 total marbles. Thus, Jude's probability of drawing a green marble is this:

$$\frac{(7-1)}{(63-1)} = \frac{6}{62} = \frac{3}{31},$$ which is answer choice F.

53. Correct answer: **E**. First, you have to know that the legs of a triangle are the two sides that are *not* the hypotenuse; in other words, the two legs are the two sides that meet at a 90° angle. That means that we can use the Pythagorean Theorem to find the missing side (the hypotenuse) and add the three together to find the perimeter of the triangle.

If you look at the answer choices, you will see that many of them are in a form that adds or multiplies a number by a square root of some kind. If you do the work on your calculator and come up with a decimal, simply try out the answer choices in your calculator to match them.

First, find the missing hypotenuse. The Pythagorean Theorem, as a reminder, says that $a^2 + b^2 = c^2$ in which c is the length of the hypotenuse:

$$a^2 + b^2 = c^2 \quad \ldots \quad 10^2 + 15^2 = c^2 \quad \ldots \quad 100 + 225 = c^2 \quad \ldots \quad \sqrt{325} = \sqrt{c^2} \quad \ldots \quad c = \sqrt{325}$$

To simplify $\sqrt{325}$, "square out" any factors of 325 that are also perfect squares. For example, $325 \div 25 = 13$, thus $\sqrt{325} = \sqrt{25 \cdot 13} = 5\sqrt{13}$. This means that the perimeter is equal to $10 + 15 + 5\sqrt{13} = 25 + 5\sqrt{13}$, which matches answer choice E.

Another option is to put $\sqrt{325}$ in your calculator and get that the length of c is 18.03. Add that to 10 and 15, and get that the perimeter of the triangle is $18.03 + 10 + 15 = 43.03$. When you put the answer choices in your calculator, you will get only one of them that equals approximately 43.03, which is answer choice E.

54. Correct answer: **H**. One way to solve this problem is to carefully add the fractions in the numerator and denominator (after carefully multiplying) by finding common denominators. Then, properly divide whatever fraction over fraction you end up with. However, I have some advice in that department:

DO NOT DO THAT ON AN ACTUAL ACT!

Put *all of this in your calculator*! This is the ACT Math mini-strategy we simply called *The Calculator*, stressing the use of your calculator to your advantage. Your pre-Algebra or Algebra teacher would have expected you to perfectly solve this kind of thing, but this isn't math class: it's the ACT. Start with the numerator, then everything in the denominator. Take steps, writing down what you've solved for thus far on occasion so that you don't make a simple mistake. Lastly, you'll probably be rounding sometimes because of the fractions, so don't expect the final answer you come up with to perfectly match to the hundredth's place the correct answer. Here's an example of what that might look like:

$$\frac{\frac{1}{6}+\left(\frac{5}{2}\cdot\frac{2}{3}\right)}{\left(-\frac{11}{12}+\frac{11}{4}\right)-\left(\frac{-3+14}{-3+15}\right)}=\frac{1.83}{1.83-0.92}=\frac{1.83}{0.91}=2.00\text{, which matches answer choice H.}$$

On a side note, if you want to solve this by finding common denominators, etc., it's not *bad* to do that, just time-consuming. That process would take me, personally, a couple of minutes. Putting it all in the calculator, on the other hand, takes me about 30 seconds.

55. Correct answer: **D**. The two expressions being described need to first be properly written out by you into a mathematical form.

First, "When x is squared and added to 4 times y, the result is 13" =

$$x^2 + 4y = 13$$

Second, "when the product of 2 and y is added to the product of negative 2 and x, the result is negative 16" =

$$2y - 2x = -16$$

Next, you are asked which of the following values of x and y is a solution for this system of equations. The only thing to do is to plug in each answer choice's x and y values and see if the equation is satisfied.

A: $x = 8;\ y = 0$

$x^2 + 4y = 13$ ... $8^2 + 4(0) = 13$ ... $64 + 0 = 13$ ... No, it doesn't satisfy; try B.

B: $x = 0;\ y = -8$

$x^2 + 4y = 13$ ... $0^2 + 4(-8) = 13$ ... $-32 = 13$ ... No, it doesn't satisfy; try C.

C: $x = 10;\ y = 2$

$x^2 + 4y = 13$ ... $10^2 + 4(2) = 13$ ... $116 = 13$ ... No, it doesn't satisfy; try D.

D: $x = 5;\ y = -3$

$x^2 + 4y = 13$ ... $5^2 + 4(-3) = 13$ ... $25 - 12 = 13$ ... Yes, it satisfies!

$2y - 2x = -16$ ... $2(-3) - 2(5) = -16$ ... $-6 - 10 = -16$ ... Yes, it satisfies!

Thus, the correct answer is D.

56. Correct answer: **F**. MC starts writing at 2:00 at a pace of 17 words per minute. She writes for 3 minutes until Clare starts writing, meaning she has already written $3 \times 17 = 51$ words.

The easiest way to conceptualize how many minutes it will take for Clare to catch MC is by thinking this: if Clare writes at 22 words per minute, and MC at 17 words per minute, then that means that every minute Clare will gain 22 – 17 = 5 words on MC. After 10 minutes (in other words, at 2:13), Clare will have gained 50 words. Though that is *close* to the 51 words that she has to gain, it isn't quite there, since we are asked to *round up* after Clare catches MC.

This means that sometime between 2:13 and 2:14 Clare will catch MC, which then rounds up to 2:14, which is answer choice F.

57. Correct answer: **B**. Triangle ECF is a right triangle, which means that we will need to use one of our trig functions (sin, cos, or tan) to find the length of EC. We know that the length of FC is 4, so what we need is either another side of the triangle, which isn't possible to find in this case, or another of the missing angles. Well, if $\angle AGD$ is 150°, then $\angle DGE$ must be 180° – 150° = 30°.

Because GD is parallel to EF, this means that $\angle FEC$ is also 30°. Now we have enough to solve for EC, but we need a trig function that uses what we know (4, the opposite angle) and what we don't know (EC, the adjacent angle), which would be tangent. For simplicity's sake, let's call the length of EC just x:

$$\tan(30) = \frac{4}{x} \quad \ldots \quad x\tan(30) = 4 \quad \ldots \quad x = \frac{4}{\tan(30)} \quad \ldots \quad x = \frac{4}{0.577} \quad \ldots \quad x = 6.93$$

Because the question asks us to round to the nearest tenth of a meter, we round down to 6.9, which is answer choice B.

58. Correct answer: **J**. There are two ways to solve this problem.

The first way is to carefully simplify. Before dealing with the fact that the expression is raised to the ½, let's treat each term within the parentheses one by one and simplify as we go:

$$\sqrt{x^4} = x^2$$

$$\sqrt[4]{x^8} = x^2$$

$$\frac{1}{x^{-2}} = x^2$$

Now, replace each term with its equivalent simplification:

$$\left(\sqrt{x^4} - \sqrt[4]{x^8} + \frac{1}{x^{-2}}\right)^{\frac{1}{2}} = \left(x^2 - x^2 + x^2\right)^{\frac{1}{2}} = (x^2)^{\frac{1}{2}}$$

When a number is raised to the ½, that is the same thing as finding the square root of that number. Thus:

$$(x^2)^{\frac{1}{2}} = \sqrt{x^2} = x, \text{ which is answer choice J.}$$

A second way to solve the problem would be to use the ACT Math mini-strategy *Picking Numbers*. This isn't a "backup" method for those who can't simplify well: *it is a strategy that the best ACT Math test takers are routinely using.* Choose a number for x, then use your calculator to help you solve. Then, apply that same x value to the answer choices to find a match. Let's pretend for this situation that $x = 2$ and see what we get when we do the math:

$$\left(\sqrt{x^4} - \sqrt[4]{x^8} + \frac{1}{x^{-2}}\right)^{\frac{1}{2}} = \left(\sqrt{2^4} - \sqrt[4]{2^8} + \frac{1}{2^{-2}}\right)^{\frac{1}{2}} = \left(\sqrt{16} - \sqrt[4]{256} + 2^2\right)^{\frac{1}{2}} = (4 - 4 + 4))^{\frac{1}{2}} = \sqrt{4} = 2$$

It turns out, that when $x = 2$, the entire expression also equals 2. Looking through the answer choices, J is then clearly correct since it is simply x.

59. Correct answer: **E**. This is one of those "sticker shock" problems, meaning just the look of it is scary. However, the mathematics within are not as scary as it may first seem. Each circle's radius is used in the perimeter twice. Thus, finding the radius of each circle is the hardest step in solving.

You are given the circumference of each circle. Recall then that the formula for the circumference of a circle is $2\pi r$. Set this formula equal to each circle to find each circle's radius:

Circle L: $2\pi r = 8\pi \quad \ldots \quad r = 4$

Circle M: $2\pi r = 12\pi \quad \ldots \quad r = 6$

Circle N: $2\pi r = 14\pi \quad \ldots \quad r = 7$

Again, each circle's radius is used twice in the perimeter of the triangle. Thus:

$\triangle LMN$ perimeter $= 2(4) + 2(6) + 2(7) = 8 + 12 + 14 = 34$ mm, which is answer choice E.

60. Correct answer: **H**. Because the odds of landing on heads or tails is the same, it is irrelevant that the coin should land on heads the first three tosses then on tails the final two. The question might as well ask for the odds of the coin landing on heads all five tosses or on tails for the first four tosses and heads for the fifth.

To determine the probability of any number of events in a row, multiply their probabilities. The odds of landing a coin on heads is $\frac{1}{2}$. Because this is the probability of each coin flip five times in a row, multiply this probability five times, like this:

$$\frac{1}{2} \cdot \frac{1}{2} \cdot \frac{1}{2} \cdot \frac{1}{2} \cdot \frac{1}{2} = \frac{1}{32},$$ which matches answer choice H.

Answer Explanations - Step 5

Correct answers:

1: C	**7: C**	**13: A**	**19: A**	**25: C**	**31: C**
2: K	**8: H**	**14: J**	**20: H**	**26: F**	**32: K**
3: E	**9: C**	**15: A**	**21: B**	**27: C**	**33: A**
4: J	**10: K**	**16: H**	**22: J**	**28: J**	
5: D	**11: D**	**17: D**	**23: D**	**29: C**	
6: F	**12: G**	**18: G**	**24: H**	**30: F**	

1. Correct answer: **C.** Here, the *Fundamental Counting Principle* is being wrapped up in the midst of a modeling problem. Here is the best way to think about this problem: if there are 5 different children that can be put in the first position, then that leaves only 4 children for the second position, which leaves 3 children for the third position, which leaves 2 children for the fourth position, which leaves one child for the fifth position. In other words, the number of ways in which this couple can line up their 5 children is:

$5 \times 4 \times 3 \times 2 \times 1 = 120$, or answer choice C.

2. Correct answer: **K.** If this question is hard to conceptualize with a variable, start out with a number (aka *Picking Numbers*). If she has $x = 3$ movies to choose from, and wants to watch 3 in a row, then how many combinations of movies are possible? Well, if $x = 3$, then there are 3 x 2 x 1 = 6 possibilities. So, which answer = 6 when $x = 3$? Try them out one at a time:

F. $3x = 3(3) = 9$, not 6.

G. $x^3 = (3)^3 = 27$, not 6

H. $x(x + 1)^2 = 3(4)^2 = 48$, not 6

J. $x^3x^2x = (3)^3(3)^2(3) = 729$, not 6

K. $x(x - 1)(x - 2) = 3(2)(1) = 6$, that's it!

3. Correct answer: **E**. This is classic, and basic, fundamental counting principle. First of all, before we do the math, if there are 80 police officers and 50 firefighters, and the mayor is choosing one of each, I think you should recognize naturally that that's a *lot* of possible combinations. But, looking at the answer choices, only one of them is greater than 131. This tells me that answer choices A, B, C, and D are designed to throw you off from the real answer.

If there are 80, from which one will be chosen, and 50, from which one will be chosen, the number of possibilities is $80 \times 50 = 4{,}000$, or answer choice E.

4. Correct answer: **J.** These license plates, we are told, feature 7 spaces for either numbers or letters. However, we also learn that the first three spaces are fixed. This leaves 4 spaces that can feature either one of the 10 numbers (0 through 9) or one of 26 letters. The fact that they *can* be repeated is important, because it makes the math easier.

If there are 10 numbers and 26 letters to choose from, that means there are 36 total characters for each space. In choosing 1 of them 4 times, we need to multiply 36 by itself 4 times in a row, thus:

$36 \times 36 \times 36 \times 36 = 1{,}679{,}616$ possibilities for license plates, or answer choice J.

5. Correct answer: **D**. We have seen these problems before. We discussed then that when the ACT asks you for the distance between two points, if you have the distance formula memorized, then that's great; you should use it. However, most of us don't, but that's OK; I think there's an easier way to find the distance between 2 points, which is to make a triangle in which the hypotenuse is the distance between two points, then use the Pythagorean Theorem (or your new knowledge of special triangles…) to find the distance between them.

Below is an expert drawing of our graphed points, made into a triangle, with the lengths of the legs of the triangles labeled:

Now, because this is a right triangle, and because we know the lengths of the two legs, we could use the Pythagorean Theorem ($a^2 + b^2 = c^2$) to find the missing length between the two points. However, this problem is occurring in a lesson on triangles that featured special triangles, and one of those special triangles was the 5-12-13 triangle, meaning this: if you have a right

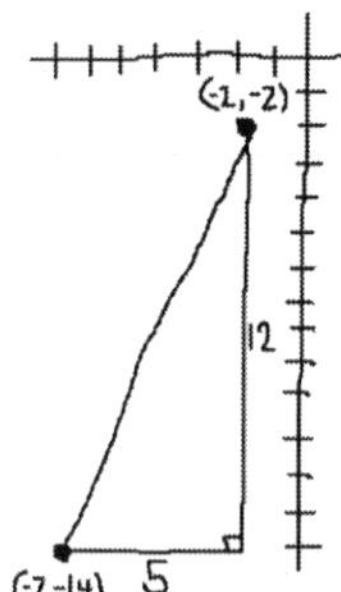

triangle with a leg of 5 and a hypotenuse of 13, you know the other leg to be 12; if you have a right triangle with a leg of 12 and a hypotenuse of 13, you know the other leg to be 5, or (most importantly for us now!) if you have a right triangle with a leg of length 5 and another leg with a length of 12, you *know* that the hypotenuse is 13.

Thus, the answer is D: 13.

6. Correct answer: **F**. This question purely tests your knowledge of the various types of triangles. First, we are told that triangle $\triangle LMN$ is an equilateral triangle, which means that all three of its sides are the same length. We are then told that angle $\angle L$ has a measure of 60 degrees. However, each angle of an equilateral triangle is the exact same (60 degrees; there is no other kind of equilateral triangle), so this measure is true of all 3 of this triangle's angles. Lastly, one of the sides, *MN*, has a length of 12mm. Again, all three sides of this triangle are the same, so every side is going to have a length of 12mm. With all of that in mind, let's get to the three statements to see which are true and which are false:

I. The first statement says that triangle *LMN* is acute, which is true; every equilateral triangle is acute, which simply means that all 3 of its angles are less than 90 degrees. TRUE

II. The second statement makes the claim that one of the triangles angles, angle *N*, is greater than 90 degrees, but this isn't possible in an equilateral triangle. FALSE

III. The third statement makes the claim that another of the triangle's sides, side *LM*, has a length less than 12 mm. Again, all three sides are going to be of equal length. FALSE

Thus, the correct answer is F; only statement I is true.

7. Correct answer: **C.** The key to this question is remembering what it means for two triangles to be *similar*; it means that their angles are all the same, and that their sides are *relative*. As you can see, side *PQ* is half the length of side *MN*; side *PR* is half the size of side *MO*; thus, it must be the case that side *RQ* is half the length of side *NO*. Because that's true, we know the three sides of triangle *PQR*, and thus we can find the perimeter (which is what the question is asking for).

$$\text{Perimeter of PQR} = (\text{Side } PQ) + (\text{Side } PR) + (\text{Side } QR) = 3.5 + 4.5 + 3.5 = 11.5$$

8. Correct answer: **H**. First, let's plug in $m = 7$ into the absolute value, and get something like this:

$$|m - 11| = |7 - 11| = |-4|$$

Remember that absolute value simply means the distance a value is away from 0 (in other words, just make it positive if it is a negative value). In this case of course, −4 is a total of 4 away from 0, which is answer choice H.

9. Correct answer: **C.** This question falls mostly into a category that we have discussed before: ACT Math *Have to Know* #6: Logical Thinking With Variables. Here, those variables are sometimes within absolute value signs, which makes them relevant for the current lesson on absolute value, of course.

We are looking for an expression that is *always* negative. Even though *j* and *k* can be any value at all (except for 0), any time that either of them is within the absolute value symbols, the result will be positive. This is going to eliminate answer choice A, since it features a positive number over a positive number. Letters B and D share a problem in that it is possible for either of them to be positive; B because if *j* is a positive value of any kind, the entire fraction will be made positive, and D because if *k* is a negative number the negatives will cancel and you will be left with a positive value.

That leaves C and E. We can eliminate E because if *j* and *k* are both negative (or if they're both positive), the fraction will be positive. Thus, by process of elimination, C is the correct answer. However, we can also see why: the absolute values of *j* in the numerator and *k* in the denominator will both be positive, but the fraction as a whole has a negative sign in front, making the expression always negative.

10. Correct answer: **K.** Just like number 9, this question falls mostly into a category that we have discussed before: ACT Math *Have to Know* #6: Logical Thinking With Variables. Here, those variables are sometimes within absolute value signs, which makes them relevant for the current lesson on absolute value.

Immediately, we can see that $|-x|$ is equivalent to x. That will probably help us as we go through the five answer choices. Let's do so one at a time.

F. This expression, if we remove the absolute value signs, is equivalent to $\frac{|x|}{|x|^2} = \frac{x}{x^2} = \frac{1}{x}$, not x.

G. This expression can be reduced like this: $-\frac{|x|^2}{|x|} = -\frac{x^2}{x} = -x$, not x.

H. This is the same as G, $-x$, not x.

J. This expression is almost 100% identical to letter F: $\frac{|-x|}{|-x|^2} = \frac{x}{x^2} = \frac{1}{x}$, not x.

K. Again, by process of elimination, we've arrived at the correct answer. However, let's work it out and reduce it down:

$$\sqrt{(-x)^2} = \sqrt{x^2} = x$$

because the square root of anything squared is simply the value itself. If you're unsure, choose a number for x and plug the above expression in your calculator and see if they're a match.

11. Correct answer: **D.** The first thing you ought to do is to convert the fraction $\frac{3}{8}$ to a decimal so that it matches up with the other two numbers; this will make it much easier to order them properly. Thus, $\frac{3}{8} = 0.375$. Now, we have our three decimals: 0.375, 0.35, and 0.04. The other little thing that might trip up some students is that, if they're not careful, they'll think that 0.04 is the largest of the 3 numbers because it starts with the number 4. However, this number has a 0 in the tens place, while the other two have the number 3 in the tens place; that makes it the smallest. Clearly, 0.375 is the largest, 0.35 is in the middle, and 0.04 is the smallest. This makes option D the correct answer in that it orders the inequalities properly.

12. Correct answer: **G.** Because all of the answer choices have solved the inequality in terms of x, we must do the same. Let's simply treat the inequality like an equation by, first, adding $4y$ to both sides:

$$-2x - 4y \leq 6y + 2 \quad \ldots \quad -2x \leq 10y + 2$$

Now is where there could be a simple mistake made. Remember: if you divide or multiply both sides of an inequality by a negative number, the sign must switch. Notice how that happens when we divide every term by -2:

$-2x \leq 10y + 2 \quad \ldots \quad x \geq -5y - 1$, which is answer choice G.

13. Correct answer: **A.** The variable, the absolute value, and the modeling story all make this problem seem much more difficult than it is (the ACT is expert at making many problems seem more difficult than they really are). All we have to do is use *Backsolving* to go one at a time through the answer choices, plug them in for c, and see which of them is *NOT* within range of the inequality.

A: $-40 \quad \ldots \quad |-40-30| \leq 45 \quad \ldots \quad |-70| \leq 45 \quad \ldots \quad 70 \leq 45$, which does NOT make sense!

Thus, the answer is A, -40, which is a value for c that falls outside the range of the inequality. If you plug in all of the other answer in for c, you will see that they all satisfy the inequality.

14. Correct answer: **J.** The first and most crucial step in this problem, of course, is actually finding the two solutions to this trinomial. Again, DON'T PANIC that you don't have the Quadratic Formula memorized; neither do I. It is very, very, very unlikely (if not impossible) that the ACT will ask you a question that requires your knowledge of the Quadratic Formula. There are easier ways to find the solutions.

The first way would be by graphing; if you don't know how, follow the steps for graphing these in the ACT Math *Good to Know* Lesson #5 on Parabolas; anywhere the parabola crosses the x-axis is a solution.

However, what I'm more likely to do is to simply factor the trinomial into two binomials and set both binomials equal to 0 to find my two solutions. This skill is important for the ACT (and has come up a lot in this book as a result). Let's do that here. Our trinomial, as a reminder, is this: $x^2 - 10x - 24$.

We need two numbers that multiply to give us -24, but add together to give us -10. These two values are -12 and 2. Thus,

$$x^2 - 10x - 24 = (x - 12)(x + 2)$$

Now, set each binomial equal to 0 to find our two solutions:

$$(x - 12) = 0 \quad \ldots \quad x = 12 \qquad \text{and,} \qquad (x + 2) = 0 \quad \ldots \quad x = -2$$

Now that we have found our two solutions (which, again, is where this parabola crosses the x-axis), we can find their mean, which just means the average:

$$\frac{12 + (-2)}{2} = \frac{10}{2} = 5 \text{, which is answer choice J.}$$

15. Correct answer: **A.** It is impossible to find the solution set (which just means the solutions) for this polynomial without first simplifying. So, this question will take three steps. Step 1, simplify and set equal to 0; Step 2, factor the resulting trinomial; Step 3, set each binomial equal to 0 (or graph it) and find our solutions.

Step 1: Simplify

$$x(x - 1) = 2x^2 + 9x + 25 \quad \ldots \quad x^2 - x = 2x^2 + 9x + 25 \quad \ldots \quad 0 = x^2 + 10x + 25$$

Step 2: Factor

Again, in factoring a trinomial (for us here, $x^2 + 10x + 25$), we need two numbers that multiply to give us the third term in the trinomial (in our case here, 25) that add together to equal the coefficient of the middle term (in our case here, 10). Those two numbers are clearly 5. Thus, we add 5 to x in our two binomials, like this:

$$x^2 + 10x + 25 = 0 \quad \ldots \quad (x + 5)(x + 5) = 0$$

Step 3: Set Equal to Zero

$$(x + 5) = 0 \quad \ldots \quad x = -5 \qquad \text{and,} \qquad (x + 5) = 0 \quad \ldots \quad x = -5$$

Because we get the same value for x, that simply means that this parabola only has 1 solution, which means that the parabola's tip touches the x-axis at $x = -5$, which makes A our correct answer.

16. Correct answer: **H.** You may notice that the shape of these three parabolas is identical; what sets them apart is simply their "height" off of the x-axis. This is determined by the final term in a quadratic, which is the y-intercept of the parabola itself. This is why the answer is H, which puts the changing z variable in the y-intercept slot.

However, if you're not fast enough conceptually to see why this question's solution is what it is, then there is a roundabout way to solve this problem. In real time, perhaps this is the type of question that you circle and come back to, but remember: there is almost always more than 1 way to solve ACT Math problems, including this one. Another way to solve it is *Backsolving*.

As a reminder, *Backsolving* simply means trying out answer choices one at a time. If you know how to graph parabolas on your graphing calculator, why not try out answer choice F with $z = 2$ and see if the resulting parabola is any of the above 3? Then move on to G, then H? This kind of flexibility and quick calculations could earn you another correct answer on the ACT Math test, but only if you have the time to do so.

17. Correct answer: **D.** To get this question correct, we must first be able to remember what the period of a wave is. The period of a wave (which is the same length as the wavelength) is the length of a wave from crest to crest or trough to trough. In other words, from the top of one wave to the top of another or the bottom of one wave to the to bottom of another. Here, we are given the data for these crests and troughs. Let's make a visual kind of chart that lists the crests and troughs, and see if we can go from there to determine the average period:

	Day 1	Day 2	Day 3	Day 4
High Tide	1:15 PM	12:30 PM	11:45 AM	11:00 AM
Low Tide	11:45 PM	11:00 PM	10:15 PM	9:30 PM

The first thing that I notice is that each tide decreases by 45 minutes each and every day, without exception. That might be enough for you to determine the answer, but let's keep going.

Remember; the period is the average distance from crest to crest or trough to trough. Crest to crest will be the time from high tide to high tide, and trough to trough will be from low tide to low tide. Let's make another little chart, this time calculating the time between each high and low tide, like this:

	Day 1 to 2	Day 2 to 3	Day 3 to 4
High Tide	23 hours, 15 min.	23 hours, 15 min.	23 hours, 15 min.
Low Tide:	23 hours, 15 min.	23 hours, 15 min.	23 hours, 15 min.

In this case, they have made the math side of things easy for us; the time between each high and low tide from one day to the next is the exact same, meaning that calculating the average period is not difficult. The average period, or the average length from high tide to high tide or low tide to low tide is 23 hours and 15 minutes, or answer choice D.

18. Correct answer: **G.** The best and fastest way to solve this problem is to conceptualize it. If sin (x), no matter what value of x you can think of, has a value up to 1 and as low as -1, and then I multiply that value by a number (in the case of our problem, c), then that value is only going to increase. For example, if $c = 3$, then the value of sin (x) is going to triple, up to a value of 3 or as far down as -3. Thus, if the "height" of the wave and the "depth" of the wave are increasing up and down as c increases, that affects the amplitude, making it "bigger."

There are only two answer choices that say that the amplitude increases, which are G and K. We can thus eliminate answers F, H, and J.

Conceptually, then, what happens to the period of the wave? Well, the period of a sin wave is simply the angles that sin is using to calculate; if the angles aren't affected, then the period will not be affected. If we were given a function of $f(x) = sin(cx)$, then the period would be stretched or narrowed as the angles change. This is why the answer is G: the period will stay the same as the amplitude increases.

19. Correct answer: **A**. As was said in the lesson accompanying this question, don't be afraid to use the *Drawn to Scale* mini-strategy on this problem if you are stuck. As was alluded to, you can even use the edge of your bubble sheet as a ruler, marking the lengths that you know to compare to the segment *BC*. Clearly, *BC* is not as long as 18 or 19; just by the looks of it, you can tell it is probably about one-third the length of AC, which is 27; that leads me to believe it is likely A or B.

However, there is an algebraic way to answer this question using the 3 values that we know (*AD, AC,* and *BD*). In words, it goes like this: $AC + BD$ is equal to the length of *AD*, but a little bit longer: the length of *BC* longer to be exact. In algebraic form, it looks like this:

$$AD = AC + BD - BC$$

In the equation above, we have 3 values that we know, and 1 that we don't, which is *BC*, which just so happens to be the value that the question asks for. Let's rewrite and solve for *BC*:

$$AD = AC + BD - BC \quad \ldots \quad 45 = 27 + 26 - BC \quad \ldots \quad -8 = -BC \quad \ldots \quad BC = 8$$

20. Correct answer: **H.** We do not have enough information given to determine in this question the exact number of students who play both a Spring and a Fall sport. However, the question doesn't ask for that. Rather, the question asks for the *minimum* number of students who play both a Spring and Fall sport.

We know there are 25 students in the class; 15 play a Spring sport, and 17 play a Fall sport. If 15 of the 25 students play a Spring sport, then that means that, so far, there are 10 students who do not yet play a sport. If we want to find the minimum number of students who play both, let's assign 10 of these students to a Fall sport. If we do that, now every student in the class plays a sport, but there are still 7 students who play a Fall sport, which means that at an absolute minimum, 7 students have to play both. This is answer choice H.

21. Correct answer: **B.** In the addition or subtraction of matrices, we simply add or subtract one space at a time with its equivalent in the other matrix. The -6 term, for example, in the top left hand corner of the first matrix will subtract from it the 10 in the top left corner of the second matrix. The resulting matrix will be of the same dimensions as the two featured in the question, like this:

$$\begin{bmatrix} -6 & 9 \\ -8 & 4 \end{bmatrix} - \begin{bmatrix} 10 & -4 \\ -1 & 0 \end{bmatrix} = \begin{bmatrix} -16 & 13 \\ -7 & 4 \end{bmatrix}$$, which is answer choice B.

22. Correct answer: **J.** All we have to do here is multiply the 3 by every term in the matrix one at a time; the resulting matrix will be of the same dimensions after it is affected: 2×2, like this:

$$3\begin{bmatrix} 0 & -2 \\ 6 & 5 \end{bmatrix} = \begin{bmatrix} 0 & -6 \\ 18 & 15 \end{bmatrix}, \text{ which is answer choice J.}$$

23. Correct answer: **D**. Matrices can be multiplied if the number of columns in the first matrix is the same as the number of rows in the second matrix. The resulting matrix, if this is the case, will be the opposite: it will be the number of rows in the first times the number of columns in the second. I remember as I'm typing this our acronym from the lesson on matrices: **CRRC**, or "Calm Rivers Reveal Crocs."

So, first we have to check if the number of columns in the first matrix matches the number of rows in the second. The first matrix has only 1 column, and the second matrix has only 1 row: so far, so good. This will mean that the resulting matrix will be the number of rows in the first matrix (3) by the number of columns in the second matrix (3).

This analysis is already enough to get the answer correct, and I would bet that if you *can* analyze the problem this well, you will probably be getting the answer fairly easily. There is only one matrix that is 3×3, which is answer choice D.

However, here is the entire thing worked out, just to be thorough:

$$\begin{bmatrix} -4 \\ x \\ 2x \end{bmatrix}[x \ \ 3 \ \ 0] = \begin{bmatrix} -4(x) & -4(3) & -4(0) \\ x(x) & x(3) & x(0) \\ 2x(x) & 2x(3) & 2x(0) \end{bmatrix} = \begin{bmatrix} -4x & -12 & 0 \\ x^2 & 3x & 0 \\ 2x^2 & 6x & 0 \end{bmatrix}, \text{ which is answer choice D.}$$

24. Correct answer: **H**. The simplest way to conceptualize this problem without making a simple mistake (which of course is what can happen if you keep it all in your head) is to convert the entire board's length into inches, get our answer, and then convert it back into feet.

Because there are 12 inches in a foot, we find the total number of inches in the board by doing this: $7(12) + 4 = 88$ inches. Since the board is cut into two equal pieces, the length of each part can be found by dividing the total length of board by two:

$$\text{Part Length} = \frac{88}{2} = 44 \text{ inches}$$

Of course, 44 inches is not an answer choice, so we need to convert it back to feet. Simply divide by 12, and any remainder is the number of inches leftover as well.

$$\frac{44}{12} = 3\frac{8}{12} = 3 \text{ feet 8 inches, which is answer choice H.}$$

25. Correct answer: **C**. When you multiply feet by feet, you get square feet; when you multiply yard by yard, you get square yards. That seems obvious, but that means that we need to use the square footage of the floor to find its dimensions in feet, then use that to find the dimensions of the floor in yards, then use that to find the square yardage of the floor. If you simply divide 14,400 by 3 (because there are 3 feet in a yard), you will get 4,800, but that is a mistake and inaccurate.

First, find the dimensions of the floor in feet. We know the square footage is 14,400 ft^2, but that doesn't mean we automatically know the dimensions of the floor. However, it doesn't matter what dimensions we come up with, as long as they are accurate. I can see that 14,400 is a perfect square (it is 120^2), so let's use that and pretend that the dimensions of the floor are 120×120.

Second, we need to convert our dimensions to yards. Since there are 3 feet in 1 yard, we just divide our dimension by 3, so a floor that measures 120 ft $\times$ 120 ft equals 40 yards $\times$ 40 yards.
Lastly, we need to find now the square yardage. Since we now know the dimension in yards (40×40), we just simply multiply one side by the other: 40 yards $\times$ 40 yards = 1,600 square yards, or answer choice C.

26. Correct answer: **F.** The first step to solving this problem is to convert 40 miles per hour into miles per minute. To do this multiply the rate we know (miles per hour) by the number of minutes per hour so that "hours" cancels and we are left with miles per minute.

$$\frac{40 \text{ miles}}{\text{hour}} \cdot \frac{1 \text{ hour}}{60 \text{ minutes}} = \frac{40 \text{ miles}}{60 \text{ minutes}} = \frac{2}{3}\frac{\text{miles}}{\text{minute}}$$

Now that we have the speed Clarence is traveling in miles per minute, we just need to multiply this rate by the 16 minutes he is traveling. This will cause minutes to cancel, leaving us with the number of miles, like this:

$$\frac{2}{3}\frac{\text{miles}}{\text{minute}} \cdot 16 \text{ minutes} = \frac{32}{3} \text{ miles} = 10\frac{2}{3} \text{ miles}$$, which is answer choice F.

27. Correct answer: **C**. The subscript following the word *log* in a log function is the base, and the number that a log function is set equal to is the exponent. Let's rewrite this in a form that might be a bit easier to understand and conceptualize:

$$\log_x 343 = 3 \quad \ldots \quad x^3 = 343$$

Now we can see that there is some number being cubed, and that number is equal to 343. You can solve this from here in couple of ways. Method 1 would be to use *Backsolving* and try out each answer one at a time to see which is the base that, when cubed, equals 343.

Method 2 is to use a calculator. Instead of starting with the x, we will start with the 343. In other words, the answer we are looking for is the cubed root of 343. There are a couple of ways to find a cubed root in your calculator. I like to raise numbers to the one-third power, like this:

$$x^3 = 343 \quad \ldots \quad (x^3)^{\frac{1}{3}} = 343^{\frac{1}{3}} \quad \ldots \quad x = 343^{\frac{1}{3}} \quad \ldots \quad x = 7$$, which is answer choice C.

28. Correct answer: **J.** The subscript following the word log in a log function is the base, and the number that a log function is set equal to is the exponent; in our question, the variable x, represents the solution to a number raised to an exponent. Like before, one helpful step is to rewrite the function so that it makes more conceptual sense.

$$\log_4 x = -3 \quad \ldots \quad 4^{-3} = x$$

Now we have a much simpler problem to work with; at least, it is simpler if you know what to do with negative exponents! Remember: if an exponent is negative, you make it positive and then flip it (either from the numerator to the denominator or vice versa), like this:

$$4^{-3} = \frac{1}{4^3} = \frac{1}{64}$$, which is answer choice J.

29. Correct answer: **C.** First, we must remember that a negative exponent needs to be made positive and then flipped from the numerator to the denominator (or vice versa), which explains what must be done with the 3^{-3} term. However, we must realize that the 3^{-3} might be in the numerator of the larger, greater fraction, but it is in the denominator of the top term; thus, you wouldn't put it in the denominator of the larger term, but the numerator of the upper term, like this:

$$\frac{\frac{1}{3^{-3}}}{3} = \frac{\frac{3^3}{1}}{3} = \frac{3^3}{3}$$

From here, you simply need to simplify, like so:

$$\frac{3^3}{3} = 3^2 = 9$$, which is answer choice C.

30. Correct answer: **F**. We need to take our time on this problem and ensure we don't make any simple mistakes. The first step is to change any variables with negative exponents into those with positive exponents by moving them from either the numerator to the denominator or vice versa. Before combining like terms, let's do this first step first:

$$\frac{a^{-3}b^2c^{-4}}{a^2b^{-2}} = \frac{b^2b^2c^1}{a^2a^3c^4}$$

Now, let's remember a couple of more rules about exponents. First, when two of the same variables raised to exponents are multiplied by one another (like we have with b in the numerator above and a in the denominator above), to combine them, you simply add their exponents together. Second, when you have two of the same variables being divided one by another, you subtract the smaller from the larger, and put the answer in the place of the larger. In the above equation, this is the case with c. You'll see how this happens as we simplify the problem above here:

$$\frac{b^2b^2c^1}{a^2a^3c^4} = \frac{b^4}{a^5c^3}$$, which is answer choice F.

31. Correct answer: **C.** If you can remember the formula of a circle, then you can get this question correct. As a reminder, the formula for the area of a circle is $(x - h)^2 + (y - k)^2 = r^2$, in which (h, k) is the center of the circle and r is the radius. Getting this question correct is as simple as plugging in the values given by the question into the equation.

If the circle is centered on $(-1, 3)$, then that means that $h = -1$ and $k = 3$. If the radius is 5, then $r^2 = 25$, thus:

$$(x - h)^2 + (y - k)^2 = r^2 \quad \ldots \quad (x + 1)^2 + (y - 3)^2 = 25$$, or choice C.

32. Correct answer: **K.** There is a LOT going on in this problem! But let's start with the ending: we are told that we are looking for circles that have an area of 64π. Recall that the area of a circle is πr^2, thus another way of saying that this circle has an area of 64π is to say that it has a radius of 8. Now, it is time to go through each of the three circles described and determine if it has a radius of 8 (aka an area of 64π).

Circle I. Because we are given the center of the circle $(-2, -2)$ and a point through which the circle passes $(6, -2)$, we have enough information to determine the radius of the circle, which is simply the distance between these two points. We have discussed on multiple occasions in this book that there is no need to memorize the distance formula (though if you have it memorized, that's great). Instead, you can simply draw a line between the two points and treat the line between them like the hypotenuse of a triangle, the length of which can then be found using the Pythagorean Theorem. However, in this case, finding the radius is much simpler.

Look at the points: they share a y value, meaning they are going to be the same "height." The line between them is going to be a straight line across $y = -2$. If you graph the points by hand, you will see what I am talking about. The distance between them, then, is simply the difference in values on the x-axis, or $6 - (-2)$, or 8. Thus, because the distance between these two points is 8, it has a radius of 8. So far, this point checks out, eliminating answer choices F and J.

Circle II. Remember that the formula for the circumference of a circle is $2\pi r$, thus if the circle described here has a circumference of 16π, it has a radius of 8. Thus, this circle also checks out, eliminating answer choice H.

Circle III. There is no need to graph this equation or any such thing; instead, realize that the formula of a circle is $(x - h)^2 + (y - k)^2 = r^2$, so all we need to look at is the last term: the r^2. Here, $r^2 = 64$, so $r = 8$, meaning it has a radius of 8. This circle, too, meets the requirements of the question.

Thus, Circles I, II, and III all have an area of 64π, which is answer choice K.

33. Correct answer: **A.** When you are given the formula for a line, such as $y = 2x - 4$, you can determine which points from a list of options are on this line by plugging each x and y value into the equation and seeing which of them satisfy. This exact same way of thinking is true of a circle. Each point that the circle goes over, when plugged into the equation of the circle, will satisfy. So, to solve this particular problem, plug in each answer choice's x and y values one at a time into the circle's equation and see which satisfies.

A. $(2, -2)$

$$(x - 2)^2 + (y - 5)^2 = 49 \quad \ldots \quad (2 - 2)^2 + (-2 - 5)^2 = 49 \quad \ldots \quad 0^2 + (-7)^2 = 49 \quad \ldots \quad 49 = 49$$

Yes, it satisfies! This is the correct answer! There is no need to go any further. However, for the sake of showing you an answer that does *not* satisfy, let's move on to answer choice B:

B. $(2, 5)$

$$(x - 2)^2 + (y - 5)^2 = 49 \quad \ldots \quad (2 - 2)^2 + (5 - 5)^2 = 49 \quad \ldots \quad 0^2 + 0^2 = 49 \quad \ldots \quad 0 = 49$$

No, 0 does not equal 49! This answer (and C, D, and E) does not satisfy. Thus, the correct answer is A.

Answer Explanations - Step 6 - Practice Test #1

Correct answers:

1: C	**11: B**	**21: E**	**31: D**	**41: B**	**51: E**
2: G	**12: J**	**22: F**	**32: K**	**42: F**	**52: F**
3: B	**13: E**	**23: D**	**33: E**	**43: B**	**53: A**
4: K	**14: H**	**24: J**	**34: H**	**44: K**	**54: G**
5: A	**15: B**	**25: B**	**35: C**	**45: D**	**55: E**
6: K	**16: H**	**26: H**	**36: J**	**46: F**	**56: K**
7: A	**17: D**	**27: A**	**37: E**	**47: C**	**57: C**
8: J	**18: F**	**28: H**	**38: J**	**48: H**	**58: J**
9: D	**19: C**	**29: C**	**39: A**	**49: D**	**59: A**
10: F	**20: G**	**30: G**	**40: G**	**50: G**	**60: K**

1. Correct answer: **C.** First, we must determine how much money Chip made from the selling of the candy bars, like this: $\$1.30 \times 28 = \$36.40$. Now, when we subtract how much money Chip had leftover after his purchase of the fishing poles, we will learn how much he actually spent on purchasing them, like this: $\$36.40 - 13.90 = \$22.50$. Lastly, we are looking for the average amount that Chip spent on the three fishing poles that he bought. We simply need to take the money spent, which we just found, and divide it by three, which will give us our final answer, like this: $(\$22.50 \div 3) = \$7.50$, which is answer choice C.

2. Correct answer: **G**. First, we need to determine the amount of hours that it took him to drive. If he left at 6:00 AM, and arrived at 10:00 PM, then that means it took him 16 hours to get to his destination. Now, the question asks for an answer in miles per hour; that's a clue to the kind of math we need to do here. Put the number of miles traveled in the numerator, and the number of hours in the denominator, then the result will be in miles over hours, or miles per hour. Thus, since we are given that he traveled 880 miles, our equation looks like this:

$$\frac{880 \text{ miles}}{16 \text{ hours}} = 55 \text{ miles per hour, which is answer choice G.}$$

3. Correct answer: **B.** In order to determine how many blocks Sylvia walked her dog today, we need to first determine how much she actually charged her client for block-walking today. What I mean is that we need to subtract the base fee of \$12 from the total charge of \$29.50, like this: $\$29.50 - \$12.00 = \$17.50$ charged for the blocks walked. If she charges \$1.25 per block, we simply need to divide this per-block charge in to the \$17.50 to determine the number of blocks walked, like this: $\$17.50 \div \$1.25 = 14$ blocks walked, which is answer choice B.

4. Correct answer: **K.** Don't let the word "translated" scare you; you can use context clues to understand that the point is simply "moved" 5 coordinate units down and then "moved" 9 coordinate units right. A simple mistake to be made would be that the moving down 5 units is mentioned first, but "up and down" on the (x, y) coordinate plane affects the y value, which is second. So, if the original point had a y value of -6, then moving down (in a negative direction) 5 would give the new point a y value of -11. Then, it is mentioned that the point is moved 9 units to the right, or in a positive direction on the right axis. The original point had an x value of 4, thus increasing it by 9 results in an x value of 13. The final answer, then, is $(13, -11)$, or answer choice K.

5. Correct answer: **A**. Adding matrices with the same dimensions is as easy as adding terms together in the same location in each matrix, the result of which will be a matrix with the same dimensions (in our case here, a 4×4 matrix). For our purposes here, the upper left corner of the first matrix has a value of 4, and the upper left corner of the second matrix has a value of -8, thus the upper left corner of the resulting matrix will have a value of $4 + (-8) = -4$. Already, we can eliminate choices B, D, and E.

Let's move to the upper right corner. The upper right value of the first matrix is 9, and the upper right value of the second matrix is 3, which means that the resulting upper right value will be $9 + 3 = 12$. Because answer choice A is the only one of our remaining options that has this value, we have done enough to conclude that it is the correct answer.

To be thorough, here is what it looks like when we add these two matrices together more formally:

$$\begin{bmatrix} 4 & 9 \\ -3 & 7 \end{bmatrix} + \begin{bmatrix} -8 & 3 \\ 4 & 0 \end{bmatrix} = \begin{bmatrix} -4 & 12 \\ 1 & 7 \end{bmatrix}, \text{ or answer choice A.}$$

6. Correct answer: **K**. We are looking in this problem for "a certain number," let's call it x, the square root of which is 7.48921. If the square root of x is 7.48911, then we simply need to square this value to find x. In other words:

$$\sqrt{x} = 7.48921 \quad \ldots \quad (\sqrt{x})^2 = (7.48921)^2 \quad \ldots \quad x = 56.08827$$

The question, however, asks us to place the number between two values, which we can do. 56.09 falls between 49 and 64, which is answer choice K.

7. Correct answer: **A**. In this problem we are given A and the midpoint of segment AB and asked to find point B. Actually graphing the two points could help you avoid simple mistakes, but if we apply the same changes that are made on the x and y axis between points A and the midpoint to the midpoint itself, we will find point B.

Point A has an x value of 2, and the midpoint has an x value of 4. That is a change of +2 on the x-axis, which means that the x value of point B will be $4 + 2 = 6$.

Point A has a y value of -4, and the midpoint has a y value of 1. That is a change of +5 on the y-axis, which means that the y value of point B will be $1 + 5 = 6$.

Thus, the coordinates of point B is (6, 6), which is answer choice A.

8. Correct answer: **J**. To find the probability that the winner is not a green car, we need to put the total number of non-green cars over the total number of cars, and simplify. If there are 20 total cars, and 16 of them are non-green (because the question states that 4 are green), then the probability that the winner of the race is not a green car looks like this:

$$\frac{\text{non-green cars}}{\text{total cars}} = \frac{16}{20} = \frac{4}{5}\text{, which is answer choice J.}$$

9. Correct answer: **D**. This is a classic Modeling-to-Algebra ACT Math problem. We have to carefully translate these words into an Algebra problem so that we can find our missing value (the number of books he had on the bookshelves last year), which we'll call x.

One key to answering this question well is realizing that 207 books "is" 30 more than 3 times x. I put quotations around the word "is" because that word is the equivalent of an equal sign in these kinds of problems. Thus, whatever equation we come up with, it will = 207.

Now for the equation on the left side of the = sign. It says that 207 is "30 more than 3 times the number." Well, "the number" is x, thus x is going to be multiplied by 3. In addition, since 207 is "30 more", then that means we are going to add 30 to it, thus:

$$3x + 30 = 207$$

Now we have an equation to solve. Subtract 30 from both sides, then divide both sides by 3:

$$3x + 30 = 207 \quad \ldots \quad 3x = 177 \quad \ldots \quad \frac{3x}{3} = \frac{177}{3} \quad \ldots \quad x = 59\text{, which is answer choice D.}$$

10. Correct answer: **F**. Most often, function questions feature only one variable, like $f(x)$. However, in this case we have two. However, the mathematics of it is still the same, no matter how many variables we have. If $f(x, y)$ is given, and we need to find $f(2, -1)$, then plug in 2 anywhere in the equation there is an x and plug in -1 anywhere there is a y in the equation, like this:

$$f(x, y) = -(x^3) + 3y = -(2^3) + 3(-1) = -(8) + (-3) = -8 - 3 = -11\text{, or answer choice F.}$$

11. Correct answer: **B**. In this problem, we need to set up an equation and solve for our missing variable, segment BC, which is possible based on what we know. The last two data points we are given is that segment AC is 21 units long and that segment BD is 24 units long. When you add those two distances together, you get a distance that is equal to all of segment AD, plus a little bit extra, but that little bit extra is BC. Thus, $AC + BD = AD + BC$. Now, we plug in what we know and solve for what we do not know (which is BC):

$$AC + BD = AD + BC \quad \ldots \quad 21 + 24 = 34 + BC \quad \ldots \quad 11 = BC\text{, which is answer choice B.}$$

Again, if you are stuck on this problem, it is a good candidate for the *Drawn to Scale* mini-strategy. First of all, just based on the *looks* of it, segment BC seems like it is about one-third of the entire line segment, AD, which is 34 units long, and only 11 is anywhere in that ballpark. You could also use your answer key as a kind of ruler, measuring out the lengths you do know along its edge and comparing it to segment BC.

12. Correct answer: **J**. The variable y in this question is used in both of the binomials that are being multiplied to equal 0, which means that there will be two values of y that make the expression as a whole equal to 0. If either of the binomials (meaning either of the terms within the parentheses) can be made to equal 0, then the expression as a whole will equal 0.

First, let's start with the first binomial: $(y + m)$. Again, if this binomial can be made to equal 0, the expression as a whole will be made to equal 0. Because we are adding m to y, then the only value for y that can make this expression equal 0 is $-m$, since $(-m + m) = 0$. So, $-m$ is one of our two values, which eliminates answer choices F, G, and K.

Second, let's move on to the second binomial: $(y - n) = 0$. Again, if this binomial can be made to equal 0, the expression as a whole will be made to equal 0. Because we are subtracting n from y, then the only value for y that makes this expression equal 0 is n, since $(n - n)$ will always = 0. Thus, n is the second of our two values. Given that our two values for y that satisfy the equation are $-m$ and n, the answer is J.

13. Correct answer: **E**. In order to determine the solutions for this expression, it needs to first be simplified by distributing the $7x$ term, adding like terms, and setting everything equal to 0. When all is set equal to 0, finding the solutions means finding the values for x that satisfy the equation, in other words finding the values of x that make the equation as a whole then equal 0. First let's simplify and set the equation equal to 0, like this:

$$x^2 = 7x(x - 0) - 54 \quad \ldots \quad x^2 = 7x^2 - 54 \quad \ldots \quad 0 = 6x^2 - 54 \quad \ldots \quad 0 = 6(x^2 - 9) \quad \ldots \quad 0 = x^2 - 9$$

You might be a little confused by that last step...where did the 6 go that was in front of the $(x^2 - 9)$ term? Well, we divided both sides by 6, and 0 divided by 6 is still 0.

Now we are left with this: $x^2 - 9 = 0$, and we have to determine what the solution set is for this expression. We have discussed elsewhere in this book how to factor a trinomial, which is a polynomial with three expressions, including an x^2 term, an x term, and a number, but here we have a binomial (only two terms in the expression) that begins with an x^2 term. However, we can easily make this into a trinomial, then factor like we are used to. To do this, we need to add a $0x$ term into the middle, like this:

$$x^2 - 9 = x^2 + 0x - 9$$

With that done, we can now factor. To factor this term into two binomials, we need two numbers that multiply to give us a -9 (our last number) and add up to give us a 0 (the middle number). Those two numbers are 3 and -3, since $3 \times -3 = -9$ and $3 + -3 = 0$. Thus:

$$x^2 - 9 = x^2 + 0x - 9 = (x - 3)(x + 3)$$

To find the solutions, set each binomial equal to 0 and solve for x. First, there is $(x - 3) = 0$, which, when solves, yields a result of $x = 3$, which is already enough to get the question correct, since E is the only option that features this as a result. However, we should also solve this for x: $(x + 3) = 0$, which, when solved, yields a result of $x = -3$, which is our second result.

However, there is another way to get this question correct, that might perhaps be even faster than the above method: *Backsolving*. Why not try out each answer choice one at a time to determine if it satisfies the equation? Of course we know that $\{-3, 3\}$ satisfies, but let me show you what it would look like *Backsolving* when you come to a number that doesn't satisfy.

Let's begin with A $\{-4\}$ and see if this is the solution for the equation. All we need to do is to plug in -4 anywhere there is an x in the equation (even without simplifying the equation!) and see if it satisfies:

$$x^2 = 7x(x - 0) - 54 \quad \ldots \quad (-4)^2 = 7(-4)(-4 - 0) - 54 \quad \ldots \quad 16 = -28(-4) - 54 \quad \ldots \quad 16 = 58? \quad \text{NOPE}$$

When you enter in -4, or any other value for x that doesn't make sense or satisfy, then you can be sure it is not a solution, which will happen with every answer choice besides E.

14. Correct answer: **H**. Because you are not given any numbers in this question or diagram (we aren't told the lengths of any segments, the measure of any angles, the perimeter/circumference or area of any shape, etc.), this is an eyeball test. In other words, you are being forced to use the *Drawn to Scale* mini-strategy in this question. Before we get to the answer, we need to recall what it means for the arc of a circle to have a degree measure. The measure of any arc of a circle (an arc, again, is a "piece" of the circumference of a circle) is equivalent to its interior angle. For example, arc JG has a degree measure that is equivalent to angle JEG in the center of the circle. To the naked eye, let's approximate the measure of each of these angles one by one and see which has the greatest degree measure.

F: Angle FKJ looks, to me, to measure roughly 45°.

G: Angle *FGH* looks, to me, to also measure roughly 45°.

H: Arc *FJ* appears to have an interior angle that measures roughly 135°, so the biggest so far.

J: Arc *JG* appears to have an interior angle that measures roughly 45°.

K: Arc *GH* appears to have an interior angle that measures roughly 45° (though there isn't an actual angle there for you to immediately visualize, you could draw it in there if it's helpful).

Thus, clearly, answer H is correct in that it appears to have the largest angle. In this kind of ACT Math question it isn't going to be close; in other words, if you're being forced to eyeball angles and to determine the biggest or smallest, the answer (if you're analyzing them correctly) is going to be obvious, as is the case here.

15. Correct answer: **B**. If two lines are parallel, they have the same slope. If two lines are perpendicular, their slopes are negative reciprocals of one another. Here, we are told that the slope of segment *EJ* is $\frac{3}{2}$, and asked to find the slope of a segment that is perpendicular to segment *EJ*. Thus, we need to find the negative reciprocal of $\frac{3}{2}$; to do so requires two steps. First, make it negative, and second, flip it upside down (take what's in the numerator and flip it to the denominator, and take what's in the denominator and flip it up into the numerator). Thus, the negative reciprocal of $\frac{3}{2}$ is $-\frac{2}{3}$, or choice B.

16. Correct answer: **H**. Because exactly half of the circle is within the triangle, we need to find the area of the circle and cut it in half. We are told that the diameter of the circle is 22, which means a radius of 11. Recall that the formula for the area of a circle is πr^2, and seeing that each answer keeps π without multiplying through, let's work on the radius squared. The area of this circle is:

$$\pi r^2 = (11)^2\pi = 121\pi$$

So, if half of the circle lies within triangle *KFI*, then dividing 121π by $2 = 60.5\pi$, or answer choice H.

17. Correct answer: **D**. There are multiple ways to solve this problem, but here is an easy way. Step 1, determine how many times $\frac{1}{5}$ can be divided into $3\frac{2}{5}$, and then Step 2, multiply that number by 14 to determine how far apart the mountains are.

Step 1:

$$3\frac{2}{5} \div \frac{1}{5} = 17$$

Step 2:

$$17 \times 14 \text{ kilometers} = 238 \text{ kilometers, or answer choice D.}$$

18. Correct answer: **F**. Don't let the fact that the number 11 is used twice confuse you. The first thing to recognize is that we are given a rate in miles per *hour*, but we want to know how far Candace will run in 11 *minutes*. I think the easiest way to solve this problem is to change the speed or rate from miles per hour to miles per minute. If there are 60 minutes in an hour, then:

$$11 \text{ mph} = \frac{11 \text{ miles}}{1 \text{ hour}} = \frac{11 \text{ miles}}{60 \text{ minutes}} = \frac{\frac{11}{60} \text{ miles}}{1 \text{ minute}} = 0.18333\frac{\text{miles}}{\text{minute}}$$

Thus, Candace can ride her bike at a rate of 0.18333 miles per minute. If we multiply that rate by the number of minutes she is going to ride (11), the minutes will cancel, and we will be left with the number of miles that Candace can ride in 11 minutes:

$$\frac{0.18333 \text{ miles}}{\text{minute}} \times 11 \text{ minutes} = 2.02 \text{ miles}$$

Because the question asks for the answer rounded to the nearest mile, we round down to 2, which is answer choice F.

19. Correct answer: **C**. This is a simple math problem dressed up in the guise of something more complicated. Simply put, one of the five answer choices will equal 7 when a value of $z = 3$ is entered, and that same answer choice will equal 28 when a value of $z = 12$ is entered. All you have to do is try out the answer choices one at a time using these two values for z (3 and 12, respectively) and see if you get the same output (7 and 12, respectively). Let's simply start with choice A and work our way through:

A: $\frac{3}{7}z = \frac{3}{7}(3) = \frac{6}{7}$, which is not 7, so move on.

B: $7z = 7(3) = 21$, which is not 7, so move on.

C: $\frac{7}{3}z = \frac{7}{3}(3) = \frac{21}{3} = 7$, which works! Now try a z value of 12 and see if the result is 28:

$\frac{7}{3}z = \frac{7}{3}(12) = \frac{84}{3} = 28$, which also works! This is why C is the correct answer.

20. Correct answer: **G**. First, realize that $\triangle WXZ$ is a right triangle, so $\angle XZW$ is 90°. That means the steps to solving this problem are as follows: 1) Find the measure of $\angle WXZ$, then 2) Subtract our two known angles from 180° to find our missing angle ($\angle VWY$).

Step 1: The angles in a line add up to 180°, which means that we simply need to subtract 114° from 180° to determine the measure of $\angle WXZ$, thus: 180° – 114° = 66°.

Step 2: Again, now that we know two of the angles of our triangle, we need to subtract these from 180° to determine the angle measure of $\angle VWY$, like this: 180° – 66° – 90° = 24°, which is answer choice G.

21. Correct answer: **E**. It is probably very tempting to think that if the stock fell by 5% three times, then went back up to where it started, that it rose 15%. But percentage questions are tricky and always require that you do the math to ensure the correct answer.

First, let's decrease \$500 by 5% 3 times. Start with \$500, then subtract 5% by subtracting \$500(0.05). Here are our three decreases:

Decrease 1: \$500 – \$500(0.05) = \$475.00
Decrease 2: \$475 – \$475(0.05) = \$451.25
Decrease 3: \$451.25 – \$451.25(0.05) = \$428.69

So, after three straight decreases of 5%, the stock is now worth \$428.69, which means it has decreased in total by an amount of \$71.31.

Now, to find the *increase*. Remember: we have to now determine the percent that the stock rose in the fourth hour when it came back to \$500. You might be tempted to find what percent \$71.31 is of \$500, but that would be inaccurate. When the stock rises in the fourth hour, it rises *from* \$428.69, so we need to find what percent \$71.31 is of this value, like this:

$$\frac{\$71.31}{\$428.69} \times 100 = 16.63\,\%$$

When rounded as the question asks for, the result is 17%, or choice E.

22. Correct answer: **F**. There are a number of ways to solve this particular problem, but I suspect the difficulty is not necessarily the math, but the *story* that the math is wrapped up in. If you remember, these kinds of math problems are called *modeling* problems and they make up a significant portion of questions on ACT day. If you are having a difficult time with these kinds of problems, try reading the last sentence first, since the last sentence always contains the actual question.

Let's identify which category he is in at the moment. If we add up his first 5 race speeds, then divide by 5, we get this: (42.50 + 45.50 + 45.00 + 51.25 + 47.75)/5 = 46.40 seconds. This means that, at the moment, he is currently outside of the Good range and in the Average range. Let's try scores one at a time and determine if adding in this particular 6th score is good enough to move him up into the Good range with an average that is 46.09 or less.

F: 44 seconds ... (42.50 + 45.50 + 45.00 + 51.25 + 47.75 + 44.00)/6 = 46.00

Thus, answer choice F is correct in that a speed of 46.00 seconds moves his average into the Good range. If you try answer choice G (or any other, since the speeds are all higher), you will get an average speed that falls in the Average category or worse. Answer G, a speed of 45.00 seconds, results in an average of 46.17 seconds, just outside of Good range.

23. Correct answer: **D**. Given that y must always be less than –2, you could start by *Picking Numbers*, inserting –3 in as y, and see what happens to the value of x. Here is what happens when we do that:

$$x = \frac{y}{y-1} = \frac{-3}{-3-1} = \frac{-3}{-4} = \frac{3}{4} = 0.75$$

Even though we are being forced to choose negative numbers for y, the equation as a whole will always end up positive, since we are dividing a negative by a negative in all circumstances. This realization eliminates options A, B, and C, leaving just D and E.

Based on our math when $y = -3$, it is easy to see that values for x that creep closer and closer to 1.00 as y gets more and more negative. For example, if $y = -99$, then we are going to get a value for x of $(-99/-100)$, or 0.99. However, the question never says that the value of y has to be an *integer*, just that it has to be lower than -2. In other words, it is possible that a value of y that equals something like -2.1 or -2.55 could give us a value for x that equals 0.71, which is why D is the correct answer.

24. Correct answer: **J**. This question is asking for the least possible number into which 21 and 49 divide evenly. It sounds more complicated than that, but all you have to do is go through the answer choices (*Backsolving*) from smallest to largest to determine which number is the smallest that both 21 and 49 can go into.

F: 7 ... Well, neither 21 nor 49 go into 7. Next.

G: 49 ... Though 49 goes into 49, 21 does not divide into 49 evenly.

H: 70 ... Neither 21 nor 49 divides into 70 evenly.

J: 147 ... (147/21) = 7, and (147/49) = 3

This means that J is the correct answer because both 21 and 49 divide into it evenly.

25. Correct answer: **B**. To determine the likelihood that Richard's ball lands in the sand trap, we have to first determine the total amount of square footage there is that his ball could land in, which is this amount:
198 + 94 + 134 + 124 = 550 square feet.

Next, we simply need to divide the sand trap's area by the total area to determine our percent likelihood:

$$\frac{134 \text{ ft}^2}{550 \text{ ft}^2} \times 100 = 24.4\%$$, which is answer choice B.

26. Correct answer: **H**. A parallelogram is a shape with 4 sides, and each pair of sides is parallel and equal. A square and a rectangle are both examples of a parallelogram because both of their pairs of sides are parallel, but you can also have parallelograms that don't feature right angles.

In this particular problem, there is enough information to determine the lengths of all 4 sides. First, if one side is 22 inches long, then, by definition, this parallelogram features a side parallel to this side with a length of 22 inches. Second, if two sides have lengths of 22 inches each, then that means that the combined length of the other two sides is 102 inches (the perimeter given in the problem) − 22 − 22 = 58 inches. If the other two sides are a combined 58 inches long, and because they are the same length because this is a parallelogram, then divide 58 by 2 and learn that each other side is 29 inches long.

Thus, our four sides are of length 22, 22, 29, and 29 inches, which is answer choice H.

27. Correct answer: **A**. There is a lot of information in this question that is unnecessary, which is a common feature of ACT Math problems. The entire question boils down to this: what is the distance between the origin, meaning point (0, 0) in the standard (x, y) coordinate plane, and point (40, 96)?

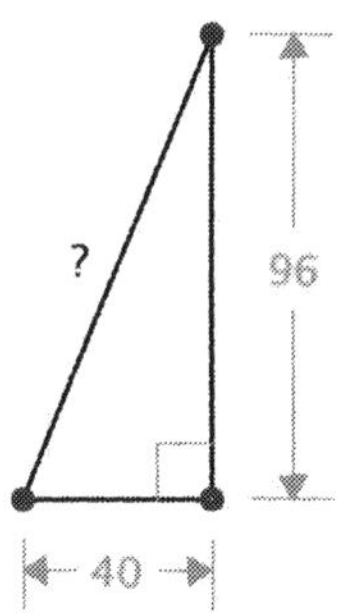

If you know the distance formula, you can certainly use it here. However, as I've discussed elsewhere in this book many times, the simplest way to solve these distance problems is to make a right triangle in which the distance between the two is the hypotenuse, then use the Pythagorean Theorem to solve.

Here is what such a triangle will look like. On the bottom, we know the length to be 40 because the question says that the ball traveled 40 feet down the first base line, and similarly we know the right side of the triangle to have a length of 96 because the question says that the ball traveled 96 feet down the third base line. Now, we can use the Pythagorean Theorem ($a^2 + b^2 = c^2$, in which c is the hypotenuse) to solve:

$$40^2 + 96^2 = c^2 \quad \ldots \quad 1{,}600 + 9{,}216 = c2 \quad \ldots \quad \sqrt{10816} = \sqrt{c^2} \quad \ldots \quad c = 104$$

Thus, answer choice A is correct: the ball traveled 104 feet.

28. Correct answer: **H**. This is a straightforward know-it-or-you-don't triangle concept problem. An isosceles triangle is one with two sides of equal length. In the case of this triangle, side *AB* and side *AC* are clearly the same length. If they have the same length, they have the same opposite angle. Because we know the angle opposite side *AC* (aka, angle *B*) is 72°, we can then deduce that the angle opposite side *AB* (aka angle *C*) is also 72°, which is answer choice H.

29. Correct answer: **C**. There are a number of ways that you could go about adding up the total cost of these bicycle orders, but I believe the easiest way to be to figure out the price of each *X*, *Y*, and *Z* bike, then multiply the cost by the number of bikes ordered.

Step 1:
- The cost of each *X* bike is: \$55 + \$20(2) + \$24 = \$119
- The cost of each *Y* bike is: \$58 + \$24(2) + \$24 = \$130
- The cost of each *Z* bike is: \$70 + \$33(2) + \$24 = \$160

Step 2: There is an order for 2 *X* bikes, 7 *Y* bikes, and 5 *Z* bikes, so if we multiply these three numbers by their respective prices, and add them together, we will get the total cost to the manufacturer:

2(\$119) + 7(\$130) + 5(\$160) = \$238 + \$910 + \$800 = \$1,948, which is answer choice C.

30. Correct answer: **G**. In order to avoid simple mistakes, let's first convert the 7 feet 3 inch board into inches. Then, when we find one-third of it, we will convert it back into feet.

If there are 12 inches in a foot, then the board is 12(7) + 3 = 87 inches long. Then, finding one-third of this board means dividing it by three, thus: (87 inches/3) = 29 inches.

Lastly, we need to convert 29 inches, which is the length of one-third of the original board, into feet. 12 inches divides into 29 2 times with 5 leftover, meaning the length of one-third of the original board is 2 feet 5 inches, or answer choice G.

31. Correct answer: **D**. Point *H*, we are told, is at point (−4, 2), but that it is reflected across the *x*-axis to point *H'*. Although the point reflects across the *x*-axis, the *x* value does not change, but rather the *y* value. This makes sense if you think about it: for the point to go "down" across the *x*-axis, the *y* value must change, and since it is a perfect reflection, the *y* value will go from 2 to – 2. Thus, *H'* rests at (−4, – 2), which is answer choice D.

32. Correct answer: **K**. Because all of the answer choices have our *x* and 21 terms in the numerator (in other words, they are not in the denominator beneath a 1), then we will have to manipulate our terms to do the same. When you move a value raised to an exponent from either the numerator to the denominator or the denominator to the numerator, you simply make the exponent negative, like this:

$$-\frac{1}{x^z} \times \frac{1}{21^z} = -x^{-z} \times 21^{-z}$$

Now notice that each term (both the *x* and the 21) share the same exponent: $-z$. This means that we can multiply the *x* and the 21 together in parentheses, and then raise the entire parentheses to the power of $-z$, like this:

$-x^{-z} \times 21^{-z} = (-x \times 21)^{-z}$, which is answer choice K.

33. Correct answer: **E**. Begin with a pretend set of 5 numbers, say {1, 1, 1, 1, 1}. Right now, the mean (aka average) is 1 and the sum is 1 + 1 + 1 + 1 + 1 = 5. The question requires that we increase the mean of the 5 numbers *by* 7, which means we have to increase the mean of our number set *to* 8. This new number set will do the trick: {8, 8, 8, 8, 8}. The sum of our new number set 40, which means that the sum of our number set has increased by 40 − 5 = 35, which is answer choice E.

34. Correct answer: **H**. We know that on Day 1 Genevieve runs 11 blocks, but the exact distance she runs on the next 3 days is to be determined by increasing the previous day's distance by (⅗), or 60%. Let's take it 1 day at a time, then add up the distances in the end. To find 60% of a number, simply multiply it by 0.6:

Day 1's distance = 11 blocks

Day 2's distance = 11 + 11(0.6) = 17.6 blocks

Day 3's distance = 17.6 + 17.6(0.6) = 28.16 blocks

Day 4's distance = 28.16 + 28.16(0.6) = 45.056 blocks, which matches answer choice H.

35. Correct answer: **C**. First, we know that the umpire in training watches 1,000 video clips of pitches and 1,000 video clips of close calls at first base, for a total of 2,000 video clips. Then, we are told that each clip lasts 8 seconds. The problem is, we are told that the umpire will be paid \$35 per hour, making this a tricky conversion. You could either determine how many hours 8 seconds is, or you could determine how much money he is paid per second; either one of these methods will work, so let's choose the second one and determine how much money he is paid per second.

If he is paid \$35 per hour, then he is paid \$35 ÷ 60 = \$0.58333 per minute (since there are 60 minutes in an hour). If he is paid \$0.58333 per minute, then he is paid \$0.58333 ÷ 60 = \$0.0097222 per second (since there are 60 seconds in a minute).

He watched 2,000 video clips at 8 seconds per video, meaning a total of 2,000(8) = 16,000 seconds of video clips. To determine how much he was paid, multiply these seconds by the amount he is paid per second to determine how much total he was paid, like this: \$0.0097222 × 16,000 = \$155.56, which is answer choice C.

36. Correct answer: **J**. Because the Retiring Umpire makes perfect calls, it is easy for us to determine how many inaccurate strike calls there were by the New Umpire, which is 393 – 319 = 74 bad strike calls. To determine what percent were in accurate, divide the number of bad calls (74) by the total number of strike calls (393 for the New Umpire), like this:

$$\frac{74}{393} \times 100 = 18.8\,\%\text{, which is answer choice J.}$$

37. Correct answer: **E**. First, we need to determine how many of each kind of clip the New Umpire incorrectly labeled. First, for the balls and strikes videos, we can compare either balls or strikes. Using strikes, we see that he mislabeled 393 – 319 = 74 videos. Second, for the safe and out videos, we can compare either safe or out. Using safe, we see that he mislabeled 502 – 421 = 81 videos. In total, then, he mislabeled 74 + 81 = 155 out of 2,000 videos. To determine the probability that one chosen clip is mislabeled by the New Umpire, simply divide 155 by 2,000. However, we are being asked for the probability that this same draw happens twice in a row. Well, if it happens once, then there are now only 154 mislabeled videos out of 1,999 that remain. To find the possibility of 2 in a row, we need to multiply these two numbers by one another, like this:

$$\frac{155}{2{,}000} \times \frac{154}{1{,}999} = 0.00597\text{, which rounds up to 0.006, which is answer choice E.}$$

38. Correct answer: **J**. The fact that David is a scientist in a lab or the fact that there is danger in the pressure of a container exceeding 255 Pascal are both irrelevant to the math of this question. Typically, one question per ACT Math test will feature an equation like the one in this problem, and you will have to solve for one of the variables. Usually the equation will feature variables that you aren't used to seeing, but again, they will give you the values of all of them but one in order to solve. Fortunately, in our case, we are being asked to solve for P, which means that all we have to do is carefully plug in all of the values on the right side of the equation. Before we get to the math below, we know this: $n = 550$, $R = 0.082$, $T = 220$, and $V = 42$.

$$P = \frac{nRT}{V} = \frac{550(0.082)(220)}{42} = \frac{9{,}922}{42} = 236.2\text{ Pascal}$$

The question asks for us to round to the nearest Pascal, which is 236, or answer choice J.

39. Correct answer: **A**. There are a number of ways to solve this problem, and most begin with simplifying the equation. However, it is possible to solve this question without doing so, which would be by using the:

Method #1: *Backsolving* mini-strategy. Where this equation crosses the x axis is a *solution*, and will result in a y value of 0. Thus, if I plug in a value of x from any of the five answer choices and get 0, that will work, then I need to try the next. If I plug in a value of x from any of the five answer choices and get a number that is not 0, then I can abandon that answer choice as incorrect and move on. I see that two of the answer choices have $x = 3$ as a potential solution, so I can evaluate two answer at the same time by trying out $x = 3$ first, like this:

$$y = \frac{-(x+3)(x^2-x-6)}{(x+2)} = \frac{-(3+3)(3^2-3-6)}{(3+2)} = \frac{(-6)(0)}{5} = \frac{0}{5} = 0\text{, which works!}$$

Now I can be confident that the answer is either A or D, since these two have a solution of $x = 3$. Let's try the other answer choice for D, which is $x = 2$, and see if it also satisfies by resulting in an answer that yields $y = 0$:

$$y = \frac{-(x+3)(x^2-x-6)}{(x+2)} = \frac{-(2+3)(2^2-2-6)}{(2+2)} = \frac{(-5)(-4)}{4} = \frac{20}{4} = 5$$, which is NOT 0, so A is correct.

Any other methods to solve begin with simplifying the equation. Notice that the equation has a trinomial that needs to be factored $(x^2 - x - 6)$; seeing that the equation has a binomial $(x + 2)$ in the denominator, it seems likely that this binomial will be canceled out with a resulting binomial after we factor the top. So, let's factor this trinomial now, then rewrite the equation and cancel what we can. We need two numbers that *multiply* to give our last term (-6), but *add* to give us our middle term (-1); these two numbers are -3 and 2, which means that our trinomial factors like this: $x^2 - x - 6 = (x-3)(x+2)$. Let's now rewrite our equation and cancel out what we can:

$$y = \frac{-(x+3)(x^2-x-6)}{(x+2)} = \frac{-(x+3)(x-3)(x+2)}{(x+2)} = -(x+3)(x-3)$$, and now we FOIL or multiply:

$$-(x+3)(x-3) = -(x^2+3x-3x-9) = -(x^2-9)$$

From here, you could also use *Backsolving* to find a solution.

Method #2: Factor and Solve. From here, we can also factor our $-(x^2-9)$ term into two binomials, set those binomials equal to 0, and solve for x both times. Some students may immediately recognize that this term is the "difference of squares", but others may notice that we went a little bit too far in our simplification and already can see what our two binomials are! Look at this again:

$$-(x+3)(x-3) = -(x^2+3x-3x-9) = -(x^2-9)$$ ... our two binomials are two steps earlier!

Thus, $-(x^2-9)$ factors into $-(x+3)(x-3)$. Now, split these into two terms, set equal to 0, and get our two solutions for x, like this:

$$-(x+3) = 0 \quad \ldots \quad -x-3 = 0 \quad \ldots \quad -x = 3 \quad \ldots \quad x = -3$$, and

$$(x-3) = 0 \quad \ldots \quad x = 3$$

Thus, our two solutions (which is where the equation crosses the x-axis are $x = -3$, and $x = 3$, or answer choice A.

40. Correct answer: **G**. Though this problem looks unbelievably complicated, let's simplify our thought as much as possible. First, recall that the amplitude of a wave is the distance between (in our case) the x-axis and the crest (or top and bottom) of a wave. Second, recall that the graph of sin normally has an amplitude of 1 (since the highest value of sin possible is 1, and the lowest value of sin possible is -1, both of which are a distance of 1 from the x-axis).

Now, it doesn't matter at all what degree measure is after the "sin" part of the equation. It looks confusing that we are working with $\sin(2x - \pi)$, but no matter what $(2x - \pi)$ is equal to, the resulting value of sin will be somewhere between 1 and -1; thus, the value after sin does not affect, at all, the amplitude of the graph of sin.

However, what is $1 \times \frac{2}{3}$? Well, it's just $\frac{2}{3}$, which means that the amplitude of the wave of sin will be "squished" down or changed so that the highest point of the wave can only reach to $\frac{2}{3}$, and the lowest point of the wave can only reach to $-\frac{2}{3}$. Either way, the resulting amplitude is $\frac{2}{3}$, which is answer choice G. Below, I put a graph of $\frac{2}{3}$sin just so you can visualize what we are talking about:

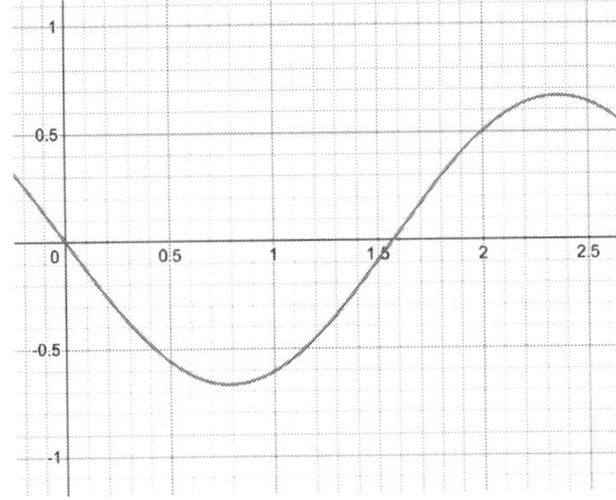

As you can see, the highest the wave gets off of the x-axis is 0.66, or $\frac{2}{3}$, and the lowest is goes down off of the x-axis is $-\frac{2}{3}$, but either way, the amplitude is now $\frac{2}{3}$.

41. Correct answer: **B**. First, plot these three points, and draw this triangle (like I've done below). Second, remember what the altitude of a triangle is; simply put, the altitude of a triangle is its height. Draw a straight line down from the uppermost point to form to 90 degree angles with the base, like the triangle shown here (the altitude is labeled x).

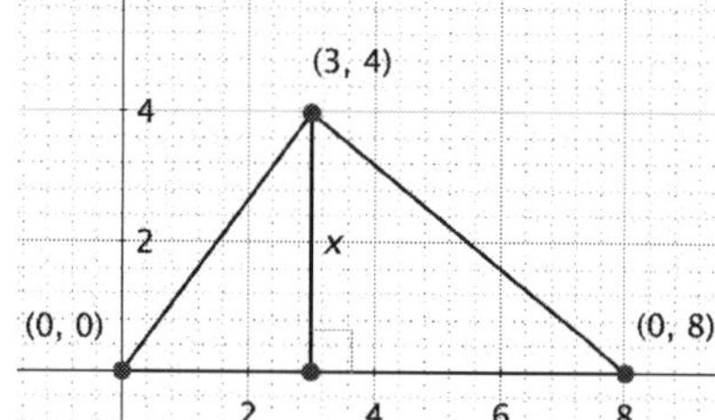

Now, fortunately, there is not any triangular math that you need to do. If all you had been told was the lengths of the three sides, then yes, you'd have some work to do. Here, because the bottom of the triangle sits on the x-axis, the height is simply how "high" the triangle goes on the y-axis, which is 4. This is why the answer is B: 4.

42. Correct answer: **F**. First, because the question asks us for how many cars are expected to be rented on any given day, let's determine how many cars are rented based on each rental rate (which we can find because we are given how many cars are in the lot, 120). To do so, multiply the rental rate by 120.

- Rental rate of 0.25 means 0.25(120) = 30 cars rented.
- Rental rate of 0.50 means 0.50(120) = 60 cars rented.
- Rental rate of 0.75 means 0.75(120) = 90 cars rented.
- Rental rate of 0.90 means 0.90(120) = 108 cars rented.
- Rental rate of 1.00 means 1.00(120) = 120 cars rented.

To find the *expected number* of cars to be rented, multiply the probabilities of each rental rate (0.10, 0.20, 0.40, 0.20, and 0.10, respectively) by the number of cars rented with that rental rate (30, 60, 90, 108, and 120, respectively) and add them together, like so:

$30(0.10) + 60(0.20) + 90(0.40) + 108(0.20) + 120(0.10) = 3 + 12 + 36 + 21.6 + 12 = 84.6$ expected per day.

The question asks us to find the number of expected cars rented to the nearest whole number, thus we round up 84.6 to 85, which is answer choice F.

43. Correct answer: **B**. The first principle to recall is that two angles in a line add up to equal 180°. Thus, we can set up an equation in which the two equations representing the angles add together to equal 180°, solve for x, then use our knowledge of x to find the value of the smallest angle.

First, adding our angles together, setting them equal to 180°, and solving for x:

$$(4x + 28) + (x + 2) = 180 \quad \dots \quad 5x + 30 = 180 \quad \dots \quad 5x = 150 \quad \dots \quad x = 30$$

Some will be tempted at this point to put that A is the correct answer, but the question asks for the value of the smallest angle, not the value of x; finding x is simply one step towards finding the right answer. The acute angle on the right, represented by the equation $(x + 2)°$, is clearly the smaller angle. Thus, if $x = 30$, then the value of this angle is $(30 + 2)° = 32°$, which is answer choice B.

44. Correct answer: **K**. This problem could conceivably be done in the head. If b decreases by 2, then that would mean the value of a will decrease by $3(2) = 6$. Then, if c increases by 1, then that would mean that the value of a will increase by $-4(1) = -4$; in other words, it would decrease by 4. A decrease of 6 plus a decrease of 4 equals a decrease of 10, which is answer choice K.

However, it might be more fitting to choose values for b and c, find a value, then decrease b by 2 and increase c by 1 and see how much the answer changes.

First, let's assume that $b = 2$ and $c = 2$:

$$a = 3b + 7 - 4c = 3(2) + 7 - 4(2) = 5$$

Second, let's decrease b by 2 (so, $b = 0$) and increase c by 1 (so, $c = 3$):

$$a = 3b + 7 - 4c = 3(0) + 7 - 4(3) = 7 - 12 = -5$$

Thus, because the difference between 5 and -5 is 10, we can know that the changes to b and c cause a to decrease by 10, which is answer choice K.

45. Correct answer: **D**. The best way to solve this problem is to draw something so that you can visualize it. For example, maybe draw 11 circles to represent the 11 rooms, and each dot put into the circle represents a person. Here, each X represents a room, and each * following it represents a person.

First, recognize that each room has to have a minimum of 2 people in it (as shown below with two * after each X).

X**	X**	X**
X**	X**	X**
X**	X**	X**
X**	X**	

Because each room has 2 people already in it, and because there are 11 rooms, then that means that there are now 90 – 2(11) = 78 people left to distribute between the 11 rooms. Because we are looking for the greatest number of rooms that can be filled with 12 people, distribute the remaining people one room at a time until it is full, then move on to the next room, like this:

X************	X************	X**
X************	X************	X**
X************	X**********	X**
X************	X**	

As you can see, there are 6 rooms that are completely filled, which is answer choice D.

46. Correct answer: **F**. One strategy for answering this question, which I believe is the fastest, begins with converting the recipe to gallons and liters, respectively, using the conversion formulas given below the problem. This would be done because the problem requires an answer using gallons and liters.

According to the conversion metrics, 1 gallon = 128 ounces, so the 400 ounces called for by the recipe equates to $\frac{400}{128} = 3.125$ gallons.

According to conversion metrics, 1 liter = 4.22675 cups, so the 5 cups of flour called for by the recipe equates to $\frac{5}{4.22675} = 1.18294$ liter.

So now we can say that the recipe calls for 3.125 gallons of water for every 1.18294 liters of flour.

The questions itself asks how many gallons are needed for 25 liters of flour. To answer this question, let's set up a cross-multiplication problem; we will let g represent the missing gallons, like this:

$$\frac{3.125 \text{ gallons}}{1.18294 \text{ liters}} = \frac{g}{25 \text{ liters}} \quad \ldots \quad 3.125(25) = g(1.18294) \quad \ldots \quad \frac{3.125(25)}{1.18294} = g \quad \ldots \quad g = 66.04 \text{ gallons}$$

At this point, you know the number of gallons needed for the larger-scale recipe. However, each of the answer choices is written in a way that does the converting that we just went through the trouble to do ourselves. The reason I believe this method is easiest is because it takes the converting out of your head where simple mistakes can be made and puts it into real numbers. Simply go through each answer choice one at a time, and determine which one also equals 66.04. This is easily accomplished with the calculator. First, let's try F:

$$\text{F:} \quad \frac{(400)(25)(4.22675)}{(5)(128)} = \frac{42267.5}{640} = 66.04$$

, which is correct; thus, F is the correct answer.

47. Correct answer: **C**. First, it must be kept in mind that you are looking for which expression or expressions are NOT equal to x. So, if any of the three does equal x, it is an incorrect answer.

I. In the numerator, x is raised to the -1 power. To change this, the x is moved to the numerator and the exponent is made positive (see below). Then, to combine like terms that are being multiplied, you add their exponents:

$$\frac{x^2}{x^{-1}} = x^2x^1 = x^{2+1} = x^3$$

, not x, which eliminates answer choice D.

II. The absolute value of a number is equal to how far it is away from a value of 0. So, the absolute value of x is going to be x, but the absolute value of $-x$ is also going to be x. This means that II equals x, which makes it an incorrect answer for this particular problem. This eliminates, in total, D, B, and E.

III. If you are stuck on the conceptualization of this problem, then choose a value for x, plug it in here, and find out what number you end up with and see if it is equal to x. In words, when you square a negative number, you get a positive square (for example, -3 squared $= 9$). Then, when you take the square root of that number, you can get two different answers: 3 or -3. However, this problem has a large negative sign out in front of it, which makes these answers (for example) now -3 or 3, respectively. Thus, this expression can equal either x or $-x$. This might be confusing, but this is why the question asks for expressions that are not *always* equal to x, which is the case here: this expression is not always equal to x because it can also equal $-x$.

Thus, the two answer that are NOT always equal to x are I and III, which is answer choice C.

48. Correct answer: **H**. There is no fancy way to get this question correct; you simply need to try out various integers until you determine how many there are that will make the equation lie between 0.480 and 0.205.

Before I start to try any numbers, I see that if a has a value of 6, then the fraction will equal 0.5. Along those same lines, because 0.200 is one-fifth, I can see that if a has a value of 15, the fraction will equal 0.2. That said, I know that I'm working, in general, with integer values between 6 and 15, but *not* 6 and 15 themselves. Let's try $a = 7$ and $a = 14$ and see if they have values that fit the problem's requirements:

If $a = 7$, then $\frac{3}{a} = \frac{3}{7} = 0.429$, which lies between 0.480 and 0.205

If $a = 14$, then $\frac{3}{a} = \frac{3}{14} = 0.214$, which also lies between 0.480 and 0.205

Thus, if 7 and 14 meet the requirements, but 6 and 15 do not, then I need to count the number of integers between (and including) 7 and 14. These are $a = 7, 8, 9, 10, 11, 12, 13$, and 14, a total of 8 integers, which is answer choice H.

49. Correct answer: **D**. The best and most mistake-free means of answering this question is to use *Picking Numbers*. Let's pretend that the average weight of his first 4 fish is 10 ounces (yes, I know that those are little fish for a bass fishing tournament, but that doesn't matter!). The question requires that we find the weight of a fifth fish that will raise the average to $a + 3$, then find how much bigger that value is than a.

So, if $a = 10$, then we need the average to rise to 13 ounces with a 5th fish. If the average after 5 fish is 13, then that means the total weight of all 5 fish is $5(13) = 65$ ounces. Remember that we already know the total weight of our first 4 fish ($10+10+10+10 = 40$ ounces), which means that the fifth fish must weigh $(65 - 40) = 25$ ounces.

If the fifth fish must weigh 25 ounces, that would mean that it weighs $(25 - a) = (25 - 10) = 15$ ounces more than a, which corresponds with answer choice D.

50. Correct answer: **G**. If two lines are intersecting, then four angles are formed. If $\angle Z$ is bigger than $\angle W$, then we can know that these two angles add up to one line, or 180°. With that in mind, we need to set up an equation that sets the addition of these two angles equal to 180°. To do so, let's call the value of $\angle W$ x for the purpose of simplicity. Here is what such an equation would look like (note: since $\angle Z$ is 1100% larger than $\angle W$, we multiply x by 11 to represent $\angle Z$).

$$\angle W + \angle Z = 180 \quad \ldots \quad x + 11x = 180 \quad \ldots \quad 12x = 180 \quad \ldots \quad x = 15°$$

Because x is $\angle W$, we know that $\angle W$ is equal to 15°, which is answer choice G.

51. Correct answer: **E**. To answer this question correctly will involve working backwards from s_4. This is because to answer the question, to find the value of s_1, you have to have the value of s_2 (because, as you can see on the right side of the equation, you need the value of $s_{(n+1)}$), and to find the value of s_2, you need the value of s_3, which is why you need the value of s_4, which is given. So, let's go one at a time, working our way down and plugging in our new value until we can solve for s_1, like this:

$s_3 = \frac{1}{2}s_{(n+1)} + |n| + 4 = \frac{1}{2}(77) + |3| + 4 = 38.5 + 3 + 4 = 45.5$ (now use this to solve for s_2)

$s_2 = \frac{1}{2}s_{(n+1)} + |n| + 4 = \frac{1}{2}(45.5) + |2| + 4 = 22.75 + 2 + 4 = 28.75$ (now use this to solve for s_1)

$s_1 = \frac{1}{2}s_{(n+1)} + |n| + 4 = \frac{1}{2}(28.75) + |1| + 4 = 14.375 + 1 + 4 = 19.375$, which is answer choice E.

52. Correct answer: **F**. Use *Picking Numbers* and choose any number less than −2, carefully solve all three expressions for a numerical value, then carefully order them from smallest to largest.

To start, let's pretend that $x = -3$. With that decided, our three expressions become:

$$-x^3 = -(-3)^3 = -(-27) = 27$$

$$-\frac{1}{x^2} = -\frac{1}{(-3)^2} = -\frac{1}{9} = -0.111$$

$$|x| = |-3| = 3$$

Now that we've done so, we can see that −0.111 is the smallest term, 3 is second smallest, and 27 is the largest. These correspond to $-\frac{1}{x^2}$, then $|x|$, then $-x^3$. So, our final inequality looks like this:

$$-\frac{1}{x^2} < |x| < -x^3$$, which corresponds to answer choice F.

53. Correct answer: **A**. In reviewing this kind of question with countless students over many years, I have learned that many students think that their graphing calculator must somehow be able to show this many decimals in one way or another, and then they need to count their way there. However, that would be both impossible and a waste of time, especially with a digit as far away from 0 as the 333rd.

Instead, realize that we have a repeating pattern of 6 digits after the decimal. So, the 6th digit will always be a 1, the 12th will always be a 1, the 18th will always be a 1, and so on: every 6th place will be a 1. We need to find a number close, but less than, 333 that is divisible by 6. Since $(330 \div 6) = 55$, we know that the 330th place after the decimal is a 1. That means that the 331st is a 7, the 332nd is a 4, and then the 333rd is a 0, which corresponds to answer choice A.

54. Correct answer: **G**. This question is a two step process. First, we need to take the amount of emails on the list and reduce it to 15% of its total, then take this new number and reduce it down to one-sixth of its total.

Step 1: 15% of 122,000 is 122,000(0.15) = 18,300 (so, 18,300 on the email list will attend the event)

Step 2: $\frac{1}{6}$ of 18,300 is $18{,}300(\frac{1}{6}) = \frac{18{,}300}{6} = 3{,}050$

So, the amount of shirts that should be printed after properly reducing the email list is 3,050, which corresponds to answer choice G, since it falls within the range of 3,000 and 3,100.

55. Correct answer: **E**. Do not be scared by the presence of the imaginary number i, which you may have either used in math class at some point or heard friends in other math classes talking about. If $i = \sqrt{-1}$, then any time there is an i^2 term that emerges as you solve, simply replace it with a −1. At least, this is how we will solve this problem at first. Then, I will show you a second, faster way.

Let's begin with the term in the numerator. As you would any other time you have two binomials being multiplied, use FOIL to multiply all of the terms, like this:

$$(-3i + 1)(2i + 2) = -6i^2 + 2 + 2i - 6i = -6i^2 - 4i + 2$$

Now that we have done that, let's replace the i^2 term with a −1 and simplify:

$$-6i^2 - 4i + 2 = -6(-1) - 4i + 2 = 6 - 4i + 2 = 8 - 4i$$

Thus, the previously-scary looking numerator has been reduced down to simply $8 - 4i$.

All that remains to do is to divide this now-simplified numerator by the term in the denominator, which is a 4.

$$\frac{8-4i}{4}=2-i$$

The 4 in the denominator can divide into both terms in the numerator, simplifying this expression all the way down to the correct answer, which is E: $2-i$.

However, I promised at the beginning of this explanation to solve this problem in a little bit of a simpler way. This requires that you have a graphing calculator. Graphing calculators have the means to type in the term i into a math equation. On the graphing calculator sitting in front of me, that would be done by hitting "2ND" then the period button at the bottom of the calculator. If you simply type in the original equation, term for term, just typing in the i whenever you encounter it, your graphing calculator will spit out the correct answer: $2-i$.

It could be that this is possible on some scientific calculators. However, the last couple of them that I looked at recently did not have this as an option. If all you have is a scientific calculator, though, just do the math like we did at first above and solve it that way.

56. Correct answer: **K**. First, recognize that the two triangles being described are *similar* triangles. In ACT Math *Good to Know* Lesson #2 on Triangles, we said that similar triangles are triangles with the same angles and equivalent sides. The question says that $\triangle ABC$ has a hypotenuse of 10, and $\triangle XYZ$ has a hypotenuse of 5. This means that each side of $\triangle ABC$ will be double that of each side of $\triangle XYZ$. Thus, this problem can be solved two ways. Either find the perimeter of $\triangle ABC$ and half it, or find the perimeter of $\triangle XYZ$ as the question asks for, which is what we will do here.

We are also told that $\triangle ABC$ has another side that is 8 inches long, which is opposite that of an angle with a measure of 53.13°. This means that $\triangle XYZ$ has a side that is 4 inches long, also opposite that of an angle with a measure of 53.13°. We now have all of the information we could possibly need to find the last side of $\triangle XYZ$. Probably the simplest way is to simply use the Pythagorean Theorem, that $a^2+b^2=c^2$, on this triangle, since we know that it is a right triangle. When we do that, and calling our missing side b, we get the following:

$$4^2+b^2=5^2 \quad \ldots \quad 16+b^2=25 \quad \ldots \quad b^2=9 \quad \ldots \quad b=3$$

We now know the three sides of the triangle: 3, 4, and 5. Thus, the perimeter is $3+4+5=12$ inches, or answer choice K.

It should be noted that there are a host of other ways to solve this problem. You might recognize right away that if $\triangle XYZ$ is a right triangle, has a hypotenuse of 5, and a side of 4, that it is then a *special* triangle, a 3-4-5 triangle, which can also be learned more about in the same *Good to Know* lesson as *similar* triangles. You can also use your knowledge of sine, cosine, and tangent to figure out any missing sides as well. All roads will lead you to the same perimeter of 12.

57. Correct answer: **C**. The best way to answer this problem is to invent two triangles (akin to the *Picking Numbers* strategy) that fit the criteria and then compare them to determine how much smaller the new triangle is compared to the original.

Let's first pretend that our original triangle has a base of 10 and a height of 10. Thus, our original triangle has an area of $\frac{1}{2}bh=\frac{1}{2}(10)(10)=50$.

Let's then create a second, smaller triangle based on the parameters in the question. First, we are told that this second triangle has a base that is increased by 10% compared to the original. To increase a number by 10%, multiply it by 1.10, like this: $10(1.10)=11$, which is the base of the second triangle. Second, we are told that this second triangle has a height that is decreased by 35% compared to the original. To decrease a number by 35%, multiply it by $(1-0.35)$, or 0.65, like this: $10(1-0.35)=10(0.65)=6.5$, which is the height of the second triangle.

Thus, our second triangle has an area of $\frac{1}{2}bh=\frac{1}{2}(11)(6.5)=35.75$.

The area of the first is 50, the area of the second is 35.75. Since we are looking for what percent smaller the area of the second is compared to the first, we first need how many units smaller it is, which is $50-35.75=14.25$. This is where many students run into difficulty: what to do with this number? Since we are comparing the decrease *to the first triangle,* we divide the first triangle by this decrease of 14.25 and multiply by 100 to get a resulting percentage, like this:

$$\frac{14.25}{50}\times 100=28.5\,\%$$

Thus the second triangle is 28.5% smaller than the original, which matches C.

58. Correct answer: **J**. To find the probability that these two die add up to a sum of 15, we need to determine the *number* of combinations that result in a 15 and divide it by the number of all possibilities.

First, let's determine the number of combinations that will result in a 15. To do so, let's begin with the 12-sided die, and work our way down one at a time to find combinations:

12-Sided Die		6-Sided Die	
12	+	3	= 15
11	+	4	= 15
10	+	5	= 15
9	+	6	= 15

Thus, there are only 4 combinations of die that will result in a total of 15.

Second, we need to determine the number of possible dice combinations. To do so, simply multiply the number of options from the first die by the number of options from the second. In other words, if there are 12 options on the first die, and 6 on the second, then the total number of pairs is $(12 \times 6) = 72$.

Third, divide the number of combinations that result in a 15 by all possible combinations to get the probability of rolling a 15, like this:

$$\frac{4}{72} = \frac{1}{18}$$, which matches answer choice J.

59. Correct answer: **A**. You would think that this problem would be as simple as dividing 5,625 by 3, which is 1,875, but that would be incorrect. You need to use the square footage to find possible dimensions of the floors, convert those dimensions to yards, then multiply to get the square yardage.

First, based on a square footage of 5,625, invent dimensions for the floors. As an example, when you divide 5,625 by 25, the result is 225, which will work for us. In other words, you can now pretend that the floors that Michael is working with have dimensions of 25ft × 225ft.

Second, convert these new dimensions into yards by dividing each dimension by 3, like this:

$$25 \text{ ft} \times 225 \text{ ft} = (25 \div 3) \text{ yards} \times (225 \div 3) \text{ yards} = 8.33 \text{ yards} \times 75 \text{ yards}$$

Third, now that we have new dimensions in yards (8.33 × 75 yards), we can multiply the two to determine the square footage:

$8.33 \times 75 = 624.75$ square yards. You might think this is *close* to answer choice A, but off by 0.25. That is true, but the deficit can be accounted for because we rounded 8.33333333333333333 (and on forever) down to 8.33; whenever you round, results will be inexact.

60. Correct answer: **K**. Before randomly doing some math, understand that this question is saying that four of the answer choices are the exact same, and only one of them is different. With that in mind, there are a few different ways to answer this problem. One way would be this: options J and K feature the exact same base (x) raised to different exponents. This means, right away, that because these are so obviously two different numbers, one of them has to be the correct answer *because* it is the one that is different from the others. Looking up at H, you can see that it results pretty simply in the ninth root of x, which is the same thing as raising x to the one-ninth power, which means that K is different, making it the right answer.

Another way to solve this problem is to use *Picking Numbers*. In this strategy, choose a number for x, plug it into the original, then plug it into the answer choices one at a time to determine the correct answer. For this strategy to work, you need to be able to find the cubed root of a number on your calculator, or even the eighteenth root, or the ninth root, and so on. Many calculators feature secondary functions that can do this, but if you aren't already versed on using the calculator in this way, then try this: to find (for example) the cubed root of a number, raise it to the $\frac{1}{3}$ power; to find (for example) the eighteenth root of a number, raise it to the $\frac{1}{18}$ power. In your calculator, type the number, then ^, then $(1 \div 18)$.

Let's assume then that x equals 27. I chose 27 because it is a number that results from another number (3) being cubed. First, I will cube this number, then find the cubed root of it 3 times in a row, like this:

$27^3 = 19{,}683$

First cubed root: $19{,}683^{\frac{1}{3}} = 27$

Second cubed root: $27^{\frac{1}{3}} = 3$

Third cubed root: $3^{\frac{1}{3}} = 1.442$

Thus, when $x = 27$, the result of the question's expression is 1.442; if you try out $x = 27$, you will get a result of 1.442 for each answer as you go, except for K, since $x^{\frac{1}{6}} = 27^{\frac{1}{6}} = 1.732$

A final way to solve would be to conceptualize the problem one step at a time. The cubed root of anything cubed is simply the number itself. Cube that number (x), and the result is $x^{\frac{1}{3}}$, then cube it one last time, and the result is $x^{\frac{1}{3} \cdot \frac{1}{3}} = x^{\frac{1}{9}}$. If you've recognized that the answer must be J or K, then this conceptualization will lead you to see that the correct answer is K, since it does *not* match the expression in the question.

Answer Explanations - Step 6 - Practice Test #2

Correct answers:

1: C	**11: C**	**21: A**	**31: D**	**41: E**	**51: D**
2: G	**12: H**	**22: K**	**32: G**	**42: H**	**52: J**
3: D	**13: B**	**23: E**	**33: A**	**43: B**	**53: C**
4: F	**14: K**	**24: G**	**34: K**	**44: J**	**54: F**
5: E	**15: B**	**25: B**	**35: A**	**45: C**	**55: E**
6: J	**16: F**	**26: F**	**36: K**	**46: H**	**56: F**
7: A	**17: E**	**27: C**	**37: C**	**47: D**	**57: B**
8: J	**18: J**	**28: F**	**38: H**	**48: K**	**58: G**
9: B	**19: D**	**29: E**	**39: D**	**49: A**	**59: A**
10: G	**20: H**	**30: H**	**40: J**	**50: G**	**60: K**

1. Correct answer: **C**. Because Elisa paid \$705 for an internet service that includes not only a monthly fee, but also a onetime fee of \$225, let's subtract this onetime fee from the total \$705 she paid, like this: (\$705 – \$225) = \$480. The remainder, in other words the \$480, is what Elisa paid for internet month by month. Since the internet costs \$20 per month, let's divide \$480 by \$20 to determine the number of weeks she paid for, like this: (\$480 ÷ \$20) = 24. Thus, Elisa has paid for 24 weeks of internet service, or answer choice C.

2. Correct answer: **G**. Recognize first that the political party has overpaid for signs. They ordered 425 signs, which made them eligible for a discount (only \$2.15 per sign), but they paid full price (\$2.50 per sign). So first, let's determine how much they paid for the signs, which is this: (425 × \$2.50) = \$1,062.50. Next determine how much the political party should have paid total, which is this: (425 × \$2.15) = \$913.75. Lastly, to determine the discount they deserve, subtract what they should have paid by what they did pay, like this: (\$1,062.50 – \$913.75) = \$148.75, which is answer choice G.

3. Correct answer: **D**. First, determine how fast the bus is traveling in miles per hour. How to do so is in the phrase "miles per hour", aka, total miles divided by total hours will result in a speed in miles per hour. So far, the bus has traveled 90 miles in 1.5 hours, so we can find the bus's speed like this:

$$\frac{90 \text{ miles}}{1.5 \text{ hours}} = 60 \text{ mph.}$$

With that done, we simply need to use the speed of the bus and apply it to the four hours that are to be traveled, like this:

$$60\frac{\text{miles}}{\text{hour}} \times 4 \text{ hours} = 240 \text{ miles}$$, which is answer choice D.

4. Correct answer: **F**. Because the restaurant only offers 1 dish that is Christopher's favorite, the odds of the waitress choosing his favorite meal is going to be 1 "over" something, or 1 "in" something. What the 1 is going to be over or out of is the total number of meal options that the waitress can choose from. If you read too quickly, you might be tempted to choose an answer choice with 17 in the denominator. But remember: there are 17 meals at the restaurant, but 5 are disqualified because they are spicy, which means that there are a total of (17 – 5) = 12 meals the waitress can choose from. This is why the answer is F: there is only a 1 in 12 or 1 over 12 chance that the restaurant will choose his favorite meal.

5. Correct answer: **E**. We need to first recognize what p is to help figure out where it should go in this particular equation. Because p is a number of students in a class, just like 21, 27, 22, 25, and 21, it is going to be added to those 5 numbers before it is affected to find an average. This narrows down our answer choices to D and E. If you look at D and E, they have the same form in that they both feature the number of students in all 6 classes (including p) being divided by a number, which will result in an average of 24. The reason E is correct as opposed to D is that answer choice E correctly divides the addition of the 6 classes by 6 to find the proper average. If I wanted to find the average of, say, 4 different numbers, I would divide their sum by the number of numbers (in this case, 4).

6. Correct answer: **J**. Let's simply plug in $x = 11$ and simplify as much as we can before we deal with the absolute value:

$$x^2 - |7 - x| - (-x) \quad ... \quad (11)^2 - |7 - 11| - (-11) \quad ... \quad 121 - |-4| + 11 \quad ... \quad 132 - |-4|$$

Now, at this point, we have to determine what to do with the absolute value. Recall that absolute value denotes how far a value is away from 0; in other words, if what is between the bars is positive keep it positive, but if it is negative, make it positive! Thus, we can finish out our solution like this:

$$132 - |-4| \quad \ldots \quad 132 - 4 \quad \ldots \quad = 128$$, which is answer choice J.

7. Correct answer: **A**. Don't let the phrasing of this question seem tricky. All you need to do is plug in $m = 16$ and solve the equation then for n, which you can do, since you would now have one equation with only one missing variable. You don't need to set the equation equal to m first. Let's plug in $m = 16$ and solve the equation one step at a time.

$$m - n = \frac{9}{4}n + 3 \quad \ldots \quad 16 - n = \frac{9}{4}n + 3 \quad \ldots \quad 13 = n + \frac{9}{4}n \quad \ldots \quad 13 = \frac{13}{4}n$$

At this point, we need to divide both sides by $\frac{13}{4}$ to solve for n. Dividing $\frac{13}{4}$ by $\frac{13}{4}$ is straightforward enough, but what about dividing 13 by $\frac{13}{4}$? To do so, reciprocate (aka flip) the fraction and multiply by 13, like this:

$$13 = \frac{13}{4}n \quad \ldots \quad \frac{13}{\frac{13}{4}} = \frac{\frac{13}{4}}{\frac{13}{4}}n \quad \ldots \quad 13 \times \frac{4}{13} = n \quad \ldots \quad 4 = n$$, which is answer choice A.

8. Correct answer: **J**. To answer this question, you have to identify which piece of the pie chart refers to chocolate. It should be enough to look at the pie and see which is the largest piece (which, we are told, is chocolate). However, we can be objective about this as well. The angles in a circle add up to 360°, so if we subtract the other three angles from this amount, we will determine the missing, chocolate angle, like this: $360° - 115° - 50° - 45° = 150°$, which is larger than any of the angles.

Do not be like many students who quickly select options like "Cannot be determined from the given information." This answer is rarely correct; what it means is that even if the world's greatest mathematicians sat down with this problem, they couldn't solve it.

Now that we know the value of chocolate's angle, finding the percentage of students who prefer chocolate is rather simple. The percent of students who prefer chocolate is the same percentage of the entire circle that the angle 150° is. If we divide 360° by 150° and multiply by 100, we will get the proper percentage, like this:

$$\frac{150°}{360°} \times 100 = 41.67\,\%$$, which can then be rounded to 42%, or choice J.

9. Correct answer: **B**. Whenever the ACT asks you to find the area of a strange shape, draw lines to break it up into smaller shapes that you know how to find the area of. In this case, you should draw a line and break it up into two smaller rectangles. If you draw a line left to right to make the left to right rectangle at the top longest, you will now have two rectangles: one of them 41 by 6, and the second 16 by 7.

Before I do the math on that, notice what I said about that second rectangle: it *won't be* 22 by 7 after you draw the left to right line creating two rectangles. You can bet that a wrong answer to this problem will be what will happen if you add the areas of two rectangles 41 by 6 and 22 by 7, but doing so will result in you double counting the area where the two rectangles meet in the upper left corner.

OK, back to our math. Like I said, drawing the left to right line results in two rectangles: one of them 41 by 6 and the other 16 by 7. To find their combined area, multiply and add, like this:

$$(41 \times 6) + (16 \times 7) = 246 + 112 = 358$$, which matches up with answer choice B.

10. Correct answer: **G**. We can't find the value of $f(g(2))$ without first finding the value of $g(2)$. To find that, let's plug in $x = 2$ into that equation, like this:

$$g(x) = \frac{x^3}{2} \quad \ldots \quad g(2) = \frac{2^3}{2} \quad \ldots \quad g(2) = \frac{8}{2} = 4$$

Now that we have $g(2)$, we can find $f(g(2))$, which is equivalent to finding $f(4)$. So, we'll plug in $x = 4$ into the f function, like this:

$$f(x) = 4x - 2 \quad \ldots \quad f(4) = 4(4) - 2 \quad \ldots \quad f(4) = 16 - 2 = 14$$, which is answer choice G.

11. Correct answer: **C**. There are two ways to solve this particular problem (at least, two simple ways). The first would be to graph what you know to visualize the missing point, like you see I've done (not so beautifully) here. Though I haven't drawn a line between A and its midpoint, you can probably get a pretty good idea where point B must be. If the line continues down and to the right, we will end up with a point in quadrant IV (the bottom right quadrant of the (x, y) coordinate plane). The points in this quadrant have a positive x value and a negative y value. Only two answer choices have these values or fall into this quadrant, which are C and E. At least C *looks* like it could be correct; E on the other hand would make our line be no longer a line. This is one way to determine that the answer is C, or (3, – 12).

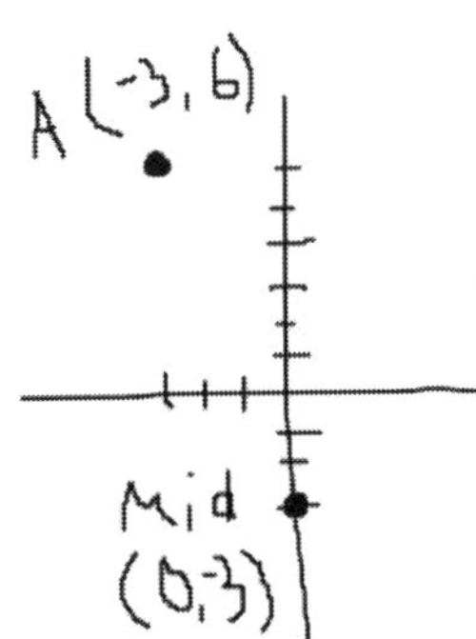

Another way to solve this problem would be to determine the x and y changes from A to the midpoint, then make the same changes from the midpoint itself, which will result in point B. On the x-axis, we move from a value of -3 to 0 from A to the midpoint, or a +3 shift on the x-axis. This means that from the midpoint to point B, there will be another +3 shift. So the x-coordinate for the correct answer will be $0 + 3 = 3$. Knowing this is already enough to determine the correct answer, since only one answer features an x-coordinate of 3. On the y-axis, we move from a value of 6 to -3 from A to the midpoint, or a -9 shift on the y-axis. This means that from the midpoint to point B, there will be another -9 shift. So the y-coordinate for the correct answer will be $-3 - 9 = -12$. Thus, our final answer after this shifting will be that the coordinates of point B are (3, – 12), which is answer choice C.

12. Correct answer: **H**. This is a question that requires caution. One of our ACT *Good to Know* math lessons was on tricky conversions. Here, we begin with how Aaron can type a certain number of words *per minute*, but we need to know how many *hours* it takes him to type a certain number of words.

Thus, let's begin by converting the number of words he can type per minute into the number of words he can type per hour. If he can type 112 words per minute, and there are 60 minutes in an hour, then he can type $(112 \times 60) = 6{,}720$ words per hour.

Now that we know the number of words per hour that Aaron can type, we need to determine how many hours it takes him to type 8,400 words. Simply divide 8,400 words by 6,720 words per hour to be left with the number of hours, like this:

$$(8{,}400 \text{ words} \div 6{,}720 \text{ words per hour}) = 1.25 \text{ hours}$$

Don't worry that the answer choices are all in fractions. Fortunately, an answer like 1.25 is easy to convert into a fraction, but that is what your calculator is for. If the answer had been a decimal that wasn't that easy to convert to a fraction, then you would simply go one answer at a time, converting the fractions into decimals in your calculator until you found a match. However, in this case, our decimal to fraction conversion isn't too difficult: $1.25 = 1\frac{1}{4}$, which matches answer choice H.

13. Correct answer: **B**. There is a technical, more difficult, algebraic way to solve this problem, which would be to create two equations with two missing variables, then solve using either substitution or elimination. If you're interested in that (which could come in handy on more difficult problems), I'll go through it after showing you the simplest way, which would simply be *Backsolving*, or going through all of the answers one at a time.

Let's start with A, and pretend that Carlos made 7 of the 2 point shots. That would mean he scored 14 points this way, leaving $(37 - 14) = 23$ points remaining for 3 point shots. Well, 23 isn't evenly divisible by 3, so it's not possible that this is the answer. Move on to B and pretend that Carlos made 8 of the 2 point shots. That would mean he scored 16 points in this way, leaving $(37 - 16) = 21$ points remaining for 3 point shots. If he took 15 shots total, and we are pretending he took 8 of the 2 point shots, that would mean he had to take 7 of the 3 point shots, which would mean 21 points. That works! Thus, the answer is B.

I promised to take you through a more technical way, which would be creating two equations with two missing variables. The missing variables would represent how many 2 and 3 point shots. Let's call 2 point shots x and 3 point shots y. We know two things about these shots, which will make up our two equations. First, we know that the total number of shots is 15, which means that $x + y = 15$. That is our first equation. Second, we know that the total number of points is 37. Because 2 point shots count for 2, and 3 point shots count for 3, our second equation is this: $2x + 3y = 37$.

There are two ways to find the missing variables from two equations. The first is **substitution**, which means solving one equation for x or y and plugging it into the other equation. For example: we know that $x + y = 15$, but we can subtract x from both sides to solve for y, like this: $y = 15 - x$. Now, I can plug in $(15 - x)$ for y in the other equation, which would leave us with only x variables, like this:

$$2x + 3y = 37 \quad \ldots \quad 2x + 3(15 - x) = 37 \quad \ldots \quad 2x + 45 - 3x = 37 \quad \ldots \quad -x = -8 \quad \ldots \quad x = 8$$

Thus, the number of 2 point shots is 8.

The second way to find the missing variables from two equations is using **elimination**. This method requires manipulating one of the equations in such a way so that when the equations are added to each other or one is subtracted from another one of the variables cancels out to 0. Because we are solving for x, we will do this to make y disappear, leaving one equation with one variable.

Because one of our equations features a $3y$ term, and the other a singular y term, let's multiply the entire second term by 3 so that the y term there becomes $3y$. Like this:

$$3(x + y = 15) \quad \ldots \quad 3x + 3y = 45$$

Now, let's subtract one equation from another, which consists in adding or subtracting like terms that are put into the same columns, canceling the y terms out to 0, like this:

$$\begin{array}{r} 3x + 3y = 45 \\ \underline{-\ 2x + 3y = 37} \\ x + 0y = 8 \end{array}$$

$x + 0y = 8$, or $x = 8$, which is answer choice B.

14. Correct answer: **K**. This is the second problem in a row in which *Backsolving* is going to be the most effective method. At first, there are 30 poker chips in the hat, 6 of which are black. This means that the current odds of drawing a black poker chip is $\frac{6}{30} = \frac{1}{5}$.

Let's go one answer at a time, starting with H: 5. If we add in 5 black chips, the odds of drawing a black go up to $\frac{6+5}{30+5} = \frac{11}{35}$, which can't be simplified further. This comes out to a little less than a third, and because we need the odds to rise all the way up to near 50%, we need more black chips.

Try J: 13. If we add in 13 black chips, the odds of drawing a black go up to $\frac{6+13}{30+13} = \frac{19}{43}$, which can't be simplified further, but we are getting closer.

Move on to K: 14. If we add in 14 black chips, the odds of drawing a black go up to:

$\frac{6+14}{30+14} = \frac{20}{44} = \frac{10}{22} = \frac{5}{11}$, which is the answer we're looking for. Thus, the answer is K.

15. Correct answer: **B**. This is the kind of question that you want to answer by using your calculator, of course. Before we enter any numbers into the calculator, however, let's work on converting 6.71×10^{-3} to a different number. The 10^{-3} simply means that the decimal point is to be moved three places to the left, or in the smaller or negative direction. Moving it once to the left will put it to the left side of the 6, as in 0.671. Moving it a second time will move it in front of the 0 that I added there, like this: 0.0671. Finally, moving it a third time will move it in front of the next 0, resulting in this: 0.00671. Thus, $6.71 \times 10^{-3} = 0.00671$.

Now, to find 4% of this number, we don't multiply it by 4; that would be finding 400% of the number. We also don't divide by 4, which would be reducing it to 25% of what it is now. We also don't multiply by 0.4, which would be to find 40% of the number. Instead, to find 4% of a number, multiply that number by 0.04, like this:

4% of $6.71 \times 10^{-3} = (0.04)0.00671 = 0.0002684$, or answer choice B.

16. Correct answer: **F**. First, this kind of question is very common in ACT Math. By "this kind of question" I mean a question in which a multi-variable equation is given, and then you are given all of the variables you need to solve the problem. Here, it is a simple case of plugging in the correct variables and doing the math correctly. The only other tricky thing about this problem is that you are given the *diameter* of the sphere, but the equation calls for the radius. Of course, the radius of a circle is half the diameter; so, if the diameter is 12, then the $r = 6$. We are also told that $h = 1$, which gives us all we need to solve:

$\pi r^2 \frac{h}{3} = \pi (6)^2 \frac{1}{3} = \pi (36)(\frac{1}{3}) = 12\pi$, which is answer choice F.

17. Correct answer: **E**. Before we can talk about finding the *product* of the two solutions for this expression, we have to figure out how to actually find the solutions in the first place. For more detail on doing this, see *Good to Know* Lesson #5: Parabolas.

To find the two solutions for a parabola (which is what this expression is), first we need to factor the trinomial into its two binomials. As a reminder, the expression we're working with is $x^2 - 10x + 21$. To factor, we need two numbers that multiply to give us our last term (21), but add together to give us our middle term (−10). Those two numbers are −3 and −7. Thus:

$$x^2 - 10x + 21 = (x - 3)(x - 7) = 0$$

Some students will be too quick and assume that the two *solutions* will be −7 and −3. That might result in the correct answer for this particular problem, but that would be a happy accident. Technically, we have to set each binomial equal to 0, then solve for x both times, which will result in our two solutions, like this:

$(x - 3) = 0$
$x = 3$

$(x - 7) = 0$
$x = 7$

Thus, our two solutions are 3 and 7. The problem however asks for the *product* of these two solutions, which means you multiply them together. Because $(3 \times 7) = 21$, the answer is E: 21.

18. Correct answer: **J**. Recall that the formula for the area of a circle is πr^2, in which r is the radius. Thus, our first step is to find the radius of this circle. Unfortunately we aren't told what the radius is, but instead we are given two equations. First, we are told that the radius is $3x - 2$, then that the diameter is $5x + 1$. Because we know that two times the radius of a circle equals its diameter, we can set up an equation in which we multiply what we know the radius to be by 2, then set it equal to the diameter. This will set up one equation with one missing variable, like this:

$$2r = d \ \ldots \ 2(3x - 2) = 5x + 1 \ \ldots \ 6x - 4 = 5x + 1 \ \ldots \ x = 5$$

However, the radius isn't 5; that's just the value of x. If the radius is $3x - 2$, then the radius is $3(5) - 2 = 13$.

Since all of the answers already feature π, then we just need to find r^2, which is $13^2 = 169$. Thus, the area of the circle is 169π, or answer choice J.

19. Correct answer: **D**. The scientific, technical jargon of this question is only a distraction; let's boil it down. If 3.20 ml is recommended for dogs weighing 70 pounds, and if the dosage decreases 0.04 ml every pound, what is the dosage recommendation for a dog weighing 42 pounds?

First, determine how many pounds fewer the 42 pound dog is: $(70 - 42) = 28$ pounds less. Next, multiply the 28 pounds by 0.04 ml, since that is the amount decreased per pound: $28(0.04) = 1.12$. Lastly, subtract 1.12 from the 3.20 baseline to get the recommended dose for a 42 pound dog, like this: $3.20 - 1.12 = 2.08$ ml, which is answer choice D.

20. Correct answer: **H**. The area of the shaded region is the width times the length, of course, but the width is y and the length is x. So, we simply have to figure those out, starting with y. The right side of the larger figure is 7, which means that the left side must also be 7. So, $y + y + 3 = 7$, or $2y = 4$, or $y = 2$. The bottom of the larger figure is also 7, which means that the top of the larger figure must also be 7. So that means that $x + x + 1 = 7$, or $2x = 6$, or $x = 3$.

So, back to our original problem. The area of the shaded portion is xy, or (2)(3), or 6, which is answer choice H.

21. Correct answer: **A**. We learned a lot about logs (aka logarithms) in *Good to Know* Lesson #10, so if you want a lot of detailed information, look there. Let's remember that logs are used to find missing exponents, and they take this form:

$$\log_{base} amount = exponent$$

So, in this problem we have the expression $\log_x 125 = 3$. Thus, what is missing is the *base* that satisfies this equation (in other words, can be rewritten as): $x^3 = 125$. Now we have an easier way to determine x: what is the cubed root of 125? In other words, what number, when cubed, equals 125?

One way to answer this question from here, of course, is to use *Backsolving*, cubing each answer to determine if it equals 125. Another easy way to find the cubed root of a number is to raise the number to the $(1 \div 3)$ power, like this:

$$x^3 = 125 \ \ldots \ 125^{\frac{1}{3}} = x \ \ldots \ x = 5, \text{ which matches answer choice A.}$$

22. Correct answer: **K**. A *greatest common factor* is a number that can equally divide into two or more numbers. For example: the greatest common factor of 10 and 100 is 10, since $(10 \div 10)$ and $(100 \div 10)$ both equal whole numbers (1 and 10, respectively).

Here, the variable a can go into both terms, and so can a b^2 term as well. This means that the greatest common factor of a^3b^2 and ab^3 is ab^2, which as the question states, also equals 24. Thus, $(a \times b \times b) = 24$.

Now that we know that, we need to use the rest of the clues to determine what b could equal. The easiest way to determine that is perhaps to use *Backsolving*. Let's start with H: 8...could b possibly equal 8 if we have to square it and then make it divisible into 24? Since $8 \times 8 = 64$, this is impossible. This is also impossible if you go one smaller and try out answer choice J: 6, since $6 \times 6 = 36$. That brings us down to K: 2. Since $2 \times 2 = 4$, which is divisible into 24, it is therefore possible for b to equal 2, making K the correct answer.

23. Correct answer: **E**. First and foremost, draw a line with fixed points and values. This will show you what can and can't be changed. In a question like this, the answer will be definitive; you don't have to worry that the correct answer is up for interpretation. Most likely, some segment will be always smaller or larger no matter what than one of our defined segments (the ones that are 8 and 10 units long).

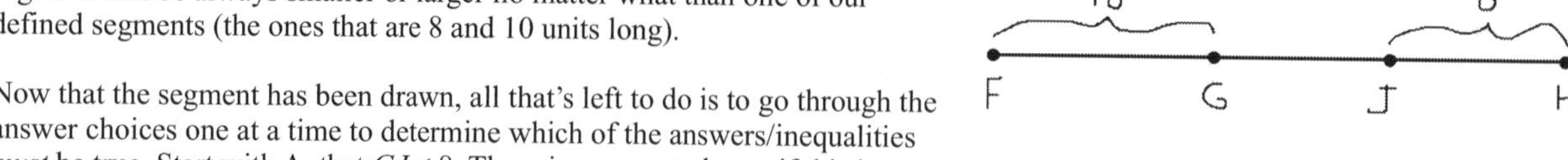

Now that the segment has been drawn, all that's left to do is to go through the answer choices one at a time to determine which of the answers/inequalities *must* be true. Start with A, that $GJ < 8$. There is no way to know if this is true or false, since the segment GJ is undefined. On the little segment I drew above, it looks a little smaller, but that's just a drawing; in reality, GJ could be 100 units long. Move on to B, that $8 > FG$. Since FG is 10 and JH is only 8, this isn't true. Move on to C, that $GH < 10$. It is possible that GH could be less than 10, but that would only be true if GJ were defined as less than 2, but because GJ is undefined, we can't be sure. Move on to D, that GJ is < 10. Again, GJ is undefined, and we have no idea how long it is. Lastly, try E, that $8 < GH$. Since GH includes JH, but also includes GJ, it always must be the case that GH is larger than JH, which makes E the correct answer.

24. Correct answer: **G**. A simplistic (I don't mean that word in a bad or negative sense!) way to solve this problem would be to draw a number line with marks one second apart. Then, you could put a dot for each bird call until you get them falling at the same number.

However, this question is essentially asking for the *least common multiple* of these two numbers, which just means the smallest whole number that they both divide into equally. With 3 and 7, it is relatively simple to find; it just so happens that when you multiply the two of them together, you get the least common multiple, which is 21, or answer choice G. With more complicated numbers, you may need to make a list of each number's multiples and find the same number, like this:

3: 3, 6, 9, **21**, 15, 21, 24, 27...
7: 7, 14, **21**, 28, 35...

Such a list makes it clear that the earliest time the two birds will call at the same time is at the 21 second mark; again, that is answer choice G.

25. Correct answer: **B**. Though the painting being described is a rectangle, this is in reality a triangle problem. We are given two sides of a right triangle, and asked to find the missing side. First, draw the triangle being described to avoid simple mistakes, as I've done below.

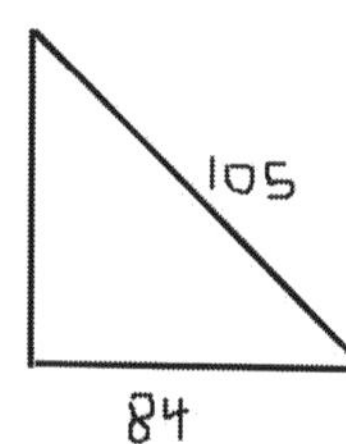

As you can see, we are simply missing the left side of the triangle, and because it is a right triangle, this means that we can use the Pythagorean Theorem to solve for the missing side. As a reminder, the Pythagorean Theorem is $a^2 + b^2 = c^2$, in which a and b are the two legs of the triangle and c is the hypotenuse. Plugging in our one leg and the hypotenuse that we know, and solving for the leg we do not know, looks like this:

$$(84)^2 + b^2 = (105)^2 \quad \ldots \quad 7{,}056 + b^2 = 11{,}025 \quad \ldots \quad b^2 = 3{,}969 \quad \ldots \quad \sqrt{b^2} = \sqrt{3{,}969} \quad \ldots \quad b = 63$$

Thus, answer choice B is correct; the height of the painting is 63 inches.

26. Correct answer: **F**. First, write the inequality as described in the question; getting it from words into a form that is more mathematically understandable will help. If 3 times n is added to -12, there is a positive result, like this: $3n + (-12) > 0$, or more simply, $3n - 12 > 0$.

Second, consider a number for n, any number, that will satisfy this inequality. The first number for n that comes into my mind to satisfy the inequality is $n = 5$, which results in this:

$$3(5) - 12 > 0 \quad \ldots \quad 15 - 12 > 0 \quad \ldots \quad 3 > 0\text{, which satisfies.}$$

From here it is plain to see that if we chose $n = 4$, we would end up with, after doing the math, an inequality that said $0 > 0$, which doesn't make any sense. Thus, any number greater than $n = 4$ would satisfy the inequality, which is answer choice F.

27. Correct answer: **C**. Most of the time, I would begin an answer explanation to this kind of question involving parabolas by explaining how to factor then simplify. This time, however, let's use this as an opportunity to first review the *Picking Numbers* strategy, then we'll solve in the traditional way.

To use the *Picking Numbers* strategy, choose a number for x that is greater than 8 (since it says "For all $x > 8$..."), so let's go with $x = 10$, which will make our math more simple. We will now plug in $x = 10$ into the original equation and see what we get:

$$\frac{(x^2 - 10x + 16)(x + 3)}{(x^2 - 5x - 24)(x - 2)} = \frac{(100 - 100 + 16)(10 + 3)}{(100 - 50 - 24)(10 - 2)} = \frac{(16)(13)}{(26)(8)} = \frac{208}{208} = 1 \text{, which is answer choice C.}$$

The more traditional route, of course and as I said, involves factoring each trinomial and then simplifying by canceling out whatever binomials may be in both the numerator and the denominator. First, let's factor the trinomial in the numerator, which is this: $(x^2 - 10x + 16)$. To factor a trinomial, look for two numbers that multiply together to give us our last term (16) which add together to give us our middle terms (-10). In this case, I see that $(8 \times 2) = 16$, but adding those terms gives me positive 10. However, $(-8 \times -2) = 16$ and add together to give me -10. Thus, this trinomial factors into these two binomials: $(x - 8)(x - 2)$.

Now, on to the binomial in the denominator, which is this: $(x^2 - 5x - 24)$. Again, we need two terms that multiply to give us the third term (-24) but which add up to the middle term (-5). These two numbers are -8 and 3. Thus, this trinomial factors into these two binomials: $(x - 8)(x + 3)$. Now, rewrite the entire equation with all known binomials:

$$\frac{(x^2 - 10x + 16)(x + 3)}{(x^2 - 5x - 24)(x - 2)} = \frac{(x - 8)(x - 2))(x + 3)}{(x - 8)(x + 3)(x - 2)}$$

As you can see, each binomial has a twin. The $(x - 8)$ term in the numerator will cancel with the $(x - 8)$ term in the denominator, and the same will happen with the $(x + 3)$ and $(x - 2)$ terms. After canceling everything, you will be left with 1, which is answer choice C.

28. Correct answer: **F**. Try out each answer choice one at a time to determine if it satisfies the inequality, taking special care to correctly use the absolute value bars; as a reminder, absolute value bars make whatever number is between them positive. With a question like this, and because ACT Math answers are almost (if not) always in numerical order from largest to smallest or smallest to largest, it is increasingly likely that the answer here will be either F or K. For no particular reason, let's try K.

Answer K has a value of \$150; let's plug in this number for m and see if it satisfies:

$$|m + \$25| \leq \$175 \;\ldots\; |\$150 + \$25| \leq \$175 \;\ldots\; |\$175| \leq \$175 \;\ldots\; \$175 \leq \$175$$

Yes, K satisfies the equation, which means it is not the correct answer, since we are looking for a number that is *not* in the range.

Now, let's try F, which gives m a value of $-\$205$:

$$|m + \$25| \leq \$175 \;\ldots\; |-\$205 + \$25| \leq \$175 \;\ldots\; |-\$180| \leq \$175 \;\ldots\; \$180 \leq \$175$$

This does not satisfy, since \$180 is greater than \$175. Thus, the answer is F: m can't equal $-\$205$.

29. Correct answer: **E**. One deceptive thing about this question is the answer choices. Only one of them is a huge number, whereas 4 of them are relatively small. However, don't let this be a problem; don't let this fool you. Let's consider a smaller situation first. If he was comfortable cooking 2 meat dishes, 2 vegetable dishes, and 2 desserts, then he'd be comfortable cooking $(2 \times 2 \times 2) = 8$ different meals. Similarly, if he can cook 80 meat dishes, 55 vegetable dishes, and 22 desserts, he is comfortable cooking $(80 \times 55 \times 22) = 96{,}800$ different meal combinations, which is answer choice E.

30. Correct answer: **H**. The simplest way to solve this problem is also a laborious one: plot the points, then consider the general slope of the line that generally passes through the points, then (if necessary) consider the y-axis of the line.

First, I have graphed the points below. You can see already that there is a kind of line that unites them all. However, the question says that there will be a line that *approximates* them, which means that it will, in general, fit the points; in other words, the line that is the answer to the question won't perfectly pass through each and every point.

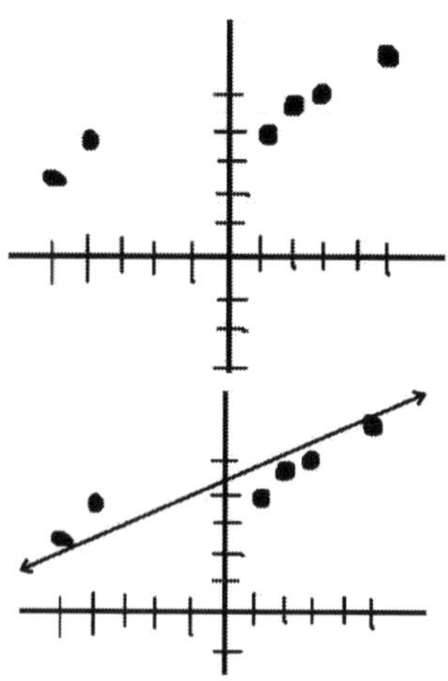

Next, consider a possible slope. On the next drawing down on the left, I've drawn in a possible line that approximates the data points. Let's recall the slope-intercept formula of a line: $y = mx + b$, in which m is the slope and b is the y-intercept (where the line crosses the y-axis). The first thing to notice is that the line has a positive slope (it has a "rise" on the positive y-axis as it "runs" left to right on the positive x-axis). This eliminates answer choices F and K, since they both have negative slopes.

The other options for slope are 3, 4, and $\frac{1}{3}$. If a slope is 3 or 4, that means it will "rise" or go up the y-axis 3 or 4 points, then "run" over 1 on the x-axis. This is NOT what our slope looks like here; it looks like the opposite (in other words, the slope is not very steep); it looks like it "runs" 3 or 4 before going up ("rise") by 1. This kind of shallow slope is fractional, which fits well with the remaining answer that has a slope of $\frac{1}{3}$. This answer choice, H, also has a y-intercept of +4, which fits fairly well with the line that I drew on top of my plotted points. For all of these reasons, H best approximates the plotted points.

31. Correct answer: **D**. This was mentioned in *Good to Know* Lesson #10, but any time a number of any kind is raised to the power of 0, the answer is 1. The only exception is 0, which, when raised to the power of 0, equals 0. Thus, this expression, as complicated as it is, is always going to equal 1 since it is raised to the power of 0; the answer then is D: 1.

32. Correct answer: **G**. Sin and cos are two trigonometric functions that rely on knowing the three sides of a right triangle. Since we are told that the $cos\ \theta = \frac{12}{13}$, and because the cos of an angle is equal to the adjacent side of an angle over the hypotenuse of the triangle, we can assume then that the adjacent side of this triangle relative to θ is 12, and that the hypotenuse of the triangle is 13.

That would leave the "opposite" side of θ, the third side of our triangle, as undefined. You may be able to quickly recognize that this is a special, 5-12-13 triangle, and thus that the third, opposite side must be 5. If you used the Pythagorean Theorem, that $a^2 + b^2 = c^2$, you would find the same.

Since the sin θ is going to equal the opposite side over the hypotenuse, we then know that the sin $\theta = \frac{5}{13}$, which is choice G.

33. Correct answer: **A**. What we know about the original picture is that it has a length of 8 and a width of 10, and thus an area of 80. Hold that thought for now.

After she cuts it, we know that the new length will be 87.5% the length of the original. To find this length, multiply the original length by 0.875. Since the original length is 8, the new length will be 8(0.875) = 7.

We now have all that we need to set up an equation to solve for the missing width, which we can call x. We are told that the new area will be 70% of the original area, which recall was 80. This means that the area of the new picture will be 80(0.7) = 56. Since we know now that the length of the new side is 7, and the area is 56, then the width can be found by solving this equation: $7x = 56$. Divide both sides by 7 and find that x, or the missing width, = 8, which is answer choice A.

34. Correct answer: **K**. Recall the formula for a circle, which is $(x - h)^2 + (y - k)^2 = r^2$, in which (h, k) is the center of the circle and r is the radius. Since the center of the circle is the origin, that means $(h, k) = (0, 0)$. This eliminates F, G, and H as answer options, since $(x - 0)^2 + (y - 0)^2$ is equivalent to $x^2 + y^2$. Lastly, the radius of the Chocolate Pie is 5.5, meaning $r^2 = 30.25$. Thus, the entire correct equation of the circle that fits this pie shape when centered at the origin is $x^2 + y^2 = 30.25$, which corresponds with answer choice K.

35. Correct answer: **A**. Since we are dealing with the area of the Chocolate Pie when compared to the area of both other pies, let's go ahead and find all three areas, recalling that the area of a circle = πr^2.

Chocolate Pie Area = $\pi r^2 = \pi(5.5)^2 = \pi 30.25 = 95.03$
Apple Pie Area = $\pi r^2 = \pi(6)^2 = \pi 36 = 113.10$
Key Lime Pie Area = $\pi r^2 = \pi(5)^2 = \pi 25 = 78.54$

Let's use *Backsolving* and try out each answer one at a time. Because we know that A is the correct answer, let's try out a wrong answer first, like B. B says that the Chocolate Pie is 121% of the Apple Pie. That would mean that when you multiply the Apple

Pie's area by 1.21, you would get the area of the Chocolate Pie. However, the area of the Apple Pie is already *larger* than that of the Chocolate Pie; multiplying it by 1.21 will only make it bigger. B can't be correct.

Now let's try A, which says that the Chocolate Pie is 84.03% of the Apple Pie. To test if this is true, multiply the Apple Pie's area (113.10) by 0.8403, and see if the result is the area of the Chocolate Pie, like this: 113.10(0.8403) = 95.04. Sure enough, that's within one hundredth of the area of the Chocolate Pie, which can be expected when decimals are being rounded (which they are here, and which is why the question requires that areas and percentages be rounded to the nearest hundredth of a percent). Thus, the answer is A; the Chocolate Pie's area is 84.03% of the Apple Pie's.

36. Correct answer: **K**. Fortunately, if you properly found the area of all three pies in the previous problem, you are one step closer to solving this problem. As the interior angles of these three pieces are to 360°, so too the area of the piece will be to the area of the pie as a whole.

Two of our pie's pieces (Piece 1 and Piece 3) are cut with interior angles of 25°. This means that these pieces are $\frac{25}{360} \times 100 = 6.94\%$ of the pie. Piece 2 is $\frac{20}{360} \times 100 = 5.56\%$ of the pie.

Now that we know what percentage of their respective pies these pieces occupy, we can determine their areas by multiplying the areas by the percentages. Recall the area of the entire Chocolate Pie is 95.03, the area of the Apple Pie is 113.10, and the area of the Key Lime Pie is 78.54 (these areas were just calculated in the previous question's answer explanation).

Piece 1 is 6.94% of Key Lime Pie's area, or 6.94% of 78.54 = 78.54(0.0694) = 5.45
Piece 2 is 5.56% of Chocolate Pie's area, or 5.56% of 95.03 = 95.03(0.0556) = 5.28
Piece 3 is 6.94% of Apple Pie's area, or 6.94% of 113.10 = 113.10(0.0694) = 7.85

Thus, Piece 3 is larger than Piece 1 is larger than Piece 2, which corresponds with choice K.

37. Correct answer: **C**. This question is testing your ability to recognize and properly use the Law of Transversals and other knowledge about angles. The first thing to note is that the segment *BD* is almost irrelevant; the only reason it is relevant is because we are told that angle $\angle ABD$ is 118° and is bisected by segment *CB*; 'bisected' means that it perfectly cuts the angle in half. This is important for us because it tells us that angle $\angle ABC$ is half of 118°, or is 59°.

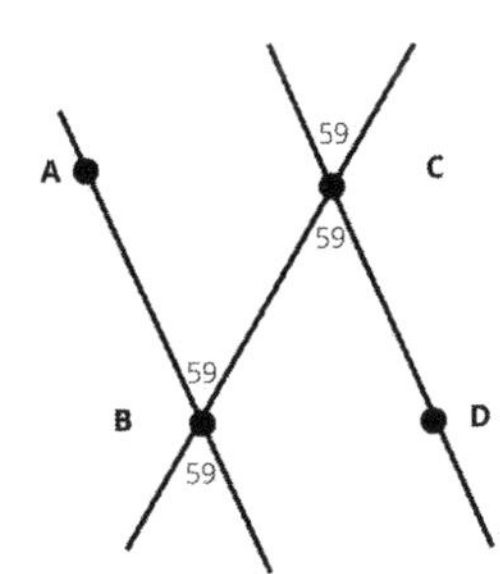

With that in mind, I've redrawn the three segments as a little bit longer. Remember what the Law of Transversals means: if two parallel lines are transversed ("cut through") with another line, then each pair of alternate interior angles are equal. Additionally, if you know even 1 of the 8 angles formed when a line passes through two others, you can determine the value of all 8 angles. Four of them will be the same, and the other four will be the same as well. Here, $\angle ABC$ is 59° as we've already determined, but that means by definition that angle $\angle BCD$ is also 59°, which is answer choice C.

38. Correct answer: **H**. Because the grass that needs replacing is in square feet, but the grass patches are sold in dimensions of inches, one or the other needs converting before we divide one by the other and determine how many grass patches are needed. It would be easier if the grass patches of 25 inches by 25 inches were converted to feet. Since there are 12 inches in a foot, then each side of each patch of grass is:

$$\frac{25 \text{ inches}}{12 \text{ inches per foot}} = 2\frac{1}{12} \text{ feet} = 2.083 \text{ feet}$$

Now, this means that each patch of grass is 2.083 by 2.083 feet. Next, we must find the square footage of each patch of grass so that we can divide them into the total square footage of the dead grass.

$$2.083 \text{ ft} \times 2.083 \text{ ft} = 4.34 \text{ ft}^2$$

Now, because we know the total square footage of the grass that needs replacing (1,350) and the square footage of each patch of grass (4.34), we simply need to divide the latter into the former to determine how many patches are needed:

$$\frac{1{,}350}{4.34} = 311.06 \text{ patches of grass needed}$$

However, the question does NOT ask for you to round the patches to the nearest integer or whole number. Instead, it asks what is the minimum number of patches needed to replace all of the dead grass. In other words, 311 is not quite enough, because there will be a small amount of grass yet uncovered (.06 patches worth). This means that you must round *up* to ensure there is enough grass purchased to cover all of the dead grass. This, of course, is 312, or answer choice H.

39. Correct answer: **D**. To answer this question, you need a proper number set, of which you can find the mean, median, mode, and range. When I say "proper number set", I mean that the numbers given need to be listed in numerical order. Below I list them in numerical order, then do the proper math to find the four values needed.

Numerical order number set: {0.05, 0.05, 0.05, 0.05, 0.06, 0.06, 0.09, 0.10, 0.11, 0.11}

Mean (average): $\frac{(.05 + .05 + .05 + .05 + .06 + .06 + .09 + .10 + .11 + .11)}{10} = \frac{0.73}{10} = 0.073$

Median (middle term, or average of 2 middle terms if even number of terms in set): 0.06

Mode (occurs the most): 0.05

Range (difference between largest and smallest term): (0.11 – 0.05) = 0.06

Thus, as you can see, it is the median and the range that are the same. This corresponds with answer choice D.

40. Correct answer: **J**. For numbers 40, 41, and 42, the absolute first thing that you should do is draw an image of the tower. Like I have done here:

Question number 40 asks us to find the height of the tower if it were to stand upright. In other words, question 40 is asking for the length of either side of the tower. If you look at the answer choices, you will see that each of them features the angle 86.03 degrees, which means we need to solve this from this particular angle.

Your first thought might be this: isn't the length of that side simply 183.25? Well, no. That is the *height* of the tower on that side; we want the length of the actual wall, which is the hypotenuse of a very tall right triangle. From the point of view of the 86.03 degree angle, we know the opposite side (which is 183.25), but again, the length of the wall is the hypotenuse of this triangle. We need to identify one of our three functions (sin, cos, tan) that uses the opposite side and the hypotenuse, which is sin. Sin, if you remember, is the opposite side over the hypotenuse. Thus, we can set up an initial equation that looks like this (let's call the length of the wall, thus the length of the hypotenuse, x):

$$\sin(86.03) = \frac{183.25}{x}$$

Now, we have to rearrange the equation to solve for x. To do so, multiply both sides by x, then divide both sides by sin(86.03), like this:

$$(x)\sin(86.03) = \frac{183.25}{x}(x) \quad \ldots \quad \sin(86.03)(x) = 183.25 \quad \ldots \quad x = \frac{183.25}{\sin(86.03)}$$

This corresponds with answer choice J.

41. Correct answer: **E**. This question has nothing to to with the actual tower, of course, but rather with Chandra's reading speed. The absolute easiest way to solve this problem is by using the *Picking Numbers* strategy from earlier in the book. Let's pretend that $x = 700$. This is simple because if she can read at 700 words per minute, and there are 350 words per page, then she can read 2 pages per minute. If she can read two pages per minute, it will take her 7.5 minutes to read 15 pages.

With that in mind, plug in $x = 700$ into the five answer choices to see which one will result in an answer of 7.5 minutes. Start with:

A: $\frac{350x}{15} = \frac{350(700)}{15} = 16{,}333\text{...not 7.5!}$

B: $\frac{x}{350(15)} = \frac{700}{350(15)} = \frac{1}{7.5}\text{...not 7.5!}$

$$C: \quad \frac{15x}{350} = \frac{15(700)}{350} = 30\text{..., not } 7.5!$$

$$D: \quad \frac{350}{15x} = \frac{350}{15(700)} = 0.03\text{...not } 7.5!$$

$$E: \quad \frac{350(15)}{x} = \frac{350(15)}{700} = 7.5\text{...that's it!}$$

Thus, the answer is E.

42. Correct answer: **H**. First, determine the volume of this new tower. The volume of a cylinder is the area of the circle of one side times the height of the cylinder. The area of a circle is πr^2, and because we know the diameter of this new tower is 50, that means the radius is 25. Thus, the area of the circle of this cylinder is $\pi r^2 = 625(3.14159) = 1{,}963.49$. Multiply this area by the height, which is 185 ft, and the result is this: $1{,}963.49(185) = 363{,}246.34$ cubic feet.

The original tower has a weight of 16,000 (2,000) pounds (since we know it weights 16,000 tons, and there are 2,000 pounds per ton). Thus, the weight of the tower is 16,000 (2,000) = 32,000,000 pounds.

Lastly, the question asks for pounds per cubic foot. Divide the pounds (32,000,000) by the cubic feet (363,246.34) to get pounds per cubic foot, like this:

$$\frac{32{,}000{,}000}{363{,}246.34} = 88.09$$, which when rounded to the nearest whole number, is 88, or answer choice H.

43. Correct answer: **B**. There are three ways to solve this particular problem. Let's go through all three ways, not because you need all three to solve one problem, but so you can find the easiest for you. I'll start with what I believe to be the easiest, then move on from there.

Method 1: Elimination - this method relies on the strange idea in Algebra that you can add equations to one another or subtract one equation from another. When you do this properly, you will be left with only one equation with only one variable. To do so, you have to manipulate at least one of the equations so that there will be canceling out. In the two equations in this problem, I see that if I multiply the second equation by 2, that the second term will be $-2y$, which, when added to the first, will result in the y terms canceling.

First, multiply the second equation by 2, like this: $2(4x - y = -29) = 8x - 2y = -58$

Second add the two equations together, like this:

$$\begin{array}{r} 3x + 2y = 14 \\ + \underline{8x - 2y = -58} \\ 11x + 0y = -44 \end{array}$$

Now, we have just one equation with one variable; only x remains. Divide both sides by 11, and learn that $x = -4$. Since only answer B says $x = -4$, we have our answer. If you needed to find y, then simply plug in $x = -4$ into either of the original equations and solve for y.

Method 2: *Backsolving* - I hope by this point that this is one of the tools in your ACT Math toolbox that you've grown accustomed to using! Try out the values of x and y one answer at a time to see if they work on BOTH equations. You can bet that at least one of the wrong answers will work for one equation, but not both.

Start with A, that $x = 2$ and $y = 4$. Plug that into the first equation: $3(2) + 2(4) = 14$ ... $6 + 8 = 14$, which works! Like I just said though, you have to now try this on the second equation, like this:
$4(2) - 4 = -29$ ... $8 - 4 = -29$ ... ??? Not quite! It doesn't satisfy.

Move on to B, that $x = -4$ and $y = 13$. Plug that into the first equation: $3(-4) + 2(13) = 14$ ... $-12 + 26 = 14$, which works! Try plugging in those two values into the second equation to see if it also works; if so, we have found our answer. If not, it's on to the next answer choice. So, plugging $x = -4$ and $y = 13$ into the second equation looks like this: $4(-4) - 13 = -29$ ... $-16 - 13 = -29$, which also works! There you have it; by *Backsolving*, we are able to show that B satisfies both equations.

Method 3: Substitution - substitution involves solving one of our equations for a variable, replacing this variable with whatever is on the other side of the equation in the other equation, then solving for the one missing variable. That sounds much more confusing than it is, so follow along to see how substitution works.

Step 1 is to choose an equation to solve for x or y. I see that there is a $-y$ term in the second equation, which will be simple enough to solve for y. Let's rearrange and manipulate it to do so:

$$4x - y = -29 \quad \ldots \quad -y = -4x - 29 \quad \ldots \quad y = 4x + 29$$

Now, we can take this value of y (which is $4x + 29$) and plug it in where there is a y in the other, first equation. This will eliminate any y's, leaving us with an equation with only x's, which can then be solved. Like this:

$$3x + 2y = 14 \quad \ldots \quad 3x + 2(4x + 29) = 14 \quad \ldots \quad 3x + 8x + 58 = 14 \quad \ldots \quad 11x = -44 \quad \ldots \quad x = -4$$

Now that we know that $x = -4$, we have enough information to solve the answer. If you need to find y, simply plug in $x = -4$ into any equation and solve for y.

44. Correct answer: **J**. First, and before we figure out what to do with the y^5 term, let's simply solve the equation in a way that isolates y^5 on one side, like this:

$$15x = 5y^5 - 25 \quad \ldots \quad -5y^5 = -15x - 25 \quad \ldots \quad y^5 = 3x + 5$$

So far, so good. To isolate the y by itself, we will need to find the fifth root of both sides. Just like the square root of anything squared is just the thing itself (the square root of 3^2 is just 3, for example), the fifth root of anything "fifthed" or raised to the power of 5 is just the thing itself. Finding the fifth root of something, though, is the same thing as raising it to the $\frac{1}{5}$ power, like this:

$$y^5 = 3x + 5 \quad \ldots \quad (y^5)^{\frac{1}{5}} = (3x + 5)^{\frac{1}{5}} \quad \ldots \quad y = (3x + 5)^{\frac{1}{5}}$$, which matches answer choice J.

45. Correct answer: **C**. First, recall that an equilateral triangle is the special type that has 3 sides of equal length, which means it also has 3 angles that are identical: all 3 angles are 60°. With this knowledge, we can "slice" an equilateral triangle in half down the height to create a new triangle that we can evaluate using sin/cos/tan. In such a case, we would know the length of one of the sides and the value of two of the angles. Below, I have created this equilateral triangle; notice that both the right and left hand sides are right triangles.

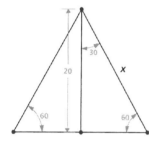

Because the area of a triangle is $\frac{1}{2}bh$ in which h is the height and b is the length of the base, we have to find what is missing which, in our case, is b. But because this is an equilateral triangle, it doesn't matter which side you rest the triangle on; it will look like this triangle here.

Now for the actual math. Notice that I have labeled the right side of the triangle with an x. This is what we need to find out that we can find the base and then the area. We need a trig function (sin, cos, or tan) that uses the side we know (that $h = 20$) and the side we need to know (the x). You could use cos from the 30° at the top, or sin from the 60° in the bottom right. Let's go with sin, like this:

$$\sin(60) = \frac{20}{x} \quad \ldots \quad x\sin(60) = 20 \quad \ldots \quad x = \frac{20}{\sin(60)} \quad \ldots \quad x = \frac{20}{0.866} \quad \ldots \quad 23.09$$

Now that we know one side is 23.09, we know that all three sides are 23.09, which means we know the base is 23.09.

Thus, the area of our triangle is $\frac{1}{2}bh = \frac{1}{2}(23.09)(20) = 230.95$. The question asks us to round to the nearest square inch, which is up to 231. This is our answer, which corresponds with answer choice C.

46. Correct answer: **H**. First, identify the first six prime numbers; as a reminder, a prime number is a number that is divisibly by only itself and the number 1. Thus, the first 6 prime numbers are 1, 2, 3, 5, 7, and 11.

The mean of these numbers is $\frac{1 + 2 + 3 + 5 + 7 + 11}{6} = \frac{29}{6}$

Second, identify the factors of 10. A numbers factors are all of the numbers that can evenly divide into it. The numbers that all evenly divide into 10, and thus 10's factors, are 1, 2, 5, and 10.

The mean of these numbers is $\frac{1+2+5+10}{4} = \frac{18}{4}$

Lastly, multiply the two together and simplify: $\frac{29}{6} \times \frac{18}{4} = \frac{522}{24} = \frac{87}{4} = 21\frac{3}{4}$, which is answer choice H.

47. Correct answer: **D**. If two matrices can not be multiplied together, it is undefined. Thus, four of these options *can* be multiplied together, and we have to figure out which ones. Fortunately, you don't have to do all of the math; if you can remember the rule about which matrices can and can't be multiplied, you can answer this question rather quickly.

The rule is this: two matrices can be multiplied together if the number of columns in the first matrix equals the number of rows in the second matrix (the columns are up and down; rows are left and right). Sometimes, just reversing the order of the two matrices makes them go from able to be multiplied to undefined. Let's go through the answer options one at a time.

Answer choice A says *AB*. Matrix *A* has 2 columns; matrix *B* has 2 rows. These can be multiplied, so this is an incorrect answer.

Answer choice B says *BA*. Matrix *B* has 1 column; matrix *A* has 1 row. These can be multiplied, so this is an incorrect answer.

Answer choice C says *DB*. Matrix *D* has 2 columns; matrix *B* has 2 rows. These can be multiplied, so this is an incorrect answer.

Answer choice D says *BD*. Matrix *B* has 1 column; matrix *D* has 3 rows. These are different, thus it can't be multiplied and is undefined and the correct answer.

48. Correct answer: **K**. First, cancel out like terms between those in the numerator and the term in the denominator. All three terms are divisible by both 2 and a^2, which will eliminate the term in the denominator entirely. It should be noted that when exponents are being divided, the exponents themselves are subtracted, not divided. For example, if I divide a^{16} by a^2, which is necessary in this step for this problem's simplification, the result is not a^8, but rather $a^{16-2} = a^{14}$. Here is the first step:

$$\frac{8a^{16} - 6a^4}{2a^2} = 4a^{14} - 3a^2$$

Now, the question becomes whether or not this term can be further simplified. There is no common factor between 4 and 3, so those will stay the same. However, there is a common factor between a^{14} and a^2, which is a^2. So, we can divide both terms by a^2 (but remember: exponents get subtracted when one is divided by another) and put it in front of parentheses, like this:

$4a^{14} - 3a^2 = a^2(4a^{12} - 3)$, which is answer choice K.

49. Correct answer: **A**. To answer this question correctly, properly identify the ratios involved and cross multiply. Before I do that, it is worth noting that it is perfectly acceptable if you want to leave these numbers as fractions, then simplify at the end. However, I'm going to convert each of these fractions into a decimal number first. This keeps me from making a simple error that can come from working these kinds of problems as fractions. This will be my first step:

$1\frac{3}{4} = 1.75$ $\qquad 2\frac{1}{8} = 2.125$ $\qquad 2\frac{1}{3} = 2.333$

Next, I want to set up my ratios and cross multiply. One way to think about this ratio is in terms of chocolate chips per butter. So, I'll put chocolate chips in the numerator, butter in the denominator, and set that equal to the same ratio with the missing butter that we need to find as *x*. Our recipe calls for a certain amount of both ingredients which (using my decimal conversions) looks like this:

$$\frac{1.75 \text{ chocolate chips}}{2.125 \text{ butter}}$$

Now, I set the ingredient amounts that Molly will use equal to this with the amount of butter we need to find labeled as *x*:

$$\frac{1.75 \text{ chocolate chips}}{2.125 \text{ butter}} = \frac{2.333 \text{ chocolate chips}}{x \text{ butter}}$$

After cross multiplying, we this equation, which we can solve for *x*:

$$1.75x = 2.125(2.333) \ \ldots \ x = \frac{4.958}{1.75} = 2.833$$

Lastly, we have to figure out which answer choice corresponds to 2.833. Only one answer choice falls between 2 and 3, which is answer choice A. Sure enough, if you put $2\frac{5}{6}$ in your calculator, you will see it is equal to 2.833.

50. Correct answer: **G**. It's important to recognize that this question is asking for the *minimum* number of athletes who play both a winter and a spring sport. There are 55 total, so let's subtract the 29 who play a winter sport. That leaves 26 football players. What's left is that 31 of them now play a spring sport. We can assume that the 26 leftover play a spring sport, but that still leaves 5 who also play a spring sport. Thus, at a minimum, at least 5 football players play both a spring and winter sport, which is answer choice G.

51. Correct answer: **D**. Though wrapped up in a very long modeling/story problem, this is really a simple probability problem. Add the number of laptops that had 0, 1, or 2 defects and divide it from the total number of laptops, like this:

$$\frac{(193 + 111 + 152)}{(193 + 111 + 152 + 105 + 53)} = \frac{456}{614} = 0.74$$

The question and answers require that we find the fraction that best approximates our probability of 0.74. Although $\frac{2}{3}$ might seem pretty close at first, letter D is spot on, since $\frac{74}{100} = \frac{37}{50}$, thus D is correct

52. Correct answer: **J**. Notice that the bottom side has a length of 5. Because every line meets at 90°, we know then that the two lines that are parallel to the bottom side also add up to 5. So far, that is 10. We also know that the two vertical sides on the right of the figure have a length of 4 + 1 = 5, so that means that each other vertical side on the left, those perpendicular to those on the right, also add up to 5. So far then, that's a total perimeter of 20. There are two sides yet to be taken into account, which are the two horizontal sides that cut into the figure from the left, each with a length of 3. Thus, the total perimeter is 26, which is answer choice J.

53. Correct answer: **C**. Simply add each day's steps without making a mistake. If you add 50 steps each day 10 times in a row, you get this list of numbers: 1000, 1050, 1100, 1150, 1200, 1250, 1300, 1350, 1400, and 1450. Add them up carefully for a total of 12,250, which is answer choice C.

54. Correct answer: **F**. The formula for the area of a parallelogram has not been discussed in this book until now since it does not fall into either the *Good to Know* or *Have to Know* categories. The formula for the area of a parallelogram is simply *bh*, in which *b* equals the length of the base and *h* equals the height from the base. This works for every parallelogram, even squares and rectangles.

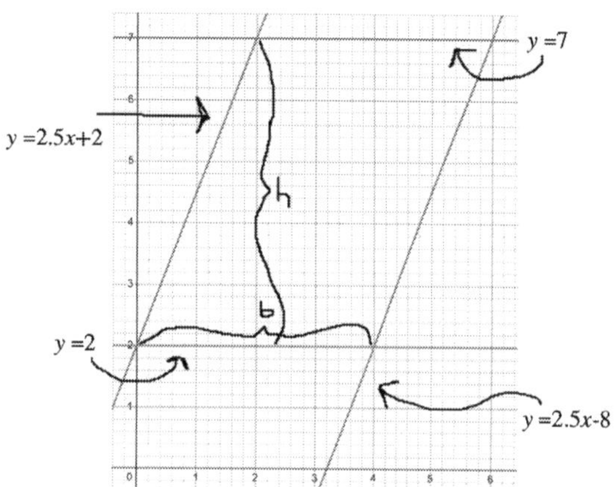

The first thing to do is to draw out the parallelogram by making a quick graph of the four lines. Two of the lines ($y = 2$ and $y = 7$) are parallel to the x-axis and stretch left to right. For the other two lines, start at their y-intercepts (+2 and −8) and plot points by the slope (they both have a slope of $2\frac{1}{2}$, which means go up on the y-axis $2\frac{1}{2}$ before going over 1 on the x-axis).

In this diagram, I've labeled the four lines. You'll notice the y-axis on the left and the x-axis on the bottom (in other words, this parallelogram is in Quadrant I of the coordinate plane), and that I've labeled the base and the height with b and h, respectively.

Now for the mathematics of it. The base, b, goes across the line $y = 2$ from an x value of 0 to an x value of 4. Thus, the base is $(4 - 0) = 4$. The height stretches from a y value of 2 to a y value of 7. Thus the height is $(7 - 2) = 5$. Since the area of a parallelogram is bh, then the area is $bh = 4(5) = 20$ square units, which is answer choice F.

55. Correct answer: **E**. There are two ways to solve this problem, but the first (factoring trinomials, canceling binomials, etc.) is tricky. Instead, use *Picking Numbers*, choose a value for *y*, and then plug it into both the expression in the question and the answers and find a match. The added difficulty is that many of the y terms are underneath a radical (in other words, you have to find the square root of y routinely), which means you'd have to choose a value of y that is a perfect square. Let's go with $y = 4$, plug it in, and see what we end up with:

$$\frac{(-\sqrt{y}-3)(y+5\sqrt{y}+4)}{(\sqrt{y}+1)(y-4\sqrt{y}-21}) = \frac{(-\sqrt{4}-3)(4+5\sqrt{4}+4)}{(\sqrt{4}+1)(4-4\sqrt{4}-21}) = \frac{(-2-3)(4+5(2)+4)}{(2+1)(4-4(2)-21})$$

Now that the radicals have been eliminated, it is simple math (taking care to avoid those simple mistakes) that simplifies from here:

$$\frac{(-2-3)(4+5(2)+4)}{(2+1)(4-4(2)-21}) = \frac{(-5)(18)}{(3)(-25)} = \frac{-90}{-75} = \frac{18}{15} = \frac{6}{5} = 1.2$$

Now, plug in $y = 4$ into the answer choices to properly determine which $= \frac{6}{5}$ or 1.2. Start with A and B, which plainly equal 2 and -2, respectively, after finding the square root of $y = 4$. Move on to C:

C: $\frac{\sqrt{y}}{\sqrt{y}+7} = \frac{\sqrt{4}}{\sqrt{4}+7} = \frac{2}{9}$, so not correct.

D: $\frac{\sqrt{y}+4}{\sqrt{y}-7} = \frac{\sqrt{4}+4}{\sqrt{4}-7} = \frac{6}{-5} = -\frac{6}{5}$, so not correct.

E: $\frac{-\sqrt{y}-4}{\sqrt{y}-7} = \frac{-\sqrt{4}-4}{\sqrt{4}-7} = \frac{-6}{-5} = \frac{6}{5} = 1.2$, which is correct!

56. Correct answer: **F**. First, remember that the graph of $\cos(x)$ has an amplitude of 1. This is because the value of cosine can only go as high as 1 or as low as -1, and either way, the wave will have a distance of 1 from the x-axis (which is the definition of amplitude). When the graph of cosine is multiplied by 3, the amplitude triples because the final output of cosine is tripling. This is enough for us to determine that the correct answer must either be G or K.

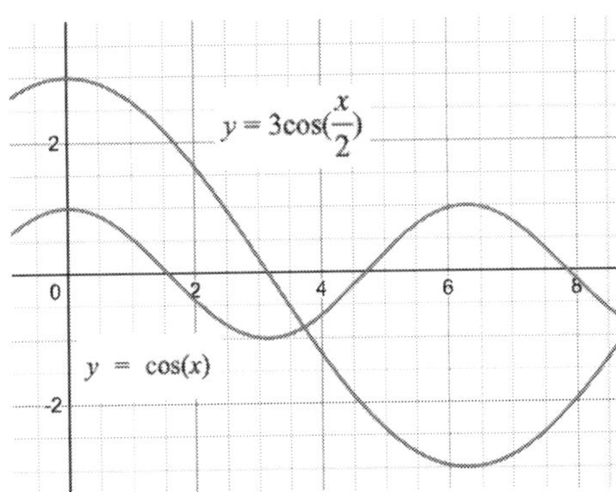

However, the question now becomes this: what happens when the value of x, which is the angle that cosine is measuring, is divided by 2? Even though the graph of cosine features a wave that relies on the value of cosine in radians (π, 2π, etc.), we can conceptualize the problem enough for us to get the correct answer if we think about it in terms of degrees.

Think about this: the x-axis of the graph of cosine is the angle that cosine is measuring, but if we cut that angle in half by dividing it by 2, then it will take *twice as long* for the wave to make a full rotation. In the graph of $\cos(x)$, the wave makes a full rotation after 360°, but if we are dividing the angles by 2, it will take twice as long; the wave will have to stretch along the x-axis to 720° before a full rotation is made. This is why the answer is F, which not only account for the new graph having 3 times the amplitude, but correctly says that the new graph will also have twice the period.

57. Correct answer: **B**. An expected outcome is NOT the same thing as the most likely outcome. The most likely outcome is that she would draw one of 36 number cards and end up winning \$10. However, the expected outcome is the result of multiplying the possible results by their individual probabilities and adding them together.

There are 4 aces out of 52 cards. The odds of drawing an ace is $\frac{4}{52} = \frac{1}{13} = 0.077$

There are 12 face cards out of 52 cards. The odds of drawing a face card is $\frac{12}{52} = \frac{3}{13} = 0.231$

There are 36 number cards out of 52 cards. The odds of drawing a number card is $\frac{36}{52} = \frac{9}{13} = 0.692$.

Now that we have determined the probabilities, we multiply each probability by each respective prize (ace=\$150, face card = \$100, number card = \$10) and add up the three. Let's do that in one big step to find the final answer:

$$\$150(0.077) + \$100(0.231) + \$10(0.692) = \$11.55 + \$23.10 + \$6.92 = \$41.57$$

Since the question requires that we round to the nearest whole dollar, we round up to \$42, which is answer choice B.

58. Correct answer: **G**. There is an extremely fast way to get this question correct. It is impossible for a rectangle to have a perimeter that is an odd number. Try any combination of numbers for a rectangle's width and length, and you'll never come up with an odd numbered perimeter. That's enough to choose choice G.

However, let's work out the mathematics of this problem as well. Essentially, we are going to have to factor out 240 in pairs and find the respective perimeters.

$240 = 240 \times 1$ = a perimeter of $(240 + 240 + 1 + 1) = 482$, which is answer choice F (so F is incorrect).

Now, I notice that the final three answers are all relatively close, so I will try to find the dimensions of this rectangle that get me in that range.

$240 = 20 \times 12$ = a perimeter of $(20 + 20 + 12 + 12) = 64$, which is answer choice J (so J is incorrect).

This guess has put me squarely between two other options, so I will try to play with the perimeter to see if these final two answer choices are possible.

$240 = 15 \times 16$ = a perimeter of $(15 + 15 + 16 + 16) = 62$, which is answer choice K (so K is incorrect).

$240 = 24 \times 10$ = a perimeter of $(24 + 24 + 10 + 10) = 68$, which is answer choice H (so H is incorrect).

By process of trial and error, we have eliminated four of the answer choices, leaving only G.

59. Correct answer: **A**. Before reading through the answer choices, think about what you know about three lines with different slopes. Each of them will cross over the other at some point; it's also possible that the three intersect at the same point. None of the three can be parallel, though two of them can be perpendicular. That said, let's go through the choices.

Choice A says that two of the lines never cross the x-axis. Well, for a line not to cross the x-axis, that means it is parallel to the x-axis with a slope of 0. If *two* lines were to never cross the x-axis, that would mean they both are parallel to the x-axis and both have slopes of 0. Because the question says that the lines have different slopes, the correct answer has already been found. A is correct because it is impossible for two of these three lines to never cross the x-axis.

60. Correct answer: **K**. First, find the volume of the original ball room. The ball room has a length of 300 ft, a width of 150 ft, and a height of 20 ft. Thus, the volume $= 300 \times 150 \times 20 = 900{,}000\ \text{ft}^2$.

Now, find the volume of the proposed, larger space. The owner wants the length to increase by 25%, thus the new length $= 300(1.25) = 375$ feet and the new width $= 150(1.25) = 187.5$ feet. Since the height of the ceiling will remain at 20 feet, the volume of the new space $= 375 \times 187.5 \times 20 = 1{,}406{,}250\ \text{ft}^2$.

Lastly, find the percent growth to the nearest 1%. To do so, first find the actual growth in square feet, which is this: $1{,}406{,}250\ \text{ft}^2 - 900{,}000\ \text{ft}^2 = 506{,}250\ \text{ft}^2$. Second, find what percent the of the original 900,000 this increase represents by division, like this:

$$\frac{506{,}250\ \text{ft}^2}{900{,}000\ \text{ft}^2} = 0.5625, \text{ or } 56.25\%$$, which, when rounded to the nearest 1%, is 56%, or answer K.

ACT Reading Explanations

Answer Explanations - Step 1

Correct Answers - Passage II:

11: B
12: F
13: C
14: H
15: B
16: G
17: D
18: J
19: A
20: H

Possible Passage Map:

Passage II

SOCIAL SCIENCE: This is an original passage about the agrarian economy of Ancient Egypt.

Until the Persian Invasion (525 BCE) introduced a cash economy into Ancient Egypt, the economy of this kingdom was an agrarian barter system, and the Nile River was its lifeblood. The river brought water and fertile soil to the cultivated fields each year, as the seasonal floods began in September. It was during these times of growth that the kingdom carried out the construction of most temples, including the Giza pyramid complex. Quarries supplied the limestone, and foreign trade supplied slaves and other minerals, but the production and redistribution of food to laborers and overseers drove the economy and brought the massive project to completion.

From the Predynastic Period (6000 – 3150 BCE) to the end of Roman Egypt (646 CE), laborers (most of whom worked the fields, while others attended to the temples, fished, or made pottery) were paid in rations and other goods. Several historical accounts mention daily food rations of bread, beer, and sometimes fish given to laborers. This could be given to individuals, but a larger allotment was given to families. For example, ten loaves of bread and two jugs of beer were given to family units, and while the amount of daily rations given to individuals depended on their status, some received less than one loaf of bread a day. Persons of higher status, such as the heads of estates, often received meat and other goods that were not available to the lower classes. In addition to these daily rations, people also received supplemental "grain wages" weekly or monthly.

The Egyptologist Toby Wilkinson describes how food was collected and redistributed under the agrarian economy: "A certain proportion went directly to state workshops for the manufacture of secondary products—for example, tallow and leather from cattle; pork from pigs; linen from flax; bread, beer, and basketry from grain. Some of these value-added products were then traded and exchanged at a profit, producing further government income; others were redistributed as payment to state employees, thereby funding the court and its projects." Taxes were paid in the form of goods produced by laborers, but only the heads of estates delivered the revenues and the surplus food to the central administration, which was led by the pharaoh. The royal residence and provincial administration centers parsed the surplus of food out to the rest of the population.

During the times of the Old Kingdom (2686 – 2181 BCE), priests of the mortuary cults owned large tracts of land exempt from taxes. Although the king was recognized as the official steward of all lands and owned much of the land, both king and priest were allowed to trade. But for the most part, the food produced on farms along the Nile River was sent to the capital, where it was redistributed through centers or used for trading with other nations. In the funerary temples, food was redistributed to the attendants from the temple offerings. When the Middle Kingdom began, more of Egypt's land, food and tombs came under the private ownership of families and estates instead of the central administration. Despite this, workers were still paid in the same way, with daily rations and grain wages.

Despite laborers being "paid" in rations, slaves were very much a part of Ancient Egypt's economy. The construction of Egyptian pyramids powered the economy, but resulted in massive transfer of wealth to the central administration and Pharaoh in particular, and the labor power and welfare of the slaves subsidized the cost of construction. Because many of the field laborers were slaves, the masters transferred the income (i.e. goods) produced by them to the wealthy without an actual increase in income. Laborers were forced to work during a period of each year that followed the ebb and flow of the Nile River (often 10 months). Soldiers were conscripted from the same pool of slaves, and travelled outside Egypt to gather minerals not found in the kingdom (e.g. copper, hardwood), whether through trade or conquest. Aside from provisions, corvée laborers were given shelter, but received few goods other than food staples.

Although money was not used until the Persian Invasion, the kingdom of Ancient Egypt denoted the value of goods based on a unit of weight: the deben. For measuring fair exchanges, stones of a set weight were placed on one end of a balance beam, and the traded good was set on the other end. Prior to the New Kingdom (1550 – 1069 BCE), deben of various materials and weights were utilized; King Userkaf, for example, possessed a gold deben. By the dawning of the New Kingdom, a copper deben became the standard, weighing approximately 91 grams.

As more silver came to Egypt from trade with the Mediterranean region, and as more gold came from the conquered region of Nubia (modern-day Sudan), more expensive goods were known to be priced based on silver or gold deben, with proportionate changes in value. For laborers, a day's work could also be valued with deben; thus the aforementioned amount of rations to be paid out would be weighted on a scale to balance with the appropriate number of deben.

11. Which of the following statements best describes how the passage characterizes the relationship between the economies of Ancient Egypt and other nations?

A. The passage suggests that nations and societies beyond the borders of Egypt had equal or greater influence within Egypt as the Pharaoh himself.
B. The passage characterizes Ancient Egypt as more isolated than other societies, but still open to trade and relationship outside of its borders.
C. The passage makes it clear that the economy of Ancient Egypt relied on a system of currency, whereas other nations were mostly agrarian.
D. The passage implies that Ancient Egypt's economy was primarily pescatarian (its laborers mostly fished the Nile River), whereas other nations relied on an almost entirely agrarian economy.

11. Correct answer: **B**. This is a macro question that requires an overall understanding of the passage to accurately get it correct. It could be that you circle this question and give it another chance when you have answered numbers 12-20 (since macro questions tend to appear most often in the first question following a passage, answering the rest of the questions could lead to a greater understanding, and thus an increased likelihood to get it correct). The reason that the correct answer is B is because the passage does indicate that Ancient Egypt is indeed more isolated (it took an invasion to have cash, for example, and reliance upon the Nile is stressed), however there are also references to interdependence with other nations (see lines 90-92, for example) and established trade. Answer choice A has no basis in truth in the passage. Answer choice C is the exact opposite of the truth (since Egypt was agrarian). Answer choice D is also the opposite of the truth; while fishing is mentioned in the passage, it is clear that the economy of Ancient Egypt was agrarian, unlike that of other nations.

12. Correct answer: **F**. Of course, you may need to go back and reread the paragraph to get this question correct; it could very well be, however, that you were able to summarize the main idea of this paragraph nicely using your Passage Map. If you need to reread the paragraph because you don't trust what you put in the margin to be perfect, that is fine; if you used active reading, you likely have the time! In summary, it looks like the fifth paragraph is about all of the different things that slaves did (labor, become soldiers, etc.). That being said, letter F nicely speaks of the various roles of slaves in Egypt's economy. Letter G might be tempting because talk of slavery might cause you, the reader, to get sympathetic, but that's not the role of this paragraph. If you put H, you were probably seeing that this answer choice mentions Egypt's military, and so does the paragraph. While that's true, that doesn't mean this is the main purpose of the paragraph. Letter J mentions slaves, but the paragraph itself makes no mention of a decision any slaves had to make.

13. Correct answer: **C**. The answer to this question is found in paragraph 2, specifically lines 25-27, which say that it is status that can determine the types of rations one may receive. To be fair, the paragraph also says that those who have families may also be receiving more rations, but that is not one of the answer choices. You may also *infer* that B, gender, and D, age, also play a role in ration distribution. Is it likely, historically speaking, that these two factors played a role in ration distribution at some point in the long history of Egypt? Of course. However, *it isn't directly stated in the passage*! Remember, to *infer* or make good guesses is deadly on the ACT. Give yourself the time to look for these answers!

14. Correct answer: **H**. Quick thinking students might see that the sentence prior to the quote (lines 30-32) sum up exactly what the quote says ("...how food was collected and redistributed...), which matches up perfectly well with the correct answer choice, H, which says the quote serves to "illustrate the cycle of food..." However, a reread of the quote (again, active read the passage to give yourself the time!) will also suffice to show you this is the case as well. Letter F may be about laborers, but that is not what the quote is primarily about. Letter G has some truth in it: of course the economy is affected by "Pharaoh's whims." However, that's not the role of the paragraph either (so don't *infer*). Letter J seems tempting and sounds good until you get to the last few words that mention Egypt becoming a cash economy, which wasn't caused by food but by foreign invasion, as stated elsewhere.

15. Correct answer: **B**. Most likely, you have never heard the word corvée. That's OK; the point of this question isn't to test your vocabulary, but to see if you can determine a likely meaning *based on context*. Thus, again, you need to go back and reread and determine the usage of this word. On a side note, this process would also be true for even the simplest words, many of which can be used in an abundance of ways. Here, the word is an adjective in front of the word *laborers* to describe them, and is featured in the last sentence of a paragraph that is entirely about the role of slaves in Ancient Egypt. Thus, this word has to do with these slave laborers. This is why the correct answer is B: forced or unpaid. It certainly isn't C or D, which essentially mean the opposite. Letter A would be a tempting choice because such laborers are certainly overwhelmed and likely depressed, but that's not what the word *means*, which is the question itself.

16. Correct answer: **G**. The word "periodic" in this question implies that there are times in which the kingdom grows, then flatlines; then growth, then flatlining; etc. Lines 4-9 speak of the Nile river flooding annually, during which time the kingdom was able to grow. This is why the answer is G. Again, you might be *inferring* to answer choice F or answer choice J. Is it likely that the growth or lack thereof of the Egyptian economy at some point in its history depended upon one of these two answers? Sure, but *it isn't stated in the passage itself*! Give yourself the time to find the correct answer.

17. Correct answer: **D**. This is a macro question that can only be answered with attention to the greater passage as a whole. If you're having trouble at first, reread your Passage Map, then cross through answer choices that are definitely false, making a decision much easier. There is truth (at least, words and phrases that at least *sound* true or almost true) in all of these answer choices. Letter A speaks of the agrarian economy, but this economy isn't traceable to the Persian Invasion: it preceded it. Letter B references a fact in the passage (that families received more rations), but that isn't the fundamental question answered by the passage (it isn't answered at all, though it can be inferred). Letter C, like B, mentions something in the passage (in this case, the deben), but again, that isn't the central question answered. Only D correctly states that the fundamental question answered by the passage has to do with the function of the economy of Ancient Egypt, which was not a cash economy.

18. Correct answer: **J**. Here, you *are* asked to infer. Again, inferring is deadly if not asked to do so, but in this case, you need to use your reasoning skills. Letter F can't be reasoned to, especially since meat and fish (especially meat) are more rarely distributed than grain. Letter G can't be inferred to because the *reason why* Pharaoh could trade freely is not because he is trustworthy, but because he's in charge! Letter H can't be inferred to because, again, it seems unlikely that soldiers are *more likely*

to make a temple offering than a government employee; there is no reason to believe this. However, because the deben was used at one point in Egypt's history to dole out rations (see lines 94-98), an inaccurate one could certainly result in unfair rationing for laborers.

19. Correct answer: **A**. The answer to this question can be found in the second paragraph, specifically lines 18-20 ("bread" and "sometimes fish") and lines 28-29 ("grain"). This is why the answer is A. While the other answer choices are mentioned throughout the paragraph, they are mentioned as being given out to other people, not laborers, and inferring to one of these other answers as also applying to laborers is a big mistake: if it's not in the passage, it isn't true.

20. Correct answer: **H**. This question references lines 21-22 in the passage, which speak of 10 loaves of bread and 2 jugs of beer being given to families. This is why the correct answer is H, since it is the only answer choice that mentions families at all.

Answer Explanations - Step 2

Correct Answers - Micro Questions - Passage III:

21: A
22: H
23: C
24: G
25: A
26: G
27: B
28: J
29: C
30: F

Possible Passage Map:

Passage III

HUMANITIES: This passage is adapted from the book *Basquiat: A Tribute* (©2019 by Robert Cliff-Hayes).

Born in 1960 to a Haitian father and a Puerto Rican mother, artist Jean-Michel Basquiat grew up in the cultural melting pot of New York City. A precocious child, Basquiat showed an early interest in the art world, making frequent trips to New York's Metropolitan Museum of Art (MoMa), where he was especially enamored by Pablo Picasso's *Guernica*, a macabre cubist masterpiece that depicted the horrors of the Spanish Civil War. At seven years old, Basquiat was hospitalized after an automobile accident, and he spent hours poring over the classic medical textbook *Gray's Anatomy*, in which he saw intricate images of the human form that would play a lasting influence on his work.

In high school, Basquiat became active in New York City's burgeoning 1970's graffiti subculture, collaborating with schoolmate Al Diaz under the alias "SAMO©" (pronounced same-oh). The pair produced anti-consumerist, satirical slogans under the SAMO© moniker, like "SAMO©...4 THE SO-CALLED AVANT-GARDE" and "SAMO©...4 MASS MEDIA MINDWASH" in what art critic Jeffrey Deitch would dub "disjointed street poetry."

It was just after this period that Basquiat became acquainted with Andy Warhol, an artist who would have a long-lasting impact on his career and aesthetic vision. Warhol was already a well-known name in the art world and beyond, having established himself during the pop art movement of the 1960s. Like Basquiat, Warhol had a style that was suffused with references to popular and consumer culture.

Soon, Basquiat began frequenting one of Warhol's favorite haunts, the Mudd Club, a night club in New York's TriBeCa neighborhood that attracted the most flamboyant celebrities of the 1980's, including David Byrne and Madonna, lending him access to the figures at the forefront of pop culture and alternative art. Still, this world was at least partially alien if not entirely foreign to the young artist, who struggled with homelessness and poverty.

For money, Basquiat sold postcard-sized drawings and hand-painted sweatshirts on the streets of New York, making at most a few dollars per sale. However, on the advice of his new acquaintances from the Mudd Club, particularly up-and-coming art curator Diego Cortez, Basquiat decided to transition from graffiti to canvas-based art.

Cortez took an active role in promoting Basquiat, arranging for him to be featured in a 1981 art show called "New York/New Wave" held at the P.S.1 Contemporary Art Center, then the epicenter of New York's alternative art movement. The show marked Basquiat's first exposure to major art dealers and curators, and the artist created a sensation with childlike, cartoony renderings of car crashes, airplanes, and crowns, accompanied by nonsensical text that paid homage to SAMO©. "Jean-Michel was the person in all the huge number of artists who stood out. I hadn't seen anything like it for ten years," P.S.1 founder Alanna Heiss would later recall.

During this period, Basquiat also began working on what would become one of his most recognizable pieces, an untitled work commonly referred to as *Skull*. Inspired by the *Gray's Anatomy* textbook that had fascinated him in his childhood, the evocative, vibrant painting is at once reminiscent of the X-ray of a head and a traditional African mask, referencing Basquiat's Afro-Caribbean heritage. Towards the edges of the canvas, disjointed, incoherent lettering alludes to the artist's SAMO© period. The work became the first of Basquiat's paintings to appear inside a gallery, marking a turning point in his career.

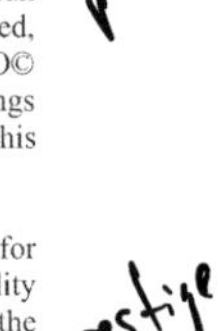

Before long, Basquiat's canvasses began to sell for $5,000 to $10,000, and the demand surpassed his ability to keep up. The artist had found success within the alternative art scene and among commercial art dealers, but he had yet to find acceptance within the art establishment—especially among the museum curators who reigned as tastemakers. That all changed in 1983, when Basquiat, just 22, became one of the youngest artists ever to be included in the Whitney Museum of American Art's prestigious Biennial Exhibition, traditionally considered the high water mark for acceptance among the arts elite.

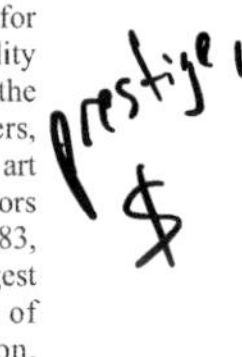

In the mid-1980s, Basquiat's relationship with Andy Warhol deepened, and the two collaborated on a show called *Warhol & Basquiat: Paintings*. Although the opening night was packed, critical reviews were overwhelmingly negative. Warhol had long faced criticism for being too overtly commercial in his work. Now Basquiat became a target as well. Vivien Raynor, the New York Times art critic, wrote of the exhibition: "the social comment implicit in [Basquiat's] previous work has now become obvious and rather silly."

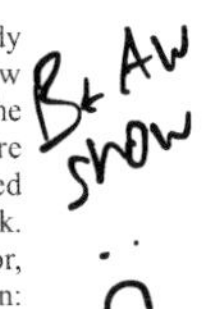

The untimely fallout from the exhibit frayed the relationship between the two artists. Tragically, no rapprochement was forthcoming, as both faced untimely deaths in the several years that followed the exhibit. Today, however, *Warhol & Basquiat: Paintings* is considered a milestone for both, but Basquiat especially: the street artist who rose from homelessness to prestige.

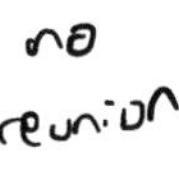

21. Based on the passage, the main reason that Basquiat became a target of criticism was primarily:

    A. his collaborative show with Andy Warhol.
    B. the fact that he lost touch with his SAMO© roots.
    C. the childlike, cartoony nature of much of his art.
    D. his failure to attend the Biennial Exhibition in person.

21. Correct answer: **A**. Is it probable that there were critics who criticized Basquiat for losing touch with his roots (choice B) or the cartoony nature of much of his art (choice C)? Of course, but *it is not stated in the passage*. This again is why you need to active read: to give yourself the time to find these answers! Answer choice D is false because there is no mention in the article that he failed to attend the exhibition. Answer choice A is correct because, according to lines 86-87, he was criticized for this show with Warhol.

22. Correct answer: **H**. This phrase is used in line 37 to describe "this world." According to the preceding sentence, "this world" is "the figures at the forefront of pop culture and alternative art." In other words, he felt detached from these more famous artists, which is why the correct answer is H. There is no indication that Basquiat felt inadequate when entering the TriBeCa neighborhood, which is why F is incorrect. Answer choice G is incorrect because there's no mention in the paragraph about Basquiat being unfamiliar with Warhol. Finally, answer J is also incorrect because, while there may have been this kind of difficulty in real life, there is no mention of it in the essay, and certainly not in the paragraph referenced by the phrase in the question.

23. Correct answer: **C**. To get this question correct, simply go back through and reread the sentences in which these words appear. When the ACT asks this kind of question, it is going to be very clear which word is being used negatively or has a negative connotation. The word "medical" (choice A) is simply being used to describe a textbook and is not used negatively. The word "advice" (choice B) has a positive connotation if anything, since the advice he gets is good and changes his career for the better. The word "rose" (choice D) also has a positive connotation, since it refers to his rising from homelessness to being a well-known artist. Lastly however, the word "target" (choice C) is correct because it refers to Basquiat being a *target* of criticism, obviously carrying a negative connotation.

24. Correct answer: **G**. This question is similar to number 23 in that you need to go back through and reread the sentences in which these words appear to determine which of them speaks to a career and/or life change by Basquiat. The word "produced" (choice F) speaks to his graffiti art, which is his first art form, so no change has taken place, which is why it is incorrect. The word "alludes" (choice H) is used to give meaning to some markings on one of Basquiat's later paintings, but it doesn't characterize a significant change in the moment. The word "faced" (choice J) has to do with Warhol's criticism and has nothing to do with Basquiat. Lastly, the word "transition" (answer choice G) is literally used to speak of his *transition* or change from graffiti to canvas art, making it the correct answer.

25. Correct answer: **A**. The mention of Basquiat's visits to the Metropolitan Museum of Art takes place in the first paragraph. In fact, in the same sentence that speaks of his visiting the museum, it says that he did so as a child. This is why the correct answer is A. It could be true that the automobile accident mentioned in the paragraph happened on the way to or from the museum, but it never says so, which is why D is incorrect. It's also of course likely true that he never graffiti'd the outside walls of the museum, but again, the passage never states this, which is why B is also incorrect. Lastly, letter C is contradicted by the passage itself, which states in line 7 that Basquiat was enamored by a macabre art piece.

26. Correct answer: **G**. Basquiat's *Skull* is described in the seventh paragraph (lines 59-70). Letter F might be tempting, but the scribbling at the edges is *not* a reference to his "cultural heritage", but rather to his earlier graffiti days. The same is true of H and J; both of these answer choices are a true detail about *Skull*, but neither is a reference to his cultural heritage. Option G, on the other hand, is correct: the fact that it looks like an African mask (line 65) is a reference to his cultural heritage (specifically, his "Afro-Caribbean heritage").

27. Correct answer: **B**. If you remember, it is towards the end of the passage that Basquiat has critics. Specifically, lines 90-92 give a quote from a critic, which states that the aspect of Basquiat's art that has "become obvious and rather silly" is his "social comment", in other words, his social message; this is why the correct answer is B. Answer choices A, C, and D all refer to true details of Basquiat's art, but none of them is spoken of in the passage as the target of criticism.

28. Correct answer: **J**. Usually, you might think you know the meaning of the word *haunts*. However, 99% of the time, such words are going to be used with a meaning that is different than the most obvious definition. This is true of this word as well. As it is used in the passage, it is a noun, not a verb, and has nothing to do with a place being haunted by a ghost (which is why H is incorrect). The fact that the word is used in the passage as a noun and not a verb also eliminates answer choice G, which speaks of *how* Andy Warhol enters a room; just because the sentence in which it is used mentions Andy Warhol, that doesn't mean that the answer has to do with him! Answer choice F is incorrect because there is no indication that the word *haunts* is being used to describe the nature of New York city business. Lastly, the correct answer is J; the word *haunts* is being used to refer to a place or a club where intriguing artists gather.

29. Correct answer: **C**. Because there are frequent references to Basquiat never forgetting his earlier days as a graffiti artist, answer choice A is incorrect (he never "dismisses" his graffiti period). Answer choice B seems tempting. However, his later artwork is *new*, even if there are small references to his graffiti days. Answer choice D is false because Basquiat did, in the eyes of the author of the article, become famous; literally the last word used to describe him is "prestige" (line 99). This leaves C, which is correct: Basquiat's later work is "memorial" in the sense that it merely pays tribute in small ways to his earlier period (see lines 66-68, for example).

30. Correct answer: **F**. Here, the question itself asks you to make an inference, meaning you need to put pieces of evidence together to reach a likely conclusion. There is no mention that Warhol had significant influence on Basquiat's fame; though they had a show together, Basquiat was already growing in fame if not already famous; this is why answer choice G is incorrect. Letter H is incorrect because the book *Grey's Anatomy* is mentioned twice: first, in the first paragraph as being read by Basquiat after his accident, but then secondly as an influence on his piece of art called *Skull*; in other words, it was useful later in life. Answer choice J is incorrect because there is no comparison of Basquiat to Pablo Picasso in the passage; if anything, it would be the other way around, since Basquiat was inspired by Picasso. Lastly, this leaves answer choice F, which is correct because lines 44-58 speak of Cortez helping Basquiat to not only decide to begin painting canvases, but he helped him to be in his first ever art show.

Correct Answers - Medium Questions - Passage IV:

31: B
32: J
33: D
34: H
35: A
36: H
37: A
38: J
39: B
40: F

Possible Passage Map:

Passage IV

NATURAL SCIENCE: This passage is adapted from the article "The Science of Spice" by Alexander Painter (©2018 by Food Science Quarterly).

Capsaicin ($C_{18}H_{27}NO_3$) is a crystalline compound found in the fruit of the genus *Capsicum* (peppers) that causes the well-known burning sensation in culinary dishes. The molar teeth of mammals can destroy the seeds, thus natural selection may have led to an increase in capsaicin, deterring mammals from eating them. Birds, which can better tolerate the sensation, disperse the plant as the seeds pass through their digestive tract intact.

Capsaicin can dissolve in fats and alcohol, but not in water. Its chemical structure has three components: an aromatic ring, a shorter lateral chain of hydrocarbons, and an organic amide bond that connects the two. The functional groups in capsaicin that cause chemical reactions are attached to the opposite sides of the double carbon bonds in the ring, making it a trans isomer. Since its extraction in 1876, researchers have studied how this colorless, odorless substance interacts with mammals. As capsaicin is an alkaloid, its unique effects on mammals give it potential as a medicine.

In various studies, capsaicin acts as an antioxidant, anticancer, and anti-inflammatory agent that can speed up metabolism and suppress the build-up of fat in our bodies. When applied to the skin, it has been shown to relieve chronic pain from different types of neuropathy and arthritis, as well as pain from rashes and psoriasis. Some of these effects are due to capsaicin's ability to bind to vanilloid receptor 1 (TRPV1), which is found in the sensory neurons. The hydroxyl (OH) group on the fourth position of the ring is especially important for its ability to bind to TRPV1. However this same binding action that results in relief can also bring pain. A heat-sensitive subunit of TRPV1 reacts to the binding by producing pain, inflammation, and a localized sense of heat. The effect is even more pronounced however when capsaicin is taken in orally because it is absorbed and reaches maximum concentration quicker than a topical cream.

Capsaicin belongs to a family of secondary metabolites known as capsaicinoids, and is the most abundant in this family, followed by dihydrocapsaicin as second most abundant. These are also the two most potent, and make up as much as 90% of the capsaicinoids found in chili peppers. There are over twenty in total. While they all share the three chemical components as described above, their chemical differences lie in the structure of the lateral chain. The compounds vary in the number of carbons in the chain (9-11), and in the number and position of double carbon bonds. For example, homocapsaicin and capsaicin have one double bond, while several others have none at all (such as nordihydrocapsaicin, homodihydrocapsaicin, and dihydrocapsaicin). Regardless of the compound, all are synthesized in peppers.

The enzyme capsaicin synthase produces capsaicin and its analogs by combining two chemicals: vanillylamine and fatty acid chains (formed from the amino acids valine or leucine). This reaction is called condensation. As the fruit matures, more capsaicinoids are produced until 40-50 days into fruit development, after which the concentration declines as the compounds degrade into secondary metabolites. The level of production is not fixed, as the concentration can vary with genetics and environmental factors. For example, water stress increases capsaicin levels. A certain fatty acid (8-methyl-noneic acid) is the limiting factor for how much of these compounds can be produced. Capsaicinoids are often produced in laboratory settings by adding the enzyme to chlorinated versions of the fatty acids and amines. Synthesis can also be achieved using traditional chemical methods, but is less effective. Using enzymes, the percent yield of capsaicinoids can be as high as 70%.

Capsaicinoids are not the only compounds in peppers that can bind to the TRPV1 receptors. Capsinoids can also do this, but do not interact with the heat-sensitive receptor subunit. Because of this, capsinoids (e.g. capsiate, dihydrocapsiate and nordihydrocapsiate) lack the pungency and sensory irritation of their analogues, but have the same beneficial effects as discussed above. Instead of an amide bond in the lateral chain, an ester bond at the same position, which lacks nitrogen and is more structurally flexible, holds these compounds. However, capsinoids are found in only a few varieties of peppers, and they exist in much lower concentrations than capsaicinoids. They are also more difficult to create in a laboratory setting because of a terminal methyl (CH_3) group in addition to the double oxygen bond found in both families of compounds.

31. According to paragraphs 2 and 3, the primary purpose of the extraction of capsaicin in 1876 and subsequent research is for:

A. veterinary purposes.
B. medical purposes.
C. culinary purposes.
D. topical purposes.

32. In the fourth paragraph (lines 38-53), the author most clearly:

F. argues for further research into the chemical differences between various capsaicinoids.
G. differentiates various capsaicinoids by the number and position of double carbon bonds.
H. lists and describes various capsaicinoids from least to most potent.
J. highlights both the differences between and similari

Step 2 32

31. Correct answer: **B**. If you reread paragraph 2, you will hear a lot about the chemical nature of capsaicin. The last sentence, however, speaks of the study of this chemical on mammals and thus its "potential as a medicine" (line 19). In addition, paragraph 3 is entirely about the use of capsaicin as a medicine. This is why the correct answer is B: medical purposes. Letter A would be tempting if you concluded that the study of capsaicin on or with mammals meant it was for animals only (thus, veterinary), but the ultimate purpose again is for people, not animals. Although capsaicin is grown in peppers, the purpose of paragraphs 2 and 3 is not to discuss how to cook the peppers (thus, culinary), which is why choice C is incorrect. Lastly, choice D is incorrect because, although paragraph 3 speaks of capsaicin being applied to the skin (thus, topical), that is part of a bigger medical discussion.

32. Correct answer: **J**. Hopefully, you are learning how to active read to as to give yourself the time to reread this paragraph. If you simply reread the first sentence of the paragraph and see that it has to do with "capsaicinoids", you'll have a hard time finding the right answer, since all four answer choices mention "capsaicinoids" in one way or another. The paragraph, upon rereading, seems to mention what some capsaicinoids have in common, and where some differ; this is why answer choice J is correct. Again, while the others mention capsaicinoids, they are all incorrect because the main idea of the fourth paragraph isn't to argue for further research (choice F), differentiate capsaicinoids by double bonds (choice G), or list capsaicinoids in order of potency (choice H).

33. Correct answer: **D**. If you answered number 31 above well, you've probably already reread this paragraph. The second half of this paragraph in particular is about the heat sensation of having capsaicin on your skin and in your mouth. The phrase "the effect that is even more pronounced" is referring to this heat effect in the mouth compared to the skin. This is why D is the correct answer. The other answer choices speak to the feeling of eating capsaicin or rubbing it on the skin, etc., but none of them truly speak to what this particular phrase is referring to: the feeling of heat in the mouth versus the skin.

34. Correct answer: **H**. Birds and mammals and their effect on the spread of pepper plants is mentioned in paragraph 1, which states that mammals destroy the seeds of pepper plants with their teeth (thus, making the seeds spicy deters this from happening), but birds eat the seeds, which pass through their digestive tract without being crushed or damaged (in other words, birds help the population spread). Letter F is thus incorrect because birds, as was just stated, are *good* for the population spread of the seeds. Letter G is incorrect because it says that mammals help the spread of the population, but as has been said, their teeth crush the seeds when consumed. Letter J is incorrect because it says *both* of these wrong things. However, letter choice H correctly states that peppers benefit from birds, but not from mammals.

35. Correct answer: **A**. In paragraph 6, you learn that capsinoids (which is stated are different from capsaicinoids) "do not interact with the heat-sensitive receptor subunit" (lines 75-76). In other words, they are less spicy. This eliminates answer choices B and C (which both state that capsinoids are "more spicy"). Letter choice D is mostly true, except for the detail about capsinoids being "not as medically beneficial," which is contradicted by line 79, which states that capsinoids "have the same beneficial effects" as capsaicinoids. This is why A is the correct answer: it correctly compares capsinoids to capsaicinoids by getting correct the three details: capsinoids are less spicy, just as medically beneficial, and more difficult to create in a lab (lines 85-86).

36. Correct answer: **H**. Again, the third paragraph discusses the medical benefits of capsaicin. Specifically, lines 30-31 state that "this same binding action that results in relief can also bring pain." It relieves pain, but also causes pain. This is why the correct answer is H: it is the only option that highlights this *bittersweet* application of capsaicin to the skin. Letters F and G are incorrect because they both state that capsaicin does not relieve pain, but that is not true. Letter J is incorrect because it falsely states that capsaicin has no side effects.

37. Correct answer: **A**. Again, hopefully you have active read to give yourself the time to reread paragraph five. Or, perhaps whatever you wrote in your Passage Map (meaning, in the margins next to the paragraph) will suffice. Upon rereading paragraph 5, you might notice that it is mostly about how capsaicinoids are produced in fruit (aka peppers) and in the laboratory. This is why the correct answer is A, since it says that paragraph five is about producing capsaicinoids naturally and artificially (aka, in peppers and a lab). Choice B is incorrect because the paragraph isn't about comparing the spice level of capsaicinoids between natural and lab production. Choice C is incorrect because the paragraph is about more than peppers' capabilities to produce capsaicinoids (and the paragraph is about how different factors affect how much capsaicin is produced; it isn't "fixed" at all). Choice D is incorrect because, though the paragraph mentions the enzyme capsaicin synthase, it is only mentioned briefly and certainly isn't the main purpose of the paragraph.

38. Correct answer: **J**. Like the previous question, hopefully you have active read to give yourself the time to reread paragraph two. Or, perhaps whatever you wrote in your Passage Map (meaning, in the margins next to the paragraph) will suffice for a summary. Upon rereading the second paragraph, you may see that it is about the chemical structure of capsaicin, but then how it was extracted for study in mammals for medicinal purposes. This is almost exactly what letter choice J says, which is why it is correct. There are elements of truth in F, but it is incorrect in that the paragraph does not "describe in detail" capsaicin's medical capabilities (that's the next paragraph). Choice G is false because the paragraph makes no warning of the chemical's spice level. Choice H is also based in partial truth, but paragraph two certainly doesn't "critique" modern understanding of capsaicin.

39. Correct answer: **B**. The correct inference here will come from a careful reread of most of paragraph five, which speaks about the various factors that affect the production of capsaicinoids in peppers. First, the paragraph states that capsaicinoids are

produced "until 40-50 days into fruit development" (line 59). This eliminates answer choices C and D, which speak of watering "before the first sign of fruit growth." The paragraph also says that capsaicinoids will increase with "water stress" (line 64); in other words, with overwatering. This eliminates answer choice A, which speaks of "underwatering." These two reasons are why answer choice B is correct, which correctly states that the peppers should be overwatered during the first 40-50 days of fruit development.

40. Correct answer: **F**. The "family of secondary metabolites known as capsaicinoids" is discussed throughout paragraph four (see lines 38-39). The paragraph mentions that there are more than 20 of them, eliminating answer choice G. Letter H is incorrect because it falsely states that capsaicin and homocapsaicin have multiple double bonds (the passage says they only have one double bond; see line 49). Letter J is incorrect because capsaicin is never mentioned as being uniquely spicy. Letter F is correct because, as we've said before, it says that there are more than twenty capsaicinoids that have different chemical structures and makeup.

Correct Answers - Micro and Medium Questions - Passage I:

1: D
2: G
3: C
4: F
5: D
6: H
7: B
8: J
9: A
10: J

Possible Passage Map:

Passage I

LITERARY NARRATIVE: This passage is adapted from F. Scott Fitzgerald's *The Great Gatsby*.

Nick Carraway is at a house party in New York with his friend Jordan Baker, and they enter into conversation about driving after a near accident.

I began to like New York, the racy, adventurous feel of it at night, and the satisfaction that the constant flicker of men and women and machines gives to the restless eye. I liked to walk up Fifth Avenue and pick out romantic women from the crowd and imagine that in a few minutes I was going to enter into their lives, and no one would ever know or disapprove. Sometimes, in my mind, I followed them to their apartments on the corners of hidden streets, and they turned and smiled back at me before they faded through a door into warm darkness. At the enchanted metropolitan twilight I felt a haunting loneliness sometimes, and felt it in others—poor young clerks who loitered in front of windows waiting until it was time for a solitary restaurant dinner—young clerks in the dusk, wasting the most poignant moments of night and life.

Again at eight o'clock, when the dark lanes of the Forties were lined five deep with throbbing taxicabs, bound for the theatre district, I felt a sinking in my heart. Forms leaned together in the taxis as they waited, and voices sang, and there was laughter from unheard jokes, and lighted cigarettes made unintelligible circles inside. Imagining that I, too, was hurrying towards gaiety and sharing their intimate excitement, I wished them well.

For a while I lost sight of Jordan Baker, and then in midsummer I found her again. At first I was flattered to go places with her, because she was a golf champion, and everyone knew her name. Then it was something more. I wasn't actually in love, but I certainly felt a sort of tender curiosity. The bored haughty face that she turned to the world concealed something—most affectations conceal something eventually, even though they don't in the beginning—and one day I found what it was.

When we were on a house-party together up in Warwick, she left a borrowed car out in the rain with the top down, and then lied about it—and suddenly I remembered the story about her that had eluded me that night at Daisy's. At her first big golf tournament there was a row that nearly reached the newspapers—a suggestion that she had moved her ball from a bad lie in the semifinal round. The thing approached the proportions of a scandal—then died away. A caddy retracted his statement, and the only other witness admitted that he might have been mistaken. The incident and the name had remained together in my mind.

Jordan Baker instinctively avoided clever, shrewd men, and now I saw that this was because she felt safer on a plane where any divergence from a code would be thought impossible. She was incurably dishonest. She wasn't able to endure being at a disadvantage and, given this unwillingness, I suppose she had begun dealing in subterfuges when she was very young in order to keep that cool, insolent smile turned to the world and yet satisfy the demands of her hard, jaunty body.

It made no difference to me. Dishonesty in a woman is a thing you never blame deeply—I was casually sorry, and then I forgot. It was on that same house-party that we had a curious conversation about driving a car. It started because she passed so close to some workmen that our fender flicked a button on one man's coat.

"You're a rotten driver," I protested. "Either you ought to be more careful, or you oughtn't to drive at all."

"I am careful."

"No, you're not."

"Well, other people are," she said lightly.

"What's that got to do with it?"

"They'll keep out of my way," she insisted. "It takes two to make an accident."

"Suppose you met somebody just as careless as yourself."

"I hope I never will," she answered. "I hate careless people. That's why I like you."

Her grey, sun-strained eyes stared straight ahead, but she had deliberately shifted our relations, and for a moment I thought I loved her. But I am slow-thinking and full of interior rules that act as brakes on my desires, and I knew that first I had to get myself definitely out of that tangle back home. I'd been writing letters once a week and signing them: "Love, Nick," and all I could think of was how, when that certain girl played tennis, a faint moustache of perspiration appeared on her upper lip. Nevertheless there was a vague understanding that had to be tactfully broken off before I was free.

Everyone suspects himself of at least one of the cardinal virtues, and this is mine: I am one of the few honest people that I have ever known.

1. It can reasonably be inferred that how much time, if any, has passed between time spent "with Jordan Baker" (line 27) and the nights out described in paragraphs 1 and 2?

A. None
B. Three or four hours
C. One or two days
D. Weeks o

1. Correct answer: **D**. The correct answer to this question is not found in the first couple of paragraphs, but rather in lines 25 and 26, which say, "For *a while* I lost sight of Jordan Baker, and then *in midsummer* I found her again." This implies that the time that has passed has been significant, not merely hours or days. This is why the correct answer is D, which correctly states that weeks or months have most likely passed.

2. Correct answer: **G**. If you reread the paragraph that this question references (lines 73-83), you will see that the narrator has a relationship with a girl (at least an implied one, which is why he signs his letter to her "Love, Nick"). This relationship he wants to break off, which eliminates answer choices F and H. However, he also says that he thinks he might love Jordan Baker, which implies he wants a relationship with her (which is also the clear motivation for why he needs to break things off with the other girl "back home"). This eliminates choice J because he does want a relationship with Baker. This is why G is correct, because only choice G identifies his feelings for the two girls correctly.

3. Correct answer: **C**. In line 65, Jordan Baker says, "Well, other people are," which serves as an excuse for her to keep driving dangerously. She is clearly not cautious, which eliminates choice A. She also is hoping that other people drive well, so she certainly doesn't distrust them; this eliminates answer choice B. While you might infer that her wealth will save her if she has a wreck or crash, the passage doesn't state it, which is why D is incorrect. Answer choice C is correct because it rightly says that the quote reveals her sense of self-importance: she does what she wants.

4. Correct answer: **F**. The "row that reached the newspapers" was an event in which she was accused of cheating. However, if she is "incurably dishonest", then it is likely that she actually did cheat. This is why F is correct: the "row" (cheating) was likely based on a true event that took place.

5. Correct answer: **D**. If you put A or B, you are making good guesses (aka, you are *inferring*). However, making *good guesses* leads to wrong answers. The question is this: which of these answer choices is definitely correct? Well, two paragraphs are dedicated to the narrator's life out on the town, where he enjoys different details, etc. This is why D is correct.

6. Correct answer: **H**. Getting this answer correct is 100% about using your time to go and find this little detail. Hopefully you used active reading to give yourself enough time over the questions to find these kinds of things. Simply, lines 55-56 state this: "Dishonesty in a woman is a thing you never blame deeply." This is why letter H is correct; there is no mention of the narrator withholding blame for her selfishness, taste in music, and certainly not her poor driving.

7. Correct answer: **B**. It is stated in lines 46-47 that Jordan Baker does *not* like men who are clever or shrewd. This instantly eliminates choice C. It also says that "she felt safer on a plane where any divergence from a code would be thought impossible" (lines 47-49). In other words, she wants stability, which is why choice A is incorrect and why choice B is, in fact, the correct answer. Though she herself is dishonest, she wants the opposite of dishonesty in a man, and there's no mention of her wanting him to be handsome (this is why D is incorrect).

8. Correct answer: **J**. The narrator mentions the look on Jordan Baker's face and what it means in lines 30-31, which say, "The bored haughty face that she turned to the world concealed something…" In other words, she is hiding something, which is why the correct answer is J.

9. Correct answer: **A**. Again, the meanings or usages of phrases or words are rarely how they seem to be out of context. You may think, "On a plane means flying through the sky," but that's not how this phrase is used in context (thus, B is false). In context, this sentence says (in abbreviated form), "Jordan Baker avoided shrewd men because she felt safer *on a plane* where any divergence from a code would be thought impossible." Here, on a plane does not mean a flat surface (thus, answer C is incorrect), and nor does it mean a higher level of thought (making D incorrect as well). Instead, this sentence is talking about the kinds of people that Jordan Baker needs to be around, which is why the answer is A: a group of people.

10. Correct answer: **J**. This is a bit of a macro question that requires an understanding of Jordan Baker's character. We know from the passage (and from thinking through previous questions) that Jordan Baker is selfish, a liar, and unconcerned with the needs of other people. Letter F is not about Jordan Baker, nor is it something seen from Jordan Baker's point of view, so it is incorrect. The same thing can be said about G and H: neither of them is about her or concerned with her point of view. Instead, the correct answer is J: she is the one who at one time borrowed a car and left the top down in the rain, a selfish act.

Answer Explanations - Step 3

Correct Answers:

Passage I:

1: A
2: H
3: D
4: F
5: A
6: H
7: C
8: G
9: D
10: H

Possible Passage Map (Passage I):

Passage I

LITERARY NARRATIVE: Passage A is adapted from the short story *The Dead* (1914) by James Joyce. Passage B is adapted from the book *Birth Night* (©2023 by Clare Josephs).

Passage A by James Joyce

She stopped, choking with sobs, and, overcome by emotion, flung herself face downward on the bed, sobbing in the quilt. Gabriel held her hand for a moment longer, irresolutely, and then, shy of intruding on her grief, let it fall gently and walked quietly to the window.

She was fast asleep.

Gabriel, leaning on his elbow, looked for a few moments unresentfully on her tangled hair and half-open mouth, listening to her deep-drawn breath. So she had had that romance in her life: a man had died for her sake. It hardly pained him now to think how poor a part he, her husband, had played in her life. He watched her while she slept, as though he and she had never lived together as man and wife. His curious eyes rested long upon her face and on her hair: and, as he thought of what she must have been then, in that time of her first girlish beauty, a strange, friendly pity for her entered his soul. He did not like to say even to himself that her face was no longer beautiful, but he knew that it was no longer the face for which Michael Furey had braved death.

The air of the room chilled his shoulders. He stretched himself cautiously along under the sheets and lay down beside his wife. One by one, they were all becoming shades. Better pass boldly into that other world, in the full glory of some passion, than fade and wither dismally with age. He thought of how she who lay beside him had locked in her heart for so many years that image of her lover's eyes when he had told her that he did not wish to live.

Generous tears filled Gabriel's eyes. He had never felt like that himself towards any woman, but he knew that such a feeling must be love. The tears gathered more thickly in his eyes and in the partial darkness he imagined he saw the form of a young man standing under a dripping tree. Other forms were near. His soul had approached that region where dwell the vast hosts of the dead. He was conscious of, but could not apprehend, their wayward and flickering existence. His own identity was fading out into a grey impalpable world: the solid world itself, which these dead had one time reared and lived in, was dissolving and dwindling.

Passage B by Clare Josephs

Given how removed Manuel had been from not only his family, but the traditions and religion of his family, it seemed unlikely that this loose "celebration" of *Dia de los Muertos*, or Day of the Dead, had any authenticity beyond the name. He recalled what he could remember about his father. There was not much there: a howling laugh, a reddened face, a farewell and a suppressed tear.

"Goodbye Manuel. Until we meet again, in this life or the next."

Had there been a crack in his voice on the words *meet again*?

Manuel trusted me with that detail, spurred in his mind in no small part from the alcohol in the cheap, canned margaritas we split 50-50. But there were more; Manuel had never spoken like this. He was quiet and reserved, observant and data driven, and smart as all get out. For all that, he was also a leaf blown by the wind; no direction, no desire, no passion to speak of, no future to fill; his compass, so to speak, was broken or missing.

Now, memories of the chocolate cake of his grandmother on his mother's side was made manifest. She refused to write down the recipe, he said. For her, that was a waste of time and a waste of ink. A little flour, an egg or two, some melted chocolate and an icing from sugar and cream cheese and more (and more and more!) chocolate. The person too helpless to bake such a simple cake would still be helpless with a detailed recipe in hand, she said.

His mother had tried to recreate the recipe for his birthday each and every year until he turned 18 and left for college. Now, for his birthday, he wasn't home.

"Today's your birthday?" I asked.

"Maybe," he replied. "Nobody knows for sure. Some say November 1st, some November 2nd. It was the stroke of midnight between the two." He paused. "'The boy who cracked open the day of the dead,' they would say."

I tried a loose "happy birthday," but Manuel did not hear me. He was lost in his thoughts. Was there something of his destiny tied up in his birthday? He, the boy who bridges the saints in heaven and those that long to get there in need of prayer. The sun was setting; birth-night was encroaching for this, my fairly new friend. It wasn't until ten or more minutes later, once the shadows of the bent and broken blinds crept up his chin and shadowed his face, that he finally broke the silence through the smile of a small child.

"Can I borrow some flour, and perhaps a few cups of sugar?"

1. In Passage A, as Gabriel is watching his wife as she sleeps he is:

A. contemplating her present and past relationships.
B. lamenting the depth of their closeness.
C. growing jealous of the man he used to be for her.
D. deepening his love of her by truly seeing her for the first time in a long time.

Step 3 43

Passage I (Literary Narrative):

1. Correct answer: **A**. Gabriel's wife falls asleep in line 6. The question is simply what he does in the next paragraphs while she is sleeping. He is certainly thinking, about both himself (lines 30-31) and about his wife and her past relationships (lines 17-20, 26-29, etc.). This is why A is the correct answer. Choice B speaks of the depth of their relationship, but there is no evidence that it is deep at all (but quite the opposite). Choice C is incorrect because his reflections on his wife's past relationship is not a relationship she had with him, but with someone else. Choice D is also incorrect; you might try to *infer* that he is falling more in love with her, but there is no evidence of that at all and it is never stated that this is the case.

2. Correct answer: **H**. Your reasoning through these answer choices is almost identical to the previous question; there is a lot of overlap between these two questions. First, the phrase "such a feeling must be love" refers to the way a man used to feel about his wife before his death; it's not about Gabriel. This eliminates answer choices G and J, which emphasize the depth of Gabriel's love for his wife. Letter F might be a tempting wrong answer because *it could very well be true based on the passage*. However, this question, again, does NOT ask you to infer to a likely or probable answer. The correct answer is H because they share an attraction (they are married, after all), but there is something missing (Gabriel admits he's not in love with her the way her previous boyfriend had been).

3. Correct answer: **D**. Go back and read the word in context. The sentence in which this word appears reads like this: "His own identity was fading out into a grey *impalpable* world: the solid world itself...was dissolving and dwindling." This world he is settling into is not bland or motionless, that isn't the indication (thus, A and B are incorrect). It certainly is not a colorful world; it even says it is "grey" (which is why C is incorrect). Choice D is correct because it says that this word means unintelligible; in other words, it can't be understood or figured out.

4. Correct answer: **F**. Hopefully, you used some active reading to save yourself enough time to reread this paragraph to get it correct. In this paragraph, Manuel is lost in thought, having previously been described as lost in life. By the end of the paragraph, he starts to smile before indicating that he is going to bake the cake of his grandmother. Choice G seems tempting because it starts off sounding true, but it ends by saying that the cake baking "catches him off guard." Whatever that is supposed to mean, that is not true here. Choice H is more descriptive of how Manuel is at the beginning of the paragraph, but is missing the character change he goes through. Choice J flips the truth and is the opposite of the correct answer (it indicates a negative character change). Choice F, on the other hand, is correct because it rightly says that Manuel goes from wandering with no direction to embracing a moment of meaning, which is exactly what the paragraph is about.

5. Correct answer: **A**. The quote referred to in the question is muttered by Manuel's father as he was leaving the house. Why he is leaving is never said, but clearly it is a difficult memory (especially because lines 51-52 indicate a crack in his voice; in other words, he is nearly crying). This is why the answer choice is A: it is a painful memory. The other answer choices all in their own way indicate that the quote is somehow a positive thing in some way, which is not true and why they are all false. You might think that answer choice D is the truth because he might be motivated by the quote. Again, if you're thinking like that, you are *inferring* when the question isn't asking you to. Just because it *could* be true doesn't make it true for the purposes of the ACT.

6. Correct answer: **H**. There is no indication that the narrator is asking Manuel any questions, making G incorrect. Answer choice J is also incorrect because it is contradicted by the passage itself (Manuel is described as quiet and certainly not talkative in line 56). The most alluring wrong answer choice is F, but it is also incorrect; while the passage indicates that the margaritas have something to do with it, the conversation is entirely about ancestors and is taking place on the Day of the Dead. This is why the correct answer choice is H: the day on which the discussion takes place.

7. Correct answer: **C**. Here, the word "recreation" is referring to creating something again, of course. The cake is discussed between lines 61 and 69, in which it is described as very difficult to recreate, so much so that the mother can't even do it (though she must come close). The grandmother thinks any good cook should be able to make it, however. Choice A is tempting, but there is no indication that the cake was made only once by the grandmother, which is why it is incorrect. Choice B says that making the cake is simple, which is just not true according to the passage. Choice D states that making the cake is easier for females; however, there is no indication in the passage that women can make it better or easier than men can. Choice C, on the other hand, correctly states that the cake is difficult to make, even though his grandmother thought it was easy.

8. Correct answer: **G**. Although the question says, "Compared to Passage A," this question is really about Passage B alone and what happens to a character within. Manuel, as has already been thought about to answer question 4 correctly, has a change for the better, eliminating choices H and J. Choice F is incorrect because he doesn't fall in love, but begins to have hope for a new future. This is why G is the correct answer.

9. Correct answer: **D**. Where these two passages overlap is that they have a theme or description of the afterlife. Again, the question itself references Passage B, but really it is about Passage A and how they are described there. If you answered question number 3 correctly, you probably already know that the dead are described as grey; they can't really be seen or figured out. This is why D is correct; the other answer choices offer a false description of the dead in Passage A.

10. Correct answer: **H**. Now we get into the true overlap of the two stories and what they have in common; they both have something to say about living life. It certainly isn't F; that may be true of one of the characters in Passage A, but it isn't true of anyone in Passage B. Choice G is actually contradicted by Passage A (lines 24-26), which makes it incorrect. Choice J states something true about Passage B and family traditions, but there is nothing about family traditions in Passage A, making it incorrect. However, answer choice H rightly states that life should be lived to the fullest, an idea present in both passages, making it the correct answer.

Passage III:

21: C
22: F
23: B
24: J
25: C
26: G
27: B
28: F
29: B
30: J

Possible Passage Map (Passage III):

Passage III

HUMANITIES: Passage A is adapted from the book *The World's Dialects* (©2014 by Keegan K Smith). Passage B is adapted from the book *A Blend of Cultures* (©1999 by Dr. DR Prouty).

Passage A by Keegan K Smith

Spanish evolves

During the reign of the Catholic Monarchs Queen Isabel and King Ferdinand, the Castile dialect from the north-central part of modern-day Spain became the official language of the country. Since its spread to Latin America through colonialism, the language has evolved into many dialects, with differences in both vocabulary and grammar. The meanings of words, verb conjugations, and pronunciations between Latin American and Castilian Spanish are distinct, as are the dialects spoken among Latin American countries.

Spain vs. L.A.

One of the clearest differences is the use of the plural form of 'you'. In Spain, the word 'vosotros' is used far more than 'ustedes'. In Latin America, the opposite is true. Both major dialects share the same word for the informal form (tú), as well as the singular formal form of 'you' (usted). However the word 'vos' is used instead of 'tú' in Argentina, Paraguay, and Uruguay. Outside of these nations, the word is seldom used aside for close friends or for those of certain social classes. For direct object pronouns that are male, Latin American nations use 'lo' while those in Spain use 'le', the latter of which is an indirect object pronoun in Latin America.

verb conjug.

Verb conjugations largely follow the same linguistic patterns, with one major exception. Contrasted with the simple past tense (e.g. "I ate"), the present perfect is used to describe a past action that continues into the present, or has happened recently (e.g. "I have eaten"). Aside from Spain, Latin American nations in the Andes Mountains prefer to use the present perfect, while other Spanish-speaking nations in the Americas (e.g. México, Costa Rica) often use the former. The conjugation between the simple past and present perfect is different. For example, infinite forms of verbs that end in –ar end instead with –ado in the present perfect.

lisp

same words w/ diff. meanings

The idea of the "Spanish lisp" is rooted in differences in pronunciation. Words that contain the letter *c* followed by the letters *e* or *i* are spoken with an 's' sound in Latin America, but in Spain it is a 'th' sound. Suffixes in Spanish can carry different meanings depending on the dialect, even if the spelling of a word is exactly the same. For example, the word 'lapicero' translates to pencil in Spain, but is a ballpoint pen in the Central America and Andes regions, and a pencil holder in Argentina. The same can be said for verbs, with some having vulgar meanings in some regions but not in others. Some vocabulary differences between Castilian and Latin American dialects are blatant, with entirely different words in Spanish referring to the same object in English. For example, the word for computer in Spain is the masculine noun (el ordenador) while it is feminine in Latin America (la computadora).

Passage B by Dr DR Prouty

Latin → Spanish

The evolution from Latin to Spanish began when the former language was introduced to the Iberian Peninsula roughly two millennia ago. The vocabulary of indigenous peoples there merged with the language to become Vulgar Latin, which was later supplemented with thousands of Arabic words spoken by the Moors. As Queen Isabel and King Ferdinand drove them out of Spain, the monarchs used the Royal Spanish Academy to establish the 'Castellano' dialect as a uniform language in both their own country and abroad as they colonized what is now Latin America.

forcing Spanish

The Spanish language itself was used as a tool of the empire. Until the 17th century, Spanish religious officials spoke and attempted conversion in local indigenous languages. From then on until the end of the 18th century, indigenous languages were suppressed and the Spanish language was used to convert the indigenous people of the Americas to Catholicism. As the Spanish Empire neared collapse in the 19th century, bilingualism throughout Latin America prevailed. When the U.S. acquired the southwestern US from Spain, they tried to eradicate both indigenous and Spanish languages through forced schooling. While some languages and cultures were lost or nearly so, ultimately they did not succeed.

use of Span. among indig.

From the southwestern U.S. to Chile, many indigenous peoples still speak their language while also speaking Spanish. The identity of Mestizaje, a Latin American term for the mixing of Spanish and Indigenous cultures, came into being. To a limited extent, Spanish and Native Americans combined their bloodlines, but this was limited by the social caste system. Most of the cultural fusion came from intermarrying tribes that used Spanish as their lingua franca, a language that makes it possible for speakers of two different native languages to communicate.

indig. words into span.

Many of the Spanish dialects throughout Latin America have adopted words and concepts from various indigenous languages, including Quechúa (the Andean region), Maya, and Nahuatl (Aztec language). Many Latin American names of fruits and vegetables are derived from these languages. For example, 'el chocolate' is derived from the Nahuatl word 'xocolatl', and the Spanish word for corncob (el elote) comes from the Nahuatl word 'elotl'. Conversely, those that still speak their native languages have mixed words from Spanish into their vocabulary.

Passage III (Humanities):

21. Correct answer: **C**. There is no blame being placed on anyone; the essay isn't accusatory, which is why answer choice A is incorrect. Choice B states that there has been little change in the Spanish language, however, Passage A is about exactly the opposite, making this answer choice incorrect. Answer choice D says that the first two paragraphs are about differences between Castilian and the Spanish monarchy's preferred form of Spanish...but these are the same thing, so there are no differences between them! This is why choice C is the correct answer: the purpose of the first two paragraphs is to introduce the spread of Spanish and how it has differed.

22. Correct answer: **F**. We are told in lines 35-38 that words that have a *ci* or *ce* in them are pronounced differently in Spain and Latin America. Out of the four answer choices, only choice F (*lapicero*) features this pair of letters.

23. Correct answer: **B**. To get this question correct, you have to likely save yourself enough time with active reading to go find it! The correct answer is simply B because it says so in lines 6-7. Castilian Spanish has spread to Latin America, but from there there have been many changes.

24. Correct answer: **J**. Answer choice F is false because that is true about persons speaking Spanish in Spain, not the Andes region (line 38). Choice G is also incorrect because "vosotros" is also true of persons in Spain (line 12). Choice H is incorrect because it is also something spoken by those in Spain (line 21). Choice J is correct because lines 28-34 state that those in the Andes region prefer the "present perfect" (line 29), which is what using -ado is (line 34).

25. Correct answer: **C**. Lines 82-85 speak of intermarrying tribes using Spanish as a mutual way to bridge their language gap. This is why the correct answer is C. Answer choice A is incorrect because this idea is never stated in the passage, which is also true of answer choices B and D: all are false because they are not stated in the passage.

26. Correct answer: **G**. The final two paragraphs of Passage B (lines 76-97) are entirely about how Spanish and native languages featured various forms of intermixing. Letter F is false because, while the first paragraph of Passage B speaks of Moorish influence over Spanish, it is false that Spanish is "unaffected by indigenous Americans." Answer H is false because it is untrue that Spanish is uninfluenced by "government influences" since it was a government (the King and Queen of Spain) that established the Castellano dialect. Answer choice J is incorrect because the Moors previously mentioned as having affected Spanish are outside influences. That leaves answer choice G, which is correct in that it rightly says that Spanish is affected by other languages.

27. Correct answer: **B**. Forcing a person to speak a certain language is described in lines 71-75. It says that "ultimately they did not succeed" in such forcing, which eliminates choices A and C. Option D states that such forcing is "necessary," which is an idea not indicated at all in the passage. This is why the answer is B: it is futile (meaning, it doesn't work) and it is discriminatory.

28. Correct answer: **F**. This entire passage is about how the Castilian form of Spanish undergoes change as it is spread through the Americas (new words, new dialects, intermixing of cultures, etc.). All of this is why F is the correct answer. Letter G is contradicted by the opening paragraph of Passage B, which indicates that Castilian Spanish was more or less established by the king and queen. Answer choice H states that it is spoken today in the Andes region, but Spanish in the Andes region is mentioned as being affected by indigenous languages (line 89), which makes it incorrect. Answer J says that Castilian Spanish is dependent on Moorish and Nahuatl influences, but Moorish influence was prior to Castilian Spanish and Nahuatl is an example of its change, making J incorrect as well.

29. Correct answer: **B**. This question is about what both passages essentially have in common; in that sense it is a macro question that requires an understanding of both. Answer choice A is incorrect because the Spanish lisp is mentioned only in Passage A, and even there there is no indication that it will make its way into English. Answer choice C is incorrect because, although it truly says that the survival of culture and language are intertwined, it then falsely adds that these things are dependent upon Latin, an idea found in neither passage. Choice D is also incorrect because it makes it seem like there is some kind of rivalry between New World Spanish and Castilian Spanish, an idea found in neither passage. This is why the correct answer is B, which rightly states that it's proper to infer that both authors would agree that culture will continue to change languages into the future, an idea they both agree on about the spread of the Spanish language according to both passages.

30. Correct answer: **J**. First, narrow down your answer to either Passage A or Passage B. The quote from this author is about the importance of maintaining language for maintaining culture. The second paragraph from Passage B, especially, is reflective of this idea, but there are elements of the maintaining of one's culture throughout Passage B as well. This is why the answer is not F or G, since they both say the quote is more reflective of Passage A. Answer choice H, however, paints the government's attempt to force language as a *success*, but Passage B contradicts this idea in lines 71-75 especially. This is why the correct answer is J, which rightly states that Passage B most closely echoes the quoted author's view because Passage B speaks often of cultural overlap.

Answer Explanations - Step 4

Correct Answers:

Passage IV (Natural Science):

31: C
32: J
33: C
34: H
35: B
36: J
37: A
38: G
39: A
40: G

Possible Passage Map:

Passage IV

NATURAL SCIENCE: This passage is adapted from the video lecture titled "Into the Deep" by Dr. Mary C Maximilian (©2014 Cambridge University).

The pelagic zone, according to oceanographers, is the area of the open ocean (often called the water column) that is divided into five regions based on depth. These five regions are similar to the layers of the atmosphere (stratosphere, troposphere, etc.), but one crucial difference is that although life is scarce within the upper atmosphere, it is relatively abundant within each of the ocean's zones. As would be expected, the prevalence of life decreases as one moves downwards. However, at all levels of the ocean, life persists: a testament to the robust and resilient nature of marine lifeforms.

The epipelagic zone is the topmost of the pelagic zone's layers. Although it is the thinnest layer of the ocean (2-3% of the ocean's water volume), this zone is home to approximately 90% of all marine life. Much of this is due to the fact that the epipelagic zone is the only layer of the ocean in which photosynthesis can occur. This means that phytoplankton such as green algae can flourish, establishing the base for a wide-ranging marine food web. Yet the significance of such phytoplankton is not limited to the ocean; they are also responsible for sequestering 40% of Earth's carbon dioxide production and producing nearly half the world's oxygen.

Below the epipelagic zone lies the mesopelagic zone, defined by the level of light penetration: it begins when only 1% of surface light can be detected. In practice, this means that the mesopelagic zone stretches from approximately 650 to 3,280 feet beneath the surface. Although this zone lacks phytoplankton, it is by no means uninhabited; it is estimated to host some 10 billion tons of animal life (for comparison, that is roughly 200 times more than the yearly catch of every fishery on Earth). Moreover, this zone contains specialized creatures such as *Gonostomatidae* (also called the bristlemouth), bioluminescent finger-sized fish thought to be the Earth's most abundant vertebrates, with their numbers estimated to be in the trillions or even quadrillions.

Beneath the pelagic zone is the bathypelagic zone, which extends downwards to 13,120 feet. It is the uppermost of the zones that receive no sunlight whatsoever. Marked by extreme pressure, some 800 times that experienced on the ocean's surface, the bathypelagic zone hosts only those organisms that have adapted themselves to the unforgiving environmental conditions, with weak musculature and skeletons. Exceedingly slow metabolisms allow bathypelagic fish to remain inactive for long periods. Most of the scarce organisms in this zone feed off "marine snow," tiny particles of organic detritus—decomposing organisms, fecal matter, and silt—that sink from higher regions.

The next zone, the abyssopelagic zone, is the largest by volume. Extending to nearly 20,000 feet beneath the surface, this zone is characterized by total darkness and near-freezing temperatures. In many parts of the ocean, the abyssopelagic zone stretches all the way to the seafloor. Here too, life finds a way; this zone features examples of every primary marine invertebrate phylum and several species of fish. Intriguingly, many such species are incredibly large, in a phenomenon known as deep-sea gigantism. For example, *Architeuthis dux* (the giant squid) can reach 30 feet in length and *Macrocheira kaempferi* (the Japanese spider crab) may grow to more than 12 feet across. Scientists propose a variety of explanations for these extreme sizes, among them cold temperatures and high levels of dissolved oxygen.

Although it extends to the ocean floor, the abyssal zone is, counterintuitively, not the ocean's lowest zone. That honor belongs to the hadal zone, confined to areas with V-shaped trenches that sink deeply into the ocean floor. The deepest of these trenches, the Pacific Ocean's Mariana Trench, stretches 7 miles downward. Historically, it was thought that no life could survive in such depths. However, it is now known that various species, such as *Hirondellea gigas* (a small shrimp-like crustacean) and *Pseudoliparis swirei* (the Mariana snailfish) are at home here, where the pressure hovers at over 15,000 psi (pounds per square inch). Still, because the abyssal zone is so difficult to explore, the full range of life within this region is still uncertain.

Much the same could be said of the entire ocean, which remains a vast, unknown expanse, less than 5% of which has been explored. What is known, however, is that the oceanic ecosystem is an embodiment of life's tenacity and adaptability, even in the face of extreme conditions. From the sunlight-drenched epipelagic zone to the crushing pressures and ink-black darkness of the hadal zone, each stratum of the sea hosts a unique array of life forms, whose very presence challenges our understanding of the limits of life while underscoring the incredible diversity of Earth's biosphere.

31. Based on the passage, as one transcends the depths from the epipelagic zone to the hadal zone:

    A. life, contrary to popular belief, becomes more abundant, not less.
    B. life gets less abundant at first, but is inexplicably most abundant in the hadal zone.
    C. life becomes less abundant, but it can be found at all layers.
    D. life becomes less abundant, and the creatures that do exist get smaller closest to the hadal zone.

32. Which of the following quotes best expresses the main idea of the passage?

    F. "These five regions are similar to the layers of the atmosphere" (lines 3-4)
    G. "Yet the significance of such phytoplankton is not limited to the ocean (lines 20-21)
    H. "the abyssa
    ocean's low
    J. "the oceani
    tenacity and adaptability" (lines 83-84)

31. Correct answer: **C**. This macro question requires you to have an understanding, of course, of the passage a whole. Specifically, this question is about the marine life that one might encounter from the top to the bottom of the ocean. Answer A says that life becomes *more* abundant, which isn't true; we learn early on in the essay that 90% of life is found in the epipelagic zone. For this reason, B is also incorrect. Answer choice D says that the creatures further down *only* get smaller. That's *probably generally* true, but the essay points out the examples of giant creatures in deep depths. Answer C on the other hand is correct because it rightly states that life becomes less abundant but exists in all layers (as the author makes sure to point out a few times).

32. Correct answer: **J**. This macro question is really about the overall purpose or thesis statement of the passage. In the case of this passage, the first and last paragraphs serve as a kind of book ends around the body paragraphs about the layers, and each of those two paragraphs makes sure to point out the abundance of life in all layers of the ocean. Letter F is probably a tempting answer, but it makes it sound like the passage is as much about the stratosphere than it is about the ocean, which of course isn't true. Letter G stresses the significance of phytoplankton, and while that is important, the essay isn't about one detail of one layer or zone. Letter H speaks too specifically to one zone. These are all reasons why J is the correct answer: it is (first of all) about the ocean as a whole and (second of all) stresses what we said about the abundance of life at all layers.

33. Correct answer: **C**. Most science passages generally are objective and dealing with established fact. Here, you are asked to identify a statement that is the opposite, something *possibly* true. This means that it is going to be a hypothesis or you'll be told it is something that only some scientists believe, etc. There is only one sentence in the passage that has this kind of language: lines 63-65. In these lines, two different ideas are proposed as causes for deep-sea gigantism, either cold temperatures or high levels of dissolved oxygen. This is why the answer is C. The other answer choices are spoken of in the passage as established fact.

34. Correct answer: **H**. Because the essay is scientific, there are no self-critical statements (meaning, things said by the author to make herself look bad) at all, which makes answer F incorrect. Choice G is incorrect for similar reasons: there are no biographical elements at all in the passage; you may think you know a lot about the author from the passage itself, which is biographical, but the *subject* of the essay is the ocean, not the author and/or her personal experiences. Answer choice J is incorrect because there are no analogies or metaphors in the passage at all. The reason the answer is H is because there are a lot of technical and scientific words used throughout the passage, from the names of the layers themselves to the scientific names of animals.

35. Correct answer: **B**. I would say this is a medium level question since it requires you to examine the paragraphs about both the bathypelagic and abyssopelagic zones. We are told in lines 51-52 that the abyssopelagic zone has the most water of all zones; this eliminates answer choices C and D. However, we are told in line 40 that the bathypelagic zone has no sunlight. Thus, a zone that is deeper in the ocean is also going to have no sunlight. This is why A is incorrect; you might think the deeper zone has *less* sunlight, but it has the *same* amount of sunlight (none at all). Thus, B is correct because it correctly compares these two zones.

36. Correct answer: **J**. This macro question requires again an overall understanding of the passage's main idea or purpose. Answer choice F speaks about correcting misunderstandings; you may think that that is true, but if that were the passage's main purpose you would also hear from the author about what those misunderstandings are in either the opening paragraph or each paragraph individually, but nothing like that exists; this is why F is incorrect. Answer choice G is similar: there is no argument for increased environmental protections for vulnerable species, thus it is also incorrect. Answer choice H starts off sounding correct, but then it mentions that these levels of the pelagic zone are being compared to those of the stratosphere, but that doesn't happen in this passage aside from one quick mention in the opening paragraph. This is why the answer is J: the passage goes through and describes each level of the water column (another name for the pelagic zone, see line 2) one at a time.

37. Correct answer: **A**. This macro question is about point of view. First of all, the passage is not written in the first-person (using pronouns such as 'I'), which eliminates answer choice B. Second of all, the passage is not written in the second-person (using pronouns such as 'you'), which eliminates answer choice D. The passage, in other words, is written in the third-person ('he', 'it', 'them', etc.) Answer choice C says that the passage is "subjective," which means that it is something like the author's personal opinions. That isn't the case. Because the information is presented as established fact (in other words, objective), the correct answer is A.

38. Correct answer: **G**. The sixth paragraph (lines 66-79) speaks about the hadal zone. Answer F is incorrect because the hadal zone's floor isn't parallel to the ocean's surface; according to line 69, it is V-shaped. Answer choice H is incorrect because the passage simply doesn't speak to how common the hadal zone is, but it is pretty clear that your local lake doesn't have a hadal zone thousands of feet beneath the surface! Answer choice J is incorrect because the hadal zone is two zones further down than the last zone to receive any sunlight at all; it is completely dark. This is why the correct answer is G: it correctly states that the hadal zone has different marine species (see lines 73-76).

39. Correct answer: **A**. The second paragraph is about the epipelagic zone. This immediately eliminates answer choice C, which proposes that the second paragraph is about introducing the essay as a whole. Answer choice B is incorrect because it makes that claim that the epipelagic zone is the "most fascinating"; this isn't a claim that the author makes, and to infer that this is the case is not a proper leap to make. Answer choice D states that the purpose is to bring awareness about phytoplankton; this might be important to do, but phytoplankton is a detail of the second paragraph, not its overall purpose. This is why the answer is A: the purpose is broadly to overview the topmost layer of the ocean.

40. Correct answer: **G**. Answer choice F proposes that the overall organization of the passage is "chronological," which means in order of time. But there is no sense of time in the passage, making it incorrect. Answer choice H states that the passage is organized to explain the differences and similarities of marine life, but while there's some description of marine life, that's not how the passage is organized or outlined. Answer choice J is wrong for this same reason: the passage is organized by layers (one paragraph per layer or ocean zone), not animals. This is why G is the correct answer: the passage is outlined by layer in order of depth from most surface-level to deepest.

Answer Explanations - Step 6 - Practice Test #1

Correct Answers:

Passage I	Passage II	Passage III	Passage IV
1: A	11: A	21: B	31: C
2: F	12: G	22: H	32: G
3: C	13: B	23: C	33: D
4: F	14: H	24: G	34: G
5: B	15: C	25: B	35: D
6: J	16: J	26: F	36: F
7: D	17: B	27: A	37: C
8: H	18: H	28: J	38: G
9: D	19: A	29: D	39: A
10: J	20: J	30: F	40: H

Possible Passage Map (Passage I):

READING TEST

35 Minutes — 40 Questions

DIRECTIONS: There are several passages in this test. Each passage is accompanied by several questions. After reading a passage, choose the best answer to each question and fill in the corresponding oval on your answer document. You may refer to the passages as often as necessary.

Passage I

LITERARY NARRATIVE: This passage is adapted from Homer's *The Odyssey*.

Ulysses has returned home in disguise after twenty years of captivity and struggle; his estate is overrun by suitors, all of whom wish to marry his wife, Penelope.

Then the old woman took the cauldron in which she was going to wash Ulysses's feet, and poured plenty of cold water into it, adding hot till the bath was warm enough. Ulysses sat by the fire, but ere long he turned away from the light, for it occurred to him that when the old woman had hold of his leg she would recognize a certain scar which it bore, whereon the whole truth would come out. And indeed as soon as she began washing her master, she at once knew the scar as one that had been given him by a wild boar when he was hunting on Mt. Parnassus with his excellent grandfather Autolycus—who was the most accomplished thief and perjurer in the whole world—and with the sons of Autolycus.

As soon as Euryclea had got the scarred limb in her hands and had well hold of it, she recognized it and dropped the foot at once. The leg fell into the bath, which rang out and was overturned, so that all the water was spilt on the ground; Euryclea's eyes between her joy and her grief filled with tears, and she could not speak, but she caught Ulysses by the beard and said, "My dear child, I am sure you must be Ulysses himself, only I did not know you till I had actually touched and handled you."

As she spoke she looked towards Penelope, as though wanting to tell her that her dear husband was in the house, but Penelope was unable to look in that direction and observe what was going on, for Minerva had diverted her attention; so Ulysses caught Euryclea by the throat with his right hand and with his left drew her close to him, and said, "Nurse, do you wish to be the ruin of me, you who nursed me at your own breast, now that after twenty years of wandering I am at last come to my own home again? Since it has been borne in upon you by heaven to recognize me, hold your tongue, and do not say a word about it to any one else in the house, for if you do I tell you—and it shall surely be—that if heaven grants me to take the lives of these suitors, I will not spare you, though you are my own nurse, when I am killing the other women."

"My child," answered Euryclea, "what are you talking about? You know very well that nothing can either bend or break me. I will hold my tongue like a stone or a piece of iron; furthermore let me say, and lay my saying to your heart, when heaven has delivered the suitors into your hand, I will give you a list of the women in the house who have been ill-behaved, and of those who are guiltless."

And Ulysses answered, "Nurse, you ought not to speak in that way; I am well able to form my own opinion about one and all of them; hold your tongue and leave everything to heaven."

As he said this Euryclea left the cloister to fetch some more water, for the first had been all spilt; and when she had washed him and anointed him with oil, Ulysses drew his seat nearer to the fire to warm himself, and hid the scar under his rags.

Then Penelope began talking to him and said: "Listen, then, to a dream that I have had and interpret it for me if you can. I have twenty geese about the house that eat mash out of a trough, and of which I am exceedingly fond. I dreamed that a great eagle came swooping down from a mountain, and dug his curved beak into the neck of each of them till he had killed them all. Presently he soared off into the sky, and left them lying dead about the yard; whereon I wept in my dream till all my maids gathered round me, so piteously was I grieving because the eagle had killed my geese. Then he came back again, and perching on a projecting rafter spoke to me with human voice, and told me to leave off crying. 'Be of good courage,' he said, 'daughter of Icarius; this is no dream, but a vision of good omen that shall surely come to pass. The geese are the suitors, and I am no longer an eagle, but your own husband, who am come back to you, and who will bring these suitors to a disgraceful end.' On this I woke, and when I looked out I saw my geese at the trough eating their mash as usual."

"This dream, Madam," replied Ulysses, "can admit but of one interpretation, for had not Ulysses himself told you how it shall be fulfilled? The death of the suitors is portended, and not one single one of them will escape."

Possible Passage Map (Passage II):

Passage II

SOCIAL SCIENCE: This passage is adapted from the article "A Nation's First Leader" by J Eggers Clyburn (©2004 by Smithsonian).

Although the Revolutionary War started well for the American troops, it was not long into 1776 that things took a turn for the worse. New York City was conquered in a mere three month period between August and November after British troops commanded by General William Howe landed in Long Island. From there, Washington, who had fled the city with some 6,000 men, was chased Southwest across New Jersey by British General Cornwallis, eventually settling near McConkey's Ferry on the Pennsylvania side of the Delaware River. Though many thousands of troops made it to the encampment safely, nearly 2,000 were in need of hospital care, and a significant number of others deserted the young army out of fear that the war had already been lost.

A brutal New England winter was imminent, and as a result, military campaigns began to slow. General Cornwallis gave up further chasing of Washington into Pennsylvania, choosing instead to establish a string of outposts from northern New Jersey to as far south as Burlington. Washington, for his part, was eager to gather other split-off American forces under the command of Generals Lee and Gates.

Washington, bolstered by reports of the casual attitudes of British soldiers, began to scheme a bold plan for a surprise attack, but morale was low. However, he was given a copy of *The American Crisis*, a pamphlet published on December 19th and written by Thomas Paine (who had also authored *Common Sense*). The pamphlet begins as such:

"These are the times that try men's souls; the summer soldier and the sunshine patriot will, in this crisis, shrink from the service of his country; but he that stands it *now,* deserves the love and thanks of man and woman. Tyranny, like hell, is not easily conquered; yet we have this consolation with us, that the harder the conflict, the more glorious the triumph."

Washington, himself inspired, ordered that the pamphlet be read to all of his troops on December 20th. This raised morale among his soldiers and went a long way in giving them the courage they needed to conquer their current and difficult living conditions as well as any wounds they may have suffered in skirmishes that Fall. On the same day, and although there had been delays, the eagerly anticipated troops of both Lee and Gates arrived in camp, raising the total number of soldiers fit for duty under the orders of the Commander of the Continental Army to 6,000.

Intelligence reports that enemy troops were planning their own eventual crossing of the Delaware River temporarily disheartened Washington. More importantly, however, these reports bolstered the Colonel's ambitious plan, which was hatched December 23rd, 1776. On the following day, the secret mission was revealed at 4:00 PM to the thousands of troops who had gathered for routine reporting, and preparations began. Vessels, such as large ferries and smaller Durham boats, were brought south from Malta Island near New Hope. On Christmas Day, Washington again reiterated that the crossing would take place that evening with an attack on a garrison of German Hessian troops fighting on behalf of the British near Trenton. But first, the crossing itself had to take place, which required that not only men but dozens of horses and artillery make safe voyages to the other side of the dangerous and icy Delaware River.

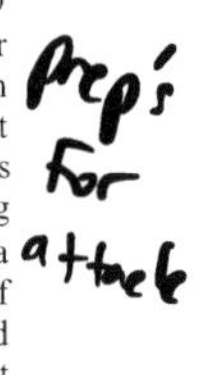

At 4:00 troops were readied with ammunition, and after sunset the crossing began. Crossings were planned to take place in waves, but the weather failed to simplify the operation. Winds blew, and what began as soft rain quickly escalated to sleet and snow. This made conditions significantly more dangerous for the men, most of whom could not swim. Finally, by 3:00 AM, all men, food, horses, and artillery had made the crossing, and no less than 1 hour later the troops were ready to march into Trenton.

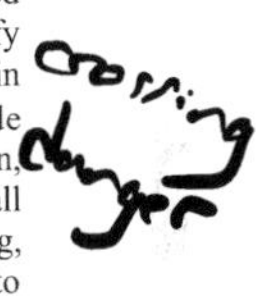

The troops were split. One half were put under the command of General Sullivan and the other half under General Greene. These garrisons took parallel roads into the city and, to say the least, caught the German troops off guard. The Hessian leadership assumed that there would be no attack on that wintry morning and had grown dull to surprise by numerous skirmishes with Americans evening after evening. Colonel Rall, leader of these troops, even spent most of the previous evening off his guard drinking and eating at the home of a Loyalist Patriot, Abraham Hunt.

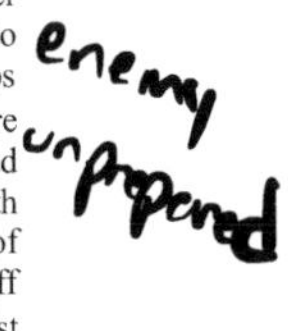

Miraculously, only 3 American troops were killed in the fight, due in large part to the unsuspecting nature of the attack. Colonel Rall was mortally wounded, as were 22 other Hessian troops. The Americans pillaged muskets, powder, and artillery, and although the return crossing back into Pennsylvania was even more dangerous than the first, they returned to camp in a celebratory mood, which was a marked difference when compared to their first arrival earlier in the month.

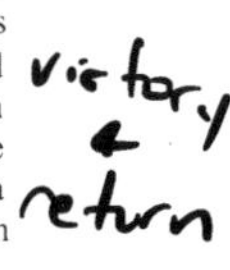

11. Those soldiers who "deserted the young army" (lines 13-14) are most nearly synonymous with which of the following?

A. "the summer soldier" (lines 31-32)
B. "eagerly anticipated troops" (line 45)
C. "enemy troops" (line 49)
D. "a garrison of German Hessian troops" (line 61)

Possible Passage Map (Passage III):

Passage III

HUMANITIES: Passage A is adapted from the book *Journeys in Anthropology: To the End of the World* (©2004 by James Thomas Todd). Passage B is adapted from the book *Art: A History of Technique* (©1997 by Lauren Thomason).

Passage A by James Thomas Todd

As not only the son of an esteemed anthropologist, but being in that profession myself, I was honored to be invited to explore the *Caverne Sous la Falaise*, a limestone cave beneath a towering cliff in Southern France. It was discovered in 2006 following an earthquake that dislodged more than 400 tonnes of rock at the base of the cliff, and was subsequently closed to the public by the government. In the last few years the cave has been opened to study to scientists, archaeologists, and anthropologists like myself and my mother who obtain a special permit from the authorities.

The entrance to the cave, a gap in the rock no more than five feet in height and three feet in width, deceived me into thinking that I would be setting foot into a small cave. Upon entering and turning on my flashlight, what was lit up was an extensive cavern with seemingly unlimited depths, crevices, and avenues. A line of paracord guided our team of half a dozen scientists through the twists and turns of these depths. Whether from darkness or danger or the time it took, what was only a hike of 75 or so meters seemed to be ten times the distance. However, it was worth it.

First, we came upon charcoal sketches of animals, and the dilapidated remains of many more. Mammoths and other mammals that are since extinct stretched up and across the limestone. While many anthropologists might attempt to explain away these ancient drawings as merely a primitive attempt to try to understand the cosmos, I wonder more about the humanity of the artist. Was he or she driven by a fundamental, human passion for art itself? Perhaps, I think, this large cave was a nursery for small children, and the sitters entertained the little ones with fascinating stories of the beasts scribbled on the walls.

We then entered a "smaller" room that took my breath away. Hundreds, or perhaps thousands, of hand prints adorned the walls. Again I wonder: are our primitive, standard explanations of the motives of cave dwellers too immature, too inhuman? No one can say for sure, but I do know that whether these hands are a way to remember ancestors or something as simple as an aesthetic pleasure, we are fortunate that they have been kept in nearly pristine condition to the present day.

Passage B by Lauren Thomason

Charcoal is, perhaps, the oldest art medium in human history. In fact, charcoal cave paintings have been discovered and studied in many parts of the world and can date back as late as 30,000 years ago (or, there is debate, perhaps even further back in time). For example, Namibia can boast of a black, charcoal drawing of what appears to be a zebra that was discovered at the Apollo Cave dating to as far back as 27,500 years ago.

However, it wasn't just ancient cave dwellers who utilized the technique. In Europe, artists beginning in the 1400's were using wallow, walnut, and grape charcoal to capture their subjects. Since then, charcoal has only grown in popularity due to its striking and deep black color and the ability of the artist to take advantage of the white canvas beneath as a contrasting method. Unfortunately, over time, many of the early pieces of charcoal art were ruined due to the flaking of the medium off of the smooth canvas. By the 16th century, artists had discovered that by dipping charcoal in a gum bath, it was less likely to flake. This process was aided by the use of a rough canvas, which forces an adhesion and prevents the fading of color or flaking over time.

Today, there are many different varieties of charcoal and methods for producing them. Compressed charcoal, for example, is pressed into the shape of a block, stick, or rectangular cube. Vine charcoal, on the other hand, is longer and thinner than the compressed variety and is produced by burning grape vines in a kiln. Despite the popularity of these two types, the most popular method of applying charcoal is via a charcoal pencil. This is simply compressed charcoal that has been enclosed in wood, like a pencil. These are especially useful when an artist needs the addition of meticulous detail in his or her art.

The method of production and the ingredients put in also have an effect on the charcoal and the final result on canvas. The softer the charcoal, the longer it had been heated.

There are also a variety of application techniques, all of which produce different effects. Blending, for example, is a technique in which the artist uses either a finger or a chamois to spread charcoal; this naturalizes the transition between darker and lighter portions of a work of art. Hatching is another technique in which an artist continually applies parallel, dark lines one after another; this can have the effect of fooling the eye to believe that a work has been filled in entirely by charcoal or give texture and dimension to a piece.

21. Which of the following statements about the *Caverne Sous la Falaise* is *least* supported by Passage A?

- **A.** There is much we do not know about our ancestors' interests and way of life.
- **B.** The cavern might have appeal to the greater public, but is of little interest to the scientific community.
- **C.** There is, from an archaeological perspective, likely much to be discovered yet unseen by modern eyes.
- **D.** Artifacts that are immovable, such as cave art, are worthy of special protection.

Possible Passage Map (Passage IV):

Passage IV

NATURAL SCIENCE: This passage is adapted from the article "Unyielding Havoc: The History and Devastating Effects of the Invasive Red Ant" by Whitney Culver (©2009 by Southeastern Science Quarterly).

The red imported fire ant, *Solenopsis invicta*, is a polymorphic species of ant native to central South America but considered an invasive species in the United States, Australia, parts of Asia, and other locations across the globe. Historically, *S. invicta* has often been confused with the black imported fire ant, *Solenopsis richteri*, a species native to southeastern South America but similarly invasive to the United States. Genetic and phenotypic research suggests a close genetic relationship between the two, so much so that hybridization or an intermixing of species occurs in areas where the two overlap (northern Mississippi, United States).

Worker ants within *S. invicta* measure between 2.4 and 6.0 mm, but larger workers or major workers are distinguishable from smaller workers by head size (0.66 to 1.41 mm in height for smaller workers, 1.35 to 1.40 mm for major workers). This difference in size, which makes them polymorphic, is indistinguishable in larvae until the fourth and final larval instar, or stage of development. The larval stages begin with an oval-shaped egg that assumes the shape of an embryo, becoming a true larva with the shedding of the shell within a week. Larvae measure approximately 3 mm in length. Upon pupation, the differences in head size between the different castes of workers becomes apparent, though both feature antennae with two or three sensilla, or sensory organs, each. In many colonies, major workers can make up as many as 35% of the total population, the function of which is to leave the colony and forage. Smaller workers care for the brood. Though worker ants can be female, only the queens, a third caste of *S. invicta*, can lay eggs.

Worker ants communicate using pheromones and semiochemicals, secreted chemical factors that trigger a social response. One example of semiochemical communication occurs when a major worker ant discovers a food source that is too heavy to carry individually. In such a situation, a worker will secrete trail pheromones alerting other ants, who synthesize the pheromones by the Dufour's gland, to the presence of the food. Similarly, when a mound is under attack, *S. invicta* will release alarm pheromones alerting the colony to the presence of a threat. Some scientists speculate the presence of a brood pheromone designed to aid workers in the segregation of brood by age and caste, resulting in care for eggs that includes antennation, licking, and grooming.

S. invicta has a natural predator in its native Brazil, a species of phorid fly of the genus *Apocephalus* also known as the ant-decapitator fly, which lays eggs in the ant's severed head. Due to the invasive nature of the ant and the havoc it can wreak on local ecosystems, scientists are studying whether or not to import a population of the phorid fly into the United States to help control the ant's spread. However, a number of insects, birds, and arachnids have learned to feed on the invasive species across the globe. The *S. invicta* that tends to be most vulnerable is the queen, which is in flight before the establishment of a new colony. In such a situation, she is particularly susceptible to being consumed by *Anax junius*, *Somatochlora provocans*, and *Tramea carolina*, all species of dragonfly native to North America, and various birds, such as the chimney swift (*Chaetura pelagica*) and the eastern kingbird (*Tyrannus tyrannus*). As many as 16 unique species of arachnid are also known to prey on *S. invicta*, including the southern black widow spider (*Lycosa timuga*) and the wolf spider (*Lycosa timuga*), the latter of which is documented to eat all three castes of the red invasive fire ant for a total of roughly 75% of its total diet.

One reason the *S. invicta* is a problematic invasive species is the effect it has on the diversity and abundance of native species, particularly arthropods and vertebrates. The Stock Island tree snail (*Orthalicus reses*), for example, is now extinct in the wild due mostly to the presence and predation of the red imported fire ant. Though interactions with mammals are rare, human beings are stung (not bitten, contrary to popular belief) by the venomous ant roughly 14 million times per year. The complex venom, fueled by the primary lipophilic alkaloid toxin *solenopsin*, usually results in mild discomfort, swelling, and itching for humans. However, because of the threat the ants pose to more susceptible populations of humans, it is important for scientists and the greater population to continue to find methods of containing this invasive species.

31. The third paragraph (lines 33-48) marks a shift in the passage from a focus on:

    A. the invasive range of *S. invicta* to the physical characteristics of *S. invicta*.
    B. the invasive range of *S. invicta* to the types of sociochemical communication among *S. invicta*.
    C. the physical characteristics of *S. invicta* to the types of sociochemical communication among *S. invicta*.
    D. the types of sociochemical communication among *S. invicta* to the physical characteristics of *S. invicta*.

32. Based on the passage, the author's use of the word "assumes" (line 21) most nearly describes the way an *S. invicta* egg:

    F. makes a characteristic decision about which of three castes of ant to enter in to.
    G. changes or takes on a new form prior to later larval growth stages.
    H. can sometimes be mistaken by worker ants for the similar-looking eggs of *S. richteri*.
    J. responds to alarm pheromones when there is an eternal threat to the colony.

Passage I

1. Correct answer: **A**. To get this question correct, it is necessary to have an understanding of the different points of views proposed in the answer choices. First-person means that the narrator is telling a story from his point of view, using the word "I" in the process. That isn't the case here, so eliminate answer choice C. Second-person means that the narrator is directing the story at "you," using that word frequently, and perhaps "we" as well. However, that isn't the case here either, which eliminates answer choice B. Third-person means that the pronouns "he", "she", "they", etc. are being used to talk *about* other people. Choice D (though it correctly says that the point of view is third-person) falsely proposes that the events are only told from the point of view of Penelope, which is incorrect (especially since she is across the room and out of the conversation at one point). This is why the answer is A: the story is third-person, but we have access to the thoughts and the actions of multiple characters (Ulysses, Euryclea, and Penelope especially).

2. Correct answer: **F**. The story begins with "the old woman" (aka Euryclea) taking hold of Ulysses's foot, then recalling how he acquired his scar on Mt. Parnassus (line 11), then the story returns to the present and Euryclea once again holding Ulysses's scarred leg in her hands (line 15). This is why the answer is F: the only reason to recall Mt. Parnassus is to give context and understanding as to the origins of the scar on Ulysses's leg.

3. Correct answer: **C**. This question essentially has two parts. First, you have to identify an initial reaction of Euryclea, then you have to pinpoint what follows this initial reaction (this is the structure of all 4 answer choices). The incident alluded to by the question takes place in lines 15-20. If you reread those lines, you see that Euryclea is certainly *not* angry or disappointed that Ulysses has returned home; this eliminates answers A and B. She certainly *is* shocked (answer C), but she could also be called astonished (answer D) as well. The differentiating factor will be what follows. Answer D says that she is astonished, which is followed by hatred and vengeance. However, that is not what is proposed in lines 19 and 20, which says directly that she feels both joy and grief. This is why the answer is C.

4. Correct answer: **F**. If you created a Passage Map of this reading passage by active reading and annotating, there is a very good chance that you have written in the margins a few words to summarize this paragraph; it could also be that you wrote next to the first half of the paragraph and a little more at the end if you thought this paragraph long enough to do so with. If you weren't lucky enough in that regard, hopefully you left yourself enough time to go back and reread this paragraph to get the answer correct. In the paragraph, Euryclea looks towards Penelope, but then Ulysses grabs her by the throat and threatens her to not tell anyone. This coincides with answer choice F. There is no indication that Euryclea is sharing this to Penelope as a memory anywhere, which eliminates choice G. There could be some truth in answer H, since it is true from the passage that he has been gone for 20 years, but in ACT Reading, you can't assume or infer an answer to be true, unless you are asked that directly. Lastly, since this paragraph and exchange end, and then Penelope immediately comes over to Ulysses to share her dream, it's impossible that the exchange caused her dream. This eliminates answer choice J.

5. Correct answer: **B**. Though it may be tempting to find an answer to this question that is deep and complicated, it is rather straightforward. In lines 59-60 Penelope reveals that she is telling Ulysses her dream so that he can interpret it. This is why B is the correct answer. In your Passage Map, you probably wrote next to that paragraph something about Penelope having a dream, directing you exactly where to look. If not, keep practicing so as to identify the main purpose of the paragraphs as you active read.

6. Correct answer: **J**. The trick to these vocabulary in context questions is not to have a previous knowledge of the meaning of the word "admit" or any other word. You very well may know what the word being asked about means, but it is about *how the word is being used in context*. That means that you have got to go back and reread the sentence in which the word is used to determine exactly *how* it is being used. The sentence the word is used in essentially says, "This dream...can *admit* but of one interpretation." If you're still unsure after reading it in context, replace the word with the answer options and see if one of them works well. If we change the sentence to say, "This dream can *allow the possibility of* (choice J) only one interpretation," then it becomes clear that this is the correct use of the word "admit" in the sentence, which is why J is correct.

7. Correct answer: **D**. There is evidence throughout the story that Ulysses and Penelope are hopefully anticipating (answer choice D) a reunion with one another. First, there is the fact that Euryclea wants to tell Penelope that her "dear husband was in the house" (lines 26-27). Secondly, there is Penelope's dream, which makes it clear that she is hopeful that the "suitors" alluded to throughout the story will be taken care of by Ulysses. Third, there is Ulysses's promise that the dream will be fulfilled by his return (lines 78-81). You may assume that they are anxious (answer A), but not that they are hopeless, and you certainly couldn't assume that they are either filled with "doubtful terror" or "melancholic dejection." There is some hope, which is why the answer is D.

8. Correct answer: **H**. There is only one character whose trustworthiness is promised, which is Euryclea. After Ulysses's threat, Euryclea says in lines 42-44 that nothing can bend or break her and that she will hold her tongue like a stone, etc. This is why the answer is H. It might be assumed that Penelope, Ulysses, or Autolycus are trustworthy, but again, you can't assume or infer anything unless the question directly asks you to do so in ACT Reading.

9. Correct answer: **D**. Since Ulysses is unrecognized, yet has made his way safely into Penelope's home (and not only that, has his feet washed and is anointed with oil (line 55), etc.), it is safe to assume (which is required in this question, since the question stem asks about something that is strongly suggested, in other words, not directly stated) that he is welcomed and treated well. In other words, he certainly isn't "ignored" (answer A), treated indifferently (answer B), or treated as a slave (answer C). Instead, he is obviously treated as an honored guest, which is why the correct answer is D.

10. Correct answer: **J**. Oftentimes, these kinds of questions are easily missed for simple mistakes. The simple mistake that students make is that they read the first clause in the answer, see that it is correct, then move on. However, the ACT is definitely going to have wrong answers that are incorrect because of the *second* clause in the sentence. Answer G is probably the easiest to dismiss; there's no direct indication to the moods of either in the last 20 years, but there are certainly hints that Penelope has missed her husband. Answer F begins well by complimenting Penelope, but what is said about Euryclea is untrue: she is definitely observant and very attached to reality to be able to identify Ulysses! Answer H also begins well, since Autolycus is described in this answer positively. However, there's no indication that Autolycus was a great outdoorsman per se, and there's also no direct indication that Ulysses "struggles mightily away from home." This leaves J, which is correct; the suitors, who are mentioned a few times, are freeloaders on the home (meaning, they are living there and living off the house without working or contributing), but Ulysses has made a great sacrifice to get back home.

Passage II

11. Correct answer: **A**. The soldiers that desert the army are afraid that the war has been lost; in other words, they don't see anything worth fighting for. These troops aren't coming back, which makes them not synonymous but antonymous (opposites) with option B, the "eagerly anticipated troops," thus B is incorrect. Though these troops leave the army, there's no indication that they become "enemy troops," and they certainly aren't the same as the "garrison of German Hessian troops" that the army attacks later; this makes C and D also incorrect. This leaves only A. Besides being correct by elimination, the quote "the summer soldier" refers to a soldier, based on the context of the Paine quote, that is a soldier when things are easy. This makes A the correct answer.

12. Correct answer: **G**. Option F seems tempting at first because the initial part of the answer is true ("was a brave and bold decision"); however, the second half ("that failed…") is false since the attack was a success. Answer H is equally false; the author certainly doesn't think that it was a foolish enterprise, especially since it was a success. Answer J correctly states that the attack was successful, but it mentions good weather and that the attack was uncoordinated (meaning, lucky or unplanned), both of which are false. Any reading of the passage indicates that G is correct: it was, in the author's point of view, heroic and to be praised because it was successful.

13. Correct answer: **B**. One of the three reasons to create a Passage Map while you actively read each passage is that, oftentimes, you will be asked about the main idea of a paragraph, in more or less words. That is the case here. You may have written next to the paragraph something like, "pamphlet + troops ↑ morale". Anything in that zone will help you to answer this question more quickly than normal. Rereading the paragraph, to be sure, is obviously still an option, which is why you active read in the first place (to ensure you have the time necessary to answer the questions). Option A might be tempting because maybe you are inferring it to be true; but remember, you can't infer in ACT Reading unless that question asks you to; there's nothing in the paragraph about how Paine should have served in the army. Answer C also has elements of truth; at one point in the essay, courage and strength are fleeing the troops, but not in this paragraph. Answer D alludes to failures in leadership, which everyone can relate to on some level, but that, again, isn't the purpose of the paragraph. Instead, the fifth paragraph is about Thomas Paine's pamphlet being read to the troops, which begins to raise morale, which is raised even higher when additional troops show up. This is why B is correct.

14. Correct answer: **H**. One of the three reasons to create a Passage Map while you actively read each passage is that, oftentimes, you will be asked about the main idea of a paragraph, in more or less words. That is the case here. You may have written next to the paragraph something like, "Germans caught off guard." Just like number 13 above, this might be enough to get this question correct. Answer F has truth in it: ordinary citizens did play an indirect role in the success of the attack through their nonstop skirmishes, but there's no indication in the paragraph that Washington recruited them, and again, you can't assume it to be true. Answer G begins truly, that "Abraham Hunt might go down in history as a patriot," but ends saying he is a traitor. Again, there's no mention of that idea in the eighth paragraph, and you can't assume it. Answer J has no validity in it whatsoever; it's an interesting thought experiment, but again, it's not in the passage and so can't be correct. This is why H is correct: it rightly says that the paragraph is about the German Hessian troops being caught off guard, which was a factor in the success of the attack.

15. Correct answer: **C**. These types of questions (in which you're given a list of facts or statements, and you have to determine which are true or false) are among the most missed in ACT Reading. However, I'd like to flip that on its head and make it simpler to you, and here's how: you need to realize that getting this question correct is *not* going to require you to go on a wild goose chase all around the passage, gathering facts from 3 or 4 different paragraphs. Instead, every time I've seen this question on previous ACT Reading passages, it has been true that all of the statements are proven true or false by one paragraph alone. Find the correct paragraph, and begin crossing out incorrect options. In this case, we need to refer to the seventh paragraph (lines 66-75), which details the dangers of crossing the Delaware River. There is no indication that British troops crossed to the American side, which eliminates I (which, in turn, eliminates A and D as options). This is where you can get smart. Looking at options B and C, both agree that II is correct, so why check it? If III ("An inability to swim") is true, then C is correct, and if IV is

true ("Skirmishes") is true, then B is correct. Line 72 says that most of the men could not swim, which makes III correct, which makes letter C the correct answer.

16. Correct answer: **J**. The only way to get this question correct is to go back and read the mentioned lines in context. In summary, the lines 11-15 mention the numbers of injured or deserted troops. Answer choice F may be a tempting answer because it is negative in tone just like lines 11-15. However, choice F speaks of losing the Revolutionary War, while this passage is about one battle. Choice G is false because that's not the purpose of the lines either. Choice H says that the focus of the lines is General Lowe, but that is also false. Answer J on the other hand proposes that the lines exist to "emphasize the dire straits of the American Army," which is of course true. This is why J is correct.

17. Correct answer: **B**. These kinds of vocabulary in context questions simply require that you go back and reread the sentence in which the word or phrase appears. This particular sentence says, "The Hessian leadership…had *grown dull* to surprise by numerous skirmishes with Americans." Obviously, the phrase "grown dull" here means that they weren't prepared for and certainly weren't anticipating an attack. This is why answer choice B is correct.

18. Correct answer: **H**. As you can see by the question itself, you are being asked to infer. Again, you can't infer in ACT Reading unless the question asks you to. To 'infer' means making an educated guess, or reaching an educated conclusion based on what you know already. The correct answer, in other words, is not going to be *directly* stated in the passage, but is a conclusion that is safe to reach *based on* the passage. Answer F might be tempting, especially because it is factually true, but inferring from something specific that happens once to then happening "dozens of occasions" is a stretch. Answer G in no way can be inferred from the passage since it contradicts the passage (Washington isn't caught off guard in the passage). Answer J can't be inferred either; though Washington did lean on his generals in the passage, to infer that he did so "too heavily" is not based on evidence. Answer choice H, on the other hand, can certainly be inferred. At the beginning of the passage, Washington retreats, only to bide his time and attack in a surprise manner; H infers that this kind of strategy is not failure if it creates opportunity. This is why H is correct.

19. Correct answer: **A**. Just like number 17 above, you are required here to go back and reread the sentence in which the word *waves* appears and come to a conclusion based on context. This particular sentence says: "Crossings were planned to take place in *waves*, but the weather failed to simplify the operation." In this case, *waves* isn't something like waves in an ocean, or someone saying hello or goodbye, or like waves on a graph, but something happening one at a time. This is why A is correct.

20. Correct answer: **J**. The Hessian colonel is mentioned in the last two paragraphs of the passage. The second-to-last paragraph speaks of him as off his guard on the evening before the attack, drinking and eating. The last paragraph speaks of him as killed in the attack. These are the only two details we have of Colonel Rall (the Hessian leader), so one of them has to be the correct answer or a major part of the correct answer. Answer F says Rall survived the attack, but as we just said, he was mortally wounded (aka killed), making F incorrect. Answer G says that Rall knew of Hunt's loyalties, but this knowledge isn't mentioned in the passage, and it *can't be inferred because the question doesn't ask you to infer*. Answer H says that Rall failed to station sentinels along the Delaware River. Again, *it can't be inferred because the question doesn't ask you to infer*. That leaves Answer J, which is obviously true: if Rall was drinking on Christmas Eve, he wasn't seriously entertaining the possibility of an attack the next morning.

Passage III

21. Correct answer: **B**. In a question that requires you to identify a statement that is *least* supported by a Passage, the answer is going to *clearly* be least supported; it's not going to be close or be a matter of opinion. That means that there is likely going to be a factually incorrect statement in one of the four answer choices that makes it definitively false, which in this case makes it the correct answer. Answer choice A is true and is supported by the passage, especially the rhetorical questions asked by the author, such as "Was he or she driven by a fundamental human passion for art itself?" (lines 30-31). Answer choice C says, essentially, that there is more to be discovered by archaeologists; besides being obviously true, it is also supported by the passage, since the passage is about an archaeological discovery made possible by happenstance. Answer choice D says that immovable artifacts deserve special protection; that is also obviously true, but is also supported by the passage in that the scientists needed a special permit to explore the cave (line 11). This leaves answer choice B, which says that the cave is not of interest to the scientific community. This is flat out incorrect, since the entire passage is about scientific interest in the cave. Thus, the correct answer is B.

22. Correct answer: **H**. Part of the theme of Passage A is the idea that there is *humanity* behind cave art. The word "dilapidated" certainly doesn't emphasize this, nor does the word "primitive". This leaves "adorned" and "pristine." The word "pristine," however, refers to the fact that the hand prints on the wall are still in good condition, which is just a lucky happenstance. On the other hand, the word "adorned" on the other hand, has a kind of sacred, beautiful, or human element to it; it implied that the handprints (which is what the walls are "adorned" with) are intentional and beautiful. This is why the correct answer is H: "adorned."

23. Correct answer: **C**. The word "smaller" is used in line 35 to compare the current room that the scientists enter into to the previous room that they were in. If the previous room is described as a "large cave" (line 31), then by putting the word *smaller* in

quotation marks, the author is saying that although the room may technically be smaller, it is still quite large. This is why the correct answer is C, which correctly identifies the current "smaller" room as "rather expansive."

24. Correct answer: **G**. This is the first question in those that are exclusively about Passage B (all previous ones, of course, are exclusively about Passage A). Hopefully, you actively read this passage, giving you the time that you need to go back and find the correct answer. Letter F is incorrect because it says that "in this time" (the "dawning of the use of Charcoal in European art") there was only one variety being used; this is incorrect, since line 54 mentions the varieties ("wallow, walnut, and grape…"). Answer choice H says that it was first "dipped in a gum bath," but this is only true of later European charcoal art (see lines 61-63). Answer choice J says that the process was "flawless", which we know isn't true, since earlier charcoal art flaked off of a smooth canvas (lines 59-61). Thus, the correct answer is G: it correctly states that early European charcoal artists were ignorant of its longevity when applied to a smooth canvas (again, see lines 59-61).

25. Correct answer: **B**. Again, hopefully you actively read, giving you the time to go back, reread lines 78-81 to get a feel for what they mean and do in the passage, and then find the correct answer choice that matches these ideas. Lines 78-81, in essence, are about producing different types of charcoal, such as softer charcoal vs harder charcoal. Do these lines then stress "the dignity of black and white art over that in color"? No, this is why A is incorrect. Do these lines push the reader to be open minded to other types of mediums besides charcoal? No, this is why C is incorrect. Do these lines then narrow the reader's expectations when it comes to charcoal possibilities? No (the opposite, actually), which is why D is incorrect. However, do these lines expand upon the "vast varieties of charcoal"? Yes, that is literally what they do; this is why B is correct.

26. Correct answer: **F**. This is a straightforward detail question that requires you to go back and find each answer. Unfortunately, this question takes more time than you might think, since it requires you to find the one that is *not* mentioned in the passage (in other words, you have to find or remember the three that are). Answer G can be found in lines 87-91. Answer H can be found in line 85. Answer J can be found in lines 73-77. This is why F is the correct answer: the method of swiping from the corner of a charcoal block is nowhere to be found in Passage B.

27. Correct answer: **A**. As with all vocabulary or phrase in context questions, you need to go back and reread the sentence in which the word *capture* appears to grasp its intended meaning. You might think you know off the top of your head what the word *capture* means (to trap or jail something or someone), but I would bet that the use of the word in the passage is *not* the most obvious usage. The sentence in which this word appears says: "In Europe, artists beginning in the 1400's were using willow, walnut, and grape charcoal to *capture* their subjects." It seems to me that this word (without yet looking at the answer choices) is being used synonymously with "draw" or "paint." This is why the answer is A, which refers to replicating "a subject on canvas" (aka, drawing them!).

28. Correct answer: **J**. This begins the series of questions that refer to or rely on both passages. Again, the Paired Passages will have some common overlap between the two passages; in this case, it is charcoal art, particularly that it has been used in cave art. Here you are asked to identify a statement that both authors agree with. Letter F might be tempting since it seems to combine messages from both. But that is exactly the problem; this idea is found in *neither* passage, let alone both. Letter G has a similar problem; nowhere is it stated or implied that limestone is ideal; limestone isn't even mentioned in Passage B. Letter H states that modern art is somehow more beautiful or valuable, but I think the author of Passage A would definitely disagree! That leaves J, which is the correct answer; both passages allude to the breaking down of charcoal art over time (Passage A speaks of it happening in a cave, while Passage B speaks of it happening on smooth canvases).

29. Correct answer: **D**. Though this question is clouded or phrased as if it has to do with both passages, that is kind of a distraction; this question is specifically and only about the rhetorical questions in Passage A and what they do for the passage overall. If you reread lines 26-31, it is obvious that the author uses the rhetorical question there to refute typical ideas of cave dwellers as primitive or lacking taste or artistic ability. This matches up perfectly well with answer choice D, which states that the rhetorical questions "cast doubt" upon these stereotypes. Choice A isn't true because there is nothing in the passage about cave art's "potential" (whatever that means). Choice B falsely says that the questions "condemn" cave dwellers, but obviously the author has nothing but praise for them. Choice C mentions varieties of charcoal, but that is an idea found or discussed in Passage B, not Passage A.

30. Correct answer: **F**. This is an interesting question; you have to, in a sense, put yourself in the shoes of the author of Passage B, who wrote a lot about different varieties of charcoal used in art and the reasons it doesn't last over time. What would that author say when standing face to face with the cave art described in Passage A? Answer choice G speaks of comparing and contrasting different animals on the walls, but that isn't the purpose of Passage B. Answer choice H tries to lure you into a false answer by speaking of a "European" perspective (since the author of Passage B wrote about European art), but the author of Passage B, as far as we know, does not provide an "anthropological" perspective (that is the role of the author of Passage A). Answer choice J speaks of a kind of historical expertise regarding cave art, but that isn't her specialty. That leaves the correct answer, which is choice F, which correctly states that the author of Passage B might speak to the type of charcoal used in the cave and how it was applied, both of which are specialties of the author of Passage B.

Passage IV

31. Correct answer: **C**. Whatever was left off with in the second paragraph is what the third paragraph shifts "from," and whatever the main topic of the third paragraph is what the paragraph shifts "to." Upon rereading the third paragraph (and upon inspection of what you annotated in the margin), it is entirely dedicated to the semiochemical communication of ants. This is what is being shifted "to," which will eliminate for us options A (which speaks of a shifting "to" physical characteristics of the ant) and D (which also speaks of the same shifting "to" physical characteristics). Answer choice B, however, speculates that what is being shifted "from" is "the invasive range" of the ant. However, the second paragraph is about the ant's physical characteristics, not its invasive range. This is why C is correct: it properly says that the third paragraph marks a shift "from" the physical characteristics of the ant (the topic/purpose of the second paragraph) to the semiochemical communication of the ant (the topic/purpose of the third paragraph).

32. Correct answer: **G**. We've discussed this before: you may think you know what the word "assumes" means, and you'd be correct. However, this word (as is true of many words in the English language) can have multiple meanings depending on how it is used. You need to, of course, go back and reread the word in the context of the sentence. The full sentence in which the word is used says this: "The larval stages begin with an oval-shaped egg that *assumes* the shape of an embryo…". Clearly, this word is being used to mean something like *takes the shape of*, or something similar. Letter F is wrong because it proposes that this word is being used to mean something like making a decision about what type of ant to be, but that is incorrect. Letter H is wrong because it proposes that this word is being used to mean something like being mistaken for something else, but that is also incorrect. Letter J proposes that *assumes* is being used to mean something like responding to an alarm, but that of course is also incorrect. Only answer choice G rightly proposes that the word *assumes* is being used to take a new shape or form (to "take the shape of"), which is why it is the correct answer.

33. Correct answer: **D**. Hopefully, you are able to identify quickly through your Passage Map and annotating which paragraph to refer to to get this question correct. The paragraph that needs to be referred to is the last paragraph (lines 71-86). Letter A is incorrect because it falsely claims that the invasive ant has been overall "beneficial", but that is contradicted by the last paragraph (especially lines 71-73). Letter choice B is also incorrect because it falsely states that it shows hybridization with native species; however, the only hybridization that is mentioned (line 10) is that between two invasive ants, not native species. Letter choice C starts out truthfully by correctly stating that the fire ant has been eaten by native species, it falsely claims that it has proven harmful to the flourishing of "non-native species," in other words, other invasive species. That's false first because the impact of invasive ants on other invasive species is never mentioned. This leaves answer choice D, which is correct; it rightly says that the fire ant has been eaten by native species (birds and spiders, for example), but that it has proven harmful to native species (the Stock Island tree snail, for example).

34. Correct answer: **G**. If you can remember this kind of detail after reading the passage actively, then I am extremely impressed. However, if you are like most, you will need to go back and find the correct answer in the passage. The paragraph to refer to is the second paragraph (lines 13-32), which details physical differences between different ants. First, let's look to see if head size (which is part of answers F, G, and J) is one physical difference between the worker and major worker castes. Sure enough, line 15 refers to their difference in head size, which eliminates answer choice H. Now, the best thing to do would be to simply keep reading until another difference became obvious, then select the appropriate answer. Sure enough, you don't need to reach much further to see that the next difference between the two types manifests in the "fourth and final larval instar" stage of development (line 19). This makes G the correct answer. Letter F is incorrect because there are more differences besides just head size. Letter J is incorrect because the paragraph later says that they have the same number of sensilla on their antennae upon pupation.

35. Correct answer: **D**. This is another example of a detail that needs finding, and it is key for you to have given yourself enough time to do so. *Solenopsis richteri* is discussed in the first paragraph (lines 1-12). Very simply, this question is asking which of the following details about the *S. richteri* is true? Choice A isn't true, since northern Mississippi is simply the area where the two type of invasive ants from South America overlap. Answer choice B isn't true either because the ability to enter into hybridization doesn't make *S. richteri* unique compared to *S. invicta* because these two species are doing it together in northern Mississippi. Answer C can't be correct either since *S. richteri* is also an invasive species (line 8). This is why D is the correct answer: *S. richteri* is native to southeastern South America (line 7), while *S. invicta* is native to central South America (lines 2-3).

36. Correct answer: **F**. First, you need to reread lines 51-55 yourself and form some kind of simple paraphrase before reading through the answer choices. I think a simple paraphrase of this sentence would be something like this: "Scientists are considering importing the phorid fly to help control ant populations/spread." Now, which answer choice best matches up with that kind of summary? For the sake of going through all of the answers, let's work backwards. Answer J proposes that the phorid fly (called *Apocephalus*) is the *only* solution to stopping the spread of the ant, but that's not in lines 51-55 and probably isn't true. Answer H is contradictory; it correctly states that the fly decapitates the ant, but falsely says that this will further the spread of the ant; this contradiction is why it is incorrect. Answer G also begins truly by indicating that the fly decapitates the ant in South America, but then it makes a claim (that the fly is unlikely to do so in invasive environments) that isn't in lines 51-55. Answer F is correct because it rightly notes that the fly might slow the ant, but scientists are cautious about introducing it (which is implied by the scientists studying whether or not to import the fly).

37. Correct answer: **C**. Unfortunately, this question sends you across the passage to find whether or not these details are true or false about *S. invicta.* Answer A is false because lines 3-5 clearly state that the ant is equally invasive in Australia and Asia as it is in the United States. Answer choice B is also false because there's no discussion of mammals eating the ant (lines 55-57 speak of insects, birds, and arachnids doing so, but not mammals). Answer choice D falsely claims that *S. invicta* are to be brought into extinction as the numbers of dragonflies increase, but there is no mention of this idea (just because there's mention that some dragonflies eat the ant, you can't then infer that the idea that the dragonfly will bring the ant to extinction). This leaves answer choice C, which is correct; it rightly proposes that the fire ant is mostly composed of smaller workers (which can be found in line 28; if major workers make up up to 35% of the ants, then that means that smaller worker ants make up 65% or more of the ants in the hive).

38. Correct answer: **G**. Again, in these vocabulary in context questions, you need to reread the word in the context it is used; you may know one or more meanings of the word *stages*, but you can't know the correct answer without a reference to the original sentence. The sentence reads like this: "The larval *stages* begin with an oval-shaped egg that assumes the shape of an embryo..." Clearly, the word *stages* is being used in this context to refer to different steps in the development process of the ant egg. This is why the correct answer is G. The other answers might be meanings of the word *stages*, but only answer choice G identifies the way it is being used in line 20.

39. Correct answer: **A**. The details about what major workers do when they encounter food is found in paragraph 3 (lines 33-47), but particularly in lines 35-41, which speak of what the ants do when they come upon food. It says that they "secrete trail pheromones" to alert other ants. Only answer choice A ("Release trail pheromones") correctly identifies what the worker ant does when it encounters food.

40. Correct answer: **H**. The venom of the red fire ant is discussed in the final paragraph of the passage, but particularly in lines 77-86. Letter F proposes that the venom of the ant isn't a threat to human beings, but the aforementioned lines speak of the threat of the venom on more vulnerable humans (lines 83-84). Letter G says that the venom is the reason why the ant is rarely eaten by birds; however, this idea is not found in the passage (certainly not in the part of the passage that discusses how many different birds eat it!). Letter J is incorrect because it falsely states that the venom is non-toxic, an idea that is contradicted in lines 79-81 especially. This leaves H, which is the correct answer; the author makes a point to say that ants do not bite, but sting (which is found in parentheses in line 78).

Answer Explanations - Step 6 - Practice Test #2

Correct Answers:

Passage I	Passage II	Passage III	Passage IV
1: B	11: D	21: D	31: B
2: G	12: J	22: H	32: F
3: D	13: D	23: A	33: D
4: J	14: H	24: F	34: G
5: B	15: B	25: B	35: C
6: H	16: H	26: J	36: F
7: A	17: C	27: A	37: A
8: J	18: J	28: G	38: H
9: D	19: C	29: C	39: A
10: H	20: F	30: H	40: F

Possible Passage Map (Passage I):

READING TEST

35 Minutes — 40 Questions

DIRECTIONS: There are several passages in this test. Each passage is accompanied by several questions. After reading a passage, choose the best answer to each question and fill in the corresponding oval on your answer document. You may refer to the passages as often as necessary.

Passage I

LITERARY NARRATIVE: This passage is adapted from the story "The Grove" by Martin J. Phillips.

That night the three returned to the property. Joey's knees bobbed up and down against the back of the driver's seat. Once deep into the grove Dillon let them take off the blindfolds. A full moon illuminated the night, and its rays pierced a few of the thick branches like silver spears.

"We have got to make this quick," Dillon said. "Janie is coming over to the house tonight when the band starts."

"I thought you said she hated fraternities," Joey said. "Why would she want to come over to our house, and while we're at it, why are we even here right now, why did I agree to this? Let's get out of here while we got the chance."

Red punched him in the shoulder and called him a wimp. "Dillon let's get on with it! It's a little bright for my liking, and besides, we do not want to keep Janie waiting."

The truck roared like a lion when Dillon slammed the accelerator. They weaved in and out and all around the arching giants and left deep tracks in the wet earth. Mud and grass were thrown into the air behind them. Joey buried his face in his hands and Red screamed with excitement. Dillon had never done anything like this, but it gave him a thrill he had rarely felt. What Janie might think, what his parents might say if they heard, was irrelevant. They drew near to the path to the creek and turned around; at least two of them had their minds set on doing more damage. After a couple of more minutes they neared the end of the cornfield on what was to them the left side of the property.

"What's that?" Dillon asked. When they were fifty feet away, they could see it more clearly. A vacant tractor was parked in the middle of their path. Dillon pressed the brake with a soft foot. Red stretched his eyes and leaned over to Joey to get a better look, whispering with concerned confidence that it had indeed been there on the way in.

Dillon adjusted his posture, easing his foot off of the brake. Like a postman he rolled down the window and reached his hand out towards the tractor, placing his hand upon the hood. He gasped and turned to his friends. "It's warm," he said. "How could it be warm?"

From behind an aged pecan tree, a shotgun's barrel emerged, followed by the limping body of the man who held it. Like an old dog he shuffled to a spot directly in front of the truck. Joey ducked and covered his head with his arms and screamed something about having told them so. Red said to run him over because they had a right to if their lives were threatened. Dillon shifted into reverse and hit the gas, but the tires only spun on their axles in the churned up mud like fireworks.

"Stop trying to be nice and go!" Red screamed.

The wheels spun. Cordia raised the gun. Red ducked beside Joey as Dillon put up his hands as if to surrender, remembering what the old man had said about being shot at in his youth. Before he closed his eyes Dillon saw a wry smile come across the old face as the gun settled on his shoulder. The moment after the weapon was fired felt like an eternity. However, no glass shattered. No one screamed or bled. Dillon cracked open his eyes like peanuts.

Pecans and branches rained down like hail, rattling the truck with a chorus of cracks and thuds. The antenna was snapped by an arm-width limb. Cordia let out a jackal's cackle and fired into the tree again with the same enthusiasm as the truck's spinning wheels. Through the open window he shouted at Dillon, "Son, just like I told you just this afternoon, turn around!" He reloaded. "Your truck's in the way of my harvest! Can't you see I'm out to farm? Turn around!" He fired into the tree twice more.

Now that Cordia had walked to one side of the path Dillon thrust the truck into drive and accelerated steadily to dislodge the tires. He drove around the old farmer as another shot was fired. More pecans landed like buckshot and a thick branch slammed into the bed and shattered a brake light. Dillon hit the gas and swiped a tree with his side mirror, which broke off and rolled to the feet of Cordia. Dillon accelerated as a final blast from the gun trumpeted a closing onslaught of pecans and branches that fell silently into the churned up tracks of mud that the college student's once prized possession had left behind. He clenched his fists, and no one spoke as the bruised and battered vehicle rumbled down the unpaved red clay and turned onto a long stretch of highway.

Possible Passage Map (Passage II):

Passage II

SOCIAL SCIENCE: Passage A is adapted from the book *England and America: A Critical Comparison* (©2012 by Edward P Block). Passage B is adapted from the book *Richard's Brother* (©1998 by Lee W. Painter).

Passage A by Edward P. Block

The American Constitution, written in 1787 and ratified in 1788, is the founding legal document of the United States, securing rights for citizens and dictating the movements of government and its system of checks and balances, among many other things. Change of this document in the form of amendments is a very strict and legal process, thus there are only 27 such amendments to the US Constitution. In the United Kingdom, such a document and process do not strictly exist.

Enacted in 1215 by King John of England, Magna Carta (originally *Magna Carta Libertatum*, meaning "Great Charter of Freedoms" in Medieval Latin) consisted of 63 clauses, most of which dealt with issues specific to King John himself. Over the next 10 years, the vast majority of these clauses would be rewritten or redacted; thus, many of the most significant changes to Magna Carta happened in the infancy of the document's influence, beginning in 1216 when Henry III, son of John, ascended to the throne. He would reissue Magna Carta more than once, most significantly in 1225 in exchange for new taxes. For a considerable time, Magna Carta was reissued by each monarch in turn and eventually solidified itself as an immovable stone in the construction of the English judicial system.

However, one clause in the original has served as a sort of bedrock of British law and an understanding of human rights the world over, most notably the Bill of Rights in the aforementioned US Constitution. It reads as such:

No free man shall be seized or imprisoned, or stripped of his rights or possessions, or outlawed or exiled, or deprived of his standing in any other way, nor will we proceed with force against him, or send others to do so, except by the lawful judgement of his equals or by the law of the land. To no one will we sell, to no one deny or delay right or justice.

This clause, number 39 in the 1215 Magna Carta, is one of only three clauses original to the document to be considered law in the United Kingdom in the present day. Much of this has to do with the organic development of British law, the courts of which may reinterpret a statute of a document such as Magna Carta from one generation to the next. On occasion, a new law may be passed by Parliament that overrules any previous legal documents, especially those issued by monarchs long ago. In modern times, the constitution of the United Kingdom, also known as the British Constitution, consists of both written and unwritten arrangements. Though uncodified into a singular body of written text or law, the piecemeal constitution of the UK does not preserve a vigilante system of justice but, quite the opposite, steadily governs the courts of Great Britain and Northern Ireland.

Passage B by Lee W. Painter

King John, the youngest of four surviving sons of King Henry II, ascended to the throne in 1199 after the death of his brother Richard, often called Richard the Lionhearted. As a young man, and being the youngest of 4 sons, he was given the nickname John Lackland because he was unlikely to inherit any land. However, John inherited at the death of his brother not only all of England and Ireland (over which he had been considered Lord for 22 years), but English-occupied France as well (including Normandy, Aquitaine, and Anjou).

Despite the signing of the Treaty of Le Goulet by both King John and Philip II, King of France, which recognized John's ownership over certain French lands, war broke in 1202 between the two sides. Though he secured early victories, John too quickly diminished funds and other military resources, and by 1204 his geographic presence on the continent was swallowed by the advances of the French King. For a decade or so and with military motives, John imposed high taxes on the citizens of England, who turned against their barons, who in turn grew increasingly angry at their king. Despite the influx in tax revenue and continental alliances, John was once and for all defeated by Philip II in 1214, permanently leaving behind the French land he had once inherited.

When John returned to England, circumstances were not much better, and his relationships with the barons continued to spoil. Despite the mutual acceptance of Magna Carta in 1215, both sides failed to live up to the document's obligations. These barons, forever known as Rebel Barons, were led by Robert Fitzwalter and others in a rebellion that led to a civil war. Louis of France, new King of France and son of Philip II, was solicited by the barons and sailed against his father's wishes to England to assist them in the war against the British King. So successful was the French army that half of England fell under French control, and Louis was proclaimed "King of England" in London by the barons themselves. After John's death, the barons softened on Louis, who was forced to sign the Treaty of Lambeth, retreat to France, and surrender any English lands and castles he claimed to be his own.

11. The author of Passage A mentions the "very strict and legal process" (lines 6-7) of amending the US Constitution primarily to:

A. solidify an argument that the American Constitution is extremely applicable in the daily lives of citizens.
B. reinforce the claim that the American Constitution is greater than that of other nations.
C. shed light on the difficulty of passing needed laws in the American legal system.
D. establish a legal system familiar to American readers so as to more easily contrast that found in the UK.

Possible Passage Map (Passage III):

Passage III

HUMANITIES: This passage is adapted from the book *A History of The Philosophical Contributions of Central and Eastern Europe* (©2020 by J. A. McAleer).

intro. to phenom.

Though some have identified phenomenology as a school or a minor branch of philosophy, it is rather something quite different, perhaps best defined as a style of thought or a method of some kind concerned primarily with the objective study of subjective experiences. This differentiates it from other fields in philosophy, such as ethics, metaphysics, logic, and epistemology. Though scientific, phenomenology is not to be confused with other subjective sciences, such as psychology or neurology, though these fields have much to say and contribute to one another.

E.H.: founder

epoché / bracketing

The founding of this philosophical style can be traced back to a professor and author named Edmund Husserl (1859-1938), an Austrian-German who taught and wrote in the late nineteenth and early twentieth centuries. Interestingly, his first published work (1891) was titled *Philosophy of Arithmetic*, a treatise on the philosophy of mathematics, the focus of which is the concept of *number* as a psychological one (thus, of subjective origin). As he grew as a philosopher, his phenomenological approach also grew, in which he noticed that in any interaction (such as one's viewing of a beautiful piece of art, the sound of far off sirens, or the witnessing of a crime or heroic achievement, for example), there are two factors to consider. First, there is the object itself (the art, the siren, the crime or achievement, etc.), which is the focus of most of philosophical inquiry. Second, there is the subject, the one doing the experiencing; this was the focus of Husserl. Using the Kantian distinction between *noumenon* and *phenomenon*, Husserl necessitated a process called bracketing or *epoché* in which the object itself (*noumenon*) is separated off or lost from focus entirely so as to unpack or gather the experience (*phenomenon*) of the subject.

E.S.: empathy

Edith Stein (1891-1942), perhaps one of Husserl's most famous students and disciples, studied under the phenomenologist at the University of Göttingen. Her focus was primarily empathy, in particular the empathetic subject and his or her experience of empathy as such. For Stein, the empathetic experience does not require a conscious or logical process, but is a result of the sense-forward or empirical experience of the other person (however unconsciously). This experience transcends a mere emotional response to another's difficulties but, as it were, puts the subject in the place of the object, as if the former were also experiencing the latter's experience. Stein, due to her Jewish background, unfortunately became a target of the Nazis, and she lost her life at Auschwitz at the age of 50.

about M.S.

Another famous phenomenologist of this era was Max Scheler (1874-1928), who was nicknamed the "Adam of the philosophical paradise." Martin Heidegger, one of the most influential philosophers of the 20th century, called Scheler "the strongest philosophical force in modern Germany, nay, in contemporary Europe and in contemporary philosophy as such." Scheler first met Husserl at the Martin Luther University of Halle-Wittenberg in 1901, but was never his student. In fact, throughout their careers, Husserl and Scheler were known to disagree on minor issues, such as the method and purpose of phenomenology itself. Nevertheless, Scheler joined the Phenomenology Circle of Munich as a professor at the University of Munich. However, he only taught there from 1907 to 1910 because he became caught up in local and university politics and subsequently lost his job. After spending time as a writer, Scheler found another teaching position at the University of Cologne, where he taught from 1919-1928.

M.S. "must love for truth"

For Scheler, philosophy at large and phenomenology in particular is not to be reduced to a sterile and value-free enterprise. Rather, participation in either requires a movement or decision of love. One can not properly gain the truth, whether metaphysical conclusions about the human person or logical conclusions about mathematics, without the precondition of love for the subject of inquiry. This definition or understanding of love served to differentiate it from the mere emotional responses or reactions to that which one loves/likes and hates. Love, as an encompassing act of the will, brings out and deepens the reality and beauty of the other, whether that be a person or, for phenomenological purposes, the object of study. Sadly, Scheler developed the habit of smoking 60 to 80 cigarettes a day near the end of his life and died of complications from a heart attack on May 19, 1928.

D.D.: critic just qualia

Phenomenology has also had its critics. Some, such as Daniel Dennett (1942 –) argue that phenomenology as a method, and thus all of its conclusions and theories, should be discarded wholesale. According to Dennett, the subject of study of phenomenology (the phenomena of the individual) is reducible entirely to *qualia*, defined as instances of subjective experience and criticized for differing from person to person. For example, the sight experience of the color red is *qualia*, but different subjects will pinpoint varied shades as the true, objective red. Thus, says Dennett, if *qualia* differ from person to person, then gathering subjective experiences of multiple individuals taints a pool of data, making it incapable of objective philosophical or scientific study.

21. The structure of the passage can best be described as an overview of phenomenology primarily focusing on:

A. contradictions in the philosophical movement that have lead to division from within.
B. the surging popularity of the method throughout various European universities, but particularly those in Austria and Germany.
C. the downfall of the movement early on, but its resurgence near the end of the twentieth century.
D. its origins and major contributors spanning the late nineteenth and twentieth centuries.

Possible Passage Map (Passage IV):

Passage IV

NATURAL SCIENCE: This passage is adapted from the article "The Rocks of Space: From Shooting Star to Museum Display" by Caitlin Richards (©2008 by Nevada Astronomical Annual Magazine).

A meteorite is a solid object originating outside of the atmosphere of earth that survives its descent to the planet's surface. More than 90% of verified meteorites are rocky, but a small percentage contain iron or nickel. Although it is estimated that as much as 120 tons of space matter (consisting mostly of space dust, or finite particles) enter the atmosphere of earth each and every day, a relatively small amount will survive the 62 mile descent from the Van Karmen line at the edge of space to the surface of the planet. This is due to the burning up of meteors in the atmosphere at temperatures as high as 2,000 degrees Kelvin (over 3,000 degrees Fahrenheit). Those that survive the descent will retain a fusion crust, a telltale meteorite sign that is often confused with desert varnish, hematite coatings, and spheroidal weathering (the process in which concentric outer layers of rock break away in pieces).

Since the early 19th century, less than 1,900 meteorites have been discovered and verified in the United States. Despite the rarity of having discovered a meteorite, thousands of persons each year seek expert classification to determine the nature of a stone they have stumbled upon. A test by a professional can help to reveal if the mineral in question is a meteorwrong (such as hematite and magnetite, both dense iron-oxides, or slag, the metallic byproduct of smelting) or one of three varieties of meteorite: stony-type, iron-type, or stony/iron-type.

While some stony-type meteorites may contain small traces of metal, they are mostly composed of minerals that contain silicates (materials made of Silicon and Oxygen). Of these stony-type meteorites, the most common is the chondrite, representing roughly 86% of all meteorite types and 88% of all stony-type meteorite samples. Chondrites originate from asteroids and are estimated to be over 4.5 billion years old (in other words, material from which the solar system formed). What separates a chondrite from an achondrite (a second, rarer variety of stony-type meteorite) is that the former has never undergone an igneous or melting phase. Almost all chondrites are composed of 33-43% SiO_2 (Silicon Dioxide), which is slightly less than most lunar (43-48%) or Martian (44-53%, with outliers on either side) rocks. Most terrestrial meteorwrongs (sandstone, quartzite, basalt, and rhyolite, among others) possess much higher concentrations of Silicon Dioxide because they contain quartz, a mineral never found in meteorites. In addition, most chondrites contain higher levels of Magnesium Oxide (MgO) that terrestrial meteorwrongs or lunar meteorites. While the percentage of MgO in Martian rocks varies greatly, that of the chondrite will likely fall between 21 and 26%, with very few outliers.

Iron-type meteorites (also known as ferrous meteorites or siderites) consist overwhelmingly of meteoric iron, an iron-nickel alloy. Typically, meteoric iron consists of two phases. The first, kamacite, typically features an isometric-hexoctahedral crystalline structure, and is composed of an iron:nickel ratio between 90%:10% and 95%:5%. Occasionally, kamacite may contain traces of cobalt or carbon, and it is not uncommon for it to intermix with the second siderite phase (taenite) in the same meteorite, forming Widmanstätten patterns, or fine interleaving of the two phases in ribbons or bands called *lamellae*. Taenite differs from kamacite primarily in iron:nickel ratio, which can vary from 80%:20% to 35%:65%. Ataxites, iron-type meteorites in which taenite is the dominant constituent, best show the opaque nature and metallic grayish color of taenite; this is a second characteristic that distinguishes taenite from kamacite, as the latter is not opaque and features a metallic luster. Most iron meteorites are believed to have originated in the cores of asteroids that melted long ago, early in their individual histories; as the asteroids melted over time, the densest elements sank to the center to form a metallic core.

Stony/iron-type meteorites, as the name suggests, are meteorites made up of nearly equal parts silicates and meteoric iron. Also known as siderolites, these meteorites are achondrites, meaning they do not contain the round grains known as chondrules that typically form as molten droplets in space before accretion into parent asteroids. Of the two types of stony/iron-type meteorites, the pallasite contains a beautiful olive-green crystal called *olivine* (a form of magnesium-iron silicate), which can also be found in the earth's mantle. Many scientists believe that the pallasite comes from the boundary between an asteroid's metallic core and silicate-rich mantle, but others maintain that the number of olivine-rich asteroids in the solar system is few, and these thus hypothesize that impact melting (when a meteorite strikes the earth) plays a direct role in the formation of olivine in pallasites.

A second stony-iron meteorite is the mesosiderite, which, as a breccia, consists of a variety of rocks (in this case, silicates and metal) cemented together by a finer material. Mesosiderites form when debris from an asteroid collision mixes together; specifically, molten metal from an asteroid core intermixes with solid fragments of silicate rocks.

31. One of the main ideas presented in the passage is that a a meteorwrong, of which there are many types,:

- **A.** is easily mistaken for a meteorite, and scientific study is mostly unable to pinpoint a difference.
- **B.** is easily mistaken for a meteorite, but scientific study can differentiate the two.
- **C.** can never be made up of or possess a significant amount of quartz.
- **D.** is rarely discovered, let alone submitted for a scientific analysis.

Passage I

1. Correct answer: **B**. This kind of question is one of those that requires a grasp of the story as a whole; at this point, rereading the passage is not an option. You must remember also that most of these answers are going to contain at least a shred of truth, or maybe be *based* on the passage, but only 1 of them is going to definitely be true. Answer choice A truthfully speaks to the reluctance of one of the three college-age students in the story, but falsely says that they won't engage in risk-taking activities (which is what the entire excerpt is about). Answer choice C proposes that the passage is about the three friends having the same opinions about things; however, whether or not that is true is debatable, and besides, that's not what this excerpt is mostly about. Answer D says that the story is about a hierarchy of friends who are mature; while it may be true that there is some kind of "hierarchy" among the three friends, they certainly aren't mature! Answer choice B is correct: it rightly proposes that the passage is mostly about the tensions among the friends and a property owner they have wronged.

2. Correct answer: **G**. This is one of the longest questions you'll ever see on an ACT test. If you can, simplify it. Here is how I would simplify this question: "Which of the quotes best reveals Dillon's personality?" Dillon has a reluctant kind of personality; he is pushed to do things he doesn't want to do by Red. Which quote shows that the most? Don't overthink it either. Upon reading answer choice F, you might think to yourself something like, "The blindfolds they are wearing are metaphors for what they don't want to do," or something like that. No; the answer isn't going to be a matter of interpretation; there is going to be a correct answer. Answer H is about Dillon tapping the brakes; again, this doesn't reveal his reluctant personality. Answer choice J is about Dillon flooring it in the pecan grove; again, this doesn't reveal his reluctant personality. This is why the answer is G, which reads, "Dillon had never done anything like this." This quote reveals Dillon's reluctant personality in that he is timid when it comes to driving through the pecan grove.

3. Correct answer: **D**. Go back and read this quote in context. In this case, the clinching of his fists is a *response* to something else; there is cause and effect, and the clenching of the fists is the effect. What is the cause? A rereading of the final passage will be enough to help you determine the correct answer. It may be that Dillon is afraid that Janie will be angry with him (answer choice A), but that is not the cause alluded to in the final paragraph. There is no indication in the final paragraph that Dillon is still afraid of the shotgun (answer choice B) or that Dillon is angry at red (answer choice C). Instead, the sentence prior to the quote about Dillon clenching his fists alludes to Dillon's truck being his "once prized possession" (line 82). This is the cause of Dillon's fist clenching, and this is why D is the correct answer.

4. Correct answer: **J**. At this point, you have probably already reasoned or had to understand that Dillon is reluctant to drive through the pecan grove. That kind of understanding was necessary to get number 2 correct, for example. What we know about Dillon is that he wants the drive over with quick (line 7), that Red is a character who pushes Dillon to start driving crazily (lines 15-18), and that "Dillon had never done anything like this" (line 24). With all of that in mind, it is clear that answer choice F is incorrect; Dillon is not portrayed as some kind of meticulous planner who thought this through. Choice G is also incorrect in that it says that Dillon is "uninfluenced by others," but certainly the opposite is true. Answer choice H is also wrong because it proposes that Janie is the source of the idea to drive the truck through the grove. This leave answer choice J, which is correct because it correctly proposes that his choice to drive the truck through the grove is dependent upon social pressure.

5. Correct answer: **B**. When Dillon begins to drive the truck through the grove, the passage says this: "What Janie might think… was irrelevant" (lines 25-27). In other words, Janie will certainly disapprove of what he is doing. This means that she certainly will not be "unfazed" (which is why answer A is incorrect) or "delighted" (which is why answer C is incorrect). Answer choice D is a tempting one, but there is no indication in the passage that Janie knows anything about the old farmer or his reputation. This is why B is the correct answer: she will certainly be "disappointed" because she will disapprove of their decision.

6. Correct answer: **H**. The best thing to do is to reread the sixth paragraph and try to pinpoint or identify its function in the narrative before reading through the answer choices. As a side note, if you were to read through the choices first, I think there's a good chance you'll cling to a partial truth in one of the answer choices, be content, and move on, none the wiser that you just got a question wrong. Upon rereading the sixth paragraph, it certainly creates suspense and serves as a bridge between the boys' driving through the grove and the farmer emerging with his shotgun. These ideas are not found in answer F, G, of J. This is why the correct answer is H: the sixth paragraph certainly creates suspense and intrigue.

7. Correct answer: **A**. The interaction that the question alludes to is not given a line reference, so you have to find it. In lines 10-18, Joey fearfully wants to leave the grove, then Red punches him in the shoulder and calls him a wimp. Letter B is not correct because it falsely says that Red is frightened, but that's true of Joey. Letter choice C is incorrect because it says that it "anticipates" that they will need to be tough, but that is a stretch and isn't directly implied or stated. Answer choice D is also incorrect because Red is not afraid, unlike Joey. Answer choice A is thus the correct answer because it rightly says that Red won't tolerate Joey's fear.

8. Correct answer: **J**. This is a straight up detail that needs to be searched out. Hopefully you used active reading to give yourself the time to look up this detail. While there are references in the passage to "a smoking gun" (answer F), "pecans and branches" (answer G), and "buckshot" (answer H), Cordia is referred to as "a jackal" (answer J) in line 66, making J the correct answer.

9. Correct answer: **D**. This is another question that likely requires you to go hunting for the correct answer. Letter C is probably the easiest to investigate, since you can pinpoint that if it is true it will be near the very end of the story. However, there is no indication in lines 83-85 that they are plotting revenge, so letter C is incorrect. Letter D is probably the next easiest to investigate, since it indicates that the trio have trespassed on this property before. Sure enough, a rereading of line 1 is enough to verify this choice as the correct answer; line 1 says that the three "returned to the property," meaning they have trespassed there before. This is why D is the correct answer. As for answer A, there is no indication that they have stolen pecans from Cordia anywhere in the story. As for answer B, there is also no indication in the story that all three friends do not want Janie to come over later.

10. Correct answer: **H**. This question requires you to infer, unlike most ACT Reading questions in which making inferences is dangerous and likely to lead to incorrect answers. When it asks you to infer, it is asking you to reach a most likely conclusion based on the data or what is said in the passage itself. In line 45 Cordia is described as "limping," but then in line 46 he is compared to an "old dog." In line 56 he is called an "old man," then in line 58 he is said to have an "old face." In other words, it is pretty clear that he is old. While it *could be true* that the mud makes it difficult to walk (answer F) or that he had been injured in war (answer G), there is not enough evidence to reach that inference. As for letter J, although it is night time, the scene is described as illuminated by a "full moon" (line 4), and Red even says that it's a "little bright" outside (line 16). These are all reasons why answer H is the correct answer; most likely, Cordia is limping and shuffling because he is elderly.

Passage II

11. Correct answer: **D**. The first paragraph of Passage A, of which this quote is a part, does something very particular for the passage as a whole. If I were to ask you about the overall meaning of the passage, you would tell me something about the British Constitution, or maybe about Magna Carta. However, the first paragraph is about the American Constitution. What this paragraph does as a whole to the passage is give the average reader something to compare the British Constitution to, since the two are very different in structure and application. This quote, about the "very strict and legal process" of the American Constitution, does this as well. Answer A is incorrect because there is no argument in the passage about the applicability of the American Constitution. Answer choice B is incorrect because there is no claim in the passage that the American Constitution is superior to others. Answer choice C is incorrect because the passage isn't about various laws that need to be passed in America. Answer choice D, on the other hand, is correct because it is true that this quote establishes something to contrast the UK system to.

12. Correct answer: **J**. We learn in line 13 that Magna Carta, which was issued by King John, had 63 clauses. However, we learn later in lines 37-39 that there are now only 3 original clauses of Magna Carta to be considered law in the UK today. Thus, letter H, which asserts that King John had an unchangeable effect, is certainly not true. We can say that G is also not true; the effect certainly wasn't delayed, since the clauses of Magna Carta came into effect immediately, then decreased in influence over time. Because Magna Carta did and does have an effect on modern law (especially the quoted clause about human rights), it also isn't true that King John had no significant effect at all, which eliminates Answer F. This leaves J, which is correct because it rightly says that John had a moderate effect on modern law.

13. Correct answer: **D**. Hopefully you active read these passages so as to give yourself enough time to research the correct answer, which can be found in lines 16-19. In that segment, it clearly states that most of the early changes to Magna Carta happened when Henry III became king. This is why D is the correct answer; the other options falsely identify the changes to Magna Carta with other persons or influences.

14. Correct answer: **H**. This is the first question that is exclusive to Passage B. The question asks for the *greatest single factor* that leads to the rebellion of the Rebel Barons. There could be dozens of factors, but only 1 most significantly led to the rebellion. Letters F, G, and J *could* all be factors in such a rebellion, but none of them are cited as a direct cause in the rebellion. It is clearly stated beginning in line 71 that John overtaxed the citizens, who turned on their barons, who turned on their king. This is why the answer is H: King John's overtaxing of the citizens of England.

15. Correct answer: **B**. This question is asking, essentially, what is the purpose of highlighting that the King of France (Louis) was declared King of England in London? It certainly isn't A; if anything, such a declaration *highlights* the lasting effect of the ongoing warfare between France and England. Answer C can't possibly be correct either; Richard the Lionhearted barely gets a mention at the beginning of Passage B, so a comparison between Louis of France and Richard is impossible and certainly not the purpose of the declaration in question. Answer D has some truth sprinkled in it: King John certainly acted on military whims, which led to this situation. However, that doesn't mean that this kind of point about English leadership is the purpose of the author including the incident. Instead, B is certainly the correct answer; the essay's focus is King John and his failures from start to finish, and this incident in London certainly emphasizes the depths of these failures.

16. Correct answer: **H**. Again, if you can't remember one of the answer choices as being true about the Rebel Barons, then hopefully you left yourself some time to go and research the correct answers by active reading! Answer choice F can be easily dismissed straight away; if they are rebelling against their king, then they certainly aren't "unfailingly obedient" to him. Answer choice G might be tempting since it speaks to a relationship between the Rebel Barons and France, but there's no indication in the passage that foreign influences "swayed" them (such as with money, promises of power, etc.). Letter J is probably the most tempting incorrect answer choice since the first clause of the sentence ("They were reluctant to obey legal documents") is true (since they, like King John, failed to live up to Magna Carta; see lines 81-82), but the second clause is definitely false because

(see the same lines) they didn't actually live up to Magna Carta. That leaves H, which is of course the correct answer; at one point they were loyal to the king, then things changed due to circumstances, then all of a sudden they were loyal to the French king.

17. Correct answer: **C**. Philip II is different than Louis; Philip II is his father. Philip II does two main things in the passage. First, he retakes French lands (in other words, lands in modern day France on the European continent) from King John (lines 69-70). Second, Philip II is opposed to his son Louis's sailing into England to conquer English land. Both of these provide evidence that he believes that England belongs to England, and France belongs to France, and encroachment of one upon the other is wrong. This means that C is certainly the correct answer. Choice A makes it sound like Philip II would also invade England if given the chance, but that's not true as we have just said. Choice B is incorrect for the exact same reasons. Answer D is also incorrect; if Philip II fought England off the European continent, then it is false to say that English presence should be expanded *onto* the European continent.

18. Correct answer: **J**. This is the beginning of the questions that, in some sense, are about both passages. This particular question is very macro, meaning it is concerned with the "big picture" of both passages, and thus a difference between them. It isn't likely that you have the time to go back and reread these passages, so don't! Let's explore the answers one at a time. Answer F is incorrect because it falsely says that Passage A focuses on "contradictions" in the British Constitution, but that isn't a focus or mentioned by Passage A. Answer choice G is incorrect because it falsely states that a "majority of the clauses of Magna Carta" are lasting; however, the opposite is stated in Passage A (see lines 37-38). Answer choice H is also incorrect because it falsely says that Passage A focuses on the monarchs' role in the modern British Constitution; however, Passage A is focused on Magna Carta's history. For what it's worth, if that's not enough for you, option H also says that Passage B focuses on French military victories, and while French military victories are an aspect of Passage B, that certainly isn't the focus. Only answer choice J correctly identifies the correct focuses of Passage A (Magna Carta's history and effect on modern British law) and Passage B (the failures of King John).

19. Correct answer: **C**. Magna Carta is an overlapping idea in both passages. If one thing is for sure about Magna Carta after reading Passage A and B, it is that it was quick to be changed and/or ignored, even by the people who enacted it! Thus, answer choice A is certainly not true; "universal" means applying to everyone (which might be true of everyone in England), but "immutable" means unchanging, which is definitely why it's false. Answer choice B states that Magna Carta is difficult to interpret, but the difficulty of interpretation is not mentioned in either passage (and remember: you can't infer to a possible conclusion in ACT Reading unless you are strictly asked to do so!). Letter D talks about it being over-the-top and lengthy; while the number of clauses in Magna Carta is mentioned in Passage A, there is no indication by either passage that it is lengthy or too long. Answer choice C, on the other hand, correctly states that both passages emphasize that Magna Carta is ignored and easily changed.

20. Correct answer: **F**. Just like number 19, this question is asking about a similarity between the two passages. Certainly letter G is false; Henry III isn't even mentioned in Passage B. Since Magna Carta was written *in* the 13th-century, it can't be true that the 13th-century was a time for "laying the groundwork" for the writing of it; this is why option H is also incorrect. Answer choice J says that the 13th-century was uninfluenced by foreigners. However, Passage B certainly stresses the effect of France on England in the 13th-century. This is why F is the correct answer: the 13th-century, as evidenced in both passages, was a time of change, yet turmoil, for England.

Passage III

21. Correct answer: **D**. This kind of overarching question requires a general understanding of the passage as a whole. Unfortunately, you don't have the time to reread this passage. On the other hand, you *should* have a Passage Map you could read over very quickly if you needed an extra bit of help to get this question correct. Answer choice A proposes that the passage focuses on the contradictions of phenomenology and then division; while there was a bit of division mentioned between Scheler and Husserl (lines 59-61), that certainly isn't the overall purpose of the passage. Answer choice B says that the primary focus of the essay is the surging popularity of phenomenology; however, there is no mention of surging popularity in the passage (in other words, no mention of the number of students, the number of professors who teach it, etc.). You might *infer* that it is growing in popularity ("surging" in popularity), but that isn't the focus of the passage as a whole. Answer choice C proposes that the focus of the essay is the early downfall then later resurgence of the movement; again, there is no mention of any downfall or resurgence. This makes D correct, which rightly says that the focus of the essay is the origins of and major contributors to phenomenology.

22. Correct answer: **H**. This answer might require you to go back and reread the paragraph about Daniel Dennett, and that would be OK to do. For Dennett, *qualia* is problematic because it is different for different people and taints a pool of data; this is why answer H is the correct answer (see line 92). Answer F can't be correct because whether or not *qualia* predate Husserl is irrelevant to whether or not it is problematic. Answer G is incorrect because, by definition, *qualia* is a subjective experience. Answer J is incorrect because *qualia* doesn't have to be only visual (it could be taste or sound, for example, based on its definition), but this also isn't mentioned in the passage.

23. Correct answer: **A**. Fortunately, this question quotes the passage and then gives you line references to follow it up. If you read beginning with the sentence that starts in line 72, you will read that one can't "properly gain the truth" without love as a

precondition. This is why answer choice A is correct. This reading of the quoted sentence ought to be enough to, at a minimum, eliminate answer choices B and C (since both are irrelevant to the idea of love). Answer D, though it uses the word "love" in it, is incorrect because it proposes that "Emotional responses" are the precondition to properly gain the truth, but according to Scheler, that isn't the same thing as love (see line 77).

24. Correct answer: **F**. This question is referring to the mention of psychology and neurology that takes place at the end of paragraph 1 (lines 7-11). If you reread those lines, you will see that the author claims that psychology, neurology, and phenomenology "have much to say and contribute to one another," meaning that each helps deepen an understanding of the other. This most closely aligns with answer choice F, which is the correct answer. Answers G, H, and J falsely claim that psychology and neurology will have a bad effect or no effect on phenomenology, which is why they are incorrect.

25. Correct answer: **B**. We have been over this: you may think you have a knowledge of the meaning of the word *Circle*, but it will almost always be used in the passage in a way that is not in line with the most obvious definition. In other words, it is very unlikely that the word *Circle* here means "a round shape" or something like that. Reread the word in the context of the sentence in which it is used, which says: "Nevertheless, Scheler joined the Phenomenology *Circle* of Munich as a professor…" Clearly, *Circle* here is being used to mean a club or a group of people with a similar interest in phenomenology. This is why the answer is B: "a group of people with shared interests" is exactly how the word *Circle* is being used.

26. Correct answer: **J**. Most likely, you will need to reread not only lines 22-23, but the rest of the second paragraph as well to answer this question correctly with confidence. Did you save yourself the time to do so with active reading? If the answer is "no," then get to work on that! The second paragraph uses "the sound of far off sirens" as an example of what affects a person. Because the sirens are outside of the person, they are objective, and because the person hears them, they are also subjective; in other words, it is an example of both *noumenon* (lines 31-32) and *phenomenon*, not only phenomenon, which is why answer choice F is incorrect. Answer choice G also says that the sirens are an example of something "subjective", but again it is being used to highlight both the objective and subjective, so G is incorrect. Answer choice H says that it is an empathetic experience, but empathy isn't discussed as a subject at all until the next paragraph (paragraph 3). This is why J is the correct answer: it rightly says that the experience of the sound of far off sirens is an example of what is needed for *epoché* (see lines 31-34), which involves separating the objective and subjective.

27. Correct answer: **A**. This question focuses on Daniel Dennett, who is discussed in detail in the final paragraph as a critic of phenomenology. Dennett, therefore, is not interested in proving the "efficacy of phenomenology" at all, which eliminates answer choice B. Upon rereading the paragraph, it is obvious that varied responses to similar sense experiences (such as the seeing the color red) "taints a pool of data" (line 97); this is why answer A is correct. Letters C and D, about their being the starting point of phenomenology and an opportunity to distinguish *phenomenon* and *noumenon*, are more likely to be true about Husserl as he and his methods are described in the second paragraph.

28. Correct answer: **G**. Hopefully you were able to active read and give yourself the time to research the answer to this question about Edith Stein, who is discussed in the third paragraph. There is no indication in the paragraph that Stein thought empathy something " to be avoided", which is why answer F is incorrect. Answer choice H proposes that empathy should be detached from others, but again, that's not mentioned in the paragraph (and would also cause empathy to not be empathy anymore), thus H is incorrect. Answer choice J states that empathy always requires a "conscious and a logical process," but that is directly contradicted in lines 40-41. However, answer choice G correctly proposes that empathy transcends emotion, which is stated in lines 43-44.

29. Correct answer: **C**. Very simply, lines 3-5 describe phenomenology as "a style of thought or a method of some kind," which is why answer choice C is correct. There is no mention of major philosophical branches (though they are listed in line 7), which means we can't say if phenomenology is one of them; this eliminates answer choice B. The passage directly states that phenomenology is not a minor branch of philosophy (lines 2-4), which is why A is incorrect. Lastly, phenomenology is also said to not be a "school" (line 2), which is why D is incorrect as well.

30. Correct answer: **H**. Certainly, Max Scheler (who is called a "famous phenomenologist" in line 50) did not reject Husserl's phenomenology wholesale, which eliminates answer choice F as an option. In addition, line 58 states that Scheler was never Husserl's student, which eliminates answer choice G. Answer choice J says that "the two never met," but this is contradicted by lines 56-58, which states they met at a university. Thus, the correct answer is H because it correctly states that the two did disagree on minor issues (see line 60), and clearly Scheler is dependent on Husserl: Husserl invented phenomenology and Scheler became a famous phenomenologist.

Passage IV

31. Correct answer: **B**. This a kind of macro question that would require a reread of much of the passage to get it correct; hopefully a remembering of the passage and a glance through your Passage Map will be enough! Nevertheless, answer choice A is incorrect; although it starts out well (saying a meteorwrong "is easily mistaken for a meteorite"), it is false that science can't pinpoint a difference (the differences is the purpose of the entire passage). Answer C is contradicted by lines 46-47, which state that meteorwrongs often contain quartz. Answer choice D is incorrect because it is contradicted by lines 21-23, which states that

thousands of persons each year submit meteorwrongs for scientific analysis. This is why B is the correct answer: meteorwrongs are easily mistaken for meteorites, and science can indeed tell a difference between the two.

32. Correct answer: **F**. Obviously, this passage is filled with hundreds of details about meteorites, but the question asks for something that is "most likely to be true" about one. The type of meteorite referenced in answer choice G is an iron-type meteorite, which are the rarer kind, which is why G is incorrect. Answer choice H is also true of iron-type meteorites (see lines 72-73), which again is the rarer kind of meteorite, so it is also incorrect. Answer choice J speaks of meteorites that are breccia (see lines 94-96), which is found in some stony/iron-type meteorites, which again are a rarer kind. This is why F is the correct answer: the chondrite is the most common type of meteorite (lines 32-35), so any authentic meteorite is most likely to be a chondrite.

33. Correct answer: **D**. There is nothing in the passage to indicate that stony-type or iron-type meteorites are lunar (meaning, from the moon). Although there is mention of lunar rocks in the third paragraph, that is simply to compare chondrites (or the most likely stony-type meteorite) to. This eliminates answer choices A and B. The difference between choices C and D is which type of meteorite originates in an asteroid's core and which originates in its mantle. Although the word "mantle" is never used to describe the outer shell of an asteroid, it is said in lines 86-88 that the mantle of an asteroid is "silicate-rich", which is true of stony-type meteorites. If that is too much of a stretch or difficult to piece together, it may be easier to refer to lines 71-74, which speaks of iron-type meteorites originating in the cores of asteroids. This is why D is the correct answer.

34. Correct answer: **G**. If something needs further research, then that simply means that the passage makes it clear that there is an unanswered question about a particular topic; maybe there is scientific disagreement about it, or maybe it is simply alluded to as a mystery. In this passage, there is only one topic that truly meets that description, which is how olivine comes to be found in pallasite meteorites; lines 85-92 clearly state that this process is a mystery and up for debate in the scientific community because there is disagreement. This is why G is the correct answer. This kind of scientific disagreement is never raised about lunar/Martian rock differences (answer choice F), the time it takes for mesosiderites to form (answer choice H), or the chemical makeup of the chondrite (answer choice J). You may be tempted to think that you could assume H to be correct, or maybe F, but again, you can't infer or assume answers to be true if they are not found in the passage.

35. Correct answer: **C**. You are told in lines 56-59 that it is a kamacite that is a type of meteorite that has at least 90% iron. As you keep reading the paragraph, you later learn the characteristics of kamacite. First, you learn that lamallae result from a combination of both iron-type meteorites, making answer choice D incorrect. You then learn that taenite (not kamacite) is opaque and has a metallic greyish color. Because these are true of taenite, and not kamacite, that makes choices A and B incorrect also. Lastly, you learn that kamacite has "a metallic luster" (line 71), which is why choice C is the correct answer.

36. Correct answer: **F**. Of course, the best way to get a question like this correct (one that asks about a particular paragraph's purpose) is to reread the paragraph. If you don't have time for that, lean on your Passage Map, using the few words you wrote in the margin to guide you towards an answer. Answer choice J says that the paragraph speaks of the faulty process of meteorite verification, but there is no mention of any such thing in this paragraph, so it is incorrect. Answer choice H says that the paragraph pinpoints great meteorite hunting locations across the United States, but there are no such details in this paragraph, so answer H is also incorrect. Choice G proposes that the paragraph transitions "from" a detailed discussion of the chemical makeup of a meteorite, but that is coming later, so G is also incorrect. Answer choice F is correct because it rightly proposes that the paragraph highlights a meteorites rarity (only so many discovered in recent memory) and introduces the three types (see the last sentence of the paragraph).

37. Correct answer: **A**. This passage discusses meteorwrongs at multiple places. First you are given a list of a few types in line 25, then again you are given a list of a few types in lines 44-45. Of the four answer choices, three of the options (B, C, and D) are all incorrect because the rock mentioned is a type of meteorite discussed at one point or another in the passage. Choice A, on the other hand, not only mentions a true meteorwrong (basalt, found in line 45), but also a true, common characteristic of meteorwrongs (spheroidal weathering; line 15), which makes it the correct answer.

38. Correct answer: **H**. The idea that 120 tons of space matter enters earth every day is not mentioned by the author to frighten people because, as the passage states in line 6, the vast majority of it is dust or fine particles; this is enough for us to conclude that choice G is incorrect. Because it could possibly be that this statistic is sobering (F), surprising (H), or jolting (J), we need to read on to decide the statistic's purpose. Letter F, after saying the statistic is sobering, then says something about man-made space debris; however, there is no mention of man-made space debris in the entire article, so F is out as incorrect. Answer choice J, on the other hand, proposes that the statistic's purpose is to get the reader's hopes up that one day he or she will find a meteorite. However, as has been said, most of that is dust, so J is also incorrect. Answer H is correct though because it correctly says that the statistic "sets the stage" for a further discussion about the rarity of meteorites (which can be discovered easily if you keep reading).

39. Correct answer: **A**. In order to get this question correct, all you need to do is go back into the passage and reread the one sentence in which the mention of igneous rock occurs. This sentence spans lines 37-40. Clearly, the mention of igneous rock is found at the beginning of this sentence, which reads, "What separates a chondrite from an achondrite…" This is why A is the correct answer. None of the other choices (B, C, and D) is listed as a purpose for the reference to igneous rock.

40. Correct answer: **F**. Again, these vocabulary in context questions require you to simply go back and reread the sentence in which the word appears, which says this: "...thousands of persons a year seek expert classification to determine the *nature* of a stone they have stumbled upon." As I've said before, you may think you know already the meaning of the word *nature*, but there are many meanings of this word and any other word that the ACT would ask you about. If you are stumped, substitute the proposed meanings into the sentence and see which fits well. Here, options G, H, and J all propose a meaning of the word *nature* that has to do with looks or "being out in nature." However, that is not how the word is being used. Instead, it is being used to describe the *essence* of a thing, which is why F is the correct answer.

ACT Science Explanations

Answer Explanations - Step 1

Correct Answers:

Passage I:	**Passage II:**	**Passage III:**	**Passage IV:**	**Passage V:**	**Passage VI:**
1: B	**5: C**	**9: C**	**13: C**	**17: C**	**21: C**
2: J	**6: F**	**10: G**	**14: F**	**18: G**	**22: J**
3: D	**7: A**	**11: A**	**15: B**	**19: D**	**23: B**
4: F	**8: H**	**12: J**	**16: J**	**20: J**	**24: J**

Passage I:

1. Correct answer: **B**. Be careful because this question asks you to refer to *Figures* 1 and 2, not *Tables* 1 and 2. There are a couple of varieties of fruit that clearly show a pretty large difference: Bloody Butcher and Juane Flamme. If you look down at Figure 2, on the other hand, there is not much difference (though there is a difference, of course) between the control and experimental groups of both Thai Hot and Ancho: this eliminates answer choices C and D as incorrect. Now, back to A and B. Both options show a pretty large difference as has been said, but it is clear from the graph that the difference is greater in Juane Flamme (with a much lower measurement in the control column), which is why B is the correct answer.

2. Correct answer: **J**. Here, you are asked to refer to Tables 1 and 2, which compare the control's fruit yield to the experimental's fruit yield. Where this question gets tricky is in the final few words: *relative to the control*. In other words, we're not looking necessarily for the *greatest* experimental yield; if we were, the answer would be California Wonder (which is why H is incorrect). Instead, as you can see, the control column yields more fruit than the experimental 100% of the time. Thus, the phrase "relative to the control" just means something like this: which experimental yield is closest to the total control yield? If you look at the second-to-last row, you'll see that Thai Hot's experimental yield (291) is *almost* the same as the control (295). Thus, answer choice J (Thai Hot) is correct.

3. Correct answer: **D**. First of all, this question is referring to *sodium concentration*, a value that is measured in Figures 1 and 2 (the graphs on the right). Second of all, the question makes it clear that there is *only 1* fruit's control yield that will result in a saltier taste (aka, the control has a higher salt concentration than the experimental yield). If you look at the figures, there is only 1 of the 6 fruits that has the white column (the control column) stretching higher than the experimental, which is Ancho. This is why the correct answer is D: Ancho. The other options (A, B, and C) all feature fruits with an experimental yield that has a higher salt concentration than the control.

4. Correct answer: **F**. This question is simple in that it simply asks you to find the fruit with the greatest sodium concentration. The difficulty is this: Figure 2's three varieties of pepper *all* have a very low sodium concentration. It may look like Thai Hot has a sodium concentration through the roof, but if you look over on the *y* axis, you'll see that the tall black bar equates to a sodium concentration of only 15. The three tomatoes in Figure 1, however, have sodium concentrations of roughly 320, 315, and 160, respectively: way higher than 15. Thus, answers H and J, because they are both peppers with low sodium concentrations, can be eliminated as incorrect. Letters F and G are both varieties of tomato as measured in Figure 1, but Bloody Butcher's black bar is slightly higher than Juane Flamme's, and the white bar is clearly higher. This is why the correct answer is F: Bloody Butcher.

Passage II:

5. Correct answer: **C**. Figure 2 displays the calculated momentum of each cart as it crosses the finish line. The question asks about Cart B, which is denoted with triangle data points in the figure. Of course, there is no data on what the momentum would be if Cart B were dropped from a height of 4.5 meters. Instead, we have to make a best guess (infer) based on the data that we do have. According to Figure 2, when Cart B was dropped from a height of 4 meters it had a momentum of something like 170 kg·m/s. When released from a height of 5 meters, it had a momentum of something like 190 kg·m/s. Thus, we need to choose an answer between these two choices. There is only one option between the two, which is C: 180 kg·m/s.

6. Correct answer: **F**. If you look at Figure 1, you'll see that as the height increases, the difference in velocity between the three cars widens. The closest that the three are (aka, the "smallest difference in velocity" occurs at the very beginning, when the three cars are dropped from a height of 1 meter. This is why the answer is F: 1 meter.

7. Correct answer: **A**. Figure 1 gives the recorded velocities for the three cars. This question is dealing however with only Cart C, which is denoted with circle data points on the figure. If you look at the trajectory of Cart C, you see a steady increase in velocity as height increases. At 5 meters, the circle is *really close* to 7.5 m/s already, so if it were released from a height of 8 meters, it seems extremely likely that it will cross the finish line at a speed higher than that. This eliminates answer choices C and D, which both say "No." Choice B states that the cart has already reached these speeds, which isn't true. This is why the correct answer is A: an increase of 1 or more m/s is expected.

8. Correct answer: **H**. This question requires you to compare the calculated velocities of carts released at various heights. To answer correctly, either circle the various data points on Figure 1 as you go or jot the rough values next to the four answer choices and simply pick the biggest. Cart A released at a height of 1 meter (choice F) has a velocity of roughly 4 m/s. Cart A released at a height of 2 meters (choice G) has a velocity of roughly 6.5 m/s. Cart B released at a height of 3 meters (choice H) has a velocity of roughly 7 m/s. Cart C released at a height of 4 meters (choice J) has a velocity of roughly 6 m/s. This is why the correct answer is H: Cart B released at 3 meters has the highest velocity of the 4 choices.

Passage III:

9. Correct answer: **C**. To get this question correct, simply look at each table and see which beakers had reached a temperature of 0 degrees after 70 minutes had elapsed. Table 1 (Beaker A)? Yes. Table 2 (Beaker B)? Yes. Table 3 (Beaker C)? Yes. Table 4 (Beaker D)? No. Three of four have reached the temperature. Because the question says what percent *had* reached a temperature of 70 degrees, the correct answer is C: 75%.

10. Correct answer: **G**. First, ensure that you are looking for data in the correct table. In this case, we are dealing with Beaker C, which is measured in Table 3. Of course, we don't have data on what the temperature was after 37 minutes had elapsed. However, we can *infer* to the correct answer by finding data points around the 37 minute mark. After 35 minutes, the temperature was 17 degrees. After 40 minutes, the temperature was 14 degrees. Thus, the correct answer must be between 17 and 14 degrees. This is why the correct answer is G: 16 degrees; it is the only answer between these two values.

11. Correct answer: **A**. Let's go through each Table one by one and see each drop in temperature over the time span between 10 and 45 minutes having elapsed. Table 1 (Beaker A) records 36 degrees at 10 minutes and 8 degrees at 45 minutes (a drop of 28 degrees). Table 2 (Beaker B) records 23 degrees at 10 minutes and 8 degrees at 45 minutes (a drop of 15 degrees). Table 3 (Beaker C) records 38 degrees at 10 minutes and 11 degrees at 45 minutes (a drop of 27 degrees). Table 4 (Beaker D) records 22 degrees at 10 minutes and 10 degrees at 45 minutes (a drop of 12 degrees). This is why the correct answer is A: Beaker A; it records the greatest drop in temperature (28 degrees) over the time span specified in the question.

12. Correct answer: **J**. This question is very similar to number 11 above. Simply go table by table and see how long it took each beaker to make the drop from 20 to 0 degrees. Beaker A (Table 1) made that drop in roughly 36 minutes. Beaker B (Table 2) made that drop in roughly 52 minutes. Beaker C (Table 3) made that drop in roughly 35 minutes. Beaker D (Table 4) made that drop in roughly 61 minutes. Thus, it clearly took Beaker D the longest to make that temperature drop, which is why J, or Beaker D, is the correct answer.

Passage IV:

13. Correct answer: **C**. According to Table 2, only foods with CT values less than 35 have a high/moderate likelihood of causing a severe peanut allergic reaction. Thus, the answer is "No," the manufacturer doesn't need this label, which eliminates answers A and B. Letter D mentions CT values "less than 50", but that scale doesn't exist at all. This is why the correct answer is C, which states correctly that a CT value between 36 and 40 means a very low possibility of causing a severe peanut allergic reaction.

14. Correct answer: **F**. According to Table 2, only foods that have a CT value of less than or equal to 29 have a high likelihood of triggering an allergic reaction. Looking at Table 1, there is only 1 food on the scale (the first one, Cereal bar I) that has a CT value that low. This is why the correct answer is F: 1.

15. Correct answer: **B**. First, determine how many foods fall in the high to moderate range. According to Table 2, only foods with a CT value of 30-35 are in this range. Looking at Table 1, there are only 3 foods that fall into this range (Cereal bar II, Cereal bar III, and Cookes with fiber). Out of these three, only 1 of them (Cereal bar III) mention peanuts on their packaging. This makes B, 33%, the correct answer, as only 1 of 3 mention peanuts on their packaging.

16. Correct answer: **J**. If you look over Table 1, there are 4 food products (Cereal bar II, Cereal bar IV, Chocolate with pistachio, and Sausage with walnut) that contain tree nuts and/or walnuts. These have CT values of 32.40, 35.90, 36.80, and ND (nonexistent), respectively. Because the ND food only contains walnuts and the other three contain tree nuts, it seems likely that anything with tree nuts will result in a CT value between 32 and 37. Only 1 of the 4 answer choices appropriately approximates such a CT value, which is answer choice J. The other answer choices simply give CT values that are much too high and not supported by the food choices in Table 1.

Passage V:

17. Correct answer: **C**. First, realize that we need to be referencing Experiment 1, and thus Table 1, which was conducted under a pH of 8 with 1mM of Trypsin. Then, it's a matter of finding the right row (left-to-right) and column (up-and-down) on the table. We are told to look at the row giving data about a substrate level of 0.09. This already eliminates answer choices A and B, both of which give absorbance values not in this row. We are also told that there has been 2 minutes of interaction. Looking across from 0.09 and down from 2 minutes, we see an absorbance value of 0.154, which makes C the correct answer. Answer choice D, 0.184, is the data point for 2.5 minutes of interaction, which is why it is incorrect.

18. Correct answer: **G**. First, realize that we need to be referencing Experiment 2, and thus Table 2, which was conducted under a pH of 6 with 1mM of Trypsin. Second, look across the row (left-to-right) for 0.15mM of substrate. The question asks for the time it would take to see an absorbance level of 0.040. However, there is no absorbance level of 0.040 in this row of the table. This means that we are going to have to approximate a time that is not actually in the table itself. After 0.5 minutes of interaction, we see an absorbance value of 0.027. After 1 minute of interaction, we see an absorbance level of 0.053. Thus, the 0.040 number is between these two, which means that our time will be between these two. If you look at the answer choices, they are all given in seconds. 0.5 minutes of course is 30 seconds, and 1 minute is 60 seconds. Thus, if our correct answer falls between these two, the correct answer must be G: 45 seconds of interaction.

19. Correct answer: **D**. The question asks for the "highest average" absorbance levels, but this is the same thing as saying, "Which substrate level results in the highest absorbance values?" The reason I say that is to remind you that the ACT Science test is not going to ask a question that requires the use of a calculator. Instead, for this question, you can simply look at the values and see which conditions are giving the highest values. First of all, the higher values are certainly coming from Table 1, which comes from Experiment 1, which was conducted under a pH of 8. This eliminates answer choices A and B, both of which propose certain conditions under a pH of 6. Answer choice C proposes a substrate level of 0.15 and D proposes a substrate level of 0.24. However, any comparison of the two reveals that there is a higher absorbance value across the board when the substrate level is 0.24. This is why the correct answer is D.

20. Correct answer: **J**. Let's begin with letter F and see if it will result in an absorbance value of 0.062. After 1 minute of a substrate of 0.04 interacting with the Trypsin under a pH of 8, the absorbance value was 0.035, but after 1.5 minutes it was 0.053; this means that after 1.25 minutes, the value would be closer to 0.043, not 0.062. This is why F is incorrect. Second, let's try G. After 1 minute of a substrate of 0.09 interacting with the Trypsin under a pH of 8, the absorbance value was 0.082, and it only gets higher from there (in other words, it isn't going to go back down to 0.062 as another 15 seconds goes by). This is why G is also incorrect. Third, let's try H. After 2 minutes of a substrate of 0.04 interacting with the Trypsin under a pH of 6, the absorbance value was 0.023, but after 2.5 minutes it was 0.027; this means that after 2.25 minutes the absorbance value would be closer to 0.025. This makes H also incorrect. Lastly (as if eliminating all three other choices wasn't enough!) let's try answer choice J. After 2 minutes of a substrate of 0.09 interacting with the Trypsin under a pH of 6, the absorbance value was 0.055, and then after 2.5 minutes, it had risen to 0.068. This means that after 2.25 minutes (between the two), the absorbance value could be expected to measure roughly 0.062, which is why choice J is the correct answer.

Passage VI:

21. Correct answer: **C**. Though the question itself is quite long, there is one student who found the greatest percentage of neutrophils in both Study 1 and Study 2, and that is Student 3. This makes answer choice C the correct answer. The other three students simply did not find a percentage of correct cells as well as Student 3 was able to.

22. Correct answer: **J**. In this question, you will have to use what you know in Tables 1 and 2 to determine how many neutrophils are present in each study. The easiest place to start is actually Study 2, since Student 3 was able to correctly identify 100% of the neutrophils. Well, if Student 3 said there were 17 neutrophils, and that is 100% correct, then there must be 17 neutrophils present in Study 2. This eliminates answer choice F as incorrect since there must be more than 17 between the two studies if there are 17 already in Study 2. Immediately here some students will think that 17 times 2 is 34, so that must be correct. However, there is no 34 option, so we must identify the correct number in Study 1 also to determine the correct amount. If you look up at Study 1, you will see that Student 1 identified 5, which is 33% correct. Well, 33% is equivalent (after rounding, of course) to ⅓. Thus, if 5 is ⅓ of the total, then there must be 15 neutrophils in Study 1. Thus, 15 + 17 = 32, which is why the correct answer is J: there are 32 total neutrophils between the two studies.

23. Correct answer: **B**. Of course, first acknowledge that the optical microscope is used in Study 1. Thus, this is where we need to apply the 47% number. If you did number 22 correctly and identified that there must be 15 neutrophils in the study, then one way to get this question correct would be to see that half of 15 (or 50% of 15) is 7.5, so the most logical whole number of neutrophils to account for 47% of the total is 7 since it is a little less than 7.5. If not, then first see that 47% is between the findings of Student 1 (who identified 5 at 33%) and Student 2 (who identified 8 at 53%). Thus, the correct answer must be either 6 or 7 neutrophils, since it is between these two values as 47% is between the two percentages. This eliminates answer choices C and D. Well, 47% is much closer to 53% than it is to 33%, so we would expect the whole number of neutrophils to also be closer to 8 than to 5. This is another reason why the correct answer is 7, or answer choice B.

24. Correct answer: **J**. The results of the optical microscope are in Table 1, which we need to compare to the results of the fluorescent microscope, the results of which are in Table 2. First, let's start with F, which proposes Student 1. However, Student 1 only found 33% of the neutrophils in Table 1, and found 76% in Table 2. This eliminates F, since Student 1 did *not* do better with the optical microscope. Second, move to G, which proposes Student 3. However, Student 3 only found 67% of the neutrophils in Table 1, and found 100% in Table 2. This eliminates G, since Student 3 did *not* do better with the optical microscope. Third, move on to H, which proposes Student 4. However, Student 4 only found 27% of the neutrophils in Table 1, and found 76% in Table 2. This eliminates H, since Student 4 did *not* do better with the optical microscope. This leaves J, which is the correct answer: each student's percentage is *lower* with the optical microscope as seen in Table 1, not higher; this is why J is the correct answer: none of the students displayed this ability.

Answer Explanations - Step 2

Correct Answers:

Passage I:	Passage II:	Passage III:	Passage IV:	Passage V:	Passage VI:
1: B	4: G	7: D	10: F	13: A	16: G
2: G	5: D	8: H	11: C	14: H	17: B
3: B	6: H	9: C	12: J	15: A	18: H

Passage I:

1. Correct answer: **B**. Answer choice A is incorrect because it states that the fruit with higher salt were watered with "groundwater aquifers," but that's true of the control (less salty) group (this is also why choice D is incorrect). Answer choice C is incorrect because the salt doesn't come from the soil they were grown in, but the water itself. This is why the correct answer is B, because it alone states that the salt comes from the alternative water source.

2. Correct answer: **G**. The word "variant" is defined in the passage as a new variety of crop; it is also stated that different variants were tested in the experiment. The variants themselves are also listed under "Tomato variant" and "Pepper variant" in Table 1 and Table 2, respectively. This is why the answer is G, the California Wonder; the other answers aren't variants of peppers or tomatoes.

3. Correct answer: **B**. The entire purpose of the experiment is to test the control and experimental groups with different water, which is why the second option (II) is false. This means that automatically that answer choices C and D are incorrect, since both include II as true. Since A and B both include I (the variants of crops tested), we only need to worry about III. However, it is stated in the second paragraph that they were grown in the same soil, which means that B is the correct answer: both I and III are true of all plants.

Passage II:

4. Correct answer: **G**. This question of course requires a rereading of the paragraphs to find the order of events. Paragraph 2 says that "velocity was *measured* as each cart crossed the finish line", and paragraph 4 says that Figure 2 shows "the *calculated* momentum." So, whatever answer is correct, it must first state that velocity was found/measured, and then that momentum was calculated. This is why the correct answer is G. Choices H and J are incorrect because, at a minimum, each of these options mentions the students making a hypothesis, but there is nothing like that mentioned in the opening paragraphs. Choice F is incorrect because it states the velocity was calculated *after* the momentum was, which is false.

5. Correct answer: **D**. Essentially, this question is asking for this: what difference is there between the 3 carts? If you think about it, if all 3 carts were the same, then they would all have the same measurements for both velocity and momentum at each of the 5 release points. Paragraph 1 mentions that they have different masses, which is why D is the correct answer; none of the other answer choices are mentioned in the experiment at all.

6. Correct answer: **H**. The question asks, essentially, this question: the acceleration due to gravity has an effect on what? Let's start with I: Mass. The mass of the three carts, however, is predetermined; *g* or the acceleration due to gravity has no effect on it. Thus, answer choice J is eliminated. That brings us to II: Velocity. In the second paragraph, we learn that the equation for velocity, $v = \sqrt{2gh}$, uses *g*. In other words, velocity depends upon the value of *g* (which eliminates choice G). At this point, you might be tempted to stop here and choose answer F: II only. However, look at the equation for momentum: $p = mv$. If velocity depends upon the acceleration due to gravity (as we've said), and momentum depends upon velocity (as you can see by this equation for momentum), then momentum is also dependent upon the acceleration due to gravity. This is why the correct answer is H: II and III (velocity and momentum) only.

Passage III:

7. Correct answer: **D**. This question of course references only the written portion of this passage. If you reread the first paragraph, you will see that that the middle few sentences state that hot water: a) Undergoes rapid evaporation, which results in b) A higher concentration of dissolved solids. Answer choices A and C are incorrect because they suppose that a *lower* concentration of dissolved solids is responsible, which is incorrect. The reason B, then, is incorrect is because it states that this higher presence of dissolved solids occurs *before* undergoing rapid evaporation, but this happens after. This is why D is correct: it puts these two steps in the proper order based on the passage.

8. Correct answer: **H**. Each of the four answer choices references the temperature of water as hot or cold. Remember that the Mpemba Effect means that hot water freezes faster than cold water. In the experiment, the "hot" water was water that had been heated to 50 degrees; the "cold" water was room temperature water (see the last line of paragraph 2). This is why the correct answer is H; the students conducting the experiment assumed or defined room temperature water as "cold"; the room temperature

water was not cooled any further before the experiment began. F is incorrect because there is no mention that 50 degrees (or the "hot" water) is boiling. G is incorrect because 30 degrees was the temperature of the "cold" water. J is incorrect because 50 degrees was the "hot" water.

9. Correct answer: **C**. Each of these four answer choice options refers to water being put into a freezer set to -18° Celsius, so that won't be the difference maker. There are 4 types of water used in the experiment: tap/purified water (2 beakers each) at temperatures of 30/50 degrees (2 beakers each). Answer options A, B, and D each refer to one of these water varieties used in the experiment. Answer choice C, on the other hand, mentions salt water, but salt water was never used in the experiment. This is why the correct answer is C: salt water was not one of the water varieties used in the study.

Passage IV:

10. Correct answer: **F**. An assumption, in this case, is going to be something arbitrarily decided by the scientists or simply assumed to be true. Letter G says that ingesting a small amount of peanut DNA can be harmful to those with an allergy, but that's not an *assumption*, but rather a fact, so G is incorrect. Letter H says that PCR analysis is used to determine the presence of a certain DNA, but that is also established fact (literally the purpose of the technique), so H is also incorrect. Choice J says that some products for sale contain traces of peanut DNA; again, this is simply true, not assumed. This leaves the answer that we skipped, answer choice F. The second paragraph states that most instances of PCR analysis stop at 40, thus, it is assumed that this is "good enough" for finding peanut DNA, which is why F is the correct answer.

11. Correct answer: **C**. Again, the last sentence of paragraph 2 states that PCR analysis stops after 40 cycles. If they can only do one a day, as the question states, then that means 40 days of cycles. However, you're also told that it can only happen on weekdays, of which there are 5 per week. 40 divided by 5 is 8, thus the laboratory would need 8 weeks maximum to determine the CT threshold of a sample, which matches answer choice C.

12. Correct answer: **J**. First, determine if a low or a high CT value is good for those with peanut allergies. You might think that a score closer to 0 is good, but that's not the case in the PCR technique; the second to last sentence in the second paragraph says, "The lower the CT value, the more likely it is that the sample contains the DNA of interest." Thus, a low score is worse for those with a peanut allergy in this case. This eliminates F and G, which both say a low score is better. Letter choice H wrongly defines what a "high" score is by stating it means *few* iterations were necessary to detect the DNA, but that's not true: a high score means lots of iterations were necessary to detect the DNA, which means that answer choice J is correct.

Passage V:

13. Correct answer: **A**. Almost immediately, we can dismiss answer choices B and D as possibilities. As you can see by each table, there are 4 substrates tested in each Experiment (eliminating choice B) and 20 different absorbance values (eliminating D). Answer C proposes the pH was the same, but the pH for Experiment 1 was 8 and the pH for Experiment 2 was 6, thus eliminating answer choice C. this is why the correct answer is A: according to the first line of each experiment, each vial contains 1mM of Trypsin.

14. Correct answer: **H**. First of all, let's look at answer choice G, which says something about "less enzymes" being in the vial. However, Trypsin is the enzyme, and we already know that there is 1mM of Trypsin in each vial, which is under the control of those conducting the experiments; thus, G is incorrect. Answer choices F and J basically say the same thing: that a higher absorbance value means, in more or less words, that the enzyme Trypsin didn't get to make product by interacting with the substrate. If two answers are synonyms, they have to be incorrect by default since there can't be two correct answers at the same time. However, there are other reasons why F and J are incorrect beyond that. Letter choice H says the opposite of this, that more substrates were catalyzed. To sort this out, look at the last line of paragraph 2, which says, "a higher absorbance value…would mean more product was made by the Trypsin." This is why the answer choice that is correct is H, which proposes rightly that more absorbance means more product created by the Trypsin when interacting with the substrate.

15. Correct answer: **A**. In the final sentence of paragraph 1, you are told that "any physical or chemical changes to an enzyme's environment, such as *changes in temperature, pH, and salt concentration*, can alter its ability to function." Plain and simple, what is italicized in this sentence are the changes that could test how Trypsin responds in its environment. Of all of the answer choices, only choice A, temperature, is listed there. The only other probable choice would be "salt concentration," but that isn't an option. This is why the correct answer is A.

Passage VI:

16. Correct answer: **G**. The differences between these two microscopes are laid out in the first two paragraphs. Choice F proposes that one difference is that the optical uses photoluminescence, but that is true of the fluorescent; this is why choice F is incorrect. Answer choice H proposes that molecules are "put into an excited state" under the optical, but again, this is true of the fluorescent; thus, choice H is incorrect. Answer choice J proposes that the fluorescent's eyepiece provides additional magnification; however, this is true of the optical (see the third sentence of the first paragraph), which is why J is incorrect. This

is why the correct answer is G: the fluorescent microscope just doesn't have as many lenses as the optical (which has 3 lenses according to the opening paragraph).

17. Correct answer: **B**. First let's identify "the part of the fluorescent microscope responsible for separating out unnecessary light." If you reread the second paragraph, you will see that this is the purpose of the filter ("The filter then works by separating…"), which comes immediately before or after two other parts of the microscope: the detector and the objective lens. This eliminates answer choices C and D, which propose this part of the microscope to be by the condenser or reflector, respectively. However, the rest of the question says that this piece is placed "relative to the path of light." Well, if you look at Figure 2, you'll see that the light goes from the bottom to the top (from the light source to the reflector to the condenser, etc.). Thus, the filter is immediately *after* the objective lens (making choice A incorrect) and immediately *prior* to the detector; this makes choice B the correct answer.

18. Correct answer: **H**. Let's simply go through these choices one at a time and determine if each one was necessary for obtaining accurate results. First, choice F proposes that it was necessary that "the antibody in Study 1…". However, that's as far as we need to go; Study 1 doesn't require an antibody because it is done under the optical microscope; it's the fluorescent microscope that needs an antibody to excite the cells. Thus, F is incorrect. Second, G proposes that it was necessary that 5 minutes was sufficient time to find the cells. However, there is nothing in the entire passage about a time limit being placed on the students; this is why G is incorrect. Next, H proposes that the antibody in Study 2 would only cause the neutrophil cells to turn green (compared to the other cells present). This is certainly true, since if other cells turned green, then the accuracy of finding neutrophil cells would be compromised (this is why H is the correct answer). Lastly, J proposes something about a prohibition on finding square cells, but square cells of this sort are mentioned nowhere in the passage; this is why J is incorrect. Thus, H is correct, as it is the only answer choice to propose a true predisposition of the studies for the sake of accuracy.

Answer Explanations - Step 3

Correct Answers:

Passage I:	Passage II:	Passage III:	Passage IV:	Passage V:	Passage VI:
1: D	4: H	7: A	10: G	13: B	16: G
2: G	5: D	8: F	11: C	14: J	17: C
3: A	6: J	9: B	12: F	15: A	18: F

Passage I:

1. Correct answer: **D**. The purpose of this experiment was to see if there were any crops that could be grown better with the saltier water than the control water from a groundwater aquifer. There is only 1 crop that shows less salt content when grown with the experimental, non-aquifer water, and that is the Ancho. If you look at Figure 2, you'll see the white bar (representing the control group) as higher than the experimental; this means the control had more salt, and thus that the experimental water didn't have a salty, adverse effect on the Ancho. This makes D the correct answer; all other choices have more salt in the experimental group.

2. Correct answer: **G**. A variety of either fruit is going to have the most "naturally" salty taste if it has the highest salt concentration under the control group (since the experimental group is grown with water that contains salt). Again, the three pepper varieties, according to Figure 2, might *look* like they have higher salt concentrations than the tomatoes, but if you look at what those bars correspond to on the *y*-axis, you'll see that the three pepper plant varieties have salt (sodium) concentrations with values of something like 10, 10.75, and 12, respectively. This is much lower than the tomatoes, which is why F and H are incorrect. Of the three tomato varieties, Bloody Butcher looks to have a sodium concentration of something like 150, while the other tomato option (choice J, Juane Flamme) has a concentration closer to 80 or so. This is why the answer is G: Bloody Butcher, since its control group has the highest sodium concentration.

3. Correct answer: **A**. A "tolerance to salt" would mean that the experimental water with heavy salt concentration did not affect the growth (aka the yield). Though some varieties still yielded a lot of fruit from the experimental column (this is true of options B, C, and D, which each had an experimental yield in the thousands), when that total is compared to the control group, it is clear that there is a significant drop off for each of these three in terms of yield from the control to the experimental. The reason the correct answer is A or Thai Hot is not because the amount of yield was the highest, but rather that because the experimental yield was fairly close to the control yield; this means that it was least affected by the salt, demonstrating the "greatest tolerance to salt in its water supply."

Passage II:

4. Correct answer: **H**. First, notice that a cart with a mass of 17 kg would be somewhere between Cart A (12.5 kg) and Cart B (21.8 kg). Thus, to get this question correct, we need to find the answer choice that gives a momentum value (NOT velocity) between Cart A's value and Cart B's value when these carts are released from a height of 4 meters. Looking at Figure 2, we see that Cart A has a momentum of about 210 kg·m/s when released from 4 meters; Cart B has a momentum of about 170 kg·m/s when released from a height of 4 meters. As is expected (and typical of the ACT), only one option is between 170 kg·m/s and 210 kg·m/s, which is answer choice H, making it the correct answer.

5. Correct answer: **D**. First, recognize that *p* means *momentum*, that "a cart weighing 12.5 kg" is Cart A, and that "a cart weighing 34.7 kg" is Cart C. Thus: what is the difference in momentum (Figure 2) between Cart A and Cart C when released from a height of 2 meters? When Cart A is released from this height, it has a momentum of roughly 150 kg·m/s; when Cart C is released from this height, it has a momentum of roughly 80 kg·m/s. That's a difference of roughly 70 kg·m/s. Answer choice D is correct because 75 kg·m/s is certainly the closest estimate out of the answer choices. Choice C, at first, might seem plausible, but a review of the data points will reveal that the real value must be much greater than merely 55 kg·m/s.

6. Correct answer: **J**. This question requires you to make a rough inference of values 4 times in a row, and choose the result that shows the *least* velocity. Typically in these kinds of questions, the correct answer is going to be most obviously correct; it isn't going to come down to a fraction of a difference. First, a cart with a mass of 10 kg is closest to Cart A's mass. Notice that the less a car weighs in this experiment, the higher its velocity (as a side note, increased mass will mean increased friction, or a slower result). Thus, choice F recommends a cart weighing 10kg released from 5 meters; this would be very fast, probably something like 11 m/s. Choice G recommends a cart weighing 10 kg released from a height of 2 meters. This would be something a little faster than Cart A at that same height, something like 7 m/s. Answer H recommends a cart weighing 15 kg (so between Carts A and B) released from a height of 4 meters; this would result in something like 8.5 m/s. Lastly, choice J recommends a cart weighing 35 kg (so almost identical to Cart C) released from a height of 3 meters. Because Cart C at this point hovers barely above the 5 m/s mark, it's safe to say that this hypothetical cart posed by choice J would have a velocity of roughly 5 m/s. Let's

review: choice F = roughly 11m/s; choice G = roughly 7 m/s; choice H = roughly 8.5 m/s; and choice J = roughly 5 m/s. Thus, J is correct because its hypothetical cart would have the slowest velocity.

Passage III:

7. Correct answer: **A**. There are a couple of details present in each of these answer choices that are irrelevant. The first is that it mentions "a gallon" of various types of water; because this amount of water is a constant for all four, it can be ignored. The second ignorable detail is that the water is put into a freezer of -18° Celsius; this is also a constant for all four answers, making it irrelevant. What matters are the other details: the temperature and type of water. It might not be noticeable right away, but the four types of water in the experiment (Beakers A, B, C, and D) are the same as these 4 choices here. Thus, the question becomes this: which type of water froze (reached 0° Celsius) the slowest? Looking back at the tables, it was Beaker D that froze the slowest, and Beaker D is filled with room temperature (30° Celsius) tap water. This is why the correct answer here is A: the gallon of room temperature tap water will freeze slower than the other 3 based on the experiment.

8. Correct answer: **F**. According to the introductory paragraph, "rapid evaporation" is what happens to hot water to make it freeze faster than cold water (thus, the Mpemba Effect). Thus, this question could be reworded to say this: which beaker had hot water and froze the fastest? Beaker A was filled with heated purified water that froze the fastest (only 60 minutes), which makes F the correct answer.

9. Correct answer: **B**. Because the water in this beaker is left at room temperature, we are going to be comparing the data points of Beakers B and D. Because this new beaker features a mixture of purified and tap water, we would expect the correct answer to be somewhere between the time it takes for Beaker B read to read 10° and Beaker D's to read 10°. Well, looking at Table 2, it takes Beaker B 40 minutes to reach a temp of 10°. Looking at Table 4, it takes Beaker D 45 minutes to reach a temp of 10°. Thus, we would expect the correct answer to fall between 40 and 45 minutes. This is why the correct answer is B: 42.5 minutes; no other answer falls within this range.

Passage IV:

10. Correct answer: **G**. Here, you are asked to find the one true statement among four. Simply go one at a time to determine if the statement is true or false about the Cookies with fiber. Answer choice F states that they have a "low to none" likelihood of causing a reaction; for this to be true (according to Figure 2), it would have to have a CT score of 36 to 40, but it doesn't (it's score is 32.25), which makes F incorrect. Answer choice H states that there's a 0% chance of causing an allergic reaction; however, this might be something you could say about a food with a CT score over 40, which this food doesn't have, so H is incorrect. Answer J states that the cycle threshold is not declared, but it is ("CT value" stands for "cycle threshold value"), thus J is incorrect because it is also false. that leave G, which states that it contains traces of peanut DNA; this is true (it just takes 32.25 cycles to find it). That's why the correct answer is G.

11. Correct answer: **C**. The number of "cycles of amplification" needed to find DNA is the same thing as the CT value. Of the foods, there is only 1 that declares that it contains peanuts (Cereal bar I), though others say peanut traces. Thus, finding the "average" of the foods that declare peanuts is easy; it's simply the CT value of Cereal bar I, well, divided by 1. In other words, the answer is 17.97 (or answer choice C).

12. Correct answer: **F**. The food that is least likely to cause a peanut allergic reaction is the food with the highest CT score (remember, the higher a CT score, the more cycles that were needed to detect the peanut DNA). Sausage with walnut, of answer choice F, is the only of the food options that has a score of "N.D.", which means (according to the final sentence of the opening paragraphs) that "there was no detection of the target DNA after 40 cycles." This is why the answer is F. Each of the other foods has a CT value, which means that the DNA was detected after a certain number of cycles of amplification.

Passage V:

13. Correct answer: **B**. First, take a look at the rows of the substrate level 0.15 at a pH of 6 (Table 2) and a pH of 8 (Table 1). What you'll notice straightaway is that the absorbance values in Table 1 are higher. Now, the answer choices state there is more or less "instances of the breaking down of amino acids into proteins" or "proteins into amino acids." If you reread paragraph 1, it doesn't speak of amino acids being broken down into proteins, but the opposite (proteins into amino acids). This eliminates answer choices A and C. The question is whether or not high absorbance values (compared to lower values) means this is happening *more* (answer choice B) or *less* (answer choice D). According to the passage, a "higher absorbance value...would mean more product was made by the Trypsin." This is why the correct answer is B: higher absorbance values means more catalyzing of proteins into amino acids by the Trypsin.

14. Correct answer: **J**. The question asks for the "best conditions for maximizing the amount of product catalyzed." Again, according to the passage, a "higher absorbance value...would mean more product was made by the Trypsin." So, we are simply looking here for the highest absorbance values possible. Straightaway, Table 1 (a pH of 8) has higher values than Table 2 (a pH of 6). This eliminates answer choices F and G. However, though both H and J propose a pH of 8, choice J is correct because it proposes a longer time period (2.5 minutes). For each substrate value, the absorbance value increases as time goes on.

15. Correct answer: **A**. This question is, perhaps, bordering on the more difficult kinds of questions you will see in Step 5 in that there are a lot of little layers to think through. First of all, the word "spectrophotometer" is just a distraction, a big word that sounds scary and more complicated; this is simply the instrument that does the measuring. To get this question correct, first compare the 1 minute values of the substrate level 0.24 at a pH of 6 and a pH of 8. At a pH of 6, we get an absorbance value of 0.090; at a pH of 8, we get an absorbance value of 0.239. Thus, a higher pH means a higher absorbance value, and a lower pH means a lower absorbance value. Because we are looking for the pH level of a vial that results in a value of 0.011 (lower than the pH of 6), we are looking for a pH level *less than 6*. This is why the correct answer is A: it gives the only pH value that is less than 6.

Passage VI:

16. Correct answer: **G**. Firstly, this question references "one of the studies," but this can only be Study 1, since this study asked students to identify "round" cell bodies. Thus, this question is essentially saying this: "In Study 1, Student 4 didn't count 4 cells that were actually neutrophils; what would her percent be if she had counted these 4?" Well, her current percentage is 27% (having identified 4 correctly), and if she had 4 more, she'd be up to 8 total. This essentially doubles her percentage. Only one answer choice is anywhere near a doubling of 27%, which is G: 53% (you might be nervous that 27% doubled should be 54%, not 53%, but the 1% difference can be accounted for because of rounding to the nearest whole number). The other three answer choices are simply incorrect percentages of what her total would be if Student 4 had 4 more correct neutrophils identified.

17. Correct answer: **C**. The question asks for the effect of photoluminescence on the two studies. Since photoluminescence is necessary for the function of the fluorescent microscope, the question is essentially asking for a comparison between how students did with the optical microscope vs fluorescent microscope. Well, it clearly had a positive increase in the sense that all 4 students were able to identify a much higher percentage of neutrophils with the fluorescent microscope in Study 2. This eliminates answer choices A and B, which indicate that photoluminescence caused the numbers to go down. Answer choice D proposes that it quadrupled some students' numbers, but even Student 4's poor percentage (27% in Study 1), when quadrupled, soars to over 100%, which is impossible. this is why D is an incorrect answer. The reason the correct answer is C is that it is true that some students' numbers were more than doubled between Study 1 and Study 2 (this is true of Student 1 and Student 4).

18. Correct answer: **F**. Between the two microscopes, it is clear that it is the fluorescent microscope (both from the descriptions of the microscopes in the written portion of the passage and Figures 1 and 2) that alters or affects light with additional steps compared to the optical microscope. However, the student's guess was that this kind of a microscope would perform more poorly, but the opposite was true. This eliminates answer choices H and J because the student was *not* correct in her guess. Answer choice G correctly says that "No," the student was not correct, but gives the wrong reason: it isn't the optical microscope that alters light more, nor does the optical microscope yield better results. This is why the correct answer is F: No, the student didn't make a correct guess, and the reason is because the microscope that alters and affects light more (the fluorescent microscope) performed better.

Answer Explanations - Step 4

Passage I:
1: C
2: F
3: D
4: G
5: D
6: J
7: A

Passage II:
8: J
9: A
10: H
11: C
12: H
13: B
14: H

Passage I

1. Correct answer: **C**. FRB 181906 is an example of a Fast Radio Burst discussed by Scientist 2. Answer choice A is tempting, but Scientist 2 says that there is another FRB (121102) that also repeats, so A can't be correct. Answer choice B is incorrect because Scientist 2 never discusses how far away any FRB is. Answer choice D is incorrect because the sentence that FRB 181906 is mentioned in contradicts this idea, saying, "...containing the energy output of hundreds of millions of stars." This is why C is correct; choice C rightly restates the position of Scientist 2 (found in the first three sentences of Scientist 2's paragraph) that all FRB's, including 181906 then, are caused by the violent merger of cosmic objects.

2. Correct answer: **F**. If you thought well through number 1 above, you should know that Scientist 2 does *not* rely on "internal disruptions of neutron stars," but rather only on merger of cosmic objects. This eliminates answer choices G and J, since both state that Scientist 2 relies on this idea. Since F and H both refer to Scientist 1, it can be taken for granted that he does believe this. Thus, the question is this: does Scientist 3 "rely on the existence of internal disruptions of neutron stars"? Well, rely means *depend*, or stated in another way, if Scientist 3 were to rely on it, it would be necessary for his argument; the question also says that this scientist relies on it to explain *all* stars. This is not the case for Scientist 3, who outright says that there are multiple origins of neutron stars. This is why the correct answer is F: only Scientist 1 is in this position.

3. Correct answer: **D**. Because Scientist 1 believes that every FRB comes from neutron stars, this discovery would not support his position. As a result, we now know that A and C are incorrect. Scientist 2, on the other hand, says that FRBs are caused by mergers of large celestial objects, thus, yes, such a discovery would support his position. Lastly, Scientist 3 says that there are all sorts of explanations for FRBs, thus such a discovery would also support his position. This is why the answer is D: the discovery of an FRB coming from the merger of two black holes would support the positions of Scientists 2 and 3.

4. Correct answer: **G**. Remember, first, what Scientist 1's main idea is, which is that FRBs come from highly magnetized and unstable neutron stars. Scientist 2, on the other hand, believes that FRB's come from celestial object mergers. Whether or not magnetars *also* release gamma rays, an FRB lasts more than a few milliseconds, or an FRB repeats once every few years is irrelevant to this particular question. This is why the answer is G: if celestial object mergers could not produce radio waves, this would crush the position of Scientist 2.

5. Correct answer: **D**. For this fact to be inconsistent with the positions of any of the scientists, it would have to disprove or run counter to one of their major premises, pieces of evidence, or overall thesis. Because it is Scientist 2 who believes that FRBs come from the merger of objects, that seems the most tempting answer (thus, I've just eliminated Scientists 1 and 3 as possibilities). However, Scientist 2 doesn't depend upon FRBs coming from within the Milky Way. In fact, the only mention of the source of an FRB puts it well outside the Milky Way itself. Although answer choice B is the most tempting wrong answer, the correct answer is D: this discovery would hurt none of the three scientists' positions.

6. Correct answer: **J**. Scientist 1 defines a neutron star as "dense remnants of massive stars that have undergone a supernova." However, it isn't only Scientist 1 that proposes neutron stars as being involved in the origins of FRBs. Scientist 2 says that their collisions with one another or black holes are FRB sources, and Scientist 3 says (essentially) that both Scientist 1 and 2 are correct about FRB origins. Thus, the correct answer is J. The other answer choices either help the position of one or two of the three scientists or none of them at all.

7. Correct answer: **A**. Scientist 1 relies on starquakes as necessary for FRBs, thus the answer must include this scientist (this eliminates answer choice C). However, Scientist 2 doesn't ever use the word "gravity," but it is pretty obvious that it is gravity that is causing these massive mergers of neutron stars and black holes. Thus, Scientist 2 also relies on gravity. Only one of the four answers includes both Scientist 1 and 2, which is A. This makes sense, since Scientist 3 agrees with both of them and their theories about the origins of FRBs.

Passage II

8. Correct answer: **J**. If you were to quickly skim the three paragraphs beneath Scientists 1, 2, and 3, you will see the letters 'DNA' in all three. Scientist 1 speaks of aging as being coded into DNA. Scientist 2 speaks of DNA mutations affecting aging. Scientist 3 speaks of the incomplete replication of the ends of DNA. Thus, all 3 of them recognize that DNA plays some kind of role in the aging process, which is why the answer is J.

9. Correct answer: **A**. Though the question may mention a new word ("thyroiditis"), this question essentially boils down to this: which scientist believes that hormonal output or hormones generally plays a role in the aging process? Scientist 1 says "hormonal changes" help to regulate the aging process, so this statement is definitely true of him. However, only 1 of the 4 answer choices proposes Scientist 1, which is answer choice A, making A the correct answer.

10. Correct answer: **H**. It is Scientist 3 who discusses the shortening of telomeres as most responsible in the aging process (see the first sentence of Scientist 3's paragraph), thus any correct answer must include this scientist. That eliminates letter F. The question now is which other scientist (or scientists) believes that "cellular damage" plays a role in aging. Well, let's look through Scientist 1 first. Upon doing so, I see nothing about "cellular damage." Scientist 1 *does* mention "decline of repair mechanisms," but there's no reason to suspect that that is the same thing as cellular damage, and it certainly isn't stated as much by the scientist. Since each answer but 1 contains Scientist 1 as an option, we now have enough information to get the question correct: the correct answer must be H. If you want to be sure, all it takes is a read of the first sentence of Scientist 2 to see that it is "the gradual accumulation of *cellular damage*" that is responsible for aging. Thus, both Scientist 2 and Scientist 3 are correct, which matches answer choice H.

11. Correct answer: **C**. Scientist 2's main idea is that cellular damage accumulates over time, which causes aging (thus, we can already see why choice D is incorrect; increasing cellular damage would cause a person, then, to age faster!). The correct answer then is going to be a medicine that slows cellular aging. Before rereading Scientist 2's paragraph with all of this information in mind, I see right away that answer choice B can also be eliminated; this idea (the shortening of telomeres) is essential to the argument of Scientist 3, not Scientist 2. That leaves A and C. Upon rereading Scientist 2's paragraph, we see in the second sentence that one cause of cellular damage is "the accumulation of cellular waste products." Thus, a medicine that would help "cells to dispose of waste more permanently" (answer choice C) would slow aging in his view. This is why C is the correct answer. As for answer choice A, the idea of hormonal production being effective would be more in line with the position of Scientist 1.

12. Correct answer: **H**. Cellular senescence is only mentioned by one of the three scientists: Scientist 3. He says, "As telomeres become critically short, cells can no longer divide and function properly, known as cellular senescence." We can eliminate answer choices F and G immediately since they both propose that cellular senescence "is necessary to slow aging," but the opposite is true: cellular senescence furthers aging. Letter choice J proposes that cellular senescence "relies on the proper functioning of telomeres," but that's not true, since cellular senescence is caused by the shortening of telomeres, not the proper functioning of them. This is why the correct answer is H: cellular senescence, according to Scientist 3, is rooted in the gradual shortening of telomeres and furthers the aging process.

13. Correct answer: **B**. There's a lot in this question to confuse you, things like CRS and other scientific jargon. However, essentially this question is asking this: which scientist thinks that the damaging of "the structure and function of molecules" has an effect on the aging process? Scientist 2 mentions a number of factors that cause damage "at the molecular level." Thus, Scientist 2 would be a correct answer, which eliminates answer choices A and C. The question now is whether or not Scientist 3 believes this. However, a rereading of the position of Scientist 3 mentions nothing about breakdowns at a "molecular" level. This is why the answer is B: Scientist 2.

14. Correct answer: **H**. Let's begin with Scientist 1. Scientist 1's claim, in essence, is that aging is genetically predetermined or coded into DNA. Thus, Scientist 1 would *not* agree with this fourth scientist's claim that aging is not genetically predetermined. That eliminates answer choices G and J, both of which refer to Scientist 1. Because both F and H say Scientist 2 agrees with the claim, there is no need to investigate it (it would be a waste of time). Thus, the only remaining question is this: does Scientist 3 agree with this claim? Well, Scientist 3 says that aging is caused, in more or less words, by the shortening of telomeres on the cellular level (aka, not genetically predetermined or coded into DNA). Thus, like Scientist 2, Scientist 3 would agree with this fourth scientist's claim. That is why the answer is H: Scientists 2 and 3.

Answer Explanations - Step 5

Correct Answers:

Passage I:	Passage II:	Passage III:	Passage IV:	Passage V:	Passage VI:
1: C	4: F	7: A	10: G	13: A	16: H
2: G	5: C	8: J	11: B	14: F	17: A
3: B	6: J	9: C	12: J	15: C	18: B

Passage I:

1. Correct answer: **C**. If you look at the various tomato variants as featured in Figure 1, the sodium concentration in the experimental group (watered with water with a high salt concentration) is always somewhere between 2 to 4 times as much as the control group. Only one answer choice falls within this range, which is answer choice C: 75 mmol is roughly 3 times larger than the 27.5 mmol when Better Boy is watered with low content salt water.

2. Correct answer: **G**. Immediately we can eliminate answer choice F, since it only shows the yield of two plants, not 3. Letters H and J either look to split the three variants evenly or to be really close to doing so. However, if you look at the three tomato plants under the control column in Table 1, there is one that is a little bigger than a second that is a little bigger than a third. This is why the answer is G: it most accurately represents the total control yield as seen in Table 1.

3. Correct answer: **B**. Bloody Butcher, when watered with a groundwater aquifer (aka the control group) yields 2,785 grams. Juane Flamme, when watered with a groundwater aquifer (aka the control group) yields 2,317 grams. So, if we have a new tomato with 50% of both, you would expect the yield to be somewhere between the two. There is only one option between the two, which is option B: 2,525 grams.

Passage II:

4. Correct answer: **F**. You may be thinking to yourself, "How am I supposed to answer this question without a calculator??? Unfair!" However, the ACT Science test will never give you a question that requires a calculator; any question that uses a mathematical step will require only a *simple* mathematical step. Here, all you need to realize to get the answer correct is that the recorded velocity on the moon will be *much lower* than the velocity on earth. If you look at Cart B's velocity in Figure 1 when released from a height of 3, you will see that it measures something near 7 m/s. There are only 2 answer choices that are even lower than 7 m/s; this eliminates right away answer choices H and J. However, answer choice G (5.05 m/s) is only *a little bit lower* than 7 m/s. If acceleration due to gravity on earth is 9.8, and on the moon it is 1.625, we need a value much lower than 7 m/s! This is why the correct answer is F: 1.15 m/s.

5. Correct answer: **C**. This is one of those rare ACT Science questions that requires you to have a previous understanding of science. Here, what is required is that you convert an answer from m/s to cm/s by first remembering that there are 100 centimeters in a meter. First, recognize that Cart B has a velocity of roughly 5.5 m/s (if you look at the answer choices, it's clear that it's velocity is 5.48 m/s). In order to calculate this same metric in centimeters per second, simply multiply the answer by 100 by moving the decimal point *to the right* twice. This results in 548 centimeters per second, which aligns with answer choice C.

6. Correct answer: **J**. Here, you are being asked to do some simple math. Again, the ACT Science test is never going to ask you a question that requires a calculator, and they are never going to give you two answer choices that are a mere fraction of a decimal apart, and one of those two is the right answer. With basic reasoning or rounding skills, the right answer will be clear. Here, you are asked to find the acceleration of Cart A as it crossed the finish line when released from a height of 5 meters, which is the velocity over the time. The velocity of Cart A when released from a height of 5 meters is roughly 10 m/s. When you divide that by 1.5 seconds, you get 6.67 m/s^2. This is why the correct answer is J.

Passage III:

7. Correct answer: **A**. The Mpemba Effect says that hot water will freeze faster than cold water. If you look at the tables to see the results of the experiment, the beaker of water that froze the fastest was Beaker A, which contained heated purified water. This *confirms* the Mpemba Effect, and thus *falsifies* the hypothesis that the Mpemba Effect would not work in purified water. This eliminates answer choices C and D, which both lead with "No." Answer choice B, however, falsely states that the water that was the first to freeze was the room temperature water. Thus, A is correct: the hypothesis was falsified because the heated and purified water was the first to freeze.

8. Correct answer: **J**. A fifth beaker, Beaker E, is put into the freezer and takes 85 minutes to freeze. This is much slower than any of the beakers in the actual experiment. Let's go through each answer choice one at a time and see if it rings true about the mysterious Beaker E. First, letter F says that it came from a "freshwater spring" (aka, pure fresh water) and was heated to 50°;

this, unfortunately, is much more like Beaker A (heated purified water) that froze quickly, so F is incorrect. Second, answer choice G says that it came from a "freshwater spring" (aka, pure fresh water) and kept at room temperature; however, this water is akin to that of Beaker B, which froze after 70 minutes, so G is incorrect. Third, answer choice H says that it came from the ocean and heated. This seems much more likely, since ocean water (like tap water in the experiment) contains minerals (like salt) that make freezing go more slowly. However, answer choice J also references salt water, but mentions that the water is "kept at room temperature." This seems much more likely to be true than H because H was heated, and heated water freezes more quickly. This is why the correct answer is J: ocean (mineral rich) water at room temperature would more than likely freeze more slowly than the others.

9. Correct answer: **C**. I have said this before: any math required on the ACT will not be difficult, but simple. By that I mean that "ballparking" your answers is always going to be good enough; the correct answer is not going to differ from wrong answers by mere decimals as they might on the ACT Math test. Now, the first step is to find the temperature of the water referenced by the question in Celsius. The beaker that contains "purified water" put in the freezer at "50°" is Beaker A. After 30 minutes had elapsed, Beaker A recorded a temperature of 17°. Now, the time has come to use the conversion formula to "calculate" this same temperature in Fahrenheit. You might now be thinking, "I can't multiply 17 × 1.8 in my head!" Me neither. Instead, I'm going to just multiply it by 2 and add 32 and approximate the correct answer. So, 17 × 2 = 34. 34 + 32 = 66°. Only one answer choice is anywhere close to this value (as expected), which is answer choice C, making it correct.

Passage IV:

10. Correct answer: **G**. Before you look at the graphs, think about the answer for yourself, then identify the graph that best fits. What do you know about the relationship between the CT value of a food and the likelihood that it will cause a reaction? Well, the higher a CT value is, the lower the likelihood. Or, to put it another way, as the CT value goes up (on the x axis of these graphs), the likelihood (the y axis) goes down. Choices H and J do not reflect this linear relationship, so they are out. Letter F is incorrect because it gets the relationship backwards; it makes it look like as CT goes up, the likelihood goes up. This is why the correct answer is G: as you move left to right on the x axis (CT value going up), the y value (likelihood of allergic reaction) goes down.

11. Correct answer: **B**. This question looks extremely complicated because it is lengthy, but the basics of it are rather simple. Essentially, this question is asking this: how many food products in Table 1 have a high to moderate likelihood of causing a reaction (a CT value of 30-35) but do NOT declare peanuts or peanut traces on the packaging. Well, there are three food products that have a CT value between 30 and 35: Cereal bar II, Cereal bar III, and Cookies with fiber. Cereal bar I does NOT declare peanuts on the packaging (that's $100,000); Cereal bar III DOES declare peanuts on the packaging (no fine); and Cookes with fiber does NOT declare peanuts on the packaging (another $100,000). That's why the answer is B: the company would owe $200,000 in fines.

12. Correct answer: **J**. This question, like the previous question, looks more difficult than it really is. It confuses you (or attempts to) with talk of half life, etc. The question is essentially this: in 1,042 years a lot of the DNA in these foods will die, so what will the CT value look like then? A CT value means how many cycles of amplification were needed to detect peanut DNA. If it took 40 cycles in the first place, then you try again 1,042 years later when the DNA is much lower, then the CT value is only going to go *higher*; in other words, it will be *way* bigger than 40 now because you will need more and more cycles of amplification to find the DNA since it has become more difficult over time. This is why the answer is J; it is the only answer that has the number of cycles increasing over 40.

Passage V:

13. Correct answer: **A**. This question requires that you have a prior understanding of pH to identify the correct answer. First, let's remember that the Trypsin functioned better in the pH 8 environment compared to the pH 6 environment. Well, the question is, is that a more basic or acidic environment? The way pH works is this: 7 is considered "neutral" (which is the pH of water). Any number lower than 7 is considered "acidic," and the closer the number gets to 0, the more acidic. Any number higher than 7 is considered "basic," and the closer a number gets to 14, the more basic. Thus, the Trypsin enzyme functioned better in a more basic environment (because pH of 8 is higher than 7, it is basic). This eliminates answer choices C and D. However, B is incorrect because it wrongly says that the absorbance levels of the more basic vials are *lower* than the more acidic, but that's not true. Answer choice A is the correct answer because it rightly states that the absorbance levels in the more basic vials (pH of 8) are *higher* than the more acidic vials (pH of 6).

14. Correct answer: **F**. As was stated in the previous explanation, this question (like #13 above) requires you have an understanding of pH on a basic level. See the previous explanation above for more detail, but essentially, a pH of over 7 is basic and a pH of under 7 is acidic. What we find in this experiment is that the more acidic vials (pH of 6 in Experiment 2) have lower absorbance values, thus lower substrates being catalyzed into product by the enzyme Trypsin. This means that the scientist's hypothesis that acidic drinks may cause lesser amino acids in the blood stream (which is what Trypsin does) *could be true*. In other words, the hypothesis is not "rejected". This eliminates answer choices H and J. Answer choice G though falsely states that the acidic vials (pH of 6 in Experiment 2) had *more substrate* catalyzed than the basic vials (pH of 8 in Experiment 1). However, that is not true. This is why the correct answer is F: the more basic vials in Experiment 1 perform better than the acidic vials in

Experiment 2; thus, the idea that acidic drinks could lower the work of Trypsin (amino acids in the bloodstream) is still possible and not rejected.

15. Correct answer: **C**. This is the third question in a row that requires that you have some kind of previous science knowledge. In science experiments, the *independent* variable is the variable that the scientists control. Here, the scientists control the substrate level, for example...and the pH of the vials...and the amount of Trypsin in each vial. This means that A, B, and D are all wrong answers. The *dependent* variable is what is being measured; it is *dependent* upon the independent variables. This is the absorbance value, which is why the correct answer is C.

Passage VI:

16. Correct answer: **H**. First, this student who is coming in late identifies 45 neutrophils when looking through the optical microscope, which means he is identifying 45 cells in Study 1 (thus Table 1). This is obviously *way more* than the actual number of neutrophils in the sample. Answer choice F proposes that he perhaps messed with the reflector, but that is only present on the fluorescent microscope (see Figure 2), which makes this answer choice incorrect. Answer choice G speaks of cells fluorescing green, but again, that is the fluorescent microscope that uses this technology, not the optical, which is why choice G is also incorrect. Answer choice J proposes that he may have "undercounted" cells, but we already know that he way *overcounted* the cells, making choice J also incorrect. That leaves H, which says that he possibly mistook each cell that he saw no matter what for a neutrophil; this is of course plausible, especially compared to the other answers, which means that H is the correct answer.

17. Correct answer: **A**. Here, what is needed is some way to differentiate "other" blood cells from the neutrophils. If they are all blue, the question is, how could a student tell the difference? Well, it has nothing to do with the color of the light, though some students will get confused with the original green light in Study 2 and choose C. But, neither C nor D is correct because they both speak of looking for a certain color light. That leaves answer choices A and B, which at first glance seem identical. There is one word of difference between them, however; A speaks of a *diameter* of 12-14 µm, and B speaks of a *radius* of 12-14 µm. If you look back at the description of what to look for in a neutrophil in the third paragraph, you'll see that in Study 1 students were supposed to look for neutrophils with a *diameter* of 12-14 µm. This makes A the correct answer and B incorrect.

18. Correct answer: **B**. Fortunately, you are told the size comparison between a meter and a µm (aka a micrometer). It is one millionth the size. To get this question correct, start with the number in micrometers. As you can see, the answer choices all feature the number 13 (which is between 12 and 14 µm, as defined by the passage as the diameter of a neutrophil nucleus). Second, move the decimal point to the left one space for every 0 that follows the number 1,000,000 (because it is one millionth of a meter). There are 6 zeros after 1,000,000, which means we need to move the decimal point to the left 6 times, adding in a 0 for every blank space. Let's do it one step at a time: 1 (13 to 1.3), 2 (1.3 to 0.13), 3 (0.13 to 0.013), 4 (0.013 to 0.0013), 5 (0.0013 to 0.00013), and lastly 6 (0.00013 to 0.000013). This is why the correct answer is 0.000013, which corresponds with answer choice B.

Answer Explanations - Step 6 - Practice Test #1

Passage I	Passage II	Passage III	Passage IV	Passage V	Passage VI
1: D	8: F	14: G	21: D	28: G	34: G
2: H	9: C	15: A	22: G	29: C	35: D
3: B	10: J	16: H	23: A	30: G	36: H
4: F	11: C	17: B	24: H	31: B	37: A
5: D	12: H	18: F	25: B	32: J	38: J
6: J	13: B	19: C	26: F	33: A	39: C
7: A		20: F	27: D		40: J

Passage I

1. Correct answer: **D**. The data for Experiment 2 is listed in Table 2. Clearly, the amount of time the ground beef is exposed to the acidic solution in the experiment is 15 minutes. Thus, it is up to you to infer what is likely to happen after an additional 5 minutes. This just means following the pattern that is being established by the data. Initially, according to Table 2, the E. coli count begins to go down to 10,000 at the 10 minute mark. However, at 15 minutes, it has begun to go up again. This trend suggests that this growth will continue, which is why the correct answer is D: greater than 15,000. None of the other three answers is supported by the actual data trends.

2. Correct answer: **H**. It is being proposed here that the ground beef samples of Experiment 3 be exposed to the vinegar solution for 10 minutes as opposed to 5, then put in the storage. Well, according to Experiment 2, after 5 minutes just in a vinegar acid reduces the E. coli count (to 15,000), but after 10 minutes the amount of E. coli is reduced even farther (to 10,000). Thus, if the beef was put in vinegar for 10 minutes before storage, it would "start" in storage with less E. coli than what really took place in Experiment 3. This means that after a day of sitting at 50 degrees, the E. coli count would have to be lower. This eliminates answers F and G. Choice J correctly says "Less," but it falsely says that this would be because the E. coli at the beginning of storage would be increased. This is why the correct answer is H: it says the count will be less and correctly identifies why this is the case.

3. Correct answer: **B**. This question simply requires that you count how many of the experiments' results had an E. coli count of 60,000 or greater. There are none of these in Table 1, there are none of these in Table 2, but there is 1 of them in Table 3 (next to 50°F). This is why the correct answer is B: 1. You may think to yourself, "but wait a second! Next to 40°F it says there is an E. coli count of 60,000!" However, the question says that a beef item would be critical if it is *over* 60,000, not 60,000 or higher.

4. Correct answer: **F**. Experiment 1 exposed the ground beef samples to radiation only. If you reread through Experiments 2 and 3 though, you will find no mention of the word "radiation," nor anything that suggests it (like, "Experiment 1 was repeated with…"). This is why the correct answer is F: only Experiment 1 used radiation.

5. Correct answer: **D**. First of all, recognize that Experiment 1 is the one that tested the E. coli count in ground beef by using radiation exposure. However, to get this question right, you need to have a previous knowledge of what direct and an indirect relationships are. A *direct* relationship means this: as one thing increases, another thing increases (like the more miles you drive, the more gas you use). An *indirect* relationship means this: as one thing increases, another thing decreases (like as the temperature increases the ice in your glass decreases). If you look back at the data in Table 1, you will see that as the time of exposure to radiation goes up (0, 5, 10, then 15 minutes) the E. coli count goes down. One goes up, one goes down: that's an inverse relationship. This eliminates A and B, which both say the relationship is direct. C though is incorrect because it states that the E. coli count *increases*, which is false. That is why the answer is D: it states that the relationship is inverse, and gives the correct reason why.

6. Correct answer: **J**. A first thing to notice would be that the final step for each answer choice is exactly the same: "then store it at 4°F for 24 hours." Because that's the same for each question, it can be ignored (which also means that Experiment 3's data can be ignored). Thus, the correct answer is going to be the combination of steps from Experiment 1 (radiation) and Experiment 2 (vinegar) that lowers the E. coli count. First, we know that the longer the beef is exposed to radiation, the lower the E. coli count. This would seem to eliminate F and G, which only propose 10 minutes of radiation compared to 15 minutes for H and J. As for H, it proposes soaking the beef then in vinegar for 15 minutes. That seems better than 10 minutes of soaking (which is what J proposes), but if you look at the data of Table 2, at the 15 minute mark the E. coli count started to increase again. This is why the answer is J: longer radiation exposure, but the perfect amount of soaking in vinegar.

7. Correct answer: **A**. This question is asking you first to find how many of the results (out of a total of 12) have been exposed to vinegar for *more than* (not equal to) 5 minutes. In Experiment 1, this was true of 0 of the samples. In Experiment 2, this was true of only 2 samples (the ones exposed to 10 and 15 minutes), and in Experiment 3 this is true of 0 samples (they had all been soaked for exactly 5 minutes). Thus, only 2 of 12 have been exposed to vinegar for greater than 5 minutes. Now, you might not be able to figure out to the proper decimal what 2 divided by 12 is equal to, but you don't have to. Remember: basic math ACT questions will never require math that needs a calculator. Instead, look at the answer choices. Choice B says 25%. However, 25%

of 12 is 3, so the actual number must be less than 3. Seeing as there is only one such answer choice, the correct answer must be A: 16.67%.

Passage II

8. Correct answer: **F**. If you look at Figure 1, you'll see that the group with the lowest amount of plants that produced beans is Group 3, the self-pollinating column. The other two, which are both larger, both include bees. Thus, it doesn't matter what type of bees you introduce to the beans (whether wild bees or honey bees); either way, the percent of plants producing beans will increase. This is why the correct answer is F: increases.

9. Correct answer: **C**. This question requires that you go through the three options one by one and see which are true. Let's start with I. "Self-pollination" literally means that no pollinators are allowed to interact with the plants, so this is true. That eliminates answer choice D, since it does not include I as a true option. Move on to II. According to Figure 1, the number of plants produced with self-pollination is certainly *not* "maximized" with self-pollination, but the opposite. This means that II is false, which eliminates answer choice B. So, either A is true (because only I is true) or C is true (because I and III are both true). To figure that out, move on to option III. If you look back at the opening paragraph, you'll see that "self-pollination" is defined as "both the egg and pollen are from the same *G. max* plant." Thus, III is also true, which means that the correct answer is C: I and III only.

10. Correct answer: **J**. This question is a bit deceiving. It asks you for the *number* of bean-producing plants from cross-pollination using honey bees (which is Group 2). You might think right away that the answer is H: 38. However, 38 is roughly the *percent* of plants that produced beans, not the number. If you look into the passage's second paragraph, you will see that 240 plants were used in each group. Thus, the correct answer is going to be way bigger than 38. Mathematically speaking, one way to reason through this question would be like this: 38% is a bit bigger than 33%; so, if 80 is 33% or one-third of 240, then the right answer will be a little bigger than that. There is only one answer choice that meets these requirements, which is answer choice J: 91.

11. Correct answer: **C**. Because it has been determined from the experiment that pollinators increase soybean yield and mass, the presence of honey bees (A), the presence of wild bees (B) and an increase in pollinators (D) would all *increase* soybean yield and mass. This is why the correct answer is C: a decrease in bees for whatever reason would lessen the percent of plants producing beans and the average mass per bean.

12. Correct answer: **H**. At first, letter choice G is the most easily dismissed, mostly because it doesn't make logical sense that a small plant would produce a bigger bean (plus, there's nothing in the passage that would help us infer to such an idea). You might be tempted, first, by answer choice F. However, there is no data on the relationship between plant size and bean size (or plant size at all), thus there's no logical way to infer to this as a reasonable conclusion. As for J, which might also be tempting, there is no information in the passage about the economics of soybeans vs other plant species, so it's impossible to infer whether or not it is a bad investment. That is why the correct answer is H: because the passage says that both wild and honey bees are good for the plants, it is reasonable to conclude that the presence of bees would be good for farmers.

13. Correct answer: **B**. Figure 2 gives the various average masses of the soybeans from different plants. Thus, it is possible that this bean weighing 179 mg could come from any of the 3 groups. However, the question asks which group is *most likely*, and because Group 2's beans average roughly 177 mg, it is definitely *most likely* that this bean comes from Group 2. This eliminates answer choices A and D. The only difference between answer choices B and C is that choice B says that Group 2 is from honey bees, and choice C says that Group 2 is from self-pollinating plants. However, Table 1 clearly states that Group 2 is from plants pollinated with honey bees, which is why B is the correct answer.

Passage III

14. Correct answer: **G**. Remember that Scientist 2's basic idea is that *Homo sapiens* evolved in one place, then moved to other places over time. It is Scientist 1 who holds beliefs more consistent with answer choice J; this is why J is incorrect. Answer choice F is incorrect because Scientist 2 makes no mention of the migration of Neanderthals or Denisovans. Answer choice H is incorrect because the answer presupposed *Homo sapiens* being there…but how can the presence of *Homo sapiens* be the cause of *Homo sapiens* living there? This is why the correct answer is G: Scientist 2 believes that *Homo sapiens* evolved in and migrated from a single point.

15. Correct answer: **A**. Scientist 1 relies on the idea that populations of *Homo sapiens* popped up independent of one another in various places from pre-human species (like *Homo erectus*, mentioned in the question). His main evidence for this is that there are strict similarities between modern humans' anatomies and the most ancient pre-human bones in the same areas. Thus, if a scientist discovers a femur bone basically identical to those in the area in modern times, this supports Scientist 1's idea. This eliminates answer choices B and D. The question then is whether or not this same discovery would help Scientist 2, but the answer there is no: Scientist 2 would need the femur bone to be more similar to the femur bones of modern Africans than modern East Asians. Thus, the correct answer is A: this femur bone would help only Scientist 1.

16. Correct answer: **H**. If a bone fragment from an early *Homo sapiens* individual in Africa was similar to that of modern Europeans, then that would support the idea that *Homo sapiens* came "out of Africa," which is the position of Scientist 2. The

question though asks if this discovery supports Scientist 1, but the answer there is "No." This eliminates answer choices F and G. Answer choice J says that Scientist 1 doesn't rely on anatomical similarities, but that is exactly what he relies on (see the second half of his paragraph). This is why the correct answer is H: Scientist 1 needs those anatomical similarities to tie *Homo sapiens* in modern times to the same locations in the past.

17. Correct answer: **B**. Scientist 2 states that *Homo sapiens* came into existence about 200,000 years ago in Africa. Thus, if a *Homo sapiens* individual were discovered in Europe even longer ago than that, then that would certainly weaken the position of Scientist 2. This eliminates answer choices A and D, since neither weakens the position of Scientist 2. Well, what about Scientist 1? However, Scientist 1 doesn't believe in the "out of Africa" hypothesis and thinks it is true that *Homo sapiens* populations popped up all throughout Africa, Asia, and Europe independently of one another. This is why the correct answer is B: this discovery would weaken only the position of Scientist 2.

18. Correct answer: **F**. Let's go through the options here backwards to see if they are something each scientist would agree with. Answer choice J, factually speaking, makes no sense: if pre-modern humanoid species' bones are indistinguishable from *Homo sapiens*, then how do you know they are from humanoid species? Answer choice H is something that Scientist 1 proposes, but not Scientist 2, so it is false. Answer choice G says that humanoid species were killed off by *Homo sapiens*, but only Scientist 1 says that outright, and it is not OK to infer that Scientist 2 believes that. Thus, answer choice F must be correct. Scientist 1 says *Homo sapiens* killed off these humanoid species, and Scientist 2 says that *Homo sapiens* "displaced and replaced" them. Either way, they lived together, which is why F is correct.

19. Correct answer: **C**. This question is really similar to the previous one, number 18. The question is about a new humanoid species, and each answer choice mentions the relationship between this species and *Homo sapiens* in one way or another. While Scientist 1 states that *Homo sapiens* killed off humanoid species and Scientist 2 states that *Homo sapiens* "displaced and replaced" them, either way, *Homo sapiens* is likely responsible for their deaths. This is why the correct answer is C. None of the other statements is something both scientists would agree with.

20. Correct answer: **F**. The main difference between Scientist 1 and 2 is not *what Homo sapiens* evolved *from*, but where that happened. This is why answers H and J are both incorrect: both of these answers rely on what *Homo sapiens* evolved from. Answer choice G states that Scientist 1 relies on DNA and Scientist 2 relies on anatomy, but that is flipped. Scientist 1 relies on anatomical comparisons between modern humans and ancient humanoid species. Scientist 2, on the other hand, relies on DNA analysis (if you quickly scan Scientist 2's paragraph, you'll see "DNA" over and over). This is why the correct answer is F: it rightly states that Scientist 1 relies on anatomical data and Scientist 2 on DNA analysis.

Passage IV

21. Correct answer: **D**. First, if you look at Figures 2 and 3, you will see that Experiments 2 and 3 more or less resulted in healthy population levels of both *P. aurelia* and *P. caudatum*. Thus, there's really not any evidence there at all to conclude that there's consuming of one another. You might be tempted to think that Experiment 1, on the other hand, shows this, since the experiment results in the precipitous decline of *P. aurelia's* population. However, just because one population declines and the other does well doesn't mean that one of them is consuming the other; there could be a whole host of reasons for this population decline, like a lack of food. This is why the answer is D: there is no direct evidence that these paramecium are willing to consume other paramecium.

22. Correct answer: **G**. If you look at the population levels for each paramecium between Experiment 2 and Experiment 3, you will see this: in both Experiments 2 and 3, *P. caudatum* (the squares on the graph) has a general increase in population. *P. aurelia* (the triangles on the graph), on the other hand, does increase in population in Experiment 2, but keeps a more-or-less steady population throughout Experiment 3. That is why the correct answer is G: *D. nasutum* (present only in Experiment 3) affects the population of *P. aurelia* more than *P. caudatum*.

23. Correct answer: **A**. This question depends on a proper analysis of Experiment 3. Clearly, because the only difference between Experiment 2 (in which both paramecium species thrived) and Experiment 3 (in which *P. aurelia* did not thrive as well) is the addition of *D. nasutum*. So, if you introduce a species that eats *D. nasutum*, then you would have to expect that the population of *P. aurelia* would increase as a result. That is why the answer is A. It certainly isn't B (which says that the population of *P. aurelia* would go down). Choices C and D are *possible*, but neither can be "reasonably expected", which is required by the question.

24. Correct answer: **H**. Simply compare the population levels at 20 days of both parameciums between Experiments 1 and 2. Start with *P. aurelia*. In Experiment 1, it has a population of roughly 35 at 20 days, and in Experiment 2 a population of roughly 60 at 20 days. So, it's population is "Greater than", which eliminates answers G and J. Now, look at *P. caudatum's* numbers. In Experiment 1, it has a population of roughly 80 at 20 days, and in Experiment 2 a population of roughly 80 at 20 days. So, it's population is "Equal to", which then eliminates answer choice F. This is why the correct answer is H: *P. aurelia's* population went up, but *P. caudatum's* stayed the same.

25. Correct answer: **B**. To answer this question correctly, simply determine the rough population levels of both paramecium combined at each of the four population points and see which is the smallest. Answer A proposes P_{20} of Experiment 1, which

shows populations of the 2 paramecium at roughly 80 and 40 for a total of 120. Answer B proposes P_{30} of Experiment 1, which shows populations of the 2 paramecium at roughly 85 and 0 for a total of 85. Answer C proposes P_{20} of Experiment 2, which shows populations of the 2 paramecium at roughly 60 and 80 for a total of 140. Answer D proposes P_{30} of Experiment 3, which shows populations of the 2 paramecium at roughly 85 and 20 for a total of 105. Thus, population levels of the paramecium is lowest (among the 4 choices) at P_{30} of Experiment 1, which is why B is the correct answer.

26. Correct answer: **F**. First, let's begin with H and J, neither of which requires the kind of inference implied by the question but a straightforward reading of Figure 3. The P_{25} and P_{30} of *P. aurelia* are relatively the same, about 20 or so, which means that neither of these is likely to be the correct answer. Answer choices F and G propose the numbers of *P. aurelia* and *P. caudatum* paralyzed in Experiment 3. Remember that Experiment 3 is essentially the exact same conditions as Experiment 2, the only difference being that a toxicyst is introduced in Experiment 3. However, a comparison of the two experiments shows that the toxicyst really had little to no effect at all on *P. caudatum*, but that the numbers of *P. aurelia* were drastically different, implying that the toxicyst killed a great number of *P. aurelia*. That's why the correct answer is F.

27. Correct answer: **D**. A "nutrient free" green algae means that the algae is no longer feeding or supplying nutrients to the two varieties of paramecium, which is in essence the exact same setup for Experiment 1 in which the two paramecium were simply placed in water. Experiment 2 ends with high population levels of *P. aurelia* and *P. caudatum*, but based on Experiment 1, what is likely to then happen when the nutrients run out? If you look at answer choice D, you'll see that it proposes the eventual sharp decline of *P. caudatum*. However, if you look at Experiment 1, *P. caudatum* did just find in the water with no nutrients. This is why the correct answer is D: this population decline of *P. caudatum* could not be reasonably inferred when comparing Experiments 1 and 2.

Passage V

28. Correct answer: **G**. For a substance to be considered *very soluble*, its m_{sv}/m_{su} value would have to be less than one. The m_{sv}/m_{su} values are found in Table 3, which you would then compare to the descriptive terms in Table 2. Looking down Table 3, there are 0 substances that have a m_{sv}/m_{su} value less than 1. Thus, the answer to the question "Was this hypothesis consistent with the results?" is no, since the hypothesis was that 1 of the substances would be "very soluble." This eliminates answer choice J. Letter F proposes that the answer is "no" because more than 1 of the substances falls into this category, but that isn't true. Letter H says there's not enough data to reach a conclusion about this, but that's not true. This is all why the correct answer is G: the answer is "no" because none of the substances fall into the *very soluble* category.

29. Correct answer: **C**. This question requires a straight reading of Table 1, the chart of the 7 substances. This chart shows the amount of each substance dissolved in 100 grams of water at varying temperatures. Simply find the column for HCl (the third substance out of seven from the left), then go down to the 60 degree row, and you'll see the number 55, which is 55 grams. This is why the correct answer is C.

30. Correct answer: **G**. If you look at Table 2, a substance is "freely soluble" if it has a m_{sv}/m_{su} value between 1 and 10. If you look at Table 3, there are only 2 substances that do not fall into this range; in other words, there are 5 that do. That means 5 of the 7 are "freely soluble," which is why the correct answer is G: 5/7.

31. Correct answer: **B**. Table 1 lists the amount of grams dissolved into 100 grams of water at different temperatures. If you look at the column for $NaNO_3$, you'll notice that at some point the concentration goes from below 100 to above 100. At 20 degrees, $NaNO_3$ has a concentration of 86 in 100 grams of water, and at 40 degrees it has risen to 105. Without looking at the answer choices, it seems most likely that $NaNO_3$ reaches *solubility equipollence* somewhere between 30 and 40 degrees. There is only one answer choice that falls into this range, which is answer choice B: 35 degrees.

32. Correct answer: **J**. "Freely soluble" means that the substance has a m_{sv}/m_{su} value between 1 and 10 (according to Table 2). If you look then at Table 3, you'll see that there are 3 substances that contain sodium. The first one, ($Na_2C_2O_4$) has a m_{sv}/m_{su} value much higher than 10. The other two substances that contain sodium ($NaNO_3$ and NaCl) are both freely soluble. This is why the correct answer is J; it rightly says that the answer is "No" (not every substance with Na is freely soluble) and gives the correct reason why (only 2 of the 3 substances have a m_{sv}/m_{su} value between 1 and 10).

33. Correct answer: **A**. If the *x* axis is degrees Celsius, then based on the graph given here we are looking for a substance that has a dissolved concentration of around 85 at 0°C, about 55 at 20°C, about 45 at 40°C, about 20 at 60°C, about 15 at 80°C, and about 10 at 100°C. The reason the correct answer is A is because, if you look at the column of concentrations under NH_3, you'll see a gradual decline in concentration as the temperature rises that roughly mirrors the values that we estimated based on the graph provided by the question. Each of the other three choices has an *increasing* concentration as the temperature goes up; NH_3 is the only of the 4 options that has a decreasing concentration as temperature rises. That is why the answer is A.

Passage VI

34. Correct answer: **G**. The two studies actually feature the same number of generations. In each study, there is a P (parental) generation, then an F_1 generation, then lastly an F_2 generation. Put simply, that is three generations, which is why G is the correct

answer. F proposes 2, which is probably a common wrong answer, but though that might be the difference in the number of generations between P and F_2, it isn't the total number of generations. Choice H is incorrect because 82 represents the total number of fruit flies observed in Study 1, not the number of generations. Choice J is incorrect because 197 represents the total number of flies of either type observed in both studies combined.

35. Correct answer: **D**. Let's go through each choice and compare each of the proposed phenotype/genotype observations to the students' expected numbers. Choice A: Table 1 says that the observed Brown eye/bb was 19, and the expectation was 20.5 (a difference of 1.5). Choice B: Table 1 says that the observed Red eye/B__ was 63, and the expectation was 61.5 (a difference of 1.5). Choice C: Table 2 says that the observed Sepia eye/ddB__ was 18, and the expectation was 21.6 (a difference of 3.6). Choice D: Table 2 says that the observed Brown eye/D__bb was 30, and the expectation was 21.6 (a difference of 8.4). Thus, Choice D has the greatest deviation, making it the correct answer.

36. Correct answer: **H**. First, understand that the question refers to the last line in Table 2, the ______ eye (phenotype) or ddbb (genotype) eye color. As you can see there, the students found 0 of them in the third generation of the study. The question is simply asking why this is the case. Letter F proposes that based on Study 1, a doubly homozygous genotype isn't possible. However, Study 1, if anything, proposes that is *is* a possibility (since there are observed bb genotype eye color flies); this is why F is incorrect. Letter G proposes that 115 flies simply wasn't enough based on expectations. However, the students only expected 1/16 of the flies to have this eye color, meaning that you'd need at least 16 flies to find 1. Because the study observes 115 flies, there are plenty to find at least 1 based on expectations; this is why G is incorrect. Let's skip to J, which proposes that there's a relationship with ddbb flies and the number of larvae that die before hatching. Is that *possible?* Sure! It could be the case that flies of this type have other issues that cause them to die before hatching. However, is that *stated* anywhere in the passage? No. This is why J is incorrect. That leaves H, which proposes that ddbb (though *genetically* a different color; a unique genotype) manifests as brown (meaning, has a *phenotype* of brown). This makes a lot of sense, since there are many more observed brown eye flies (30) than was predicted (21.6). This is why H is the correct answer.

37. Correct answer: **A**. The purpose of the studies was to compare expectations of eye color both genetically (genotype) and in terms of looks (phenotype), but the only way to get the genotypes "mixed up" enough with various alleles (B, b, D, d in the study) was to study across three generations. This is why the correct answer is A, to ensure enough allele intermixing for diversification worth studying. Choice B is incorrect because it proposes an idea (about sample sizes helping avoid a certain margin of error) that is not found anywhere in the experiment. Choice C is incorrect because it proposes something about creating a population at F_2 that with 100% homozygous alleles, but the purpose of F_2 is the opposite. Choice D is incorrect for a couple of reasons, but one of which is that the sepia eye type is only relevant to Study 2, not Study 1, which also utilized flies across 3 generations.

38. Correct answer: **J**. In order for this one sheep to have black wool when all of its parents and grandparents had white wool, it must have a genotype of, first of all, recessive genes; white is clearly the dominant gene in this family tree. This eliminates answer choices G and H, both of which propose that this black sheep inherited a "dominant black wool gene." Secondly, in genetics, if one dominant gene is present in the genotype, the phenotype will manifest as that dominant (or white) gene. This means that what is needed is *not* a "heterozygous" genotype, because that would result (according to the definition given in the passage) in 1 dominant gene and 1 recessive gene, which would result in white wool. This eliminates answer choice F. Thus, what is needed is a "homozygous" genotype, meaning containing nothing but recessive genes. That is what answer choice J proposes, which is why it is correct.

39. Correct answer: **C**. In genetics, and in these two studies, all that is necessary for the manifestation of a dominant genotype is the presence of 1 dominant allele. For example, if you look at Table 1 (which was about the fruit fly, which is what the question is about) in F_2 at the Red eye row, you'll see the capital B followed by blanks (__). This is because it doesn't matter what follows this dominant allele (whether dominant or recessive); it will be the determining factor for the eye color. This is why the correct answer is C. More research into the role of the second allele is unnecessary because it will have no effect on the observed numbers.

40. Correct answer: **J**. First of all, notice that there are 4 total observations made in Study 2 (more specifically, 3 observed numbers and 4 expected numbers). This eliminates answer choices F and G as options, since neither shows 4 different colors on its two pie charts. The question now is which pair of pie charts between H and J accurately represents the numbers. However, there is a bit of a shortcut to making these comparisons, and that is this: there are 0 observed ddbb genotype flies in Table 2, which means that they will not have a slice of the pie chart. Under the observed column, you'll clearly see that choice H has 4 slices as if all 4 genotypes have observations, but choice J only has 3. This is why the correct answer is J: it correctly (and accurately, for that matter) gives 3 slices of the pie chart to the observed numbers and 4 slices to the expected numbers.

Answer Explanations - Step 6 - Practice Test #2

Passage I	Passage II	Passage III	Passage IV	Passage V	Passage VI
1: B	7: D	14: H	20: H	27: C	34: H
2: F	8: J	15: D	21: B	28: F	35: A
3: B	9: C	16: F	22: F	29: A	36: F
4: G	10: G	17: C	23: C	30: H	37: A
5: D	11: D	18: J	24: H	31: B	38: J
6: G	12: J	19: B	25: B	32: J	39: A
	13: A		26: F	33: C	40: G

Passage I

1. Correct answer: **B**. Again, you are never going to be asked a mathematics question on the ACT Science test that requires a calculator. This means that general estimations and basic math are going to be enough for you to get the question correct. In this question, notice that Figure 1 shows that 88% of the organisms in the lake are bacteria, but that Figure 2 shows the types of bacteria. As far as bacteroidetes go, they are 33% or ⅓ of the bacteria, or 33% of 88% of all organisms in the lake. Well, what's 88% divided by 3 (aka, ⅓ of 88%)? Well, $3 \times 30\% = 90\%$, so the correct answer is going to be a little less than 30%. This is why the correct answer is B: 29%.

2. Correct answer: **F**. The passage states this about hypersaline (really salty) lakes: "This type of environment is not suitable for the majority of living microorganisms, as extremely high salinity levels are often toxic to cells." Thus, as the question states, if salinity or salt levels go *down*, you can expect the presence of other types of organisms to go *up*. Thus, the percent occupied by bacteria overall will go down. This eliminates answer choices H and J, which both state that the percent of bacteria would increase. Answer choice G correctly says that the overall percent of bacteria would decrease, but it wrongly states that this would be due to the fact that other life would fail to survive, but the opposite is true. Thus, choice F is correct because it says that the bacteria levels would decrease because other life would be able to survive and thrive in the lake as the salt levels went down.

3. Correct answer: **B**. Ordering species of organisms from lowest to highest percentage occupation level would be much easier if one of the options was 'bacteria' since, according to Figure 1, they occupy 88% of the lake. However, that isn't the case; instead you are given individual bacteria names. Before we answer the question, let's go ahead and list the 5 named organisms from lowest to highest percentage of occupation levels in the lake: 1) Archea; 2) Eukaryota; 3) Firmicutes; 4) Proteobacteria; 5) Bacteroidetes. Now, because each list has 4 organisms, any list that does *not* begin with either archea or eukaryota as the first is going to be incorrect; this eliminates C and D as potential correct answers. Choice A begins with archea and eukaryota, but then falls apart with it lists proteobacteria ahead of firmicutes. This is why the correct answer is B: although it does not list archea first, the remaining 4 are listed in correct order from lowest to highest percentage occupation levels.

4. Correct answer: **G**. Because the passage makes clear that Mars does *not* presently have any lakes, we can eliminate answer choices H and J, both of which speak of lakes in the present tense. That leaves F and G which both speak of radiation and temperatures. The passage says this in the second sentence: "While current conditions on Mars include freezing temperatures and high radiation levels…" These conditions match up with choice G: low temperatures and high radiation make for a lifeless Mars.

5. Correct answer: **D**. If you look at the pie chart in Figure 1, you'll see that there is a slice of Uncharacterized life that represents 5% of the diversity in the lake. Because the question asks "*At most*"…, we can hold that it is possible that this fungus makes up up to 5% of the total life population of the lake. That is why the correct answer is D: 5%.

6. Correct answer: **G**. Because the hypersaline lake on earth is made up of bacteroidetes more than proteobacterias, it is safe to conclude that it is more likely that an ancient Martian lake contained a bacteriodete (if anything!). This eliminates answer choices H and J. In addition, the passage states of course that if a lake had existed on Mars, it would have been hypersaline. This is why the correct answer is G: unlike answer choice F (which speaks of a lake with little or no salt), answer choice G proposes that if any lake were present on Mars in the past it would have been a hypersaline lake.

Passage II

7. Correct answer: **D**. The "two weeks" referred to in this question is not the condition of any of the three experiments. Rather, this is between the use of some wild caught owls immediately in Experiment 2 and the use of other wild caught owls after being in captivity for one month. In Experiment 1, the owls ate 0.9 yellow geckos (see Figure 1) over 24 hours on average. In Experiment 2, the owls ate 0.7 yellow geckos (see Figure 2) over 24 hours on average. Thus, if the owls had been kept in captivity right between the two lengths of these experiments, it is safe to assume that they would eat 0.8 (right in the middle) yellow geckos on average over a 24 hour period. This is why the correct answer is D.

8. Correct answer: **J**. This question is going to require you to do a little bit of basic math. Add up the number of geckos eaten in Figure 1, then do the same things with Figure 2 and 3, and see what the progress is on the number of geckos eaten over the three

experiments. Figure 1 shows an average of 0.9 + 0.8 + 0.7 + 0.5 + 0.5 = 3.4 geckos eaten. Figure 2 shows an average of 0.7 + 0.5 + 0.6 + 0.4 + 0.4 = 2.6 geckos eaten. So far, that's a decrease, which eliminates answer choices F and H, both of which propose an increase. Then finally, Figure 3 shows 1.0 + 0.4 + 0.7 + 0.6 + 0.6 = 3.3 geckos eaten. Thus, the number of geckos eaten goes back up from Figure 2. This is why the correct answer is J, which properly says that the numbers first go down, then up again.

9. Correct answer: **C**. First, understand this this question asks for which color is *least likely* to be found thriving in the habitat of the owl. In other words: which of the following colors is most likely to be eaten by the owl? Second, recognize that getting this question right will require reference to the correct pool of data. You don't need to reference all three figures (which would actually be bad). Instead, see that Figure 1 is the best data to use because the owls in the experiment were put into the habitat the same day they were caught (in other words, they're more wild than the others). The two color geckos in Experiment 1 that are eaten the most are yellow and white, which is why the correct answer is C; a yellowish-white gecko is most likely to be eaten in the wild, and thus least likely to thrive.

10. Correct answer: **G**. You might be tempted to select "Yellow" because its bar on the bar graph is the tallest. However recall that the bar on the bar graph is in reference to how many geckos are eaten. Thus, it is *least likely* that yellow would be the last remaining gecko since it's the most likely to be eaten. Thus, all we have to do is to look at Figure 3 and find which gecko is eaten the least. This is the white gecko, of which only 0.4 are consumed per 24 hours. This is why the correct answer is G: white.

11. Correct answer: **D**. Let's go through each of these options one at a time and determine if they are true or false. Answer choice A is incorrect because it falsely claims that the owls eat less the longer they're in captivity; this is true for the change from Experiment 1 to 2, but after that (Experiment 3) their appetite starts to pick up. Answer choice B is incorrect because it falsely states that there is no difference in the amount that wild and captive owls eat; while there's not too much difference between the number of geckos eaten between Experiment 1 and Experiment 3, there is a big drop in the middle (which also uses captive owls, though only for a month). Answer choice C is incorrect because it falsely states that captive owls eat more than wild ones; however, the experiment in which the owls ate the most is Experiment 1, which used wild owls. Answer choice D, on the other hand, correctly states that wild owls eat more than captive ones; if you compare the numbers from Experiment 1 to Experiment 2, you'll see that the wild ones definitely eat more, and they even eat slightly more than the owls in Experiment 3.

12. Correct answer: **J**. Let's go through each answer choice one at a time to determine if it contains an assumption that is true. Answer choice F says that the variety of species eaten by the owl is an assumption made by the scientists. However, only one animal species, the gecko, is used in the experiment, and it is not *assumed* that owls eat geckos, but established fact. Answer choice G proposes that is is assumed that the amount eaten by wild/captive owls is the same; however, that's not an assumption of the experiment, but the very *purpose* of the experiment. Answer choice H proposes that it is assumed that the owls hunt less when there's no competition for food. However, again, the amount of geckos eaten is the *purpose* of the experiment, not an assumption. That leaves answer choice J, which proposes that it is assumed that 24 hours is enough time to measure eating habits. This is of course true, since all of the data is based on the owls' eating habits over 24 hours. This is why the correct answer is J.

13. Correct answer: **A**. This question, though it is long, is essentially asking you to see what kind of change is most likely as the owls in Experiment 3 become more like the owls in Experiment 1. The greatest and most obvious difference in the data is that the owls of Experiment 3 do *not* eat very many white geckos compared to Experiment 1 (though the yellow, grey, purple, and brown are all relatively close to Experiment 1's numbers). This is why the correct answer is A: most likely, captive owls would eat more white geckos compared to what happens in Experiment 3.

Passage III

14. Correct answer: **H**. This question is as straightforward as it looks. Sampling site #1 has a depth of 1.30 meters, a temperature of 15.5 degrees, and a pH level of 7.97. There is another site that has these exact same characteristics, which is answer choice H: Sampling site #3.

15. Correct answer: **D**. First, understand that a direct relationship is one in which as one value goes up, another value goes up also (or as one value goes down, another goes down). For example, there is a direct relationship between how much you exercise and how in shape you are: if exercise goes up, how in shape you are goes up. There is only 1 direct relationship among the four options, and that is the relationship between the water depth and the pH levels. As depth goes "up" or gets deeper (such as Sampling site 2 to Sampling site 3 to Sampling site 5 to Sampling site 6), the pH levels also go up. That is why the correct answer is D. As for the others, there might be individual examples of each of these relationships, but none of them are shown to be true across all 6 sampling sites.

16. Correct answer: **F**. Let's go one by one and determine the truth or falsehood of the four answer choices. Letter F proposes that Tables 2 and 3 indicate that EDC's are harder to remove from sediment compared to water. This is true, making F the correct answer. Table 2 gives a much higher concentration range of EDC's in sediment, and Table 3 shows a much higher half-life for EDC's in sediment. Thus, F is the correct answer. Choice G proposes the opposite, that removing EDC's from the water is more difficult, but it was just shown how this was false. Choices H and J propose that there is no overlap of the concentration ranges of EDC's in water and sediment, respectively; however, Table 2 shows that both of these overlaps exist (see BPAF and BPB, for example); thus, H and J are also incorrect.

17. Correct answer: **C**. This question requires you to develop an understanding of the relationship between the concentration ranges in water and sediment of various EDC's as given in Table 2. There are two things to notice: first, the concentration range in water is simply *smaller* (both in its minimum value and range) compared to the concentration range in sediment. For the purposes of the questions, this eliminates answer choices A and B (both of which propose a sediment concentration smaller than the water concentration in the question). The second thing to notice about the patterns in Table 2 is that there is always overlap in the range (like overlapping circles) values. Answer choice D does not have this overlap; its minimum value (4,459) is the uppermost value of the water concentration range in the question (4,459). This is why the correct answer is C: this possible sediment concentration range is bigger than the water range and overlaps with it as well.

18. Correct answer: **J**. The fact that the question proposes removing BADGE from "Sampling site #5" is irrelevant; in other words, the correct answer does not depend on the sampling site at all. Instead, it depends on the half-life of BADGE as presented in Table 3. According to Table 3, BADGE has a half-life of 540 in sediment. Some might get this question incorrect because they use the half-life in water, but that is a mistake. We know that Sampling site #5 has sediment because the second paragraph of the passage says so (and Table 2 gives a minimum BADGE present in any body of water at 4,290, so all sites must have BADGE present). Nevertheless, half-life means the amount of time for half of the EDC to disappear or dissolve. Well, after 540 days then 50% would be gone, then after another 540 days, 50% of what's remaining (25% of the total) would then disappear. Thus, for a total of 75% of BADGE to disappear would take 540 + 540 = 1,080 days. This is why J is the correct answer.

19. Correct answer: **B**. To get this question correct, you have to see the little asterisk (*) under Table 1, which says "note: the deeper the stream, the lower the concentration of EDC's in water." In other words, the *less deep* the stream, the higher the concentration. This hypothetical stream is less deep or shallower than any stream in the study. If you look at the range of BPA concentration in water, you'll see that the range is 298 - 3,620. The 3,620 amount, based on the asterisk, *must* refer to the shallowest sampling site (Sampling site #4). This means that a sampling site that's slightly shallower (in our case, a depth of only -0.15m) must have a BPA concentration a little higher than this. This is why the correct answer is B: 4,200. The other three options are all much to small (choice A) or much too large (choices C and D).

Passage IV

20. Correct answer: **H**. In Scientist 1's paragraph, she states that Io is in a "gravitational tug-of-war", so we know for sure that Scientist 1 believes that gravity plays a role in Io's volcanoes. This eliminates answer choices G and J. Scientist 2 though also believes that gravity plays a role; she speaks of "extreme competitive gravitational pulls", etc. That is why the correct answer is H: both scientists believe the gravitational pull in both directions has an effect on Io.

21. Correct answer: **B**. Scientist 2 is the only of the two scientists who speaks of molten rock being a part of the lava flows or volcanic activity on Io (Scientist 1 believes it is all sulfur). This is why the correct answer here is B: only Scientist 2's position is consistent with the hypothetical finding about friction melting rock proposed by the question itself.

22. Correct answer: **F**. If you reread Scientist 1's position, you will see in the 4th sentence that the gravitational pulls of both Jupiter and the Galilean moons play a role in its volcanic activity; this eliminates answer choices H and J from contention as correct answers. The 5th sentence discusses how sulfur can flow at lower temperatures. Thus, answer choice G is also incorrect as sulfur too plays a role in Io's extreme volcanic activity. Letter F is correct because, although the size of Io compared to Earth is mentioned by Scientist 1, it is never presented as a factor directly related to the volcanic activity. This is why F is the correct answer.

23. Correct answer: **C**. Because Scientist 1 proposes that the lava on Io is entirely sulfur, we would expect those plumes to fly highest. This eliminates answer choices A and B, neither of which get this part of the inequality correct. Scientist 2 proposes in his theory that Io's volcanoes possess not only sulfur, but also molten rock. This would mean that these plumes would be lesser than Scientist 1's plumes of course, but because Earth's plumes contain no sulfur and only rock, we'd expect Earth's to be the smallest. This is where D goes wrong: it proposes that Scientist 2's Theory of Io would generate plumes the same size as Earth's. This is why C is the correct answer: Scientist 1's plumes would be higher than Scientist 2's, which would be higher than Earth's.

24. Correct answer: **H**. Scientist 1 says about ⅔ the way through his paragraph that Io's volcanoes are "characterized by extensive flows of molten sulfur," so this proposition is certainly true of him. That eliminates answer choices G and J. Next, although Scientist 2 believes that Io's lava contains at least some molten rock, she says in the final sentence, "Though sulfur is undeniably present on the planet, both in volcanic flows and plumes..." Thus, it is both scientists who believe that the volcanoes of Io contain sulfur, which is why the correct answer is H: Both Scientist 1 and Scientist 2.

25. Correct answer: **B**. Both Scientist 1 and Scientist 2 believe that Jupiter's gravitational pull (and thus, its size) has an effect on the volcanoes. If something were to change about Jupiter's size, it could perhaps weaken both of their positions simultaneously, but it wouldn't weaken only Scientist 2's position. This means that C and D are both false. Answer choice A proposes that a lower melting point of rock would weaken Scientist 2, but that would actually help her, seeing as she proposes that there is rock in Io's magma and that Io's surface temperatures are low due to its distance from the sun. This means that B is correct, and it is correct

because if sulfur can "build upon itself," then that means that the necessity that Io's volcanoes contain rock goes down, which weakens Scientist 2.

26. Correct answer: **F**. Since Scientist 1 proposes that only sulfur flows from Io's volcanoes, and sulfur is yellow, then we first need an answer consistent with Scientist 1 proposing a yellow flume. This eliminates answer choices H and J. Scientist 2, if you remember, believes that the lava flowing from Io's volcanoes consists of sulfur (yellow) and magma (red), which means that Scientist 2 would expect to see an orange plume in a high definition photo. This is why the correct answer is F: it rightly says that Scientist 1 would expect a yellow plume (sulfur) and that Scientist 2 would expect an orange plume (sulfur and magma).

Passage V

27. Correct answer: **C**. This question asks you to find which resistor caused the greatest voltage drop in the Trials 2-4. The resistor that causes the greatest voltage drop is also, by definition, going to be the resistor with the highest resistance in ohms. If you look at Table 2, the resistor with the highest resistance is R3. This eliminates answer choices A and B, since these two answers give the wrong resistors under Trial 2. If you look at Table 3, you'll notice that it is R2 that has the highest resistance. This is now enough for us to get the question correct, since choice D lists R3 as having the highest resistance for Trial 2. This is why the correct answer is C; only choice C properly notes that R3, R2, and R3 have the highest resistance (caused the highest percent of voltage drop) in Trials 2-4, respectively.

28. Correct answer: **F**. Again, the ACT Science test is never going to ask you to perform math that would require a calculator. If you can do basic or rudimentary math you will end up at or near the correct answer most of the time if not always. Here, you are asked to look for the second resistor (R2) in the series in Trial 4. Specifically, you're looking for its percent of voltage drop. If you look at Table 4, you'll see that R2 is responsible for a voltage drop of 1.081 out of 12 total volts. You may not be able to calculate that this is approximately 9% in your head, but you can certainly see that this percentage is less than 100% (choice J), 91% (choice H) and even 33% (choice G). This is why the correct answer is F: 1.081 out of 12 volts is approximately 9% of the entire voltage drop in Trial 4.

29. Correct answer: **A**. The idea that the voltage drop would necessarily double if resistance is doubled is not supported by Trials 1-4. Why not? Well, look at Trial 1: each resistor has a resistance of 100 ohms, resulting in a voltage drop of 4.0 volts. Then look at R2 in Table 2; its resistance has now doubled to 200 ohms, but the voltage drop is the same (4.0 volts). This is because voltage drop is relative to the value of the other resistors. This means that both C and D, both of which say "Yes", are incorrect. Choice B is incorrect also because although it says "No," it gives a false reason why: there isn't a "direct relationship" between resistance and voltage drop (because it depends on the value of the resistance of the other resistors in the series). This leaves A, which correctly says that the answer is "No" for the proper reason: the effect of a resistor depends on the other resistors' values.

30. Correct answer: **H**. Fortunately, you are given here a little definition of an independent variable as a part of the question itself. To be thorough, an *independent* variable is what scientists (or whoever is doing the experiment) controls or changes. In this case, the student is changing the value of the resistance of each resistor in each trial. This means that F and G are incorrect, and the correct answer must be H or J. The *dependent* variable of an experiment is that which is measured; its value *depends* upon the value of the independent variable. In this case, it is voltage drop that is being measured or is dependent upon the resistance. This means that the correct answer is H: resistance is independent (changed) and voltage drop is dependent (measured). As for the 12V power supply, it is neither changed nor measured, but constant.

31. Correct answer: **B**. This question is asking you to look at Tables 1-4 and identify the resistors that are, basically, really effective or big compared to the other two in the series; so "big" that they account for 50%+ of the voltage drop in their series. Instead of looking through the answer choices one by one, let's look through the 4 trials and tables and find if any resistors are responsible for this kind of voltage drop. In Trial/Table 1, the resistors all had the same value (100 ohms), account for an even voltage drop in all 3. Thus, we can reject that one. In Trial/Table 2, R3 accounts for a voltage drop of 6.0, which is exactly 50% of the voltage drop in the series. However, the question says the we are looking for a voltage drop of *over* or *more than* 50%. Thus, we can also reject Trial 2. In Trial/Table 3, R2 causes a voltage drop of 6.75, which is more than 50% of the series. Thus, this is one correct answer. This is already enough to answer the question correctly, since only one of the four answer choices includes R2 of Trial 3 as an option, which is answer choice B. Just to verify, answer choice B also proposes that R3 of Trial 4 also accounts for a more than 50% drop in voltage. Sure enough, if you investigate Table 4, you will see that R3, being so large, accounts for over 90% of the voltage drop in that series.

32. Correct answer: **J**. *Kirchoff's Law* is just that: a law. There's not going to be such a thing as an "exception" unless stated so by the passage (which it doesn't). Having an exception to a law would be like having an exception to 2 + 2 = 4. Thus, you need to right away realize that the answer is "No." This eliminates answer choices F and G. As for answer choice H, it says something about not having voltage taps means there's no voltage divider, but all the voltage taps do is to measure the voltage drop (or, you might say, measure *Kirchoff's Law* working). Whether or not you measure it, the law is still working. This is why the answer is J, which rightly says "No," but also that the law is independent of the number of resistors or voltage.

33. Correct answer: **C**. By this point you may have noticed that the total voltage drop is equivalent to the voltage of the circuit. Trials 1-4 are all conducted with a 12V circuit, and the total voltage drop by each resistor, when added up, equals 12V. Thus, if

there were four resistors, this idea would still apply. If each resistor has equal resistance, then they will have the same voltage drop (no matter the value of the resistance). In this case, with 4 resistors, each will cause a voltage drop of 3.0 volts (because 3 × 4 = 12), which is why the correct answer is C.

Passage VI

34. Correct answer: **H**. This question is essentially asking you to identify the one factor that didn't affect how long it took the rats to finish the maze. Answer choice F proposes whether or not the rat had caffeine, but that certainly *did* affect the rats' finish times. Answer choice G proposes the new location of the platform in Trial 3, but this also certainly affected finish times; if it wouldn't have affected the times, the scientists wouldn't have moved it. Answer choice J proposes the opaque water, but that of course does affect rat times because they can't see the platform under such water. That leaves answer choice H, which is of course correct; how fast rats swim relative to mice is irrelevant to their finish times.

35. Correct answer: **A**. The opening portion of this question (about rats not being exhausted by a swim under 100 seconds) just means that the rats in Trial 3 did not swim more slowly than in Trial 1 due to being tired (something else was affecting them). Let's work backwards through the answers to identify them as true or false. Answer D proposes that caffeine doesn't make a difference in performance, but that is certainly not true (just look at the differences between Trial 1 and 2). Answer choice C proposes that caffeine has a *negative* impact on performance, but that is also not true; the rats in Trial 1 (with the caffeine) swam faster than those in Trial 2. Answer choice B proposes that a rat gets better after caffeine wears off, but that isn't true; the rats in Trial 3 performed much poorer than the rats in Trial 1. This leaves A, which is correct, since it rightly states that a withdrawal from caffeine must account for the poor performance of the rats as seen in Trial 3 compared to Trial 1.

36. Correct answer: **F**. This question is asking you to compare rats' performance in Trial 3 to Trial 1 (since both trials use the same rats). If you look at the four answer choices, you'll realize that this comparison only needs to be made in regards to four of the rats: Rat 4, Rat 5, Rat 6, and Rat 8. Let's find the difference in performance between trials for all four, then compare to find the greatest drop. Rat 4's Trial 1 time was roughly 52 seconds; its Trial 3 time was roughly 95 seconds (a performance drop of roughly 43 seconds). Rat 5's Trial 1 time was roughly 65 seconds; its Trial 3 time was roughly 85 seconds (a performance drop of roughly 20 seconds). Rat 6's Trial 1 time was roughly 70 seconds; its Trial 3 time was roughly 85 seconds (a performance drop of roughly 15 seconds). Lastly, Rat 8's Trial 1 time was roughly 53 seconds; its Trial 3 time was roughly 55 seconds (a performance drop of roughly 2 seconds). By far the greatest drop is seen in Rat 4 (43 seconds), making F the correct answer.

37. Correct answer: **A**. Trial 3 was performed 1 hour after the caffeine dosage. If the trial were repeated with a 15 minute rest, we would expect the result to be somewhere between the Trial 1 result and the Trial 3 result. Rat 3, according to Figure 1, completed Trial 1 with a time of about 38 seconds. According to Figure 3, Rat 3 completed Trial 3 with a time of about 67 seconds. Thus, we would expect the correct answer to be within this range. This eliminates answer choices C and D right away as they are both outside of this range. Answer choice B looks at first like an option, since it begins with 60 seconds on the low end. However, it ends with 70 seconds on the high end, which would already be outside our range; not only that, after a wait of only 15 minutes we would expect the time to be closer to the 38 second mark. This is why the correct answer is A: between 40 and 60 seconds is the best estimate for Rat 3 to finish the test after a 15 minute wait based on its times as given in Figures 1 and 3.

38. Correct answer: **J**. This question is essentially asking you for the average of the 8 times given to you in Figure 2 (since the rats in Trial 2 were never administered caffeine). As always, a rough estimate is enough. This is especially true when it comes to this question, since it is difficult to tell exact times off of the figures. If you make close guesses, then find an approximate average, you'll be fine. However, another, faster way to answer this question (which is how I would ballpark it) is to draw a line across the x axis that approximates the average. This will work because the answer choices are pretty far apart, so just getting it close will be good enough. To me, because there are 5 points above 75 seconds (though 2 of them, Rats 13 and 14, are really close to 75) and 3 points below, it seems that the average will be roughly 75 seconds. However, "75 seconds" isn't an option, but 1.25 minutes and 75 seconds are the same thing. This is why the correct answer is J: 1.25 minutes.

39. Correct answer: **A**. This question requires you to compare Rat 1 in Trial 1 with Rat 9 in Trial 2, and so on 8 times. Let's do this one at a time and determine if any of the rats that did not consume caffeine (aka Trial 2) would have won the race. If a rat from Trial 2 wins (which is the number we're looking for, I'll italicize and underline it. Rat 1 vs Rat 9: <u>*Rat 9*</u> (no caffeine) was faster! Rat 2 vs Rat 10: Rat 2 was faster. Rat 3 vs Rat 11: Rat 3 was faster. Rat 4 vs Rat 12: Rat 4 was faster. Rat 5 vs Rat 13: Rat 5 was faster. Rat 6 vs Rat 14: Rat 6 was faster. Rat 7 vs Rat 15: Rat 7 was faster. Rat 8 vs Rat 16: Rat 8 was faster. Thus, only once (Rat 9) was the rat with no caffeine in Trial 2 faster than its competitor in Trial 1. This is why the correct answer is A: 1 of 8.

40. Correct answer: **G**. Two of these rats (Rat 9 and Rat 11) are from Trial 2, which means they don't really have an "average" in any difficult sense because they only did the maze once; their one time is their average. Rat 11 did the maze in about 60 seconds. Rat 9 did the maze in about 55 seconds (so this eliminates answer choice F: Rat 11). As for Rat 4, it did the maze in Trial 1 in a time of about 50 seconds, then did the maze in Trial 3 in about 95 seconds, which gives him an average of something like 73 seconds. Because this is much slower than Rat 9, answer choice H is thus incorrect. Lastly, as for Rat 2, it ran the maze in Trial 1 in a time of about 85 seconds, then did the maze in Trial 3 in about 95 seconds, which gives him an average of about 90 seconds. Because this is much slower than Rat 9, answer choice J is thus incorrect. This is why answer choice G is the correct answer: Rat 9's average time was faster than any of the other three options.

Score Conversion

Do not count on this chart for perfect accuracy, but rather as an estimation as to how you might perform on the ACT. The chart itself, and your scores, are approximate. Even the ACT uses a different chart for each test! Find your score on any practice test (the "raw" score, or how many answers you scored correctly) and follow it to the ACT Scaled Score in the left or right columns. If you add all 4 scaled scores (English, Math, Reading, and Science) and divide by 4, round to the nearest whole number to get your approximate ACT score.

ACT Scaled Score	**English** Raw Score	**Math** Raw Score	**Reading** Raw Score	**Science** Raw Score	**ACT** Scaled Score
36	**73-75**	**58-60**	**40**	**39-40**	**36**
35	71-72	56-57	38-39	37-38	35
34	**69-70**	**54-55**	**37**	**36**	**34**
33	68	53	36	35	33
32	**67**	**51-52**	**34-35**	**34**	**32**
31	66	49-50	33	—	31
30	**65**	**48**	**32**	**33**	**30**
29	64	46-47	31	32	29
28	**63**	**44-45**	**30**	**31**	**28**
27	61-62	41-43	—	—	27
26	**60**	**39-40**	**29**	**30**	**26**
25	57-59	37-38	28	28-29	25
24	**55-56**	**35-36**	**26-27**	**26-27**	**24**
23	52-54	33-34	25	25	23
22	**49-51**	**31-32**	**23-24**	**23-24**	**22**
21	46-48	30	22	22	21
20	**43-45**	**28-29**	**20-21**	**20-21**	**20**
19	41-42	26-27	19	19	19
18	**40**	**24-25**	**18**	**17-18**	**18**
17	37-39	21-23	16-17	15-16	17
16	**34-36**	**17-20**	**15**	**13-14**	**16**
15	30-33	13-16	14	12	15
14	**27-29**	**10-12**	**12-13**	**11**	**14**
13	25-26	8-9	11	10	13
12	**23-24**	**6-7**	**10**	**9**	**12**
11	20-22	5	8-9	8	11
10	**17-19**	**4**	**7**	**7**	**10**
9	14-16	—	6	6	9
8	**12-13**	**3**	**5**	**5**	**8**
7	10-11	—	—	4	7
6	**8-9**	**2**	**4**	**3**	**6**
5	6-7	—	3	—	5
4	**5**	**1**	**2**	**2**	**4**
3	3-4	—	—	1	3
2	**2**	—	**1**	—	**2**
1	0-1	0	0	0	1

About the Author

Philip J Martin studied Industrial and Systems Engineering and Philosophy at Auburn University before earning his Master's Degree in Theology from the Franciscan University of Steubenville. He has been a classroom teacher for more than a decade, won a Nappie Award for his teaching in 2022, and has taught thousands of hours of ACT prep in person to hundreds of different students. He is the author of *The ACT English System, The ACT Math System, The ACT Reading System, and The ACT Science System* and the creator of *The ACT System*, a systematic approach to ACT prep that puts first-things-first by teaching content and strategy from most to least important. Along the way, he has earned multiple awards for his short fiction and has published poetry, non fiction, and fiction in print, including a collection of short stories titled *Ephphatha* published by Full Quiver Publishing. Today, he lives and writes from beautiful Daphne, AL with his lovely wife and children.

Made in the USA
Columbia, SC
26 September 2024